Sixth Edition

SCHOOL LAW AND THE PUBLIC SCHOOLS
A PRACTICAL GUIDE FOR EDUCATIONAL LEADERS

Nathan L. Essex
University of Memphis

PEARSON

Boston   Columbus   Indianapolis   New York   San Francisco   Hoboken
Amsterdam   Cape Town   Dubai   London   Madrid   Milan   Munich   Paris   Montreal   Toronto
Delhi   Mexico City   São Paulo   Sydney   Hong Kong   Seoul   Singapore   Taipei   Tokyo

Vice President and Editorial Director: Jeffery W. Johnston

Senior Acquisitions Editor: Julie Peters

Program Manager: Megan Moffo

Project Manager: Mary Beth Finch

Editorial Assistant: Andrea Hall

Executive Product Marketing Manager: Christopher Barry

Executive Field Marketing Manager: Krista Clark

Procurement Specialist: Deidra Skahill

Senior Art Director: Diane Lorenzo

Cover Designer: Carie Keller, Cenveo

Cover Art: Shutterstock/Jerry Sliwowski

Media Project Manager: Allison Longley

Full-Service Project Management: Kailash Jadli/ Aptara®, Inc.

Composition: Aptara®, Inc.

Printer/Binder: Edwards Brothers

Cover Printer: Edwards Brothers

Text Font: Times 10/12

Every effort has been made to provide accurate and current Internet information in this book. However, the Internet and information posted on it are constantly changing, so it is inevitable that some of the Internet addresses listed in this textbook will change.

Library of Congress Cataloging-in-Publication Data

Essex, Nathan L., author.
 School law and the public schools : a practical guide for educational leaders / Nathan L. Essex, University of Memphis.—Sixth edition.
    pages cm
  ISBN 978-0-13-390542-7—ISBN 0-13-390542-X   1. Educational law and legislation—United States.
2. School management and organization—Law and legislation—United States.   3. Student records—Access control—United States.   I. Title.
  KF4119.E84 2016
  344.73´071—dc23

                                                                                2014024890

10 9 8 7 6 5 4 3 2 1

ISBN 10:   0-13-390542-X
ISBN 13: 978-0-13-390542-7

ABOUT THE AUTHOR

Nathan L. Essex is professor of Educational Law and Leadership at the University of Memphis and President of Southwest Tennessee Community College. He received a B.S. degree in English at Alabama A&M University, an M.S. degree in Educational Administration at Jacksonville State University, and a Ph.D. degree in Administration and Planning at The University of Alabama.

Essex's interests include law, educational policy, and personnel administration. He has served as consultant for more than a hundred school districts and numerous educational agencies. He served as a policy consultant with the Alabama State Department of Education for twelve years and received numerous awards in recognition of his contributions in the field of education. He is the recipient of the Truman M. Pierce Award for Educational Leadership and outstanding contributions that advanced the direction of education in the state of Alabama; the Academic Excellence Award, in recognition of professional achievement and academic excellence in the research, service, and teaching of education; Capstone College of Education Society, Academic Excellence Award, The University of Alabama; the Distinguished Service Award— *Who's Who in the State of Tennessee;* The University of Memphis Distinguished Administrator of the Year 1995–96; "Educator on the Move," The University of Memphis; Phi Delta Kappa, the President's Award for Leadership and Service to the Community, Youth Services, Inc.; *Who's Who in Corporate Memphis, Grace* Magazine; President Bush's Community Service Award; Alpha Beta Gamma, President of the Year 2004; and Community Hero, Memphis Grizzlies; just to name a few. Essex has published numerous articles, book chapters, and newsletters on legal issues. Many of his works appear in *The Administrator's Notebook, The Horizon, Compensation Review, The Clearinghouse, The American School Board Journal, American Management Association, Community College Review, Education and Law,* and many other professional journals. He is highly sought by educators at all levels to share his knowledge and expertise regarding legal issues that impact public schools.

Dedicated to my wife Lorene, and my children, Kimberly, Jarvis, and Nathalie. They have been and continue to be my inspiration and my greatest fans.

CONTENTS

PREFACE

How do educational leaders respond to the legal challenges facing their organizations in a highly litigious society? How do they ensure that their organizations are achieving their mission without unduly restricting the constitutional rights and personal freedoms of their students and staff? How do leaders know when they are operating within the law? How can they build and foster an organizational culture that places high value on the personal rights and uniqueness of each individual? These are issues this book addresses. The courts expect educational leaders to possess the necessary knowledge and skill that will enable them to meet legal challenges that impact their organizations.

School Law and the Public Schools: A Practical Guide for Educational Leaders, Sixth Edition, is based on the premise that educational leaders and policy makers must be knowledgeable of the law that governs the operation and conduct of their organizations as they face a highly litigious society. Increasingly, educational leaders need to exercise discretion in making sound and legally defensible decisions that affect students and school personnel under their authority. They need to guide the development and execution of sound and well-developed policies, rules, and regulations governing many aspects of their operation. Educational leaders must ensure that they possess the legal knowledge necessary to accomplish these important administrative tasks successfully.

NEW TO THIS EDITION

The basic intent of this sixth edition is to better equip educational leaders and policy makers with relevant and timely information that will assist them in meeting legal challenges while minimizing legal exposure as they execute their defined duties and responsibilities in a highly litigious environment. The goal of the sixth edition is to provide comprehensive and practical information regarding relevant and emerging contemporary issues that impact the organization and administration of public schools. An additional goal is to better prepare educators at all levels to perform their professional duties within the boundaries of the U.S. Constitution, statutory law, case law, and school district policies. Information included in this edition will focus on practices that are legally defensible as well as those that are not. Knowledge of existing and emerging legal issues will enable educational leaders to exercise discretion in addressing the myriad legal issues they face on a daily basis. Increasingly, school leaders are expected to operate within the context of well-defined policies, rules, and regulations governing all aspect of their organizations. This edition will ensure that they possess the legal knowledge necessary to accomplish their essential administrative tasks successfully. The sixth edition includes the following additions and revisions:

- New addition to chapter on *legal framework* to include searching case law and the trial process
  - Guidance in identifying and researching cases and a visual depiction of how the trial process works
- Revised chapter on *religion* includes a discussion of prayer at legislative meetings, religious banners at football games, and legislation on acknowledging Christmas in schools
  - Includes an in-depth discussion of all issues relating to the Exercise Clause of the First Amendment
- *Search and Social Media*
  - Provides guidance regarding the extent to which school personnel may or may not search cell phones of students in public schools
- Use of *electronic devices* by students and teachers
  - Provides guidance regarding academic advantages of electronic devices in the classroom for instructional purposes

- Procedures for *Evaluating Threats*
  - Includes steps that should be taken to properly assess and respond to threats in schools
- *Legal Liability and Hazing*
- *Zero Tolerance and Due Process*
  - Discusses the issue regarding the fairness of zero tolerance policies in the context of Fourteenth Amendment applications
- *English Language Learners and Special Education*
  - Examines the issues surrounding misclassification of English learners into special education based on English language deficiencies
- *Multitiered System of Support*
  - Discusses the tiered learning system as a mechanism to improve learning outcomes for all students including students with special needs
- *Liability at Bus Stops*
  - Discusses the legal limits of school or district liability regarding student activities at bus stops
- *School Liability and Technology Use by Students*
  - Provides guidance for school personnel regarding potential liability for negligence in failing to monitor how students use technology in schools
- *Digitizing Student Records*
  - Discusses advantages and precautions that should be exercised by school personnel regarding digitization of student records and student privacy issues
- *Student Complaints and FERPA*
  - Discusses the extent to which students are covered under FERPA when they register complaints regarding their teachers
- *Teachers' Use of Facebook and Other Social Media*
  - Discusses the dangers associated with teachers' use of Facebook and other social media and the inherent problems associated with communicating with students
- *Transgender Teachers*
  - Discusses the rights afforded transgender teachers and how they should be treated in schools
- *Unwed Pregnant Teachers*
  - Discusses the rights of pregnant teachers and the privileges they should be afforded in schools
- *Genetic Information Discrimination Act*
  - Defines actions that are discriminatory with respect to requesting or requiring disclosure of genetic information regarding a prospective employee or his/her family members when rendering an employment decision
- *Vague Interviews*
  - Provides guidance regarding the appropriateness or inappropriateness of certain inquiries during the interview process
- *Retention of Personnel Data*
  - Provides insight relative to the length of time in which certain personnel records should be maintained for legal purposes
- *School Leader Evaluation*
  - Provides guidance with respect to factors that might be considered in assessing leadership effectiveness
- *Teaching Evaluation*
  - Provides information regarding myriad factors to be considered in assessing teacher effectiveness

- *Documentation of Teacher Performance*
  - Discusses methods of recording vital information regarding teaching performance as a means of assisting teachers in improving performance

- *Insubordination Steps*
  - Provides a systematic and legally defensible process for determining whether a teacher's conduct constitutes insubordination.

- *Documentation of Teacher Misconduct*
  - Discusses legal steps that should be considered in determining teacher misconduct

- *McKinney-Vento Homeless Assistance Act*
  - Provides guidance regarding the liberty interests of homeless students to attend public schools and the support systems that are required to ensure that they are provided an opportunity to succeed.

- *Common Core Standards*
  - Provides an overview of Common Core Standards to include objectives, outcomes, and opposition regarding these standards

This book is organized and written in a style that facilitates ease of reading even for individuals who have little or no legal background. Significant court cases are carefully selected to address issues that are most relevant to effective practice. The text begins with an in-depth focused discussion of the development of the U.S. Constitution and major legal issues, followed by relevant constitutional, statutory, and case law. Legal citations are used to support and enhance the discussion of these issues, and a section on searching case law and the trial process also is included. Legal references supporting the topics under discussion are found on each page, thus enabling the reader to easily ascertain the legal sources of authority related to those particular topics.

One unique and salient feature of this text is its focus on the development of administrative guides that relate to major issues discussed in each chapter. These guides provide leaders with information pertinent to directing their day-to-day decisions and actions as they encounter a wide array of legal challenges within their organizations. No attempt was made to review or include a significant number of state statutes or interpretations because variations are numerous from state to state. The primary focus of this text involves legal sources or developments that have significant implications for effective educational leadership throughout public schools in the United States. A significant component of the book is the inclusion of case studies at the end of each chapter that provide meaningful application exercises for educational leaders, thus allowing them to make sound and legally defensible decisions.

The book concludes with appendices that include selected amendments of the U.S. Constitution, as well as an expanded glossary of important legal terms to assist the reader and provide relevance to the body of the text. *School Law and the Public Schools,* Sixth Edition, provides a practical and useful resource guide for educational leaders and is aimed at increasing their knowledge and awareness of the complex legal issues that impact their organizations. It will enable them to more effectively perform their legal duties and meet the requirements of reasonableness as they move their organization toward their mission.

The *Instructor's Manual with Test Items* is available online to adopters. Please contact your local Pearson representative for access.

ACKNOWLEDGMENTS

I would like to express my heartfelt appreciation to my administrative assistant, Carol Brown, for the countless hours spent preparing this document. Her energy, enthusiasm, encouragement, and support far exceeded my expectations. For her untiring efforts, I am eternally grateful.

I would also like to express my appreciation to my wife, Lorene, and my children, Kimberly, Jarvis, and Nathalie, for their love, support, and encouragement during the writing of this text. Their support provided me inspiration to persevere through the completion of this project.

I express gratitude to my daughter, Nathalie, an attorney, for her editorial research and technical assistance, which aided me greatly in the production of this book.

I would also like to thank the following reviewers for their time and input:

Brett Geier, University of South Florida; Susan Sostak, Loyola University Chicago; Joe Flora, University of South Carolina; Terry McDaniel, Indiana State University, and Richard "Kent" Murray, The Citadel.

Last, I express appreciation to my administrative team, friends, and colleagues for their support and encouragement during the writing of this sixth edition.

To my staff, colleagues, and family, I am immensely grateful.

— N.L.E.

Chapter 1

Legal Framework Affecting Public Schools

SOURCES OF LAW

Public schools as governmental agencies must operate within the boundaries of law at the local, state, and federal levels. Therefore, school personnel are expected to perform their prescribed duties within a framework of law. A number of legal sources affect the administration and operation of schools.

Bill of Rights and the Fourteenth Amendment

The Bill of Rights represents the primary source of individual rights and freedoms under the U.S. Constitution. The first ten amendments to the Constitution are viewed as fundamental liberties of free people because they place restrictions on the government's powers to intrude on the fundamental rights of all citizens. These restrictions simply mean that the government cannot exercise certain powers in relationship to free people. For example, the government cannot pass laws prohibiting the freedom of speech. Consequently, citizens may speak freely within the boundaries of the Constitution without undue interference by the government. At its inception, the Bill of Rights limited only the federal government's powers and not those of state government, which meant that each state relied on its own bill of rights to limit state powers.

However, this changed with the adoption in 1868 of the Fourteenth Amendment, which guarantees that due process of law and fundamental fairness are applied to the states. The Fourteenth Amendment stipulates, "No State shall make or enforce any law which shall abridge the privileges or immunities of citizens of the United States; nor shall any State deprive any person of life, liberty, or property, without due process of law; nor deny to any person within its jurisdiction the equal protection of the laws." Fourteenth Amendment provisions are considered federal law and are enforced by state or federal courts operating within their proper jurisdictions.

Before the adoption of the Fourteenth Amendment, very few controls were placed on state governments if they failed to abide by their own bills of rights. Relief could be sought only in the state courts without any certainty that these courts would enforce their own states' bills of rights. Federal courts had no authority to enforce a state bill of rights that was solely under the jurisdiction of state courts. By virtue of the Fourteenth Amendment, that authority is now **vested** in the federal courts.

Along with due process and equal protection provisions, the most formidable freedoms contained in the Bill of Rights include freedom of speech, press, assembly, and religion as well as freedom from unreasonable searches and protection against self-incrimination. Thus, the first ten amendments now apply to encroachment by state government. Because public schools are agents of the state, they are subject to the provisions of the Bill of Rights, which means that school officials must recognize and respect the constitutional rights of students and school personnel. Failure to do so will result in infringement of constitutionally protected rights and possible legal challenges through the courts.

The Federal Constitution

The Constitution of the United States is the basic law of the land. It provides a framework of law in which orderly governmental processes operate. The Constitution thus becomes the primary source of law. All statutes enacted at the federal, state, and local levels as well as state constitutions, local regulations, and ordinances are subordinate to the Constitution.

The U.S. Constitution is distinguishable in its provision to protect the fundamental rights of all citizens of the United States. Inherent among these rights are those involving personal, property, and political freedoms. Although the Constitution does not make reference to education, it impacts the operation and management of schools, particularly with respect to amendments, which protect the individual rights of students, faculty, and staff.

One salient feature of the Constitution is the provision that calls for the separation of powers involving the executive, judicial, and legislative branches of government. The precept of separated powers provides each branch with the proper checks and balances on the powers of other branches.

Key Amendments

Several amendments to the U.S. Constitution have a direct bearing on the operation of public schools, namely the following:

The **First Amendment** addresses basic personal freedoms of students and school personnel involving speech, press, assembly, and religion.

The **Fourth Amendment** addresses rights to privacy and protects students and school personnel from unreasonable intrusion into their person or property.

The **Fifth Amendment** provides protection against self-incrimination in cases when the individual's life, liberty, or property is in jeopardy.

The **Eighth Amendment** does not directly apply to school discipline but has been referenced by parents and students in cases involving corporal punishment where there is an **allegation** of cruel and unusual punishment by school personnel. The intent of the Eighth Amendment is to protect individuals against cruel and unusual punishment involving those who have committed criminal offenses.

The **Tenth Amendment** reserves education as a state function, thus placing the primary responsibility for public schools on individual states.

The **Fourteenth Amendment** addresses the due process rights of students and school personnel to ensure that equal protection under the laws and fundamental fairness occur in matters involving deprivation of liberty and property.

State Constitutions

Based on the Tenth Amendment to the U.S. Constitution, powers not delegated to the United States by the Constitution, nor prohibited by it to the states, are reserved to the states respectively. Because education is not mentioned in the Tenth Amendment, it is left to states to control. Therefore, state constitutions represent the basic source of law for individual states and generally require legislative bodies to perform various functions, including establishing systems of public education. They prescribe funding and operational schemes for public schools. State constitutions also restrict the powers that legislative bodies may exercise.

State constitutions often address the same subject matter found in the U.S. Constitution, such as due process, individual rights and freedoms, and separation of church and state. State constitutions may exceed coverage granted by the U.S. Constitution but may not fail to meet the basic requirements of the Constitution or contradict it in any manner. Thus, a state statute may be in direct conflict with both federal and state constitutions or may violate one and be in compliance with the other. In all cases, federal and state constitutions prevail.

Statutes

Statutes represent acts of the legislative branch of government. The word *statute* is derived from the Latin term *statutum,* meaning "it is decided." Statutes are the most abundant source of law affecting public schools. School district policy, rules, and regulations generally are based on statutory law. Because education is considered a state function by virtue of the Tenth Amendment, courts tend to support the view that state legislatures should exercise power over public schools. It is only when statutes conflict with the U.S. Constitution, federal law, or state constitutions that a challenge is brought to the courts. In short, statutes are always subject to review by the judicial branch of government to determine their constitutionality. Statutes represent the most effective means of developing new law or changing old laws.

State legislators grant local school boards the authority to adopt and enforce reasonable rules and regulations necessary for the operation and management of schools. When challenged, school officials must be able to demonstrate that a legitimate state interest is met by enforcing a particular rule or regulation, especially in cases where individual freedoms are restricted.

Court or Case Law

Case law is generally reflected in judge-made or common law, as distinguished from statutory law. **Common law** consists of the **judgments**, opinions, and decisions of courts adopting and enforcing preceding usages and customs. Frequently, case law relies on past court decisions, which are called *precedents.* This practice is derived from the rule of law known as *stare decisis,* a Latin term meaning "let the decision stand." This doctrine requires courts to observe legal precedents established in previous cases in the same jurisdictions in making future decisions involving the same or similar subject matter and factual circumstances. Although courts generally rely on precedent, they are not absolutely bound by it in rendering a decision. Factual circumstances may be sufficiently different to warrant a different decision, even when the subject matter is similar. Moreover, the rationale used in reaching the decision may not be viewed as applicable to the particular case under review. Federal courts, in their rulings, have contributed to a significant body of case law, which affects the development of educational policies governing the administration and operation of public schools.

Case law is sometimes viewed as unsettled law because occasionally courts render conflicting rulings within their jurisdictions. Thus, a ruling by a federal, district, or appellate court only affects educational policymakers in that particular jurisdiction. Consequently, what is actually practiced, accepted, and enforced varies by time and place regardless of precedent. For example, if a Florida court sets a precedent, schools in Connecticut are not bound by the decision because they are not located in the same jurisdiction. The U.S. Supreme Court is the single court whose decisions affect the organization and administration of public schools across the nation. Even so, in many instances state and federal appellate decisions are not followed due, in large measure, to the fact that the Supreme Court has no ability to hear every conceivable issue relating to schools.

Researching Case Law

A case is a written decision issued by a court.[1] Federal and state courts publish their decisions in reporters. These reporters are organized chronologically. This system provides a methodology to research case law relevant to student conduct as well as permissible teacher and administrative action. The most effective means of understanding the context of a case and its application is to read the case in its entirety. The facts and the **holding** (the court's decision) of the case provide key information that will be helpful in understanding the genesis of the law in a particular area.

There are free legal research sites such as Lexis-Nexis, Westlaw, and FindLaw. Each of these sites provides an opportunity to conduct case research by citation, case name, and subject matter. These sites typically provide access to post-1990 court opinions with the exception of United States Supreme Court opinions, which typically are accessible to the public. Access to any case law prior to this time may require a paid membership. Access to these sites provides an opportunity to read and gain a better understanding of the law on any particular subject matter of interest.

LOCATING A CASE BY CITATION.   *New Jersey v. TLO* will be used as an example in the following discussion to illustrate how to conduct case research.

A standard three-part citation indicates where to find the case:

Volume Number	Reporter	Page Number
469	US	325

Simply entering this citation into a search box will enable the researcher to easily locate any case that is being researched. Another research option is locating the case style (name of court, case number, and names of plaintiffs and defendants) or case name.

FINDING A CASE BY CASE NAME.   Enter in the find by name or case name search box:

New Jersey v. TLO

Case names are organized by party names. The plaintiff is listed first and the defendant second. Entering the style or name of a case will also facilitate the location of the case desired.

LOCATING A CASE BY TOPIC.   The *New Jersey v. TLO* decision centered on searches in public schools. Because this is a Supreme Court decision, a simple word search of "public school searches and United States Supreme Court" will reveal the decisions of the Supreme Court relating to public school searches.

State Agencies

State legislatures in virtually all states have created administrative agencies to execute various laws and policies governing public schools. One of these agencies typically includes state boards of education. The legislature generally prescribes the duties and scope of authority delegated to state boards. Members of each state board of education are either appointed by the governor or elected by popular vote by citizens within the state. Conflicts frequently arise with state boards of education based on the separation of the executive, legislative, and judicial branches of government. The legislature is prohibited from delegating its powers to an administrative agency.

For example, the legislature in the state of Illinois commanded the superintendent of public instruction to prepare specifications for minimum requirements to conserve the health and safety of students. The specifications developed by the superintendent of instruction were challenged by the board of education under a claim that they were unconstitutional. The board sought injunctive relief against their enforcement. The circuit court granted relief. The superintendent appealed the decision. The Supreme Court of Illinois held that the statute was a proper delegation of administrative authority to the superintendent. However, the superintendent's specifications, which preempted the entire field of school safety and purported to strike down all local codes and ordinances relating to school safety, were invalid. Only the legislature had the power to preempt local codes and ordinances regarding school safety.

STATE BOARDS OF EDUCATION.   The state board of education may exercise broad or limited powers, based on legislative authorization. Public schools generally are placed under the control of the state board of education. In this capacity, the state board of education determines, to some degree, the direction of education in its state and also functions as a planning and evaluative body that functions immediately below the legislature. Through delegated power, the board may develop policies covering an array of legal issues such as, among others, health and safety, minimum requirements for teacher licensure, graduation requirements for students, rights of students with disabilities, and student disciplinary practices. The courts generally recognize the board's authority based on state statute to regulate student and school personnel conduct as long as its actions are not **arbitrary** or capricious.

In general, most state boards have six legal powers in common. They (1) establish certification standards for teachers and administrators, (2) establish high school graduation requirements, (3) establish state testing programs, (4) establish standards for accreditation of school districts and teacher and administrator preparation programs, (5) review and approve the budget of the state education agency, and (6) develop rules and regulations for the administration of state programs.[*]

State boards of education may not abrogate responsibilities delegated to them by state statutes. The courts are reluctant to impose their judgment regarding decisions that are made within the state board of education's designated authority unless there is evidence of arbitrary and capricious acts or a violation of an individual's constitutional rights. In such cases, the courts will intervene to determine whether the evidence supports constitutional violations. In reviewing the action of an administrative board, one court has held that it will go no further than to determine (1) whether the board acted within its jurisdiction, (2) whether it acted according to law, (3) whether its action was arbitrary, oppressive, or unreasonable and represented its will rather than its judgment, and (4) whether the evidence was such that it might reasonably make the order or determination in question.[2]

In addition to state boards of education, each state has a state department of education, which is headed by a state superintendent or chief state school officer (CSSO). State departments are the professional arm of the CSSO. These departments consist of specialists in virtually all areas relating to education. They provide consultation and advice to local school districts, the state board, and the CSSO. State departments generally are depositories for massive amounts of research data and strategic reports collected from local school districts. Much of these data consists of reports necessary to ensure that the state is in compliance with federal and state **mandates** and to facilitate education planning at the state and local levels. Among other duties, the state department of education conducts research on school practices, develops short- and long-term plans for educational outcomes, enforces state and federal law, evaluates districts for accreditation, evaluates statewide testing programs, and monitors compliance of state-approved curriculum.

Local School Boards

Local school boards impact education policy and the administration of public schools. The school board exercises general supervision over the schools within its district. However, its broader role involves the formulation of school district policy. Consequently, it is viewed as a policy-making body. School district policy is generally based on state statute. If consistent with state and federal laws, state and federal constitutions, and court rulings, school district policies are considered to be legally enforceable.

The local school board has a responsibility to formulate a vision that defines the future it envisions for the district. Certain goals, objectives, and measurable outcomes may be included as integral components of the board's vision.

The vision of the school district is closely aligned with the district's mission. The mission generally defines the basic purpose of the district and the core values embraced by the district as

[*]Reprinted with permission from 2009 Education Commission of the States, "Equipping Leaders, Advancing Ideas," 700 Broadway, #1200, Denver, CO 80203-3460.

it moves toward achieving its mission. Virtually all districts have formulated standards of performance for both students and teachers that in general are closely aligned with state standards related to No Child Left Behind provisions. Certain performance measures are established to determine the extent to which specified standards are met. The board has a leading responsibility for formulating goals that contribute to student achievement and continuous improvement of all educational programs. The board typically functions as the appellate body involving faculty, staff, and students when legal issues emerge involving recommended sanctions such as suspensions, expulsions, and dismissal.

The board is responsible for the formulation of policies, rules, and regulations that provide direction for the administration and operation of schools. The board is viewed as a corporate body. Therefore, individual board members have no power beyond the power that is granted to the full board by the legislature. Consequently, individual school board members are not free to formulate policy or to act independently of the board as a whole. School board members are considered public school officers and are granted powers by the legislature that are essential to the execution of their duties and responsibilities. The board is typically advised by its attorney and strives to act within legal boundaries established by the U.S. Constitution, state constitutions, state and federal statutes, and relevant court decisions affecting the school district.

The size of school boards varies and is generally determined by state statute. The number of school board members is typically odd to prevent a pattern of tie votes. Board members are either appointed or elected. School boards generally consist of five to seven members, although some districts may have fewer than five or more than seven.

One very significant duty of the school board involves the selection of its superintendent, unless the board operates in one of the few states where the superintendent is elected by citizens within the district. The relationship between the superintendent and the school board is best described as a legislative–executive one within which the board formulates policy and the superintendent executes policy. The board delegates certain duties and responsibilities and holds the superintendent accountable for performing them. The board evaluates the effectiveness of its policies and may revise or delete existing policies or formulate new ones based on district needs.

The board also adopts an annual budget covering personnel, instruction, student services, transportation, facilities, equipment, and materials needed to meet desired educational outcomes. Professional and support personnel are employed by the board based on the superintendent's recommendation. If the board has defensible grounds, it has the latitude to accept or reject personnel recommendations. Terms and conditions, salary schedules, and overall staffing and evaluation policies are determined by the board.

Because the board is accountable to the public, it is expected to operate in an open and transparent manner. Thus, school board meetings are viewed as open meetings, as virtually all states have enacted "sunshine laws" that allow citizens to attend open meetings and be informed of actions taken by the board. Citizens may request an opportunity to be included on the board's agenda during a regular board meeting in order to speak on issues that are of concern to themselves or the community at large. Citizens may also access school board minutes because they are considered public records.

School boards may hold executive sessions to discuss sensitive matters such as employee discipline, **contract** issues, or attorney–board consultation. Only board members may attend these meetings. The intent of these meetings is to protect the confidentiality of sensitive information or potentially damaging information that may injure a person's good name or reputation. Consequently, all items discussed during executive sessions are confidential and should not be divulged by board members.

School boards are expected to be accountable to the general public and specifically to their communities for what occurs in the district regarding school safety, student achievement, teaching performance, financial management, and other areas of importance. In recent years, the No Child Left Behind Act has changed the culture of schools through the enactment of initiatives aimed at an assessment of year-to-year student progress based on statewide assessment measures.

The school board has a leading responsibility for establishing high quality standards and system priorities centered on enhancing student achievement. Not only is it expected to establish high-quality performance standards, but it also has a responsibility to create an environment and climate within which excellent teaching and learning occur. Therefore, the board must ensure to the greatest degree possible that proper resources are provided to achieve desired district outcomes and that funds are administered responsibly.

SCHOOL BOARD POLICIES.   School board policies represent a basic source of law for school personnel as reflected in the rules and regulations governing the total operation of schools. School board policies are legally defensible as long as they do not conflict with the federal or state constitutions, federal or state statutes, or case law. Once these legal requirements are met, the school board as the delegated policy-making body at the local level may not violate its own policies. A school board is legally required to adhere to its own policies. Failure to do so may result in legal challenges by those adversely affected by the board's actions.

THE U.S. SYSTEM OF COURTS

The judicial system consists of federal and state courts. The organization of the courts at both levels is essentially the same: trial courts, intermediate courts of appeal, and the highest court, which is the U.S. Supreme Court. State constitutions usually prescribe the powers of state courts as well as their jurisdiction. Irrespective of the level, courts are limited only to cases or legal conflicts presented to them for resolution. Courts cannot take it upon themselves to decide on the constitutionality of a statute or a policy unless a **suit** is brought challenging the legality of that particular statute or policy.

The courts usually perform three types of judicial functions when they are called on to act. They (1) settle controversies through applying basic principles of law to specific factual circumstances, (2) interpret legislative enactments, and (3) determine the constitutionality of legislative or administrative mandates. When applying principles of law to specific situations, the courts may find that principles of law are vague or ambiguous. In such cases, the courts must rely on legal precedent for direction.

In interpreting statutes, the courts, through their analogies and rulings, may actually affect the definition of the legislation by assigning meaning to it. When determining the constitutionality of statutes, courts make the presumption that such statutes are constitutional. Consequently, those who challenge the legality of the statute must assume the burden of proof to demonstrate otherwise. The Supreme Court in Florida addressed this issue as follows:

> We have held that legislative acts carry such a strong presumption of validity that they should
> be held constitutional if there is any reasonable theory to that end.... Moreover, unconstitu-
> tionality must appear beyond all reasonable doubt before an act is condemned. ... If a statute
> can be interpreted in two different ways, one by which it will be constitutional, courts will
> adopt the constitutional interpretation.[3]

Federal Courts

Federal courts typically deal with cases involving federal or constitutional issues ("federal questions") or cases in which the parties are residents of different states ("diversity of citizenship"). The federal court system includes district courts, **appellate courts**, and the Supreme Court. There are ninety-five federal district courts in the United States. At least one federal court is found in each state; larger states, such as New York and California, have as many as four. Federal courts usually hear cases between citizens of different states and cases involving **litigation of federal statutes**.

Federal appellate courts are represented by circuit courts of appeal. The thirteen federal circuit courts include eleven with geographic jurisdiction over a number of states and territories, one for the District of Columbia, and one involving three specialized federal courts. Table 1.1 and Figure 1.1 identify the geographic areas associated with each circuit.

Many judges sit on the various courts of appeals; for example, the Sixth Circuit Court of Appeals has fourteen judges and eight "senior" judges available to sit in panels of three judges. The primary function of the appellate court is to review the proceedings of lower courts to determine whether errors of law (as opposed to facts) were committed, such as procedural irregularities, constitutional misinterpretations, or inappropriate application of rules of evidence. Panels of

TABLE 1.1	Jurisdiction of Federal Circuit Courts of Appeal
Circuit	**Jurisdiction**
1st	Maine, Massachusetts, New Hampshire, Puerto Rico, Rhode Island
2nd	Connecticut, New York, Vermont
3rd	Delaware, New Jersey, Pennsylvania, Virgin Islands
4th	Maryland, North Carolina, South Carolina, Virginia, West Virginia
5th	Louisiana, Mississippi, Texas
6th	Kentucky, Ohio, Michigan, Tennessee
7th	Illinois, Indiana, Wisconsin
8th	Arkansas, Iowa, Minnesota, Missouri, Nebraska, North Dakota, South Dakota
9th	Alaska, Arizona, California, Guam, Hawaii, Idaho, Montana, Nevada, Northern Mariana Islands, Oregon, Washington
10th	Colorado, Kansas, New Mexico, Oklahoma, Utah, Wyoming
11th	Alabama, Florida, Georgia
DC	Washington, DC
Federal	Washington, DC (specialized courts)

Source: Administrative Office of the U.S. Courts. (n.d.). *Court Locator.* USCourts.gov. Retrieved September 14, 2010, from http://www.uscourts.gov/courtlinks

FIGURE 1.1   U.S. Courts: The Federal Judiciary

SOURCE: Administrative Office of the U.S. Courts. (n.d.). *Court Locator.* USCourts.gov. Retrieved September 14, 2010, from http://www.uscourts.gov/courtlinks

judges for appellate courts hear oral arguments from the appellant and the appellee, examine written arguments, vote, and render a ruling. The appellate court may also, based on its finding, **remand** the case to be retried by the lower court.

State Courts

State courts are the part of each state's judicial system with the responsibility of hearing cases involving issues related to state constitutional law, state statutes, and common law. Many education cases are heard in state courts because they do not involve a federal question. The structure of state courts is similar to those found in the federal courts: courts of general juris-diction, courts of special jurisdiction, courts of limited jurisdiction, and appellate courts. The names of these courts vary among the fifty states, but all states have at least three to four tiers of courts.

State statutes generally prescribe the types of cases that must be heard by the various courts within a state. Discretionary jurisdiction involves cases in which a party files **a petition** to the state supreme court seeking redress. It is then left to the court to use its discretion (or **discretionary power**) in deciding to accept or reject the case. It is important to understand that state courts play a vital role in addressing many issues involving the administration of public schools.

COURTS OF GENERAL JURISDICTION.   Courts of general jurisdiction are often referred to as dis-trict or circuit courts. Their jurisdiction covers most cases except those held for special courts. In many instances, decisions of these courts may be appealed to intermediate appellate courts or even to the state supreme court. Areas adjudicated by these courts include civil, criminal, traffic, and juvenile issues.

COURTS OF SPECIAL JURISDICTION.   Courts of special jurisdiction hear legal disputes on special matters. They are generally referred to as trial courts with *limited* jurisdiction and may be called municipal, justice of the peace, probate, small claims, or traffic court.

INTERMEDIATE APPELLATE COURTS.   Intermediate appellate courts have emerged over the past three decades to hear **appeals** from trial courts or certain state agencies. Their primary role involves reviewing proceedings from trial courts to determine whether substantive or procedural errors occurred in applying the law. In a sense, their duties are similar to those of the highest court within the state; however, the primary difference between the two courts is discretion: The intermediate court has less discretion in accepting cases than does the high-est or state supreme court. Many, but not all, of the cases heard by the intermediate courts are mandatory.

APPELLATE COURTS.   Appellate courts represent the highest courts within the state. They are considered courts of last resort. In forty-four states, these are referred to as the state supreme courts. These courts have some discretion in accepting cases, but they must hear mandatory cases based on appeal and decide on the merits of each.

See Figure 1.2, which depicts the progression of a case through the U.S. court system.

THE TRIAL PROCESS.   There are five essential stages to a trial. These stages are as follows:

1. **Pleadings stage** involves a **complaint** filed by the plaintiff and an answer to the complaint by the defendant. The defendant may also file **a motion** rather than an answer requesting that the court dismiss the case, or may require the plaintiff to further clarify the intent of the case.

2. **Pre-trial stage** is designed to seek resolution of issues that can be resolved prior to the trial. Issues are identified that are in dispute and must be resolved at trial versus issues that are not in dispute.

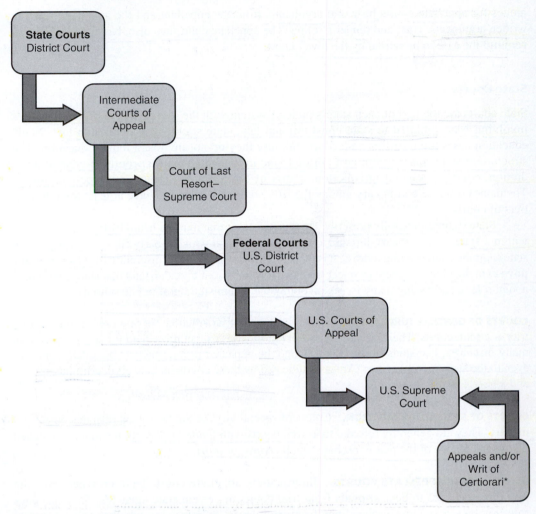

FIGURE 1.2   Case Progression Through the Court System

*A writ of certiorari is a discretionary review granted or denied by the U.S. Supreme Court.

③ **Motions** are used by attorneys to request that the court initiate a specific **action** by issuing an order to resolve a dispute. **Summary judgment** is an example, where the court decides to settle a dispute or dispose of a case promptly without conducting full legal proceedings because no issue, material, or facts exist that support a **cause of action**.

④ **Discovery stage** entails gathering evidence by attorneys from the plaintiff and defendant, which involves inspecting relevant documentation and interviewing individuals who are aware of the circumstances leading to the lawsuit. Depositions are taken and interrogatories also are initiated.

⑤ **Trial stage** consists of jury selection. If a jury is involved (as opposed to a bench trial) from a pool of potential jurors, jurors are questioned to determine their suitability to serve impartially. The judge and counsel for both the plaintiff and defendant are involved in this process. When a jury is seated, opening statements are made by the plaintiff's and defendant's attorneys. Closing arguments are also made by each attorney when the trial concludes. The judge provides specific instructions to the jury regarding the evaluation of the case prior to its deliberations.

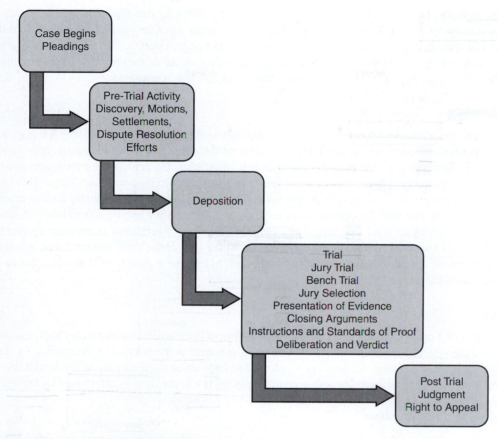

FIGURE 1.3   Trial Progression

 Post-trial stage consists of a verdict rendered by the jury and a ruling by the court. The party, either plaintiff or defendant, may appeal for the case to be heard by a higher court.

Steps involving pre-trial, discovery, and motions may be completed concurrently or inter-changeably depending upon the circumstances within the case.

See Figure 1.3 for components of the trial progression process.

ANALYSIS OF AN APPELLATE COURT OPINION

Court proceedings are concluded with a written opinion setting forth the decision of the court on an issue under review by the court. These opinions consist of a set of components designed to facilitate an understanding of the court's ruling. The most common elements include the name of the case, the year in which the case was decided by the court, the appellant's contention, the appellee's defense, the procedure by which the case reached the court, the facts giving rise to the case, the ruling of the court, the court's rationale for the ruling, and the final disposition on the issue.

Case (Citation)

Cases are usually named for the parties involved in the controversy. The party initiating the suit at the trial court level is referred to as the **plaintiff**. The party against whom the suit or action is brought is called the **defendant**. The plaintiff's name comes first, followed by the defendant's (e.g., *Baker v. Owen*). If the case is appealed, the party initiating the appeal who was not supported at the first level becomes the **appellant**, and the other party becomes the **appellee**. In this instance, the appellant is listed first and the appellee last (e.g., *Owen v. Baker*). Even though it may take as long as several years before all legal remedies are exhausted in a particular case, the year in the case citation indicates the time when the decision was rendered.

Procedure

The initiator of the suit (plaintiff) files a complaint seeking **relief** by the courts for alleged improper actions taken by the defendant or failure on the defendant's part to meet certain legal standards. In either case, the plaintiff contends that an indefensible act has been attributed to the defendant. The party against whom a complaint is filed responds to the complaint with a rationale as to why certain actions were or were not taken. The defendant attempts to justify actions taken in regard to the plaintiff. In appellate decisions, an explanation may be given as to how the case reached the appellate level. An appeal or a petition for a *writ of* **certiorari** is the most common means used to bring a case to a higher court level. At the U.S. Supreme Court level and in some state courts of appeals, the writ of certiorari is used to remove a case from a lower court to a higher court for review.

Facts

The facts of a case describe the specific details leading to the conflict or controversy that resulted in the case reaching the court. The facts describe the nature of the conflict as determined by the evidence presented during the actual proceeding. The facts are at issue only at the lower trial court level, not at the appeals stage. Appellate courts apply the law to the facts as determined by the trial.

Ruling and Justification

The ruling of the court, made manifest in the form of the written decision or opinion of the court, represents the court's response to the issue presented for its review. The ruling is usually accompanied by a justification detailing the basis on which the ruling was made. The ruling usually includes statements covering primary facts and the major conclusions reached by the courts. *Stare decisis*— the following of precedents—is an important component of all court decisions.

Disposition

The **disposition** follows the ruling of the case that determines whether the plaintiff or the defendant was supported by the courts in the dispute. Once the victor is determined, the court reaches a conclusion and orders that some action be taken consistent with its ruling. If the plaintiff wins, the court will prescribe a **remedy** for the **damages** suffered by the plaintiff. It may be in the form of an order compelling the defendant to compensate the plaintiff for damages or an **injunction** prohibiting the defendant from continuing a certain practice deemed to be unjust. If the defendant is upheld, the case may be dismissed with an order that the plaintiff pay court fees and other legal fees associated with the case. In some instances, the case may be passed to an appellate court to determine the proper remedy. The appellate court may uphold the lower court decision, reverse the lower court decision, or modify the decision in some manner. The court may also remand the case back to the lower court for further proceedings based on its review of the case.

THE U.S. SUPREME COURT

The U.S. Supreme Court is the highest court in the land. Unlike lower courts, there is no appeal beyond the decision of this court. The Supreme Court's ruling can be overturned only by an amendment to the U.S. Constitution. Nine justices, including a chief justice, comprise the High Court. To avoid political infringement, they are appointed to life terms.

Interestingly, the Supreme Court first convened in New York in 1790 and adjourned because it had nothing to do. It decided only fifty-six cases over a ten-year period, with very few of the cases having any real significance. Cases reach the Supreme Court primarily in two ways: on appeal and by writ of certiorari. The Supreme Court's review occurs in the following manner:

On Appeal (A Review by Right)

From State Courts
1. Where a state court has held a federal statute or treaty provision unconstitutional
2. Where a state court has upheld a state law or state constitutional provision arguably in conflict with the U.S. Constitution, laws, or treaties

From Federal Courts of Appeals
1. Where a federal law or treaty is held unconstitutional
2. Where a state law or state constitutional provision is held invalid because it conflicts with a federal law, treaty, or constitutional provision

From Federal District Courts (direct appeal to Supreme Court)
1. Where a federal statute having a criminal penalty is held unconstitutional
2. Where judgment has been rendered to enforce antitrust laws, the Interstate Commerce Act, or Title II of the Federal Communications Act
3. Where a three-judge district court grants or denies an injunction **restraining** enforcement of state statutes or federal statutes, or orders of certain federal agencies

On Certiorari (A Discretionary Review Granted or Denied by Vote of the Supreme Court)

From State Courts
1. In cases involving federal questions where the decision supported a federal claim made under federal law or constitutional provisions

From Federal Courts of Appeals
1. Where a decision interpreted or applied the Constitution or various federal laws

or

2. Where state laws or state constitutional provisions have been challenged in conflict with federal law where the court of appeals upheld the state provisions.[4]

Decisions reached by the Supreme Court are group decisions that presumably produce stability. Justices work collectively but independently to arrive at decisions. The High Court meets for thirty-six weeks, commencing on the first Monday of each October and ending during the week of July 7. The justices spend their time listening to lawyers' arguments, discussing court business, writing or studying opinions, and reading **briefs** submitted by attorneys. Each justice works six days a week, eight to ten hours each day. Court is open four days each week from Monday through Thursday. During this time, the justices listen four hours each day to oral arguments. Each case is given only one hour to argue its position, with the plaintiff and the defendant receiving thirty minutes each to make their points. The Court recesses for two weeks to allow the justices to perform their important duties relating to the business of the Court.

U.S. Supreme Court Ritual

On Fridays at 11:00 A.M., the justices meet in a conference room (which is lined with books from floor to ceiling at a marble fireplace). They meet under a painting of the great chief justice John James Marshall, the fourth chief justice of the United States, and shake hands, showing harmony of aims. Justices are called to chamber by a buzzer five minutes before 11:00 A.M.

Seated at the head of the table is the chief justice; directly across from him at the other end of the table sits the Senior Associate Justice. The rest sit on either side of the table according to rank in seniority, descending in seniority away from the chief justice. The most recently appointed justice serves as a "messenger," carrying messages in and out of the conference room. Discussion of issues passes from justice to justice according to seniority. After discussion, a vote is called—four votes bring a case to the Court; five votes dispose of it. If a justice disqualifies himself or herself and the vote is four to four, the lower court decision stands. Justices vote in reverse order, from least senior to most senior.

After voting, the case is assigned to a justice to write an opinion. Writing is assigned by the chief justice if he voted with the majority; if not, then the next most senior justice performs this task. When the opinion is written, it is disseminated to other justices for their concurrence (**concurring opinion**) or dissention (**dissenting opinion**); they also look for weaknesses. Frequently, the opinion is rewritten by the original author, sometimes as many as twenty-five times. It is then filed in Open Court.

U.S. Supreme Court Decisions

U.S. Supreme Court decisions include three citations that are often referred to as **parallel citations,** which means that the same case can be found in three different sets of documents. These sources are as follows:

1. *United States Reporter* (U.S.), the official reports of Supreme Court decisions
2. *Supreme Court Reporter* (Sup. Ct. or S.Ct.), published by West Publishing Company
3. *United States Supreme Court Reporter* (L. Ed.), published by Lawyers Cooperative Publishing Company

Parallel citations are illustrated in the following example: *Baker v. Carr,* 369 U.S. 186, 82 S.Ct. 691, 7 L. Ed. 2d 663 (1992). In the first citation, 369 refers to the volume in the *United States Reporter;* 186 refers to the page where the case can be found. In the second citation, 82 refers to the volume of the *Supreme Court Reporter;* 691 refers to the page where the case can be found. In the third citation, 7 refers to the *Lawyer's Edition* volume, 2d refers to the second edition, and 633 refers to the page where the case can be found. The 1992 inside parentheses denotes the year in which the decision was rendered. Any of these three sources may be used to locate a U.S. Supreme Court case.

LEGAL INFORMATION RETRIEVAL SYSTEMS

The two primary legal information retrieval systems are Westlaw and LexisNexis. Both are important sources for legal research and tools for legal professionals and practitioners.

Westlaw cites case law, state and federal statutes, and administrative **codes** as well as law journal reviews that may be found at the Westlaw legal research service. Westlaw contains more than 40,000 databases. These databases are indexed to the West Key Number System, which is Westlaw's Master Classification System of law in the United States. *The National Reporter System* is published by West and is the most prominent set of reporters. West publishes the following reporters containing decisions of the federal courts: (1) *Supreme Court Reporter* includes decisions of the United States Supreme Court, (2) *Federal Reporter* includes decisions of the various courts of appeals, and (3) *Federal Supplement* includes decisions of the various district courts. In addition to the West reporters, *United States Reports* is an official reporter for the U.S. Supreme Court. The Westlaw website may be accessed at http://web2.westlaw.com.

LexisNexis provides legal content from newspapers, magazines, and legal documents. This database contains public records, unpublished opinions, and legal news. LexisNexis services are found on two websites. One website, Lexis.com, is referenced for legal research, whereas Nexis.com is intended for corporations; local, state, and federal government; and professionals in academia. The Lexis database contains all current U.S. statutes and laws, nearly all published case opinions, and virtually all publicly available unpublished opinions.

Administrative Guide

Legal Framework

1. The U.S. Constitution is the fundamental law of the land. State laws and school district policies or administrative practices may not conflict with any constitutional amendments.
2. When developing school policies, the U.S. Constitution should be considered the primary source of law. Statutes should be considered the second primary source of law if they are consistent with the Constitution. If not, case law becomes the second primary source, with statutes becoming the third primary source.
3. Because education is a state function, state statutes create local school districts and establish all requirements that school districts must meet. Statutes are subject to review by the judicial branch of government to determine their constitutionality.
4. With the exception of U.S. Supreme Court decisions, school leaders must adhere to court rulings affecting their respective states and circuits for administrative guidance.
5. Local school boards as policy-making bodies are responsible for formulating districtwide school policy.
6. The courts will not permit local school boards to violate their own policies once they are determined to be legally defensible.

Resources

Supreme Court decisions may be located on the following websites:

westlaw.com

loislaw.com

lexisnexis.com

findlaw.com

supremecourt.gov

CASE STUDY

Local School Board Policies

Review your local school board policies with a focus on statutory law:

- Are your local policies consistent with state and federal law?
- Do they meet current and future needs?
- When were they last revised?
- Do you see policy voids—areas that should be covered, but are not covered?
- What recommendations would you make if you were provided an opportunity to improve these policies for the following?
  a. Relevance
  b. Legal defensibility
  c. Appropriateness based on need
  d. Codification

Endnotes

1. This definition of case may be located at: www.lawschool.cornell.edu/library/whatwedo/researchguides/basics.cfm#11
2. *Board of Education of the City of Rockford v. Page*, 211 N.E. 2d 361 (Ill. 1965).
3. *Hobbs v. County of Moore*, 267 N.C. 665, 149, S.E. 2d 1 (1966).
4. Arval A. Morris, *The Constitution and American Education* (St. Paul, MN: West Publishing, 1974). Reprinted with permission.

Chapter 2

Religion and the Public Schools

The Fourteenth Amendment, a key component of the U.S. Constitution, focuses on the rights and privileges of citizens of the United States in the provision that states:

> All persons born or naturalized in the United States, and subject to the jurisdiction thereof, are citizens of the United States and of the State wherein they reside. No State shall make or enforce any law which shall abridge the privileges or immunities of citizens of the United States; nor shall any State deprive any person of life, liberty, or property, without **due process** of law; nor deny to any person within its jurisdiction the equal protection of the laws.

Although the Fourteenth Amendment prohibited infringement on the rights of U.S. citizens, the Constitution as a whole made virtually no reference to religious liberties of U.S. citizens when it was ratified by the states. The only exception was a religious-test provision that prohibited states from imposing religious tests for federal offices. This provision became the last clause of Article VI of the Constitution. The omission of religious liberties in the Constitution was defended by James Madison, which led Thomas Jefferson to convince him that a religious provision was needed in the Bill of Rights. The uncertainty of whether religious rights were **implied** in the Constitution was sufficient to justify the need for a Bill of Rights protecting religious freedoms. Madison then introduced a series of proposals that included amendments aimed at preventing encroachment by government into the rights and liberties of all citizens. These proposals, presented to the House of Representatives, eventually became the Bill of Rights. Noticeable among these rights was the separation of church and state, which guarantees religious freedoms and prohibits the establishment of religion by the government.

Although religious freedoms are addressed in the Bill of Rights, conflicts involving church and state interactions have intensified over the past decade, as numerous challenges have been levied against public schools regarding certain questionable religious practices. Courts increasingly have been called on to determine the constitutional validity of these practices.

The tension between church and state issues relates to the requirement that the government maintain a neutral position toward religion. In 1879 in the landmark case *Reynolds v. United States,* the U.S. Supreme Court invoked Thomas Jefferson's view that there should be a wall of separation between church and state.[1]

The First Amendment serves as the basis for delineating certain individual religious rights and freedoms as well as governmental prohibitions regarding religion. The First Amendment to the U.S. Constitution states, "Congress shall make no law respecting an establishment of religion, or prohibiting the free exercise thereof; or abridging the freedom of speech, or of the press; or the right of the people peaceably to assemble, and to petition the Government for a redress of grievances."

Although the initial intent of the First Amendment prohibited Congress from making laws supporting religion or prohibiting individuals from exercising their religious rights, the U.S. Supreme Court, in a compelling decision, *Cantwell v. Connecticut,* held that this prohibition, aimed at Congress, also applied to the states.[2] The Fourteenth Amendment made the First Amendment applicable to state action, thus providing the same constitutional guarantees to citizens against state infringement of their religious rights by prohibiting the establishment of religious practices in public schools.

The First Amendment contains two essential clauses regarding religion: the Establishment Clause and the free exercise clause. The *Establishment Clause* prohibits the state from passing laws that aid a religion or show preference for one religion over another; the *free exercise clause* prohibits the state from interfering with individual religious freedoms. In a non–educational-related free exercise case involving Oregon's Department of Human Services, Alfred Smith and Glen Black were dismissed from their jobs because they violated a term of employment by ingesting the drug peyote. The State of Oregon considered the controlled substance to be a hallucinogen as classified by the Federal Controlled Substances Act. Both **respondents** are members of the Native American Church, which uses peyote in a sacramental ritual. They applied for unemployment compensation through the state and were denied based on having lost employment through misconduct. The lower court held that peyote can be criminally prohibited. Both respondents appealed the state's decision, relying on the free exercise clause of the First Amendment because the use of peyote was considered a religious ritual. The U.S. Supreme Court held that the free exercise clause of the First Amendment made applicable to the state does not prevent the State of Oregon from including a religiously inspired peyote use in its criminal prohibition of the drug. Therefore, the state may deny unemployment benefits to all users, including users of religious content. The High Court's conclusion was that the respondents' belief does not excuse them from acting lawfully as determined by a valid state law.[3] In an educational setting, the combined effect of the establishment and free exercise clauses compels public schools as state agencies to maintain a neutral position in their daily operations regarding religious matters. This means that the state can neither aid nor inhibit religion—it must adhere to the principle of neutrality. The intent of the Establishment Clause was clearly enunciated in the famous *Everson* case, in which the U.S. Supreme Court stated:

> The "establishment of religion" clause of the First Amendment means at least this: Neither a state nor the Federal Government can set up a church. Neither can pass laws which aid one religion, aid all religions, or prefer one religion over another. Neither can force nor influence a person to go to or to remain away from church against his will or force him to profess a belief or disbelief in any religion. No person can be punished for entertaining or professing religious beliefs or disbeliefs, for church attendance or non-attendance. No tax in any amount, large or small, can be levied to support any religious activities or institutions, whatever they may be called, or whatever form they may adopt to teach or practice religion. Neither a state nor the Federal Government can, openly or secretly, participate in the affairs of any religious organizations or groups and vice versa. In the words of Jefferson, the clause against establishment of religion by law was intended to erect "a wall of separation between Church and State."[4]

Since the *Cantwell* decision, which held that the Fourteenth Amendment makes the First Amendment applicable to state action, the Establishment Clause has significant implications for the administration of public schools.

The Establishment Clause essentially raises concerns in instances where school personnel act as government officials. When school officials are not acting in this capacity, the Establishment Clause does not restrict their religious freedom. Freedom of speech, freedom of association, and freedom of religion protect school personnel just as they protect the religious activities of other citizens. The courts have used the Endorsement and Coercion Tests in some instances to gain a clearer interpretation of the Establishment Clause of the First Amendment.[5] The Endorsement Test is typically relied on in cases where the government is engaged in activities involving free expression, as would be the case in situations regarding prayer at graduation exercises, religious symbols on government property, and religious content in school curricula. This test was advocated by Justice Sandra Day O'Connor when she raised the issue as to whether a particular government action amounts to an endorsement of religion. According to Justice O'Connor, a government action is invalid if it creates a perception in the mind of a reasonable observer that the government is either endorsing or disapproving religion. Her concern grew out of the *Lynch v. Donnelly* case in which she suggested that the Establishment Clause prohibits the government from endorsing religion in any manner.[6]

Under the Coercion Test, the government does not violate the Establishment Clause unless it provides direct aid to religion in a manner that would tend to establish a state church or it coerces people to support or participate in religion against their will. Under this test, the government would be allowed to erect religious symbols such as the Nativity Scene standing alone in a public school or other public building at Christmas. This test, however, is subject to varying interpretation, as was the case in *Lee v. Weisman* when Justices Kennedy and Scalia applied the same test and reached different results.[7] The Coercion Test was a product of Justice Kennedy's dissent in the *County of Allegheny v. ACLU* case that affects a person's standing in a political community. His concern was whether a specific government action conveys a message to non-subscribers that they are outsiders, rather than full members of the political community, and a different message to subscribers that they are, in fact, insiders favored by the community. The Endorsement Test has on occasion been merged into the *Lemon* Test.[8]

An interesting Establishment Clause decision was rendered when the U.S. Supreme Court let stand a decision by lower courts that a school district's Islam program did not violate the Establishment Clause of the First Amendment. Prior to the Court's order denying review, the U.S. Court of Appeals, Ninth Circuit, held that the program activities were not "overt religious exercises that raise Establishment Clause concerns." The action was brought by two families who alleged that a middle school world history teacher asked them to choose Muslim names, learn prayers, simulate Muslim rituals, and engage in other role-playing exercises. The Ninth Circuit held that the school district and individual school employees were entitled to qualified immunity "because they did not violate any constitutional right, let alone a clearly established one."[9]

SCHOOL-SPONSORED PRAYER

The issue of prayer in public schools was addressed in a landmark case in the early 1960s by the U.S. Supreme Court. Prior to this time, prayer was routinely offered in public schools across the nation and generally supported by the courts. In spite of the landmark *Engle* decision banning prayer in public schools, school prayer continues to be challenged by Congress, state legislatures, and citizens as they persist in seeking creative ways to support prayer in the nation's schools. For example, in 1996 a Republican congressman prepared an amendment to the Constitution designed to allow prayer in public schools. Representative Ernest Istook of Oklahoma indicated that he introduced a fifty-two-word "Religious Freedom Amendment" before Congress. Americans United for Separation of Church and State and other opponents were strongly opposed to such a measure and cited the harmful impact it would have for minority religions. This proposal represents just one example of congressional efforts to return prayer to public school. Prayer will continue to be a hotly contested issue, as it has quickly become one of the most highly debated topics in the United States today.

The U.S. Supreme Court first addressed prayer in public schools in the famous *Engle* case. A local board of education, acting under authority of a New York State law, ordered a brief non-denominational prayer to be said aloud by each class, in the presence of a teacher, at the beginning of each school day. The prayer had been composed by the state board of regents, which also had established the procedure for its recitation. Those children not wishing to pray were excused from this exercise. Parents brought action to challenge the constitutionality of both the state law that authorized the school district to mandate the use of prayer in public schools and the school district's action of ordering recitation of this particular prayer. State encouragement of the regular recitation of prayer in the public school system is unconstitutional. The High Court held that the statute authorizing prayer recitation in the public schools is in direct violation of the First Amendment prohibition of a state establishment of religion.[10]

In November 1996, the U.S. Supreme Court refused to revive a 1994 Mississippi statute that authorized voluntary student prayer at assemblies, sports events, and other school activities.

The High Court, without comment, allowed the lower court ruling to stand, which found the law unconstitutional and disallowed its implementation. Interestingly, the state did not, in its appeal to the Supreme Court, address the merits of the law itself but rather argued that the plaintiffs who challenged the law had no legal **standing** to do so. The state further argued that the law should not have been barred before it was actually enforced.

The lower court rejected both arguments, holding that the law violated the Establishment Clause of the First Amendment. This law was enacted by legislators after Bishop Knox, a high school principal, defied his superiors by permitting students to pray daily over the school's public address system. As a consequence, Knox was fired by the school board, but this was later reduced to a suspension due to widespread public support for his actions. The Mississippi law called for nonsectarian and nonproselytizing student-initiated prayer and voluntary prayer during school activities and events. This practice was challenged by the American Civil Liberties Union. Both the district court and the U.S. Court of Appeals for the Fifth Circuit barred this practice on the grounds that the state was endorsing a religion. However, the lower court let stand a previous ruling that allowed student-led voluntary prayer at graduation ceremonies.

The *Jones v. Clear Creek Independent School District* case (discussed later in this chapter) represented a major step for school prayer proponents. The Fifth Circuit Court held that nonschool-sponsored, student-initiated prayer at graduation ceremonies did not offend the First Amendment prohibition regarding separation of church and state. The court viewed this practice as an exercise of students' First Amendment rights to free speech, which did not create excessive entanglement between the church and state.[11] Also, under the No Child Left Behind Act, school districts are required to certify in writing to their state agencies that no local district policy prevents or denies participation in constitutionally protected prayer in their public schools. This requirement is a condition to the receipt of NCLB funds.

SCHOOL-SPONSORED BIBLE READING

In 1963, the U.S. Supreme Court addressed the constitutionality of the practice of Bible reading in public schools. Two similar cases reached the Supreme Court during the same period of time. *Abington School District v. Schempp* involved a challenge regarding the validity of a Pennsylvania state statute that required the reading of ten verses of the Bible without comment at the opening of each school day. A companion case, *Murray v. Curlett,* challenged the actual practice of daily Bible reading in the schools of Baltimore, Maryland.

In the former case, several members of the Unitarian Church brought suit against the state to prohibit the state from enforcing the statute, as it was contrary to their religious beliefs and in violation of the First Amendment. The legislature attempted to defend its practice by making provisions for students to be excused with parental consent, if the practice offended them.

The facts surrounding the *Murray* case were similar to those in the *Schempp* case, with the exception that no state statute was involved. The Supreme Court, in addressing both cases, ruled in an 8–1 decision that these Bible-reading practices were unconstitutional. The Court found these practices to be an advancement of religion and a clear violation of the separation of church and state. Justice Tom C. Clark, speaking for the majority, stated, "It is no defense to urge that the religious practices here may be a relatively minor encroachment on the First Amendment. The **breach** of neutrality that today is a trickling stream may all too soon become a raging torrent and, in the words of Madison, 'It is proper to take alarm at the first experiment on our liberties.'"[12]

The Supreme Court invoked the *primary effect test* to determine the impact of the statute and practice relating to each case. The primary effect test raises the question of whether the primary purpose of a law or practice has the effect of advancing or inhibiting religion and creating excessive entanglement between church and state. If the response to these questions is affirmative, the principle of neutrality has been breached and the act is considered to be an impermissible establishment of religion and a violation of the First Amendment. The Court did, however, indicate in the *Schempp* case that the use of the Bible as a historical, literary, ethical, or philosophical document is permissible if a secular purpose is clearly served.

SILENT PRAYER AND MEDITATION

In recent years, attempts also have been made by state legislatures to support some form of state-sponsored voluntary prayer or meditation in public schools. Their efforts, however, have been largely unsuccessful. Numerous challenges to these types of statutes or practices have been led by opposing parents and citizens. Their challenges cover a full range of school activities, such as meditation and prayer at school-sponsored athletic events and graduation ceremonies, both of which are discussed later in this chapter.

The U.S. Supreme Court, in 1985, responded to the silent meditation and prayer issue by their ruling in *Wallace v. Jaffree*. The case was initiated in 1982 by the father of three elementary students who challenged the validity of two Alabama statutes: a 1981 statute that allowed a period of silence for "meditation or voluntary prayer," and a 1982 statute authorizing teachers to lead "willing students" in a nonsectarian prayer composed by the state legislature. After a lower court found both statutes unconstitutional, the U.S. Supreme Court agreed to review only the portion of the lower court decision invalidating the 1981 statute that allowed "meditation or voluntary prayer." The Court concluded that the intent of the Alabama legislature was to affirmatively reestablish prayer in the public schools. Inclusion of the words "or voluntary prayer" in the statute indicated that it had been enacted to convey state approval of a religious activity and violated the First Amendment's Establishment Clause.[13] However, student-initiated meditation that is not endorsed by school officials will not likely violate the Establishment Clause so long as the school does not set aside moments or prescribe that students should do so and no disruption to the educational process occurs. Student-initiated meditation is considered to be a form of mental reflection exercised by students. Students may meditate to relax before taking an exam or to relieve stress they experience during the school day.

PRAYER AT SCHOOL EVENTS

Student-Led Prayer at Public School Events

In a significant development, a federal court of appeals held that the U.S. Supreme Court ruling in the *Santa Fe* case does not prevent students in Alabama from discussing religion in public schools or praying publicly, as long as such activities are voluntary. This ruling is significant in that it represents the first interpretation by an appeals court of the Supreme Court's *Santa Fe* decision. The recent circuit court ruling upholds its earlier decision permitting voluntary student-led prayer at public school events. In an earlier action, the Eleventh Circuit Court overturned a federal district court ruling that limited religious expression by students in DeKalb County, Alabama. The High Court asked the circuit court of appeals to reassess its decision based on its ruling in the *Santa Fe* case. The circuit court has stated in its most recent ruling that its decision was not in conflict with the High Court's ruling in *Santa Fe* based on voluntary prayer in Alabama as contrasted with school-sanctioned, student-led prayer in Texas.[14]

The Eleventh Circuit ruling was an outgrowth of a suit filed by the plaintiff Chandler in Alabama, who challenged the practice of offering prayer at school-sponsored events. He specifically objected to the practice of offering student-led prayer at athletic contests. The *Santa Fe* and *Chandler*[15] cases appear to represent opposite sides of the same constitutional coin. For example, *Santa Fe* prohibits school-sponsored prayer, whereas *Chandler* condemns school censorship of prayer.

The Alabama case was initially filed by the American Civil Liberties Union on behalf of DeKalb County educator Michael Chandler, who challenged religious practices in public schools. The essence of the recent Eleventh Circuit ruling is that students do not shed their religious rights when they enter the schoolhouse door. The circuit court rejected the argument that prayer is forbidden by the First Amendment and supported the concept of free speech as guaranteed by the

First Amendment. What does this ruling really mean? For now, it means that any student-led group in the Eleventh Circuit may engage in voluntary prayer at school events. However, school personnel may not direct or supervise students who initiate religious expression.

It is interesting that in its ruling the appeals court adopted the High Court's language in stating that nothing in the Constitution prohibits prayer. In the aftermath of the Eleventh Circuit ruling, what are the implications? Although this ruling affects only public schools in Alabama, Florida, and Georgia, it means that in those states, at least for now, school valedictorians, regardless of their belief or faith, may voluntarily pray at graduation ceremonies. It also allows student athletes to voluntarily engage in prayer at an athletic contest as long as school officials remain completely neutral. The Eleventh Circuit Court ruling reopens the debate on the legality of voluntary prayer by students at school-sponsored events. At issue are the free expression rights of students and the free exercise of their religious beliefs versus the Establishment Clause of the First Amendment. The First Amendment does not prohibit student-initiated private prayer. Based on the free exercise clause, students have the right to pray voluntarily any time and any place as long as it is private, strictly voluntary, and does not infringe on the rights of others. However, what is prohibited by the First Amendment is institutionally sponsored public prayer, which is an obvious violation of the Establishment Clause of the First Amendment. School officials should clearly understand this important distinction. This debate will likely persist as states continue to seek ways to address religion in public schools.

Prayer at Athletic Contests

Any type of school-sponsored prayer at athletic contests is deemed to be a violation of the First Amendment. The principle of neutrality mandates that public schools remain neutral in all matters relating to religion. For a number of years, a prevailing view was that prayer could be offered at athletic events as long as attendance was not compulsory. If attendance were voluntary, with prior knowledge that prayer would be offered, the offended person could simply avoid attending the event during the short time period in which prayer was to be offered. This view has not been accepted or supported by the courts in recent years, however. When public schools allow prayer to be offered at school events, they are placing the weight and influence of the school in support of a religious activity—an impermissible accommodation to religion and an obvious violation of the Establishment Clause. In recent years, courts have been fairly consistent in holding that prayer at football games and other athletic events violates the Establishment Clause of the First Amendment. The following case reflects the sentiment of the courts regarding prayer at athletic events.

The *Jager* case arose in Georgia when a high school student complained to his principal about invocations at home football games. The student indicated that invocations were in conflict with his religious beliefs. Invocations were delivered, in large part, by Protestant clergy and had been practiced since 1947. The school had adopted an "equal access" plan that provided for the random selection of the invocation speaker by the student government.

The student filed suit against the district, seeking **declaratory relief** regarding the selection process and to prohibit the offering of invocations at home football games, as both practices were in violation of the First Amendment clause. The district court held for the school district. The student appealed to the U.S. Court of Appeals for the Eleventh Circuit.

The court of appeals applied the *Lemon* Test to determine whether the invocations violated the Establishment Clause, based on a case involving aid to parochial schools, which will be discussed later in this chapter. According to the *Lemon* Test, for such practices to be held constitutional they need to have a *secular purpose* that *neither advances nor inhibits religion,* and they *do not create excessive entanglement between the state and religion.*[16] The court held that the equal access plan had no secular purpose and did, in fact, promote religion in violation of the Establishment Clause, even though it did not involve excessive entanglement with religion. The circuit court reversed the district court's decision, holding for the student.[17] Based on the ruling in the *Jager* case, public school officials are well advised to refrain from the use of prayer at any school-sponsored event.

Prohibition of prayer at school events was given a major thrust when the U.S. Supreme Court in a 6–3 ruling in *Santa Fe Independent School District v. Jane Doe* banned student-led prayer at athletic contests, graduations, and other school-sponsored events.[18] This ruling challenged previous lower court decisions permitting student-led prayer at graduation exercises in *Jones v. Clear Creek Independent School District* and *Adler v. Duval County School Board in Florida* (both discussed later in this chapter).

The U.S. Supreme Court decision stemmed from a case that was initiated in Santa Fe, Texas. Santa Fe's high school implemented a policy that allowed the school's student council chaplain to deliver a prayer over the public address system before each home varsity football game. This practice was challenged by respondents, Mormon and Catholic students, under the Establishment Clause of the First Amendment. Although the suit was pending, petitioner school districts adopted a different policy, which authorized two student elections: the first to determine whether invocations should be delivered at home games and the second to select the spokesperson to deliver them. After students held two elections authorizing such prayers and selecting a spokesperson, the district court entered an order modifying the policy to permit only nonsectarian, nonproselytizing prayer. Before the revised policy was implemented, the Fifth Circuit held that even as modified by the district, the policy was invalid because it violated the Establishment Clause of the First Amendment. The district argued, unpersuasively, that the messages delivered at football games are private student speech, not public speech. The district also argued that it did not coerce students to participate in religious observances.

In its ruling against the district, the U.S. Supreme Court stated, "The delivery of a message such as an invocation on school property at school sponsored events over the public address system by a speaker representing the student body under the supervision of school faculty based on school policy that implicitly encourages public prayer is not properly characterized as private speech."[19]

Various district and circuit courts rendered decisions that made it possible, prior to the recent U.S. Supreme Court ruling in the *Santa Fe* case, for states to decide if they wanted to support student-led prayer at graduation ceremonies. With this landmark *Santa Fe* ruling, states no longer may decide if voluntary student-initiated prayer may be offered at school events. According to the Court's ruling, this is an impermissible act that violates the Establishment Clause of the First Amendment.

The High Court noted further that this case demonstrates that student views are not unanimous on the issue of prayer and that the Establishment Clause's purpose is to remove debate over this kind of issue from governmental supervision and control. Although the ultimate choice of student speakers is attributable to students, the district's decision to hold this constitutionally problematic election is clearly a choice attributed to the state. The argument by the district that no coercion is involved lacks merit. Students who participate in band, cheerleading, and football

Administrative Guide

Prayer, Bible Reading, and Silent Meditation

1. School-sponsored prayer is illegal and cannot be justified based on First Amendment prohibitions.
2. School-sponsored Bible reading in public school is an illegal activity. However, the Bible may be used as an instructional document to meet a secular purpose.
3. Silent meditation or any other type of devotional activity sanctioned by schools will not be supported by the courts.
4. Invocations at school-sponsored athletic activities violate the Establishment Clause of the First Amendment.
5. Private voluntary prayer by a student is permissible under the free exercise clause of the First Amendment.

are sometimes mandated to attend the athletic events for class credit. The Constitution demands that schools not force on students the difficult choice between whether to attend these games or risk facing a personally offensive religious ritual.

VOLUNTARY PRAYER AT COMMENCEMENT EXERCISES

As previously discussed, the constitutionality of prayer in public schools was seriously challenged in 1962 in the landmark *Engel v. Vitale* case in which the U.S. Supreme Court struck down the daily recitation of prayer over a school's public address system. This landmark ruling banned prayer in any form in all school activities across the nation, based on a violation of the Establishment Clause of the First Amendment. In spite of this 1962 ruling, prayer at graduation ceremonies remains controversial.

For example, in a leading case in California, two taxpayers challenged the inclusion of religious invocations, benedictions, and other religious rituals at public high school graduation ceremonies. The invocations and benedictions were delivered by a Protestant minister or a Catholic priest, and all contained religious content. Summary judgment was granted on behalf of the taxpayers. The district appealed to the California Court of Appeals. The appellate court reversed the trial court's ruling, which resulted in an appeal by the taxpayers to the California Supreme Court.

The court ruled that the practice of including religious invocations and benedictions at high school graduation ceremonies conveyed a powerful message that the district approves of the content of prayers offered and favored one religion over others. Because Christian denominations and non-Christians are many and varied, respect for all of these groups requires that the state not place its stamp of approval on any particular practice. The court further stipulated that public school graduation ceremonies involving prayer cannot be in harmony with the First Amendment's command for neutrality. Therefore, the court of appeal's judgment was reversed.[20]

However, in another significant development, the U.S. Supreme Court let stand a stunning appeals court decision permitting student-initiated, student-led prayer at the Clear Creek Independent School District's graduation ceremonies in Texas. In this decision, a federal appeals court ruled that a Texas school district's policy of allowing each high school senior class to decide whether to offer student-initiated and student-led prayers at its graduation ceremony does not violate the First Amendment ban on the government's establishment of religion.

Prayer at graduation ceremonies will continue to be a highly sensitive and controversial issue. During the last several years, courts have become increasingly active in responding to issues involving religion in public schools. School officials no longer enjoy the freedom they once had in planning school programs based solely on community values and standards. During the 1950s, religious controversies were not viewed primarily in terms of constitutional rights but rather in terms of community sentiment. However, the courts in recent years have abandoned community sentiment in favor of constitutionality. The Supreme Court's position in *Jones v. Clear Creek Independent School District,* however, may provide an opportunity for communities to decide if they wish to have students assume the decision-making role. For now, at least, under certain conditions, voluntary student-led prayer at graduation ceremonies may be permissible. This is a major victory for proponents of prayer and perhaps an end to some of the controversy involving graduation ceremonies.

Landmark Rulings

Prior to the U.S. Supreme Court ruling in the *Santa Fe* case, a three-judge panel of the U.S. Court of Appeals for the Fifth Circuit ruled that the Clear Creek Independent School District's policy did not violate the Establishment Clause of the First Amendment, nor did it conflict with the Supreme Court's ruling in a 1992 Rhode Island case in which the High Court ruled that a

Providence middle school principal violated the Establishment Clause by inviting a rabbi to deliver a prayer at a promotion ceremony.[21] From the Court's view, the administrator's involvement suggested that the school was compelling students to participate in a religious exercise. However, the significance of the more recent *Jones v. Clear Creek Independent School District* case in Texas is that it creates a way to include prayer in graduation ceremonies without creating conflict with the Supreme Court's previous decisions.

In the Rhode Island case (*Lee v. Weisman*), the three-part Establishment Clause test set forth in the *Lemon* case[22] was used by the Supreme Court in ruling against the school district. Under the *Lemon* Test, a state practice that is challenged as unconstitutional must meet the criteria that it has a secular purpose, that its practices neither advance nor inhibit religion, and that it does not foster excessive entanglement between the state and religion. The student-initiated prayer in the *Clear Creek* case obviously met the *Lemon* Test, because the school played no role in offering the program and had no influence on the student who led the prayer.

The *Clear Creek* case reached the court in 1987 when the district's policy was challenged in federal court by two students. The Federal District Court and the Fifth Circuit Court of Appeals upheld the district's policy. The two students appealed to the U.S. Supreme Court, which **vacated** the Fifth Circuit Court's original ruling and asked the court of appeals to reconsider the case in light of the *Lee v. Weisman* decision. The three-judge panel unanimously concluded that the Clear Creek policy allowing for student-initiated prayer did not fail the so-called Coercion Test set forth in the Rhode Island case. The Supreme Court declined to review the federal court of appeal's decision, thus allowing student-initiated voluntary prayer at graduation ceremonies to be considered constitutionally permissible in the Fifth Circuit.[23]

The clear distinction between these two cases lies in the difference between student-initiated and school-initiated prayers. When the school initiates a prayer, it creates excessive entanglement and advances religion, both of which violate the basic tenets of the First Amendment. When students voluntarily do so without involvement of the school, excessive entanglement is not evident.

Impact of Ruling

An earlier decision of the U.S. Supreme Court to let stand the U.S. Court of Appeals for the Fifth Circuit decision created opportunities for every state in the country to make an independent judgment regarding student-led graduation prayers, although the Fifth Circuit ruling affects only Texas, Louisiana, and Mississippi. In the Texas case, the district's policy did not mandate prayer but merely made provisions for one should the seniors agree. The prayer, if supported by students, would be led by a student volunteer and be nonsectarian and nonproselytizing in nature. The reality of the Texas decision is that students could do what the school officials could not. It was not surprising to observe other states following the Texas decision.

In fact, a case arose in Florida during the same year in which the *Clear Creek* ruling was handed down by the Fifth Circuit Court. In *Adler v. Duval County School Board,* a Florida school board revised its graduation exercise policy by allowing the graduating class discretion to choose opening and closing remarks of two minutes or less to be delivered by a student volunteer selected by the class. The policy required that the student volunteer prepare the message without supervision or review by the school board. Senior classes at ten schools voted for prayer; seven other senior classes voted for a secular message or no message.

A group of graduating seniors and their parents filed suit against the board in the district court of Florida, alleging violation of their rights under the First Amendment. The court applied the familiar *Lemon* Test and held that the policy did not violate the *Lemon* criteria of having the primary effect of advancing religion or excessively entangling the school district with religion. Evidence revealed that the policy had a secular purpose of safeguarding the free speech rights of students participating and refraining from content-based regulations. The policy was held to be neutral, involving no coercion of students by school officials.[24]

These two cases may very well serve as precedents for other states as they approach the legalities of prayer at graduation ceremonies.

Student-initiated prayer is permissible based on free speech rights of students so long as it is not endorsed by school personnel and school personnel do not participate in the prayer. Designated school officials should not set aside a time period in which students participate or encourage students to engage in prayer. Student-initiated prayer should not disrupt the educational activities of the school. Student-initiated prayer may involve an individual student or a group of students. Examples include student-initiated prayer during club meetings; daily, weekly, or monthly prayer around the flagpole; before, during or after school; offering grace before a meal in the cafeteria; or silent prayer in class prior to taking an exam.

Significant challenges have emerged involving free speech rights of students in religious matters. The following represents recent litigation regarding religion and free speech:

1. The U.S. Supreme Court declined to hear an appeal regarding religious murals. In this case, the principal invited a student leadership class to organize a mural project to decorate panels that had been placed around an area of the school under renovation. Some students painted references to Jesus, prompting the principal to request that they be painted over due to disruption to the educational process. One student's mother sued on her daughter's behalf, alleging that painting over the mural amounted to censorship and subjected her daughter to ridicule based on her religious beliefs. The federal district court and subsequently the U.S. Court of Appeals for the Eleventh Circuit held that the principal had editorial control over the murals because they were school-sponsored speech that could be considered a part of the curriculum.[25]

2. An Ohio federal district court held that school officials violated a student's free speech right when they prohibited him from wearing a T-shirt that expressed his religious views on sensitive social issues such as abortion and homosexuality.[26]

3. A California district court held that a student suspended for wearing a T-shirt condemning homosexuality may sue his school district for violating his First Amendment rights to free speech, free exercise of religion, and freedom from establishment of religion but not for Fourteenth Amendment rights to equal protection.[27]

4. The U.S. District Court for the Eastern District of Michigan held that a high school's refusal to permit a student to voice opposition to homosexuality during a panel discussion on religion and homosexuality during a student assembly violated her rights to free speech, equal protection, and freedom from state establishment of religion.[28]

5. The U.S. Court of Appeals for the Eleventh Circuit remanded a case to the district court to determine if an Alabama school board violated a student's free speech when his principal disciplined him for refusing to recite the Pledge of Allegiance.[29]

Prayer at School Board Meetings

School boards that open their meetings with prayer are violating the Constitution's First Amendment Establishment Clause. The Sixth Circuit Court of Appeals relied on a series of prayer cases in rendering its decision. A school board started a practice of inviting clergy to offer prayer at its meetings. Later, one of the board members who was a minister began offering prayers at subsequent meetings. This practice was challenged by a student and a teacher who frequently attended board meetings. The federal district court upheld the board's practice, finding that the meetings resembled legislative sessions rather than school events and relied on the 1983 U.S. Supreme Court ruling that allowed official prayers at the beginning of a state legislative session. The student and teacher appealed to the Sixth Circuit, which ruled that board meetings were held on school property, were regularly attended by students, and did not resemble legislative sessions. The court further emphasized that board meetings had a function that was uniquely directed toward students and school matters, making it necessary for students to attend such meetings on many occasions. The Sixth Circuit Court stated that prayer at school board meetings was potentially coercive to students in attendance. The Circuit Court reversed the district court's ruling, holding that prayer has the tendency to endorse Christianity through excessively entangling the board in religious matters.[30]

Prayer at Legislative Meetings

The U.S. Supreme Court at the time of the writing of this text is debating whether public prayer at a New York town's board meeting is permissible. In *Galloway v. Town of Greece*, two local women are challenging the practice of including an opening prayer during monthly meetings.[31] This practice is overwhelmingly Christian in nature. The women argued that officials repeatedly ignored their request to modify or eliminate the practice or make it more inclusive. The opening prayer has been offered since 1998 on a volunteer basis by accepting anyone who wishes to come and volunteer to offer prayer.

A federal appeals court in New York found the board's policy to be an unconstitutional violation of the Establishment Clause. Interestingly, the nation's legislature has offered similar prayers since the nation's founding. Moreover, the U.S. Supreme Court begins its public session by invoking a traditional statement that ends with "God save the United States and this honorable court." The Obama Administration has joined conservative states and federal lawmakers in urging the Supreme Court to tolerate prayer during governmental meetings. It appears that the High Court is not necessarily interested in banning prayer based on comments made by various justices. Subsequently, a divided court ruled that legislative bodies such as city councils can in fact begin their meetings with prayer, even if it plainly favors a specific religion. This 5–4 decision is landmark in that it opens the door for every governmental body in the United States to offer prayer before its meetings. However, the sharp disagreement among the Justices evolved around the view that the majority ruling could encourage public bodies to provide more freedom for religious expression in their ceremonial prayers and less concern regarding objections of religious minorities. The High Court's five conservatives suggested that legislative prayers need not omit references to a specific religion—the prayers in question often invoked Jesus Christ and the resurrection. Those who pray before legislative meetings should be "unfettered" by what government officials find appropriate according to the High Court.

Administrative Guide

Prayer at School Events

In light of the court rulings regarding prayer at graduation ceremonies, it would be prudent for administrators to develop carefully drawn guidelines to minimize legal challenges in this area, such as the following:

1. Develop legally defensible guidelines that are supported by the U.S. Supreme Court decision addressing student-initiated prayer at athletic contests and other school events.
2. Do not rely on customs and community expectations when encouraging student-initiated prayer at school events.
3. Student-initiated prayer is probably permissible at school events when not endorsed by school officials.
4. School officials should respond judiciously if alerted that school personnel are encouraging students to offer voluntary prayer at school-sponsored events.
5. Voluntary student-led prayer will likely pass court scrutiny when it is initiated solely by students without involvement of school personnel.
6. Prayer at school board meetings violates the Establishment Clause, creates excessive entanglement, and cannot be justified on the basis that such meetings are similar to legislative sessions rather than school events.

AID TO PAROCHIAL SCHOOLS

Public aid to parochial schools has created numerous legal questions and conflicts. School districts have been challenged on issues involving the awarding of free textbooks, transportation, tax credits, and auxiliary services. Many of these issues have received mixed reviews by the courts.

In cases where evidence reveals that the aid directly benefited the child rather than the parochial school, courts have been permissive in allowing certain types of aid under the *child benefit theory*. This theory is valid if parochial children are the primary beneficiaries of a public-supported service provided for all children. Conversely, if the aid serves to benefit primarily parochial schools, it will be deemed impermissible and a violation of the First Amendment. When state activities cannot be clearly separated from religious activities, excessive entanglement occurs, thus preventing a clear line of separation between the two.

The issue of aid to parochial schools continues to be contested, as strong advocates as well as opponents are involved in the debate. Advocates have requested the U.S. Supreme Court to reverse its 1985 decision that disallows public school teachers from providing Title I remedial instruction in parochial schools. The New York City Public Schools and Roman Catholic parents sought reconsideration of the 5–4 High Court decision in the *Aguilar v. Felton* case[32] in which the court held that it was an unconstitutional establishment of religion for public school teachers to provide remedial classes in religious schools. This ruling created enormous costs incurred by the district through the purchase of mobile classrooms and leasing land to house them. These groups charged that these funds, roughly $14 million used to purchase mobile classrooms and lease land, could be better spent to support the Title I program.

An appeal in the *Agostini v. Felton*[33] case arose when the New York City School Board filed a motion asking a federal judge to be relieved from the 1985 *Felton* ruling. The National Committee for Public Education and Religious Liberty argued that it would be more feasible for the district to send private school students to Title I school sites for instruction. There was no dispute that private school students are eligible for Title I services; how they can best be served is the disputed issue.

The district judge upheld the use of mobile classes and ruled that the U.S. Supreme Court's decision could not be overturned. The U.S. Court of Appeals for the Second Circuit heard the board's appeal, agreeing with the district court's ruling that the U.S. Supreme Court's decision could not be overturned. However, on need, the case was readdressed by the High Court. In a rather rare and surprising move, the Court revised its previous decision in *Aguilar* by ruling in a 5–4 decision that the Constitution does not prohibit Title I from serving eligible religious school students on their premises. The legal significance of the Supreme Court's decision is that church–state barriers to Title I services no longer exist. These services can be provided to parochial students without offending church–state constitutional prohibitions.

The *Lemon v. Kurtzman* and *Early v. Dicenso* cases are perhaps the most significant early cases involving state aid to parochial schools. These cases arose when Rhode Island and Pennsylvania laws providing assistance to parochial schools, their students, and their teachers were challenged by various citizens and taxpayers. Rhode Island implemented an educational assistance program designed to assist private and parochial schools. This program provided supplemental teacher salaries for teachers who taught secular instruction in parochial schools. Pennsylvania enacted a similar statute but included assistance in purchasing supplies and textbooks in secular subjects.

Citizens in both states sought declaratory relief regarding practices that violated the First Amendment. The Pennsylvania District Court dismissed the complaint, whereas the Rhode Island court ruled that the practice was unconstitutional. The U.S. Supreme Court subsequently held that a law providing a state subsidy for nonpublic-school teachers' salaries is unconstitutional, even when the funds are paid only to teachers of secular subjects. The High Court also struck down a state law that reimbursed nonpublic schools for expenses incurred in teaching secular subjects. Justice Burger, speaking for the majority, stated, "The First Amendment not only prohibits the passing of laws establishing religion but it also prohibits passing of a law respecting such establishment."

This ruling referenced the famous *Lemon* Test (discussed previously in this chapter) in deciding on the constitutionality of certain practices involving public and parochial schools. Based on the *Lemon* standards, it was determined that a law must meet the following criteria to be legally valid regarding religion:

1. It must have a secular purpose.
2. It must neither advance nor inhibit religion.
3. It must not create excessive entanglement.[34]

As aid to parochial schools continues to be challenged, the following examples illustrate the courts' responses to certain practices:

1. Tuition reimbursement to parents of parochial school children is deemed unconstitutional.[35]
2. Shared time and community education programs for parochial school students violate the First Amendment.[36]
3. State financing of auxiliary services and direct loans for instructional equipment and materials for parochial schools is a violation of the First Amendment.[37]
4. Tax deductions for parents of parochial school children do not violate the First Amendment.[38]
5. Free public transportation for parochial school students does not violate the First Amendment.[39]
6. Free textbooks for parochial school students at state expense do not violate the First Amendment.[40]

Aid to students in religious schools received major impetus in a recent development in *Mitchell v. Helms,*[41] in which the U.S. Supreme Court ruled that a federal program that placed computers and other instructional equipment in parochial school classrooms did not violate the constitutional separation of church and state. Reversing an appeals court decision in a Louisiana case, the justices upheld, 6–3, a federal program that has distributed educational equipment and other materials to public and private schools since 1965. This practice was challenged by respondents who argued that direct nonincidental aid to religious schools is always impermissible. They further argued that the purpose of the direct/indirect distinction is to prevent subsidization of religion.

Concluding for the majority justices, Clarence Thomas, Antonin Scalia, and Anthony Kennedy supported the view that Chapter II of the Education Consolidation and Improvement Act of 1981, as applied in Jefferson Parish, is not a law respecting an establishment of religion simply because many of the private schools receiving Chapter II aid in the parish are religiously affiliated. Furthermore, Chapter II does not define its recipients by reference to religion. Aid is allocated on the basis of neutral, secular criteria that neither favor nor disfavor religion and is made available to both religious and secular beneficiaries on a nondiscriminatory basis.

Also, Chapter II does not result in governmental indoctrination of religion. It determines eligibility for aid neutrally, making a broad array of schools eligible without regard to their religious affiliations or lack thereof. Thus, it is not problematic that Chapter II could be fairly described as providing "direct" aid. Finally, the Chapter II aid provided to religious schools does not have an impermissible content. The statute explicitly requires that such aid be secular, neutral, and nonideological.

Religious Symbols

Public schools may not display religious exhibits or other visual materials. It may be appropriate, however, for public school teachers to acknowledge and explain the various holidays of all cultural and religious groups as a unit in cultural heritage or some other related subject, as long as a secular purpose is served.

Public school teachers should refrain from the use of religious symbols or pictures, even in conjunction with discussing the various holidays. A case could be made that the presence of the crucifix creates a religious atmosphere in the classroom. The presence of any type of religious symbol or picture would violate the principle of neutrality. Pictures of religious events may also create a religious atmosphere.

Religious Displays

Certain types of displays may be permitted in public school settings. For example, the City of Las Cruces, New Mexico, and its school district did not violate the Establishment Clause by incorporating three crosses into city and school district logos. The imagery was based on the city's history and was not intended to endorse Christianity. The city and school district used a logo consisting of three interlocking crosses surrounded by a sun. The logo appeared on a sculpture, a mural at an elementary school, and on school maintenance vehicles. Resident taxpayers brought separate federal district court actions against the Las Cruces Public Schools and the City of Las Cruces challenging the use of a Christian symbol on the logo. The court held the district did not use the logo on school maintenance vehicles to proselytize. No evidence indicated the district's stated purpose for using the insignia on school maintenance vehicles was insincere. The judgment was **affirmed**.[42] In addition, it is permissible to employ seasonal decorations, such as snow, pine trees, wreaths, eggs, or bunny rabbits. These are considered merely reflections of the joy and merriment associated with various holidays, as long as they are not used to meet a sectarian purpose.

Public schools may not erect any type of religious display on school property. However, in 1963, one such display was held by a district in New York to be a mere passive accommodation of religion.[43] This court supported the erection of a nativity scene on school grounds. The posture of the courts today would not support such a **finding**. It is indisputable that the presence of a nativity scene on school property violates the separation of church and state by demonstrating preference of one religion over another and is in clear violation of the Establishment Clause of the First Amendment. In fact, a different ruling occurred in *Washegesic v. Bloomingdale Public Schools* in which the Sixth Circuit Court of Appeals held that a portrait of Jesus Christ that had been hanging outside the principal's office in the hallway for thirty years was unconstitutional because it constituted the government's endorsement of religion and an Establishment Clause violation.[44]

Ten Commandments

Two early court decisions, one at the federal district level and the other by the U.S. Supreme Court, held that posting of the Ten Commandments in a public school is unconstitutional. North Dakota passed a law requiring the display of a placard that contained the Ten Commandments of the Christian and Jewish religions. The statute called for this display to be located in a conspicuous place in every classroom in public schools. The district court ruled that this practice violated the Establishment Clause of the First Amendment.[45] Interestingly, the State Supreme Court of Kentucky in *Stone v. Graham*[46] reached a tie decision regarding a statute that required posting the Ten Commandments in public school classrooms. The tie proved to be insignificant, when the U.S. Supreme Court in a 5–4 decision held that this practice was unconstitutional and a violation of the Establishment Clause of the First Amendment.

The U.S. Supreme Court issued split decisions in two cases involving the Ten Commandments on government property. It held in *McCreary County, Kentucky v. American Civil Liberties Union of Kentucky* that framed copies on the walls of two Kentucky courthouses were illegal and amounted to an accommodation to religion and a violation of separation of church and state.[47] In a contrasting case, *Van Orden v. Perry* in Texas, the High Court held that a monument erected in 1962 served a less blatant religious purpose and served educational and historical purposes.[48] In addition, it was located among other secular and educational markers on the grounds of the state capitol. The decisive vote was cast by Justice Stephen Breyer, who noted that the granite statue had stood for more than forty years without a complaint, whereas the framed copies posted in Kentucky sparked legal challenges as soon as they were posted. Those who opposed posting the Ten Commandments argued that the first four or five commandments made sole reference to Jewish and Christian religions, which made them offensive to non-Judeo-Christians. They argued further that these postings violate the principle of separation of church and state. The courts, at most levels, tend to support the view that posting of isolated religious text and symbols in public buildings is a violation of separation of church and state and further violates the principle of neutrality to which governmental or state agencies such as public schools must adhere.

Posting Religious Mottos and Expressions

In recent developments, state boards of education across the country are developing resolutions supporting the posting of the Ten Commandments in public school buildings. These resolutions are strongly opposed by the American Civil Liberties Union. The view held by opponents of this practice is that such postings amount to a government endorsement of religion. State officials respond by suggesting that such postings teach civility as well as proper moral and ethical values badly needed by children.

Some state officials are supporting policies calling for posting the words *In God We Trust* in public schools as a motto that has been on U.S. currency since 1864. These efforts will undoubtedly result in legal battles as they are embraced by other school districts across the United States. For example, Colorado's State Board of Education voted to urge schools to post *In God We Trust* in buildings throughout the state as a means of celebrating national heritage, traditions, values, and civic virtue.

Opponents are charging that the board is attempting to use a familiar and generally accepted phrase to inject religion into public schools. The resolution calls for the Colorado State Board of Education to encourage the appropriate display of this national motto in school buildings. Congress approved this phrase during the nineteenth century in response to a request from the clergy. The U.S. Supreme Court has never addressed this issue. However, several appeals courts have allowed its use on coins, suggesting that it does not amount to a government endorsement of religion. These developments point to the ongoing tension that exists between issues relating to separation of church and state and the level of emotions surrounding these issues. Only time will reveal how the courts will address these emerging conflicts.

Religious Banners at Football Games

A district court judge upheld cheerleaders' use of religious banners at football games after the school district in Kountze, Texas banned the displays. Consequently, cheerleaders may continue to display their Bible verse banners at football games. The judge held that the display did not violate the Constitution. The cheerleaders captured national attention when they sued the school district in a case that pitted freedom of expression rights against the separation of church and state clause in the federal Constitution. One of the banner displays read, "If God is for us, who can be against us? Romans 8:31." Evidence in this case revealed that religious messages displayed on run-through banners did not and will not create an establishment of religion in the Kountze community.

The cheerleaders' suit was aided by the conservative Texas-based Liberty Institute who argued that the ban violated both the cheerleaders' religious and freedom of expression rights. The essential difference that likely led to the decision favoring the cheerleaders is that the school district was not promoting religion, which would be an Establishment Clause violation. The cheerleaders received no coercion by the district to display the banners. They did so by privately promoting their own views. The Anti-Defamation League criticized the ruling by indicating that football games are a quintessential school event. Cheerleaders are a key part of that event. The league suggested further that the decision flies in the face of clear U.S. Supreme Court and other rulings. It was suggested that the banners conveyed the message that the school supports and promotes one religion over another. The school district has filed an appeal and is seeking further clarification from the judge. The community unanimously supported the banners. If this ruling stands, it will be interesting to see if other cheerleader groups around the country will be inclined to display religious banners at their football games.[49]

USE OF SCHOOL FACILITIES BY RELIGIOUS STUDENT GROUPS

The use of school facilities by student religious groups continues to create friction between students and school officials. Considerable tension has mounted in recent years between administrators and student religious groups regarding access to school facilities during the school day. At issue is the growing debate regarding the viability of the Equal Access Act. Does the act, in fact, provide free access to student religious groups? Are students' First Amendment rights violated when access is denied? Under what circumstances may student religious groups be denied access?

Congress attempted to address these issues when it passed the Equal Access Act in 1984 for the express purpose of providing student religious clubs equal opportunities to access high school facilities as enjoyed by other noncurricular clubs. Under federal statute, it is unlawful for any public secondary school receiving federal financial assistance that has created a "limited open forum" to deny access to student-initiated groups on the basis of the religious, political, or philosophical content of their speech. A limited open forum exists when an administrator allows one or more noncurricula-related student groups to meet on school premises during noninstructional time.[50]

Before the passage of this act, the U.S. Court of Appeals for the Second, Fifth, Tenth, and Eleventh Circuits had routinely denied access to student religious clubs. With the passage of this act, controversy still exists regarding its interpretation. For example, do school administrators have the right to deny students access, and do students have a constitutional right to be provided access? Based on the intent of the act, it would be unlawful for a student religious group to be denied use whereas other noncurricular student groups were not. If the school claims not to have a limited open forum, there likely would not be an infringement of students' personal rights. Perhaps the most controversial issue to date is the question of exactly what constitutes a limited open forum. With increasing frequency, administrators appear to be taking the position that limited open forums do not exist in their schools as a means of disallowing free access to student religious clubs.

A limited open forum is established whenever a public school grants an offering to or opportunity for one or more non–curriculum-related student groups to meet on school premises during noninstructional time. The following conditions should apply:

   a. The meeting should be voluntary and student-initiated.
   b. There is no sponsorship of the meeting by the public school.
   c. Employees of the school are present at religious meetings only in a nonparticipatory and supervisory capacity.
   d. The meeting does not materially and substantially interfere with orderly conduct and educational activities within the school.
   e. The meeting is not controlled by any persons or groups not affiliated with the school.

In summary, then, if a school official allows any noncurricular student club to use school facilities, then student religious groups also must be allowed equal access. The viability of the Equal Access Act has been debated across the nation, including cases in Texas, Nebraska, Washington, Pennsylvania, and Virginia.

Legal Precedents

As administrators deal with student religious clubs, their actions should be guided by a sense of fundamental fairness and respect for the First Amendment rights of others. The U.S. Supreme Court earlier bypassed an opportunity to set an important precedent in this area in 1986 when it declined on technical grounds to review a Bible-study case, *Bender v. Williams Sport.*[51] By failing to hear this case, the Supreme Court left the issue to be decided by the lower courts, thereby failing to create uniform compliance across the country and address the constitutionality of the law itself. However, the Supreme Court did address the issue in 1990. Between 1986 and 1990, a number of lower court decisions were rendered in various states across the country. Following is a brief description of those decisions.

In a 1988 case, *Mergens v. Board of Education of the Westside Community Schools,*[52] the district judge ruled that an Omaha district did not create an open forum for student speech and, thus, did not need to allow a Bible student club to meet at the high school.

Rossford high school students had a band that performed mostly Christian songs. The father of one student was a school board member and the band's manager. He sought approval for a band performance at a school-wide assembly during school hours. The district superintendent first approved the performance but cancelled it after a school attorney warned of Establishment Clause problems. Band members sued the school district in a federal court, asserting that their appearance was cancelled because of disapproval of their Christian message.

The court rejected the band members' claim that the assembly was a public forum in which the district had to maintain viewpoint neutrality. The assembly was not a "forum" of any kind, and for that reason, the district was not subject to any neutrality requirement. The school district "was entitled to exercise editorial control" over it. When the school itself was the speaker, educators were entitled to exercise greater control to assure the views of speakers were not erroneously attributed to the school. The school district could impose a ban against the band members because of their Christian religious identity. The court awarded pretrial judgment to the school district.[53]

In 1992, in yet another case, *Clark v. Dallas Independent School,*[54] a U.S. district judge ruled against a prayer group whose meetings grew into loud revivals involving proselytizing of other students. In his ruling, the judge indicated that the Equal Access Act may, in fact, violate the First Amendment Establishment Clause.

To avoid the label of limited open forums under the Equal Access Act, many districts either have refused to permit any extracurricular clubs access or have created extremely broad definitions of precisely what is curriculum related. This, then, allows schools to maintain school-based clubs without recognizing religious clubs.

On appeal, the U.S. Supreme Court addressed the equal access issue in the *Board of Education of Westside Community Schools v. Mergens.* The High Court was faced with deciding whether the Equal Access Act prohibited Westside High School from denying a student religious group access to school facilities and, if so, whether the act violated the Establishment Clause of the First Amendment.

Students at Westside were provided more than thirty clubs from which to choose, all of which met after school. Membership was voluntary, and a club sponsor was required for each club based on board policy. Board policy further stipulated that no club or organization shall be sponsored by any political or religious organization or by any organization that denies membership based on race, color, creed, gender, or political belief. Mergens, a student, petitioned Westside High for permission to conduct a religious meeting on school premises. Her request was denied on the basis that the meeting would violate the Establishment Clause. A suit subsequently filed by Mergens contended that the denial violated the Equal Access Act. The school responded by indicating that the act was unconstitutional and did not apply to the school. The district court held for Westside in supporting the denial. However, the court of appeals reversed the district court's decision, holding that the act was constitutional and that Westside was in violation of the act.

The case reached the Supreme Court when the district appealed. Justice Sandra Day O'Connor, speaking for the majority, affirmed the court of appeals' ruling by stating that the Equal Access Act constitutionally prohibits a limited open forum from denying a student group's request to use school facilities based on the religious content of their meeting. The act intended to grant equal access to secular and religious speech. Because the meeting occurs during noninstructional time and limits school official participation, the Equal Access Act creates no substantial risk of excessive entanglement. The court of appeal's ruling was affirmed.

Based on the High Court's ruling, schools that provide a limited open forum may not permit certain groups to use school facilities while denying others. Once a limited forum is established, it must be equally accessible among all student groups, and it may not be restricted based on religious, political, or philosophical ideologies. Schools may bar such clubs if those schools have a closed forum in which no clubs are allowed to use school facilities during noninstructional hours. Whether the school district maintains a limited open forum or a closed forum is left to the discretion of the school district, unless otherwise determined by state statute. Once the decision is reached regarding either of these options, consistency and fairness must prevail, as the option chosen is executed by the district. In a significant case involving the use of school facilities by a student club, the Court declined to review a Ninth Circuit decision that held a school district did not violate the U.S. Constitution when it denied recognition to a student club based on its name—Truth—and its restriction of voting membership to those who professed belief in the Bible and Jesus Christ. The Ninth Circuit found the restrictions inherently excluded non-Christians, in violation of school district nondiscrimination policies.[55]

Issues involving religious freedom are highly charged emotionally, and thus the Equal Access Act continues to be a stormy matter, with no indication that this will change in the foreseeable future. As administrators deal with student religious clubs, their actions should be guided by a sense of fundamental fairness and respect for the First Amendment rights of others. These actions should not be taken simply because the courts mandate them but rather because fair administration is right and proper.

Administrators should ensure that criteria, rules, and regulations governing student clubs are carefully drawn and communicated to all students. Ideally, student representatives should be involved in the policy development process. All efforts should be made to provide equal protection for all groups, regardless of philosophical ideology. The only way this can be achieved is through a strong conviction and commitment to fairness for all students irrespective of differences that might exist regarding their religious or moral beliefs.

Administrative Guide

Equal Access

1. Do not allow some student clubs with similar noncurricular functions to meet on school premises while denying other religious clubs this same privilege, especially where there are ideological differences between the administration and the student groups.
2. Avoid denying religious clubs access based on personal or philosophical disagreement with the clubs' objectives.
3. Do not establish extremely broad definitions as to what is considered curriculum related in an effort to ban religious clubs.
4. Avoid classifying all other clubs as curriculum related irrespective of function and disallowing the same classification for religious clubs.
5. School authorities should consult the district's legal counsel regarding any questionable religious activities in their school.
6. High school student religious clubs may be allowed to use school facilities if the school supports a limited open forum. They cannot be denied use if other noncurricular groups are permitted to use facilities before or after the school day.

USE OF SCHOOL FACILITIES BY OUTSIDE RELIGIOUS GROUPS

Many local school districts, in an effort to be responsive to their communities, provide access to school facilities for various public organizations during noninstructional hours. This accommodation is typically viewed as a positive gesture and one that is consistent with the view that schools serve as centers for community activities. In most instances, minimal conflict arises between local school officials and community organizations over the use of school facilities.

However, one area that often creates controversy, friction, and even legal challenges involves the use of school facilities by community-based religious groups. Legal challenges by these groups usually involve allegations that school officials' denial of access to district facilities amounts to a violation of their freedom of expression and equal protection rights under the laws.

School officials respond that the district must maintain a clear separation between religious activities and state activities based on First Amendment prohibitions.

When *denying* access to religious groups, are school officials, in fact, infringing on the group's free exercise and freedom of expression rights? How far can school districts go to accommodate religious organizations? How do district officials respond to the needs of religious groups without violating First Amendment prohibitions involving church–state relations? How do they respond to challenges by other citizens who contend that the use of school facilities by religious groups offends the community? School district officials find themselves in a precarious position when they attempt to make reasonable accommodations to religious groups without offending the Establishment Clause of the First Amendment, which prohibits staff support of religious activities.

Relevant Cases

The following cases illustrate the court's position on the use of school facilities by religious groups. A community church, through its minister, requested the use of a school facility for regular Sunday services and was told that district policy prohibited the use of school facilities for any religious purpose. The policy stated that district facilities shall be open to public, literary, scientific, recreational, or educational meetings or for discussions on matters of public interest. Although the portion of the policy dealing with religious activity was later removed, the church was denied access. The church contended that an open forum existed based on the language in the policy and that the denial violated their right to free speech and assembly.

The court did find that the district's community use policy created an open forum. *However, it held that the practice of excluding religious organizations from holding religious services in its facilities was justified. The court ruled that religious services held on a regular basis would violate the Establishment Clause.*[56] This violation provided a compelling reason to justify the content-based restriction of the open forum.

In contrast, the court supported a religious organization in the *Gregoire v. Centennial* case,[57] when the Centennial School District developed a facilities use policy prohibiting religious activities within its buildings. A district court **enjoined** the policy, thus allowing the plaintiff to use a school auditorium to hold a magic show after which an evangelical message was given. The school district then altered its policy to include a list of organizations that were allowed to use school facilities. This new policy also included a prohibition on religious services as well as the distribution of religious materials. The plaintiff requested to use the facility again if it were open to the public, claiming that facilities are open forums and prohibitions against religious activities violated equal protection, free speech, and the exercise clause of the First Amendment. The court held that the new policy still created a prohibition against religious activity and a violation of the plaintiff's free speech and free exercise rights. The court noted that the list of other groups who could use facilities created an open forum. Once created, the plaintiff cannot be denied access based on content of speech.

In a landmark case involving use of school facilities by a religious group, *Bronx Household of Faith v. Community School District No. 10* (1997),[58] the U.S. Supreme Court rejected an appeal from an evangelical Christian church that had sought to use a middle school gymnasium in New York for religious services. This religious group contended that the school district should not be permitted to ban the use of the gym by religious groups while allowing other community groups to use it. According to the plaintiffs, this amounted to **discrimination**.

By policy, the New York City Board of Education permits rental of schools for a variety of community purposes, including religious discussions, but prohibits their use for religious services. The Bronx Household of Faith challenged this rule in federal district court. The district court ruled for the school district. On appeal, the U.S. Court of Appeals also ruled for the school district. In its ruling, the appeals court indicated that the use of school facilities by community groups created an open forum rather than a traditional public forum. Under First Amendment freedoms, government restrictions on speech in a public forum are held to very strict scrutiny. However, in a limited open forum, such as a public school, the government can restrict speech if it makes reasonable and *viewpoint-neutral* distinctions among speakers. Further, public school officials reasonably might wish to avoid the appearance of sponsoring religious services. Because the U.S. Supreme Court rejected an appeal, the appeal court's decision stands.

Finally, in the *Lamb's Chapel v. Center Moriches School District* case (1993)[59] involving a closed forum, an evangelical Christian church applied on four occasions for approval to use public facilities of a local high school for various nonsecular functions, including family-oriented films with a Christian perspective. Each request was denied by school officials because the proposed functions were church related and had religious connotations. School officials relied on a New York State law that bars the use of district facilities for religious purposes. The minister of the church brought legal action against the district, claiming First and Fourteenth Amendment violations—freedom of speech and equal protection of the law, respectively. The Second Circuit Court of Appeals held that the facilities were not deemed open forums; therefore, the church's First and Fourteenth Amendments rights were not abridged. However, the U.S. Supreme Court unanimously ruled that the district's rule was unconstitutional as applied to the film series. The Court acknowledged that the district, like a private owner of property, could have preserved its property for the use to which it was dedicated and need not have permitted any after-hours use of its property. However, once the district voluntarily made its facilities available for use by after-hours groups, it could not enforce rules designed to exclude expression of specific points of view. School officials must remain viewpoint neutral in approving use of school facilities by community groups. The Court further concluded that to permit Lamb's Chapel to use the facilities would not violate the Establishment Clause because it would have neither the purpose nor primary effect of advancing or inhibiting religion and would not foster excessive entanglement with religion.

Use of School Facilities by Community Groups

Local school boards, either through implied powers or specific authority, have the capacity to formulate policies governing the use of school facilities within their districts. By policy or practice, school officials may permit public groups to use school facilities during noninstructional hours as long as their activities do not interfere with normal school operations. Unless otherwise prescribed by state statute, districts are not required to provide facilities to community groups. It is within the discretion of school boards to determine if the district will support an "open forum." An open forum is present when the district allows community groups to use its facilities during noninstructional hours. If supported, the district may not discriminate against any community group based on philosophical or ideological differences. The district must remain *viewpoint neutral* in accommodating these groups. However, if the district chooses a closed forum, then no community groups are allowed to use facilities. Under an open forum, districts may prescribe certain policies regarding the use of their facilities with respect to maintenance, safety, and overall operations. Reasonable fees may also be imposed to cover costs associated with opening, closing, cleaning, and generally maintaining facilities during use by community groups. A closed forum, however, is a place that traditionally has not been open to public expression. Restrictions on access by school districts will generally be upheld as long as such restrictions are viewed as reasonable and not based on speech content. Closed forums may not be used to suppress a particular viewpoint. School officials must remain viewpoint neutral. School district officials may opt to support a limited open forum or a closed forum as long as their policies are applied consistently and they remain viewpoint neutral.

Right to Deny Access

School districts may deny access to community groups even when an open forum exists in instances where there is evidence of abuse or destruction of property. Willful violation of district policy or local or state laws also may result in denial of use. If the facility is used for subversive activities aimed at carrying out unlawful objectives, access may be justifiably denied. In addition, criminal charges may be levied against guilty parties depending on the circumstances surrounding each case. Activities conducted in school facilities that pose a threat to public safety may also be curtailed. The district should have approved written policies that address all aspects of facility use by community groups. All approved policies governing the use of district facilities must be applied fairly and consistently with all groups, including religious groups.

When conflict arises over denial of school facilities by school officials, it will usually involve either freedom of association, freedom of expression, or equal protection challenges. School districts will normally be supported by the courts in cases involving denial based on issues pertaining to unlawful acts, threats to health or safety, and destruction of school property. They generally will not be supported in matters involving free speech and association or equal protection violations. When challenges arise, the courts will examine all relevant facts surrounding the particular case and will determine if a substantive right is in question.

Administrative Guide

Use of Facilities by Outside Religious Groups

1. School districts must allow religious groups access to their facilities if other nonreligious groups are permitted to use them.
2. School officials are not expected to allow religious groups to use facilities for regular religious services, even when an open forum is established by the district.
3. School districts are not required to accommodate religious groups under a closed forum policy.
4. In the absence of religious services, school officials must remain *viewpoint neutral* in permitting religious groups to use facilities under an open forum.

RELIGIOUS ACTIVITIES AND HOLIDAY PROGRAMS

The observance of holy days by public schools is clearly an unconstitutional activity if conducted in a devotional atmosphere. The First Amendment prohibits states from either aiding religion or showing preference for one religion over another. Public schools may not celebrate religious holidays. No worship or devotional services nor religious pageants or plays of any nature should be held in any school. However, certain programs may be conducted if a secular purpose is clearly served.

For example, the district court upheld a school's Christmas program in South Dakota when certain parents challenged the religious content of a Christmas program that was sponsored, based on school district policy. The district's policy was challenged on the grounds that it violated the Establishment Clause of the First Amendment. The U.S. District Court of South Dakota held for the school district in ruling that the performance of music containing religious content does not within itself constitute a religious activity, as long as it serves an educational rather than a religious purpose.[60]

Schools, however, are prohibited from the use of sacred music that occurs in a devotional setting. This type of music may be sung or played as a part of a music appreciation class, as long as a secular purpose is served. School choirs and assemblies may be permitted to sing or play holiday carols, as long as these activities are held for entertainment purposes rather than religious purposes. A religious music case arose in Washington State based on public complaints regarding religious music at graduation. A Washington school district received complaints regarding religious music selections at a 2005 high school graduation ceremony. As the 2006 graduation approached, administrators rejected the school wind ensemble's selection of "Ave Maria," believing it created a risk of new complaints. They requested that the ensemble make another selection. A student member of the wind ensemble sued the school district and superintendent for constitutional violations. A federal district court held that the district did not violate the student's rights. On appeal, the U.S. Court of Appeals, Ninth Circuit, held that instrumental music was "speech" for First Amendment analysis purposes. Schools are not considered public forums for speech unless they are opened up by officials for indiscriminate use. A limited public forum for expression had been opened in this case because of the district's tradition of allowing seniors to select the music for their graduation ceremonies. In a limited public forum, restrictions can be based on subject matter, so long as distinctions are reasonable in light of the purpose of the forum. Here, the school district acted reasonably to avoid repeating the prior year's controversy. The court affirmed the judgment for the district.[61]

Merry Christmas Bill

The Texas legislature passed the Merry Christmas Bill in 2013, which protects Texas's right to acknowledge traditional holidays on school grounds. There was a view in Texas that children have been denied the opportunity to enjoy the activities and joy of celebrations in their school whether Christmas, Hanukkah, Kwanzaa, or others. This bill protects Texas public schools from legal challenges while stressing that freedom of religion is not the same as freedom from religion. It also removes legal risks of saying "Merry Christmas" in schools while extending protection to traditional holiday symbols such as a menorah or a nativity scene so long as more than one religion and secular symbol are reflected. The motivation for this bill arose when a Republican representative discovered that his son's school had erected a "holiday tree" in December for fear that mentioning Christmas could prompt litigation.

Released Time for Religious Instruction

Releasing public school students for religious instruction has not been a major issue in recent years. Public school officials are aware that a very fine line separates church and state relationships. Landmark rulings prohibiting prayer, Bible reading, and financial aid to parochial schools have heightened awareness among public school officials of the need to adhere to the principle of neutrality regarding their role in religious matters affecting the operation of public schools.

Prior to these landmark decisions in the 1960s, it was not an uncommon practice in some districts to observe teachers of religious instruction entering public schools to teach religious classes for students whose parents granted consent. This practice involved virtually all denominations. Because no public school funds were involved in teaching these classes, the commonly held view was that such practices were an acceptable accommodation to parents and students who wished to participate in religious instruction.

However, in a leading Illinois case, the U.S. Supreme Court held that offering religious instruction on a released-time basis in public schools was unconstitutional. The case arose when the board of education initiated a program that permitted representatives of various religious groups to provide religious instruction during the school day on a voluntary basis. McCollum, a private citizen and a parent, challenged this practice as a violation of the Establishment Clause of the First Amendment and sought declaratory relief.

The school district stressed the point that no school resources were involved and those students who did not wish to participate in religious instruction were allowed to move to some other location in the building for secular instruction. Class attendance records were maintained by religious instructors. However, the facts revealed that school property was utilized for religious instruction and a close relationship had emerged between the school and religious organizations. The state trial court upheld this practice. The state supreme court affirmed the trial court's ruling.

However, the U.S. Supreme Court reversed that decision, holding that "the state may not permit religious teaching on tax-supported public school property during regular school hours." This practice aids religion through the implementation of compulsory attendance laws and was deemed to be a violation of the First Amendment, which created a wall of separation between church and state that must be respected.[62]

In a later case with a slightly different slant, the U.S. Supreme Court upheld a released-time program involving religious instruction. This case involved a New York City program that permitted public schools to release students during the school day to attend religious instruction at religious centers at locations around the city. All administrative activities were coordinated by the religious organization, which assumed full responsibility for transportation and attendance reporting.

Zorach, a citizen of New York, filed suit, challenging this practice as a violation of the First Amendment's ban on separation of church and state. Zorach further charged that normal school activities ceased while students were transported to religious centers and that public school teachers were required to monitor students released to attend these centers.

The U.S. Supreme Court upheld this practice by stating that the city may permit public school students to attend religious centers during school hours because no compulsion is involved and no public school resources are expended. Parents decide whether their children will attend religious centers, and because this program is voluntary public schools do no more than make a mere scheduling accommodation. The Court held that this practice did not violate First Amendment prohibitions.[63]

Although both programs were voluntary in nature, the obvious difference between these two cases rests on one important fact: In the *McCollum* case, the school utilized resources in the form of classrooms during the school day, whereas in the *Zorach* case no public tax-supported resources were involved. In a more recent development, the U.S. Court of Appeals for the Tenth Circuit held a released-time program unconstitutional that allowed students to attend religious seminars and receive public school credit for classes that were viewed as denominational in nature.[64]

Teaching the Bible in Public Schools

Many school officials shy away from endorsing Bible teaching for fear of inviting lawsuits. School students, however, learn beyond rudimentary knowledge of the Bible. For example, Shakespeare's works contain numerous references to the Bible. Mark Twain's works also contain biblical references.

Although the use of the Bible in school for religious purposes is unconstitutional, some public schools across the nation are introducing Bible classes into the curriculum. There is strong advocacy for and against teaching the Bible in public schools. Many critics of public schools who support Bible teaching cite the decay of moral values as a leading cause of serious discipline problems and gross disrespect for authority.

Some educators believe that knowledge of the Bible is critical to understanding the best literary works as well as historical and contemporary speech and writing. Those educators who oppose teaching the Bible in public school contend that it promotes a specific Christian interpretation and runs the risk of teachers indoctrinating students to a religious belief. In spite of opposition, the Bible may be taught in public schools as a part of the school's curriculum if it is not associated with any form of worship and it is taught objectively as a part of a secular program. In fact, the U.S. Supreme Court ruled in an early case, *Stone v. Graham,* that the Bible may be used constitutionally as an appropriate study of history, civilization, ethics, or comparative religion.[65] In supporting this view, a national council on Bible curriculum in public schools was formed by congressmen, legislators, and attorneys across the nation to ensure that reliable information and legal support of schools' right to teach the Bible as an elective are ensured.

The tension between church and state persists, as reflected by ongoing litigation involving the use of the Bible in public schools. For example, in *Gibson v. Lee County Board of Education* plaintiffs challenged the practice of teaching the Bible in public schools by contending that the specific curricula adopted by the school board did not present the Bible objectively as part of a secular program in education.[66] They argued further that the school district's intent in officially offering and preparing to teach courses entitled Bible History: Old Testament and Bible History: New Testament is designed to promote religion generally and Christianity specifically, resulting in excessive entanglement. The court noted, using the *Lemon* criteria, that no government act or practice can be upheld under the Establishment Clause unless it (1) was adopted for a secular purpose, (2) has a primary effect that neither advances nor inhibits religion, and (3) does not foster an excessive government entanglement with religion.[67] Plaintiffs argued that the Bible history curricula adopted failed all three tests.

The court held for the school district based on its view that the district satisfied the secular purpose requirement by adopting a curriculum that was modified on the advice of the school board's legal counsel. The court also noted that the teachers for the proposed Bible history class had been properly instructed on how and what to teach and what not to teach. The court concluded that it could not evaluate the second and third *Lemon* requirements without some record of classroom instruction involved in teaching the Bible history classes.

In a contrasting case, *Wiley v. Franklin,* a federal district court found that the account of the resurrection of Jesus Christ as presented in the New Testament constitutes the central statement of the Christian religious faith.[68] The court further found that the only reasonable interpretation of the resurrection is a religious interpretation. The court noted that counsel for the defendants recommended the deletion of references to the resurrection, as well as many other modifications to the proposed Bible History II curriculum. The court found that plaintiffs had established a substantial likelihood of success on merits regarding the Bible History II curriculum adopted by the school board.

Finally, in a significant ruling, a federal district court ruled in *Elrod v. Burns* that an infringement of plaintiff's First Amendment rights guaranteed by the Establishment Clause, even for minimal periods of time, constituted irreparable injury.[69]

Administrative Guide

Bible Teaching

1. The Bible must be taught objectively and in a strictly secular manner.
2. Teachers should not create a devotional (religious) atmosphere when teaching the Bible.
3. Teachers assigned to teach the Bible as part of the school's secular program must be properly instructed on how and what to teach.
4. School officials should formulate policies governing Bible teaching through the involvement of teachers, students, and, where appropriate, parents and community leaders.
5. Bible-teaching policies should be communicated effectively to teachers, students, and parents.

Intelligent Design and School Curriculum

Intelligent design (ID) is a controversial concept that suggests that certain features of the universe, including living things, exhibit characteristics of a product derived from an intelligent cause rather than a natural selection. Advocates of ID believe that the concept has equal status with other current scientific theories regarding the origin of life. Supporters of this theory believe that the ultimate designer of living things is God. This concept has invited legal challenges regarding its inclusion in public school curricula.

For example, the *Kitzmiller v. Dover Area School District* lawsuit arose in Dover, Pennsylvania, to challenge a policy formulated by the Dover school board requiring students to be introduced in a ninth-grade biology class to the intelligent design theory along with the theory of evolution.[70] The school district revised the science curriculum to include a unit that explores the gaps or problems in the theory of evolution along with an introductory unit on intelligent design. A high school teacher testified that she and her colleagues refused to read a statement regarding intelligent design in class because they failed to view the concept as a viable scientific alternative to the theory of evolution. Eleven parents, joined by the American Civil Liberties Union of Pennsylvania, filed suit and challenged the board's policy. Based on the policy, a four-paragraph statement would be read to biology students describing evolution as not being factual while introducing intelligent design. The issue presented to the court centered on whether teaching intelligent design is constitutionally permissible. Plaintiffs asserted that the Dover School Board identified intelligent design as a means of inserting Christian beliefs into science classes. The school board contended that its policies simply promoted scientific inquiry. Plaintiffs argued that intelligent design is not a science and should not be taught in public schools because it violates the Constitution. The defendant school board filed a motion for summary judgment. The U.S. district court denied the motion for summary judgment. In what is referred to as the Scopes case of the twenty-first century, U.S. District Judge John E. Jones, III, ruled that it is unconstitutional to teach intelligent design, a concept critical of Darwinian evolution theory, in public classrooms. The court's decision is binding only on the parties involved in this case, but it may impact how certain subjects, such as biology, are taught.

The basis of this decision centers on a view that intelligent design has religious connotations and thus violates the separation of church and state, specifically the Establishment Clause of the First Amendment. The judge's decision will not likely weaken the interest in intelligent design.

Administrative Guide

Intelligent Design

1. Advocates of intelligent design argue that it is not based on the Bible, is a scientific theory, and should have equal status with other scientific theories. However, this view has not received significant support by the scientific community.
2. The theory of intelligent design suggests that certain features of the universe and of living things are best explained by an intelligent cause rather than a natural selection.
3. Intelligent design asserts that physical and biological systems in the universe result from a purposeful design by an intelligent being rather than from chance or undirected natural causes.
4. A district judge in Pennsylvania has ruled in *Kitzmiller v. Dover* that teaching intelligent design is unconstitutional because it carries religious connotations.
5. Unless ruled unconstitutional by a federal court in its jurisdiction, the decision regarding inclusion of intelligent design into the school's curriculum is left to the discretion of school boards because the U.S. Supreme Court has not addressed its legality.

Theory of Evolution

Darwin's theory of evolution subscribes to the view that all life is related and has descended from a common ancestor. From a scientific perspective, the theory of evolution is not viewed as a hunch or a guess but rather a fact. Evolution is considered to be a well-substantiated explanation of the origin of man. It is based on the view that life evolved from nonlife in a purely naturalistic fashion with some modifications. The evolution theory supports the notion that complex creatures evolved from more simplistic ancestors over time. In essence, random genetic mutations became part of an organizational genetic code. These beneficial mutations were preserved and passed on to the next generation to facilitate their survival in a process referred to as natural selection. Many scientists believe that evolution is the force that connects all biological research. Thus, biologists consider biological evolution to be a fact based on historical evidence. According to biologists, it is indisputable that major life forms currently on Earth were not represented in the past. In fact, most life forms of the past are not living today. The important question facing scientists does not appear to be whether evolution occurred but rather what mechanisms facilitated its occurrence. Thus, the debate among scientists focuses only on the details of how evolution occurred rather than whether it occurred.

Some people reject evolution, however, for religious purposes. They tend to oppose evolution as a fact as well as mechanism theories associated with it. Still others reject evolution theory because it conflicts with the Creationists who support the view that each species on Earth was placed here by a divine being.

Teaching the Theory of Evolution

Classroom instruction regarding evolution theory has resulted in legal challenges. In the past, many states banned evolution from school curricula based on the belief that it was in direct conflict with the biblical version of creation. For example, the U.S. Supreme Court, in *Epperson v. Arkansas,* examined the constitutionality of an Arkansas law that rendered it illegal for teachers to teach this theory.[71] The court concluded that Arkansas law could not be defended as an act of religious neutrality. The law did not attempt to ban curricula in schools and universities regarding all discussions of the origin of man but rather a particular theory because it was thought to conflict with the biblical account. The court found the law to be unconstitutional. The *Epperson* case summarily prevented legislatures from banning the teaching of evolution in public schools. The court based its decision on the view that evolution is a science rather than a secular religion. The *Epperson* case was significant in providing a clear distinction between science and secular religion.

Interestingly, in the famous *Scopes* "Monkey Trial" in 1927, the Tennessee Supreme Court upheld a law that prohibited the teaching of any theory that conflicted with the Genesis version of creation.[72] Following the *Epperson* ruling, creationists attempted to support laws that provided equal emphasis on biblical accounts of creation during times in which evolution was taught in public schools. This issue was settled in 1987 in Louisiana in *Edwards v. Aguillard* when the U.S. Supreme Court invalidated Louisiana's statutes that called for equal time for creation science whenever evolution was introduced into the curriculum.[73] The court concluded that such law unconstitutionally advanced religion and represented a clear violation of the Establishment Clause.

In a related case, a federal district court in Georgia held that a school district's application of stickers to science textbooks cautioning about the scientific validity of the theory of evolution violates the Establishment Clause of the U.S. Constitution.[74] The court also ruled that the stickers violate the Georgia constitution. For years, Cobb County School District maintained a policy that the origins of life must only be taught in elective courses and never as part of the required science curriculum. Although this policy did not expressly refer to evolution, it was implemented for the purpose of avoiding conflict with a large segment of the school district's residents whose religious beliefs are inconsistent with the theory of evolution. However, in 2001 the school board decided to strengthen evolution instruction and bring the district into compliance with statewide curriculum requirements. Part of this process involved adopting new science textbooks. When members of the community, identified as creationists, submitted a petition objecting to evolution being taught "as fact rather than theory," the idea of affixing stickers to the textbooks was produced by school district legal counsel. "This textbook contains material on evolution. Evolution is a theory, not a fact, regarding the origin of living things. This material should be approached with an open mind, studied carefully, and critically considered." In the fall of 2002, the school district began affixing the stickers to all science textbooks that discussed the origins of life. A group of parents sued, alleging that the stickers violated the U.S. Constitution's Establishment Clause. The district court addressed the Establishment Clause challenge by applying the three-pronged test enunciated in *Lemon v. Kurtzman.*[75] Under the *Lemon* test, a government action passes First Amendment muster if (1) it has a secular purpose, (2) its principal or primary effect is neither to advance nor to inhibit religion, and (3) it does not create excessive entanglement of government with religion. The court noted that the second and third prongs have merged into a single "effect" inquiry. Addressing the purpose prong, the district court found that the board's purpose was to assuage members of the community who opposed the teaching of evolution based on their religious beliefs. Although this purpose is intertwined with religion, the court held that it was valid and secular because the presentation of evolution was not unnecessarily hostile. Fostering critical thinking was also a valid secular purpose. The court did not find that these purposes were merely a "sham" for promoting religion. Turning to the "effect" prong, the court noted that the disclaimer language must be analyzed to determine if it "conveys a message of endorsement or disapproval of religion to an informed reasonable observer." The court concluded that the sticker fails to satisfy the effect prong because a "reasonable observer" would interpret it as sending a message to "those who oppose evolution for religious reasons that they are favored members of the political community" and "to those who believe in evolution that they are political outsiders." A reasonable observer would be aware of the heated debate and therefore would view the sticker as endorsing "the viewpoint of Christian fundamentalists and creationists that evolution is a problematic theory lacking an adequate foundation."

In a related case, *Freiler v. Tangipahoa Parish Board of Education*, the board of education adopted a policy mandating that a disclaimer be presented prior to any discussion of evolution in biology indicating that the theory of evolution should be presented to inform students of the scientific concept and is not intended to influence or dissuade the biblical version of creation or any other concept.[76] The district was sued by parents for violating the Establishment Clause of the U.S. Constitution and was supported by the U.S. District Court and the Fifth Circuit Court of Appeals. The district appealed to the U.S. Supreme Court, who in a 6–3 decision declined to hear the case, thus allowing the lower court court decision to stand.

Administrative Guide

Theory of Evolution

1. Evolution theory suggests that all life is related and has descended from a common ancestor.
2. Historically, evolution theory had been banned from public school curriculum based on a view that it conflicted with the biblical version of creation.
3. The U.S. Supreme Court, however, in *Epperson* prevented lawmakers from banning the teaching of evolution in public schools, holding that evolution is a science rather than a secular religion.
4. Biological evolution is considered to be a fact based on historical evidence by biologists.
5. The prevailing debate among biologists revolves around details of how evolution occurred rather than whether it occurred.
6. The evolution theory provokes controversy between the scientific community and certain evangelical and fundamentalist Christian religious groups based on their attempts to prevent the teaching of evolution by having it replaced with teaching from their religious traditions.
7. The decision regarding the inclusion of evolution theory is left to the discretion of the school board.

Distribution of Religious Materials

Public school personnel are not permitted to distribute religious materials on school premises. Such practice would be a clear violation of the Establishment Clause. Public school officials also may not allow religious groups to distribute religious materials on school grounds. Support of such practices would suggest that the school embraces religion and could suggest preference of one religion over another. Again, the principle of neutrality demands that schools assume a neutral position, neither supporting religion nor prohibiting individual students from exercising their religious rights. Two cases illustrate the courts' posture regarding the distribution of religious materials.

One case involving the distribution of religious material arose in Florida when an elementary school student brought religious pamphlets to distribute to her classmates. The school district's policy vested the superintendent with power to restrain the distribution of any materials unrelated to school courses in the public schools. When the elementary student requested, through her teacher, to be allowed to distribute the pamphlets, they were confiscated and carried to the principal, who subsequently destroyed them, indicating that he could not permit the distribution of religious material at school.

The student and her mother filed suit in the U.S. district court, seeking a preliminary injunction against enforcement of the policy. The court held that the motion was premature and that the policy had never been applied by the school. The Eleventh Circuit Court affirmed the district court's decision. The district court then addressed the student's request for a permanent injunction against enforcing the policy. The court discerned that the policy was a content-based prior restraint ban on free speech that could be justified only with a showing that the literature would materially or substantially disrupt the operations of the school or infringe on the rights of other students.

In the absence of this showing, the school district's policy, as expected, could not be supported under the law. The First Amendment to the U.S. Constitution prohibits the government from inhibiting the free exercise of religion. There was no evidence that the distribution of the religious pamphlets interfered *materially* or *substantially* with school operations. The court held for the student by issuing a permanent injunction against the enforcement of the policy and also awarded nominal damages and attorney fees.[77]

The other leading case, *Tudor v. Board of Education,*[78] arose in New Jersey, where the highest state court struck down an attempt by Gideons International to distribute the Gideon Bible throughout the public schools. Distribution of the Bible was expressly approved by the board of education. Approval was based on parental requests that Bibles be distributed to their children. The court, in assessing this practice, determined that the Gideon Bible was sectarian, based on testimony of representatives of various faiths, many of whom did not accept part or all of the Gideon Bible. The court also considered testimony from psychologists and educators who affirmed that the distribution of permission slips for parental consent would create subtle pressure on all children to accept the slips. Furthermore, the distribution of the Bible, as embraced by the school, would signify that school officials had given the Bible their stamp of approval, thus creating increased tension among other religious groups.

The court, in its ruling, found the practice to be unconstitutional in that it showed preference of one religion over others, thus violating the Establishment Clause. The Fifth Circuit Court of Appeals unanimously agreed with the New Jersey district court's ruling in the related *Meltzer v. Board of Public Instruction of Orange County.*[79]

In yet another case involving the distribution of the Bible, a Nebraska school board member withdrew his son from school and resigned from his position on the board when his son was given a Gideon Bible in the school's hallway. The distribution was clearly in violation of unwritten district policy, which permitted distribution of Bibles to fifth-graders on the sidewalk and off school premises once per year. The school employed an open forum policy, which made sidewalks available to any group after school hours. The facts revealed that distribution was voluntary, as students were reminded over the school's public address system that they were not required to accept a Bible. On the following day, students received Bibles in the hallway. Although there was no evidence that the district played any role in this activity, the board member filed suit in the U.S. district court under 42 U.S.C. § 1983.

The court held that the district played no role in the hallway distribution and that its open forum was valid because it had a neutral purpose that neither advanced nor inhibited religious groups. It further noted that no groups had ever been denied access to the sidewalk and that no district resources were involved. The court granted summary judgment for the district.[80]

Pledge of Allegiance

LANDMARK CASE.   A landmark case challenging the daily ritual of reciting the Pledge of Allegiance emerged in the Ninth Circuit Court in California regarding the constitutionality of the inclusion of the words *under God.* The final outcome of the ruling in this case has had a profound effect on public schools, on state and federal governments, and on U.S. citizens in general. Forty-nine states have filed briefs supporting the Pledge of Allegiance.

This case arose when Michael R. Newdow, an atheist, filed a suit on behalf of his eight-year-old daughter challenging the inclusion of *under God* in the pledge. A panel of the U.S. Court of Appeals for the Ninth Circuit in San Francisco created quite a controversy when it ruled 2–1 that the inclusion of *under God* was an unconstitutional establishment of religion by the government.

Although Newdow does not have legal custody of his daughter, the court held that he has legal standing to raise the challenge on behalf of his daughter, who has not been named in court papers. The defendants are the Elk Grove Unified School District, the State of California, the U.S. Congress, and President George W. Bush. The eight-year-old girl's mother, Sandra Banning, has publicly confirmed that her daughter has no religious objection to reciting the pledge in school. Newdow and Banning, the child's parents, have never been married. Both held informal custody of their daughter until February 2003, after which time sole custody was awarded to Ms. Banning. A California Superior Court barred Newdow from naming his daughter as defendant.

U.S. Circuit Judge Alfred T. Goodwin wrote the original opinion against the constitutionality of the pledge and also stated that the mother had no power as sole legal custodian to insist that her child be subjected to unconstitutional state action. U.S. Circuit Judge Ferdinand F. Fernandez, who dissented, agreed only on the issue of legal standing. Subsequently, a larger panel of Ninth Circuit judges heard this case and supported the decision of the three-judge panel. This case has been appealed to the Supreme Court.

The George W. Bush administration defended the words *under God* in the Pledge of Allegiance and asked the Supreme Court to uphold the daily recitation of the pledge. The administration's rationale was that reciting the Pledge of Allegiance is a patriotic exercise and not a religious testimonial. In addition, the administration said that the reference to "one nation under God" in the Pledge of Allegiance is an official acknowledgment of what all students may properly be taught in school regardless of their religious affiliation. Jay Sekulow, chief counsel of the American Center for Law, filed court appeal or court papers on behalf of members of Congress.

On June 14, 2004, the U.S. Supreme Court overturned the Ninth Circuit Court's decision on technical grounds and preserved the contested phrase "one nation under God" in the Pledge of Allegiance. The Supreme Court ruled that Newdow, the plaintiff, had no legal standing to challenge the pledge because he was not the custodial parent of his then ten-year-old daughter and could not legally represent her. This ruling failed to address whether the inclusion of the reference to God was an impermissible practice involving an unconstitutional blending of church and state. Consequently, the U.S. Supreme Court's ruling did not prevent a future lawsuit challenging the inclusion of the phrase "one nation under God" in the pledge. In fact, another challenge has emerged by Newdow and others who oppose the Pledge of Allegiance.[81]

Interestingly, a federal judge in San Francisco has held subsequent to Newdow's initial challenge that reciting the Pledge of Allegiance in public schools is unconstitutional. The case, identical to his earlier challenge, was brought by Newdow but this time on behalf of three unnamed parents and their children. U.S. District Judge Lawrence Karlton ruled that this pledge's reference to "one nation under God" violates students' right to be "free from a coercive requirement to affirm God." Judge Karlton indicated that he was bound by the precedent established by the Ninth U.S. Circuit Court of Appeals, which ruled in favor of Newdow in 2002 by holding that the pledge is unconstitutional when recited in public schools.

Karlton issued an order preventing the reciting of the pledge at Elk Grove Unified School District, Rio Linda, and Elverta joint elementary school districts in Sacramento County where the plaintiffs' children attend school. The judge's order will not extend beyond these districts unless affirmed by a higher court, at which time the ruling would be extended to the nine states within the Ninth Circuit. At least for now, millions of schoolchildren who desire to do so may continue to recite the Pledge of Allegiance in public schools because the U.S. Supreme Court decision in the *West Virginia State Board of Education v. Barnette* case in 1943 held that public school officials may not require students to salute and pledge allegiance to the flag.[82] These activities must be strictly voluntary.

Although it is difficult to predict the outcome of this case, it appears that the U.S. Supreme Court may presumably address criteria similar to those used in the *Lemon* case:

Does the pledge have a secular purpose?

Does it advance or inhibit religion?

Does it create excessive entanglement?

In addition, the court may likely consider that reciting the pledge is optional, as decided in 1943 in *West Virginia State Board of Education v. Barnette,* in which the U.S. Supreme Court held that public school officials may not require students to salute and pledge allegiance to the flag.[83] After the events of September 11, 2001, the United States has become strongly united around patriotism, which will no doubt have some impact on the ultimate ruling. Added to these developments is the fact that *In God We Trust,* found on U.S. coins, has been held to be a national slogan and not the government's endorsement of religion. It will be interesting to observe the outcome and impact of this case. However, in a recent decision, a federal appeals court in the Ninth District upheld the use of the words *under God* in the Pledge of Allegiance as well as *In God We Trust* on U.S. currency. The court rejected arguments that these phrases violate the separation of church and state. The Ninth Circuit Court of Appeals decision was a response to Michael Newdow's claim that these references to God were unconstitutional and infringed on his religious beliefs. Religious issues continue to invoke conflict and highly charged emotional responses as reflected by the volume and diversity of litigation surrounding religion. Issues involving religion remain unsettled. Consequently, absolutes are difficult to identify.

Administrative Guide

Religious Activities

1. School-sponsored holiday programs are permitted if they are not conducted in a religious atmosphere.
2. Released time for religious instruction may be allowed if evidence reveals that no public school resources are involved. Use of public school resources violates the Establishment Clause of the First Amendment.
3. School districts may find it difficult to justify the posting of the Ten Commandments or other references to God as meeting a purely secular purpose.
4. Religious pageants, displays, or symbols will not meet the constitutional requirements of neutrality by school officials. Statues or pictures may be used to teach art forms if taught as a secular activity.
5. The distribution of religious material by external groups is illegal if the distribution occurs on school premises. However, a student may be allowed to distribute religious pamphlets if the distribution does not interfere with normal school activities or create material or substantial disruption.
6. School authorities must respect the free exercise rights of students, unless the exercise of those rights violates the rights of others or disrupts the educational process.
7. School authorities must refrain from any activity that would create an unclear line of separation between school activities and religious activities.
8. School authorities should consult the district's legal counsel regarding any questionable religious activities in their schools.
9. Aid to students attending religious school in the form of computers and equipment is permissible as part of a general program designed to enhance overall educational opportunities of all students.
10. Students may not be compelled to recite the Pledge of Allegiance based on their right to freedom of expression.

RELIGIOUS FREEDOMS INVOLVING TEACHERS

The First Amendment guarantees religious freedom to all citizens. Title VII of the Civil Rights Act of 1964 further prohibits any forms of discrimination based on religion. Therefore, it is unlawful for a school district to deny employment, dismiss, or fail to renew a teacher's contract based on religious grounds. Teachers, like all citizens, possess religious rights that must be respected. As with all rights, religious rights are not without limits. Because teachers are public employees and schools must remain neutral in all matters regarding religion, reasonable restraints affect the exercise of religious rights in the school setting. However, teachers are completely free to fully exercise their religious rights outside of normal school activities.

For example, teachers may not refuse to teach certain aspects of the state-approved curriculum based on religious objections or beliefs. Although the courts recognize the existence of the teacher's religious rights, they also recognize the compelling state interest in educating all children. One court held that education "cannot be left to individual teachers to teach the way they please." Teachers have no constitutional right to require others to submit to their views and to forgo a portion of their education they would otherwise be entitled to enjoy.[84] In short, teachers cannot subject others, particularly students, to their religious beliefs or ideologies; they, too, must remain neutral in their relationship with students.

Religious Rights of Teachers in the School Environment

Based on the free exercise of religion, it is reasonable to conclude that teachers should be afforded the right to informally engage in religious speech with their colleagues, including prayer or Bible study, at times when teachers are allowed to meet with their colleagues for other forms of expression. However, no organized prayer meetings, informal religious speech, or Bible discussion should occur. These should be activities protected by the free speech clause as long as they occur in a private area where students cannot observe or participate in them. Such activities ideally should occur before or after school. It is difficult to determine precisely how the courts would view these activities, because this issue has very rarely been presented to the courts.

In one of the rare cases involving the use of school facilities by teachers for religious meetings, a teacher brought suit against the school board, its members, and the superintendent, seeking an injunction against banning religious meetings by teachers on school property. The U.S. District Court for the Southern District of Indiana granted the school district a motion for summary judgment. The teacher appealed. The court of appeals held that teachers had no right under the First Amendment free speech clause to hold prayer meetings on school property before students arrived and the school day began. The court observed further that school officials had consistently applied a policy prohibiting the use of school facilities for religious activity. The teacher contended that the school was an open forum in that it was used for meetings on other subjects. The court found her claim to be clearly erroneous.[85] Teachers generally should have a right to express themselves to other teachers while on school property during noninstructional times as long as students are not involved and the expression only involves willing teachers. Teachers should be cautious that their speech is not construed as harassment of another teacher who does not wish to be involved in these discussions. Therefore, willing parties would be important in this instance. As previously stated, this issue has not been decided conclusively by courts; however, it appears that the First Amendment should provide some degree of protection to teachers regarding their right to express personal views on religion in conversation with their peers, just as they would on other topics. Until these issues are addressed by the courts, it is difficult to determine precisely how the courts might rule.

Use of Religious Garb by Teachers

The wearing of religious garb by public school teachers has created legal questions regarding freedom of expression rights versus religious violations based on dress. It has been well established that public school districts may not legally deny employment opportunities to teachers based on their religious beliefs or affiliation. However, the wearing of religious garb by public school teachers raises the issue of whether such dress creates a sectarian influence in the classroom.

Many state statutes prohibit public school teachers from wearing religious garb in the classroom. Some legal experts believe that the mere presence of religious dress serves as a constant reminder of the teacher's religious orientation and could have a proselytizing effect on children, because they are impressionable, particularly those in the lower grades.

Conversely, public school teachers advance the argument that religious dress is a protected right regarding freedom of expression. The courts, however, have clearly established the position that the exercise of one person's rights may not infringe on the rights of others and that public interest supersedes individual interests. Further, prohibiting a teacher from wearing religious dress does not adversely affect the teacher's belief. It merely means that teachers cannot exercise their beliefs through dress during the period of the day in which they are employed. There is no interference outside the school day. Thus, a teacher is free to exercise full religious rights and freedoms outside normal hours of employment. The courts have not reached total consensus on this issue, as can be discerned through the following analysis.

In a significant case, the Pennsylvania Supreme Court supported the authority of a local board of education to employ nuns as teachers and to permit them to dress in the custom of their order.[86] Subsequent to the Pennsylvania decision, the legislature enacted a statute prohibiting the wearing of any religious dress as insignia by public school teachers representing any religious order. The constitutional validity of this statute was upheld by the Pennsylvania Supreme Court, noting that the law was not passed against belief but rather against acts as teachers in performing their duties.[87]

Another court disqualified all nuns from teaching in public schools on the grounds that their lives were dedicated to teaching religion.[88] Recent court interpretations seem to suggest that religious dress that creates a reverent atmosphere and may have the potential to proselytize, thereby creating a sufficient sectarian influence, violates the First Amendment neutrality clause.

A related case involving free speech and religion arose in Pennsylvania. A teacher at an intermediate school was suspended for wearing a cross on a necklace to school. The Pennsylvania legislature passed a "religious garb law" that prohibited teachers from wearing religious clothing to public schools. Brenda Nichol was suspended after being informed by her principal that wearing the cross in a visible manner violated school policy. She subsequently filed a suit claiming that the policy violated her rights because jewelry containing religious symbols was banned whereas other jewelry was not.[89]

The district court agreed and held that the school district had engaged in viewpoint discrimination that could not be justified as serving a compelling state interest. The court relied on the U.S. Supreme Court's reasoning in *Good News Club v. Milford Central School*[90] that religious-based restrictions on expression of speech demonstrate hostility toward religion and violate the principle of neutrality. The court rejected the district's claim that impressionable young children would be indoctrinated by the presence of the religious necklace. The court held that Ms. Nichol's subdued expression of her religious faith outweighed the district's concern.

Administrative Guide

Religious Freedoms

1. Wearing of religious garb by teachers may be disallowed if their dress creates a reverent atmosphere or has a proselytizing impact on students.
2. The religious rights of teachers must be respected, as long as they do not violate the Establishment Clause of the First Amendment by creating excessive entanglement in the school.
3. School officials must make reasonable accommodations for teachers regarding observance of special religious holidays, as long as such accommodations are not deemed excessive or disruptive to the educational process.
4. Teachers should not be coerced to participate in nonacademic ceremonies or activities that violate their religious beliefs or convictions.
5. In cases involving the performance of their nonacademic duties, teachers may be requested to present documentable evidence that a religious belief or right is violated.
6. No form of religious discrimination may be used to influence decisions regarding employment, promotion, salary increments, transfers, demotions, or dismissals.

CASE STUDIES

Teachers and Devotional Activities

You are a principal of a vibrant school located in an industrial city of 300,000 people. It has been reported that a group of your teachers are holding devotional activities in the teacher's lounge during their break.

Discussion Questions

1. How do you respond to this news?
2. Is it permissible for teachers to hold devotional activities during school hours on school premises? Why? Why not?
3. What action, if any, would you take?
4. How do you think the courts would view this practice in the context of the Establishment Clause?
5. How do you think the courts would view your decision?
6. What is the basis for your response?

Religion and Student Expression

Jean Riley is the principal of a small elementary school in a metropolitan school district. One of her best teachers asked her first-graders to make a poster depicting things for which they were thankful. One student made a poster expressing thanks for Jesus. Posters were displayed in the school's hallway. The student's poster was removed but later returned in a less prominent place. The next year, the student was chosen to read a story to the class. The student selected an adaptation of a biblical story.

Discussion Questions

1. Should the student be permitted to read his biblical story? Why or why not?
2. What is the legal issue surrounding both the poster and the biblical story?
3. What legal risks does the school incur (if any) if it permits both of these activities?
4. What legal risks does the school incur if it denies both of these practices?
5. How would the courts likely rule on this case? Provide a rationale for your response.

Use of Facilities by Religious Groups

Gayle Dixon is the principal of a midsize, progressive, metropolitan high school located in the Mid-South. The school maintains an open forum, thereby allowing noncurricular groups to use facilities during noninstructional times, including student religious groups. A Bible club has requested the use of school facilities, but Dixon learned that the club's charter allows only Christians to be club officers. In her mind, this provision of the charter is discriminatory. Based on this provision, she rejected the club's request to use school facilities. The club filed suit.

Discussion Questions

1. Does the club have legitimate grounds to file suit? Why or why not?
2. Is Dixon justified in rejecting the club's request to use school facilities? Why or why not?
3. Does the Bible club have the right to specify that only Christians may be club officers? Why or why not?
4. If you were the principal, would you handle this situation any differently?
5. How do you think the court would rule in this case? Provide a rationale for your response.
6. What are the administrative implications of this case?

Use of Facilities by the Community

A midwestern school district approved a policy allowing open access to its facilities by the public as long as public use did not interfere with school activities. The community has a history of deep religious convictions. A group of graduating seniors and their parents arranged for a baccalaureate ceremony sponsored by the community. The ceremony was to be held in a school gymnasium. Verbal authorization was granted by school district officials. One month later, the district approved a new policy, which prohibited the group from using the gym.

Discussion Questions

1. Does the board's action constitute a breach of duty to honor its verbal authorization? Why or why not?
2. Does the district have a right to change its policies after giving verbal authorization for use of the gym? Why or why not?
3. Does the district's action amount to a breach? Why or why not?
4. What is the legality of reversing a policy that has been approved and executed for an extended period of time?
5. Would the district's action constitute discrimination against the students, their parents, and the community?
6. What might the district's defense be in this situation?
7. How would the court likely rule on this issue? Provide a rationale for your response.
8. What are the administrative implications?

Note: The board is the legal body for the district.

Student Response Sheet _____

Professor _____   Student _____

Course _____   Date _____

Title of In-Basket Exercise _____

Reaction:

_____

_____

_____

_____

_____

_____

_____

_____

_____

_____

_____

_____

_____

_____

_____

_____

_____

_____

_____

_____

_____

_____

_____

_____

_____

_____

Endnotes

1. *Reynolds v. United States,* 98 U.S. (8 OTTO) 145 (1879).
2. *Cantwell v. Connecticut,* 310 U.S. 296 (1940).
3. *Employment Division, Department of Human Resources of Oregon v. Smith,* 444 U.S. 872 (1990).
4. *Everson v. Board of Education of the Township of Ewing,* 330 U.S. 1, 15 (1947).
5. Source: First Amendment Center.
6. *Lynch v. Donnelly,* 465 U.S. 668 (1984).
7. *Lee v. Weisman,* 505 U.S. 577 (1992).
8. *County of Allegheny v. American Civil Liberties Union,* 492 U.S. 573 (1989).
9. *Ecklund v. Byron Union School Dist.,* 549 U.S. 942 (U.S. cert. denied 10/2/06).
10. *Engel v. Vitale,* 370 U.S. 421, 82 S.Ct. 1261 (1962).
11. *Ingebretsen v. Jackson Public School District,* 864 F. Supp. 1473 (S.D. Miss. 1994).
12. *School District of Abington Township v. Schempp; Murray v. Curlett,* 374 U.S. 203, 83 S.Ct. 1650 (1965).
13. *Wallace v. Jaffree,* 472 U.S. 38, 105 S.Ct. 2479 (1985).
14. *Santa Fe Independent School District v. Jane Doe,* 120 S.Ct. 2266; 147 L. Ed. 2d 295 (2000).
15. *Chandler v. Siegelman,* 230 F.3d 1313 (11th Cir. 2000).
16. *Lemon v. Kurtzman,* 403 U.S. 602 (1971).
17. *Jager v. Douglas County School District,* 862 F.2d 824, 11th Cir. (1989).
18. *Santa Fe,* op. cit.
19. Ibid.
20. *Sands v. Morongo Unified School District,* 809 P. 2d 809 (Cal. 1991).
21. *Lee v. Weisman,* 505 U.S. 577 (1992).
22. *Lemon v. Kurtzman,* op. cit.
23. *Jones v. Clear Creek Independent School District,* 977 F.2d 963 (5th Cir. 1992).
24. *Adler v. Duval County School Board,* 851 F. Supp. 446 (M.D. Fla. 1994).
25. *Bannon v. School District of Palm Beach County,* 387 F.3d 1208, 1214 (11th Cir. 2004).
26. *Nixon v. Northern Local District Board of Education,* 383 F. Supp. 2d 965 (S.D. Ohio 2005).
27. *Tyler Chase Harper v. Poway Unified School District,* 345 F. Supp. 2d 1096 (S.D. Cal. 2004).
28. *Hansen v. Ann Arbor Public Schools,* 293 F. Supp. 2d 780, 797 (E.D. Mich. 2003).
29. *Holloman v. Harland,* 370 F.3d 1252 (11th Cir. 2004).
30. *Coles v. Cleveland Board of Education,* 1999, WL 144262 (6th Cir. 1999).
31. *Galloway v. Town of Greece,* 681 F.3d 20 - Court of Appeals, 2nd Circuit 2012.
32. *Aguilar v. Felton,* 473 U.S. 402 (1985).

33. *Agostini v. Felton,* 473 U.S. 402, 105 S.Ct. 3232, 87 L. Ed. 2d 290 (1985).
34. *Lemon v. Kurtzman* and *Early v. Dicenso,* 403 U.S. 602, 91 S.Ct. 2105 (1971).
35. *Sloan v. Lemon,* 413 U.S. 825, 93 S.Ct. 2982 (1973).
36. *School District of the City of Grand Rapids v. Ball,* 473 U.S. 373, 195 S.Ct. 3216 (1985).
37. *Meek v. Pittenger,* 421 U.S. 349, 95 S.Ct. 1753 (1975).
38. *Mueller v. Allen,* 463 U.S. 388, 103 S.Ct. 3062 (1983).
39. *Everson,* op. cit.
40. *Cochran v. Louisiana State Board of Education,* 281 U.S. 370 (1930).
41. *Mitchell v. Helms,* 120 S.Ct. 2530; 147 L. Ed. 2d 660; 68 (2000).
42. *Weinbaum v. City of Las Cruces, New Mexico,* 541 F.31 1017 (19th Cir. 2008).
43. *Lawrence v. Buchmuller,* 40 Misc. 2d 300, 243 N.Y.S. 2d 87, 91 (Sup. Ct. 1963).
44. *Washegesic v. Bloomingdale Public Schools,* 33 F.3d 697 (6th Cir. 1994).
45. *Ring v. Grand Forks School District No. 1,* 483 F. Supp. 272 (N.D. 1980).
46. *Stone v. Graham,* 599 S.W. 2d 157 (Ky. 1980).
47. *McCreary County, Kentucky v. American Civil Liberties Union of Kentucky,* 354 F.3d 438 (2005).
48. *Van Orden v. Perry,* 351 F.3d 173 (2005).
49. Source: *Los Angeles Times,* May 8, 2013.
50. 20 U.S.C. § 4071 (1988).
51. *Bender v. Williams Sport,* 106 S.Ct. 1326 (1986).
52. *Mergens v. Board of Education of the Westside Community Schools,* 496 U.S. 226 (1990).
53. *Golden v. Rossford Exempted Village School Dist.,* 445 F.Supp.2d 820 (N.D. Ohio 2006).
54. *Clark v. Dallas Independent School,* 806 F. Supp. 116 (N.D. Texas 1992).
55. *Truth v. Kent School District,* No. 8-1130, 2009 WL 1835191 (U.S. cert. denied 6/29/09).
56. *Wallace v. Washoe County District* (1988).
57. *Gregoire v. Centennial School District,* 907 F.2d 13; 66 1378-70, 1382 (3rd Cir. 1990).
58. *Bronx Household of Faith v. Community School District No. 10,* 127 F.3d 207 (2nd Cir. 1997).
59. *Lamb's Chapel v. Center Moriches School District,* 508 U.S. 384, 124 L. Ed. 2d 352, 113 S.Ct. 2141 (Sup. Ct. 1993).
60. *Florey v. Sioux Falls School District,* 464 F. Supp. 911 (D.S.D. 1979).
61. *Nurre v. Whitehead,* 580 F.3d 1087 (9th Cir. 2009).
62. *People of State of Illinois ex rel. McCollum v. Board of Education of District No. 71, Champaign County, Illinois,* 333 U.S. 203, 68 S.Ct. 462 (1948).
63. *Zorach v. Clauson U.S. Supreme Court,* 343 U.S. 306, 72 S.Ct. 679 (1952).

64. *Lanner v. Wimmer,* 662 F.2d 1349 (10th Cir. 1981).

65. *Stone v. Graham,* 599 S.W. 2d 157 (Ky. 1980).

66. *Gibson v. Lee County Board of Education,* F. Supp. 2d 1426; 1998 U.S. Dist. LEXIS 2696; 11 Fla. LawW. Fed. D 503 (1998).

67. *Lemon v. Kurtzman,* 403 U.S. 602, 612-613, 29 L.Ed. 2d 745, 91 S.Ct. 2105 (1971).

68. *Wiley v. Franklin,* 468 F. Supp. 133, 150 (E.D. Tenn. 1979).

69. *Elrod v. Burns,* 427 U.S. 347, 49 L. Ed. 2d 547, 96 S.Ct. 2673 (1976).

70. *Kitzmiller v. Dover Area School District* (ruling in January 2006).

71. *Epperson v. Arkansas,* 393, U.S. 97 (1968).

72. *Scopes v. State,* 289 S.W. 363, 364 (TN 1927).

73. *Edwards v. Aguillard,* 482 US 578 (1987).

74. *Selman v. Cobb County School District,* 390 F. Supp. 2d 1286 (N.D. Ga. 2005).

75. *Lemon v. Kurtzman,* op. cit.

76. *Freiler v. Tangipahoa Parish Board of Education,* 185 F.3d 337 (5th Cir.) (1999).

77. *Johnson-Loehner v. O'Brien,* 859 F. Supp. 575 (M.D. Fla. 1994).

78. *Tudor v. Board of Education of Borough of Rutherford,* 14 N.J. 31,100 A. 2d 857 (1953), cert. den., 348 U.S. 816, 75 S.Ct. 25, 99 L. Ed. 664 (1954).

79. *Meltzer v. Board of Public Instruction of Orange County,* U.S. Court of Appeals, 5th Cir. (1978), 577 F.2d 311, cert. denied, 439 U.S. 1089 (1979).

80. *Schanou v. Lancaster County School District No. 160,* 863 F. Supp. 1048 D. Neb. (1994).

81. *Newdow v. United States,* 315 F.3d 495 (C.A. 9, 2002).

82. *West Virginia State Board of Education v. Barnette,* 319 U.S. 624, 63 S.Ct. 1178, 1943.

83. Ibid.

84. *Palmer v. Board of Education of the City of Chicago,* 603 F.2d 1271, 1274 (7th Cir. 1979), cert. denied, 444 U.S. 1026, 100 S.Ct. 689 (1980).

85. *May v. Evansville,* 787 F.2d 1105 (97th Cir. 1986).

86. *Hysong v. Gallitzin Borough School District,* 164 Pa. 629, 30 A. 482 (1894).

87. *Commonwealth v. Herr,* 229 Pa. 132 78 A. 68 (1915).

88. *Harfst v. Hoegen,* 349 Mo. 808, 163 S.W. 3d 609.

89. *Nichol v. Arin Intermediate Unit 28,* 268 F. Supp. 2d 536 (W.D. Pa. 2003).

90. *Good News Club v. Milford Central School,* 202 F.3d 502 (2nd Cir. 1999).

Chapter 3

Student Rights and Restrictions

School officials are granted broad powers to establish rules and regulations governing student conduct in the school setting. These powers, however, are not absolute. They are subject to the standard of *reasonableness*. Generally, rules are deemed to be reasonable if they are necessary to maintain an orderly and peaceful school environment and advance the educational process. The courts—in determining the enforceability of policies, rules, and regulations—require evidence of *sufficient justification* by school authorities of the need to enforce the policy, rule, or regulation. Because students enjoy many of the same constitutional rights as adults, courts have been very diligent in ensuring protection of their constitutional rights.

Although school rules are necessary to ensure proper order and decorum, they should not be so broad and nebulous as to allow for *arbitrary and inconsistent interpretation.* Fundamental fairness requires that students know what behavior is required of them by school officials. They should not be expected to conform to rules that are vague and ambiguous in meaning or application. Rules should be sufficiently definite in providing students with adequate information regarding expected behavior. They should be stated in such a manner that students of average intelligence are not necessarily required to guess at their meaning. *It is important to remember that a fair and reasonable exercise of administrative authority will withstand court scrutiny.*

Further, in determining whether policies or regulations are fair and reasonable, it is necessary to assess them in the context of their application. Whether a rule or regulation is legally defensible depends on the fact situation.

The concept of **in loco parentis** (in place of parent) has permitted school officials to promulgate rules that allow them to exercise a reasonable degree of control over students under their supervision. This concept, however, is not without limits. School authorities and teachers do not fully occupy the place of the parent. *Their control or jurisdiction is limited to school functions and activities.* Although *in loco parentis* is considered a viable concept, it does require prudence on the part of school officials and teachers. Prudence in this instance implies that school authorities' actions must be consistent with those of the average parent under the same or similar circumstances. Generally, if administrative actions conform to this norm, they are judged to be reasonable. Although children are subject to reasonable rules and regulations promulgated by school officials, they do enjoy personal rights that must be recognized and respected by school officials.

In the landmark 1960s *Tinker* case, the U.S. Supreme Court for the very first time held that *students possess the same constitutional rights as adults and that these rights do not end at the schoolhouse door.*[1] This ruling by the High Court significantly altered the relationship between school officials and students. The *Tinker* ruling clearly mandated that professional educators respect the **civil rights** of students in the school. In cases where student rights are restricted, school officials must demonstrate a *justifiable or legitimate reason* for doing so. In these instances, the burden of proof justifiably rests with school officials. For example, school officials may restrict the rights of a student if they are able to demonstrate that such a restriction is necessary to maintain order and proper decorum in the school. A student's rights also may be restricted if the exercise of those rights infringes on the rights of others. In short, no rights are absolute but, rather, are subject to reasonable restrictions that must be justified by school officials.

The development of a legally defensible code of student conduct represents one method of ensuring that the rights of students are protected. The student code should be developed through the involvement of school personnel, parents, citizens, and even students, where appropriate. A final step should include a review by the school district's attorney to validate the code's legality. Once approved and adopted, policies should be disseminated, periodically reviewed, and revised as needed.

FREEDOM OF EXPRESSION

Freedom of expression is derived from the First Amendment to the U.S. Constitution, which provides, in part, "Congress shall make no law . . . abridging the freedom of speech, or of press or of the rights of peoples to peacefully assemble." The *Tinker* case confirmed that students are entitled to all First Amendment guarantees, subject only to the provision in which the exercise of these rights creates **material** and substantial disruption in the school. An excerpt from *Tinker* pointed out the following:

> School officials do not possess absolute authority over their students. Students in school as well as out of school are "persons" under our Constitution. They possess fundamental rights which the State must respect. . . . In our system, students may not be regarded as closed-circuit recipients of only that which the state chooses to communicate. They may not be confined to the expression of those sentiments that are officially approved. In the absence of a specific showing of constitutionally valid reasons to regulate their speech, students are entitled to freedom of expression of their views.[2]

Stated differently, the First Amendment to the Constitution guarantees freedom of speech to U.S. citizens, including students in public schools. This freedom, however, does not include a license to exercise such rights in a manner that creates *material or substantial disruption to the educational process*. These were the criteria applied by the Supreme Court in determining whether regulations prohibiting student expression were constitutionally valid.

The *Tinker* case is viewed as the leading case in addressing speech as symbolic expression. This case emerged when three public school students wore black armbands to class in protest of the government's policy in Vietnam. All were suspended. There was no evidence that substantial interference with school work or school discipline had resulted or could reasonably have been predicted to result from the students' conduct. School authorities did not prohibit the wearing of other symbols with political or controversial significance, but were interested in suppressing students' expressions of opinion about a specific subject, the Vietnam War. The students sought a court order restraining the officials from disciplining them and contending that the suspensions were unconstitutional. The U.S. Supreme Court held that it is unconstitutional to discipline students for the peaceful wearing of armbands or for other symbolic expressions of opinion unless it can be shown that material interference with, or substantial disruption of, the school's routine did or would occur. The peaceful wearing of armbands is an expression of opinion entitled to protection under the First Amendment, which is made applicable to the states by the Fourteenth Amendment. Because students are "persons" under the Constitution, school officials may constitutionally infringe on students' First Amendment rights only when the particular expression of opinion proscribed would materially and substantially interfere with the operation of the school and the rights of other students to learn. Mere apprehension of disturbance is not a sufficient basis for such action on the part of school authorities.[3]

To gain a clearer view of the nature of the litigation involving freedom of expression in the *Tinker* case, a contrasting Fifth Circuit Court of Appeals case, *Blackwell v. Issaquena County Board of Education,* emerged in Mississippi when a principal banned the wearing of political buttons in response to a disturbance by students noisily talking in the corridor when they were scheduled to be in class. Those students wearing the buttons were found pinning them on other students who objected. Class instruction deteriorated into a state of general confusion and a breakdown in discipline. Students were warned during an assembly program not to wear the buttons. This warning was repeated on the following day. Violators were subsequently suspended. As the suspended students left campus, they attempted to influence other nonviolators to leave with them. The court held for the board of education, upholding the principal's action as reasonable, based on the factual circumstances surrounding these incidents. The Fifth Circuit justices reasoned that it is always within the province of school authorities to provide by regulation for the prohibition and punishment of acts calculated to undermine the school's routine: "This is not only proper in our opinion, but it is necessary."[4]

As illustrated by this case, evidence of material and substantial disruption forms sufficient grounds to limit freedom of expression. The significant difference, however, in viewing these two cases is that there was no evidence of disruption in *Tinker* but there was considerable evidence of disruption in *Blackwell.* Consequently, the principal's action was not justified in the former case but was well justified in the latter. The importance of this distinction is evident when a valuable constitutional right is involved. In these instances, decisions must be made on a case-by-case basis.

A landmark case involving freedom of expression by students was heard by the U.S. Supreme Court in 1986.[5] This case arose when a male student at Bethel High School delivered a speech nominating a fellow student for elective office before an assembly of over six hundred peers, many of whom were fourteen-year-olds. Students were required to attend the assembly or report to study hall. In his nominating speech, the student referred to his candidate in terms of an elaborate, explicit sexual metaphor, despite having been warned in advance by two teachers not to do so. During the speech, a counselor observed students' reactions, which included laughter, graphic sexual gestures, hooting, bewilderment, and embarrassment. The student was called into the assistant principal's office and notified that he had violated a school rule prohibiting obscene language or gestures. When he admitted to the assistant principal that he had deliberately used sexual innuendo in his speech, he was informed that he would be suspended for three days and that his name would be removed from the list of candidates for student speaker at the school's commencement exercises.

The student brought suit against the school in a U.S. district court, claiming that his First Amendment right to freedom of speech had been violated. The district court agreed and awarded him $278 as compensation for deprivation of his constitutional rights based on two days of suspension and $12,750 in litigation costs and attorney's fees. The court also ordered the school district to allow the student to speak at commencement. The U.S. Court of Appeals, Ninth Circuit, rejected the school district's appeal and held that the district had failed to prove that the speech had interfered with or disrupted the educational environment. On further appeal by the school district, the U.S. Supreme Court ruled that although public school students have the right to advocate unpopular and controversial views in school, that right must be balanced against the schools' interest in teaching socially appropriate behavior. A public school may legitimately establish standards of civil and mature conduct. The Court in ruling for the district observed that such standards would be difficult to convey in a school that tolerated the "lewd, indecent and offensive" speech and conduct that the student in this case exhibited.

Interestingly, in a later case, the U.S. Supreme Court limited the impact of its student expression decision in *Tinker*. An example of speech that is inconsistent with the school's mission may be found in the *Morse v. Frederick* case.[6] Joseph Frederick was a student at Douglas High School in Juneau, Alaska. During an Olympic torch relay event, he held up a fourteen-foot-long banner that read "Bong Hits 4 Jesus." Even though he was standing on a public sidewalk rather than on the school grounds, high school principal Deborah Morse suspended Frederick for ten days for violating the school's policy against promoting illegal substances at a school-sanctioned event. In response to his suspension, Frederick brought suit against the school, alleging that his First Amendment right to free speech was violated.

The Ninth Circuit Court of Appeals held for Frederick in ruling that Morse violated his right to free speech by suspending him from school. The school district appealed to the U.S. Supreme Court. In June 2007, the U.S. Supreme Court ruled in a 5–4 decision that the school had a right to discipline students who presented messages that conflicted with stated anti-drug policies even when there is an absence of disruption in the school.

In a related case, an Illinois student who opposed a student "Day of Silence" wore a T-shirt stating: "Be Happy, Not Gay" and "My Day of Silence, Straight Alliance." A school official made him ink out the phrase "Not Gay." To avoid discipline, he did not wear the shirt the next day. The student sued school officials, arguing that the First Amendment permitted his expression. A court refused to issue an order allowing him to wear the T-shirt, and he appealed. The U.S. Court of Appeals, Seventh Circuit, found the school's ban of "Be Happy, Not Gay" under a rule forbidding derogatory comments about race, ethnicity, religion, gender, sexual orientation, or disability to be reasonable. However, the slogan was a play on words that was not derogatory. The message was not targeted and "only tepidly negative." It was highly speculative that the T-shirt would provoke harassment of homosexuals. While the student failed to qualify for an order suspending the school rule pending the outcome of his lawsuit, he could wear the shirt on a preliminary basis.[7]

Another significant case involving student expression and social media arose in Florida. A senior high school student created a group of students on Facebook who had been taught by the same teacher as she had been. The group's purpose was to voice their dislike for the teacher. Evans posted a message indicating that this teacher was the worse teacher she had ever met. This posting appeared on the page of other students who supported the teacher and debased Evans for creating the group. The page also included a picture of the teacher. The posting was made after school hours from Evans' home computer. Bayer, the principal, suspended Evans for three days and forced her to move from advanced placement into lesser-weighted honor courses. Her notice of suspension stated that she was suspended for bullying, cyberbullying/harassment toward a staff member.

Evans alleged that she engaged in an off-campus activity in a nonviolent and nonthreatening public forum and that punishment resulted in an unjustified stain on her academic reputation. She further contended that Bayer's action violated her First and Fourteenth Amendment rights. She sought an injunction enjoining Bayer from maintaining records relating to her suspension on her permanent school record. She also sought nominal charges as well as attorney fees. Bayer's primary argument is that qualified immunity shielded him from litigation and that he had an obligation to discipline students for potentially disruptive behavior. The court held that qualified immunity did not shield Bayer from injunctive relief. Further, it held that the speech was off campus, although accessed on campus, and could not be handled as on-campus speech. It was no longer accessible when Bayer learned of it. Additionally, there was no evidence presented that suggested that disruption was present on campus. Having determined that Bayer did not have qualified immunity, he was subjected to the possibility of paying attorney's fees. Bayer's motion to dismiss was denied. The plaintiff's request for an injunction was dismissed without prejudice.[8]

Administrative Guide

Freedom of Expression

1. School officials may restrict freedom of expression where there is evidence of material and substantial disruption, indecent or offensive speech, violation of school rules, destruction of school property, or disregard for authority. In each case, students must be provided minimal due process before any punitive action is taken.
2. Buttons, pamphlets, and other insignia may be banned if the message communicated is vulgar or obscene or mocks others based on race, origin, color, sex, or religion. They may also be banned if their content is inconsistent with the basic mission of the school. School policies that address these issues should be developed and communicated to students and parents.
3. To justify the prohibition of a particular form of expression, there must be something more than a mere desire to avoid the discomfort and unpleasantness associated with an unpopular view. Such action is arbitrary, capricious, and indefensible.
4. The time, place, and manner of the distribution of pamphlets, buttons, and insignia may be regulated by school officials. Prohibiting distribution in class during regular school hours or in the corridors between classes is considered reasonable.
5. Unsubstantiated fear and apprehension of disturbance are insufficient grounds for restricting the right to freedom of expression.

Protests and Demonstrations

Protests and demonstrations are considered forms of free expression. Thus, students are afforded the right to participate in these activities under certain conditions. As long as these activities are peaceful, do not violate school rules, and do not result in destruction of school property, protests and demonstrations are allowed. Because school officials are charged with protecting the health and safety of all students and providing an orderly school environment, they may regulate the time, place, and manner of conducting these activities. Such regulations, however, are considered to be mere conditions rather than prohibitions.

School officials should anticipate that minor disruption may occur in response to disagreement or opposite points of view regarding various issues in schools. The courts concur that *minor disruption must be tolerated by school officials.* Only when school officials demonstrate that a particular form of expression has caused or will likely cause material and substantial disruption might they justifiably restrict students' rights to free speech.

In a tragic case involving alleged protest retaliation, a California student and three others walked out of their middle school with the intent of participating in protests against pending immigration reform measures. The middle school vice principal allegedly threatened them harshly with discipline upon their return calling them "dumb, dumb and dumber" and warning them of the possible legal consequences of their truancy. He also allegedly threatened them with a $250 fine and juvenile sentencing, which did not occur. After returning home on the day of the discipline, the student committed suicide, leaving a note that stated, "I killed myself because I have too many problems. . . . Tell my teachers they're the best and tell [the vice principal] he is a mother f#@(-)ker." The student's estate sued the school district, vice principal, and others for constitutional and state law violations. The case reached the U.S. Court of Appeals, Ninth Circuit, which found that no First Amendment retaliation claim could be based on threats of discipline if it was based on a lawful consequence that was never administered.

The policy of disciplining truancy violated no First Amendment rights, even if the students sought to leave for expressive purposes. Further, the vice principal's words were not a form of corporal punishment, and nothing indicated that he had a retaliatory or discriminatory motive. Finally, because the suicide was not foreseeable, the estate failed to show **negligence**. The court affirmed the judgment.[9]

Administrative Guide

Protests and Demonstrations

1. Demonstrations that deprive other students of the right to pursue their studies in an orderly and peaceful environment can be disallowed.
2. Students engaged in demonstrations and protests cannot obstruct the corridors or prevent free movement among students who are not participants in these activities.
3. Any activities associated with demonstrations and protests that result in disrespect for authority, destruction of property, violation of school rules, or any other unlawful activities may be banned.
4. An activity involving students' right to freedom of expression cannot be banned on the grounds that it creates discomfort or conflicts with the views of school officials.

School-Sponsored Newspapers

Courts generally hold that a school publication is responsible for providing a forum for students to express their ideas and views on a variety of topics of interest to the school community. Although the newspaper is intended to represent a forum for student expression, those responsible for its production should be mindful of their obligation to embrace responsible rules of journalism. The school newspaper should reflect editorial policy and sound judgment of student editors who operate under the guidance of a faculty advisor.

Although faculty advisors are generally assigned the responsibility of monitoring material written for the student newspaper, in reality their primary responsibility should involve advice with respect to form, style, grammar, and appropriateness of material, recognizing that *the final decision for printed material rests with student editors.*

Thus, student editors under the guidance of their advisors should be free to report the news and to editorialize, but at all times they must adhere to the rules of responsible journalism. A faculty advisor may not be punished, demoted, or dismissed for allowing to be printed constitutionally protected material that may prove distasteful to school officials. When justified, school administrators may exercise *limited review* of school-financed publications as long as they spell out, in policy, the reason for the review, the time frame involved, the person(s) responsible for reviewing the material, and specifically what material will be reviewed. Administrators should not abuse the review process by employing unreasonable time frames and unnecessary time delays to suppress material deemed to be personally objectionable. Students are afforded the right to express views and ideas that do not materially and substantially affect the operation of the school. The review process, if employed, should always be guided by a sense of fairness and openness. Broad censorship by school officials is not permitted and is in violation of the free speech rights of students. In light of these precautions, however, students' free speech rights are not without limits. *Material that is libelous, vulgar, obscene, or mocks others on the basis of race, origin, sex, color, or religion is impermissible.* In cases where the newspaper is produced by students as part of their school curriculum, school officials may regulate content that is inconsistent with the basic educational mission of the school.

A newspaper produced as part of the school's curriculum may not enjoy the same privileges as one that is produced outside the school's curriculum. Although in both cases, the paper is intended to serve as a forum for student expression, more latitude is extended when the paper is not considered to be part of the school's curriculum. For example, if the newspaper is not deemed part of the curriculum, greater freedom should be granted to student editors in reporting the news as long as there is no evidence of disruption or **defamation**. Also, school authorities would likely incur less risk of lawsuits if the school's paper is not considered part of the curriculum. However, if it is considered part of the curriculum, then school authorities must be allowed to exercise *reasonable control* over newspaper content because they may be subject to liability for defamation involving libel.

Although administrators may exercise greater authority in monitoring student press, particularly school-sponsored newspapers, caution should be exercised not to violate student rights in the process. For example, there should be sufficient evidence to demonstrate that the content of the publication does in fact create a disruptive influence on the school's program and is inconsistent with the mission of the school. In the absence of such evidence, censorship would be inappropriate and unjustified. Even the leading *Hazelwood* case and decision do not imply that administrators may arbitrarily suppress or censor student speech.[10]

Although the U.S. Supreme Court's decision in *Hazelwood* provides greater latitude for administrators, courts generally still accept the notion that a school publication has the responsibility for *leading opinions, provoking student dialogue, and providing a forum for a variety of student opinions.* Administrators must be mindful of the intended purpose of student publications and be guided by respect for the freedom of expression rights of students.

In *Hazelwood School District v. Kuhlmeier,* the U.S. Supreme Court reached a landmark decision. The *Hazelwood* case originated in the spring of 1983 when a high school principal in St. Louis, Missouri, district prevented the school publication *Spectrum* from publishing articles that profiled three pregnant students. The publication also quoted other students on the reasons for their parents' divorces. The principal was concerned that the identity of three pregnant girls might be revealed through the feature in the paper. He also believed that the article's reference to sexual activity and birth control were inappropriate for some of the younger students at the school. Finally, he felt that the divorced parents of the students who were identified in the article should have been provided an opportunity to respond to the remarks made by their children or to consent to the publication of the article.

Student editors claimed that the principal's actions amounted to prior restraint of free press and a denial of due process, constituting both First Amendment and Fourteenth Amendment violations. In May 1985, a federal district judge ruled that because the paper was produced as part of the school's journalism curriculum, it was not a public forum entitled to the same degree of First Amendment protection accorded to student speech carried out independently of any school-sponsored program or activity. This court held that the principal needed only a reasonable basis for his action. However, the U.S. Court of Appeals for the Eighth Circuit reversed the federal district court's ruling in a 2–1 decision, stating that the *Spectrum* was a public forum intended to be a marketplace for student expression and not simply part of the school's journalism curriculum. Because the paper was considered a public forum, the principal's actions were subject to the same free speech standards established by the *Tinker* case.

In reviewing all circumstances related to this particular case, the U.S. Supreme Court reversed the Eighth Circuit Court of Appeals in ruling that the principal did not violate students' free speech rights by ordering certain material removed from an issue of the student newspaper. The Court concluded by stating the following:

> We cannot reject as unreasonable Principal Reynolds' conclusion that neither the pregnancy article nor the divorce was suitable for publication in the *Spectrum.* Reynolds could reasonably have concluded that students who wrote and edited the article had not sufficiently mastered those portions of the Journalism II Curriculum that pertained to the treatment of controversial issues and personal attacks, the need to protect the privacy of individuals whose most intimate concerns are to be revealed in the newspapers and "the legal, moral and ethical restrictions imposed upon journalists within the school community."[11]

The *Hazelwood* ruling has important implications for student newspapers that are part of the school's curriculum in that restrictions may be placed on them based on reasonable grounds.

Administrative Guide

Student Newspapers

In light of the Eighth Circuit Court's posture, school authorities would be well advised to consider these suggestions to avoid legal challenges regarding school-sponsored student newspapers:

1. Through the involvement of representative students, teachers, and other interested persons, formulate a set of legally defensible policies governing publication of the school's newspaper.
2. Choose responsible student editors who will exercise high standards of responsible journalism.
3. Be aware that administrative prerogatives vary based on whether the student newspaper is considered to be an open forum or a curriculum-based publication.
4. Emphasize to student editors that they have primary responsibility to see that the newspaper is free of libelous statements and obscenity. In addition, remind them that newspapers are subject to the law of libel.
5. Develop regulations that prescribe procedures to be followed in the event that prior review is warranted. These should include the following:
   a. A definite period of time in which the review of materials will be completed
   b. The specific person to whom the materials will be submitted
   c. What specific materials are included for review
6. Do not impose policy restrictions on school-sponsored publications that cannot be defended on reasonable grounds.
7. Consult the school district's legal advisor in cases where there is uncertainty regarding the appropriate administrative action to be taken when controversial subject matter is proposed by students.

Nonschool-Sponsored Newspapers

Nonschool-sponsored newspapers are those not endorsed by the school but printed at students' expense away from school premises. These publications may not be totally prohibited by school officials. Restrictions, however, may be imposed regarding the time, place, and manner of distribution. Such restrictions are recognized as conditions, not prohibitions, affecting freedom of press. Students also may be required to remove any debris in the area after papers are distributed. Thus, students have the right to distribute "underground" newspapers as long as the distribution does not interfere with normal school activities or create material disruption. The school assumes no responsibility to assist with the publication or distribution of such newspapers and generally is not held **liable** for the content of the newspapers. Students who are responsible for producing the newspapers are held accountable for any libelous material printed in the newspaper.

Generally, broad censorship of nonsponsored newspapers is not permitted, but *material that is libelous, is clearly obscene, or would lead school officials to forecast a material and substantial disruption of the educational process or violate the rights of others may be suppressed.* This point was illustrated in *Bystrom v. Fridley High School Independent School District,* in which the Eighth Circuit Court of Appeals supported a school rule that prohibited publication of material that was pervasively indecent and vulgar, even though there was some subjectivity involved in the interpretation of content in the newspaper.[12]

One should be mindful, however, that the courts require stricter standards to be met when school officials attempt to restrict free speech before it actually occurs. In all instances, legitimate and defensible reasons for suppressing material must be clearly demonstrated. For example, in the *Burch v. Barker* case, which involved an underground newspaper, the Ninth Circuit Court of Appeals held that the school rule involved was too broad and vague, giving school officials unlimited discretion in exercising prior restraint. Further, such policy was unconstitutional for lack of specificity for distribution and approval procedures. Most significant, however, was that the school policy was unduly broad concerning the content-based requirements for exercising prior restraint.[13]

Administrative Guide

Nonschool-Sponsored Student Publications

1. Defensible policies should be developed that cover all aspects of student publications. These policies should be carefully crafted and communicated to students and their parents. Fundamental fairness should be the guiding principle in developing these policies.
2. School policies regarding nonschool-sponsored publications should not be written using broad and vague language so as to provide unlimited discretion in exercising prior restraint measures by school officials.
3. School officials must establish proof of disruption of a material and substantial nature before they can initiate disciplinary action against students. Disciplinary actions must meet the standards of fundamental fairness.
4. Actions by school officials are justified when there is evidence that the publication encourages disregard for school rules and disrespect for school personnel.
5. If the publication contains vulgar or obscene language, ridicules others, or violates policies on time, place, and conditions for distribution, disciplinary action by school officials is generally supported by the courts.
6. School officials may not be held accountable for content in a nonschool-sponsored newspaper. Student editors are responsible for their own acts of libel.

Censorship

Limited review of school-sponsored publications may be permitted, but *broad censorship* is not. School officials' commitment to sponsor a student publication should reflect a commitment to respect personal rights associated with freedom of expression. School officials have the option to decide whether they wish to finance a school-sponsored publication. Once a decision is made to support an open forum for student ideas, broad censorship powers may not be imposed. School officials must be mindful that students are afforded the right to express their ideas and criticisms when these expressions do not materially and substantially interfere with proper decorum in the school. However, as previously stated, material that is vulgar, libelous, or indisputably obscene may be prohibited. The U.S. Supreme Court defined *obscenity* as material that describes or portrays hard-core sexual conduct specifically described by state law and that lacks serious literary artistic, political, or scientific value. *Miller v. California* was a landmark court decision in which the U.S. Supreme Court redefined its definition of obscenity from that of utterly without social redeeming value to that which lacks serious literary, artistic, political, or social value, a three-pronged test referred to as the Miller Standard. The court did not support Miller's claim of freedom of expression rights violation when he was charged with sending out brochures and books that graphically depicted sexual activity using the following three-prong test that set limits on certain forms of expression:

1. Whether the average person, applying contemporary community standards (not national standards, as some prior tests required), would find that the work, taken as a whole, appeals to the prurient interest;
2. Whether the work depicts or describes, in a patently offensive way, sexual conduct or excretory functions specifically defined by applicable state law; and
3. Whether the work taken as a whole lacks serious literary, social, artistic, political, or scientific value.[14]

As one may discern, obscenity matters are typically influenced by state and local community standards. The courts generally hold that constructive criticism of school policy or practice is permitted, but material that falls in the area of personal attacks on school personnel is not.

DRESS AND APPEARANCE

A prevailing view seems to be that issues involving dress should be left to the decisions of state courts. The U.S. Supreme Court has consistently declined to address this issue. Student dress as a form of free expression is not viewed as significantly as most other forms of free expression. There is, however, a First Amendment freedom associated with it.

Dress may be regulated if there is a defensible basis for doing so. However, school regulations that violate students' rights by being vague, ambiguous, and failing to demonstrate a connection to disruption will not meet court scrutiny. Dress regulations based on fashion or taste as a sole criterion will not survive court scrutiny. School officials, however, may within reason prescribe rules governing student dress and appearance with an emphasis on *reasonableness*. Emphasis on reasonableness centers around well-established facts that (1) students have protected constitutional rights and (2) students' rights must be weighed against a compelling need to restrict their rights. In fact, the courts are now requiring school officials to demonstrate the reasonableness of their rules before the courts will even elect to decide whether constitutional rights of students are violated.

Dress is generally viewed as a form of self-expression reflecting a student's values, background, culture, and personality. Thus, a student must be provided opportunities for self-expression. Therefore, restrictions on student dress are justified only when there is evidence of material or substantial disruption of the educational process. Violation of health and safety standards or cases where unusual attention is drawn to one's anatomy are also justifiable reasons to restrict certain types of dress. In most cases, courts tend to respond favorably when community sentiment is expressed regarding dress standards.

The following restrictions have been upheld by the courts regarding dress and appearance:

1. School regulations necessary to protect the safety of students (e.g., wearing of long hair or jewelry around dangerous equipment in laboratories)
2. School regulations necessary to protect the health of students (e.g., requiring students to keep hair clean and free of parasites)
3. Rules prohibiting dress that does not meet standards of the community (e.g., dressing in a manner that calls undue attention to one's body)
4. Dress that results in material and substantial disruption to the orderly administration of the school (e.g., wearing T-shirts containing vulgar, lewd, or defamatory language based on race, color, gender, national origin, or religion)

A challenge to a district's dress code policy arose in Kentucky when the U.S. Court of Appeals for the Sixth Circuit ruled that a middle school's dress code does not violate student rights to freedom of expression or **substantive due process**.[15] The dress code also does not violate parents' substantive due process right to control the dress of their children. Highlands Middle School adopted a dress code designed to improve safety, discipline, and academic achievement. Robert Blau sued Fort Thomas School District on behalf of himself and his daughter Amanda, a student. Along with several state constitutional and statutory claims, Blau alleged that the district's dress code violated Amanda's right to freedom of expression and her substantive due process right to dress as she chooses, as well as his own substantive due process right to control his child's dress. The federal district court granted the district's motion for summary judgment, rejecting all of the Blaus' claims. The Sixth Circuit affirmed. The appellate court first held that the case was not moot, despite Amanda's subsequent advancement to high school, because the Blaus sought not only to strike down the dress code but also to be awarded monetary damages. The court noted that although the school clearly has the legal authority to enforce its dress code, the difficult question presented by the case was whether the First Amendment even covers this kind of claim. The court concluded that it does not. Amanda's claim demonstrated nothing more than a "generalized and vague desire to express her middle-school individuality." The court then addressed whether the dress code nonetheless was unconstitutionally overbroad on its face because it suppressed a substantial amount of protected conduct engaged in by those other than the plaintiffs. The court found that the dress code satisfied the U.S. Supreme Court's three-prong test for upholding regulations restricting expressive conduct: It (1) is unrelated to the suppression of expression, (2) "furthers an important or substantial government interest," and (3) "does not burden substantially more speech than necessary to further the interest." The court stressed that the plaintiffs were unable to demonstrate that the dress code suppressed a substantial amount of protected conduct. Addressing Amanda's claim that the code's prohibition of blue jeans in particular violated her substantive due process rights, the court concluded that the right to wear blue jeans is not a fundamental right entitled to heightened protection. The Sixth Circuit concluded that Blau has no fundamental right to exempt his child from the dress code.

Administrative Guide

Dress and Appearance

1. Local school dress codes developed by the school should be approved by the board of education. Faculty, students, parents, and citizens should be involved in the formulation of such regulations.
2. Policies and regulations governing dress should be communicated and discussed with students and parents.
3. Dress codes will be supported by the courts only when there is evidence that they are reasonable.
4. Dress and appearance restrictions based on taste, style, and fashion rather than health, safety, and order will not pass court scrutiny.
5. Appearance that does not conform to rudiments of decency may be regulated.
6. Dress that is considered vulgar or that mocks others on the basis of race, gender, religion, color, or national origin may be prohibited.

Health and Safety Issues

Schools are vested with broad and implied powers designed to protect the health, safety, and welfare of students. Therefore, school officials may promulgate reasonable rules and regulations necessary to address health and safety concerns of students. Thus, situations involving certain types of dress that pose a threat to the safety and well-being of students may be regulated. For example, if students are wearing excessively long hair that poses a threat to their safety in vocational shop classes or other laboratory settings, school officials may take appropriate steps to regulate hair length. Similarly, if fancy jewelry is worn that poses a potential threat to safety when students are engaged in shop, activity, or physical education classes, similar measures may be taken to regulate the type of jewelry worn.

Students may be required to wash long hair, for hygienic purposes. For example, if certain types of fungi are associated with dirty, long hair, a student may be required to take appropriate steps to rectify the problem. Other hygienic issues related to dress where there is clear evidence that a problem exists may be addressed by school officials. In every case, efforts should be made to ensure that the dignity and personal rights of students are protected. If there is evidence that reasonable dress codes are developed using these standards, the courts are less inclined to intervene, particularly when representatives of the community have been included in the development of dress codes.

Controversial Slogans

Slogans worn on T-shirts, caps, and other items that are in direct conflict with the school's stated mission may be regulated. Those expressions that violate standards of common decency and contain vulgar, lewd, and otherwise obscene gestures also may be regulated. In instances where disruption occurs or where there is a reasonable forecast that disruption might occur, school officials may take appropriate action to rectify the situation. These actions are particularly relevant when the content of such expressions mocks others based on race, gender, color, religion, language, sexual orientation, or national origin.

A leading case emerged in the U.S. District Court in Massachusetts. Two minor high school students in *Pyle v. The South Hadley School Committee* sued the school committee, challenging a school policy that prohibited them from wearing on school premises either of two T-shirts, one offering a suggestive sexual slogan and the other bearing slang references to male genitals.[16] They sought injunctive relief, alleging that their First Amendment rights were violated with respect to freedom of expression. They further declared that T-shirts are not horribly offensive when compared to other influences in society.

Female students had frequently commented to their English teachers about the sexual harassment environment in the school and how a lack of sensitivity to harassment adversely affected their ability to learn. One T-shirt bore the following: "Coed Naked Band" and "Do It To The Rhythm." Another included the slogan "See Dick Drink, See Dick Die, Don't Be A Dick." These slogans were deemed to be suggestive and vulgar, based on the school committee's findings. Further, these statements interfered with the school's mission and were demeaning to women. The district court upheld the school's official position, based on the findings of the committee.

In short, banning controversial slogans will generally be upheld in the presence of sufficient evidence of disruption or if the message is offensive to others based on race, gender, color, religion, or national origin. As in this case, a school should have policies that address these issues as well as an impartial committee to review these incidents on a case-by-case basis.

In a subsequent case involving potentially offensive expressions, *Scott v. School Board of Alachua County,* the U.S. Court of Appeals for the Eleventh Circuit held that a high school principal's unwritten policy banning the display of Confederate flag symbols on school grounds is constitutional.[17] The court, relying on *Tinker v. Des Moines*[18] and *Bethel School District v. Fraser,*[19] concluded that the principal's policy could be justified either on the grounds that displaying Confederate symbols is potentially disruptive or that the Confederate flag can be perceived as a highly offensive symbol of racism. Two students at Santa Fe High School in Alachua County, Florida, were suspended for displaying a Confederate flag on school grounds after previously being directed by the school's principal not to do so. The students filed suit in federal district court, claiming violation of their First Amendment free speech rights. The district court dismissed the students' suit, finding that the principal's ban could be upheld on two grounds. First, under the standards enunciated in *Tinker,* school officials can censure speech when "they reasonably fear that certain speech is likely to 'appreciably disrupt the appropriate discipline in the school.'" Second, even if the threat of disruption is not immediate, under *Bethel,* public schools as part of their educational mission have the authority to prohibit vulgar and offensive symbols from public discourse. Addressing the issue of whether the school district presented evidence sufficient to satisfy the *Tinker* standard, the Eleventh Circuit concluded that testimony from school officials established the race-based nature of fights at the high school in the months prior to the ban. Regarding the question of whether the flag could be viewed as "highly offensive," the court conceded that the Confederate flag could be viewed merely as a symbol of "Southern heritage." However, it suggested that it is equally true that it can be viewed as a symbol of racism and white supremacy. As a result, the Eleventh Circuit found that it is not unreasonable for school officials to ban such divisive symbols in order to fulfill their essential mission of teaching students of "differing races, creeds and colors to engage each other in civil terms rather than in 'terms of debate that is highly offensive or highly threatening to others.' "

SEARCH AND SEIZURE

The Fourth Amendment to the U.S. Constitution provides protection of all citizens against unreasonable search and seizure. This amendment provides, in part, that "the right of people to be secure in their persons, houses, papers and effects against unreasonable searches and seizures, shall not be violated, and no warrants shall be issued, but upon probable cause."

Because students enjoy many of the same constitutional rights as adults, they are granted protection against unreasonable search and seizure. The major challenge facing school officials involves the task of delicately balancing a student's individual right to Fourth Amendment protection against the duty to provide a safe and secure environment for all students.

To search or not to search a pupil's locker, desk, purse, and automobile on school premises presents a perplexing problem for educators. Basic to this issue is the question of precisely what constitutes a *reasonable search.* The reasonableness of the search becomes the critical issue in cases where students claim personal violations based on illegal searches.

Most authorities point out the distinction between searches of a student's person and searches that involve lockers and desks. The major distinction, of course, is that lockers and desks are considered to be school property. Consequently, school officials are provided greater latitude in searching lockers and desks than they are a student's person.

The underlying command of the Fourth Amendment is that searches and seizures be deemed reasonable. Thus, if students are to be searched, the search must be reasonable. What, then, constitutes a reasonable search? A reasonable search is one that clearly does not violate the constitutional rights of students. What is reasonable will depend on the context within which a search takes place.

Reasonable Suspicion

School officials need only reasonable suspicion to initiate a search. This standard is less rigorous than the requirement of probable cause. What exactly constitutes reasonable suspicion? *Reasonable suspicion* is based on information received from students or teachers that is considered reliable by school officials. As long as the informant is known rather than anonymous and the information provided seems credible, courts will generally find little difficulty supporting administrative actions based on reasonable grounds.[20]

Consequently, school officials may search if reasonable suspicion is established as the primary basis for the search. The courts have declared that *in loco parentis* cannot stand alone without reasonable suspicion. One court stated: "A school teacher, to a limited extent at least, stands *in loco parentis* to pupils under her charge. The *in loco parentis* doctrine is so compelling in light of public necessity and as a social concept antedating the Fourth Amendment, that any action including a search taken thereunder upon reasonable suspicion should be accepted as necessary and reasonable."[21]

From the courts' view, reasonable suspicion is the key ingredient in legalizing school searches. When an educator is operating under reasonable suspicion in school-related searches, no constitutional violation is in question. This issue was settled in the landmark *New Jersey v. T.L.O.*

case in 1985, when the Supreme Court reaffirmed that searches conducted by school authorities are indeed subject to standards of the Fourth Amendment;[22] however, the **warrant** requirement in particular is unsuited to the school environment. According to the High Court, requiring a teacher to obtain a warrant before searching a child suspected of an infraction of school rules would unduly interfere with the maintenance of the swift, informal disciplinary procedures needed in the schools. This is the only case involving school searches in which the U.S. Supreme Court has made a ruling.

This case arose when a teacher, on discovering a 14-year-old student smoking cigarettes in a school lavatory in violation of a school rule, took her to the principal's office. When the girl denied that she had been smoking and claimed that she never smoked, the assistant vice principal demanded to search her purse. After finding a pack of cigarettes, he noticed a package of rolling papers commonly associated with marijuana. His further search uncovered some marijuana, a pipe, plastic bags, a fairly large amount of money, and writings implicating her in drug dealing. Subsequently, the state brought delinquency charges against the student. The student moved to suppress the evidence and her subsequent confession, which she argued, was tainted by an unlawful search. The High Court held that the Fourth Amendment does not require school officials to obtain a warrant or show probable cause before searching a student who is under their authority; rather, the constitutionality of the search depends on its reasonableness in two steps: (1) under ordinary circumstances, the search of a student at its inception requires reasonable grounds for suspecting the search will turn up evidence that the student has violated either the law or the rules of the school; (2) the scope of the search must be reasonably related to the objectives of the search, the age and sex of the student, and the nature of the infraction. Further, the scope of the search must be limited to the incident at hand. In other words, a sweep search of all students in hope of turning up evidence of contraband or violation of rules would be illegal. Neither may a particular student be searched because he or she created a reasonable suspicion of violation of some unparticular rule, nor may any student be searched because of a particular violation by an unknown person. There should be *individualized* suspicion, referring to both the individual student and the individual violation.[23]

The case of *A.H. v. State* illustrates the consequences of not meeting the reasonable suspicion standard by school officials. A Florida appellate court held that a school administrator's search of a student's wallet was unconstitutional. The court concluded that no facts, even combined with rational inferences, warranted the search. A.H. was purchasing a uniform from his physical education teacher when the teacher noticed that the student's speech was slurred. Believing A.H. to be under the influence of drugs, the teacher reported his suspicions to the assistant principal. The assistant principal, along with a school resource officer, took A.H. to an empty office. After having him empty his pockets, the assistant principal searched his wallet and found a substance later identified as marijuana. The court found that the search was based on the teacher's "gut feelings," which alone did not support a reasonable suspicion that a search would turn up drugs. Because the search was not "justified at its inception," it violated A.H.'s Fourth Amendment right to be free from unreasonable government searches.[24]

In a similar case, the U.S. Court of Appeals for the Eighth Circuit held that an Arkansas school district's policy of conducting random, suspicionless searches of students and their belongings violated students' Fourth Amendment right to freedom from unreasonable search and seizure. The school district failed to demonstrate the required "special needs" to justify conducting searches in the absence of individual suspicion.

Jane Doe, a high school student, was charged with and convicted of misdemeanor drug possession after marijuana was found in her purse during a random search of students' purses, book bags, and backpacks. The search was initiated based on a school policy placed in the student handbook indicating that book bags, purses, backpacks, and similar containers permitted on campus for the convenience of students are at all times subject to random and periodic inspection by school officials. The court rejected the school district's reliance on the decision in *Vernonia School District v. Acton* that upheld the constitutionality of random, suspicionless drug testing of student athletes.[25] The court found that unlike student athletes in *Vernonia* and students participating in extracurricular activities, the general student body had not voluntarily ceded a larger portion of its privacy interests by participating in optional activities. The court stated that whatever privacy interest students have in their personal belongings is wholly obliterated by search practices initiated by school officials because all such belongings are subject to search at any time without notice, individualized suspicion, or any other apparent limit regarding the extensiveness of the search. The intrusion by school officials was more severe than that in *Vernonia* because the sanctions imposed on student athletes was simply exclusion from activities whereas students in this case faced criminal sanctions.[26]

Another case that emphasized reasonable suspicion occurred when a Massachusetts school administrator saw three students in a parking lot when they should have been in class. A search of one student yielded a small bag of marijuana. A juvenile court denied his motion to suppress the marijuana evidence and found him delinquent. On appeal, the Supreme Judicial Court of Massachusetts explained that reasonable suspicion is not a hunch or "unparticularized suspicion," but instead requires commonsense conclusions about human behavior. In this case, the student has recently been truant and failed to bring his mother to a meeting to discuss it. School officials had no evidence he possessed contraband or had violated a law or school rule. The court rejected the argument that the search was appropriate based on the student's truancy. A violation of school rules, standing alone, would not provide reasonable grounds for a search unless the specific facts of the violation created a reasonable suspicion of a violation. As there was no information of an individualized nature that the student might have contraband, any search was unreasonable at its inception, and the court vacated the juvenile court order.[27]

Search and Social Media

In a defining 2–1 decision, the Sixth Circuit Court of Appeals ruled that a school administrator's search of text messages on a student's cell phone was unreasonable and violated the student's Fourth Amendment rights. Gabriel was a troubled student who began having disciplinary issues as a freshman at Owensboro Public School. During the school year, he informed school officials of prior illegal drug use as well as predispositions to anger and depression, including suicidal thoughts. In March of 2009, after walking out of a meeting with the high school's prevention coordinator, Gabriel went to Assistant Principal Smith's office where he told her that he was worried about the same things as when he first expressed to her his suicidal thoughts. Assistant Principal Smith was worried about Gabriel and subsequently checked his cell phone to determine whether there was any other indication he was thinking about suicide. Gabriel visited a treatment center later that day where it was recommended he be admitted for one to two weeks.

Six months later in September of 2009, Gabriel was caught texting in class in violation of the school's no-cell phone policy. Gabriel's teacher confiscated the phone and brought it to Assistant Principal Brown, who read four text messages, reportedly to see whether there were any issues that might lead him to hurt himself or others.

G.C. then filed suit against Owensboro Public School in federal district court, alleging violations of his First, Fourth, and Fifth Amendment rights and state law. He amended his complaint to include a claim under § 504 of the Rehabilitation Act. The district court granted Owensboro Public School summary judgment on all federal claims and declined to exercise supplement jurisdiction over the state law claims.

The Sixth Circuit panel reversed the lower court's grant of summary judgment to Owensboro Public School on G.C.'s due process and Fourth Amendment search claims, and remanded the case to the district court. It affirmed the district court's grant of summary judgment on the § 504 claim.

The majority concluded: "The defendants have failed to demonstrate how anything in this sequence of events indicated to them that a search of the phone would reveal evidence of criminal activity, impending contravention of additional school rules, or potential harm to anyone in the school." It also rejected Owensboro Public School's contention that the claim failed because G.C. had not established that he suffered any harm as a result of the search.[28]

Student Desks

Student desks are subject to search if school officials meet the standard of reasonableness. Desks should never be searched based on a mere hunch; rather, reliable information must lead school officials to believe that school rules have been violated or that the health or safety of students is threatened. In all cases, searches should be based on clearly written policies that inform students that desks are subject to search if reasonable suspicion is established. School policies should spell out the conditions and circumstances under which desk searches will occur. Again, wider discretion is provided school officials in searches involving school property.

Student Lockers

School officials must meet the same standard of reasonableness in relation to student lockers regarding the search of student desks. Because student lockers provide privacy for students, oftentimes there is a greater tendency to expect students to harbor items that violate school rules or items that involve criminal activity. *This view alone does not justify an indiscriminate search.* Again, students should be informed that lockers will be searched if reasonable suspicion is established to justify a need to search. If a search of a student's locker becomes necessary, the student and at least one other school official should be present to ensure that proper procedures are followed. The student affected should open the locker in the presence of school officials. This student may also request the presence of another student if he or she wishes. In no cases except extreme emergencies, such as a bomb threat, should an indiscriminate search be initiated. Barring an emergency, indiscriminate searches of students' lockers are *indefensible* and *illegal.*

For example a Pennsylvania court invalidated a locker search by school officials who discovered marijuana cigarettes in a jacket pocket. The student was observed getting a pack of cigarettes out of his locker and giving it to another student. The assistant principal confiscated the cigarette and the pack and searched the locker. The court found, consistent with the *T.L.O.* standards, that students do have a reasonable expectation of privacy in a jacket taken to school. Once the cigarettes were confiscated, no reasonable basis aroused suspicion that more would be in the locker. Retrieving the cigarettes formed the pretext for a search for drugs in violation of the Fourteenth Amendment.[29]

Book Bags

Searches involving book bags tend to be extremely complex, due to the intrusive nature of the search itself. A more extensive and intrusive search will likely require stronger evidence to establish reasonable suspicion. At least one court has stated that "we are also of the view that as the intrusiveness of the search intensifies, the standard of Fourth Amendment reasonableness approaches probable cause, even in the school context."[30]

In *Desilets v. Clearview Regional Board of Education,* a New Jersey case involving book bag searches of students engaged in a field trip, the Superior Court of New Jersey held that the search of students' hand luggage was justified under the Fourth Amendment, based on a legitimate interest of school administrators and teachers in preventing students from taking contraband on field trips. This case arose when the parents of a junior high school student sued the board, superintendent, and principal, alleging that search of their child's book bag before he boarded the bus violated his Fourth Amendment rights. Brian was a tenth-grader participating in a voluntary field trip. Permission slips were sent to parents, indicating that hand luggage would be searched based on board policy. Brian's mother testified that she read the slip before signing it. Based on prior knowledge of the search, students had an opportunity to remove any items that, although not necessarily illegal, were personal to the student.

The court held for the school board by stating that the search was justified at its inception by the unique burden placed on school personnel in the field trip context and that the search limited to hand luggage was reasonably related to the school's duty to provide discipline, supervision, and control.[31] This decision reflects a more liberal view of the court regarding search, but it should not be viewed as a license to conduct unwarranted and more intrusive searches.

Automobiles

School officials may search student automobiles parked on school property if the standards of reasonable suspicion are met. Students and parents should be informed by school or district policy that automobiles are subject to reasonable search if there is a legitimate basis for doing so. For example, if a school official receives information from a reliable source who indicates that a student's automobile contains illegal items in violation of school rules, the official may request that the automobile be searched. Procedures similar to the search of student lockers should be followed—that is, having the student and another witness available during the actual search.

If the student's automobile is parked on nonschool property, *probable cause* must be established, involving law enforcement officials who are required to present a warrant prior to the initiation of a search. Again, parents should be informed of the impending search so as to allow them the opportunity to initiate any steps they deem necessary in this situation. If illegal items such as drugs or weapons are discovered, they are admissible in a court of law. In one compelling case involving search of a student's automobile for drugs, the assistant principal observed that the student had glassy eyes, a flushed face, slurred speech, the smell of alcohol, and an unsteady gait. These observations formed the basis to search the student's automobile under the concept of reasonable suspicion. The court found ample evidence to support reasonable suspicion.[32]

Strip Searches

Strip searches should be avoided except under extreme circumstances involving the health and safety of other students. Historically, courts have not viewed strip searches by school officials very favorably because they are considered the most intrusive forms of all searches. There should be a strong sense of urgency accompanying a strip search that involves an immediate threat to health, safety, and order in the school. Remember, as one court previously stated, "We are of the view that as the intrusiveness intensifies, the standard of the Fourth Amendment reasonableness approaches probable cause even in the school context."[33] Thus, when a teacher conducts a highly intrusive invasion, such as a strip search, it is reasonable to approach the probable cause requirement.

Only school personnel of the same gender should be involved in intrusive searches, and extreme caution should be taken to ensure, as much as possible, that the student is not demeaned or embarrassed during this process. Unless there is an extreme sense of urgency, it might be advisable to isolate the student, keeping him or her under observation, and to consult with the student's parents or legal guardian.

Although probable cause should be closely linked with strip searches, courts in recent years seem more inclined to allow strip searches in certain situations. Among these are a reasonable suspicion that the student is in possession of something that is illegal, against school regulations, or harmful to the health and safety of other students.

An example of the lack of sufficient information to justify a strip search is found in *Cales v. Howell Public School,* in which a female student was forced to remove her jeans and submit to a visual inspection of her brassiere. The court ruled the fact that the student had ducked behind a car and had given a school security guard a false name was insufficient to establish reasonable suspicion. The court held that without further specific information, the school had no more reason to believe that the girl was hiding drugs than to believe that she was skipping class, stealing hubcaps, or engaging in other types of illegal activities.[34]

In one of the more revealing cases involving strip search, the court held for school officials. In *Cornfield by Lewis v. School District No. 230,* a student who was subjected to a strip search brought action against the school district, teachers, and dean, alleging violation of his constitutional rights. The lower court granted summary judgment in favor of the teacher and dean. The student appealed. The Court of Appeals for the Seventh Circuit held that the strip search was reasonable under the Fourth Amendment.

This case arose when Brian, a student enrolled in a behavior disorder program at the high school, was observed outside the building, in violation of school rules. Further, he was reported by an aide and corroborated by another teacher to have been well endowed by virtue of an unusual bulge in his crotch area.

Brian was boarding the bus when he was taken aside by the teachers and the dean, who believed that the bulge was drugs. When asked to accompany them to the office, Brian became agitated and yelled obscenities. Permission was sought from Brian's mother to conduct the search. The parent refused to grant permission. The search was, in fact, conducted in the locker room by requesting that Brian strip and put on a gym uniform. Visual inspection took place, but no body cavity search occurred. No drugs were found.

The court held that "privacy rights of students versus the need of the school to maintain order does not require strict adherence to probable cause standards." However, a nude search by an official of the opposite sex would violate the standard of excessive intrusion. The court held for the school district.[35] This case represents a rare exception to the traditional views held by the courts. School officials should *not* view this case as a license to arbitrarily initiate a strip search.

A more recent strip search case involving a search of Savanna Redding by officials in Safford Unified School District was addressed by the U.S. Supreme Court.[36] Redding was searched based on a claim by a fellow student that she was given a prescription drug as well as over-the-counter drugs in violation of the school's zero tolerance policy. Redding was questioned by the principal and an assistant and subsequently strip-searched by the school's nurse who required her to pull her bra out to the side while shaking it and also to pull out the elastic on her underwear. No pills were found. The High Court assessed the degree of intrusion against the strength of the allegation and held that the search violated Redding's Fourth Amendment rights against unreasonable intrusion. The mere possibility that she might be hiding something in her underwear did not justify that level of intrusion. Its ruling did not fundamentally change the manner in which searches are analyzed by the courts. The High Court concluded, based on *T.L.O.* standards, that the scope of a search is permissible only when measures adopted are reasonably related to the search's objective and are not excessively intrusive in light of the child's age and gender and the nature of the offense.

In a related case, a federal district court approved of a settlement arising from the strip search of two Alabama middle school students for $10 in missing cash.[37] The school board admitted no wrongdoing but agreed to a $15,000 cash settlement. The board's insurer paid the amount, which included an award of attorneys' fees and the costs of mediation. One of the students was allowed to transfer to a different school. The court held $3,900 for each student from the settlement in accounts until they turn age nineteen.

Involvement of Law Enforcement Officials

When law enforcement officials enter the school to conduct a search, the search must be preceded by a *warrant.* If a warrant is issued, strong evidence involving probable cause should be established. Reasonable suspicion would not apply in searches involving law enforcement officers unless officers were assisting school officials with disciplinary action. In such a case, reasonable suspicion will likely be adequate. Typically, when law enforcement officers are involved in a school search, facts and circumstances based on trustworthy information are sufficient in themselves to warrant a person of reasonable caution to believe that some type of illegal activity or crime has been committed.

Before police officers initiate a search of a student, parents or legal guardians should be contacted immediately by school officials and informed of the situation. Parents may wish to be present during the search process. In any case, parents should always be informed prior to any action taken by law enforcement officials. When parents cannot be reached, contact attempts must be documented to verify that a **bona fide** effort was made to reach them. Documentation should include, at a minimum, time of day, the number(s) called, and witnesses.

If parents cannot be reached or elect not to be present during the search, a school official should accompany the officer(s) and serve as a witness during this process. Details of this activity should be communicated to parents immediately so that they are knowledgeable of the circumstances involving the search and the resulting action taken by law enforcement officials based on the search. Students and their parents have consistently challenged searches by police officers on school property.

In a *Miranda* case, a Boston middle school student showed a clear plastic bag containing over 50 bullets to other students. The school resource officer confiscated the bullets and later conducted a pat-down search that yielded no further evidence. The officer then read the student his *Miranda* warnings and asked him to disclose the location of his gun. The student said he did not have a gun. His mother and grandmother arrived at school, and the officer continued questioning the student without informing the adults of the student's *Miranda* rights. After an expulsion **hearing** the same day, the student led the officer to the gun, which he had hidden in a yard in a residential area. In juvenile delinquency proceedings, the judge found the resource officer had unlawfully failed to provide the student *Miranda* warnings in the presence of an interested adult, as required by state law. The case reached the Supreme Judicial Court of Massachusetts, which noted that the juvenile court judge refused to apply the "limited public safety exception" to *Miranda* established by the U.S. Supreme Court in *New York v. Quarles*. Here, the student was only 13 years old.[38]

Juvenile suspects under 14 may not **waive** their *Miranda* rights in the absence of an interested adult, such as a parent. However, the resource officer here was faced with an emergency that threatened 890 middle school students and area residents. He reasonably found an immediate need to question the student. The student's possession of 50 bullets was enough to support the inference that a gun was in close proximity. This was a valid reason to invoke the public safety exception to *Miranda*. Accordingly, the court reversed the juvenile court order.[39]

In a contrasting case, students who were seized, handcuffed, transported, and detained at a municipal building in response to a threatening letter found on school premises brought suit against the school district and the city alleging deprivation of their Fourth Amendment and Fourteenth Amendment rights. Defendants moved to dismiss for failure to state a claim of action. The district court held that students' Fourth Amendment protections against unreasonable search and seizure were not violated, given the magnitude of the potential threat posed by the letter. This fact, coupled with school authorities' apparent belief that the students were associated with the suspected letter writer because they congregated in the same area of the school, was sufficient to justify the action taken by the school district.[40] Lower courts have generally applied the *T.L.O.* standards in cases where school officials initiated searches with minimal involvement by law enforcement officers.

DRUG AND ALCOHOL TESTING

Drug and alcohol use affects the health and safety of a significant number of students across the United States. Many are beginning to use these substances at a younger age than did others their age in previous years. For example, in the year 2000 the use of marijuana on a trial basis rose by 3 percent among students in grades four through seven, representing an increase from 250,000 children to roughly 480,000 who experimented with drugs. Because of this steady increase in drug use among students, the courts have become more lenient in their rulings supporting school authorities. Controlling drug and alcohol use by students presents a formidable challenge for school authorities, thus leading a number of districts to consider seriously or actually implementing drug testing programs.

Drug Testing

Drug testing programs have already been initiated in the private sector and by state and federal governmental agencies. These programs were designed to combat drug use and promote safety and personal health.

The U.S. Supreme Court ruled on two drug testing cases in 1989. One case involved the testing of railway employees; the other involved testing of customs service employees. The High Court ruled that a drug test, irrespective of the method, constitutes a search. Although the Court recognized that these programs constituted a search, both searches were upheld, based on the government's compelling interest in promoting public safety through minimizing rail accidents and protecting the public against certain agents who carried firearms. In neither case was individual suspicion necessary nor required to justify the testing program.

Until the mid-1990s, no case involving drug testing in public schools had been litigated by the U.S. Supreme Court. *Vernonia School District v. Acton,* however, reached the Supreme Court when the Ninth Circuit Court reversed the district court's holding for the school district.[41] School officials in Oregon formulated a district policy based on the belief that some athletes had been smoking marijuana and using other drugs. They also believed that drugs were a major factor in the formulation of rowdy student groups carrying such names as "Big Elk" and "Drug Cartel." Under the district's policy, all student athletes were required to provide a urine sample at the beginning of the season for the particular sport in which they participated. Random tests were conducted among selected athletes. Athletes who tested positive were offered the choice between counseling and weekly testing or suspension from athletics for the current and subsequent seasons.

James Acton, a seventh-grade student who wished to join the football team at Washington Grade School, challenged the policy. Because his parents refused to sign the consent form for drug testing, he was suspended from athletics. There was absolutely no evidence that James used drugs. The district court rejected the family's claim of unreasonable intrusion in 1992, but the Ninth Circuit reversed the district court's decision. The school district based its decision on the landmark *New Jersey v. T.L.O.* case, in which the court ruled that school officials had greater latitude to search students in the school environment in order to maintain orderly conduct. The Supreme Court held for the school district.

Supreme Court Justice Antonin Scalia, writing for the majority, stated that the Vernonia School District's program was reasonable and constitutionally permissible for three reasons. First, students, especially student athletes, have low expectations for privacy in communal locker rooms and restrooms where students must produce their urine samples. "School sports are not for the bashful," Scalia wrote. He stated further that it was clear from the court's earlier cases that school officials could generally exercise a degree of supervision and control over students that could not be exercised over free adults. Second, Justice Scalia said the testing program was designed to be unobtrusive, with students producing their samples in relative privacy and with the samples handled confidentially by an outside laboratory. Finally, the program served the district's interest in combating drug abuse. "It seems self-evident to us that drug use, of particular danger to athletes, is effectively addressed by making sure that athletes do not use drugs."[42]

The Supreme Court, in this case, adopted a sympathetic view of the problems encountered by school districts with respect to drug use by student athletes. In addition, the Court placed great importance on the "role model" image of the student athletes. It also emphasized that student athletes should not expect complete privacy—a price that must be paid to participate in athletic programs.

Administrative Guide

Drug Testing Student Athletes

1. Initiate a districtwide program on drug education, stressing the harmful effects of drugs and the benefits of abstaining from the use of drugs.
2. Develop school and district policies prohibiting the use and/or possession of drugs on school grounds, indicating specific actions that will be taken when students are found guilty of violating school and district policy.
3. Develop a full due process procedure to ensure that there is a fair and impartial opportunity for student athletes to present their side of the issue if accused of drug use.
4. Involve teachers, parents, student athletes, health officials, and community citizens in formulating school and/or district policies regarding drug testing programs that are reasonable and legally defensible.
5. Provide support in cases where students are found guilty of drug use. This is a time when students need as much support as possible.
6. Develop and maintain open relationships with parents so that frequent communication can occur, especially in cases where there is a suspicion that a student may be involved with drugs.
7. Do not use the recent Supreme Court decision as a license to treat students unfairly. If a drug testing program is adopted for athletes, be certain that there is a need to adopt such a program.

Alcohol and Breathalyzer Testing

School officials may, based on school or district policy, administer breathalyzer testing where there is an immediate concern regarding students under the influence of alcohol during voluntary school-sponsored events. Arguably, students who are under the influence of alcohol pose a safety risk to themselves and to others if they drive automobiles to school events. In cases involving the use of breathalyzers, sworn police officers or trained district officials should administer tests to students who voluntarily attend school-sponsored events after reasonable suspicion has been established.

If school officials have reasonable suspicion that the student is under the influence of alcohol, they will likely succeed in initiating a breathalyzer test to any student. As indicated previously, school officials or their designees must be trained and certified by law enforcement officers to accurately and effectively administer tests with the use of a quality commercial breathalyzer. Reasonable suspicion may be established if school officials detect the smell of alcohol on a student or observe behavior that might suggest a student is intoxicated, such as slurred speech or impaired motor control. Reasonable suspicion also may be established when a reliable person informs school officials that he or she has either observed another student consuming alcohol or smells a detectable odor of alcohol on a fellow student. School officials should exercise caution and be able to establish the basis for determining reasonable suspicion.

There has been no preponderance of litigation involving the use of breathalyzers in public schools. However, two cases illustrate the courts' position regarding their use. The state supreme court of New Jersey was called on to evaluate the constitutionality of a high school random drug and alcohol testing program.[43] The program applied to all students who participated in athletic and nonathletic extracurricular activities or who possessed school parking permits. Students who tested positively for drug or alcohol use were temporarily suspended from their school activities or were required to relinquish their parking permits. They were also required to seek treatment if necessary. They were not prosecuted or exposed to criminal liability. The state supreme court held for the district in concluding that the *Vernonia* case, a similar case, was upheld by the U.S. Supreme Court. Therefore, this school district does not offend the Constitution in implementing its drug or alcohol program. A factor that supported the school district's program was a documented survey that revealed that a third of the student body in the upper grades used illegal drugs and 40 percent of the students in the same grades had been intoxicated within the survey's prior twelve-month period.

In a contrasting case, school officials in Indiana established a substance abuse awareness committee to develop a plan for reducing student use of alcohol, tobacco, and other drugs. After receiving the committee's report, the district created a drug testing investigation committee composed of students, parents, and school personnel to study drug testing as a method of reducing student substance abuse. The committee recommended a random suspicionless student alcohol and drug testing program. The district implemented a program that required students who participated in extracurricular activities, including athletics, to submit to a random suspicionless urinalysis. After students attended a drug education class, students and their parents were required to sign a written consent form. Refusal to do so barred a student from participating in extracurricular activities. Students who sought parking permits on school property were subjected to the same testing. Other categories for testing involved students and staff who volunteered to participate in the random program and students who were tested based on reasonable suspicion. No parking permits were issued without a signed consent form from the student and parent. Students who returned forms were assigned numbers, which were placed in a pool and randomly selected. Health professionals conducted tests in private restrooms. Students and their parents challenged the suspicionless program. The district filed for summary judgment, and the students responded with a cross motion for summary judgment, which was granted by the trial court. The court found that the testing program violated the search and seizure clause of the state constitution. Meanwhile, the Seventh Circuit Court of Appeals issued an opinion in 2000 that found the policy to be constitutional under the Fourth Amendment, except for drivers who used nicotine. Three months later, this court issued a unanimous opinion in *Linke v. Northwestern School Corporation* that required individual suspicion before students could be tested.[44] Based on this finding, the trial court granted summary judgment for the students, finding that these two cases were indistinguishable. The case was appealed by the district to the state supreme court. Without consolidating these two cases, the Indiana Supreme Court ruled against random suspicionless drug testing. It was not relevant to the court that the complaining student had graduated, the fact of which was the strategy sought by the district to have the case dismissed.[45]

Administrative Guide

Alcohol Use/Breathalyzers

1. School officials will find it increasingly difficult to initiate a random suspicionless alcohol or drug test without significant documented evidence that alcohol and drug use presents a serious problem for public schools.
2. Reasonable suspicion provides a legitimate basis to initiate random alcohol and drug tests.
3. All tests should be administered by trained professionals using high-quality commercial equipment.
4. Faulty readings used as a basis to deprive a student are not legally defensible and violate equal protection rights of students.
5. School districts should develop policies that address the consequences for refusing to submit to defensible alcohol/drug tests. These policies should be reviewed by the board's attorney before they are publicized.
6. Students and parents alike should receive copies of the district's policies regarding drug and alcohol testing.
7. Meetings should be scheduled by the district to discuss the policies and respond to questions raised by students or parents.

Use of Canines

The use of canines by school officials has received mixed reviews from the courts, which appear to be almost evenly divided on this issue. However, with the growing incidence of drugs and violence in schools, the courts may eventually reach some level of consensus regarding this issue.

The Seventh Circuit Court in *Doe v. Renfrow* held in a questionable decision that school officials stood *in loco parentis* and had the right to use dogs to seek out drugs. In this particular case, school officials, in cooperation with local police, detained 2,700 junior and senior high school students in their classrooms while canines walked through classroom aisles and sniffed students. When the dogs alerted their trainers to a student, that particular student was searched. In total, fifty students were searched. One student was subjected to a strip search after the initial search produced no drugs. The court held that school officials had a reasonable basis for believing that students had drugs in their possession when the canines led them to a particular student.[46]

In a similar ruling, the Tenth Circuit Court of Appeals in *Zamoro v. Pomeroy* held for the school in its use of dogs in exploratory sniffing of lockers. The court noted that the school gave notice at the beginning of the school year that lockers may be periodically inspected and furthermore that lockers were jointly possessed by both students and the school. Because school officials are charged with the responsibility to maintain a safe and orderly school environment, it was necessary for them to inspect lockers even though a slight Fourth Amendment infringement was involved.[47]

In two different rulings, the federal district court in *Jones v. Latexo Independent School District* held that the use of dogs was too intrusive in the absence of individual suspicion. In this case, dogs were used to sniff both students and automobiles. Because students did not have access to their cars during the school day, school officials' interest in using dogs to sniff cars was minimal and unreasonable.[48]

In a related case, *Horton v. Goose Creek Independent School District,* the court held that the use of canines to sniff lockers and cars did not constitute a search. Further, school officials may employ canines to search students if there is reasonable cause, but the intrusion on dignity and personal security that accompanies this type of search cannot be justified by the need to prevent alcohol and drug abuse when there is no individualized suspicion. Therefore, such a search is unconstitutional. This court seems to support the use of canines, if there is a legitimate basis to do so, but ruled that such measures cannot be justified in the absence of individualized suspicion involving canines. In short, mass searches are not permitted.[49]

In a more recent case, a challenge to a canine search arose when a former high school student brought § 1983 action against the school district, school officials, and law enforcement officers, alleging that a dog sniff at school violated his Fourth Amendment right to be free from unreasonable search and seizure. The U.S. District Court for the Eastern District of California entered summary judgment for the school district. The student appealed. The court of appeals held that the plaintiff lacked the standing to seek injunctive relief. The student also failed to support official capacity claims against defendants, which included an inability to establish that a dog sniff of high school students was a Fourth Amendment search and that a random and suspicionless dog sniff search of a student was unreasonable under the circumstances. The plaintiff was a former high school student. Because he was no longer a student at high school or at any other school in the school district subsequent to the time of dog-sniffing incident, he was not supported by the court. Summary judgment was granted to the school district.[50]

In *B.C. v. Plumas Unified School District,* a related canine case, an expelled high school student filed a suit against various school defendants alleging that his constitutional rights had been violated. The basis for this challenge involved a search of his truck that revealed the presence of a knife on school grounds and resulted in his expulsion. The student alleged that his substantive rights were violated. In determining the reasonableness of the search, the court made a twofold inquiry: first, whether the search was justified at its inception, and second, whether it was reasonably related in scope to the circumstances that justified the search in the first place. The court held that where a school official has reasonable grounds to believe a search will disclose evidence that a student has violated a school rule, the initiation of a search is justified. The court further held that a search of the student's truck was permissible after a canine duly trained and certified in exploratory sniffing alerted officials to the truck. The alert, although not a search, gave school officials reasonable grounds to suspect that a search of the truck would uncover evidence of a rule violation. The court held for the district.[51]

In a slightly different case, the Supreme Court ruled in *Florida v. Harris* that the police may use drug detection dogs to conduct searches without a warrant even when the dog finds drugs they are not trained to detect. The Florida Supreme Court ruled that the search was unlawful because the state failed to provide field performance records to establish the dog's reliability. The U.S. Supreme Court unanimously reversed this ruling in an opinion written by Justice Elena Kagan, rejecting the Florida court's "inflexible checklist" of necessary evidence in favor of a more flexible common sense standard. A ruling upholding the Florida court's requirement may have effectively limited the use of drug sniffing dogs by law enforcement, which has escalated in recent years regarding locker sweeps, parking lots, and occasionally student backpacks.[52]

Administrative Guide

Search and Seizure

1. A student's freedom from unreasonable search should be carefully balanced against the need for school officials to maintain order, maintain discipline, and protect the health, safety, and welfare of all students.
2. Factors such as the need for the search, the student's age, history, and record of behavior, the gravity of the problem, and the need for an immediate search should be considered before initiating a search.
3. A school search should be based on reasonable grounds—that is, believing that something contrary to school rules or significantly detrimental to the school and its students will be produced by the search.
4. The information leading to school searches should be independent of law enforcement officials. Searches involving law enforcement officials must be accompanied by probable cause and a search warrant.
5. Although the primary purpose for the search should be to secure evidence of student misconduct for school disciplinary purposes, it may be contemplated under certain circumstances that criminal evidence may be made available to law enforcement officials.
6. Strip searches should be avoided except where imminent danger exists. Such searches can be justified only in cases of extreme emergency where there is an immediate threat to the health and safety of students and school personnel. In such cases, school authorities should be certain that their actions are fully justified and that they have convincing information to support this more intrusive search.
7. School personnel should conduct the search in a private setting. At best, a search is a demoralizing experience; care should be taken to minimize embarrassment to the student as much as possible.
8. The magnitude of the offense, the extent of the intrusiveness, the nature of the evidence, and the background of the student involved should be considered before a search is initiated.
9. A pat-down search of a student, if justified, should be conducted by a school official of the same sex and with an adult witness of the same sex present, if possible. Personal searches conducted by persons of the opposite sex can be very risky.
10. Arbitrary searches or mass shakedowns cannot be justified as reasonable and are illegal.
11. The use of canines should be avoided unless sufficient evidence justifies the need to employ these methods. Serious incidents that pose an imminent threat to students' safety should form the basis for such action.

USE OF CELL PHONES AND ELECTRONIC DEVICES

The use of cell phones by public school students has increased in frequency and popularity in recent years. Students find these devices to be affordable and convenient sources of communication both on and off school premises. It is estimated that nine in ten students own cell phones. Although no significant legal challenges have reached the courts regarding the school district's authority to restrict or prohibit their use, the courts would likely support school officials' decision to do so unless there is evidence that a First Amendment right is in jeopardy, which is unlikely.

If cell phones and/or other electronic devices are prohibited by policy, all allowable exceptions should be filed and readily available should school officials need to retrieve them if challenged by parents raising questions regarding preferential treatment. In the absence of compelling evidence that electronic devices are needed by students, school officials will likely succeed without court intervention, as long as they consistently adhere to their own policies and demonstrate no evidence of disparate treatment among students regarding permission to use these devices. A number of states have currently formulated policies prohibiting the use of cell phones in public schools and stated expected consequences for policy violators and exceptions granted for special use. School officials, however, appear to be moving toward relaxing policies that prohibit the use of cell phones.

An example of a policy violation involving cell phones occurred when a Delaware student used his cell phone at a school assembly, in violation of the school code of conduct. He refused to surrender his phone to a staff member. The principal asked him four times to hand it over. The principal told the student he would have to accompany him to the office. The student still refused to move. The principal attempted to escort him from the assembly by the elbow. The student struggled, pushed the principal, and stepped on his foot. After being removed from the assembly, he continued to use his cell phone. The student remained disruptive in the school office. He also threatened other students and teachers. He was arrested. The school board expelled the student for the rest of the school year and assigned him to an alternative school. The state board of education affirmed the action, and the student appealed to a state superior court.

The court held the state board could overturn a local board decision only if it was contrary to state law or state regulations, was not supported by substantial evidence, or was arbitrary and capricious. The court found sufficient evidence that the student had pushed the principal and stepped on his foot. The student had intentionally and offensively touched the principal in violation of the school code. Expulsion with referral to an alternative program was not disproportionate to the misconduct.[53]

There is some disagreement among school leaders regarding the use of cell phones in schools. Many districts banned cell phones after September 11, 2001. Other districts banned them prior to that, based on a view that students used them for drug and gang activities. However, most schools allow students to carry cell phones for safety purposes in light of the school shootings that have occurred across the country. The current focus appears to be centered around safety by proponents for cell phone use in schools. They contend that students are able to contact parents or law enforcement officials in the event of an emergency as students did during the Columbine tragedy. However, there is concern regarding the adverse impact of cell phone use by students in emergency crisis situations based on the potential for challenges related to rumor management. School officials who oppose cell phone use cite disruption, a lack of focus by students, and too much socialization affecting students' learning opportunities.

The National School Safety and Security Service is a Cleveland, Ohio–based leading national consulting firm specializing in school security and school emergency/crisis preparedness, training, school security assessments, and school safety. It opposes the use of cell phones in school and cites the issues in Table 3.1 in support of its position.

There also have been reports of cheating by students who take pictures of exams and send them to their classmates. In addition, there is concern that students can use cell phones to capture other students using the restrooms or disrobed in dressing rooms. Obviously, all these activities are prohibited in schools.

It is well established that school officials may prohibit any practice that creates material or substantial disruption to the educational process. School districts may minimize legal challenges where there is evidence that the use of cell phones creates disruption or that the devices are used for improper purposes. School officials are given the authority to maintain a safe and orderly

| **TABLE 3.1** | Cell Phone Detraction Involving School Safety and Crisis Preparedness |

1. Cell phones have been used for calling in bomb threats to schools, and, in many communities, cell calls cannot be traced by public safety officials.
2. Student use of cell phones could potentially detonate a real bomb if one is actually on campus.
3. Cell phone use by students can hamper rumor control and, in doing so, disrupt and delay effective public safety personnel response.
4. Cell phone use by students can impede public safety response by accelerating parental and community arrival at the scene of an emergency during times when officials may be attempting to evacuate students to another site.
5. Cell phone systems typically overload during a real major crisis (as they did during the Columbine tragedy, World Trade Center attacks, etc.), and usage by a large number of students at once could add to the overload and knock out cell phone systems quicker than may normally occur. Since cell phones may be a backup communications tool for school administrators and crisis teams, widespread student use in a crisis could thus eliminate crisis team emergency communications tools in a very short period of critical time.

Source: Reprinted with permission from Kenneth S. Trump, M.P.A., President, National School Safety and Security Services, Cleveland, Ohio, http://www.schoolsecurity.org

environment to facilitate teaching and learning. Consequently, they may prohibit any practice that affects proper order and decorum because learning cannot occur in a disruptive environment. When school officials provide evidence that cell phones create a disruptive influence in the school and are abused by students, most typically involving texting among students, they will likely succeed in prohibiting student possession of these devices on school premises. This prohibition will not likely offend the personal rights of students. If cell phones are allowed, harsh penalties should be imposed on students who violate school or district policy that prohibits texting during classroom instruction.

If cell phones are banned, school boards, through district policy, may allow special exceptions in cases where such devices are needed for medical emergencies involving students with a chronic illness or other special circumstances that warrant their use. School officials should examine the need for these devices on a case-by-case basis and demonstrate flexibility in allowing students to use them under special and justifiable circumstances. Such exceptions should be reflected by school district policy and require proper documentation by parents or medical experts that these devices are necessary and essential under certain conditions.

The debate regarding whether cell phones should be allowed in public schools is currently being addressed by allowing their use in the classroom in a number of school districts. For example, Wiregrass Ranch High School in Wesley Chapel, a Florida suburb near Tampa, is one of a growing number of U.S. schools that is abandoning traditional policies of cell phone prohibition and incorporating them into class lessons. In fact, it is estimated that roughly 73% of teachers use cell phones for classroom purposes. For example, Spanish vocabulary has become a digital scavenger hunt. Notes are copied with a cell phone camera. Text messages serve as homework reminders. Students appear to be highly motivated to use their cell phones as a learning tool. These phones function as small computers where students initiate Internet searches and e-mail their teachers for clarification regarding assignments. They may be very practical in districts that do not possess a sufficient number of computers for all students. The use of cell phones for teaching and learning appears to be influencing school officials to reexamine their cell phone use policy based on the percentage of teachers who incorporate cell phones into their classroom instruction.

U.S. Supreme Court and Cell Phones

In two significant non–educational-related cell phone development cases, the U.S. Supreme Court heard two different cell phone cases in April 2014. At issue are privacy rights versus prerogatives that law enforcement officials may take in enforcing the law. The High Court accepted two cases involving different technologies. One involved a Massachusetts individual's old-style flip phone and the other involved a smart phone. At least six courts have held that the Fourth Amendment permits such searches while three other courts have held that it does not.

Both defendants as well as privacy groups are alleging that modern cell phones contain personal information that has historically received protection from undue intrusion. In one of the two cases, the High Court accepted a federal appeals judge's decision that suggested that cell phones contain a vast amount of information that traditionally has been maintained at home such as photographs, videos, written and audio messages, texts, e-mails, voicemail, calendars, appointments, and web searches as well as financial and medical information. Lower courts appear to be split regarding the application of constitutional protection against unreasonable search. These cases arose when police initiated a search of a criminal suspect's cell phone without a warrant. The other case involved criminal prosecution that used information confiscated without a warrant. The legal issue facing the High Court is whether a search for such information after a defendant is arrested violates the Fourth Amendment of the U.S. Constitution. In a rare unanimous decision, the U.S. Supreme Court ruled that police need warrants to initiate a search of cell phones of people they arrest. Chief Justice Roberts stated. "The fact that technology now allows an individual to carry such information in his hand does not make the information any less worthy of the protection for which the founders fought." This landmark ruling will likely apply to searches of tablets and laptop computers based on privacy protection for U.S. citizens.

Administrative Guide

Cell Phones and Other Electronic Devices

1. Do not arbitrarily ban the use of cell phones and other electronic devices by students unless there is sufficient evidence of disruption or improper use.
2. If permitted, develop specific guidelines governing the conditions under which these devices may be used.
3. If not permitted for general use, allow for exceptional cases involving medical emergencies or other special circumstances that warrant the use of these devices.
4. Policies or guidelines should always be guided by a sense of fairness and due consideration for the unique and personal needs of students.

MOBILE DEVICES IN THE CLASSROOM

iPads and Kindles as classroom educational tools have become increasingly popular as teachers seek new strategies to motivate students to learn. There are numerous applications that may be used to enhance student performance. For example, the eBook reader is designed to allow teachers to load several books for students to read with the ability to respond to questions regarding a book through the use of a word processor on the iPad. The iWork application allows students to use word processing, create slide shows, presentations and spread sheets. iPads may also be used as video cameras, audio recorders, and multimedia notebooks for students' creations. Applications are available for students in lower grades that are designed to allow students to create and express ideas.

The use of iPads is endless regarding the range of learning activities that enhance student growth and performance. They may be used to improve mathematics, writing, spelling, and skills and allow teachers to move away from the front of the classroom and permit students to work more collaboratively. Teachers may also use iPads to make assignments, evaluate students' work, or reteach a unit of instruction. Students may use iPads to take notes and review content in preparation for exams. iPads, when used properly, have the potential to create an engaging and collaborative learning environment. School policy should address any restrictions that apply to the use of iPads including consequences in cases where students fail to comply. Students' use of iPads should be monitored by teachers to ensure that they are used properly. In no instance should iPad use create material or substantial disruption to the educational process. Further, iPads should not be used to harass or intimidate other students or staff with inappropriate or threatening messages.

Kindle has emerged as another popular learning device among teachers for classroom use. This device minimizes reliance on printed textbooks. Kindle is an e-reader that has the capacity to store hundreds of books that can be downloaded and copied as needed. It has the potential to increase interest in reading among students by providing easy access.

Administrative Guide

iPad Usage

1. If iPads are permitted, they should be used for instructional purposes only.
2. School or district policy should provide proper guidance regarding the use of iPads in the school setting.
3. Consequences should be imposed for students who violate the school's use policy.
4. Teachers should monitor iPad usage to ensure that students are conforming to school or district policy.
5. The use of iPads may not create material or substantial disruption in the school setting.
6. Students may not use iPads to harass, intimidate, or threaten other students or staff.
7. Kindles offer increased opportunities to enhance students' interest in reading.

DUE PROCESS

The due process clause of the Fifth Amendment applies to the federal government, whereas the Fourteenth Amendment applies to the states. Essentially, both prohibit the government from depriving a person of life, liberty, or property without due process of law. Due process requires fundamental fairness, fair processes, and fair procedures.

Due process of law includes four aspects: procedural, substantive, Vagueness Test, and Presumption Test. These tests are applied by the courts in addressing various forms of discrimination. For example, the Vagueness Test protects those who allege discrimination from arbitrary or capricious acts by an employer. Laws or policies are considered vague if a person of common intelligence has to guess at their meaning. The degree of vagueness allowed by the U.S. Constitution is contingent on the nature of the legislation and the consequences that follow. Laws involving substantive due process are held to higher standards than those addressing less important penalties.

Procedural Due Process

Procedural due process guarantees that a prescribed set of steps will be followed that allows students and school personnel an opportunity to seek redress for alleged violations before any action is taken against them. It is based on the concept of procedural fairness. At a minimum, it includes an individual's right to be adequately notified of pending charges or proceedings and the opportunity to be heard during these proceedings. The extent or degree of due process will be a function of the seriousness of the deprivation regarding an individual's life, liberty, and property. Due process is designed to prohibit arbitrary and capricious action by school officials as they provide leadership for the daily operations of public schools.

Due Process of Law

Both the Fifth Amendment and Fourteenth Amendment to the U.S. Constitution provide protection against arbitrary and unfair treatment of individuals by the government. The Fifth Amendment applies to the federal government, whereas the Fourteenth Amendment applies to the states. Both amendments prohibit all levels of government (federal and state) from unfairly depriving an individual of life, liberty, or property without due process. The Bill of Rights ensures that these protections apply to both federal and state governments.

Because public schools are state agencies, the Fourteenth Amendment applies to the operations of public schools. Therefore, school officials must comply with due process provisions of the U.S. Constitution. Due process essentially guarantees fundamental fairness in relationship to students and school personnel. It ensures that all legal proceedings will be fair and that individuals will be provided notice of proceedings and an opportunity to be heard before school officials act to deprive them of life, liberty, or property. The application of due process is divided into two aspects: procedural and substantive. These aspects are applied most often in cases involving student suspension (minimal due process) and expulsions (full due process). (See Chapter 10 for a discussion of minimal and full due process.) Both aspects are applied to teachers and other school personnel in cases involving dismissal.

Substantive Due Process

Substantive due process ensures that a valid reason exists before an individual is deprived of life, liberty, or property and that the means used to achieve this objective are reasonable. Taken together, both procedural and substantive requirements must be met to comply with all constitutional requirements regarding fundamental fairness. The boundary between substance and procedure is not always clearly determined. The U.S. Supreme Court has held for much of its history that due process must include limits not only on how people are placed on trial (procedures) but also on what kind of control officials can have over individuals (substance).

Substantive due process in a public school context ensures that students will not be subjected to arbitrary or capricious acts by school officials regarding the exercise of their personal rights. School officials must be pursuing a compelling state objective, and their action must be necessary to achieve it. An example of a compelling act would involve the health, safety, and welfare of faculty and students in public schools. The Constitution guarantees due process because it expands the personal freedoms of individual citizens. Substantive due process protects individual rights such as freedom of speech, assembly, and religion. Furthermore, substantive due process guarantees that a student's freedom or property cannot be taken without appropriate justification irrespective of the procedures that are used in the process.

Vagueness Doctrine and Presumption Standard

The *vagueness doctrine* stems from the Fourteenth Amendment requirement of fundamental fairness. In the public school context, a student should not be penalized for behavior that he or she could not reasonably understand to be prohibited. Students must reasonably understand what behavior is expected of them by school officials.

The *presumption standard* places restrictions on the power of the state to deprive an individual of liberty or property without sufficient factual evidence to justify its action. In the school context, school officials must have a definitive basis before they initiate measures to deprive students of their liberty or property interests. The presumption test requires the state to clearly demonstrate that it has a legal and/or logically defensible basis prior to depriving or restricting a student's rights. Presumption of innocence is embedded in several provisions to the U.S. Constitution, such as the right to remain silent and the right to a jury.

The application of due process is not absolute but depends on circumstances that surround a particular situation. Although due process requires fundamental fairness, it is not always easy to determine fairness. Fairness varies based on the specific circumstances surrounding each case. The seriousness of the potential deprivation impacts the level and intensiveness of the process that is applied in each case. The courts, in an effort to address the various conditions that impact deprivation of liberty on property interests, rely on a test that emerged in *Mathews v. Eldridge* to determine the appropriateness of procedures that should apply in a given situation. The courts focus on the private interest that will be impacted by an official action against an individual followed by the risk of an erroneous deprivation of the individual's liberty or property interest and lastly the government's interest including the fiscal impact that would be placed on the government if an alternative procedure were applied.[54] When these factors are considered, the courts are better able to determine the appropriate level and/or intensity of due process that is required in any given situation.

The significance of substantive and procedural requirements is that both provisions must be met by school officials to succeed in meeting the basic requirements of the Fourteenth Amendment.

An example of a procedural due process violation is illustrated in the *Gault* case, which occurred in Arizona in 1967. Gerald Gault, a juvenile, had been found guilty of making an obscene phone call. The typical punishment for an adult committing the same offense would have been a $50 fine. But because Gerald was considered a juvenile, he was remanded by the court to the state reform school for a period of up to six years.

The U.S. Supreme Court held that Gault had been committed to the industrial school without the benefit of procedural due process. The High Court also noted that the Arizona law regarding juveniles contained several deficiencies: (1) No appeal of the conviction was provided, (2) no written charges of the alleged crime were presented during the hearing, and (3) protection against self-incrimination had been denied.

In overturning the verdict, the Supreme Court stated the following: "Where a substantial penalty is involved, a juvenile, like an adult, is entitled to due process of law."[55] The impact of the *Gault* ruling was significant in its broad and liberal application. This decision defined how school officials must respond to students in disciplinary hearings and guaranteed that no student shall be denied personal rights under the Fourteenth Amendment.

Another leading U.S. Supreme Court case, *Goss v. Lopez,* determined that students facing suspensions of up to ten days or less were entitled to oral or written notice of charges, an explanation of the evidence to be used against them, and an opportunity to present their side of the issue. This case arose when Lopez, a high school student in Columbus, Ohio, was suspended from school with at least seventy-five other students who were connected to a disturbance in the school cafeteria. The disturbance followed a disagreement with school administrators regarding which community leaders would be permitted to speak during the school's assembly program. Polarization rapidly deteriorated into a disturbance, which resulted in suspensions during Black History week. The suspensions were to last ten days.

No hearing took place prior to or after the suspension. Consequently, Lopez had no opportunity to affirm or deny his participation in the disturbance. A state law required the principal to notify parents within twenty-four hours of a suspension for up to ten days, and such notice must provide the reason(s) for the suspension. No other forms of due process were required. Neither notice of charges, opportunity to be heard, chance to confront witnesses, nor right to further appeal was required. Lopez filed suit. His case, along with others, was heard by a three-judge federal district court, which found the state's law unconstitutional. The administrators appealed to the Supreme Court, where the lower court's decision favoring the students was upheld.

The administrators sought to have the Court affirm its contention that because there is no federal constitutional right to a free public education, there is no corresponding federal constitutional right requiring the application of due process procedures to suspensions from public schools. Justice Byron White, writing for the Court, said that because the state had extended the right to attend public schools to students, including Lopez, that right is a legitimate property interest protected by the due process clause of the Constitution and that the state "may not withdraw that right on grounds of misconduct, absent fundamentally fair procedures to determine whether the misconduct has occurred." At the least, students facing a short suspension from school, not exceeding ten days, and thereby facing loss of "a protected property interest must be given some kind of notice and afforded some kind of hearing." White's statement noted, in part, that although Ohio may not be constitutionally obligated to establish and maintain a public school system, it has nevertheless done so and has required its children to attend. Those young people do not "shed their constitutional rights" at the schoolhouse door.

The Supreme Court also noted the existence of a liberty interest stemming from charges of misconduct leveled against the students involved. The Court stated:

> If charges are sustained and duly recorded, they could seriously damage students' standing in the school as well as interfere with future opportunities to pursue an education or employment. It is apparent that the right claimed by the state to determine unilaterally without due process that misconduct has occurred collides with the requirements of the Constitution.[56]

The implications of this decision for practitioners suggest that, for school suspensions of up to ten days, a student must be given notice of the misconduct as well as an opportunity for a hearing regarding the misconduct. Such notice and hearing may occur almost immediately after the infraction, and only "rudimentary" procedures are required. The hearing need only be an explanation of the evidence against the student after he or she is told the nature of the charges and is provided an opportunity to tell his or her side of the story. In case the student's presence on the premises poses a continuing threat or danger, the student may be immediately removed from school, with the notice and hearing following whenever practicable.

For suspensions of more than ten days (and expulsions), obviously more than rudimentary due process procedures must be observed. However, the Supreme Court has not currently addressed this situation, and case law **precedents** are conflicting among the various circuit courts of appeals. A prudent school leader, however, should err on the side of providing students an opportunity for full protection of due process, including but not limited to the following:

1. Notice of charges
2. Prior notice of hearing
3. Right to legal counsel at all appropriate stages
4. Hearing before impartial party
5. Right to compel supportive witnesses to attend
6. Right to confront and cross-examine adverse witnesses and/or to view and inspect adverse evidence prior to hearing
7. Right to testify on one's own behalf
8. Right to have a transcript of proceedings for use on appeal

Administrative Guide

Due Process

1. The essential focus of due process is fundamental fairness.
2. Due process provides a remedy for students against arbitrary or capricious acts by school officials.
3. The level of due process is a function of the seriousness of the threat to deprive students of their liberty or property interests.
4. Procedural or substantive due process singularly is of no value to school officials, unless the requirements of both aspects are met when they contemplate depriving students of liberty and property interests.
5. Fairness is not always absolute. What constitutes fairness in one situation may be totally unfair in another. The courts use a balancing test to determine the appropriateness of the procedures that should apply in a given situation.

CORPORAL PUNISHMENT

Corporal punishment remains a highly controversial topic in the United States today. Perhaps no other legal issue in education has drawn as much criticism as the use of physical punishment in public schools. Those who support corporal punishment contend that it will cause changes in student behavior, teaching students self-discipline and respect for authority. Those who oppose corporal punishment view it as a legalized form of child abuse, which conveys to students that violence is an acceptable method of resolving problems or disagreements. Irrespective of the views supporting or opposing corporal punishment, the courts still view corporal punishment as an acceptable form of discipline when administered in a reasonable manner. Although corporal punishment is considered to be an acceptable form of discipline by the courts, school personnel are increasingly facing charges of assault and battery, prosecution, and even termination of employment for abusive acts against students.

Corporal punishment usually involves the use of physical contact for disciplinary purposes. As a disciplinary tool, this type of discipline is not uncommon within school systems in the United States. In fact, twenty states currently allow corporal punishment to be used as a means of discipline. Interestingly, the courts, under the concept of *in loco parentis*, have sanctioned reasonable corporal punishment by school personnel, but no laws except those in one state protect school personnel who administer it.*

Every industrialized country in the world—except the United States, Canada, and one state in Australia—now prohibits school corporal punishment.

The question of the constitutionality of corporal punishment was reaffirmed in the landmark case *Ingraham v. Wright,* where the U.S. Supreme Court ruled that even severe corporal punishment may not violate the Eighth Amendment prohibition of cruel and unusual punishment.[57] This case arose when Ingraham and another student from the Dade County, Florida, public schools filed suit after they had been subjected to paddling. State law allowed corporal punishment if it was not "degrading or unduly severe" and if it was done after consultation with the principal or other teacher in charge of the school. Paddling was considered a less drastic form of punishment than suspension. For violating a teacher's instructions, Ingraham received twenty licks while he was held over a table in the principal's office. He required medical attention and missed school for several days.

Because this paddling was probably "unduly severe," on hearing the evidence and appeals the High Court found no constitutional violation. According to Justice Lewis Powell, "The schoolchild has little need for the protection of the Eighth Amendment." It is more appropriately applied in the case of the criminally convicted and thereby involuntarily confined. A student is always free to leave the premises and return home at the end of the day. "The child brings with him the support of family and friends and is rarely apart from teachers and other pupils who may witness and protest any instances of mistreatment."[58]

Although the court declined to declare corporal punishment as used in the context of public schools to be a violation of the cruel and unusual proscription or due process under federal law, it did state that paddling students deprived them of liberty interests protected by the Constitution. Although not required by law, but in the spirit of fairness, *rudimentary due process* should be applied before corporal punishment is administered. However, there is no requirement that there be a formidable load placed on school officials in administering corporal punishment. Thus, state and local school districts are left to decide for themselves what is required. When corporal punishment is approved by state law or local rules, a brief explanation of the wrong charged and an opportunity to hear the student's comments are probably all that are necessary to comply with due process requirements prior to paddling a student. Again, a prudent policy would require that an adult witness be present and that parents' wishes concerning this form of punishment be considered, if not respected.

In addressing the issue, the U.S. Supreme Court referred to traditional common law:

> The use of corporal punishment in this country as a means of disciplining schoolchildren dates back to the colonial period. It has survived the transformation of primary and secondary education from the colonials' reliance on optional private arrangements to our present system of compulsory education and dependence on public schools. Despite the general abandonment of corporal punishment as a means of punishing criminal offenders, the practice continues to play a role in the public education of schoolchildren in most parts of the country. Professional and public opinion is sharply divided on the practice, and has been for more than a century. Yet we can discern no trend toward its elimination. The Eighth Amendment does not apply to the administration of discipline through corporal punishment to public school teachers and administrators.[59]

---

*The Alabama legislature passed a teacher immunity bill, Act #95-53, that provides immunity for teachers to use corporal punishment or otherwise maintain order when exercising such authority within their local boards.

In spite of this ruling, federal courts have subsequently ruled that excessive corporal punishment violates the substantive due process clause of the Fourteenth Amendment. The courts, however, have fallen short of determining exactly when corporal punishment becomes excessive.

Although the *Ingraham* case upholds the legality of corporal punishment as an acceptable means of controlling student behavior, local school district policy in many cases has seriously limited its use. Nevertheless, according to a recent survey conducted by the National Center for the Study of Corporal Punishment and Alternatives in Schools, at least two million U.S. schoolchildren are physically punished each year.

Reasonable Punishment

Poor decisions regarding the use of corporal punishment by school officials may result in civil damage suits or even criminal prosecution for assault and battery. Corporal punishment, when permitted, should be used only as a *last resort* measure. Every reasonable method should be employed prior to its use. Working very closely with teachers, parents, or guardians to resolve a child's deviant behavior is viewed as a more positive alternative.

If corporal punishment is employed, students should be informed beforehand of specific infractions that warrant its use. When administered, the punishment should be reasonable and consistent with the gravity of the infraction. Corporal punishment should never be administered *excessively or with* **malice**.

In the past, numerous suits have alleged that children were struck with double belts, lacrosse sticks, baseball bats, electrical cords, bamboo rods, hoses, and wooden drawer dividers. Other suits have alleged that children were kicked, choked, and forced to eat cigarettes. Such acts by school personnel are totally indefensible. None of these practices meets the test of reasonableness established by today's courts. The right to discipline students is subject to the same standards of reasonableness as would be expected by the average parent.

The courts have advanced two standards governing corporal punishment of students: The first is the reasonableness standard—punishment must be exerted within bounds of reason and humanity. The second is the good faith standard—the person administering the punishment must not be motivated by malice and must not inflict punishment wantonly or excessively.[60]

In a rather interesting case, *Baker v. Owen,* the U.S. Supreme Court affirmed the judgment of a three-judge panel of the U.S. District Court in North Carolina, which upheld the administration of corporal punishment over a parent's objection. In this case, Russell Baker, a sixth-grade student, was paddled for violating an announced rule against throwing kickballs except during the designated play period. Russell's mother had requested that her son not receive corporal punishment because she was opposed to it. Despite her objection, Russell was corporally punished for his disobedience. In her suit, the parent alleged violations of the child's right to procedural due process and that the paddling amounted to cruel and unusual punishment, thus violating the Eighth Amendment. The court held for the teacher.[61]

The court identified procedural safeguards that should be invoked to meet minimal standards of due process: (1) Specific warning must be given about what behavior would result in corporal punishment, and evidence must exist that other measures attempted had failed to bring about desired behavioral modifications, (2) administration of corporal punishment must take place in the presence of another school official, and (3) on request, a written statement must be given to parents regarding reasons for the punishment and the name of the official witness.

Further, it was held that the two licks administered by the teacher with an instrument that was somewhat longer and thicker than a foot ruler involved no lasting effect or discomfort and was not in violation of the Eighth Amendment involving cruel and unusual punishment.[62] Interestingly, another court has ruled that there is no constitutional violation when a school district complies with a minor's wish for corporal punishment rather than follows the parent's preference for suspension.[63]

Minimal Due Process

Before corporal punishment is administered, school officials should have formulated rules that provide students with adequate notice that specific violations may result in the use of corporal punishment. These rules should be published and disseminated to parents and students. Further, the student who is to be punished should be informed of the rule violation in question and provided an opportunity to respond. A brief but thorough *informal hearing* should be provided so as to allow the student the opportunity to present his or her side of the issue. On request, parents or guardians must be provided a written explanation of the reasons for the punishment and the name of the school official who was present to witness the punishment. These conditions would satisfy minimal due process requirements. Because the student's property rights are not involved, an extensive, full due process procedure is not warranted.

Excessive Punishment

School officials must exercise extreme caution to ensure that corporal punishment is not deemed excessive. Excessiveness occurs when the punishment is inflicted with such force or in a manner that is considered to be *cruel and unusual*. Excessiveness also occurs when no consideration is given to the *age, size, gender, and physical condition or to the student's ability to bear the punishment*.

Assault and battery charges are normally associated with allegations of excessive punishment. Both are classified as intentional **torts**. An **assault** involves "an overt act or an attempt to inflict immediate physical injury to the person of another. The overt act must be a display of force or menace or violence of such a nature as to cause reasonable apprehension of immediate bodily harm."[64] The person accused of an assault must have the ability to execute it. All of the elements found in this definition must be present to sustain an assault charge. An assault occurs when a person has been placed in fear for his or her immediate safety. A **battery**, on the other hand, is a successful assault that involves actual physical contact.

From the school official's perspective, when corporal punishment is administered in a rude and malicious manner, using poor judgment regarding the excessive nature of the punishment, assault and battery charges may be imminent, especially if there is a view that the official *intended* to harm the student. Intent is an important element involving a battery. The person who inflicts the harm must be perceived as purposely doing so. Stated differently, the official's contact with the student must be intentional. Of course, once corporal punishment is administered, school personnel may find it difficult to refute that this form of punishment was not inflicted in an excessive manner intended for and directed at the student. Although *in loco parentis* allows school officials to administer corporal punishment, their actions must be considered reasonable and necessary under the circumstances.

An example of excessive, rude, and malicious punishment is demonstrated in one of the most blatant cases involving the use of corporal punishment. This case arose in Georgia when a fourteen-year-old freshman varsity football player, Durante Neal, alleged that his teacher and coach violated his right under the due process clause to be free from excessive corporal punishment.

During football practice, Royonte Griffin, another football player, slapped Neal in the face. Neal reported the incident to Coach Ector, who allegedly told him that he needed to learn how to handle his own business. Neal then picked up a weight lock and placed it in his gym bag. After practice, he was again approached by Griffin. Neal pulled the weight lock out of his bag, hit Griffin in the head, and then placed the lock back in his bag. Then both began to fight. During the fight, Coach Ector and the principal, Herschel Robinson, were in the immediate area. Neither teacher nor coach attempted to stop the fight. Coach Ector dumped the contents of Neal's bag on the ground while repeatedly shouting "What did you hit him with?" Ector told Neal that he would be hit with the same object he used to hit Griffin. Ector took the same weight lock and struck Neal in his left eye. As a result of the blow, Neal's eye was knocked completely out of its socket, leaving it destroyed and dismembered. Neal's eye was hanging out of his head as he experienced severe pain, but neither Ector nor Robinson stopped the fight.

Neal sued Ector, Robinson, Superintendent Dolinger, and the Fulton County School Board under 42 U.S.C. § 1983, claiming that Ector's use of corporal punishment was so excessive as to shock the conscience and violate his Fourteenth Amendment substantive due process rights. Neal further charged that the school board, superintendent, and principal were liable for failing to properly train, instruct, and supervise Coach Ector. The district court held for the school district.

On appeal, the board's motion for summary judgment was declined by the Eleventh Circuit Court of Appeals, which held that Ector's conduct did constitute corporal punishment. The court then addressed the issue of whether corporal punishment, regardless of its severity, rose to the level of a substantive due process claim. In doing so, the court referred to the leading corporal punishment case, *Ingraham v. Wright,*[65] and disagreed with the district court's interpretation of it. The Fifth Circuit ruling in *Ingraham* declined to suggest that corporal punishment could not rise to the level of a constitutional violation. It further held that the facts in both cases were too different to arrive at the same conclusion. The court of appeals examined (1) the need for the punishment, (2) the relationship between the need and amount of punishment administered, and (3) the extent of the injury inflicted. The court concluded that the plaintiff had stated a claim of action and that Ector went too far in using an obviously excessive amount of force that presented a reasonably foreseeable risk of serious bodily injury. The circuit court ruled that the plaintiff had adequately alleged a violation of his right under the Fourteenth Amendment to be free from excessive corporal punishment. The district court's judgment dismissing the case was reversed and remanded for further proceedings consistent with the court's opinion.[66]

The legal consequences of administering corporal punishment in an excessive and unreasonable manner are also illustrated in the following case. Demario Jones, a student at Eutaw High School in Alabama, was summoned to Principal James Morrow's office for disciplinary reasons. Demario claimed that he was struck in the head, back, and ribs with a metal cane, which resulted in a knot on his head as well as migraine headaches. He filed suit alleging that the principal used excessive force in violation of his substantive due process rights.[67] The court rejected Principal Morrow's argument that his use of corporal punishment did not rise to the level of a constitutional violation. The Eleventh Circuit Court found that the repeated striking of a defenseless student with a metal cane met the criteria of excessive force. The U.S. Court of Appeals for the Eleventh Circuit held that a principal who repeatedly struck a student with a metal cane is not entitled to qualified immunity from the student's substantive due process claim of excessive force. The court further held that the force used presented a foreseeable risk of serious bodily injury to the student.

Administrative Guide

Corporal Punishment

1. Corporal punishment should not be used except for acts of misconduct that are so antisocial and disruptive in nature as to shock the conscience.
2. School officials should not expect the courts to support malicious and excessive physical punishment of students.
3. The punishment must not be inflicted with such force or in such manner as to be considered malicious, excessively cruel, or unusual.
4. Reasonable administration of corporal punishment should be based on such factors as the gravity of the offense and the age, size, gender, and physical ability of the child to bear the punishment.
5. If a student professes a lack of knowledge regarding the rule violation or innocence of the rule violation, a brief but adequate opportunity should be provided to explain the rule and to allow the student to speak on his or her behalf.
6. Whenever possible, students should be provided punishment options for deviant behavior. Corporal punishment should never be administered when the child is physically resisting.
7. Attempts should be made to comply with a parent's request that corporal punishment not be administered on the child with the understanding that the parent assumes responsibility for the child's behavior during the school day.

SCHOOL SUSPENSION

School suspension is a legal form of discipline for students who violate school or district policy that often involves issues relating to school safety. In-school suspensions are growing in popularity in many school districts, whereas other school districts continue to rely on out-of-school suspensions. Race, ethnicity, and socioeconomic status often are factors that have an impact on school suspensions. There appears to be a close relationship between socioeconomic status, race, and ethnicity and the rate of suspensions. A larger number of minority students of lower socioeconomic status are suspended yearly than are other students.

School suspensions require that *substantive and procedural* provisions of due process be met. Due process of law is a fundamental right guaranteed to citizens of the United States under the Fourteenth Amendment of the Constitution. This amendment provides, in part, that "no State shall . . . deprive any person of life, liberty or property, without due process of law." Basically, due process is a course of legal proceedings following established rules that ensure enforcement and protection of individual rights. The guarantees of due process require that every person be entitled to the protection of a fair trial. The essential element of due process is *fundamental fairness,* which means a fair hearing, a fair trial, and a fair judgment.

For example, the court of appeals of North Carolina held that a school district denied a student due process by refusing to allow him to be represented by an attorney at a disciplinary hearing.

Administrative Guide

Suspension

1. Adequate notice must be provided to students and parents regarding the existence of rules governing student behavior. These should be clearly communicated to all affected by their implementation.
2. A record should be compiled that includes the following information:
   a. The infraction allegedly committed
   b. The time of the alleged infraction
   c. The place where the alleged infraction occurred
   d. Those person(s) who witnessed the alleged act
   e. Previous efforts made to remedy the alleged misbehavior
3. Students facing suspension should, at minimum, be provided some type of notice followed by a brief informal hearing.
4. Students should be provided either oral or written notice of charges against them and the evidence school authorities have to support the charges, and should be provided an opportunity to refute the charges.
5. Because permanent removal is not intended, no delay is necessary between the time notice is given and the time of the actual hearing. In most instances, school officials may informally discuss alleged misconduct with students immediately after it is reported.
6. During the hearing, the school official should listen to all sides of the issue. Adequate time should be provided for students to present their side of the issue without interruption.
7. Parents or guardians should be informed of the hearing and provided written notification of the action that results from the hearing. At a minimum, the written notice should include the following:
   a. The charge(s) brought against the student
   b. A description of the available evidence used to support the charge(s)
   c. The number of days suspended
   d. A determination of whether the suspension is an in-school or out-of-school suspension
   e. A list of other conditions that must be met before the student returns to school (e.g., a conference with parent or guardian)
   f. A statement that informs parents or guardians that the suspension can be appealed to the district's pupil personnel director or a designee
8. Parents or guardians should be informed by phone of the suspension, followed by written notification, which should be promptly mailed, preferably by registered mail on the day of the hearing.

The district disciplined the student for violation of its sexual harassment policy. Its policy specifically forbade attorneys from appearing at hearings on behalf of students. The court of appeals affirmed a trial court judgment for the student, ruling the district denied him due process. The facts were in dispute and the student was entitled to full hearing rights for a long-term suspension, including the right to be represented by counsel in *In re Roberts* (2002).[68] The state Supreme Court dismissed the board's appeal in *In re Roberts* (2003),[69] as did the U.S. Supreme Court.[70]

EXPULSION

Unlike suspension, expulsion is considered one of the more severe forms of discipline because it involves long-term separation from the school district or, in some instances, permanent separation. Expulsion usually involves more serious offenses or rule violations than does suspension. In recent years, a significant number of expulsions have been linked with weapons violations. With continued gang presence in schools and frequent incidents of violence, school officials will continue to be challenged to maintain safe schools.

Expulsion is typically used by school districts to discipline students who commit serious infractions. Because expulsion is considered to be a form of discipline that deprives the student of the right to attend school, it must be preceded by a formal hearing in which the student is afforded full Fourteenth Amendment rights involving due process and equal protection privileges.

Because the threat of expulsion is so serious, students and parents should be aware of the types of infractions that may result in expulsion. These infractions should be identified by school and district policy. In addition, they should be clearly communicated to students and parents to ensure that there is no misinterpretation regarding the intent and substance of expulsion policies. Parents, students, citizens, and school personnel should be involved in the development of expulsion policies, recognizing that the board of education has the ultimate authority for approving such policies.

School officials may expel a student for a serious infraction that could potentially pose a threat to school safety even when law enforcement officials find no basis to prosecute the student. The following case in Indiana illustrates this point: The Indiana Court of Appeals upheld the expulsion of a student for his off-campus threat to carry out a mass shooting at school, even though law enforcement officials refused to charge him with a crime. Spencer Sherrell, a student at Tri-Central High School, informed two friends while off campus that he was going to "get his dad's gun in Indianapolis, bring it to school, start with seventh grade, and work his way up." Shortly after being informed of this, the principal and assistant principal interviewed Spencer, who admitted that he had made the threat and that this violated school rules. Law enforcement officers also interviewed Spencer but decided his threat did not constitute an "unlawful act." Therefore, no criminal charges were filed. The school board, however, voted to expel Spencer for the remainder of the school year. The board relied on a state law allowing schools to suspend or expel a student for engaging in unlawful activity on or off school grounds if (1) the unlawful activity reasonably may be considered an interference with school purposes or an educational function or (2) the student's removal is necessary to restore order or protect persons on school property. Spencer filed suit, alleging that the board's action was arbitrary and capricious because the board lacked statutory authority to determine that his threat constituted "unlawful activity." He contended that only law enforcement officials have the authority to make this determination. The court emphasized that Spencer had conceded that the board had the authority to determine whether a student's conduct met the statutory test. The court concluded that it would defy common sense to suggest that a prosecutor must determine whether the conduct was unlawful before a disciplinary hearing can proceed. Spencer's claim was without merit.[71]

In virtually every state, the board of education is the only body with legal authority to expel students. The board is responsible for holding the expulsion hearing and meeting all rudiments of due process consistent with the Fourteenth Amendment. Any errors along procedural or substantive grounds usually will result in the student being supported by the courts.

The *Dixon v. Alabama State Board of Education* case, involving expulsion of higher education students, illustrates how students' Fourteenth Amendment rights were violated by school officials.

The *Dixon* case involved a group of higher education students who were expelled without due process provisions. Although this case involved expulsion in a higher education institution, it has application to due process rights of all public school students. Students at Alabama State University in early 1960 engaged in off-campus sit-in demonstrations in a privately owned cafeteria in the county courthouse. The students were expelled by the university without opportunity to appear at a hearing on the basis that they had violated their "contract" with the university to adhere to certain standards of conduct. University officials failed to consider that the students involved had a constitutional interest in attending the state school. According to tradition, discipline involving students, even behavior off campus, was permitted without regard to whether the students had a constitutional interest that could not be deprived without due process of law. This tradition was based on the theory that students should behave properly as ladies and gentlemen and that their conduct should not reflect adversely on the reputation of the institution. During this time, this view was consistent with the *in loco parentis* concept widely used in K–12 schools, both public and private, where school officials could act as arbitrarily as parents in meting out discipline.

The court decision held, contrary to the contract theory tradition, that students in a state-supported college or university do hold a constitutional right not to be expelled without some appropriate and fair due process, such as notice of charges and the opportunity for some form of hearing.[72] *Dixon* is significant for K–12 public school officials because it represents the first time public school administrators were challenged for arbitrarily enacting and enforcing rules without consideration to act with some degree of fairness toward students.

Wood v. Strickland is another significant case regarding school officials who failed to observe procedural guidelines. The outcome resulted not only in a ruling on behalf of the students but also a ruling in which individual board members were informed that they could be liable for damages resulting from the violation of students' constitutional rights. This case involved three female high school students, all sixteen-year-old sophomores. All three girls admitted mixing three bottles of 3.2% beer into a soda pop punch, bringing it to a school function, and serving the mixture, apparently without noticeable effect, to parents and teachers.

Following the spread of rumors, the students were called in and confessed to what they had done. The board of education thereafter held a meeting to which neither the students nor their parents were invited. Despite a plea for clemency by the school's principal, the board decided to expel the girls for the remainder of the year—a period of three months.

The board did not attempt to prove that the particular mixture involved was "intoxicating," stating that its prohibition had been meant to include *any alcoholic beverage.* At a second board meeting two weeks later, at which time the students were represented, the board refused to withdraw its action "because the rule prescribed a mandatory expulsion for the offense." The students, through their parents, brought action to block the board's decision. Their petition was later amended to include financial damages against the board members as individuals under the Civil Rights Act of 1871 (42 U.S.C. Sec. 1983).

The district court originally favored the school board on the grounds that the board members were immune from damages, but the court of appeals reversed, holding that the board's failure to present any evidence that the punch was, in fact, "intoxicating" was a violation of the plaintiffs' constitutional rights.

On appeal, the U.S. Supreme Court, by a 5–4 vote, stated that malicious intent was not always required to hold a public official liable for damages: Justice Lewis Powell, writing in the majority, stated:

> Ignorance of what a student's constitutional rights are *will not always* serve as a defense in such cases. . . . School officials are entitled to a "qualified" privilege against damages for wrongful acts while *acting in good faith.* However, school board members will not be considered *absolutely immune* to such payment if they *knew,* or *reasonably should have known,*

that the actions they took would violate the constitutional rights of a student, just as if they took the action with *malicious intention* to cause deprivation of some right to which the student is *entitled*.[73]

As one can see, a lack of awareness of students' constitutional rights will not pass court scrutiny, especially when it is evident that school authorities should have been aware of these rights.

Administrative Guide

Expulsion

These steps, if implemented correctly, will meet the standards of due process and fundamental fairness while ensuring that the constitutional rights of students are protected.

1. Students, parents, or legal guardians should be informed based on school or district policy of specific infractions that may result in expulsion. They should also be informed of their Fourteenth Amendment rights regarding substantive and procedural due process.
2. In cases of serious misconduct for which serious disciplinary measures may be imposed, the student is entitled to written notice of the charges and a right to a fair hearing. Written notice must be furnished to the students and parent or guardian well in advance of the actual hearing.
3. At a minimum, the following procedural steps should be considered:
   a. Written notice of charges
   b. Right to a fair hearing
   c. Right to inspect evidence
   d. Right to present evidence on student's behalf
   e. Right to legal counsel
   f. Right to call witnesses
   g. Right to cross-examination and to confrontation
   h. Right against self-incrimination
   i. Right to appeal

Table 3.2 summarizes the significant differences between school suspension and expulsion.

STUDENT DISCIPLINE FOR OFF-CAMPUS BEHAVIOR

The courts have long held the view that the seriousness of an offense, rather than the place in which the offense occurs, determines the right to punish perpetrators of the offense. If the act tends to immediately and directly affect proper discipline and decorum in schools or make them less effective, the jurisdiction of the teacher extends beyond the school to acts committed away from school.[74]

A court in Iowa addressed the authority of schools to control acts committed away from school and after regular hours:

> If the effects of acts committed beyond school hours reach within the school room during school hours and are detrimental to good order and the best interest of students, it is evident that such acts may be forbidden. The view that acts committed within the authority of the school board and teachers for discipline and correction must be done within school hours, is narrow, and without regard to the spirit of the law and the best interests of our common schools.[75]

The court's position in *Burdick* was reinforced in subsequent rulings. In an early case in Arkansas, the court held that the board of education had the authority to suspend a pupil who was drunk and disorderly on the streets of the village on Christmas Day.[76]

In a similar ruling, the court supported a teacher for punching a student who was found guilty of harassing small girls on their way home from school. The fact that the offense was committed after the perpetrator had reached home and was on the premises of his parents did not negate the teacher's authority.[77]

TABLE 3.2	Summary of Differences Between School Suspension and Expulsion
Suspension	**Expulsion**
• May result in suspension	• May result in expulsion
• Short-term in nature, ten days or less, typically three days or less pending a parental conference	• Long-term in nature, may be indefinite or permanent based on nature of infraction
• Informal hearing	• Prior written notice required informing student of alleged infraction and his/her rights under due process, including time and place of formal hearing
• Oral or written notice regarding alleged offense	
• Opportunity to refute charges by student	• Full due process provisions (all procedural steps) mandatory
• Nonadversarial in nature	• Legal counsel permitted
• Suspension of student by school principal possible after providing minimal due process	• Expulsion case heard by full school board or designated body
• In-school suspension, an option based on district policy	• Fair, impartial expulsion decision by school board
• Legal counsel typically disallowed	• Expulsion decision to the courts by student or parents allowed
• Designed to correct student behavior without depriving him/her of an educational opportunity	• No requirement for other districts to enroll student
• Written notice to parents and superintendent required	

It is important that school officials formulate valid discipline policies governing student behavior after school hours away from school. These policies should be sufficiently definite so that students and parents understand their intent. For example, a vague policy prohibiting the consumption of alcohol prior to the school day was struck down by the court based on the fact that it was overly broad and left to arbitrary interpretation. "Prior to the school day" could be interpreted as minutes, hours, or days before attending school. It is important that policies outlined be precise enough to provide clear guidance to students. Even so, the courts do not hold school officials to the same stringent requirements as would be required in criminal statutes.[78]

In an unpublished, *per curiam* decision, the U.S. Court of Appeals for the Fourth Circuit ruled that a Virginia school district's code of conduct that allows school officials to discipline students for off-campus conduct under certain circumstances is not unconstitutionally vague.[79] The Fourth Circuit also rejected claims that the code violated the disciplined student's rights to substantive due process and equal protection. Jeremy Collins was expelled from school by the Prince William County School Board after he participated with several other students in exploding bottle bombs off campus. After a hearing, the school board voted to expel Jeremy for having violated the student code of conduct provision regarding off-campus offenses. The board concluded that his conduct resulted in disruption to the school system because of the inordinate amount of time school staff, teachers, and administrators had to devote to the investigation and discussion of the incident. Jeremy sued in federal district court, alleging that the board had violated his substantive due process and equal protection rights. He also claimed that the provision of the code was unconstitutionally vague because it failed to inform him adequately that his off-campus conduct could subject him to expulsion. The district court dismissed the suit, rejecting the due process claim by finding that there was ample evidence to support the board's decision and rejecting the equal protection claim by concluding that Jeremy was treated no differently than other similarly situated students and that the board's action was rationally related to a legitimate governmental interest. The district court also dismissed the vagueness claim. The Fourth Circuit affirmed the dismissal of the substantive due process and equal protection claims on the same grounds. However, the appellate court addressed the vagueness claim in somewhat more detail. Citing *Bethel School District No. 403 v. Fraser,* the court determined that because schools need to impose disciplinary sanctions for a wide range of unanticipated conduct that disrupts the educational process, school disciplinary codes need not be as detailed as criminal codes.[80] Addressing the code's off-campus provision in light of *Fraser,* the court concluded that it provided Jeremy "sufficient notice . . . that his use of explosive devices off-site could result in a disruption to the school significant enough to warrant his expulsion from school."

CLASSROOM HARASSMENT

Harassment is a form of sexual discrimination. The U.S. Supreme Court, in a stunning 5–4 decision, ruled that public schools may be sued for failing to deal with students who harass their classmates. LaShonda Davis was allegedly the victim of a prolonged pattern of sexual harassment by a fifth-grade classmate. LaShonda's teacher as well as the principal had been informed of these allegations but did not promptly investigate them.[81] This landmark decision, hailed as a victory by sexual harassment protection groups, raises a number of interesting questions: How will it affect the operation and management of schools? Will it create insurmountable problems of supervision for teachers and principals? Will every adolescent gesture made against a classmate trigger a need for the school to respond? Has the High Court invoked a federal code of conduct that regulates behavior typically associated with adolescence? These are complex issues facing school leaders as they attempt to address harassment issues in their schools.

The Supreme Court's Decision

Justice Sandra Day O'Connor, writing for the majority in *Davis,* attempted to clarify these complex issues by indicating that lawsuits are valid only when the harassing student's behavior is so severe, pervasive, and objectively offensive that it denies the victim equal access to an education guaranteed by federal law. She further suggested that harassment claims are valid only when school administrators are clearly unreasonable and deliberately indifferent toward the alleged harassing conduct, which obviously means that they must have been aware of such conduct and did nothing to address it. However, liability charges may be made even if a teacher is the only one aware of the harassing behavior. An excerpt from the High Court's majority opinion states the following:

> We consider here whether a private damages action may lie against the school board in cases of student-on-student harassment. We conclude that it may, but only where the funding recipient acts with deliberate indifference to known acts of harassment that are so severe and pervasive and objectively offensive that they effectively bar the victim's access to an educational opportunity or benefit. . . .
>
> We stress that our conclusion . . . does not mean that recipients can avoid liability only by purging their schools of actionable peer harassment or that administrators must engage in particular disciplinary action. . . . School administrators will continue to enjoy the flexibility they require. . . .
>
> Courts . . . must bear in mind that schools are unlike the adult workplace and that children may regularly interact in a manner that would be unacceptable among adults.

A Dissenting Opinion

Based on the majority ruling, school leaders need not fear lawsuits unless they are deliberately indifferent to reported cases of harassment. The High Court's decision is not intended to restrict administrative flexibility in managing schools. Because this case resulted in a 5–4 ruling, there were obviously dissenting opinions.

Dissenting Justice Anthony Kennedy stated that the majority's decision will result in the diversion of scarce resources from educating children and that many school districts, desperate to avoid Title IX peer harassment suits, will adopt whatever federal code of student conduct and discipline the Department of Education sees fit to impose on them.

Danger Signals

Nonetheless, it appears that school leaders are not liable unless they knew of the harassing behavior and failed to take reasonable steps to respond. One issue, however, that might complicate this finding is whether evidence suggests that school leaders should have known of the harasser's conduct. For example, if it is common knowledge among students and teachers that harassing behavior is occurring in specific situations, it may be increasingly difficult for school leaders, when challenged, to claim to be unaware of it.

School leaders may receive notice of harassment in a variety of ways. According to the Office for Civil Rights (OCR), school officials should know of alleged sexual harassment when a student files a grievance or complains to a teacher about a classmate's behavior. They should also pay attention when a student, parent, or other individual contacts the principal or teacher regarding allegations of harassment. In these instances, the student who has been subjected to harassing conduct has met the notice requirement under OCR guidelines. It then becomes the responsibility of the principal or a designee to respond appropriately.

In a related case, the Eleventh Circuit ruled that female students were not entitled to private damages for student-on-student sexual harassment under Title IX because the harassment did not systematically deprive them of access to educational opportunities.[82] The case involved three second-grade girls at North Toledo Blade Elementary School (Florida) who were subjected to verbal and physical harassment by a male classmate. Because the U.S. Supreme Court and other U.S. Circuit Courts of Appeals have not provided controlling authority on the issue of actual notice to school officials, and because the required finding of "deliberate indifference" by school officials is intertwined with the notice issue, the court resolved the case solely on the basis of whether the harassment was so severe, pervasive, and objectively offensive that it systematically deprived the girls of access to the educational opportunities available at the school. Although the behavior was persistent and frequent and included sexually explicit and vulgar language and offensive touching, the court concluded that it was not so severe as to result in such systematic deprivation. The court pointed out that none of the students' grades suffered and that no change in their classroom demeanor was observed. Although

Administrative Guide

Classroom Harassment

1. Formulate district policies and procedures to address sexual harassment for employees and students. Be certain that everyone—faculty, students, and staff—understands these policies and the consequences for violating them.
2. Establish a zero tolerance policy so that everyone understands the school's position on issues involving harassment.
3. Provide staff development programs periodically for faculty and staff to familiarize them with all aspects of harassment and specific behavior considered to fall in the harassment category.
4. Encourage faculty and students to report all violations through a well-defined, developed, and publicized grievance procedure.
5. Provide educational programs for students on classroom harassment and school sanctions associated with harassment conduct.
6. React swiftly and judiciously to complaints filed by students, faculty, and staff so that everyone knows that the institution takes harassment seriously.
7. Create an environment where students and school personnel feel comfortable in honestly reporting complaints of harassment free of any form of reprisal.
8. Protect the confidentiality of those filing complaints to the greatest degree possible. Professional reputations can be damaged if charges prove to be false.
9. Create and maintain a school climate characterized by mutual respect and consideration of others.
10. Based on a recent Supreme Court decision in the *Gebser* case, students who are sexually abused by teachers cannot recover monetary damages from school officials unless officials knew of the harassment and were in a position to act and failed to do so.[83]

they all testified that they were upset by the harassment, the court noted that they apparently were not upset enough to report the harassment to their parents until months had passed.

In an unusual case that never reached a court, a six-year-old student in Colorado was suspended for two days for sexual harassment because he kissed a girl on her hand. He returned to school after a national wave of negative publicity. The school dropped the sexual harassment claim against him. The student had a crush on the young girl. The charge was subsequently changed to misconduct.

CHILD ABUSE

In virtually all states, teachers are required to report suspected cases of child abuse and neglect to the appropriate agency. School districts, based on state statutes, have procedures for filing these reports. The procedures vary among the states. Forty-nine states have mandatory reporting requirements for teachers. If no evidence supports findings of abuse, teachers will not be liable. Immunity is granted in virtually every state when reports are made by teachers in good faith. Laws in most states penalize individuals who fail to report child abuse and neglect. Failure to report abuse is a misdemeanor that generally carries a fine up to $1,000 and a jail sentence. A recent development in Ohio illustrates the negative effect of not reporting possible child abuse.

An Ohio superintendent, two coaches, and a principal were charged by a grand jury that investigated whether other laws were broken in the rape of a drunken 16-year-old girl by two football players. The special grand jury, convened in Steubenville, had investigated whether adults like coaches or school administrators knew of the rape allegation but failed to report it as required by state law. An elementary school principal and a strength coach are charged with failing to report possible child abuse. A former volunteer coach faces several misdemeanor charges, including making false statements and contributing to underage alcohol consumption. A judge convicted two Steubenville high school football players of raping the West Virginia girl after an alcohol-fueled party in August 2012 following a team scrimmage. School personnel are strongly advised to immediately report suspected cases of child abuse to the appropriate agency. Failure to do so may prove costly, as illustrated in this case.

Teachers and school leaders should be vigilant in observing and interacting with students so that unusual behavior by their students may be detected. Some visible observations may include difficulty in walking or sitting, unexplained bruises, swellings and a pattern of frequent injuries, welts, withdrawal and isolation from classmates, wearing certain types of clothing to conceal injuries, hygiene problems, dirty clothing, inappropriate clothing based on weather, pattern of habitual tardiness or absenteeism from school, preoccupation, look of sadness, a lack of engagement in classroom instruction, and fear of returning home after school. Child abuse is not always apparent. Teachers and school leaders must be observant and very knowledgeable of abuse regarding their students and behavioral patterns to detect any changes in behavior or appearance that might create a cause for concern.

One of the most flagrant child abuse cases regrettably involved a special education teacher in *Evans vs. Antioch Unified School District* in California. Parents of the children involved alleged that the special education teacher slapped, pinched, and verbally abused her students and school administrators failed to report the abuse to authorities. Some of the students were classified as nonverbal with autism in a kindergarten class. The parents sued the district and five employees. Internal district documents did in fact reveal that district officials attempted to conceal abusive behavior by the teacher. Allegations against the teacher included using the back of her hand to hit a child in the mouth, yelling at nonverbal students at close range, pinching a 7-year-old autistic child's nipple to get him to follow instructions, using derogatory terms such as "retard," picking a child's nose and forcing him to eat it, and driving her knee into a child's back as she restrained him on the ground. One parent observed bruises on her son's neck and face and was told by school leaders not to report her findings. Other employees observed the abuse and failed to report it. The Antioch School District announced that it will pay $8 million dollars, the largest amount ever reported, to families of eight kindergarten special education students based on the teacher's abuse and the failure by school administrators to report abuse suspicions to proper authorities.

The Childhelp National Child Abuse Hotline (1-800-4-A-Child) was established in 1982. The hotline is staffed 24 hours a day, 6 days per week, with professional crisis counselors who provide assistance, support, information, and references. The hotline receives calls from at-risk children, parents in distress who need crisis intervention. The hotline is a valuable resource, particularly for school personnel and other professionals who are required by law to report suspected cases of child abuse.

Administrative Guide

Child Abuse

1. Teachers, based on their frequent interactions with students, are expected to detect signs of potential child abuse.
2. Most states have imposed a duty on teachers and school leaders to report suspected cases of child abuse to the appropriate agencies.
3. Teachers and school leaders may face criminal liability for failure to report suspected cases of child abuse.

PREGNANT STUDENTS

The courts have generally held that pregnant students may not be denied the opportunity to attend school and must be afforded equal protection under the law as well as due process of the law.

School officials have attempted to withdraw pregnant students from school based on knowledge that such students have become pregnant, whereas others have specified a particular time for withdrawal. Many of these rules have been successful in the past. However, the courts have become increasingly amenable to declaring these rules invalid. The commonly acceptable practice is that the student's physician may prescribe the time at which the student should withdraw for health and safety reasons. On withdrawal, school officials must provide appropriate home-based instruction. When cleared by the attending physician after childbirth, she may return to school and be entitled to the same rights and privileges afforded other students. She cannot be denied participation in school activities, events, or organizations during her pregnancy or after her pregnancy, unless participation is disallowed by her physician or school officials can demonstrate a legitimate reason to limit her participation.

In a Kansas case, the board of education attempted to exclude a married student from school. This student married after discovering her pregnancy, before the child was born. She was abandoned by her husband shortly after their marriage. After giving birth, she attempted to reenter school. The court ruled that the board had acted in an arbitrary and capricious manner in attempting to exclude the student from school, stating that the student should not be prevented from securing an education that would better prepare her to meet the challenges of life.[84]

MARRIED STUDENTS

Married students have the right to attend public schools. Any rules designed to exclude married students from attending school are invalid and in violation of Fourteenth Amendment rights—namely, equal protection under the law. School board rules that prohibited married students from permanently attending public schools were invalidated by the courts during the late 1920s and early 1930s. They suggested even then that there must be a showing of immorality, misconduct, or a deleterious effect on other students.[85] School rules that required students to withdraw from school for a one-year period after marriage were invalidated by the court.[86] Further, the court established the position that a sixteen-year-old married student has the right to attend public school, even when she has a child.[87]

Married students are considered to be **emancipated** (free of parental authority and control and free to make independent decisions) and not subject to compulsory attendance laws. Thus, a married or minor student cannot be coerced to attend school. These students attend as they wish to do so and may not be denied an opportunity to participate in extracurricular activities.

Administrative Guide

Pregnant and Married Students

1. Pregnant and married students are afforded the same rights as all other students enrolled in public schools, and they may not be prohibited from attending school.
2. To justify any attempt to restrict their attendance, compelling evidence must demonstrate that the presence of married or pregnant students creates disruption or interference with school activities or a negative influence on other students.
3. The pregnant student's physician is authorized to determine when the student should withdraw from school and when it is feasible for her to return.
4. Home-based instruction should be offered for students who have withdrawn from school due to pregnancy.
5. A heavy burden of proof rests with school officials in instances where attempts are made to exclude either pregnant or married students from participating in regular and extracurricular activities.
6. The courts are unanimous in invalidating school rules that prohibit married or pregnant students from attending school.

CASE STUDIES

Student Protest for Poor Treatment

A group of students in Cloverdale School has staged a protest regarding the general treatment of students by both teachers and administration. They have camped out on the school lawn.

Discussion Questions

1. Under what conditions would such action be considered legal?
2. Under what conditions would such action be considered illegal?
3. What action should school officials take in the cases described in questions 1 and 2?
4. Write a set of defensible guidelines that should be followed by school personnel in dealing with student protest and demonstration.

Student Publication and Censorship

Brian Dickerson, a student editor in a northeastern upper-middle-class school district, wrote a review in the student newspaper on a movie that was rated "R." The review did not contain any vulgar or offensive language. School officials censored the review on the basis that it might pose a danger to students' health. Brian's parents sued on his behalf, claiming First Amendment violations.

Discussion Questions

1. Do Brian's parents have a legitimate cause of action? Why or why not?
2. Can school officials censor material that they believe is harmful to students?

3. What evidence is needed to justify censorship? (Be specific.)
4. How do you think the court would rule in this case?
5. Provide a rationale to support your response to question 4.
6. What are the administrative implications suggested by this case?

Search of Student Involving Protruding Object

Jim Robinson is a tenth-grade teacher. While walking down the hall, he spotted a suspicious object protruding from a student's pocket. The student has a history of misbehavior. He asked the student to empty his pocket, but the student refused.

Discussion Questions

1. Does the teacher have grounds to make such a request?
2. Does the student have a right to refuse to obey the teacher's request?
3. Should physical force be used to identify the object?
4. Would such a search be legal?
5. What guidelines would you suggest school personnel follow in matters involving student search in situations such as this one?

Off-Campus Search

Students were informed that drugs and alcohol were banned during their participation in an overnight school-sponsored trip. The principal smelled marijuana in the hallway where students had congregated at the hotel.

Discussion Questions

1. Does the smell of marijuana justify a search of each student's room? If yes, why? If no, why not?
2. Has reasonable suspicion been established by the principal? If yes, why? If not, why not?
3. Can the principal legally request that hotel personnel provide him access to each student's room? If yes, why? If not, why not?
4. Does inspection of students' room constitute a breach of student privacy? If yes, why? If not, why not?
5. Is the principal justified in punishing guilty students when they are away from school after school hours? If yes, why? If not, why not?

Corporal Punishment over Student's Objection

Carl Palmer, principal of Carbondale Middle School, became very upset with Walter Johnson for being disrespectful to several of his teachers. Palmer explained to Walter that because of his actions, he (Palmer) must administer corporal punishment based on school policy. When the principal proceeded to get his instrument to administer the punishment, Walter told Palmer that he was not going to hit him with anything. Other students, faculty, and staff in the outer office heard him say this.

Discussion Questions

1. What is the dilemma facing Palmer?
2. Should Palmer proceed with his plan to administer the punishment? Why or why not?
3. Does the student have the right to decide his punishment?
4. Is the principal creating a problem maintaining respect and discipline when others heard Walter refuse to accept punishment?
5. If the principal decides to administer punishment, what steps should he follow to ensure legal defensibility?
6. What should the principal's decision be in this situation?
7. What should be the basis for his decision?

Student Suspension for Misconduct

Kelvin Brooks is an eighth-grade student at Summerville Middle School, which is located in an affluent southern community. He has committed various acts of misconduct, including skipping class, excessive tardiness, and smoking cigarettes on school property. It is necessary that Kelvin be suspended for five days based on his conduct.

Discussion Questions

1. Write a suspension letter to Kelvin's parents informing them of the suspension. Include evidence in the letter that minimal due process requirements were met.
2. Develop a suspension form that you feel meets the requirements of due process.
3. Outline a defensible suspension procedure that will meet court scrutiny.
4. Identify viable options other than suspension that may be considered.
5. What advantages might your options provide Kelvin that would not otherwise be provided under a five-day suspension?

Expulsion for Assault of a Student

Larry Smith, principal of Farley Middle School in an upscale community in the Northeast, recently recommended to his superintendent that a student, Susan Brown, be expelled for the remainder of the year for various acts of misconduct, including disrespect of authority and physically attacking a student who refused to loan her money.

Discussion Questions

1. What type of evidence is needed to sustain a recommendation of expulsion?
2. Outline a legally defensible procedure that should be followed in this situation, including the rights to which Susan is entitled.
3. If the student's parents challenge the expulsion, how do you think the courts would respond to the procedure you outlined?
4. Provide a rationale for your response to question 3.
5. How does expulsion differ from suspension with respect to due process consideration? (Be specific.)

Endnotes

1. *Tinker v. Des Moines Independent Community School District*, 393 U.S. 503, at 511, 89 S.Ct. 733, 21 L. Ed. 2d 731 (1969).
2. Ibid.
3. Ibid.
4. *Blackwell v. Issaquena County Board of Education*, 366 F.2d 749 (5th Cir. 1966).
5. *Bethel School District v. Fraser*, 478 U.S. 675, 106 S.Ct. 3159, 93 L. Ed. 2d 549 (1986).
6. *Morse v. Frederick*, 439 F.3d 1114 (9th Cir. 2006).
7. *Nuxoll v. Indian Prairie School Dist. #204*, 523 F.3d 668 (7th Cir. 2008).
8. *Evans v. Bayer*, 684 F. Supp.2d 1365 (S.D. Fla. 2010).
9. *Corales v. Bennett*, 567 F.3d 554 (9th Cir. 2009).
10. *Hazelwood School District v. Kuhlmeier*, 484 U.S. 260, at 276; 108 S.Ct. 562; 98 L. Ed. 2d 592 (1987).
11. *Hazelwood School District v. Kuhlmeier*, op cit.
12. *Bystrom v. Fridley High School Independent School District No. 14*, 822 F.2d 747 (8th Cir. 1987).
13. *Burch v. Barker*, 861 F.2d 1149 (9th Cir. 1988).
14. *Miller v. California*, 413 U.S. 15 (1973).
15. *Blau v. Fort Thomas Pub. Sch. Dist.*, 401 F.3d 381, 395-96 (6th Cir. 2005).
16. *Pyle v. The South Hadley School Committee*, 861 F. Supp. 157 (D. Mass. 1994), 55 F.3d 20 (1st Cir. 1995).
17. *Scott v. School Board of Alachua County*, 324 F.3d 1246 1248-49 (11th Cir. 2003).
18. *Tinker v. Des Moines*, op. cit.
19. *Bethel v. Fraser*, op. cit.
20. *In re Gault*, 387 U.S. 1; 875 S.Ct. 1428; 18 L. Ed. 2d 527 (1967).
21. *People v. Jackson*, 65 Misc. 2d 909, 319 N.Y.S. 2d 731 (1971).

22. *New Jersey v. T.L.O.,* 469 U.S. 809; 105 S.Ct. 68; 83 L. Ed. 2d 19 (1984).

23. Ibid.

24. *A.H. v. State,* 846 So.2d 1215 (Fla. App. 5 Dist., Jun 06, 2003).

25. *Vernonia School District v. Acton,* 115 S.Ct. 2386; 132 L. Ed. 2d 564 (1995).

26. *Doe v. Little Rock District,* 380 F.3d 349 (8th Cir. 2004).

27. *Comwlth. of Massachusetts v. Damian D.,* 752 N.E. 2d 679 (Mass. 2001).

28. *G.C. v. Owensboro Pub. Sch.,* No. 11-6476 (6th Cir. Mar. 28, 2013).

29. *In re Guy Dumas, a minor,* 515 A.2d 984 (Pa. Super. CT. 1986).

30. *Bellnier v. Lund,* 438 F. Supp. 47 (N.D. N.Y. 1977).

31. *Desilets ex rel. Desilets v. Clearview Regional Board of Education,* 265 N.J. Super. 370 (App. Div. 1993).

32. *Shamberg v. State,* 762 P. 2d 488 (Alaska App. 1988).

33. *M.M. v. Anker,* 607 F.2d 588 (2d Cir. 1979).

34. *Cales v. Howell Public Schools,* 635 F. Supp. 454 (E.D. Mich. 1985).

35. *Cornfield by Lewis v. Consolidated School District No. 230,* 991 Vol. II F.2d 1316 (7th Cir. 1993).

36. *Safford Unified School District # 1, et al. v. April Redding,* U.S. LEXIS 4735 (June 25, 2009).

37. *Parker v. Dallas County Board of Educ.,* No. Civ. A. 04-0684-BH-M, 2005 WL 2456981 (S.D. Ala. 2005).

38. *New York v. Quarles,* 467 U.S. 649 (1984).

39. *Comwlth. v. Dillon D.,* 448 Mass. 793, 863 N.E. 2d 1287 (Mass. 2007).

40. *Stockton v. City of Freeport, Texas,* 147 F. Supp. 2d 642 (2001).

41. *Vernonia School District v. Acton,* 115 S.Ct. 2386; 132 L. Ed. 2d 564 (1995).

42. Ibid.

43. *Joye v. Hunterdon Central Regional High School Board of Education,* 176 N.J. 568; 826 A. 2d 624. 2003 Lexis 687.

44. *Linke v. Northwestern School Corp.,* 734 N.E. 2d 252, 259 (Ind. App. 2000).

45. *Penn-Harris Madison School Corporation v. Tianna Joy,* 678 N.E. 2d 940; Ind App Lexis 815 (2002).

46. *Doe v. Renfrow,* 475 F. Supp. 1012 (N.D. Ind. 1979).

47. *Zamoro v. Pomeroy,* 639 F.2d 662 (10th Cir. 1981).

48. *Jones v. Latexo Independent School District,* 499 F. Supp. 223 (E.D. Tex. 1980).

49. *Horton v. Goose Creek Independent School District,* 690 F.2d 470 (5th Cir. 1982).

50. *B.C. v. Plumas Unified School District,* 192 F.3d 1260, 138 Ed. Law Rep. 1003 (Cal. 1999).

51. *Bundick v. Bay Independent School District,* 140 F. Supp. 2d 735, 154 Ed. Law Rep. 183 (S.D. Texas 2001).

52. *Florida v. Harris,* 133 S.Ct. 1050 (2013).

53. *Jordan v. Smyrna School Dist. Board of Educ.,* No. 05A-02-004, 2006 WL 1149149 (Del. Super. Ct. 2006).

54. *Mathews v. Eldridge,* 424 U.S. 319 335 96 S.Ct. 893, 903 (1976).

55. *In re Gault,* 387 U.S. 1; 875 S.Ct. 1428; 18 L. Ed. 2d 527 (1967).

56. *Goss v. Lopez,* 419 U.S. 565; 955 S.Ct. 729; 42 L. Ed. 2d 725 (1975).

57. *Ingraham v. Wright,* 430 U.S. 651; 97 S.Ct. 1401; 51 L. Ed. 2d 711 (1977).

58. Ibid.

59. Ibid.

60. Ibid.

61. *Baker v. Owen,* 395 F. Supp. 294 (M.D. N.C. 1975).

62. Ibid.

63. *Woodward v. Los Fresnos Independent School District,* 732 F.2d 1243 (5th Cir. 1984).

64. *State v. Ingram,* 237 N.C. 197, 74 S.E. 2d 532 (1953).

65. *Ingraham v. Wright,* op. cit.

66. *Neal v. Fulton County Board of Education,* 229 F.3d 1069; U.S. App. (2000).

67. *Kirkland v. Greene County Board of Education,* 03-10583 (11th Cir. Dec. 7, 2003).

68. *In re Roberts,* 563 S.E. 2d 37 (N.C. Ct. App. 2002).

69. *In re Roberts,* 576 S.E. 2d 327 (N.C. 2003).

70. *Buncombe County, North Carolina, Board of Educ. v. Roberts,* 124 S.Ct. 103 (2003).

71. *Sherrell v. Northern Community School Corporation,* 801 N.E. 2d 693 (Ind. App. 2004).

72. *Dixon v. Alabama State Board of Education,* 186 F. Supp. 945; reversed 294 F.2d 15; cert. denied, 368 U.S. 930, 825 S.Ct. 368 (1961).

73. *Wood v. Strickland,* 420 U.S. 308; 95 S.Ct. 992; 43 L. Ed. 2d 214 (1975).

74. *Balding v. State,* 4 S.W. 759 (Tex. 1887).

75. *Burdick v. Babcock,* 31 Iowa 562 (1871).

76. *Douglas v. Campbell,* 116 S.W. 211 (Ark. 1909).

77. *O'Rourke v. Walker,* 128 Atl. 25 (Conn. 1925).

78. *Claiborne v. Beebe Sch. Dist.,* 687 F. 1358 (E.D. Ark. 1988).

79. *Collins v. Prince William County School Board,* 142 Fed. Appx. 144 (Not selected for publication in the Federal Reporter), 2005 WL 1655027 (4th Cir.[Va.]), 201 Ed. Law Rep. 487, 4th Cir.(Va.), Jul 15, 2005.

80. *Bethel v. Fraser,* op. cit.

81. *Davis v. Monroe County Board of Education,* 526 U.S. 629; 119 S.Ct. 1661; 143 L. Ed. 2d 839 (1999).

82. *Hawkins v. Sarasota County School Board,* 322 F.3d 1279, 1288 (2003).

83. *Gebser v. Lago Vista Independent School District,* 524 U.S. 274; 118 S.Ct 1989; 141 L. Ed. 2d 277.

84. *Nutt v. Goodland Board of Education,* 128 Kan. 507, 278 P. 1065 (1929).

85. *McLeod v. State,* 122 So. 77 (Miss. 1929).

86. *Board of Education of Harrodsburg v. Bentley,* 383 S.W. 2d 387 (Tex. 1967).

87. *Alvin Independent School District v. Cooper,* 404 S.W. 2d 76 (Tex. 1966).

Chapter 4

National Security and School Safety

HOMELAND SECURITY

National security and safety have taken center stage since the tragic events of September 11, 2001. The United States has initiated a terrorist alert system based on guidelines formulated by the Department of Homeland Security, which was created by HR 5005 in the 107th Congress and signed into law on November 26, 2002, by President George W. Bush. Since the alert system was created, the United States has vacillated between orange (high risk) terror alert and yellow (elevated) terror alert.

Concurrently, the wave of violence that has struck public schools, resulting in injury and death of students, faculty, and school leaders, has prompted increased attention to school safety. National security and school safety have profoundly affected the administration and operation of public schools as measures have been initiated by school officials to respond to national threats to the safety of students, faculty, and staff. This chapter addresses safety and security issues at both the national and local school district levels.

School safety has become a major issue facing communities throughout the nation. In light of the terrorist attacks on September 11, 2001, and subsequent threats to U.S. security, what role should schools play in creating and maintaining a safe environment conducive to learning? Since the events of September 11, 2001, many school districts have collaborated with local law enforcement agencies to address issues involving safety. It is now common knowledge that public schools, like many other establishments, are vulnerable to various threats to safety. In addition, school officials must incorporate into their plans responses to natural disasters such as hurricanes, tornadoes, and earthquakes. When natural disasters strike, schools may be called on to provide temporary shelter for evacuees as well as food and medical assistance. Contingency plans should consider all anticipated or foreseeable events so that schools may be proactive rather than reactive.

USA PATRIOT ACT

The USA PATRIOT Act (commonly known as the Patriot Act) was enacted by Congress after September 11, 2001, and expressly authorized U.S. law authorities to investigate and preempt potential terrorist acts in the United States and around the world. This act is a revision of the Foreign Intelligence Surveillance Act (FISA). This enhanced legal authority also may be used to detect and prosecute other alleged potential crimes. The Patriot Act defines *terrorism* as an activity that results in coercion or intimidation involving the government and American citizens. These activities involve violation of criminal law as well as endangerment of human life.

Public schools fall under the jurisdiction of this act. The Federal Bureau of Investigation (FBI) may obtain a court order without probable cause from a secret court for the production of any tangible resources (books, records, paper documents, or other items) for an authorized investigation to protect against terrorism or clandestine intelligence activities. Information relating to Internet usage, including e-mail addresses, may also be monitored. Information may also be obtained by the FBI under the Family Educational Rights and Privacy Act (FERPA). Amendments to FERPA permit educational agencies and institutions to disclose, without the consent or knowledge of the student or parent, personally identifiable information from the student's educational records to the attorney general of the United States or designee in response to an *ex parte* order in connection with the investigation of prosecution of terrorism crimes. FERPA, as amended under the Patriot Act, does not require a school official to record a disclosure of information from a student's record when the school makes that disclosure pursuant to an **ex parte** order (by or for one party). Critics of this act claim that it is not necessary, and it allows U.S. law enforcement to infringe on free speech, freedom of the press, human rights, and rights to privacy. The aspect of this act most hotly contested between Democrats and Republicans involves provisions that allow the government to invade the privacy rights of U.S. citizens as it conducts intelligence activities, specifically with respect to accessing telephone and Internet records.

Controversy also has arisen over the government's expanded powers under this act. Congress has expressed concern regarding the FBI's aggressive acts of accessing private phone and financial records of ordinary citizens. One view among some lawmakers is that the FBI's actions are approaching abuse of powers. The government's expanded powers highlight the risks of balancing national security against individual rights. Under the Patriot Act, the FBI issues more than 30,000 national security letters permitting investigations each year, which represents a hundred-fold increase over historic norms. These security letters, which were initially used in the 1970s, allow access to citizens' phone and e-mail records as well as their financial information and the Internet sites they access. The Patriot Act removed the stipulation that records sought be those of someone under suspicion.

The Patriot Act was reauthorized by Congress in March 2006 following a hotly contested debate over national security and civil liberties (see Figure 4.1). The act makes it easier for FBI agents to monitor phone calls and e-mails, to search homes, and to obtain business records of terrorism suspects, activities that are at the center of debate regarding the continuation of the act. Although this act continues to evoke criticism and debate, the Senate has passed a one-year extension of key provisions of the act. The bill goes to the House for consideration.

NO CHILD LEFT BEHIND AND SCHOOL SAFETY

Under the No Child Left Behind (NCLB) Act, school safety also has become a major priority for local school districts, which must provide assurances that plans are on file regarding steps schools will initiate to maintain safe and drug-free environments. In March 2003, Secretary of Education Rod Paige announced that $30 million was available in fiscal 2003 to assist school districts in improving and strengthening emergency response and crisis management plans.

The National School Safety Center (NSSC) was created to provide assistance in combating school safety problems so that schools can be free to focus on the primary job of educating the nation's children. It was established by presidential directive in 1984 as a partnership between the U.S. Department of Justice and the U.S. Department of Education. It has since become a private, nonprofit organization serving school administrators, teachers, law officers, community leaders, government officials, and others interested in creating safe schools throughout the United States and internationally.

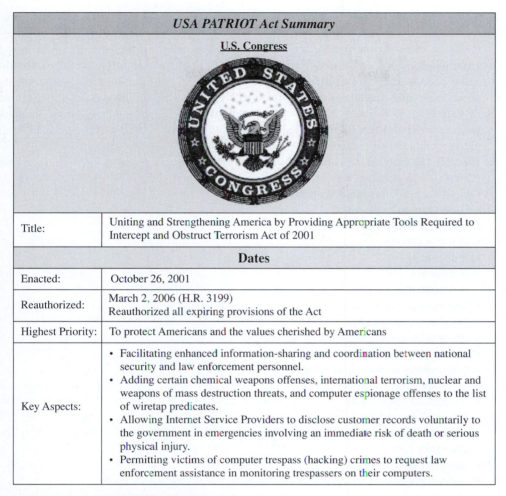

	USA PATRIOT Act Summary
	U.S. Congress
Title:	Uniting and Strengthening America by Providing Appropriate Tools Required to Intercept and Obstruct Terrorism Act of 2001
Dates	
Enacted:	October 26, 2001
Reauthorized:	March 2, 2006 (H.R. 3199) Reauthorized all expiring provisions of the Act
Highest Priority:	To protect Americans and the values cherished by Americans
Key Aspects:	• Facilitating enhanced information-sharing and coordination between national security and law enforcement personnel. • Adding certain chemical weapons offenses, international terrorism, nuclear and weapons of mass destruction threats, and computer espionage offenses to the list of wiretap predicates. • Allowing Internet Service Providers to disclose customer records voluntarily to the government in emergencies involving an immediate risk of death or serious physical injury. • Permitting victims of computer trespass (hacking) crimes to request law enforcement assistance in monitoring trespassers on their computers.

FIGURE 4.1   USA PATRIOT Act Summary

SOURCE: FirstGov.gov ™ is the U.S. government's official web portal: Office of Citizen Services and Communications, U.S. General Services Administration 1800 F Street, NW, Washington, DC 20405

The NSSC has developed guidelines to enhance safety for each of the groups identified above. Schools are free to develop guidelines that exceed those suggested by the safety center. Minimal guidelines pertaining to the roles of schools in homeland security are as follows:

1. **In the school's mission statement, identify the context for which the school wishes the academic learning to take place,** using phrases like "to learn in a safe and secure environment free of violence, drugs, and fear." Such phrases enhance the school's legal position to create and enforce policies that promote a safe, caring, and disciplined school climate. A statement of this nature can have a powerful effect on the validity and credibility of the school's efforts to create and preserve a safe environment. The context for student learning should focus on student outcomes as the most significant priority. The school's assessment process should impact the school's priorities; consequently, the assessment process must consider outcomes and student learning experiences that contribute to the desired mission and vision of the district. An understanding of student learning experiences may be best accomplished by examining the context for learning, which involves school mission, the learning environment, student outcomes, and relevant learning experiences.

2. **Identify a specific procedure for evaluating and responding to threats.** Every campus should have a series of threat assessment protocols so that school officials can effectively work with mental health and law enforcement professionals in handling circumstances that could result in potential violence or harm. School officials should make certain students are involved in the planning process. For the most part, students are the best information resources for inside threats. Recent studies by the Secret Service revealed that in the vast majority of student shootings, other students on the campus were aware that the event might occur. Having a tip line or safe reporting mechanism in place for students is critical.

3. **Identify the potential disasters that could occur based on the school's setting and climate.** Such disasters may include the following:
   * Civil unrest/demonstrations/rioting
   * Bomb threats/explosions
   * Intruders/unauthorized visitors
   * Hostage takings
   * Sniper attacks
   * Extortion
   * Assault/battery/rape
   * Weapons possessions
   * Drug abuse/trafficking
   * Gang-related violence/drive-by shootings
   * Kidnappings/abductions
   * Child abuse/neglect/molestation
   * Life-threatening illness
   * Accidental injury or death
   * Intentional injury or death
   * Utility failures
   * Chemical spills
   * Automobile accidents
   * Natural disasters: earthquake, flood, tornado, fire, hurricane, tsunami
   * Mass transit disasters: falling aircraft/train derailment/bus accidents

4. **Control campus access.** Minimize the number of campus entrance and exit points used daily. Access points to school grounds should be limited and supervised on a regular basis by individuals who are familiar with the student body. Campus traffic, both pedestrian and vehicular, should flow through areas that can be easily and naturally supervised. Delivery entrances used by vendors also should be checked regularly. Parking lots often have multiple entrances and exits, which contribute to vandalism and defacement of vehicles and school property. Vehicular and pedestrian access should be carefully controlled. Perimeter fencing should be considered. Bus lots should be secured and monitored. Infrequently used rooms and closets should be locked. Access to utilities, roofs, and cleaning closets should be secured.

5. **Identify specifically assigned roles and responsibilities.** Specific policies and procedures that detail staff members' responsibilities for security should be developed. These responsibilities may include monitoring hallways and restrooms, patrolling parking lots, and providing supervision at before-school and after-school activities. Specific roles and responsibilities should also be assigned for times of crisis, including the appointment of a crisis team.

6. **Identify whom to call in a crisis.** Maintain an updated list of whom to call in case of various kinds of crises. Develop a close working partnership with these emergency responders. When a crisis occurs, school officials do not have the time or luxury to determine who handles chemical or biological disasters or who handles bomb threats. Know the extent of services offered by these agencies. Determine what to do when an emergency

responder is not immediately available. Develop a close working partnership with law enforcement officials. If feasible, become acquainted with school security before there is a crisis. Develop a memorandum of understanding as to the role of a police officer on campus. Determine in advance who will lead, who will follow, and how searches, interrogations, and other issues will be handled. Create a close working partnership with mental health professionals who can assist school officials in evaluating and assessing potentially dangerous students who may threaten or intimidate others. The counselor or psychologist also can be an important partner in the aftermath of a crisis.

7. **Provide cultural awareness and sensitivity training for all members of the school community.** It is important to consider the impact of cultural influences on a school community's ability to create and maintain safe, secure, and peaceful schools. Cultural influences will directly affect the information, strategies, and resources that will be used in safe school planning. Sensitivity to cultural influences also applies to creating a plan to manage and respond to a crisis.

8. **Establish an emergency operation communication system.** In addition to campus intercoms and two-way radios, it is important for school officials to be able to communicate with law enforcement and outside telephone providers, including with cell phones.

9. **Implement a uniform school crime-reporting and record-keeping system.** When school administrators know what crimes are being committed on their campus, when they are committed, where a crime is committed, and who is involved, this knowledge becomes extremely useful in determining the types of strategies and supervision that should be implemented. In addition, it is important to conduct some level of crime analysis to determine what, if any, links exist among various aspects of criminal activity on the campus.

Procedures for Evaluating and Responding to Threats

School safety must be a leading priority in public schools in order to create a safe, peaceful, and effective learning environment. To achieve this objective, specific strategies should be developed to respond to potential threats involving safety. These strategies minimally include the following:

1. Develop a comprehensive school safety program based on district policy that focuses on a positive teaching and learning environment.

2. Establish a broadly based threat assessment team consisting of teachers, administrative staff, students, safety professionals, mental health professionals, and community leaders that focuses on threat assessment, prevention, and intervention strategies.

3. Develop a comprehensive list of possible safety threats to the school with appropriate action **abatement** strategies to respond rapidly to these threats.

4. Follow leads regarding individuals who may be contemplating violent acts.

5. Develop and implement district policies that focus on assessment and intervention involving students whose behavior poses a safety threat to the school.

6. Solicit assistance and intervention by parents as appropriate.

7. Develop proper strategies to minimize and/or eliminate the potential threat based on the type of threat and the potential risk involved.

8. Elicit the assistance of law enforcement officials, mental health professionals, and social service professionals based on the perceived risk to safety.

9. Provide support for potential offenders such as counseling, anger management, and opportunities to succeed in school.

10. Act decisively based on school policy to deal with offenders considering a full range of options such as alternative programs, referrals to appropriate external agencies, and suspension and/or expulsion.

11. Provide comprehensive and continuous training for school personnel regarding school safety.

12. Create an environment of trust and respect that permeates the culture of the entire school.

Preparing for National Emergencies

Schools might wish to begin a process of learning and staying informed about potential national security threats, preparing for emergencies, and responses during an attack. In view of Department of Homeland Security recommendations, it is especially important to focus added attention to the possibility of the following kinds of disasters.

- Bomb threats/explosions
- Suicide bombings
- Intruders/unauthorized visitors
- Biological/radiological attacks
- Utility failures
- Mass transit disasters: falling aircraft/train derailment/bus accidents

It is necessary to continually review and revise district crises plans accordingly. Visit the U.S. Department of Homeland Security website at dhs.gov/dhspublic for more information.

HANDLING VIOLENCE IN SCHOOLS

It is important that all school personnel, school officials, and teachers understand that elementary school violence is everyone's responsibility. Teachers can no longer assume that they are only responsible for students to whom they are assigned. It is important for teachers to be visible and observant in the hallways, on school grounds, and during extracurricular activities. If they notice signs of disruptive behavior, appropriate steps must be taken to address deviant behavior consistent with school or district policy.

Students should not be permitted to harass or intimidate other students or to make discriminatory or derogatory comments in classrooms or on school property. Setting expectations for appropriate behavior can be pivotal in reducing violence in schools. It is important for all school personnel to become aware of danger signs that may lead to violence. If a student displays significant mood swings, becomes irritable, loses interest in school work, or becomes obsessed with violent games, these may signal that some type of intervention is needed.

An environment or school climate should be established that encourages students to express concerns or views regarding school violence. Building open and positive relationships with students may entice them to privately convey information regarding planned acts of violence by classmates. Teachers should convey alternative ways in which discord may be resolved so that students learn to resolve conflicts and control anger. Teaching respect for others and building a community-oriented school climate can be important in minimizing school violence. Involving parents through openly sharing observations regarding their child's behavior may also be helpful in addressing student conflicts. Handling school violence is important to health, safety, and a vibrant learning environment and should be viewed as a team approach involving school officials, teachers, and parents.

Hazing

Hazing in public schools is a significant problem that may result in serious injury to students who are victims. It may also result in legal challenges for school personnel. Public schools are deemed to be safe places by the courts where teaching and learning occur. Thus, school personnel have a leading responsibility to protect the safety of students under the functional custody of their schools. Hazing is often viewed as abusive, harassing, and a humiliating form of initiation into a group. Hazing, if unchecked, poses a potential threat to student safety. School personnel have a primary responsibility to create and maintain safe school environments free of hazing. Hazing has become so prevalent that it has prompted forty-two states to pass legislation banning it. In spite of anti-hazing laws, hazing continues to occur among athletes, peer groups, gangs, and other schools, clubs, and organizations. Hazing creates stress, anxiety, intimidation, and often results in serious physical and emotional harm to victims. Well-defined policies prohibiting hazing and proper procedures for reporting hazing coupled with vigilance by school personnel in monitoring student activities may greatly reduce hazing incidents and minimize lawsuits.

School officials and teachers must be proactive in addressing potential threats to students' safety based on reported incidents of hazing in their schools. Under the concept of liability, school personnel must be able to foresee that students' safety may be threatened if they are victims of hazing. Foreseeability, in this instance, is defined as the school personnel's ability to predict or anticipate that a hazing activity may prove harmful to students either physically or emotionally who are victims. Once a hazing activity becomes foreseeable, prudent steps must be taken to prevent harm to students by eliminating hazing promptly. There are instances in which the courts expect school officials and school personnel to be aware of harmful activities in their schools. For example, if it is common knowledge among students that hazing is occurring in the school's clubs and other student organizations, professional educators are expected to be aware of such activity and take prudent steps to address the hazing activity. Failure to do so can result in lawsuits for negligence.

To control hazing, it must be viewed as a school–community effort with active involvement (engagement) of school officials, teachers, parents, and community leaders. For example, school officials and teachers, especially coaches and club advisors, should discuss with students specifically what actions constitute hazing and the dangers associated with it as well as the consequences that will follow if they are found guilty of initiating or participating in hazing activities. They should also convey to students that hazing activities must be reported promptly through a well-defined reporting process without fear of reprisal or retaliation based on school or district policy.

Parents and community leaders should work closely with school leaders and teachers to reinforce the school's position on hazing. Parents should discuss the inappropriateness of such behavior and the punishment their children will face at home if they are involved in initiating or participating in hazing activities in school.

Administrative Guide

Hazing

1. Hazing should be clearly defined so that students, faculty, club advisors, coaches, and parents are aware of specific acts that constitute undesirable behavior by students involved in school organizations and athletic teams.
2. The school board should adopt policies that clearly establish that hazing either on or off school property is strictly prohibited.
3. Penalties should be clearly established for violations of anti-hazing policies including denial of permission for student organizations to operate on school property and/or civil penalties or criminal penalties as appropriate.
4. Teachers, students, and parents should be informed of proper procedures for reporting incidents of hazing on and off school premises and be assured that there will be no retaliation or reprisals brought against them for reporting these incidents.

Bullying

Bullying is associated with many acts of violence in public schools. It generally involves intentional cruel behavior between the person who exhibits this behavior and the students who are victims of bullying behavior. Bullying may involve physical or verbal acts intended to harass, intimidate, or create anxiety and fear among victims. There is often a pattern of repeated antisocial behavior toward others, but bullying may also involve a single incident. Bullying can create a hostile school and classroom environment and occasionally result in serious injury or death, as

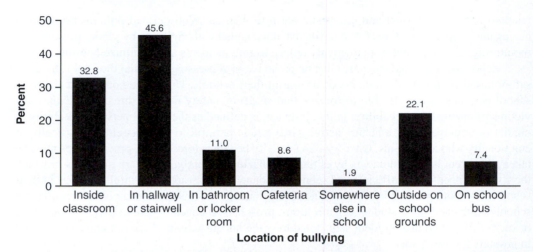

FIGURE 4.2   Among students ages 12–18 who reported being bullied at school during the school year, percentage who reported being bullied in various locations: 2011

NOTE: "At school" includes the school building, on school property, on a school bus, or going to and from school. For more information, please see appendix A. Location totals may sum to more than 100 because students could have been bullied in more than one location.

SOURCE: U.S. Department of Justice, Bureau of Justice Statistics, School Crime Supplement (SCS) to the National Crime Victimization Survey, 2011

has been seen in a number of school shootings, including the tragedies in Littleton, Colorado (Columbine High School); Williamsport, Pennsylvania; and Santee, California. In other cases, victims of bullying may respond violently after repeated acts of violence have been committed against them.

School or district policies are typically formulated to address bullying. Some of these policies are categorized as anti-bullying policies. Fair, consistent, and firm enforcement of anti-bullying policies is necessary to minimize bullying and contribute to a safe school environment. The percentage of students bullied at various locations in the school is reflected in Figure 4.2.

According to a survey funded by the U.S. Department of Justice, the largest percentage of children who reported being physically bullied over the past year occurred in the hallway and stairwell. Based on these statistics, more focused supervision of students may be needed. Figure 4.3 depicts the percentage of students bullied based on school characteristics. Rural schools experienced the highest percentage followed by urban schools.

A bully, depending on the circumstances, may be charged criminally if he or she exceeds age twelve. Bullying may begin among adolescents with simple joking behavior that escalates into physical contact based on relationships. Although simple joking and physical contact may be acceptable among friends, similar behavior may not be acceptable if positive social relationships do not exist. The key issue involving bullying centers around the relationship between the bully and the victim and the intent of the person who exhibits bullying behavior. Generally speaking, there is a power difference between the bully and the victim, such as physical size, popularity in school, or the ability to intimidate others or ostracize them socially. The intent of bullying is to create stress or a sense of helplessness among victims. The effects of bullying can be devastating to the victim and may linger for years after bullying incidents occur because bullying tends to embarrass and humiliate victims.

Bullies, particularly those who engage in physical and verbal abuse, tend to be known by all students because of their behavior. Many times victims of bullying, out of fear or desperation, feel a need to protect themselves or strike back, which most often results in victims responding with violence. Other victims may resort to self-inflicted injuries to escape bullying behavior.

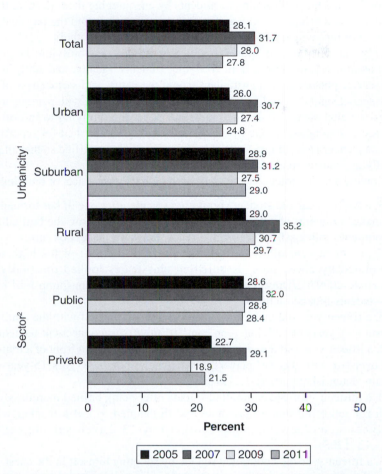

Selected school characteristics

Total: 28.1, 31.7, 28.0, 27.8
Urban: 26.0, 30.7, 27.4, 24.8
Suburban: 28.9, 31.2, 27.5, 29.0
Rural: 29.0, 35.2, 30.7, 29.7
Public: 28.6, 32.0, 28.8, 28.4
Private: 22.7, 29.1, 18.9, 21.5

■ 2005 ■ 2007 □ 2009 ■ 2011

FIGURE 4.3 Percentage of students ages 12–18 who reported being bullied at school during the school year, by selected school characteristics: Various years, 2005–2011

[1]Refers to the Standard Metropolitan Statistical Area (MSA) status of the respondent's household as defined in 2000 by the U.S. Census Bureau, Categories include "central city of an MSA (Urban)," "in MSA but not in central city (Suburban)," and "not MSA (Rural)." These data by metropolitan status were based on the location of households and differ from those published in *Student Reports of Bullying and CyberBullying: Results From the 2011 School Crime Supplement to the National Crime Victimization Survey*, which were based on the urban-centric measure of the location of the school that the child attended.

[2]Sector of school as reported by the respondent, These data differ from those based on a matching of the respondent-reported school name to the Common Core of Data, Public Elementary/Secondary School Universe Survey and Private School Survey, as reported in *Student Reports of Bullying and CyberBullying: Results From the 2011 School Crime Supplement to the National Crime Victimization Survey*.

NOTE: "At school" includes the school building, on school property, on a school bus, or going to and from school.

SOURCE: U.S. Department of Justice, Bureau of Justice Statistics, School Crime Supplement (SCS) to the National Crime Victimization Survey, 2005–2011

These issues alone point to the seriousness of bullying in public schools. Consequently, schools need to establish, maintain, and enforce strong anti-bullying policies to protect students and embrace an ongoing safe and peaceful school environment. Students, because they know who the bullies are, can assist in deterring bullying if they feel secure and believe that they will be protected by teachers and school officials once they report bullying behavior. It is the school's responsibility to ensure that students are protected when they report bullies. Therefore, any anti-bullying program must focus on greater student supervision, talking openly with students about the school's climate, and listening to students by encouraging them to share their feelings regarding student relationships. Faculty and staff must also understand the physical, emotional, and social impact of repeated acts involving bullying of students by others.

It is likely that no standard approach can properly address bullying; however, school officials must assume a leadership role in educating students, faculty, and staff, including bus drivers, food service personnel, and custodians, about the nature and seriousness of bullying in the context of school safety. In addition, they should, in conjunction with parents, teachers, and staff members, develop clear policies and guidelines regarding bullying to inform students of required and acceptable behavior. Guidelines should also be established for reporting bullying behavior. Consequences for continued acts of bullying should be specified so that all students are aware that bullying is unacceptable behavior.

The following acts of violence were associated with excessive acts of bullying:

- In 2013, a twelve-year-old student committed suicide after one of her tormenters continued to make comments about her online and bragged about how she bullied the student. (nola.com/news/index.ssf/2013/10/fla_girl_14_brags_on_facebook.html)
- In 2012, a fifteen-year-old leapt to his death from the roof of his high school after being taunted by classmates, as horrified classmates looked on. (dailymail.co.uk /news/article-2099802/Drew-Ferraro-Bullied-teen-took-running-jump-roof-high-school-dozens-students-looked-on.html)
- In 2013, a fifteen-year-old male student shot and killed himself with the family's shotgun after sustaining years of bullying. (cnn.com/2013/09/02/us/connecticut-teen-suicide)
- In 2012, a fifteen-year-old female student jumped to her death in front of a train after being bullied over sex with football players. (nydailynews.com/new-york/15-year-old-throws-front-train-staten-island-article-1.1191808)
- In 2013, a thirteen-year-old committed suicide after being bullied mercilessly and called a snitch for reporting that a classmate had threatened to kill a teacher with a knife. (nydailynews.com/news/national/georgia-boy-13-driven-suicide-called-snitch-article-1.1311208)
- In 2013, a fifteen-year-old committed suicide by shooting himself in the chest. His suicide note stated that he was tired of life and was killing himself because he was being bullied at school. The day before, he had participated in a class on bullying and viewed a video where the student being bullied went home and committed suicide. (fox8.com/2013/10/18 /a-day-after-a-class-on-bullying-a-student-commits-suicide)

Administrative Guide

Bullying

1. Schools are often targets for bullying.
2. Students who engage in bullying are power seekers.
3. Bullies tend to convince others to exclude a certain person from the social group.
4. Bullying can and most often leaves physical, emotional, and psychological scars for the victim.
5. Violence by victims may be an outgrowth of bullying behavior.
6. Bullying is not necessarily a function of social, cultural, or financial boundaries.
7. School officials have an obligation to establish a climate in which physical aggression and bullying are not permitted to gain popularity in schools.
8. Schools or the school districts should develop a zero tolerance policy toward bullying behavior and communicate this policy to students and parents.
9. Eliminating bullying is the responsibility of school leaders, teachers, staff, parents, and students as well.

Cyberbullying

Cyberbullying involves the use of electronic devices to send or post hurtful, embarrassing text or images intended to create anxiety, intimidation, or emotional distress in another person. Cyberbullying may involve a pattern of continuing unwelcome e-mails to others who have indicated that they wish to have no contact with the sender. More serious forms of communication may involve hate speech, threats, sexually offensive content, or messages designed to ridicule the victim. Posting false statements also falls within the spectrum of offensive communication. In some instances, an individual's personal or sensitive information may be disclosed for the purpose of defaming or embarrassing the victim. A continued pattern of these types of communications constitutes cyber stalking. Figure 4.4 provides data regarding the percentage of students who experienced cyberbullying based on selected cyberbullying problems.

MEGAN MEIER CYBERBULLYING PREVENTION ACT.   Megan Meier committed suicide after a classmate and her mother fabricated an online account attributed to a fictitious sixteen-year-old boy to whom Megan was attracted. Megan thought messages were cordial and inviting at the outset but later turned negative about her and were communicated to her friends along with bulletins suggesting that she was a bad person.

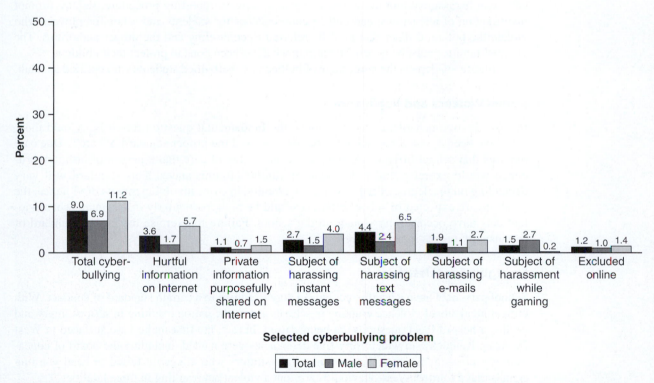

FIGURE 4.4   Percentage of students ages 12–18 who reported being cyberbullied anywhere during the school year, by selected cyberbullying problems and sex: 2011

*Interpret data with caution. The coefficient of variation (CV) for this estimate is between 30 and 50 percent.

NOTE: "Cyberbullying" includes students who responded that another student had posted hurtful information about them on the Internet; purposefully shared private information about them on the Internet; harassed them via instant messaging; harassed them via Short Message Service (SMS) text messaging; harassed them via e-mail; harassed them while gaming; or excluded them online. Cyberbullying types do not sum to total because students could have experienced more than one type of cyberbullying.

SOURCE: U.S. Department of Justice, Bureau of Justice Statistics, School Crime Supplement (SCS) to the National Crime Victimization Survey, 2011

Based on Megan Meier's unfortunate suicide incident stemming from cyberbullying through a social network website, in 2009, H.R. 1966, known as the Megan Meier Cyberbullying Prevention Act, was introduced in Congress. The intent of this act is to amend the federal criminal code to impose criminal penalties on anyone who transmits in interstate or foreign commerce a communication intended to coerce, intimidate, harass, or cause substantial emotional distress to another person, using electronic means to support severe, repeated, and hostile behavior. A subcommittee hearing was held on September 30, 2009. The bill is pending in the House as of this writing.

Jeffrey Johnston Stand Up for All Students Act

Jeffrey Johnston was a strapping, quiet honors student who loved video games. He was the one student who stood up for friends. He grew weary of being called a "faggot" and "fat and ugly." He was beaten down by cyberattacks that made him question his sexuality and lose his circle of friends.

Jeffrey kissed his mother good night, closed his bedroom door, and hanged himself in his closet. He was discovered by his mother and brother the next morning. In Jeffrey's honor, his mother was relentless in energizing a committee of students, educators, and legislators that resulted in the Jeffrey Johnston Stand Up For All Students Act in Florida.

The Jeffrey Johnston Stand Up For All Students Act, passed by a rarely unified Florida Legislature in 2008, requires all school districts to institute anti-bullying policies that specifically ban harassment and intimidation, create a diligent reporting procedure, require prompt investigation of allegations, and outline consequences for students and school employees who violate the policy. Bullies also must be referred to counseling and the proper authorities. The victims' families must be notified regarding what has been done to protect their children.

Figure 4.5 depicts the percentage of bullied or cyberbullied students who notified an adult.

School Violence and Negligence

In cases involving violent acts in schools, the fundamental question raised is, "Could these acts have been avoided had school officials exercised the proper standard of care?" Due care requires that school officials exercise the same degree of care that a person of ordinary prudence would exercise under the same or similar circumstances. This standard will vary depending on the degree of risk involved. Certainly, in cases involving threats of violence, the level of care expected of school officials would be high, particularly in instances where violent acts have occurred previously in the school. Failure to exercise the proper standard of care usually results in negligence.

Emerging Legal Issues

School personnel have a legally recognized duty to adhere to a certain standard of conduct. With critical incidents of violence erupting in schools across the nation resulting in serious injury and deaths, a host of legal questions are being raised. In fact, the first major case surfaced in West Paducah, Kentucky, in which forty-five defendants were named, including the board of education as well as numerous teachers and administrators who allegedly failed to heed warning signals that a fourteen-year-old would carry out a violent act resulting in three fatalities.

In this case, plaintiffs contended that the suspect wrote violent class papers involving shooting students and detonating bombs at school, yet no action was taken by the teacher to inform school officials of the suspect's violent stories. Failure to do so, according to the plaintiffs, constitutes negligence. Given the seriousness of these charges, coupled with continuous acts of violence, school personnel are facing a serious dilemma. How far are teachers and administrators expected to go in responding to students' work that contains violent content? Are there legal consequences when they do so? What are the consequences when they fail to respond? These are perplexing questions with no simple answers.

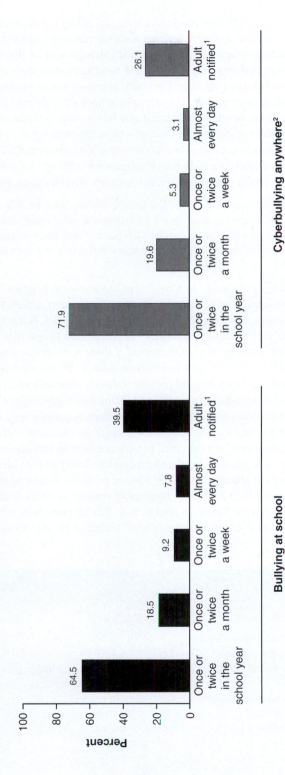

Bullying at school

Percent

Once or twice in the school year: 64.5
Once or twice a month: 18.5
Once or twice a week: 9.2
Almost every day: 7.8
Adult notified[1]: 39.5

Cyberbullying anywhere[2]

Once or twice in the school year: 71.9
Once or twice a month: 19.6
Once or twice a week: 5.3
Almost every day: 3.1
Adult notified[1]: 26.1

FIGURE 4.5 **Percentage distribution of students ages 12–18 who reported being bullied at school and cyberbullied anywhere during the school year, by frequency of bullying and percentage of students who notified an adult: 2011**

[1]Teacher or other adult at school notified.

[2]"Cyberbullying" includes students who responded that another student had posted hurtful information about them on the Internet; purposefully shared private information about them on the Internet; harassed them via instant messaging; harassed them via Short Message Service (SMS) text messaging; harassed them via e-mail; harassed them while gaming; or excluded them online.

NOTE: "At school" includes the school building, on school property, on a school bus, or going to and from school. Detail may not sum to totals because of rounding. For more information, please see appendix A.

SOURCE: U.S. Department of Justice, Bureau of Justice Statistics, School Crime Supplement (SCS) to the National Crime Victimization Survey, 2011

FREEDOM OF EXPRESSION: PROHIBITIONS AND SCHOOL VIOLENCE

Students are afforded certain constitutional rights in the school setting, including freedom of expression, rights to a degree of privacy, protection against cruel and abusive treatment, and equality of treatment. They also are afforded constitutional protection against infringement of these rights, unless school officials can demonstrate that they had a legitimate need to restrict their rights, in which case the burden of proof rests with school officials. Certainly, concerns involving health and safety of students would justifiably fall in this category. For example, school officials may prevent a student from bringing a dangerous weapon to school because it obviously poses a threat to safety. Administrative action can be taken without offending the student's constitutional rights to privacy. The issue, however, that is not as clearly discernible is one involving self-expression. Under what conditions may school officials restrict a student's right to self-expression without violating his or her constitutional rights? The landmark *Tinker* case discussed in Chapter 3 provides some guidance:

> To justify a prohibition of a particular expression or opinion, school officials must be able to show that their action was caused by something more than a mere desire to avoid the discomfort and unpleasantness that always surrounds an unpopular viewpoint. There must be facts that might reasonably lead school authorities to forecast a substantial disruption or a material interference with school activities.[1]

Based on the Supreme Court's ruling in *Tinker,* to what extent can a student's right to express violent content in a class paper be restricted? Can school officials take disciplinary action against a student for writing such a paper without violating the student's rights? Probably not. Is it reasonable to prohibit student writings containing violent themes, and does this prohibition necessarily prevent violence? School officials may restrict writings on violent themes if there is evidence connecting such writings with serious acts of disruption or threats to safety in school. Without a reasonable connection between the two, school officials may be hard pressed to justify their actions as reasonable. School officials would likely be at no risk if, on receiving information regarding a student's violent writing, they conferred with the student to determine whether there was cause for concern.

School violence will continue to plague U.S. schools, although incidents of violence in public schools are declining. School personnel are expected to take reasonable and prudent steps to safeguard the safety of all students. They have a legal and professional duty to provide quality supervision and to be certain that they are able to reasonably foresee possible danger to students. When they do so, they are expected to act in a prudent manner to protect students under their supervision and avoid costly liability charges based on negligence. School personnel who properly execute their legal duty will succeed in minimizing acts of violence in schools and limit potential liability charges.

Administrative Guide

School Violence

1. Heed warning signs exhibited by disruptive students.
2. Follow up on threats made against one student by another.
3. Create an open and comfortable school climate in which students can anonymously report potential problems.
4. Implement a defensible zero tolerance policy on violent behavior in school.
5. Prohibit taunting of students by others.
6. Design programs/activities to engage all students for success in school.
7. Counsel with students who are viewed as "misfits" by their peers.
8. Act swiftly but fairly to deal with disruptive or violent acts in school.
9. Hold workshops on violence and liability for school personnel.
10. Stress school safety through education and increased security.

Gangs

Gang activities declined in mid-1990 through early 2005. Currently, the United States is facing a resurgence of gang activity.

LEGAL CHALLENGES RELATED TO SCHOOL GANGS.   When violent acts based on negligence by school personnel result in injury to students, liability claims are likely. These claims are made when school personnel fail to adequately foresee that students may be harmed through violent acts.

When injury occurs in a negligent situation, school personnel have breached their legal duty to protect students under their supervision. Although school personnel are not expected to guarantee that students are never harmed, they are expected to ensure that reasonable measures have been taken to prevent foreseeable injury.

Because negligence is based in part on foreseeability, gangs constitute a potential legal threat to school personnel. In schools and communities where gangs are present, it is foreseeable that violence will erupt if their activities go unchecked. In these cases, the standard of care becomes greater for school personnel. Thus, they must take extra precautions to prevent violence and foreseeable injury.

School leaders are expected to monitor gang behavior in school and respond swiftly to information that suggests that gang activity is escalating. In searching for appropriate strategies to prevent gang activity, it is helpful to learn as much as possible about gangs and their members. By keeping in touch with gang activity, school leaders may become more aware of friction between gangs and move to mediate problems before they escalate into violence.

GANG CHARACTERISTICS AND MEMBERSHIP.   Gangs are best described as groups of individuals involved in unusually close social relationships. They share a common collective identity expressed through a gang name. Gangs adopt certain symbols or signs and claim control over a certain turf or territory. These organized groups are often involved in drugs, weapons trafficking, and other forms of criminal activity. They can create fear among other students and increase the level of violence in schools.

Gang members are typically young teenage males of similar ethnic or racial backgrounds. Loyalty is expressed through adherence to a strict gang code. Camaraderie is solidified through participation in group activities that are often antisocial, illegal, violent, and criminal. Goals, identified roles, and responsibilities are clearly established and defined, often unspoken but understood. The chain of command is hierarchical and respected by members. In recent years, gangs have attracted younger members (as young as eight and nine years old) and have also shown a growth in the number of female members.

Youths join gangs for various reasons, including peer pressure, neglect, economic reward, a sense of identity, the desire for excitement, the need for recognition or acceptance, and lack of appropriate involvement. Gang members show strong loyalty to their gang and will do whatever is necessary to be initiated into the gang, including committing violent crimes.

Gangs are forces that are challenging schools and communities across the nation. School leaders, however, have an especially important role to play as gang violence has quickly become a part of public schools' vocabulary.

See Figure 4.6 regarding reporting of youth gang problems by law enforcement officials. In addition, factors influencing local gang violence are shown in Figure 4.7.

GANG DRESS.   Gang members tend to wear specific apparel or colors to convey gang affiliation. Where gang activity has been prevalent in the school or community and there is clear knowledge that certain types of dress are associated with disruptive gang activity, school officials may prohibit such dress. In all cases, this prohibition should be preceded by school policies that clearly communicate the need to regulate certain types of dress.

In most cases, the pattern or style of dress is generally chosen by gang leaders. As pressure is exerted by parents, law enforcement officers, and school officials, gangs will often change

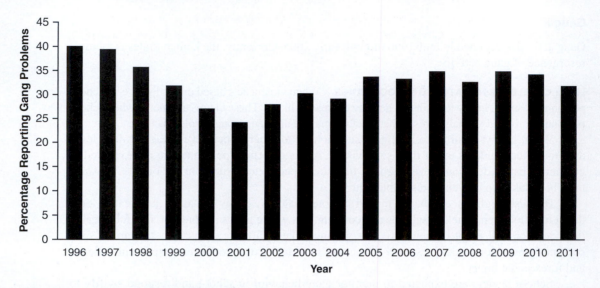

FIGURE 4.6   Percentage of Local Law Enforcement Agencies Reporting Youth Gang Problems, 1996–2011
SOURCE: U.S. Department of Justice, Juvenile Justice Fact Sheet, Office of Justice Programs, Office of Juvenile Justice and Delinquency Prevention, September 2013.

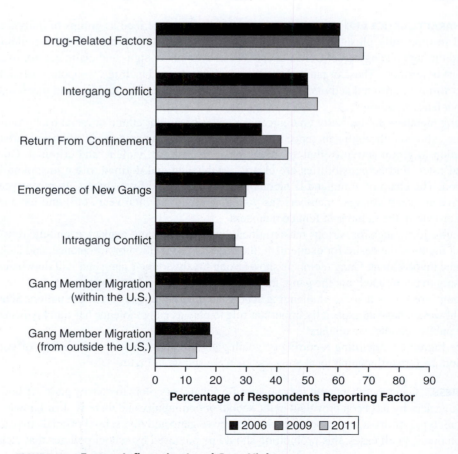

FIGURE 4.7   Factors Influencing Local Gang Violence
SOURCE: U.S. Department of Justice, Juvenile Justice Fact Sheet, Office of Justice Programs, Office of Juvenile Justice and Delinquency Prevention, September 2013.

their appearance to become less recognizable. Today, many gang members wear professional sports team jackets, caps, and T-shirts, making it difficult to identify them. Because school officials are responsible for protecting students from potential danger, they may take reasonable steps to minimize gang presence in school. On the other hand, school officials should provide opportunities for all students to succeed in school and feel that they are important members of the school's family. In many cases, the lack of success in school and a feeling of alienation contribute to gang affiliation.

DUTY OF CARE AND GANG VIOLENCE.   Based on foreseeability, school personnel are expected to exercise the standard of care that any other reasonable professional would exercise under the same or similar circumstances. This standard of care will vary depending on the gravity of the particular situation. If school officials are aware of gang presence in their schools, there is a greater expectation for monitoring gang activity; consequently, the standard of care is higher based on prior knowledge of gang presence. In all cases, the courts expect school personnel to exhibit behavior that conforms to the standard that a reasonable, mature, and intelligent person would meet, given the gravity of the situation. Anything short of this expectation may result in liability charges.

Limiting and eliminating gang activity is a community-wide problem. Every group has a vital role to play if violence is to be controlled in schools. The school's role involves education, swift and aggressive action in response to acts of violence, defensible policies and procedures distinguishing misbehavior from criminal acts, removal of graffiti, and a close working relationship with law enforcement agencies. Parents' role involves talking with their children early and regularly about gangs, alcohol and drug use, violence, and at-risk behavior as well as searching for warning signs, such as sudden changes in their child's moods, a drop in grades, sudden alignment with new friends, a change in dress, unaccountable sums of money, and other signs that might merit stronger intervention. Community residents' role involves removing graffiti in their communities, reporting any suspicious gang activity to law enforcement units, and partnering with the school in addressing gang activity.

Gang violence will continue to plague public schools, even as national trends show an increase in gang activity. In addition, more weapons are associated with gang activity and a greater use of firearms than was the case in the past. School leaders are expected to become proactive in taking appropriate steps to eliminate gang activity while providing protection for all students under their care. Simultaneously, they are also expected to create and maintain an environment where effective teaching and learning can occur. These are challenges that place school leaders in difficult and sometimes conflicting roles.

Administrative Guide

Liability and Gang Violence

1. School leaders are responsible for recognizing gang activity in schools.
2. Efforts should be made to ensure that school personnel have knowledge of gang identification strategies as well as gang management techniques.
3. Policies and procedures should be established to address gang violence in the school.
4. A system should be implemented to report suspected gang involvement and activity to proper law enforcement gang units.
5. A schoolwide safety plan should be developed to protect students, faculty, and staff against violence.
6. Parents, community leaders, and citizens should be involved collaboratively in addressing serious incidents of violence stemming from gang activity.
7. School leaders must follow through on threats made by gang members.
8. Gang issues should be included in classroom discussion and lessons.
9. A mediation process should be developed to resolve conflict between rival gangs.
10. Dress related to gang activity may be banned by school officials.

SCHOOL UNIFORM DRESS POLICIES, SCHOOL SAFETY, AND STUDENTS' FREEDOM OF EXPRESSION RIGHTS

Many school officials, in their desire to create and maintain safe schools, have developed uniform dress code policies for students. These policies are intended to provide easy identification of students, eliminate gang dress, promote discipline, deter theft and violence, prevent unauthorized visitors from intruding on campus, and foster a positive learning environment. Although there is no consensus regarding the effectiveness of school uniforms, their use is increasing in schools throughout the United States as part of an overall program to improve school safety and discipline. For example, school districts in Georgia, Indiana, Louisiana, Maryland, Tennessee, Utah, and Virginia have enacted school uniform regulations. Many large public school systems, including Baltimore, Cincinnati, Detroit, Los Angeles, Miami, and New York, have schools with either voluntary or mandatory uniform policies; generally in elementary and middle schools. In addition, many private and parochial schools have required uniforms for several years.

As school leaders draw school uniform policies, it is prudent that they be mindful of the freedom of expression rights of students. Policies that do not recognize these rights are risky at best and may result in legal challenges and unnecessary legal costs to school districts. School officials should be assured, within limits, that the First Amendment rights of students are protected as they strive to create and maintain safe schools. As discussed in Chapter 3, students' rights must be recognized and respected.

EARLY LEGAL CHALLENGES.   With frequent acts of violence in public schools, schools are moving swiftly and aggressively to enforce uniform dress policies. Early legal battles have already surfaced in Mississippi over dress codes and religious freedoms, involving the rights of students to wear clothing with religious symbols to school. Officials in Harrison County, Mississippi, backed off on the same day from enforcing a regulation that prohibited a Jewish student from wearing a Star of David necklace to class based on its policy of prohibiting students from wearing anything that could be viewed as a gang symbol. A similar case arose in Van Cleave, Mississippi, when a local board of education banned students from wearing clothing with Christian symbols based on the school's mandatory uniform policy. In this case, two students wore T-shirts stamped with the words "Jesus loves me." The basis for implementing the mandatory uniform policy was safety. After an unsuccessful appeal to the school board, parents of the two students filed a suit in the U.S. district court challenging the legality of a policy that prohibits free expression of their children's religious beliefs. These early legal cases may suggest a lack of some degree of sensitivity to the First Amendment rights of students as school uniform policies are drafted.

Administrative Guide

School Uniforms

1. Involve parents, teachers, community leaders, and student representatives in drafting school uniform policies.
2. Make certain that students' religious expressions are preserved in relation to uniform dress codes.
3. Make certain that students' freedom of expression rights are protected within reasonable limits as uniform dress standards are established.
4. Make financial provisions for economically disadvantaged students regarding mandatory uniforms.
5. Enforce school uniform policies fairly and consistently.
6. Implement school uniform policies as a component of an overall school safety program.
7. Present uniform policy drafts to legal counsel for review.
8. Review and revise school uniform policies as the need arises.

ZERO TOLERANCE AND SCHOOL SAFETY

School safety has become a leading priority for school leaders as they respond to a wave of violence that has struck public schools throughout the United States. Although schools are still considered safe places, limiting violence has become a part of public schools' agenda. Many districts have initiated a zero tolerance policy in an effort to reduce school violence. Opponents are raising questions as to whether school leaders are going too far and moving too swiftly with a "one strike, you're out" approach. They also are questioning whether school leaders' actions are reasonable and legally defensible.

Zero Tolerance

Zero tolerance is not new. It emerged during the 1990s, aimed primarily at students who concealed weapons and drugs on school grounds. In fact, President Bill Clinton provided a major boost when he signed the Gun Free School Act of 1994, which mandates expulsion of students who bring a weapon to school. This federal statute affects each state that receives federal funds and requires local educational agencies to expel from school for a period of not less than one year any student who is found to have brought a weapon to school under the jurisdiction of the local school district. However, the statute does provide the chief administrator of the district the latitude to modify the expulsion requirement for students on a case-by-case basis.

In a leading case involving zero tolerance, the Fifth Circuit affirmed the assignment of a Mississippi honor student to an alternative school after a cup of beer was found in a car she had parked in a school lot. Her parent had left the beer in the car, and she did not know about it. She appealed the transfer decision to the school board and a federal court, without success. She withdrew from school and obtained a GED. The Fifth Circuit held that however misguided the school district might have been for applying its zero-tolerance policy, the case had to be dismissed. The Supreme Court has observed that public education relies upon the discretion and judgment of school and board members. An alternative school assignment implicated no constitutional rights.[2]

In a related case, a Florida student who was suspended for violating a school's zero-tolerance policy against weapons possession had no right to appeal the school board decision to the state court system. The Court of Appeal of Florida held the case was properly dismissed because the Florida Administrative Procedure Act does not permit court review of a suspension order. The court rejected the student's assertion that he could appeal his suspension because he faced a possible expulsion. Instead, only a hearing that results in an actual expulsion is available for court review.[3]

Zero Tolerance and Due Process

Zero-tolerance policies tend to ignore constitutionally protected rights of students because these policies tend to operate under an automatic presumption of guilt. Under zero tolerance, the student's past record of behavior is not considered, and the seriousness of the offense and the impact the behavior has on order and decorum are not considered. These issues are important in ensuring fundamental fairness for implicated students. If the presumption of guilt is automatic, students are denied an opportunity to explain their side of the issue or face an accuser—both of which are important dimensions of procedural due process. Substantive due process is also unmet in zero tolerance policies, which essentially means that a valid reason must exist before a student is deprived of his liberty right to attend school and further that means used to deprive the student are reasonable. The presumption of guilt without meeting substantive and procedural provisions conflicts with constitutional safeguards regarding students' due process rights. Procedural and substantive safeguards become most critical in student suspension and expulsion cases.

Recent Zero Tolerance Practices

Because zero tolerance has emerged in a number of districts, students have been affected in ways that raise questions regarding the legal defensibility of these approaches. The following incidents reflect recent zero tolerance practices:

- A fifth-grade student drew a bloody vampire for his art class assignment. He was told that he could not return to school unless he passed a psychological test.[4]
- A first-grader was disciplined for smacking a classmate's bottom on the playground, and the police were summoned to the school.[5]
- One of the most unfortunate outcomes of zero tolerance occurred in Tennessee. Dustin Seal, then a high school senior, was expelled after authorities at his high school discovered a three-inch knife in his car. The knife did not belong to Dustin. A friend who left the knife in Dustin's car claimed responsibility for it. The administration, however, did not change its position. Dustin became depressed and withdrawn after his expulsion. He was distraught because he had done nothing wrong. However, he was not allowed to return to school. Dustin's parents sued the school district and took the case all the way to the Supreme Court, winning at every step. But by the time the Court sent the case back to the local level for Dustin to claim damages, he was too exhausted to continue fighting. He settled for $30,000. Six months later, Dustin placed a pistol under his chin and pulled the trigger. He was twenty-two years old. Almost two years after his son's suicide, Dennis Seal sued the Knox County School Board for wrongful death, claiming that Dustin's suicide was a direct result of his expulsion.[6]
- Students have been suspended from school for possession of Midol, Tylenol, Alka Seltzer, cough drops, and Scope mouthwash—contraband that violates zero tolerance and anti-drug policies.[7]
- A ten-year-old student at a school in Colorado was expelled because her mother placed a small knife in her lunchbox to cut an apple. When the student realized the knife might violate the school's zero tolerance policy, she turned the knife in to the teacher, who told her she had done the right thing.[8]

Based on controversial zero tolerance practices in the state of Florida, the legislature amended state law to limit the use of zero tolerance policies. School boards must now define criteria for reporting acts to law enforcement agencies. Policies must also define acts that pose a threat to school safety and those that are petty acts of misconduct.

In an interesting development, the Obama Administration has pressed schools in the United States to abandon overzealous discipline policies that result in students going to court rather than the principal's office. Attorney General Holder indicated that the problem most

---

Administrative Guide

Zero Tolerance

1. Do not use zero tolerance solely to rid the school of disruptive students.
2. Involve teachers, parents, community leaders, and student representatives in the formulation of zero tolerance policies.
3. Draft policies with recognition that students possess constitutional rights.
4. Do not move too swiftly with the assumption that zero tolerance is a cure-all for student misconduct.
5. When it becomes necessary to expel students for an extended period of time, seek alternative educational opportunities.
6. Consider the student's history of behavior in school, the seriousness of the offense, and the immediate need to act before determining punishment.
7. Make certain that the student's substantive and procedural process rights are addressed in all disciplinary matters.

often stems from well-intentioned zero-tolerance policies that inject the criminal justice system into school matters. The government's investigation also revealed that a disproportionate number of African-American students were disciplined more harshly and more frequently than were white students. While not binding, schools are encouraged to train school personnel in classroom management, conflict resolution, and approaches to de-escalate classroom disruption. The Administration acknowledged that there is a challenge in achieving the proper balance to maintain safe and orderly conduct. The Administration indicated further that it would attempt to negotiate voluntary settlements if school discipline policies are found to violate civil rights laws. For a full discussion of guiding principles regarding school climate and discipline, visit the following websites:

> ed.gov/about/offices/list/ocr/letters/colleague-201401-title-vi.pdf
>
> ed.gov/policy/gen/guid/school-discipline/guiding-principles.pdf

METAL DETECTORS

Metal detectors have grown in use and popularity as school officials seek to maintain a safe and orderly school environment. To date, no legal challenge has reached the Supreme Court regarding the use of detectors. However, several cases have emerged at the district court level. In *Thompson v. Carthage School District,* a school bus driver noticed fresh cuts in a seat cushion and reported such to the principal, who ordered that all male students in grades six through twelve be searched, based on school policy. Additional information indicated that drugs were present in the school. The students were searched using metal detectors. If the detector sounded, the student was patted down. One student was searched and crack cocaine was found. He was subsequently expelled. That student filed suit, alleging wrongful expulsion. The district court ruled for the student. However, the appeals court reversed the district court's decision by indicating that the exclusionary rule compromises school safety and held that the search was justified from its inception, based on reasonable suspicion and inferences.[9]

A number of other cases involving metal detector screening arose through challenges by plaintiffs regarding the legality of this practice in public schools. In one case, *In re F.B.,* a student was found to be in possession of a knife in a Philadelphia school. He was later arrested based on the results of metal detection screening. A motion was filed by the student, attempting to suppress the evidence that had been seized. He claimed that the search was unreasonable and that no individual suspicion existed to justify the search at its inception. The court applied the reasonable factor found in the *T.L.O.* case and held that the search was justified at its inception based on the high incidence of violence in Philadelphia schools. The court ruled further that the search was reasonable and legally defensible because school officials had no way of knowing whether students had weapons prior to entering the building.[10]

A similar case, *People v. Pruitt,* arose in Chicago involving a metal detector screening conducted in the public schools by city police of Chicago. During the screening process, it was discovered that a student was in possession of a loaded 38-caliber pistol. He was subsequently arrested. The validity of the search was deemed appropriate by the court. The court again referred to the Fourteenth Amendment test of reasonableness established in the *T.L.O.* case. The court held that the action was justified at its inception based on a record of violence in the schools.[11]

In another case, *People v. Dukes,* the New York City Board of Education formulated guidelines regarding the use of metal detectors in a high school to be used by a special task force that included police officers. Scanning posts were established in the main lobby of the school based on guidelines. All students who entered the building were randomly subject to search, based on the length of waiting lines. During the screening process, a student was found to be in possession of a switchblade knife and subsequently charged with a misdemeanor. The student challenged the charge and attempted to have the evidence suppressed. The court held that the administrative action was reasonable. In so finding, the court assessed the degree of intrusion versus the severity of damages and the need to conduct the screening at its inception. The court concluded that the search was reasonable and that the school had a compelling interest to provide a safe and secure school.[12]

The use of metal detectors, like other intrusive methods, must be justified as reasonable and necessary to meet a legitimate school objective. In these cases, maintaining a safe and orderly school environment was considered a legitimate school objective. There should be, in all cases, *significant* or *compelling* evidence to suggest that metal detectors be used. If a school has a chronic history of drug use and violence involving the use of weapons, the courts will likely support the use of metal detectors as a means of combating these problems. If metal detectors are employed by school officials, students should be informed before the procedure is implemented that they are subject to this type of screening. Such information should be included in school or district policy and clearly communicated to students and parents. In no instance, except extreme emergencies, should students be surprised by the use of metal detectors. Also, if detectors are used, the methods employed in using them must be reasonable and not designed to degrade students.

Administrative Guide

Metal Detectors

1. Metal detectors should be used only when there is evidence of student behavior that poses a threat to the health and safety of students in the school. Students and parents should be informed beforehand that metal detectors will be employed and should be informed of the reasons for employing this method, barring an emergency situation.
2. If metal detectors are used to achieve a legitimate school interest, then use will likely be supported by the courts.
3. Students and parents should be informed through a legally defensible school policy regarding the use of metal detectors.
4. Students and parents should not be surprised by the use of metal detectors, except in unusual circumstances.
5. If school officials' acts are reasonable regarding the use of metal detectors, they will generally receive minimal resistance from parents.

CASE STUDIES

Gang Violence Involving a Shooting Incident

Bobby Holbrook was an eleventh-grade student enrolled at Lanier High School in an inner-city community. Holbrook had just left the main building after school and was outside congregating with other students when several youth wearing red gang colors associated with a group called Bloods surrounded him. One of the gang members swung at Holbrook, which caused him to run into the street. When he ran, another gang member pulled a gun and shot him. Holbrook was an excellent student with no history of involvement with gangs. It was later learned that Holbrook was mistaken for another person. During the time of this incident, the principal, Wilma Myers, was supervising students who were boarding buses at another exit in the building. Holbrook's parents filed suit, claiming negligent supervision on the part of a school official.

Discussion Questions

1. Do the parents have a legitimate claim? Is so, why? If not, why not?
2. Should the school be held liable for Holbrook's injury?

3. What facts must be known before a determination is made regarding school officials' liability? (Be specific.)
4. Under what conditions would school officials be liable for the injury?
5. Under what conditions would school officials not be liable for the injury?
6. What are the administrative implications suggested by this case?

Bullying

Bobby Parker is well known as a school bully. He has consistently been observed hitting other students and taunting and threatening them in ways that create fear and turmoil in your school. You have disciplined Bobby for these acts, including suspension and detention, and counseled with his mother, who is a single parent, and warned Bobby that a continuation of his behavior will result in harsher disciplinary measures. Bobby has continued to exhibit bullying behavior. In addition, teachers report increased incidents of bullying in the school.

Discussion Questions

1. What might be the consequences of acts of bullying in your school regarding the following?
   a. School safety
   b. Student morale
   c. School climate
2. Outline what you believe to be an appropriate intervention plan to address bullying in your school and specifically what action you will take to address Bobby Parker's behavior. (Be specific.)

Gang and Student Dress

A large high school in the northeastern United States initiated a policy prohibiting the wearing of gang symbols such as jewelry, emblems, earrings, and athletic caps. This policy was developed based on gang activities that were prevalent in the school. Bill Foster, who was not involved in gang activity, wore an earring to school as a form of self-expression and a belief that the earring was attractive to young ladies. He was suspended for his act. Consequently, he filed suit.

Discussion Questions

1. Were Bill's freedom of expression rights violated in this case? Why or why not?
2. Was his suspension justified? Why or why not?
3. Should Bill have been permitted to wear the earring, because he was not involved in gang activity?
4. As principal, what factors would you weigh in determining whether Bill would be permitted to wear an earring? (Be specific.)
5. Would the court support Bill? Why or why not?
6. Would the court support school officials? Why or why not?
7. What are the administrative implications suggested by this case?

Zero Tolerance

You are a newly appointed superintendent in a suburban school district of 40,000 students. You have very strong feelings about the misapplication of zero tolerance as it is currently implemented in the district.

Discussion Questions

1. Write a presentation that you would make to your school board in an attempt to influence them to abolish zero tolerance.
2. What salient points would you stress as a basis to eliminate the practice?
3. What constitutional issues would you include?
4. What options would you offer if the school board considers your request?

Cyberbullying

A group of ninth-grade female students threatened another student through a series of cyberbullying communications. The victim was also portrayed as a person who was having multiple affairs with student athletes. The mother of one of the student athletes was aware of this but failed to act. The victim attempted suicide but was found by her mother and rushed to the hospital.

Discussion Questions

1. Because these incidents occurred off campus, can the principal intervene in this situation?
2. Was it significant that one parent was aware but failed to act?
3. Can these students be disciplined for their behavior? Why? Why not?
4. Should the school simply allow the victim's parent to handle this situation through law enforcement officials? Why? Why not?
5. What is the solution to this problem?

Endnotes

1. *In re Gault,* 387 U.S. 1; 875 S.Ct. 1428; 18 L. Ed. 2d 527 (1967).
2. *Langley v. Monroe County School Dist.,* 264 Fed. Appx. 366 (5th Cir. 2008).
3. *D.K. v. Dist. School Board of Indian River County,* 981 So.2d 667 (Fla. Dist. Ct. App. 2008).
4. *Savannah Morning News,* October 31, 2008.
5. *Education Week,* Vol. 27 No 41, June 11, 2008.
6. *Seal v. Morgan,* 229 F.3d 567 (6th Cir. 2000).
7. USA Today Education News, April 13, 1999.
8. Ibid.
9. *Thompson v. Carthage School District,* U.S. App. Lexis 15461 (8th Cir. 1996).
10. *In re F.B.,* 658 A. 2d 1378 (Pa. Super. 1993).
11. *People v. Pruitt,* 662 N.E. 2d 540 (III. App 1 Dist. 1996).
12. *People v. Dukes,* 580 N.Y.S. 2d 850 (NY City Crim. Ct. 1992).

Chapter 5

Individuals with Disabilities

In 1975, Congress enacted P.L. 94-142, the Education for All Handicapped Children Act (EAHCA), based on findings that supported the need for the act. Congress discerned that more than eight million children in the United States with disabilities had needs that had not been fully met. Roughly four million of these same children had not been provided appropriate educational services that allowed them to receive an equal educational opportunity. Even more startling was the realization that over one million children with disabilities had not received any type of public educational opportunity. Many of those who did receive some form of public education were unable to receive the full benefits of an educational experience because their disabilities had not been discovered. In many instances, parents were forced to seek assistance for their children outside the public school arena, often at great expense and inconvenience to their family.

Based on these findings, Congress realized that it was in the nation's best interest for the federal government to intervene and work collaboratively with states in addressing the needs of children with disabilities throughout the country. This intervention was presented in the form of the EAHCA, which has undergone a number of amendments since its inception. In 1990, it was referred to as the Individuals with Disabilities Education Act (IDEA). In 2004, the act was amended and became known as the Individuals with Disabilities Education Improvement Act (IDEIA). Although the act has been amended on a number of occasions, its primary purpose has remained intact.

The number of children who have been classified as disabled has increased steadily. This growth trend highlights the importance of improving services to meet the needs of these children and providing equal access to educational opportunities.

Individuals with disabilities are protected by three significant federal statutes: the IDEA, the Americans with Disabilities Act of 1990 (ADA), and the Rehabilitation Act of 1973, Section 504. These statutes were enacted to protect individuals with disabilities from discrimination and to provide them equal access to educational opportunities, facility utilization, and employment opportunities in public school settings.

Two leading cases focused major attention on the needs of children with disabilities during the early 1970s: *The Pennsylvania Association for Retarded Children v. Commonwealth* and *Mills v. Board of Education.* In the *Pennsylvania* case, a district court ruled that the state's children with mental retardation were entitled to a free public education and, whenever possible, should be educated in regular classrooms rather than classrooms that were isolated from the normal school population. The court stated:

> A free public program of education and training appropriate to the child's capacity, within the context of a presumption that, among the alternative programs of education and training

required by statutes to be available, placement in a regular public school class is preferable to placement in a special public school class. Further, placement in a special public school class is preferable to placement in any other type of program of education and training.[1]

The *Mills* case challenged the exclusion of children with disabilities from the District of Columbia public schools, which resulted in the denial of a publicly supported education. In rendering summary judgment for the plaintiff, the court stated:

> No child eligible for a publicly supported education in the District of Columbia shall be excluded from a regular public school assignment by a rule, policy or board policy unless such child is provided adequate alternative educational services consistent with the child's needs which may include special education or tuition grants. Further, if the child is to be reassigned or provided other alternatives, procedural due process shall be required.[2]

These two cases, coupled with political pressures nationwide regarding children with disabilities, resulted in the passage of federal legislation by Congress, which culminated in the adoption of the Rehabilitation Act of 1973 and the subsequent passage of the EAHCA. The EAHCA provided federal funds and extensive regulations designed to provide equal access and a free, appropriate education for children with disabilities. With the passage of new laws and amendments, numerous modifications and extensions have resulted in major improvements for these children.

INDIVIDUALS WITH DISABILITIES EDUCATION ACT OF 1990 (IDEA) AND THE INDIVIDUALS WITH DISABILITIES EDUCATION IMPROVEMENT ACT OF 2004 (IDEIA)

Mandatory Requirements

As stated previously, the IDEA succeeded P.L. 94-142, the EAHCA of 1975. Congress passed the IDEA to define clearly the responsibilities of school districts regarding children with disabilities and to provide a measure of financial support to assist states in meeting their obligations.

The IDEA essentially guarantees children with disabilities, ages three to twenty-one, the right to a free, appropriate education in public schools. This act also establishes **substantive** and **procedural due process** rights, which are discussed later in this chapter. Under the Child Find component of this act, each state is required to identify, locate, and evaluate all children with disabilities ages birth to twenty-one years who are in need of early intervention or special education services.

Congress passed historic legislation on November 19, 2004, reauthorizing the IDEA. President George W. Bush signed the IDEIA of 2004 into law on December 3, 2004. The amended act contains a number of significant changes that are referenced in subsequent sections of this chapter.

The IDEIA is a federal law that ensures that eligible children with disabilities between the ages of three and twenty-one or until graduation receive a free, appropriate public education (FAPE) consistent with their individual needs. (*A free, appropriate education,* as defined under Section 504, includes regular or special education and related services designed to meet the individual needs of students consistent with the provisions involving evaluation, placement, and procedural safeguards.) The EAHCA (P.L. 94-142) represents an earlier version of the current IDEIA. The reauthorized act permits federal funding to assist states and local communities, which provide varying degrees of special education services to over six million students. The new provision regarding early intervention services allows local education agencies (LEAs) to allocate up to 15 percent of their total IDEIA funding to offer services to students prior to being identified as having a disability. This provision is optional and does not require LEAs to engage in such an activity.

This act also establishes *substantive* and *procedural due process rights,* which are discussed later in this chapter. To meet eligibility requirements, a state must develop a plan to ensure a free, appropriate education for all children with disabilities within its jurisdiction. Each state must establish goals that address graduation rates and dropout rates as well as other factors the state may determine.

In addition, each state must formulate a policy that ensures certain due process rights for all children with disabilities. The state's plan should include its goals and a timetable for meeting these goals, as well as the personnel, facilities, and related services necessary to meet the needs of children with disabilities. The state's plan also must include a well-designed system for allocating funds to local school districts.

The new act provides new formulas for allocating funds to state and local education agencies that include the number of children ages three through five and six through twenty-one years receiving special education and related services, and the average per pupil expenditure in the United States based on the current fiscal year.

In turn, each local district must submit an application to the state, demonstrating how it will comply with the requirements of the IDEA. District plans must be on file and available for review by citizens on request.

An earlier challenge reached the U.S. Supreme Court regarding a free, appropriate education in the *Rowley* case.[3] In New York, parents of a child who was nearly totally deaf brought suit against school administrators for failing to provide their child with a qualified sign language interpreter for all her academic classes. The school district had provided the child a hearing aid as well as additional instruction from a tutor. A U.S. district court, in a decision upheld by the U.S. Court of Appeals, Second Circuit, ruled that even though the child was performing better than average in her class and was advancing easily from grade to grade, she was not performing as well academically as she would have without her disability. Because of the disparity between her achievement and her potential, the court held that she was not receiving a FAPE as provided by the EAHCA. However, the lower courts' decisions were reversed by the U.S. Supreme Court, which held that the EAHCA is satisfied when the state provides personalized instruction with sufficient support services to allow the child with disabilities to receive educational benefits from that instruction. The High Court held that the Individualized Education Plan (IEP) required by the EAHCA should be reasonably calculated to enable the child to achieve passing marks and advance from grade to grade. The act does not require the school to provide a sign language interpreter as requested by this child's parents. The act was not intended to guarantee a certain level of education but merely to open the door of education to children with disabilities by means of special educational services. In addition, the decision noted that a state is not required to maximize the potential of each child who is disabled commensurate with the opportunity provided children who are not disabled. This landmark decision established the standard for determining the proper interpretation of free, appropriate education.

The IDEA requires each state to allocate federal funds first to children with disabilities who are not receiving any type of education and subsequently to children with the most severe disabilities within each disability category. The IDEA further stipulates that, to the fullest extent possible, children with disabilities must be educated with children who are not disabled. In principle, no child with disabilities may be excluded from receiving a FAPE. The statute does not require such a child to demonstrate that he or she will benefit from special education as a condition to receiving educational services. With the wide array of disabilities, the IDEA does not require equality of results; it merely requires that children with disabilities benefit from instruction.

In another leading case, *Timothy W. v. Rochester, New Hampshire School District,* the court addressed the issue of whether a district may require a child to demonstrate a benefit as a condition prior to participation in special education.[4] Timothy had multiple physical handicaps and was profoundly mentally retarded. He suffered from complex developmental disabilities, cerebral palsy, cortical blindness, and a seizure disorder. Appropriate services were requested by his mother and refused by the Rochester School District on the grounds that Timothy's disability was so severe that he could not benefit from an education. Because the district felt that the child could not benefit from special education, Timothy was not entitled to one.

After seven years of proceedings, evaluations, and expert testimony, there was difference of opinion regarding Timothy's ability to benefit from any educational program. The district court ruled for the school district, based on its review of materials, reports, and testimony that Timothy was incapable of benefiting from special education. The district court relied quite heavily on *Board of Education of Hendrick Hudson Central School v. Rowley*[5] in concluding that a child is not entitled to a public education unless he or she can benefit from it. The district court, however, misjudged *Rowley,* which focused on the *level* and *quality* of programs and services rather than the actual criteria for access to programs.

The First Circuit Court, in reversing the district court's ruling, observed that the IDEA specifically recognizes that education for children with severe physical disabilities is to be broadly defined to include basic functional life skills as well as traditional academic skills. The primary question facing the school district, according to the circuit court, was to determine, in conjunction with Timothy's parent, what constitutes an appropriate IEP for Timothy.

The judgment of the district court was reversed, and the case was remanded to the circuit court, which retained jurisdiction until a suitable IEP was developed. Timothy was entitled to an interim placement until the final IEP was developed and agreed on by all parties. The district court also was instructed to address the question of damages that were assessed against the school district.

As this case illustrates, no child with disabilities may be excluded from receiving a FAPE. Furthermore, no child with disabilities may be required to demonstrate that he or she will benefit from special education as a condition precedent to receiving appropriate services.

NATIONAL COUNCIL ON DISABILITY

On January 25, 2000, the National Council on Disability (NCD), an independent federal agency of fifteen members appointed by the U.S. president and confirmed by the Senate, released its report entitled "Back to School on Civil Rights." The council's purpose is to promote policies, programs, practices, and procedures designed to ensure equal opportunity for individuals with disabilities irrespective of the nature and severity of their disability. Based on NCD's finding, every state was out of compliance with the IDEA to some degree. More than half of the states failed to ensure compliance in a majority of the key compliance areas.

A compliance issue was addressed in *Gaskin v. Commonwealth of Pennsylvania.*[6] The *Gaskin* case involved a **class action** suit that was settled in lieu of litigation. A **civil action** was filed by plaintiffs on June 30, 1994, against the Pennsylvania Department of Education. The suit alleged that the department failed to assume that members of the class would be educated with students who did not have disabilities to the maximum extent appropriate and those included in the regular classroom were not provided supplementary aids and services needed to benefit from participating in the regular education classroom—all in violation of federal statute. This settlement affected 280,000 special education students in Pennsylvania. The agreement mandated training and technical assistance along with monitoring and compliance regulations that required local school districts to offer a full continuum of support service that allows students with disabilities to be educated in regular classrooms.

Functional Exclusion of Disabled Children

Two practices tend to create additional challenges for children with disabilities: exclusion from educational programs and misclassification based on improper assessment. Both practices may result in functional exclusion of disabled children. **Functional exclusion** occurs when disabled children receive a highly inappropriate placement that denies them the opportunity to receive an appropriate education. Both of these practices generally result in legal challenges. In recent years based on the IDEA, considerable progress has been made regarding inclusion of disabled students. Unfortunately, errors continue to occur regarding proper classification and placement.

Consequently, school officials should exercise caution to ensure that classification and placement of disabled children are executed properly.

Interpretation and Identification of Children with Disabilities

The term *children with disabilities* is defined by the IDEA as those who meet the following conditions:

> Mental retardation, hearing impairments which include deafness, speech or language impairment, visual impairment including blindness, learning disabilities, brain injury, emotional disturbance, orthopedic impairments, autism, traumatic brain injury, specific learning disabilities and other impairments who by reason of such conditions need special education and related services.[7]

Teacher Qualifications

All special education teachers are included under the definition of No Child Left Behind (NCLB). They must earn a special education certificate or pass a state licensing exam and possess a license to teach special education. Licensure or certification must not have been waived on an emergency or provisional basis, and the teachers must have earned at least a bachelor's degree.

Prereferral Intervention

Regular classroom teachers have the responsibility of identifying students who may need special services in order to receive the full benefits of an education. This function should be executed before any formal assessment or special programming occurs. In short, the teacher must raise the question after carefully working with the student over a reasonable period of time and examining the student's work to determine whether he or she needs special assistance beyond that which is provided in the regular classroom. This question should emerge after continuous and multiple efforts have failed to meet the needs of the student through the regular classroom program.

Deficiencies in academic performance, as well as those related to social and interpersonal behavior, may be evident during the teacher's work with and observation of the student. After the regular classroom teacher has worked with a student and appears convinced that the student needs special assistance, a request should be made in the form of a *referral.* Virtually all school districts have well-developed policies and procedures regarding referrals. Although the procedures vary from district to district, usually there is some type of referral form used by the regular teacher when a student is deemed to need special services. This form should be as inclusive as possible in providing relevant information needed to conduct a formal assessment of the student if needed. Data requested on the referral form may include the student's name, present grade level, age, gender, standardized test scores, local test data, strengths and weaknesses in key subject areas, reading ability, behavior and relationships with fellow students, pertinent family data, and teaching methods or strategies that have been successful, as well as those that have been unsuccessful.

English Language Learners and Special Education

It is important that limited English proficient (LEP) students not be referred for special educational services based on limited English proficiency. Unless these students fall into categories of disabilities covered by IDEIA, they should not be referred to receive special education. Inappropriate referrals can create stigmas for students and impede their ability to achieve at high levels. If an LEP student meets one or more of the disabilities required for special education services, then the student should receive the same treatment that any other English-speaking student receives with respect to diagnosis and proper placement.

Experts presume that, statistically, a similar proportion of students will qualify for special education services irrespective of their ethnicity. However, there is a view that students with

English language challenges are disproportionately represented in special needs categories, particularly in the learning-disabled category. This may be attributable to LEP students being assigned strictly on the basis of limited English speaking capabilities. It is critically important that proper interventions be implemented along with multitier instructional strategies to prevent inappropriate referrals and placement. Effective and appropriate assessment and placement procedures should be implemented to ensure that LEP students are properly educated. No single assessment measure should determine a student's placement. Multiple assessment tools should be used to determine appropriate placement for English Language Learners. School leaders should monitor the quality and effectiveness of programs provided for LEP students and consider the short- and long-range effects that improper diagnosis and placement can have on this group of students.

In 1998, Proposition 227 was passed, which required all California schools to teach LEP students in special classes that are taught in English, effectively eliminating bilingual classes. It further required that LEP students move from special classes to regular classes when they acquire a proficient knowledge of English. The intent of the bill was to educate limited proficiency students in a rapid one-year program. State government was required to allocate 50 million dollars each year for ten years to support the program. California has perhaps the highest population of limited English speaking students. According to the findings of a study initiated by the California Department of Education, there has been a slight decrease in the performance gap between English Learners (ELs) and "English Only" students; however, it has remained virtually constant in most subject areas for most grades. When former ELs reclassified to Fluent English Proficient students are included in the cohorts of ELs, this pattern in the performance gap is very similar. These data might suggest that English Learners were not overly represented in special education programs.

Response to Intervention

Response to Intervention (RTI) involves a combination of assessments and interventions used to provide early, effective assistance and support to children who are experiencing difficulty learning. RTI is also referred to as a data-based process of diagnosing learning disabilities. The RTI method is frequently used as an alternative to identifying learning disabilities, which requires children to demonstrate a notable inconsistency between their IQ and academic achievement as determined by standardized tests. The RTI more clearly describes the Specific Learning Disability (SLD) category of the IDEIA of 2004.

RTI minimizes academic failure based on early intervention, regular progress reports, and intensive research-based instructional interventions for children who continue to experience difficulty. Students who do not respond to effective interventions are more likely to experience learning disabilities that require special education. RTI may also be used to assist teachers in reducing student failures by identifying appropriate interventions when children exhibit an inability to achieve learning objectives.

Multi-tiered System of Support—Response to Intervention

This instructional system of support is designed to improve learning outcomes for all students and was initiated in the 2004 Reauthorization of the Individuals with Disabilities Education Improvement Act (IDEIA). Response to Intervention consists of a multitier approach to improving students' performance outcomes. This system focuses not only on students with disabilities but also on any students who experience learning or behavioral difficulties. RTI incorporates a scientific, research-based intervention strategy to identify students who need support to enhance learning outcomes. Intervention includes intense assessment of student strengths and weaknesses and classroom instruction. While this system is designed to enhance learning outcomes for all students, a particular focus involves minority students who face challenges regarding academic performance. Tiered instruction focuses on flexible tiers for education: **Tier One** typically includes core instruction for all students with the objective of raising achievement levels of all students; **Tier Two** provides intensive individualized instruction based on students who do not demonstrate acceptable levels of proficiency at Tier One; and **Tier Three** involves intense instructional interventions to improve students' academic progress. It may or may not involve special needs students. The objective of Response to Intervention is to identify and implement alternative strategies for grouping students who experience learning difficulties, thereby reducing the number of students who are categorized as learning disabled. These strategies should reflect research-based best practice academic interventions. The success of this intervention system is based on dedicated faculty and staff who believe that students are capable of learning and performing academically. Classroom instruction must be differentiated, of high quality, research based, multidimensional, and data driven to enhance student outcomes. Instructional leadership and engagement by the school leader is critical to the success of Response to Intervention, as it requires a collaborative approach involving school leaders, faculty, parents, and appropriate external agencies to facilitate student success. The multitier instructional process represents the core of a Response to Intervention model. The instruction that occurs related to student outcomes and assessment data drives the intervention process.

If a formal assessment procedure is contemplated, the student's parent must grant consent to do so and must be informed of personal rights under due process. Teachers should approach the referral process with great care, because it affects the student's education, consumes time and district resources, and may result in stigmatizing a student. It is not uncommon for districts to hold prereferral conferences to discuss concerns regarding the student's academic and social performance. These meetings will usually involve the referring teacher, a special education professional, the principal, the counselor, and, in many instances, the parent. Such meetings might be used as an intermediate measure to discuss the implementation of new and different strategies regarding the student's academic and social performance. During this time, an evaluation period should be established to assess the student's progress before a formal assessment is contemplated and decisions made regarding the need for special services. It is highly desirable to employ some type of intervention prior to implementing a formal assessment process. This measure, if implemented appropriately, may reduce *overreferrals and misclassifications* and result in the best education program for the student, particularly when new strategies and interventions are implemented and evaluated over a reasonable period of time.

In each case, school officials should ensure that the school's review process is consistent with state and federal regulations and that whatever action is taken is in the best interest of the student. If it is determined that the student's problem stems from a disability, a classification is agreed on during the conference in which the parent is present. Once agreement is reached on the classification, this information is passed on to a committee, which, along with the parent, will engage in developing the student's IEP. The parent must sign the IEP and approve any placement outside the regular classroom.

Thus, school districts are required to evaluate every child with disabilities to determine the nature of the disability and the need for special education and related services. Prior to this evaluation, each district must forward to the child's parent a written notice, in the parent's native language, describing the proposed evaluation process. Parental consent must be sought prior to the actual evaluation.

The new act establishes a sixty-day timeline from receipt of parental consent for an evaluation regarding eligibility, determination of eligibility, and the educational needs of the child. If consent is not provided, the district must initiate an impartial hearing through a hearing officer to secure approval to conduct the evaluation.

Once approval is granted, the evaluation must be fully objective and free of any form of bias. The meeting should be conducted, in the child's native language, by a multidisciplinary team qualified to assess a wide range of skill areas. Every effort must be made to ensure that only validated tests designed to assess specific areas of need are utilized. This evaluation process should occur in a timely fashion and address each area of the child's suspected disability.

No single test should be used as the sole criterion for determining disabilities; rather, a battery of appropriate tests designed to assess areas of suspected disabilities should be used. The child's strengths and weaknesses should be identified during this process, because these will determine, to a large extent, the nature of his or her individualized program.

The reauthorized act adds language regarding a child's SLD by stating that a local educational agency may use an evaluation process to determine if a child responds to scientific research-based intervention as a part of the required evaluation procedures when addressing specific learning disabilities.

A parent or legal guardian who is dissatisfied with the evaluation may secure an independent evaluation at the school district's expense, unless the hearing officer agrees with the district's assessment. In either case, reevaluation of each child with disabilities should minimally occur every three years.

Alternative Assessment

Under the IDEIA, states have the option of testing up to two percent of their students using alternate assessments based on modified standards. This flexibility is designed to provide an option for students who are able to make progress toward grade-level standards but may be unable to reach them at the same time as their peers.

This flexibility is separate from another provision that permits 1 percent of students with severe cognitive disabilities to take alternative assessments and be counted as proficient under NCLB. These provisions combined affect roughly 30 percent of students with disabilities and are significant because schools must demonstrate that students with disabilities and other subgroups are making adequate yearly progress under NCLB.

Individualized Educational Program Requirement

Under IDEIA 2004, the requirement by IEP teams to spell out short-term objectives is no longer required for most children. Short-term objectives are required only for children who are taking alternative assessment standards. The NCLB standards restrict the assessments to students with the most significant cognitive disabilities. Under NCLB, grade-level standards and alternative achievement standards are aligned with state standards. The amended law authorizes the secretary of education to approve proposals from up to fifteen states to allow local school districts to develop a multiyear IEP for a maximum of three years with parental consent. This provision limits participation by not requiring an annual IEP review. Also, comparable services as described under the IEP must be provided by a new school district if a child transfers into that district during the school year in the same state.

When the evaluation results are produced, an IEP must be designed for each child with disabilities. This process usually involves one or more meetings in which the child's teacher, parent, and special education representative for the district are present to review and discuss evaluation results for children with significant cognitive disabilities. It is also recommended that a representative from the evaluation team be present to respond to questions and interpret results. If feasible, this person may be represented by the child's teacher or the special education supervisor. At a minimum, each IEP should include the following:

1. A statement detailing the child's present level of educational performance
2. A statement of annual goals, as well as short-term instructional objectives
3. A description of specific educational services to be provided and a determination as to whether the child is able to participate in regular educational programs
4. A description of transitional services to be rendered if the child is a junior or senior in high school, to ensure that necessary services are provided when the child leaves the regular school environment or reaches 16 years of age, or beginning not later than one year before the child reaches the age of majority under state law

5. A description of services to be provided and a timetable for providing these services
6. An explanation of relevant criteria and procedures to be employed annually to determine if instructional objectives are or have been achieved

An IEP dispute was addressed in *Florence County School District v. Shannon Carter.*[8] Shannon entered school as a functionally illiterate child due to dyslexia and attention-deficit/ hyperactivity disorder (ADHD). She was reading at fifth-grade level and had frequent bouts of depression. The school district developed an IEP after Shannon tested and qualified for special education services. According to the IEP, Shannon would progress from 5.4 to 5.8 grade level in reading and from 6.4 to 6.8 grade level in math. She would make four months of academic progress after a year of special education.

Shannon's parents felt that the IEP was inadequate to meet her needs and requested a more extensive program for her so that she would be able to read at a high school level on graduation. Florence County refused Shannon's parents, who then placed Shannon in Trident Academy, a private school that specialized in educating children with dyslexia and other language learning disabilities. The parents then requested a due process review, which was denied. The parents sued the district for tuition costs. The U.S. district court ruled for Shannon. Florence County appealed the decision to the U.S. Court of Appeals for the Fourth Circuit, arguing that four months of progress were appropriate and that Trident Academy was not a state-approved school. The district further argued that Shannon's parents were not entitled to reimbursement. The court of appeals unanimously held for Shannon. The case was appealed to the U.S. Supreme Court, which ruled in a 9–0 decision for Shannon. This case illustrates that the courts will not hesitate to rule in cases regarding IEP conflicts involving due process denials. In this case, the burden of proof was placed on the school district to demonstrate that the IEP was free, appropriate, and adequate to meet the educational needs of Shannon Carter. In a related IEP case, the parents of a Texas student with disabilities disagreed with the district's proposed IEP for grade two and placed her in a private school. They sought due process and obtained a ruling from the hearing officer, who indicated that the district did not make an appropriate placement. Thus, the parents were entitled to tuition reimbursement. By the time the administrative ruling was issued, the school year was nearly over. When the district appealed to a federal court, the parents did not seek tuition reimbursement for another school year. As a result, when the court ruled on the case over a year later, it held that they were not entitled to tuition reimbursement. However, the Fifth Circuit reversed the decision, finding that another year of tuition was due under the stay-put provision.[9]

Equal Access to Assistive Technology for Students with Disabilities

The Technology-Related Assistance for Individuals with Disabilities Act Amendments of 1994 provide financial assistance to states to support systems changes that assist in the development and implementation of technology-related support for individuals with disabilities. The act further ensures timely acquisition and delivery of *assistive technology devices,* including equipment and product systems commercially acquired, modified, or customized that are used to increase, maintain, or improve functional capabilities of a child with disabilities. Assistive technology does not include a medical device that is surgically implanted or the replacement of that device.

Technology assistive services are also included in this act and involve any service that directly assists a child with a disability in the selection, acquisition, or use of an assistive technology device. These services may include (1) purchasing, leasing, or otherwise providing for the acquisition of assistive technology by the child; (2) selecting, designing, fitting, customizing, adapting, applying, maintaining, repairing, or replacing assistive technology devices; (3) coordinating and using other therapies, interventions, or services with assistive technology devices, such as those associated with existing education and rehabilitation plans and programs; (4) training or technical assistance for the child or, where appropriate, the family of such child; and (5) training or technical assistance for professionals (including individuals providing education and rehabilitation services), employers, and other individuals who provide services to, employ, or are otherwise substantially involved in the major life functions of the child.

Personal Data Assistants for Disabled Students

Personal data assistants (PDAs) are also used for students with disabilities under the Technology-Related Assistance for Individuals with Disabilities Act. PDAs are very versatile personal computers that may be used to take notes and serve as communication devices. These devices are small and compact but offer state-of-the-art technology applications such as touch screens and handwriting recognition. PDAs that are specifically designed for disabled students incorporate aural output and Braille display as well as Braille keyboards to accommodate visually impaired students. Another group of PDAs is designed to take notes for students who have visual acuity problems but may also possess other types of disabilities that prevent them from functioning effectively in the classroom. These devices are considered related services that allow disabled students to participate in regular classrooms consistent with their individual education programs. PDAs are also designed to serve as electronic dictionaries, spell checkers, grammar checkers, and thesauruses. These devices are quite useful to individuals with learning or visual disabilities in that they allow students to access print material either through synthesized speech or in an audio format.

As a part of assistive technology service, training for teachers, employers, administrators, and/or any other persons who are dealing directly with student disabilities must be accommodated. Training needs may include:

1. An understanding of federal law—Section 504, ADA, and/or the IDEA/IDEIA
2. An understanding of their responsibilities in providing accommodations
3. An understanding of the rights of the child with disabilities
4. An understanding of how accommodations and modifications should be provided

Program Review and Changes

Each IEP must be reviewed and revised annually, if necessary, to ensure that the continuing needs of the child are met. If changes are contemplated, the child's parent or legal guardian must be notified. If either objects to the proposed changes, an impartial hearing must be held to resolve the conflict. If this process proves unsuccessful, the parent or guardian may appeal to the state agency and subsequently to the courts if a resolution is not reached at the state level. This appeals process is designed to ensure fundamental fairness and to meet the requirements of due process, as spelled out in the ADA.

Under the newly reauthorized act, a member of the IEP team shall not be required to attend all or part of the IEP meeting if the parent (in writing) and the LEA agree that the team member's attendance is not necessary because the member's area of curriculum-related services is not being modified or discussed during the meeting. If changes to the IEP are necessary after the annual meeting for a school year, the parent and the LEA may agree not to convene an IEP meeting to make the changes but instead may develop a written document to amend or modify the current IEP.

There is an ongoing conflict between parents of disabled children and school districts regarding where the burden of proof resides in IEP disputes. One such debate—*Schaffer v. Weast*—was heard by the Supreme Court on November 14, 2005.[10] On February 22, 2005, the U.S. Supreme Court agreed to resolve the division among circuit courts regarding where the burden of proof should be placed—on parents or school districts—during special-education due process hearings. In 1998, the administrative law judge placed the burden of proof on the parents and ruled for the school district on the merits of the child's IEP. In 2000, the district court reversed the administrative law judge's ruling by holding that the burden of proof resides with the school district and remanded the case for further proceedings. In 2004, the U.S. Court of

Appeals for the Fourth Circuit reversed the district court's ruling on the burden of proof issue by placing the burden on the parents and remanded the case. The burden was placed on the parents who initiated the special education due process hearing, thus creating a split among circuits. There was no consensus among the circuit courts. Three circuit courts assigned the burden of proof to parents, whereas four other circuit courts assigned the burden of proof to the school district. Under the reauthorized IDEIA, lawsuits filed by parents that are considered frivolous assign legal fees, including cost of court, to the parents. The U.S. Supreme Court issued its ruling in this case on November 14, 2005. In a 6–2 decision, the Court held that the burden of proof in an administrative hearing challenging an IEP is properly placed on the party seeking relief.

States have not been consistent in addressing issues regarding burden of proof in these hearings. This important decision by the High Court will apply to all school districts throughout the nation and will bring clarity and consistency regarding the burden of proof in due process hearings.

EDUCATION-RELATED SERVICE REQUIREMENT

A related service is viewed as one that must be provided to allow the child with disabilities to benefit from special education. The U.S. Supreme Court ruled that clean intermittent catheterization (CIC) is a related service not subject to the "medical service" exclusion of the IDEA. The parents of an eight-year-old girl born with spina bifida sued their local Texas school district after it refused to provide CIC for the child at school. The parents tried to force the district to train staff to perform the procedure. After a U.S. district court held against the parents, they appealed to the U.S. Court of Appeals, Fifth Circuit, which reversed the district court ruling. The district then appealed. The Supreme Court affirmed the ruling of the court of appeals that CIC is a supportive related service, not an excluded medical service.

A more compelling case, *Cedar Rapids Community District v. Garret F.,* involving related service arose in Iowa.[11] When Garret F., a student with disabilities, requested that the school district provide services to meet his physical needs based on the fact that he is a wheelchair user and ventilator dependent, Garret contended that these related services are necessary to allow him to receive a free, appropriate education designed to meet his needs. The school district refused to provide continuous one-on-one nursing care, arguing that these services are medical rather than related services. An administrative law judge ruled that the IDEA required the district to provide the needed service and bear the financial responsibility for all of the disputed services, discovering that similar services were currently being provided for other disabled students. The federal district court and the Eighth Circuit Court of Appeals affirmed this decision, concluding that *Irving Independent School District v. Tatro*[12] provided a two-step analysis of the related service definition that was satisfied in this case. First, he requested services that were supportive services because Garret could not attend school without them. Second, these services were not excluded as medical services under *Tatro.* Services provided by a physician other than diagnostics and education are subject to the medical services exclusion; however, services that can be provided by a nurse or qualified lay person are not. The U.S. Supreme Court heard this case and held for Garret, thus requiring the district to provide nursing services during school hours to allow Garret to benefit from a FAPE.

As illustrated by these cases, school districts will be required to provide simple medical procedures under the category of related services when such procedures do not require complex mastery and the services are necessary for the child to benefit from an appropriate special education program.

Least Restrictive Environment

The IDEA embraces the notion that children with disabilities be placed, when appropriate, in educational settings that offer the least amount of restrictions. This view is supported by the philosophy that children with disabilities should be educated under normal classroom conditions with children who are not disabled. The primary objective is to provide children with disabilities an opportunity to interact, socialize, and learn with "regular" students, thus minimizing the tendency to become stigmatized and isolated from the school's regular program. There is also inherent value in providing nondisabled students an opportunity to increase awareness of the many challenges faced by children with disabilities and to sensitize them to their unique needs. Thus, the least restrictive provision of the act mandates the inclusion of students with disabilities in regular classrooms. This provision is clearly established in the regulation that states:

> To the maximum extent possible handicapped children in public, private or other institutions should be educated with children who are not handicapped and that separate schooling or other removal of handicapped children from the regular educational environment should occur only when the nature or severity of the handicap is such that education in regular classes with the use of supplementary aids and services cannot be achieved satisfactorily.[13]

This regulation is designed to ensure that students with disabilities be provided the broadest range of opportunities, based on the least restrictive environment (LRE) provisions. The interpretation of precisely what constitutes the *least restrictive environment* has led to conflicts as well as litigation. Generally, when a child with disabilities is not involved in regular classroom instruction, the district must demonstrate through the evaluation and IEP process that a segregated facility would represent a more appropriate and beneficial learning environment. Because the law indicates a strong preference for inclusion, the burden of proof rests with educators to demonstrate that their decisions are not arbitrary or capricious regarding the placement of a child with disabilities. The statute does not mandate inclusion in each case involving such a child, but it does require that inclusion be used to the fullest extent possible and as appropriate based on the unique needs of the child with disabilities.

The LRE is a relative concept. What constitutes the LRE for one child might be totally inappropriate for another. For example, a regular classroom placement might be restrictive and inappropriate if the child's instructional and social needs cannot be adequately met. Because there is such wide variation of needs among students with disabilities, there is no ideal way to provide appropriate educational services to such children. Given the variations among these students, a range of placement options must be provided, which might include but are not limited to the following possibilities:

- Regular class with support from regular classroom teachers
- Regular class with support instruction from special teachers
- Regular class with special resource instruction
- Full-time special education class in regular school
- Full-time special school
- Residential school
- Homebound instruction

The particular placement options should be determined by the needs of the child who has disabilities and the type of environment that will best meet his or her educational and social needs.

A Pennsylvania student with autism spectrum disorder had a behavioral crisis while in a private school funded by the district. A reevaluation led to an evaluation report that used boilerplate language, listing generic goals and principles that might work for any child rather than specifying the student's needs and issues. The IEP also contained much of that boilerplate language. When the parents sought due process, a hearing officer determined that both the IEP and the private school placement were inappropriate. The case reached a federal court, which agreed that the IEP and the private school were inappropriate. A new IEP would have to be developed.[14]

Many courts, in addressing the LRE requirement, rely on *Oberti v. Board of Education of Clementon School District*.[15] The case evaluated whether the district made reasonable efforts to accommodate a student in regular class if appropriate supplemental aids and services were provided and the probable negative impact for other students if the student with disabilities remained in the regular classroom.

Circuit courts have been particularly divided on what criteria should be used in determining LREs:

- Self-contained classroom represented LRE for a Down syndrome student.[16] (The courts relied on Oberti criteria.)
- A categorical classroom placement is the most appropriate for one Down syndrome student even when the program is not located in the child's neighborhood.[17] (The courts did not apply Oberti criteria.)
- The regular classroom provided an unsatisfactory placement for a student with Rett syndrome.[18] (The courts relied on Oberti criteria.)
- Educational benefits must be balanced against factors such as disruptive influence, costs, and effect on students.[19] (Relied in part on Oberti criteria and in part on cost–benefit analysis.)

Inclusion of Children with Disabilities

Inclusion is an extension of the traditional concept of *mainstreaming.* Its intent is to ensure, as much as possible and when appropriate, that children with disabilities are placed in regular classrooms. Inclusion is seen as one mechanism designed to ensure that all children receive a free, appropriate education in an effort to maximize their learning potential.

Implicit in this concept is the notion that some educational benefit is conferred on students with disabilities when they attend public schools. A child's evaluation results, which are used to develop the IEP, would ultimately determine the nature of the placement. Because the IEP is tailored specifically to meet the needs of the child with disabilities, it must be reasonably calculated to enable the child to receive the benefit of instruction.

Inclusion also is valuable in integrating children with disabilities into the regular school program. Many educators feel that all children—disabled and nondisabled—benefit from this arrangement. Although many educators support inclusion as a way of placing children with disabilities in the most ideal educational environment, many others feel that inclusion places these children in nonsupportive environments, eliminating valuable time from their learning activities. This may be particularly critical in environments where the classroom teacher is not properly trained to work with children who have disabilities. The preparation of teachers to meet the needs of these children is critical, because inclusion is an important component of the IDEA that supports equal access for children with disabilities.

Under the concept of inclusion, regular classroom teachers in schools across the country are challenged to meet the needs of students with disabilities. In many instances, teachers are unprepared to do so. Because the IDEA specifies that students with disabilities be provided an FAPE in the LRE based on each student's IEP, there is an affirmative obligation placed on schools to serve the needs of these students. If teachers are not prepared to meet these needs, a legal issue may emerge regarding both *academic injury* as well as *physical injury* to the student.

With increasing frequency, regular classroom teachers are called on to meet academic needs and perform related services such as catheterization, suctioning, colostomy, and seizure monitoring when students with disabilities are placed in regular classrooms. If teachers are unable to perform these vital services effectively, resulting in injury to the child, liability charges may be forthcoming, depending on the nature of the injury and factors leading to such injury. Thus, not only are classroom teachers expected to meet the academic needs of children with disabilities, but they may also be expected to provide special education services during the inclusion period.

School districts, then, have the responsibility of ensuring that a *reasonable standard of care* is met when regular teachers work with students who have disabilities. This means that districts must be properly prepared to meet the diverse needs of such students, which may be accomplished through systematic and continuous training as well as appropriately developed policies and procedures regarding the teacher's role in relation to students with disabilities. These procedures should be monitored on a systematic basis and altered as the need arises. Failure to adhere to these precautions may form the grounds for liability suits for physical injury, as well as threats of educational malpractice if parents of children with disabilities allege that academic injury resulted from the teacher's lack of skill or fidelity in performing professional duties.

Length of School Year

Numerous lawsuits have emerged regarding the adequacy of the length of the school term in relationship to the needs of children with disabilities. There appears to be some evidence that supports the view that these children regress more quickly when they are without education and services than do students without disabilities. Based on this view, the courts have been quite liberal in granting requests for continuous or yearlong schooling for children with disabilities, as illustrated by the following case.

A mother requested the school district to provide a summer program, including transportation, for her child with severe disabilities. Her request was denied. The mother appealed the district's decision to the Texas Education Agency. A hearing examiner ruled on her behalf. The school district then filed suit, seeking review in U.S. district court. The court found that the student, having been without a structured summer program, suffered significant regression regarding the knowledge gained and skills learned during the school year. The U.S. court of appeals agreed with the district court's decision in holding that if a child with disabilities experiences severe or substantial regression during the summer months in the absence of an appropriate summer school program, the child is entitled to year-round services. Because the child in this case would suffer significant regression, he was entitled to summer instruction. The court further found that the request for transportation was reasonable because the mother was a full-time employee, and it would not create an undue burden on the school district to provide transportation.[20] Also, attorney's fees were awarded to the parent, based on the Handicapped Children's Protection Act, which makes this provision if parents or guardians are successful in their litigation against state or local agencies.

Residential Placement

The matter of whether or not a child with a disability should be placed in a residential facility tends to provoke controversy between parents and school district officials. Residential facilities are typically expensive and, in most cases, more restrictive for the child. However, the IDEA requires such placement where there is sufficient evidence that residential placement is necessary to provide special education and related services to the child with disabilities. In such cases, the costs related to residential placement must be covered by the local school district. If residential placement is the only means by which a child receives services for educational purposes or educational benefits when there is evidence that such placement also provides noneducational benefits, the school district or the state is not relieved of its financial obligations to cover the costs related to the placement.

For example, the parents of an Oregon child were awarded reimbursement for expenses incurred when they decided to place their child in a residential facility after his behavior deteriorated severely in the public school placement. Experts testified that the child could only benefit from a twenty-four-hour, seven-day-a-week, completely consistent environment. The school had a duty to place the child in the most appropriate educational placement and failed to do so.[21]

In a contrasting case, the school district decided that a child with chronic schizophrenia and disabilities could no longer attend day programs because of episodes of aggressive behavior. When the district could not identify a proper residential facility in state, it recommended one in the closest state, over the parents' objection. The court held for the parents when it was determined that the child was denied appropriate education in accordance with his current IEP by his placement in an out-of-state facility close to home. The student was awarded compensatory education for the years he had been inappropriately placed.[22]

Public school districts are required to pay private school tuition and related expenses in cases where the district fails to offer an appropriate special education program to a student with a disability. This concept was reinforced by the U.S. Supreme Court in the *Burlington* case, in which the father of a child with learning disabilities became dissatisfied with his third-grade son's lack of progress in a Massachusetts public school system.[23] A new IEP was developed for the child, which called for placement in a different public school. The father, following the advice of specialists at Massachusetts General Hospital, unilaterally withdrew his son from the school system, placing him instead at a state-approved private facility in Massachusetts. He then sought reimbursement for tuition and transportation expenses from the school committee, maintaining that the IEP was inappropriate. The state Board of Special Education Appeals (BSEA) ruled that the proposed IEP was inappropriate and that the father was justified in placing his son at a special school. The BSEA ordered the school committee to reimburse the father for tuition and transportation expenses. The committee appealed to the federal courts. A U.S. district court held that the parents had violated the status quo provision of the Education of the Handicapped Act (EHA) by enrolling their child in the private school without approval. Thus, they were not entitled to reimbursement. However, the U.S. Court of Appeals, First Circuit, reversed the district court's ruling, and the committee appealed to the U.S. Supreme Court.

In affirming the court of appeals' decision, the Supreme Court ruled that parents who place a child with a disability in a private educational facility are entitled to reimbursement for the child's tuition and living expenses *if* a court later determines that the school district has proposed an inappropriate IEP. Reimbursement could not be ordered if the school district's proposed IEP were later found to be appropriate. The Supreme Court observed that to disallow reimbursement claims under all circumstances would be contrary to the EHA, which favors proper interim placements for children with disabilities.

Private School Placement

The IDEA requires each state to provide special education and related services to all children with disabilities. Each state must ensure, to the greatest degree possible, that children with disabilities enrolled in private schools receive an appropriate education. Local school districts may provide services in a public school setting or opt to cover the cost of services in private schools. In either case, services must be comparable in quality in both settings. The statute makes a distinction between those who are placed in a private school based on their IEPs versus those whose parents voluntarily place them in private schools. The child who is voluntarily placed in a private school by his or her parent(s) has lesser entitlement than the child placed in a public school. If an FAPE is provided for the child with disabilities based on the IEP and the child is placed in a private school based on the parent's desire, the district is under no obligation to cover the costs incurred in such placement. However, if the child's IEP calls for a private school placement, the district is obligated to cover all costs associated with such placement.

A reimbursement challenge occurred in Oregon when a student with ADHD and depression made progress in school but engaged in defiant and risky behavior at home. Her parents sought a more restrictive placement for her, but the school district ruled it out because she was earning good grades when she did her work. Her parents unilaterally placed her in a residential facility, but she was expelled for having sex with another student. Her parents then placed her in an out-of-state facility and sought tuition reimbursement, which the Ninth Circuit denied. It held that the student did not require residential placement for any educational reason. She was not disruptive in class and was well regarded by teachers.[24]

In another case, an adopted student in Maryland with learning disabilities and emotional disturbance exhibited suicidal tendencies and clinical depression. Her IEP team placed her in a private special education day school. She later self-mutilated and attempted suicide. Her parents placed her in a residential school, even though a school psychologist found that she should be placed in a therapeutic school for students with serious emotional issues. The parents sought reimbursement, but a federal court and later the Fourth Circuit ruled against them. The placement was based on the parents' desire to ensure the student did not harm herself. It was not made for educational reasons and was not the least restrictive environment because she made progress in the day school when her mental health issues stabilized.[25]

These two cases illustrate that parental decisions regarding placement of their children will not be supported if the students' IEPs do not reasonably justify private placement.

ISOLATION AND RESTRAINT LAWS FOR STUDENTS WITH DISABILITIES

A number of states have passed legislation governing isolation and restraint practices for students with disabilities. These laws were enacted to ensure equal protection and to protect the safety of students with disabilities. These statutes govern the circumstances under which isolation and restraints may occur. They include maximum time periods involved, particular types of isolation that may be used, condition of isolation rooms, supervision that must be provided during isolation, and approval by school officials prior to utilizing isolation measures. Some statutes also require parental notification.

Basic objectives of most isolation and restraint laws are as follows:

- To protect students receiving special education services from unsafe and unwarranted uses of isolation and restraint measures;
- To facilitate positive behavioral strategies and support measures in classrooms that result in positive outcomes for special needs students;
- To ensure that fundamental fairness is applied in all classroom activities involving students;
- To ensure that school personnel comply with state laws governing the use of isolation and restraint measures; and,
- To ensure that teachers who serve special education students are equipped and prepared to protect disabled students, themselves, and other students from physical harm.

Based on restraint laws, the following areas are generally addressed. The use of chemical restraints, noxious substances, isolation or seclusion, mechanical restraints, and any form of life-threatening restraints on a student receiving special education services. "Chemical restraint" generally refers to a medication that is prescribed to restrict a student's freedom of movement to control extreme violent misbehavior. Chemical restraints are medications used in addition to, or in replacement of, a student's regular drug regimen to control extreme or violent behavior. The medications related to the student's regular medical regimen are not generally considered chemical restraints, even if their purpose is to treat ongoing behavioral symptoms. Typically, the administration of a chemical restraint should be permissible when administered for therapeutic purposes under the direction of a physician and with the parent's or guardian's consent. "Noxious substance" typically denotes any defense substance such as Mace, tear gas, pepper spray, and other defense sprays. "Isolation" or "seclusion" typically involves the confinement of a student alone in a room or an area where the student is physically prevented from leaving. This definition is not limited to instances in which a student is confined by a locked or closed door. Isolation does not include time-out, a behavior management procedure in which a student is placed in a different and less rewarding setting for a brief period of time. School personnel should not use isolation or restraint as punishment or to coerce a student to respond in a certain manner or to simply make the teacher's job easier. "Mechanical restraint" refers to a device or equipment, including ambulatory restraints, that hinders movement in an emergency situation. Examples include handcuffs, straps, tape, and other similar devices. Mechanical restraint does not typically include the use of restraints for medical immobilization, adaptive support, or medical protection. "Physical restraint" involves manual restraint by school personnel that restricts a student's freedom of movement such as a choke hold or any act that applies pressure on a child's chest that may result in impeding breathing.

A student receiving special education services should be restrained or isolated only if such restraint or isolation is provided for the student's individual education program (IEP). However, the student, based on district or state statutes, may be restrained or isolated in emergency situations if it is necessary to protect the physical safety of the student or others. School personnel should remain in the physical presence of any restrained student and continuously observe a student who is in isolation or being restrained to monitor the health and well-being of the student even when such action is not required by statute or district policy. If school personnel impose restraints or isolation in an emergency situation, the school should immediately contact appropriate school personnel who are designated under state statute or district policy to authorize the isolation or restraint measure. School personnel authorized by statute or district policy should assess and evaluate the student's condition within a reasonable time after the intervention. The student's parent or guardian should be notified, orally or by written communication on the same day the isolation or restraint occurred. If the student's individualized education program (IEP) does not provide for the use of isolation or restraint measures for the behavior precipitating certain action by the school or if school personnel are required to use isolation or restraint over an extended period of time as determined by statute or district policy, then an individual education program meeting should be convened following the use of isolation or restraint with a focus on positive behavior interventions. The use of physical holding restraints may not be prohibited if it is brief and designed to calm or comfort a student, to assist a student in completing a task, or to prevent any impulsive behavior that threatens the student's immediate safety. Parents should be promptly notified when isolation or restraint measures are applied to their children.

The U.S. Department of Education has developed fifteen principles that it recommends to be used as a foundation for policies and procedures in public schools. These principles stress the need to prevent the use of restraints and seclusion and that any behavioral intervention must be consistent with the child's right to be treated with dignity and freedom from abuse. These principles support the All Students Safe Act passed in 2010.

There have been reports of student deaths involving physical or prone restraints in Michigan, Texas, Georgia, Tennessee, and other states when isolation and restraint methods are used. Prone restraints appear to be most controversial when the student is required to lie on his or her stomach (prone) under pressure, which, in many cases, affects the capacity to breathe and has resulted in student deaths. Some state statutes prohibit prone restraint altogether. Suicide deaths also have been associated with students who were isolated in a dark locked room. In other cases, students indefensibly were reported to have been placed for punitive reasons in dark janitor closets and small plywood boxes. The type of restraints used may trigger the IEP team's review of the student's placement to determine if a change in placement is required with parental involvement. There have been cases in which serious injury or deaths have resulted from physical restraints. An important dimension of employing approved isolation restraint measures is training of all teachers who are involved in implementing these measures. Isolation and restraint laws are designed to protect students with disabilities from abuse, injury, and in some instances death.

The following examples illustrate the serious consequences of employing isolation and restraint measures:

- A fourteen-year-old middle school student in Texas was killed when his teacher held him down, ignoring his plea, "I can't breathe, I can't breathe." Knowing that the student had a mental illness, other disabilities, and was sensitive to food issues because he had been denied food when he was younger, the teacher sought to punish his aggressive behavior by refusing to allow him to eat lunch. When the student tried to leave the classroom to go to the lunchroom, the use of deadly restraint by the teacher ensued.

  Source: cnn.com/2008/US/12/17/seclusion.rooms

- A thirteen-year-old student in Georgia hanged himself in a small concrete-walled, locked seclusion room by using a cord provided by a teacher to hold up his pants. The eighth-grader had pleaded with his teachers that he could not stand being locked within the small seclusion room for nine hours at a time. The student had threatened suicide in school a few weeks before his death.

Source: cnn.com/2008/US/12/17/seclusion.rooms

- A Tennessee mother alleged in a federal suit against the Learn Center that her 51-pound nine-year-old autistic son was bruised when school instructors used their body weight on his legs and torso to hold him down before putting him in a "quiet room" for four hours.

Source: cnn.com/2008/US/12/17/seclusion.rooms

- Eight-year-old Isabel Loeffler, who has autism, was held down by her teachers and confined in a storage closet when she pulled out her hair and wet her pants at a Dallas County, Iowa, elementary school. A judge found that the school had violated the girl's rights.

Source: cnn.com/2008/US/12/17/seclusion.rooms

- A fourteen-year-old male diagnosed with post-traumatic stress syndrome and attending a Texas public school was killed when a 230-pound teacher placed the 129-pound child face-down on floor and laid on top of him because he did not stay seated in class, causing his death. The student's death was ruled a homicide but the grand jury did not indict the teacher. The teacher currently teaches in Virginia.

Source: gao.gov/new.items/d09719t.pdf

- The parents of a nine-year-old male diagnosed with a learning disability granted permission to the school to use the time-out room, but only as a last resort. The school placed the child in the room repeatedly for hours at a time for offenses such as whistling, slouching, and hand waving. The mother reported that the time-out room smelled of urine and her child's hands became blistered while trying to escape. The jury awarded the family $1,000 for each time the child was placed in the room.

Source: gao.gov/new.items/d09719t.pdf

DISCIPLINING STUDENTS WITH DISABILITIES

It has long been held that children with disabilities may not be punished for conduct that is a *manifestation* of their disability. However, they may be disciplined by school authorities for any behavior that is not associated with their disability, using regular disciplinary procedures, as reflected in school policies. In situations where certain types of discipline are warranted, an effort must be made to ensure that the punishment does not *materially* and *substantially* interrupt the child's education. School expulsions, suspensions, and transfers are examples that fall into this category.

Expulsion

Expulsion represents the most serious form of punishment because it results in permanent separation from the school district for the student. Two early cases addressed the issue of discipline and a change in placement regarding expulsion and long-term suspension of children with disabilities. The first case, *S-1 v. Turlington,*[26] involved expulsion of nine high school students in Hendry, Florida. In separate actions, these students were expelled for various acts of misconduct. One student, S-1, requested a hearing to determine whether his behavior was associated with his disability. The other eight made no such request.

School officials had determined in S-1's case that his conduct was not related to his disability because he was not seriously disabled. S-1 brought suit, claiming that his rights had been violated under the EAHCA. The district court issued an injunction against the state, which was appealed by Turlington, the state superintendent of education.

The issue addressed during the appeal was whether a child with mild retardation could be expelled without a hearing to determine if the conduct for which the student was expelled was related to his disability. The Fifth Circuit Court ruled for S-1 by stating that a student with retardation may not be expelled without a hearing to determine whether the conduct exhibited by the child was related to his or her disability.

The court was not receptive to the state's claim that the other eight students requested no hearing. The court stated that those eight must be provided a hearing prior to expulsion proceedings to make the determination regarding disability-related behavior. The act places an obligation on school officials to make this determination. Even when a determination is made that the conduct exhibited by the child is unrelated to his or her disability, school officials must also be mindful that long-term suspensions or expulsion are tantamount to a change in placement, thus triggering a need for implementation of full procedural safeguards and stay-put provisions.

A leading case, *Stuart v. Nappi,* addressed this issue. Kathy Stuart was diagnosed with serious academic and emotional difficulties that stemmed from complex learning disabilities and limited intelligence. She also had a record of behavioral problems.

A meeting of the planning and placement team (PPT) was held in February 1975, at which time Kathy was diagnosed as having a major learning disability. The PPT recommended that Kathy be scheduled on a trial basis in the special education program for remediating learning disabilities and that she be given a psychological evaluation. Although the PPT report specifically stated that the psychological evaluation should be given "at the earliest feasible time," no such evaluation was administered.

At the beginning of the 1976–1977 school year, Kathy was scheduled to participate in a learning disability program on a part-time basis. Her attendance continued to decline throughout the first half of the school year. By late fall, she had completely stopped attending her special education classes and had begun to spend this time wandering the school corridors with her friends. Although she was encouraged to participate in the special education classes, the PPT meeting concerning Kathy's program, which had been requested at the end of the previous school year, was not conducted in the fall of 1976.

On September 14, 1977, Kathy was involved in schoolwide disturbances that erupted at Danbury High School. As a result of her involvement in these disturbances, she received a ten-day disciplinary suspension and was scheduled to appear at a disciplinary hearing on November 30, 1977. The superintendent of the Danbury schools recommended to the Danbury Board of Education that Kathy be expelled for the remainder of the 1977–1978 school year at this hearing.

Kathy's attorney requested a hearing with the Danbury Board of Education to review Kathy's special education program and successfully obtained a temporary restraining order that enjoined the board from conducting the hearing. Evidence revealed that Kathy's program had not been reviewed in nine months by the PPT review committee, nor had the school developed a new special program for her. In ruling for Kathy, the court stated:

> The expulsion of handicapped children not only jeopardizes their right to an education in the least restrictive environment, but is inconsistent with the procedures established by the Handicapped Act for changing the placement of disruptive children. The Handicapped Act prescribes a procedure whereby disruptive children are transferred to more restrictive placements when their behavior significantly impairs the education of other children. Thus, the use of expulsion proceedings as a means of changing the placement of a disruptive handicapped child contravenes the procedures of the Handicapped Act. After considerable reflection, the Court is persuaded that any changes in plaintiff's placement must be made by a PPT after considering the range of available placement and plaintiff's particular needs.[27]

The importance of the parameters of this decision should be clearly understood. Children with disabilities are neither immune from a school's disciplinary process nor are they entitled to participate in programs when their behavior impairs the education of other children in the program. School officials may exercise at least two options in this situation. First, school authorities can take swift disciplinary measures, such as suspension, against disruptive children, disabled or not. Second, a PPT can request a change in placement to a more restrictive environment for children with disabilities who have demonstrated by disrupting the education of other children that their present placement is inappropriate. The IDEA thereby affords schools both short-term and long-term methods of dealing with children with disabilities who exhibit behavioral problems.

Schools may use their normal disciplinary procedures to address behavior of such students, if that behavior is nondisability related. As emphasized earlier in the *S-1 v. Turlington* case, school authorities may not discipline a student with disabilities for behavior that is a manifestation of his or her disability.

Because certain types of disciplinary measures may involve removal of children with disabilities from their placement, care must be taken to ensure that proper procedural guidelines are followed. As established in the *Stuart v. Nappi* case, suspension of a student with disabilities is tantamount to a change in placement, thus triggering the stay-put provision of the IDEA. These decisions may involve transfers, suspensions, and expulsions. The stay-put provision of the IDEA requires that children with disabilities remain in their current placement pending the completion of the IEP review process. However, under the 2004 reauthorization the stay-put provision is eliminated for alleged violations of a school code that may result in a removal from the student's current educational placement for more than ten days.

There has been some debate as to what constitutes a change in placement. This question has been addressed by a number of courts, resulting in several definitions. In *Concerned Parents v. New York City Board of Education,* the court ruled that a change in placement occurs when there is a change in the general education program in which the student is enrolled, as opposed to mere variations of it.[28]

In yet another case, *Tilton v. Jefferson County Board of Education,* the Sixth Circuit Court interpreted a change of placement as occurring when the modified or revised program is not comparable to the program established in the original IEP. Irrespective of the precise definition, such change triggers both the procedural and stay-put provisions of the IDEA. Procedural protections are obviously designed to ensure that the required legal proceedings occur in the manner prescribed by statutes, whereas the stay-put provisions allow students to remain in their placement during the impartial hearing or subsequent appeals. When there is agreement between the parent and school authorities, the child remains in the current placement, even though it may not be deemed the most appropriate one at that time.[29]

If either the parent or the school authorities wish to temporarily change the placement before the appeals process is exhausted, a *court order* must be ascertained to effect this change. If a decision is reached that a child's placement should be changed, special education and related services cannot be discontinued. The child must receive educational support.

Suspension

School suspension is one of the most common forms of punishment used to remove disruptive students from the school environment. It is particularly useful as a disciplinary tool in cases where there is an immediate threat to health and safety of the child with disabilities or other children in the school. A temporary suspension may be justified in cases that fall into this category. School authorities have disagreed considerably regarding the limits of their authority to temporarily remove disabled children during emergency situations when the health and safety of other students are threatened.

In a compelling case, *Honig v. Doe,* the U.S. Supreme Court responded to this issue.[30] This case involved two students who were emotionally disturbed and had been suspended indefinitely for violent conduct related to their disabilities, pending the results of an expulsion hearing. Doe had a history of aggressive behavior, particularly when he was ridiculed by other students. The facts revealed that Doe choked a fellow student with sufficient force to leave visible neck abrasions. He also kicked out a window while being led to the principal's office. The other student, Smith, experienced academic and social difficulties and had a tendency to respond with verbal hostility, stealing, extorting money from classmates, and making sexual overtures to female students.

Both students filed suit, contending that the suspensions and proposed expulsions violated the stay-put provision of the IDEA. The district court ruled for the students and was later affirmed by the court of appeals. The case was reviewed by the U.S. Supreme Court. The fundamental issue confronting the High Court was whether the stay-put provision of the act prohibits states from removing children from school for violent or disruptive conduct stemming from their disability. Justice William Brennan, writing for the majority, reasoned that, under the act, states may not remove students with disabilities from classrooms for violent or disruptive conduct stemming from their disabilities. The language in the IDEA clearly prohibits such action while any proceedings are pending. The court cannot render an exception to this provision, as the plaintiff suggested.

Schools, however, may use their normal procedures in dealing with students who endanger themselves or others. Students who pose an immediate threat to school safety may be temporarily suspended for up to ten days without an inquiry into whether the student's behavior was a manifestation of a disability. This type of suspension, consistent with an earlier case, *Goss v. Lopez,* involving nondisabled students, is considered to be a short-term suspension that allows school authorities the freedom to punish a student with disabilities by removing him or her from the classroom in anticipation of further action that might involve long-term suspension, movement to a more restrictive environment, or, as a last resort, expulsion.

The significance of this ruling is that the High Court does not interpret short-term suspension as a change in placement, and therefore does not trigger the need for elaborate procedural requirements associated with the act.[31] However, it is important to note that long-term suspensions and expulsion do constitute a change in placement and may not be used if the student's conduct is associated with a known disability. In extreme situations involving safety risks, school districts may seek a court order that permits them to initiate a temporary change of placement. In either case, educational services should be provided during the suspension.

Because the burden of proof to determine whether a student's misconduct is a manifestation of a disability rests with the school district, there must be clear and objective evidence to support the district's actions. A highly skilled and trained team of knowledgeable professionals must be charged with making this determination. Although there is some disagreement among the courts regarding whether educational services should be provided during long-term suspension of students with disabilities, the U.S. Department of Education has adopted the position of the Fifth Circuit Court by suggesting that services should be provided to those students who are serving long-term suspensions.

INDIVIDUALS WITH DISABILITIES EDUCATION ACT OF 1997

Amendments Regarding Discipline

Under the IDEA Amendments of 1997, discipline with respect to suspension, manifestation, and *interim alternative educational settings (IAES)* is addressed. These amendments are designed to provide greater flexibility to school districts without violating the rights of students who are disabled. Based on these amendments, the following provisions apply.

DISCIPLINE AND OPTIONAL SANCTIONS. When a student violates a school rule or code of conduct that is uniformly applicable to all students, the LEA, acting through the student's IEP team, may take one of several actions:

1. Place the student in an interim alternative educational setting or other setting for up to ten days, provided, however, that it also may use the same sanction for students who do not have disabilities (stay-put provision applies)
2. Suspend the student for up to ten days, provided that it also may use the same sanction for students who do not have disabilities (stay-put provision applies)

3. Place the student in an IAES for up to forty-five days, provided that it also may use the same sanction for students without disabilities, if the student carries a weapon to school or to a student function or illegally uses drugs or sells or solicits the sale of a controlled substance at school or a school function (for weapons and drug discipline, stay-put rule does not apply)
4. Request a hearing officer to place a dangerous student into an IAES for up to forty-five days (if the officer agrees, the stay-put rule does not apply)

PRE/POSTSANCTION IEP REVIEW, BEHAVIOR MODIFICATION PLAN, AND FUNCTIONAL ASSESSMENT. Before it takes any disciplinary actions or within at least ten days after it does so, the LEA must convene the IEP team to take one of two actions:

1. If the LEA has not already conducted a *functional behavioral assessment* and implemented a *behavioral intervention,* then the IEP team must develop an assessment plan to address the student's behavior; or
2. If the LEA has already developed such a plan and put it into the student's IEP, then the team must review the plan and modify it, as necessary, to address the behavior for which the student was disciplined.

PREMANIFESTATION DETERMINATION ACTION. Before it imposes any sanction (placement in an IAES, placement in another setting, suspension for up to ten days, or placement in an IAES for up to forty-five school days for weapons, drug violations, or dangerousness), the IEP team and any other qualified personnel must:

1. Notify the student's parents of the decision and of the student's and parents' procedural safeguards.
2. No later than ten days after making the decision, review the relationship between the student's disability and the student's behavior.

MANIFESTATION DETERMINATION REVIEW. When conducting the manifestation determination review, the IEP team must determine that the behavior was *not* a manifestation of the disability if it complies with two requirements:

1. It first considers, in terms of the behavior, all relevant information, including evaluation and diagnostic results, information supplied by the parents, observations of the student, and the student's present IEP and placement.
2. After considering these matters, the team must determine that:
   • The student's IEP and placement were appropriate and the LEA provided special education, related services, supplementary aids and services, and behavior intervention strategies consistent with the IEP and placement.
   • The disability did not impair the student's ability to understand the impact and consequences of the behavior.
   • The disability did not impair the student's ability to control the behavior.
   • The amended act grants school personnel the authority, on a case-by-case basis, to consider unique circumstances when deciding whether to prescribe a change in placement for a child with disabilities who violates a student code of conduct.
   • The amended act also shifts the burden from the school (to demonstrate that the behavior resulting in disciplinary action was not a manifestation of the child's disability) to the parent (who must prove that the child's behavior was substantially related to his or her disability).

If the team determines that the behavior was *not* a manifestation of the disability, then the LEA may:

1. Apply to the student the same sanctions that it may apply to students without a disability, but it may not terminate altogether the student's access to an FAPE (no cessation).
2. Ensure that the student's disciplinary and educational records are transmitted for consideration by the person making the final disciplinary decision (e.g., a school principal).

APPEAL FROM DISCIPLINARY ACTION.   A parent may appeal (to an impartial hearing officer) the determination concerning "no manifestation" or any discipline-related placement decision.

1. The hearing must be expedited and must be conducted before an impartial hearing officer.
2. The hearing officer must determine whether the LEA has demonstrated that the student's behavior was not a manifestation.

During the hearing, the hearing officer may place the student in an appropriate IAES for up to forty-five days, but only if:

1. The officer determines that the LEA has demonstrated by substantial evidence (defined as "beyond a preponderance of the evidence") that maintaining the student's current placement is substantially likely to result in injury to the student, other students, or staff.
2. The officer considers the appropriateness of the student's current placement.
3. The officer considers whether the LEA has made reasonable efforts to minimize the risk of harm in the student's current placement, including the use of supplementary aids and services.
4. The officer determines that the IAES allows the student to continue to participate in the general curriculum and to continue to receive those services and modifications that will enable the student to meet IEP goals as well as services and modifications that address the sanctioned behavior to ensure that it does not recur.

PLACEMENT DURING APPEALS.   The student remains in the IAES pending the decision of the hearing officer, for up to forty-five days, unless the parents and LEA agree otherwise.

PROPOSED NEW PLACEMENT (FOLLOWING IAES).   If the LEA places the student in an IAES and then proposes to change the student's placement after the IAES placement expires, and if the parents challenge this proposed change in placement, the general rule is that, during the pendency of the hearing on the parents' challenge, the student remains in the placement that existed before the interim placement. This rule, however, will not apply, and an exception to it exists, if the LEA maintains that it is dangerous for the student to be in that placement and if it also requests an expedited hearing. To determine whether the student will return to the original placement, remain in the alternative setting (converting it from an interim to a permanent placement), or be placed in another setting, the hearing officer must make the same four findings of fact and then decide on the placement.

PREEMPTIVE STRIKE.   To gain the protections of the IDEA's disciplinary safeguards, a student who previously was not entitled to the protections of the IDEA may assert that he or she is entitled to special education and related services and to the special procedural and other safeguards of the IDEA if the LEA had knowledge that the student was a student with a disability before the misconduct occurred. The LEA is deemed to have known that the student had a disability if:

1. The parent expressed concern in writing to the LEA that the student is in need of services.
2. The parent has requested a nondiscriminatory evaluation.
3. The student's behavior or performance has demonstrated that he or she needs those services.
4. The student's teacher or other school personnel have a concern regarding the student's behavior or performance and have expressed that concern to the LEA's special education director or other personnel.

If, however, none of these conditions exists and the LEA has no knowledge or is not charged with knowledge that the student has a disability, then it may subject the student to the same discipline as any other student who engages in comparable behavior. If the student is evaluated during the time he or she is subjected to disciplinary measures, the LEA must expedite the evaluation.

If the LEA determines that the student is in need of special education and related services, it must provide those services in accordance with the IDEA. The student, however, must remain in the educational placement determined by the school authorities pending the evaluation.

REPORTING CRIMINAL BEHAVIOR AND REFERRING TO LAW ENFORCEMENT AND JUDICIAL AGENCIES.   The LEA may report any crime committed by a student to the appropriate authorities. The IDEA does not prevent those authorities from exercising any of their duties to enforce state or federal criminal law. If it files a report, the LEA must provide copies of the student's special education and disciplinary records to the authorities with which it filed the report of a crime.

TRANSMITTING STUDENT INFORMATION.   The state may require the LEA to include in the student's file a statement of any current or previous disciplinary action taken against the student. This information may be transmitted to educators to the same extent as such information is transmitted for students without disabilities. This statement may include a description of the student's behavior that required disciplinary action, a description of the disciplinary action taken, and any other information that is relevant to the safety of the child and others. If the state adopts a disclosure policy and the student transfers from one school to another, the student's records must include a copy of his or her original IEP and a statement of current or previous disciplinary action taken against the student.

The significance of the changes is that the IEP serves as the link between the nondiscriminatory education (NDE) and the LRE placement. These amendments make this connection more explicit. There is also a very strong component of the LRE found in the IEP.

DISCIPLINE AND BEHAVIOR ARE NOW LINKED.   The IEP "special factors" provision requires the IEP team to include appropriate strategies, including positive behavioral interventions, strategies, and support to address (i.e., prevent and remediate) behaviors that impede the student's or others' learning. These behaviors undoubtedly include those for which the student may be disciplined. Thus, the present *harmful effects* rule (the student may not be placed in a program where there will be harmful effects to the student, other students, or staff) is not retained, but a *prevention of harmful effects* rule is substituted.

In addition, the IEP team must consist of a regular educator whose input includes determining appropriate positive interventions and strategies.[32] The 1997 amendments should provide greater flexibility for school officials without violating the personal and due process of students with disabilities, as well as their parents.

Attention-Deficit/Hyperactivity Disorder and Federal Protection

A growing number of children with ADHD are enrolled in public schools. Three federal statutes—the IDEA, Section 504 of the Rehabilitation Act of 1973 (RHA), and the ADA—cover children with attention-deficit/hyperactivity disorder.

Under the IDEA, ADHD-eligible students must possess one or more specified physical or mental impairments, and it must be determined that they require special education and related services based on these impairments. ADHD alone is not sufficient to qualify a child for special education services unless it impairs the child's ability to benefit from education. Children with ADHD may be eligible for special education services if they are found to have a specific learning disability, be seriously emotionally disturbed, or possess other health impairments.

Section 504 provides education for children who do not fall within the disability categories covered under the IDEA. This statute further requires that an FAPE be provided to each eligible

Administrative Guide

Student Disabilities

1. School districts should ensure that children with disabilities in their districts be provided equal access to a public education. Failure to provide appropriate special education may result in a court injunction as well as mandatory compensatory education.

2. A lack of funds should not be used by school districts as the basis to deny children with disabilities a public education.

3. School districts should be certain that they clearly understand the difference between medical services and related services.

4. A well-organized and coordinated staff development plan should be developed to prepare all teachers to work effectively with children who are disabled. These activities should be coherent, continuous, and well supported by the district.

5. School personnel should be aware of possible liability challenges if they fail to perform certain related services properly.

6. Parental rights must be respected and addressed in matters relating to evaluation and IEP development.

7. Children with disabilities should not be disciplined for behavior that is associated with their known disabilities.

8. Long-term suspension, if necessary, will trigger the need for change of placement requirements, but in virtually no cases should children with disabilities be without educational services. School officials should become familiar with the new IDEA amendments regarding discipline of such students and be certain that the amendments are incorporated into district policy.

9. School districts may be assessed attorneys' fees under the Handicapped Children's Protection Act, if a parent prevails in a suit for a violation of the IDEA.

10. A state education agency or local education agency that prevails based on a frivolous or unreasonable complaint by a parent without cause or against the attorney of a parent who continues to litigate after the litigation clearly becomes frivolous, unreasonable, or without foundation may be awarded attorneys' fees.

11. The burden of proof rests with the school district in determining whether misbehavior by a student with disabilities is attributed to the disability.

12. School districts should ensure that architectural barriers do not prevent or otherwise qualify individuals who are disabled from receiving services or participating in programs or activities provided by the district.

13. School districts may be required to provide educational services beyond the regular school year, depending on the student's unique needs.

child who is disabled but does not require special education and related services under the IDEA. The act stipulates the following:

- Parents are guaranteed the right to contest the outcome of an evaluation if a local district determines that a child is not disabled under Section 504.
- The local district is required to make an individualized determination of the child's educational needs for regular or special education or related aids and services if the child is determined to be eligible under Section 504.
- Implementation of an IEP is required.
- The child's education must be provided in the regular classroom unless it is shown that the education in the regular classroom with the use of supplementary aids and services cannot be achieved satisfactorily.
- Necessary adjustments must be made in the regular classroom for children who qualify under Section 504.

The education program requirements of the RHA, although not as detailed, are fairly consistent with those of the IDEA. The RHA and the ADA are similar regarding basic provisions.

The RHA regulates organizations that receive federal funds, whereas the ADA covers virtually all public and private schools with the exception of private religious schools. Receipt of federal funds is not associated with the ADA. Although these two laws overlap, the requirements are essentially the same for both. Fundamental to both laws is the requirement that children with ADHD and other disabilities not be treated differently based solely on their disability.

Section 504 Rehabilitation Act of 1973

Under Section 504 of the Rehabilitation Act of 1973, schools must guarantee that programs, services, and activities are accessible and responsive to the needs of individuals with disabilities when the district's programs and activities are considered in their entirety. Students who qualify under 504 are provided an Individual Accommodation Plan (IAP). The IAP identifies a student's disability and his/her access to the school's regular education program. The school's regular program should be accessible to the student to the greatest degree possible.

A disability is defined as a physical or mental impairment that substantially limits one or more major life activities. Major life activities may include but are not limited to caring for oneself, performing manual tasks, seeing, hearing, eating, sleeping, walking, standing, sitting, reaching, lifting, bending, speaking, breathing, learning, reading, concentrating, thinking, communicating, interacting with others, and working. Also included are the operations of major bodily functions such as the immune system, special sense organs and skin, digestive, genitourinary, bowel, bladder, neurological, brain, respiratory, circulatory, cardiovascular, endocrine, hemic, lymphatic, musculoskeletal, and reproductive functions.

A student qualifies for 504 services based on an assessment by a student support team to determine if a student has a disability that substantially limits one or more major life activities. Based on the student's disability, he/she must not be limited in ability to access the regular educational program and may or may not require special educational services. Appropriate interventions must be noted in the Individualized Accommodation Plan. The IAP team consists of the student's parent or legal guardian; the student's teacher; the student, when appropriate; and an administrative representative. The team must ensure that proper documentation is present to specify teaching practices, the nature of the student's disability, and student-specific individualized interventions and accommodations. Periodic evaluations and an annual review of the student's plan must be conducted with appropriate changes implemented based on student data.

The ADA Amendments Act of 2008

Amendments to the ADA signed into law on September 25, 2008, clarify and reiterate who is covered by the law's civil rights protections. The ADA Amendments Act of 2008 revises the definition of *disability* to more broadly encompass impairments that substantially limit a major life activity. The amended language also states that mitigating measures, including assistive devices, auxiliary aids, accommodations, and medical therapies and supplies (other than eyeglasses and contact lenses) have no bearing in determining whether a disability qualifies under the law. Revisions also clarified coverage of impairments that are episodic or in remission that substantially limit a major life activity when active, such as epilepsy or post-traumatic stress disorder. The amendments became effective on January 1, 2009.

The amended act expanded major life activities to include but not be limited to operation of major bodily functions—"immune system, normal cell growth, digestive, bowel, bladder, neurological, brain, respiratory, circulatory, endocrine, and reproductive functions." Episodic or in remission limitations must be considered as if they are active. In the past, individuals whose condition was in remission or whose limitations were episodic have not been covered by the ADA, depending on how long that person's limitations were in an active state. This meant that a person with, for example, mental illness, might not be entitled to accommodations in the workplace when his or her condition was active because he or she did not meet the ADA's definition of disability. Congress addressed this issue in the Amendments Act by stating that "an impairment that is episodic or in remission is a disability if it would substantially limit a major life activity when active." Lastly, the act rejected the requirements enunciated by the U.S. Supreme Court in *Sutton v. United Airlines*[33] and *Toyota v. Williams*,[34] holding that correctable illnesses such as vision and carpal tunnel syndrome did not qualify under the ADA for accommodations. The amendments now cover a whole new population of employees who were not classified as disabled and who did not meet the definition of having a disability under the current ADA. The statute also provides that impairments that are episodic or in remission must be assessed in their active state. The new requirements will result in additional individuals to whom employers will need to offer reasonable accommodations in the workplace.

Table 5.1 represents a summary of significant changes to the IDEA Reauthorization Act (IDEIA) of 2004.

TABLE 5.1 Summary of Significant Changes to the IDEA Reauthorization Act of 2004	
1997	**2004**
Teacher Qualifications	**Teacher Qualifications**
Special Education Teachers did not fall under NCLB's definition of highly qualified teacher.	All special education teachers fall under NCLB definition and must possess a special education certificate or pass a state licensing exam; must not have had a waiver based on emergency, temporary, or a provisional basis and must have earned a bachelor's degree.
Funds	**Funds**
Funding Formula did not include per pupil expenditures in the United States based on current fiscal year.	Funds are allocated to state and local educational agencies for special education and related services based on per average pupil expenditure in the United States during current fiscal year.
Eligibility Determination	**Eligibility Determination**
Timeline for parental consent for determination of eligibility was not established.	A 60-day timeline is established from receipt of parental consent for evaluation regarding a determination of eligibility and the educational needs of the child.
Transition Services	**Transition Services**
Transition services did not specify age of children with disabilities.	Transition services are required when a disabled child reaches age 16.
Individual Education Program	**Individual Education Program**
School personnel in all school districts are required to review and revise the IEP annually. Short-term objectives are required of all children with disabilities as a component of the IEP.	The Secretary of Education is authorized to approve proposals for up to 15 states to allow school districts to develop a multi-year IEP for a maximum of 3 years with parental consent. The IEP may not necessarily be reviewed annually. Short-term objectives are no longer required except for children who are meeting alternative assessment requirements and/or students with the most significant cognitive disabilities.
Related Services	**Related Services**
Provisions of the IEP did not require that comparable related services be provided a child with disabilities who transfers to another school district within the same school year. Examples of related services include transportation, medical services, counseling services, psychological services, physical therapy, speech pathology, audiology, and occupational therapy.	Comparable related services must be provided a disabled child who transfers to a new school district in his/her state within the same school year. Services are expanded to include nursing and interpreting services.

(Continued)

TABLE 5.1   (*Continued*)

1997	2004
Manifestation	**Manifestation**
The burden of proof rests with schools to show that behavior resulting in disciplinary action was not a manifestation of the child's disability.	The burden shifts from schools to parents who must demonstrate that the child's behavior was not substantially related to his/her disability.
Placement	**Placement**
Allows limited discretion to schools to determine placement for children with disabilities who violate a student code of conduct.	School personnel may consider on a case-by-case basis the unique circumstances when deciding whether to prescribe a change in placement for a child with disabilities who violates a code of conduct.
Attorneys' Fees	**Attorneys' Fees**
Attorney fees are awarded to parents who file a substantive complaint regarding their rights or the rights of their child with a disability.	A state or local educational agency may be awarded attorneys' fees if they prevail based on frivolous or unreasonable complaints by parents or attorneys who continue to pursue a frivolous complaint.
Stay Put	**Stay Put**
Students with disabilities are permitted to remain in their current placement pending an appeal regarding violations involving drugs, weapons, or other dangerous activity.	Stay Put Provision is eliminated for alleged violations of a school code that may result in a removal from student's current educational placement for more than 10 days under the 2004 reauthorization.
IEP Team Attendance	**IEP Team Attendance**
All IEP team members are required to attend the annual program review meeting.	A member of the IEP team shall not be required to attend all or part of the IEP meeting if the parent (in writing) and the LEA agree that the team member's attendance is not necessary because the member's area of curriculum or related services is not being modified or discussed during the meeting.
IEP Meeting	**IEP Meeting**
If changes to a child's IEP are necessary after the annual IEP meeting, the IEP committee is required to meet to amend the current IEP.	If changes to the IEP are necessary after the annual meeting for the school year, the parent and the LEA may agree not to convene an IEP meeting to make the changes, but instead develop a written document to amend or modify the current IEP.
Learning Disabilities	**Learning Disabilities**
A battery of appropriate tests are used during the evaluation process to determine if a child has a disability.	Local educational agencies may use an evaluation process to determine if a child responds to scientific research-based intervention as a part of the required evaluation procedures when addressing specific learning disabilities.
Mandatory Requirements	**Mandatory Requirements**
Mandatory services do not address graduation rates, dropout rates, or other relevant factors as determined by states.	Each state must establish goals that address graduation rates, dropout rates, as well as other factors each state may determine.

Administrative Guide

Americans with Disabilities

1. The ADA prohibits employment discrimination by employers with fifteen or more employees.
2. School districts should develop nondiscriminatory policies regarding individuals with disabilities.
3. School districts should not segregate or limit job opportunities for individuals based on their disabilities.
4. School districts may not utilize and promote standards that have a discriminatory effect or perpetuate discrimination against people with disabilities.
5. Employment or employment benefits may not be denied to individuals who have a relationship with people who are disabled.
6. School authorities may not deny employment to individuals with disabilities to avoid providing reasonable accommodations.
7. Selection tests or standards may not be used that screen out individuals with disabilities unless school authorities can demonstrate that they are job related.
8. School districts must utilize standards that identify the skills of the person with disabilities rather than his or her impairments.
9. School districts should take appropriate measures to protect the confidentiality of medical records regarding individuals with disabilities.
10. School districts may be assessed **compensatory damages** and **punitive damages** for deliberate acts of discrimination against individuals with disabilities.
11. Physical and mental impairments must be bona fide and meet the full requirements of ADA to receive coverage.

CASE STUDIES

Student Disability and Inclusion Decisions

David Sterns is a first-year principal of a middle school in an upper-class community in the eastern United States. The district has an outstanding reputation for its academic programs. Sterns admittedly is not as familiar with all issues involving disabled students as a more experienced administrator might be. The parents of a moderately mentally retarded student requested that their daughter be placed in the regular classroom on a full-time basis. Sterns was only willing to place her in regular education classes for nonacademic subjects and into special education classes for academic courses. The parents are upset with his decision.

Discussion Questions

1. Is Sterns justified in his decision? Why or why not?
2. Is the request by the parents a reasonable one? Why or why not?
3. What does special education law suggest with respect to inclusion?
4. What process should be initiated to respond to the parents' request?
5. How would the law apply in this case?
6. What are the administrative implications of this case?

A Disabled Student and Related Services

Debbie Young is a seasoned high school principal. She served as a special education teacher and as an assistant principal in a progressive, affluent school district in the South. She is approached by the parents of a severely disabled tenth-grade student, Jonathan, requesting that a full-time nurse be provided under the label of "related services." Jonathan has multiple disabilities requiring constant care by a specially trained nurse. He is profoundly mentally disabled, has spastic quadriplegia, and has a seizure disorder. Young refuses the parents' request due to extraordinary expense and a view that the school is not the most appropriate placement for Jonathan.

Discussion Questions

1. Is Young's decision defensible? Why or why not?
2. Is the parents' request reasonable under the law? Why or why not?
3. Is the provision of a nurse a related service if it is necessary for Jonathan to receive an appropriate education? Why or why not?
4. How do you think a court would rule in this case? Provide a rationale for your response.
5. What are the administrative implications of this case?

Student with Disabilities Reported to Law Enforcement

A student with disabilities in a small high school in a very close-knit community shared her prescribed medication with another student, which resulted in the assistant principal reporting her to the police, although the student showed no signs of having been harmed by the medication.

Discussion Questions

1. How would you assess the assistant principal's action?
2. Is his action justified? If so, why? If not, why not?
3. Were other options available to the assistant principal? If so, please identify and provide a rationale for these options.
4. Does the child with disabilities have a valid legal claim against the assistant principal? If so, why? If not, why not?
5. How do you feel the courts would view school leaders sharing their investigation results with law enforcement agents?

Isolation and Restraint

One of your most effective teachers with sixteen years of experience has used unorthodox disciplinary practices to curtail misbehavior involving middle school students with disabilities. You were informed of her methods by another teacher. The teacher allegedly used isolation and restraint measures that could create safety risks for students.

Discussion Questions

1. How would you respond to this development?
2. If these allegations are deemed to be valid, what action would you take?
3. Are disciplinary measures appropriate for the teacher? Why? Why not?
4. What might be the consequences for you and the teacher if you fail to act?

Endnotes

1. *The Pennsylvania Association for Retarded Children v. Commonwealth* 334 F. Supp. 1257 (E.D. Pa. 1971), 343 F. Supp. 279 (E.D. Pa. 1972).
2. *Mills v. Board of Education of District of Columbia,* 348 F. Supp. 866 (D.D.C. 1972).
3. *Board of Education of Hendrick Hudson Central School v. Rowley,* 458 U.S. 176, 102 S.Ct. 3034, 73 L. Ed. 2d 690 (1982).
4. *Timothy W. v. Rochester, New Hampshire School District,* 875 F.2d 954 (1st Cir. 1989).
5. *Board of Education of Hendrick Hudson Central School v. Rowley,* 458 U.S. 176 (1982).
6. *Gaskin v. Commonwealth of Pennsylvania,* No. 94-CV-4048 (E.D. PA).
7. 20 U.S.C. § 1400 (C) (1988).

8. *Florence County School District v. Shannon Carter,* 510 U.S. 7, 114 S.Ct. 361, 126 L. Ed. 2d 284 (1993).

9. *Houston Independent School Dist. v. V.P.,* 582 F.3d 576 (5th Cir. 2009).

10. *Schaffer v. Weast,* 377 F.3d 449 (4th Cir. 2005).

11. *Cedar Rapids Community District v. Garret F.,* 526 U.S. 66 (1999).

12. *Irving Independent School District v. Tatro,* 468 U.S. 883, 104 S.Ct. 3371 (1984).

13. 20 U.S.C.A. § 1412 (5) (B); 34 C.F.R. §§ 300–551.

14. *A.Y. and D.Y. v. Cumberland Valley School Dist.,* 569 F. Supp. 2d 496 (M.D. Pa. 2008).

15. *Oberti v. Board of Education of Borough of Clementon School District,* 995 F.2d 1204 (3rd Cir. 1993).

16. *T.W. v. Unified School District No. 259,* Wichita, KS, No. 04-3093, 136 F.3d, Appx. 122 (10th Cir. 2005).

17. *McLaughlin v. Holt Public School Board of Education,* 320 F.3d, 663 (6th Cir. 2003).

18. *Beth B. v. VanClay,* 282 F.3d 493 (7th Cir. 2002).

19. *Clyde K. v. Puyallup School District No. 3,* 35 F.3d 1396 (9th Cir. 1994).

20. *Alamo Heights Independent School District v. State Board of Education,* 790 F.2d 1153 (5th Cir. 1986).

21. *Ash v. Lake Oswego School District No. 7J,* 766 F. Supp. 852 (D. Or. 1991).

22. *Todd D. by Robert D. v. Andrews,* 922 F.2d 1576 (11th Cir.), 67 Ed. Law Rptr. 1065 (1991).

23. *Burlington School Committee v. Department of Education of Massachusetts,* 471 U.S. 359, 105 S.Ct. 1996, 85 L. Ed. 2d 385 (1985).

24. *Ashland School Dist. v. Parents of Student R.J.,* No. 1 v. B.S., 82 F.3d 1493, 1499 (9th Cir. 1996).

25. *Shaw v. Weast,* 364 Fed.Appx 47 (4th Cir. 2010).

26. *S-1 v. Turlington,* 635 F.2d 343 (5th Cir. Unit B Jan), cert. denied, 454 U.S. 1030 (1981).

27. *Stuart v. Nappi,* 443 F. Supp. 1235 (D. Conn. 1978).

28. *Concerned Parents v. New York City Board of Education,* 629 F.2d 751 (2d Cir. 1980), cert. denied, 449 U.S. 1078 (1981).

29. *Tilton v. Jefferson County Board of Education,* 705 F.2d 800, 804 (6th Cir. 1983).

30. *Honig v. Doe,* 484 U.S. 305, 108 S.Ct. 592 (1988).

31. Ibid.

32. 20 U.S.C. Sec. 1415 (g) (k).

33. *Sutton v. United Airlines, Inc.,* 527 U.S. 471; 119 S.Ct. 2139; 144 L. Ed. 2d 450 (1999).

34. *Toyota v. Williams,* 534 U.S. 184 122 S.Ct 682, 651 L.Ed2d615; (2002).

Chapter 6

School Personnel and School District Liability

School districts as well as school officials and employees may incur liability for their tortious acts, when these acts result in injury to students. A *tort* is an actionable or civil wrong committed against one person by another independent of contract. If injury occurs based on the actions of school personnel, liability charges may be imminent. Liability may result from deliberate acts committed by another or acts involving negligence.

Students who are injured by school district personnel may claim monetary damages for their injury resulting from either intentional or unintentional torts. They also may, under certain conditions, seek injunctive relief to prevent the continuation of a harmful practice. Tort law further provides an opportunity for injured parties to bring charges when facts reveal that they received injury to their reputations.

In school settings, a tort may involve a class action suit affecting a number of school personnel, especially in cases involving negligent behavior. A tort may also involve actions brought against a single teacher, principal, or board member, depending on the circumstances surrounding the injury and the severity of the injury.

Educators commit a tort when they violate a legally imposed duty that results in injury to students. Before the court will allow recovery, it will determine factually where the actual fault lies and whether liability claims are justified based on the circumstances in a given situation.

THE SCHOOL AS A SAFE PLACE

Schools are presumed to be safe places where teachers teach and students learn. The prevailing view held by the courts is that prudent professional educators, acting in place of parents, are supervising students under their care and ensuring, to the greatest extent possible, that they are safe. This doctrine is designed to provide parents reasonable assurance that their children are safe while under the supervision of responsible professional adults.

In fact, educators have been assigned three legal duties by the courts under *in loco parentis* (in place of parents)—to instruct, supervise, and provide for the safety of students. Although there is little expectation that students will never be injured, there is an expectation that school personnel will exercise proper care to ensure, to the greatest extent possible, that students are protected from harm.

When an unavoidable injury occurs, there is generally no liability. However, when injury is based on negligence, there are grounds for liability charges. School personnel, based on their legal duty, are expected to foresee that students may be injured under certain circumstances. Once a potential danger has been determined, reasonable steps are necessary to prevent injury. In liability cases, courts will seek to determine whether school officials knew or should have known of an impending danger and whether appropriate steps were taken to protect students. For example, when school officials receive information regarding a threat made to a student, they are expected to investigate to determine whether there is imminent danger involved. Failure to do so may lead to liability charges. Simply stated, there is no defense for failure to take reasonable steps to prevent foreseeable injury to students in school. Of course, prudent action is not required in the absence of foreseeability. It would, however, be difficult for school officials to make the case that they were unaware of a potentially dangerous situation when students and teachers were aware of it.

In loco parentis places an affirmative obligation on all certified school personnel to take necessary measures to ensure that the school environment is safe and conducive for students. Although the courts, in general, have fallen short of ruling that students have a constitutional right to be protected from harm, at least two courts have been willing to address this issue.

In the *Hosemann v. Oakland Unified School District* case, a California Superior Court judge ruled that Oakland public schools have an *affirmative duty* to alleviate crime and violence on school campuses.[1] This case involved two students, a theft, and an assault. The facts surrounding the case may not be as important as its outcome. This ruling represented the first one in which a court interpreted a state constitutional amendment that grants students and staff an "inalienable right" to attend campuses that are safe, secure, and crime free.

Subsequently, in the *Doe v. Taylor* case involving sexual abuse of a female student, the court exonerated the superintendent but not the principal, who should have known of the girl's constitutional right to be protected from sexual abuse. The court further held that a public school administrator in Texas had a duty to protect students from hazards of which he knew or should have known while students were under the school's functional custody.[2] These two cases fall short of holding school officials to a strict constitutional standard regarding safe campuses, but they do open the arena for further debate regarding the obligation school officials have in providing safe campuses, especially in light of the high incidence of crime and violence in public schools today. It would not be surprising to see courts become more stringent in their rulings involving school safety, as school violence continues to be present in the nation's public schools.

LIABILITY OF SCHOOL PERSONNEL

School personnel are responsible for their own tortious acts in the school environment. Liability involving school personnel normally falls into two categories: intentional and unintentional torts. *Intentional torts*—such as assault, battery, libel, slander, defamation, false arrest, malicious prosecution, and invasion of privacy—require proof of intent or willfulness; whereas an *unintentional tort*—such as simple negligence—does not require such proof of intent or willfulness. In each case, liability charges may be sustained if the facts reveal that school personnel acted improperly or failed to act appropriately in situations involving students.

Individual Liability

In certain situations, school personnel may be held individually liable for their actions that result in injury to a student. Individual liability will not usually occur unless the plaintiff can demonstrate that a school employee's action violated a clearly established law and that the employee exhibited a reckless disregard for the rights of the plaintiff.[3]

The Supreme Court held in the *Davis* case that officials are shielded from liability for civil damages if their conduct does not violate clearly established statutory or constitutional rights of which a reasonable person would have known at the time of the incident.[4] School personnel are not liable under the Civil Rights Act of 1871, Section 1983, unless they exhibited reckless disregard for the constitutional rights of students. As discussed in Chapter 3 in the *Wood v. Strickland* case, school board members may be held individually liable for damages under Section 1983 of the Civil Rights Act of 1871 when they violate the constitutional rights of students.

The U.S. Supreme Court clarified the conditions under which recovery for damages may be awarded in *Carey v. Piphus,* where two students were suspended for twenty days.[5] One was suspended for smoking marijuana on school property during school hours and the other for wearing an earring in violation of a school rule to discourage gang activity in the school. The court ruled that both students had been suspended in violation of the Fourteenth Amendment. Furthermore, school officials were not entitled to qualified immunity from damages. It was clear that they should have known that a lengthy suspension without a hearing violated due process of law. Therefore, liability is probable when students' constitutional rights are willfully violated by school officials.

An interesting case arose in Mississippi where the U.S. Court of Appeals for the Fifth Circuit held that a school district and its officials are not liable for a racially motivated attack during a high school football practice that resulted in a serious eye injury to an African American player.[6] Terry Priester, a high school athlete, argued that the coaching staff's actions and omissions constituted a conspiracy among the coaches and his assailant to deprive him of his federal civil rights under § 1983. He alleged that head coach Rick Cahalane derided him with racial epithets in front of teammates. As a result, Terry's assailant felt free to abuse him verbally and physically, often using the same derogatory terms. The eye injury occurred during a full-contact blocking drill, when the assailant stuck his hands through Terry's face mask and gouged his eye. The Fifth Circuit rejected Terry's attempt to demonstrate a conspiracy in order to establish that the assailant's actions amounted to state action. It concluded that Terry was unable to establish any of three exceptions to the general rule that the state's failure to protect an individual from private violence does not violate the individual's due process rights. The court dismissed Terry's argument that the coaches were state actors by virtue of the "special relationship" between students and teachers. The "special relationship" exception to the general rule applies only when a person is confined or restrained against his or her will by governmental order or the exercise of state power. The court also disposed of the "state-created danger" exception on the grounds that Terry had failed to raise this argument on appeal. Last, regarding the "fair attribution" exception, the assailant's actions were not fairly attributable to the state because there was no evidence of agreement between the coaches and the assailant for the assailant to attack Terry.

Vicarious Liability

Because school districts are deemed to be employers of teachers, districts also may be held vicariously liable for the negligent behavior of their employees. Under the old theory of **respondeat superior**, the master is responsible only for authorized acts of its servants or agents. As applied in **vicarious liability**, the board rather than the principal is held liable for the tortious acts of its teachers, even though the board is not at fault. There is a requirement, under vicarious liability, that the teacher is acting within the scope of his or her assigned duties. This concept is most prevalent in cases involving negligence where class action suits are brought not only against the teacher but also against the school district for alleged negligence by the teacher.

Foreseeability

Foreseeability is a crucial element in liability cases, especially in cases involving negligence. *Foreseeability* is defined as the ability of the teacher or administrator to predict or anticipate that a certain activity or situation may prove harmful to students. Once determined, the expectation is that prudent steps will be taken to prevent harm to students. Failure to act in a prudent manner may result in liability claims. Whether an injury is or is not foreseeable is a question of fact that is determined by a jury when deciding if liability should be imposed.

In many instances teachers and administrators are *expected to foresee* the potential danger associated with an activity or condition in the school. For example, if teachers or administrators observe broken glass panes in entry doors or in classrooms, it is foreseeable that a student, while entering the building or the room, might sustain an injury if contact is made with the broken glass. In this instance, school personnel have an obligation to warn students of the impending danger and to exercise caution to ensure that students are not injured in this potentially dangerous condition. Thus, the broken panes should be reported to the proper authority and repaired promptly.

Similar expectations would occur in situations involving defective playground equipment, loose stair rails, or other *nuisances* (unsafe conditions) present in the school environment. Also, if two students are observed fighting, it is foreseeable that one or both might sustain an injury. In this case, school personnel are obligated to take appropriate steps to prevent harm to the students involved, without harming themselves in the process.

Nuisance

A **nuisance** is any dangerous or hazardous condition that limits free use of property by the user. The existence of such a condition may require school personnel to exercise extra care to ensure that students are protected from possible harm. The implication suggested here is that school districts have an obligation to maintain safe premises for students under their supervision. School district personnel have the responsibility to inform students of unsafe conditions and to take steps to counsel students away from dangerous situations. Reasonable measures should be taken to remove or correct hazardous conditions as soon as they become known.

In some instances, the question of attractive nuisance arises. An *attractive nuisance* is a dangerous instrument or condition that has a special attraction to a less mature child who does not appreciate the potential danger and who could be harmed. The standard of care increases in attractive nuisance cases. An attractive nuisance claim will be supported if the evidence suggests one or more of the following:

1. Those responsible for the property knew or should have known that children would be attracted to the hazardous condition.
2. The responsible party knew that the hazardous condition posed an unreasonable risk to children.
3. Children, because of their youth, were unaware of the risk.
4. The utility to the owner of maintaining the risk and the cost of eliminating it were slight, as compared to the risk to children.
5. The owner failed to exercise reasonable care in eliminating the risk.[7]

Premises liability is based on the expectation that owners and possessors of buildings and grounds have a duty to their guests to maintain the premises in a reasonably safe condition. Negligence or failure to routinely inspect buildings or grounds to ensure that they are safe could result in injury to students, and claims of liability could be brought against the district and school personnel who have supervisory responsibilities. Negligence is usually not sustained unless school personnel carelessly created a hazardous condition or allowed it to continue after being informed of the existence of such a hazard.

Negligence claims may be supported, however, if the evidence reveals that school personnel should have been aware of the hazard and were not diligent in responding to it. According to one court, it is unreasonable to expect that school personnel be required to discover or instantly correct every defect that is not of their own creation.[8] Reasonable action is required in cases involving nuisances. The courts have not required school personnel to ensure that premises are safe at all times. If reasonable measures, such as routine and periodic inspections and repairs occur, unanticipated or unexplained accidents usually will not create liability charges against school personnel.

In most states, the level of care expected of those who oversee property is related to people who enter the property. These people are divided into three groups: invitees, licensees, and trespassers.

INVITEES.   An **invitee** is one who is present on the premises by invitation of the owner. There is an expectation that the property is safe for invitees. They should be protected from known hazards or those that should be known by the owner. Owners have an obligation to inspect the property to ensure that it is safe for invitees.

Aside from students and employees, invitees might include those who are on the school campus to conduct business (e.g., salespersons, parents, or community citizens who are invited to attend public school functions). There is no absolute duty to ensure that invitees are safe. Invitees also have a responsibility to exercise reasonable actions to care for themselves. If they observe a dangerous condition, the expectation is that they utilize necessary measures to protect themselves from harm.

Obviously, the degree of care regarding students would vary with age and maturity. If the student is mature enough to appreciate the danger and commits an act that results in injury, school personnel may succeed with *contributory negligence claims* against the student. If the student is not mature enough to appreciate the danger and incurs injury, based on unsafe conditions, successful liability claims may be brought against school officials.

LICENSEES. A **licensee** is a person who has the *privilege* to enter school property. School officials have a duty to warn licensees of any impending dangerous conditions found on school grounds and to take reasonable steps to protect them from harm. Licensees might include salespersons or community groups using school facilities but not by invitation. School officials must be aware that licensees are on school grounds. If their presence is unknown to school officials, it would be unreasonable to expect them to meet the standards as mentioned. Licensees generally assume risks in cases where the owner is unaware of any known hazards; they take the property as they find it.

TRESPASSERS. A *trespasser* is one who enters school property without consent. There is normally no obligation to protect trespassers who enter the property illegally. There is no duty of care owed trespassers, even in cases where dangerous conditions exist.

This would not hold true for students who return to campus after school hours to use playground equipment. School officials, in this case having knowledge that students return, must ensure that the equipment is in good repair and that known hazards on school grounds have been promptly corrected and students forewarned of their existence. In cases involving trespassers, school officials cannot *willfully or wantonly* harm the trespassers or *deliberately create* conditions to harm them. Such actions would not meet court scrutiny.

In sum, a property owner owes an invitee the duty of exercising reasonable care, a licensee the duty of not increasing danger, and trespasser the duty of not engaging in willful or wanton conduct.

Because of their duty, teachers and administrators have a higher *standard of care* and are expected to *foresee* an accident more readily than would the average person. One of the fundamental questions raised by the courts in a case involving injury to a student is whether the teacher or principal knew or should have known of the potential for harm to students. After an examination of facts, if the judge or jury determines that either should have known of the impending danger and failed to act appropriately, liability charges will likely be imposed. On the other hand, if the facts reveal that school personnel reasonably foresaw the potential danger associated with an activity or situation and took reasonable steps to remedy the danger, no liability would likely be imposed, even if injury occurred. Factual circumstances would determine if liability claims are warranted.

The other question the court would raise involving student injury is whether the injury could have been avoided had the teacher or administrator acted prudently. School personnel may not use the defense that they were unaware of the impending danger associated with a certain activity that resulted in injury to a student in cases where they should have been aware of such a danger.

Liability Involving Students and Bus Stops

The school bus and bus stops are generally viewed as extensions of the school for disciplinary purposes. Consequently, all school rules and regulations pertaining to student conduct also apply to student conduct at bus stops and on the bus. The school or district should have formulated student discipline policies, rules, and procedures governing student conduct at bus stops and on school buses. These policies, rules, and procedures, including consequences for specific infractions, should be clearly communicated to students and their parents. The school may use its normal disciplinary procedures involving misconduct at bus stops and school buses as they apply in the school setting.

Early courts have established that the seriousness of an offense rather than the place in which it occurs determines the right to punish the perpetrators. (See a full discussion in Chapter 3 regarding Student Discipline for Off-Campus Behavior.) Liability charges usually will not be levied against school leaders regarding student behavior at bus stops. School liability may apply when students actually board the bus. However, school leaders should respond to bus stop incidents when they are informed of these activities based on school or district policy. It is foreseeable that students may be injured under certain circumstances. Once foreseeability is established, reasonable action must be taken by school leaders and parents with the cooperation of bus drivers to prevent harm to students. School leaders and parents must ensure to the greatest extent possible that students at bus stops and on school-sponsored transportation are protected from foreseeable harm. In *Francis v. School Board of Palm Beach County*, the Florida Supreme Court held that school boards are not insurers of school safety. A school board's duty of care to students regarding transportation extends from when a bus picks up the student at a bus stop to when they reach the school door. This stems from the board's custody of the student.[9]

School Liability and Use of Technology by Students

In the modern age of technology, the use of electronic devices by students in public schools has escalated. Based on district policy, students may or may not access cell phones and other electronic devices during regular school hours. However, it is becoming apparent that these devices, if used properly, may enhance student achievement and assist teachers as an instructional tool. Students' use of technology throughout the school, in hallways, cafeterias, and other locations may create liability challenges for school leaders if they are aware that the use of technology by students has created a harmful effect on other students such as cyberbullying, texting, and sexting. Schools or school districts should develop, implement, and communicate technology use policies and vigorously enforce penalties against students who violate policies. Parents should be contacted and made aware of policy violations involving their children. School personnel have a leading responsibility to provide a safe educational environment for all students. If students are harmed by other students through cyberbullying or sexting and school personnel fail to respond to this type of behavior, then liability charges may be imminent. Questions that will likely be raised by the court include, were school personnel aware of this potentially harmful behavior or should they have been aware of it? Subsequently, what action was taken in response to the harmful act? Failure to act could result in liability challenges against school personnel.

Parental Access to School Premises

The distinction is clear between **trespass** and *parental access* to public school property. Parents have a legal right to visit schools, meet with teachers or administrators, and attend school-sponsored activities held on and off campus before and after normal school hours. Inherently, parents are afforded the privilege to do so. Unlike a trespasser who enters school property without permission, parents have the right to enter school premises. Consequently, school officials share responsibility for their safety. Unless the parent has exhibited behavior that has posed a threat to the safety of administrators, teachers, students, and staff, or the parent has consistently violated school policy and procedures regarding school visitations, the privilege to visit is maintained. If the parent has been issued a court order that bars school visits, he or she may be guilty of trespassing if the parent enters school grounds without permission or privilege. School officials have no official duty of care to trespassers found on school grounds, whereas such duty is expected for those who have a right or privilege to be there. This duty ensures that the property is safe for parents and others who are authorized, and many times invited, to visit school premises.

When parents visit schools, there is an obligation to address unsafe conditions prior to their arrival. Because they come by invitation, they must be protected from known hazards on campus. If unsafe conditions are found on school premises, visible warnings should be located in these areas, informing parents that potentially dangerous conditions exist and that caution should be exercised as they approach these areas. These steps will lessen the possibility of liability suits involving school officials and the school board.

INTENTIONAL TORTS

As explained previously, torts fall into two categories: intentional and unintentional. An *intentional tort* results from a *deliberate act* committed against another person. It may or may not be accompanied by malice. When there is no intent to harm another person but one proceeds intentionally in a manner that infringes on the rights of another, a tort has been committed. The law grants to each individual certain rights that must be respected by others. If by action or speech these rights are violated, resulting in injury, a tort has been committed.

The most common forms of intentional torts affecting school personnel include assault, battery, defamation, libel and slander, mental distress, false imprisonment, and trespassing on personal property.

Assault

An *assault* is an offer to use force in a hostile manner that causes apprehension. The person being assaulted normally must feel a degree of immediacy, in the sense that the one committing the assault will execute it promptly and has the apparent capacity to do so. An assault involves a threat to inflict harm to another person's body in an offensive manner. Each of the elements identified in the definition must be present to sustain assault charges. Therefore, all elements and facts relating to an alleged assault must be examined in detail to determine whether the assault is valid.

An assault is a tort committed against a person's mind, causing fear and apprehension for his or her safety. It may be verbal or exhibited through actions. The important issue in cases involving assault is that *no physical injury is necessary*. The mere *fear* for one's personal safety is sufficient to establish an assault.

Battery

A *battery* occurs when physical contact actually takes place. In practice, a battery is a successful assault. It involves *unwelcomed and unprivileged* body contact involving another person. This contact is normally considered to be *hostile and unlawful*. The assault generally precedes the battery. It is not uncommon for these two to be combined when charges are brought against the perpetrator.

Assault and battery affect teachers, administrators, and students in the school environment. Every person is responsible for his or her actions in cases involving assault and battery. Teachers and administrators are not only responsible for their own acts of assault and battery, most notably in instances involving the administration of corporal punishment, but also may be liable if they observe a student being assaulted or battered by others and fail to exercise proper steps to prevent injury. Charges may also be brought against teachers and administrators if they fail to act when it is foreseeable that one student may injure another based on threats and no action is taken to prevent possible injury.

Typically, cases involving a battery include an intent to make contact with another person. School personnel most commonly are charged with assault and battery when evidence indicates that they administered corporal punishment with malice or excessive force. The type of instrument used as well as considerations regarding the age, size, gender, and physical condition of the student also may be factors.

ASSAULT AND BATTERY INVOLVING PHYSICAL FIGHTS.   Assaults may be associated with physical fights when the actions of the person who initiates the fight are intended to place another person in apprehension of bodily harm. Assaults usually take the form of threats to inflict bodily harm to another, which causes the person assaulted to be apprehensive and fearful of injury. If physical contact is actually made in the form of a physical fight, the person who initiated the fight may be charged with assault and battery. The injured student may file suit against school personnel for damages resulting from injuries received in a physical attack by another student when there is evidence that they had prior knowledge that the student had been threatened prior to the actual physical attack. Under these circumstances, it is foreseeable that a physical attack might result in serious injury to the student who received the threat. School personnel have an obligation to take precautions to prevent physical attacks on students.

School officials may also be liable if two students mutually engage in a physical fight when there is prior knowledge that physical contact will occur. Again, it is foreseeable that one or both students might incur serious injury when engaged in physical confrontation. Prudence requires that all preventive measures be taken by school officials to prevent assaults and physical attacks involving students. Failure to do so may prove costly if injury results from offensive contact associated with physical contact involving students.

Defamation

Defamation occurs when false statements are made about another person. These statements generally tend to harm a person's good name or reputation or subject the person to hatred, contempt, or ridicule. To succeed in sustaining defamation charges, evidence must demonstrate that defamatory statements were communicated to a third party. If no third party is involved, there is no defamation. The most common forms of defamation are libel and slander.

Defamation derives from the belief that people have a right to expect their reputations to be free of false or malicious statements made by others. Teachers and administrators must be aware of liability claims that may stem from committing acts of defamation. Although school personnel enjoy what is referred to as a *qualified privilege,* this privilege does not permit them to make statements that do not meet the requirement of good faith. Certain statements are privileged if made in good faith and within the scope of the educator's duty.

Therefore, school personnel who expect to be protected by qualified privilege must not make false statements regarding students or colleagues with *malice* or the *intent to harm.* Statements made must be true and based on reasonable grounds. *Truth* as a defense against charges of defamation is valid only with absence of malice. School personnel do not have the right to publicize information regarding a student or colleague with the intent to maliciously injure that person, even if the statements are true.

The teacher's lounge appears to be one of the most popular places to spread rumors about students and colleagues. School personnel must understand that "off the cuff" statements about others that might injure someone's reputation or good standing in the school may form grounds for liability. Many times, teachers inadvertently share very sensitive information regarding a student's background, home conditions, or family history that may prove damaging to the student. Personal information regarding a student's record should be used exclusively by the teacher to assist the student in providing the best educational experiences possible and not shared with others who have no need to have access to this information. School personnel will experience difficulty making the claim that no harmful intent exists when very personal and sensitive information is shared with others who have no need to know. If the student affected is able to demonstrate that he or she has been harmed, held in low esteem by teachers, or shunned by others as a result of these comments, the student may have grounds for personal damages.

LIBEL AND SLANDER.   Defamation falls into two categories: libel and slander. **Slander** is considered oral defamation, whereas *libel* is considered written defamation. Both include statements or communication that result in injury to a person's reputation, good name, or standing in the school or community. As previously stated, a third party must be privileged to this communication to establish defamation. The burden of proof rests with the person who claims injury. If claims are successful, they will usually result in monetary damages. However, four categories of slander are considered defamatory on their own merits. The person affected by these statements need not prove damages when statements are made regarding *criminal behavior, professional or job incompetency, possession of a contagious disease* (e.g., AIDS), and *unchastity in a woman.* The very nature of these statements may result in injury to one's good name, reputation, or esteem or may cause others to ostracize the affected person. (See Chapter 7 for a discussion of libel and slander.)

DEFENSES AGAINST DEFAMATION

The most common defenses cited against defamation are privilege, good faith, and truth.

Privilege

Because education is of great public interest, courts have generally recognized the importance of statements made by school personnel in executing their official duty. They enjoy some degree of freedom as long as they have an interest in the information and act in good faith. It is important to remember that qualified privilege is not without limits. Certain statements must be made within the scope of the educators' duty. One court stated that qualified privilege is established where there is no evidence that statements were made based solely on personal spite, ill will, or culpable recklessness or negligence.[10] In this instance, there is no recovery. When educators operate within these parameters, they will generally be supported by the courts. However, if they act unreasonably with indefensible motives, there is no protection, and they are open to legal challenges.

Good Faith

Good faith is essential in establishing a qualified privilege. Educators only enjoy qualified privilege when there is evidence that they acted in good faith and without an intent to harm others. As previously cited, statements should also be made within the scope of their official duties. Again, these statements should be based on reasonable grounds and not motivated by ill will or spite. Because educators occupy professional positions that influence the lives of children, there is an expectation that their actions are guided by good faith. Educators should always demonstrate sensitivity and a concern for protecting the personal rights and interests of students when responding to requests for information involving students.

Since the passage of the Freedom of Information Act in 1966, statements attributed to public school officials while serving in their official capacities are subject to disclosure. Students are not required to waive their rights to examine statements made about them by school personnel. In fact, they have the option to examine these statements, if they so choose. Qualified privilege will be supported if statements are reasonable and made without malice in one's official professional capacity.

Truth

Truth is generally considered a defense against charges involving defamation. In other words, if the person making the statement is doing so based on information believed to be accurate and reasonable, courts will generally recognize these statements as being nondefamatory in nature. However, if there is evidence that malice was involved, statements that are true will not be supported as a defense. For example, educators are frequently called on to provide references for students as well as colleagues. Inquiries may be made regarding personal traits, personality, and overall fitness.

Educators should be very careful not to express opinions about students or colleagues that might be damaging without having the qualifications to make such statements. Any statements regarding another's mental, psychological, or emotional status are very risky and should be avoided. Educators should only provide reasonable information based on good faith for which they are qualified to make. Even though truth is a defense against defamation claims, it is not absolute. If statements are made about another that will automatically result in injury to that person's reputation, truth may not be a reasonable defense. Statements involving marital status, sexual preference, or contagious diseases—even if they are true—may result in defamation charges, if individuals against whom these statements are made can prove that they were damaged.

Mental Distress

Charges of mental distress usually arise when one exhibits conduct that exceeds the acceptable boundaries of decency. It is a form of tort liability that is construed to create mental anguish of a serious nature. Historically, it has been difficult to prove mental distress in the absence of some type of physical injury. This situation has changed in recent years, however.

School personnel may be charged with mental distress if there is evidence that their behavior or conduct was calculated to cause serious emotional distress for students. School personnel typically are charged with inflicting mental distress when they use an unreasonable and unorthodox method of discipline designed to embarrass students or cause them to be ridiculed or humiliated in the presence of their peers. Punishing students by requiring them to walk around the building with books on their heads, standing for long periods of time with one foot raised, standing and facing the corner of the room, or placing students in a locked closet are examples of actions that may cause mental distress and that might prove difficult to defend as reasonable actions.

As stated in Chapter 3, courts will allow school personnel to discipline students as long as the discipline is reasonable and consistent with school or district policy. Many legal experts believe that actions by school personnel designed to embarrass students may be more damaging than physical harm. A student's self-esteem may be seriously damaged at a time when it should be growing and expanding. This is not intended to suggest that teachers or administrators cannot admonish a student in the classroom or hallway in front of his or her peers. This issue was clearly addressed in *Gordon v. Oak Park School District No. 97,* which involved a verbal lashing administered to a student by the teacher. The Illinois Appellate Court held that such action by the teacher did not result in the teacher's being held liable. The court recognized that within the broad delegation of parental authority, a teacher has the right to verbally chastise a student.

The teacher, however, may be held liable if the evidence reveals that there was an intentional act committed with the intent to humiliate or degrade when it is accompanied by proof of wantonness or malice.[11] The implication suggested in this case is that disciplinary methods that are deemed necessary should be carried out in a *reasonable manner,* providing the greatest degree of respect for the student.

An illustration of what a teacher might face when poor judgment is exercised is found in the *Celestine v. Lafayette Parish School Board* case. A teacher was dismissed when it was determined that poor judgment and a lack of educational purpose resulted in the teacher's requiring students to write a vulgar word 1,000 times in the presence of their classmates as a disciplinary measure for having uttered the word.[12] In many cases, students will rebel when they feel embarrassed by the action of the teacher or principal in the presence of their peers.

Another troublesome incident involving poor judgment of a teacher occurred recently when a Fairfax County private school teacher was found guilty of assault charges when she taped a student's hands and mouth with masking tape as punishment for waking other students during nap time. A similar incident occurred in a Florida middle school where a teacher taped two students to a desk and a wall with masking tape. This teacher resigned after the parents filed a complaint. Mental distress is a relatively new tort, but one that should be taken seriously by school personnel. (Defamation is also discussed in more detail in Chapter 7 regarding student records.)

False Imprisonment

If a student is confined by school personnel, there should be a reasonable basis for doing so and the confinement must be viewed as reasonable. *False imprisonment* occurs when a student is detained illegally by the teacher or the principal. It is considered an *intentional tort*. If a student is wrongfully detained for an unreasonable period of time for offensive behavior that does not warrant detention, a tort has occurred. False imprisonment is not considered a major liability issue, but it is one that could prove difficult for school personnel, if evidence shows that detention was in violation of school or district policy and carried out with malice toward the student. Thus, school or district policy should serve as a guide in these situations.

Teachers and administrators may detain students and prevent their participation in playground activities, recess, and certain other extracurricular activities. They may detain students after school if the offense is clearly one that warrants detention and if parents are aware of the planned detention so that proper arrangements can be made to transport the student after the detention period has ended. Students should never be denied lunch breaks as a form of punishment.

In Virginia, a Fourteenth Amendment claim regarding detention arose in which the U.S. Court of Appeals for the Fourth Circuit declined to require that school officials notify parents prior to detaining their child or to ban detentions of a certain length when school officials are investigating a serious allegation of student misconduct.[13] The court held that school officials did not violate a parent's Fourteenth Amendment right to due process by failing to notify her that her child was being detained and questioned, initially by school administrators and later by local police. The court concluded further that the detention of the student was necessary to investigate reports that she possessed a weapon and did not violate her Fourth Amendment right to freedom from unreasonable seizures.

On the Wednesday before the Thanksgiving holiday, several students at Colonial Elementary School in Botetourt County, Virginia, reported that M. D. brought a gun to school. Acting on the reports, an assistant principal detained M. D. for questioning, during which M. D. allowed the assistant principal to search her book bag and classroom desk. When no gun was found, M. D. was released to go home. However, on the Monday after the holiday, the assistant principal and principal continued the investigation by reinterviewing students. One student claimed he saw M. D. dispose of the gun in the woods adjacent to the school. School officials contacted local police and detained M. D. for further questioning. M. D. later claimed that during questioning by both the police and school officials, she requested them to contact her mother, but they failed to do so. After the police failed to recover the gun, they ended the questioning and contacted M. D.'s mother. M. D. and her mother sued the school administrators, the school board, and sheriff's department officers in federal district court, which dismissed both the due process and the illegal seizure claims. The Fourth Circuit affirmed this decision, rejecting the plaintiffs' contention that detention required parental notification. Such a rule, the court held, would lead to "over-constitutionalizing disciplinary procedures" and interfere with the well-established judicial principle of allowing school officials leeway to maintain order on school premises and provide a safe environment. Addressing the due process claim, the court concluded that the federal "constitution does not impose a duty of parental notification before the pupil's disciplinary detainment" while the student remains under the school's guardianship. As to the Fourth Amendment claim, the court determined under the standard established by the U.S. Supreme Court in *New Jersey v. T.L.O.*[14] that school officials had reasonable grounds to believe M. D. had brought a gun to school in violation of the law and school rules and that, based on the account given by the student witness, M. D.'s detention was reasonable in scope.

Trespassing on Personal Property

Trespassing on personal property is a tort that involves confiscating or interfering with the use of a student's personal property without proper authority. This is not an area that normally generates legal action but, rather, one that school personnel should be mindful of because it most commonly involves teachers and administrators.

This intentional tort occurs frequently when school personnel confiscate various items from students during the school day. Many of these items may be in violation of school rules, may create disruption, or may cause harm to the student in possession of the item or to other students.

Teachers and administrators have the right to confiscate such items, but they do not have the right to keep or retain them for an unreasonable period of time. If such an item is considered dangerous, the student's parent or guardian should be contacted and informed of the potential danger. Arrangements should be made with the parent or guardian to ensure that the item is not returned to the student.

Nonthreatening items should be returned to the student as soon as possible, with instructions not to return them to school. If the item is not in violation of school policy, dangerous, or disruptive to the educational process, school personnel have no right to confiscate the item. Even in instances where confiscation is justified, the property belongs to the student and should not be detained and discarded at the end of the year simply because the teacher or administrator failed to remember from whom it was confiscated or merely decided rather arbitrarily that the item(s) should not be returned. In no case should the student's property be damaged or destroyed by school personnel. Generally, no serious charge stems from this type of tort, but it is important that school personnel project the image of respect for the personal property of others and fundamental fairness in their dealings with students in the school.

UNINTENTIONAL TORTS

An *unintentional tort* is a wrong perpetrated by someone who fails to exercise the proper degree of care in doing what is otherwise permissible (i.e., acts negligently). Negligence is perhaps the most prevalent source of litigation involving injury to students. Many cases regarding negligence in school settings are class action in nature, implicating teachers, principals, and boards of education. Defendants in these cases are usually released from the suit if facts reveal that they played no significant role in the injury.

Negligence is generally viewed as the failure to exercise a reasonable standard of care that results in harm or injury to another person. Most negligence cases involve civil wrongs, although there may be instances in which the accused faces both civil and criminal charges. In cases involving wanton negligence, such as injuries sustained by others based on violation of traffic laws, criminal charges may be appropriate, depending on the specific circumstances relating to the injury.

For example, when charges of negligence are sought by an injured student, certain requirements must be met. The student bringing the charges must be able to prove that four elements were present. Failure to establish each of the following elements invalidates charges of liability:

Standard of care: The teacher or principal owed a legal duty to protect the student by conforming to certain standards.

Breach of duty: The teacher or principal failed to meet these standards (duty of care).

Proximity or legal cause: The student must be able to demonstrate *proximate cause* (i.e., that a causal relationship existed between the breach of duty and the actual injury sustained by the student).

Injury: The student must prove actual injury based on a breach of duty by the teacher or principal.

Standard of Care

Standard of care is an important concept in cases involving liability of school personnel. It requires that school personnel exercise the same degree of care that other professional educators holding similar positions would exercise under the same or similar conditions. This standard of care will vary depending on particular circumstances. The level of care due students changes based on the age, maturity, experience, and mental capacity of students, as well as the nature of the learning activities in which they are involved.

For example, the standard of care for teachers of kindergarten or early primary grade students is usually higher than that for teachers of senior high students, due to differences in age levels, maturity, and experience. Likewise, the standard of care for a chemistry laboratory teacher or a physical education teacher is greater than that for an English teacher, based on the nature of the activities and the potential danger faced by students who are engaged during the instructional period.

As the Indiana Supreme Court stated, the standard of care that may be adequate when dealing with adults generally will not be sufficient when dealing with students. The court observed, "The relationship of school pupils and school authorities should call into play the well-recognized duty in tort law that people entrusted with children or others whose characteristics make it likely that they may do somewhat unreasonable things have a special responsibility recognized by the common law to supervise their charges."[15]

Courts are aware that children do not possess the same level of maturity, insight, caution, and knowledge as do adults and, therefore, may not be judged by the same standard of care required by adults. This realization by the courts places a higher standard on educators to ensure that they are exercising the level of maturity and judgment that will be viewed as prudent. Standard of care becomes an important consideration in determining whether school personnel are liable in specific situations involving students under their supervision.

The courts do not expect educators to assume unreasonable personal risks to prevent all conceivable harm to students. To do so would amount to an insurer's role. However, there is an expectation that educators exhibit behavior that meets the standard that a reasonable, mature, and intelligent person would meet in the same or similar situation. Interestingly, state statutes vary regarding the standard of care prescribed for educators. Many states simply require that this standard be that of a reasonable parent. Illinois law, however, requires willful and wanton misconduct by educators—a much more liberal standard than is found in most other states. Failure to meet a prescribed duty of care resulting in injury to students may result in liability. However, liability would not exist in situations in which accidents occurred that were unavoidable or unforeseeable. The courts simply expect educators to exercise reasonable judgment in their dealings with students to ensure to the greatest degree possible that they are protected from harm. The following case illustrates what can occur when a reasonable standard of care and foreseeability is not met.

Two New York sisters were assaulted and injured by a group of students and nonstudents as they attempted to leave their high school after classes. Prior to the assault, one of the sisters had been threatened by one of the guilty students. This incident had been reported to a teacher, who failed to take any action. One of the sisters attempted to enter the security department to report the assault and found it closed. The sisters filed a lawsuit against the city of New York and the city board of education, alleging negligent supervision. At trial, evidence indicated that no security officers were at their posts during the time of the assault. The jury returned a verdict of $750,000 for one of the sisters and $50,000 for the other against the city and the board of education. The court granted the school board's motion to set aside the verdict and dismiss the complaint. However, the New York Supreme Court, Appellate Division, reversed this decision.

The court of appeals found sufficient evidence to establish liability for negligent supervision. The evidence revealed that the teacher was aware of the assault and the school's security policy had not been enforced at the time of the assault. Schools have a duty to adequately supervise students and are *liable for foreseeable injuries related to inadequate supervision.* The court affirmed the appellate division's decision.[16] As can be seen from the *Mirand* case involving the two sisters, failure to exercise due care in situations involving students can be very costly. Reasonable and prudent actions by the teacher and security office would likely have prevented harm to the assault victims.

Breach of Duty

Breach of duty is determined in part based on the nature of the activity for which the educator is held responsible. Various school activities require different levels of supervision. The question normally posed by courts regarding breach is whether the conduct of school personnel met the standard of care required in a given situation. The second issue involves a determination as to whether school personnel should have foreseen possible injury. The fact that a student is injured in a given situation does not necessarily imply that a breach of duty has occurred. School personnel are not insurers against all possible harm to students. They are, however, expected to take prudent steps, based on their duty to students, to prevent harm when it is reasonably foreseeable that students might be harmed. Failure to act in this instance would constitute a breach of duty.

The following case illustrates an unsuccessful breach of duty claim by a student. A New Hampshire school administrator and guidance counselors were not liable for the suicide of a student with learning disabilities who had experienced problems at his middle school.[17] During the student's seventh-grade year, a teacher's aide overheard him say that he "wanted to blow his brains out." She reported this information to the guidance counselor who called the student's mother. She offered to pick up her son at school, but the counselor said he was "okay now" and sent him back to his class. Without informing the mother, the guidance counselor had the student sign a contract for safety. However, she took no other action in response to the suicide threat. The next day, the student was reported to the vice principal and suspended for tipping a desk, being rude, and calling another teacher a bitch. After the suspension, the student returned home, went to his room, and hanged himself. His mother later sued the school administrator, a teacher, and the guidance counselor in state court for negligence, intentional infliction of emotional distress, and wrongful death. A state superior court dismissed the case. The mother appealed. The appellate court held that schools have a special relationship with students entrusted to their care and as such they have a duty of reasonable supervision—and not a duty that extends so far as to prevent the student's suicide in this case. A duty to prevent a suicide may exist in a jail or juvenile detention facility but not at school. As a result, the judgment was affirmed.

Proximate Cause

Proximate cause occurs when a causal relationship existed between the breach of duty and the actual injury sustained by the student. If a student is injured and the injury is not related to the teacher or administrator's failure to exercise the proper standard of care, no liability is involved. *There must be evidence that links the injury directly to failure of educators to act prudently in a given situation.* One issue courts would likely raise is whether the actual injury was based on the teacher or administrator's behavior. If the evidence reveals that the teacher or administrator's behavior played a direct and substantial role in the injury, proximate cause has been established.

For example, if a teacher is absent from the classroom for a brief period of time and an injury occurs in the teacher's absence, was the injury directly related to the teacher's absence—that is, could the injury have been avoided had the teacher been present? If a student is accidentally stuck with a pencil when he is pushed by another student attempting to use the pencil sharpener in the teacher's absence, might this injury have been avoided if the teacher had been present? Could she have prevented one student from pushing the other and causing his injury? Was this act reasonably foreseeable? Had there been prior pushing incidents involving students using the pencil sharpener? If the response to these questions is yes, then proximate cause has likely been established. There is no set rule for determining when an act is sufficiently connected to an injury. An analysis of facts and circumstances surrounding the injury would be factors considered by the courts.

Injury

If no harm or injury is suffered by a student, there is no liability. To establish liability, evidence must reveal that actual injury resulted either from acts committed by school personnel or their failure to act prudently in a given situation. The person claiming injury must demonstrate that he or she received an injury and that some compensatory damages are related to the injury. The courts will normally award compensatory damages, except in cases of wanton or willful negligence, in which case punitive damages may be considered.

A case involving class action liability arose in Indiana. Nick King, a student at North Central High School, was brutally beaten by four other students in the school's parking lot.[18] Nick sued Washington Township and Northeast Security Company, a company hired by the district to provide security on school grounds to prevent negligence. The Indiana Supreme Court ruled for the student in holding that both the school district and security firm could be held liable for failure to take reasonable steps to provide adequate security against criminal acts of third parties. The court held that the district cannot be sued for failure to prevent crime but may be held legally responsible for failure to take reasonable safety precautions. Finally, the court concluded that the security firm could be held liable for negligence in carrying out its contractual obligation to the district. This case illustrates that negligence is negligence even when external contractual firms are involved. The lack of proper security by the school district and negligence by the security firm were linked to this severe injury received by the student.

DEFENSES FOR NEGLIGENCE

Various defenses are used by school personnel to reduce or eliminate the impact of liability charges. These defenses are used, even in cases where the four elements of negligence (listed previously) are present.

Contributory Negligence

If the evidence reveals that a person claiming injury exhibited conduct that fell below a reasonable standard, liability charges against school personnel may be abrogated. If, by action or decision, the student contributed to any injury received, the courts may find school personnel innocent of liability charges under many state laws.

The following examples illustrate cases where students were found to be contributorily negligent:

1. A student was found guilty of contributory negligence when he was injured by a flare-up of certain chemicals that he mixed together with the knowledge that they were dangerous.[19]
2. A high school student was injured while running in the dark after the lights went off in the school building.[20]
3. After convincing their chemistry teacher to allow them to acquire some potassium chlorate, two students were injured after knowingly mixing the potassium chlorate and powdered sugar, producing an explosive charge.[21]
4. A student was injured when he stole an oxidizing agent from the school's science lab, which resulted in a fire at his home, causing serious burns to his legs.[22]

Contributory negligence is probably the most common defense employed in charges of negligence. When a teacher or administrator is charged with negligence, neither will be assessed monetary awards when contributory negligence is proven. However, there is a common law presumption regarding the incapacity of students to be contributorily negligent. Common law **precedent** suggests that a child under the age of seven years cannot be charged with contributory negligence. With children between the ages of seven and fourteen years, there is a reasonable assumption that they are incapable of contributory negligence. A child beyond the age of fourteen years may be assumed to be contributorily negligent, depending on the facts surrounding the injury.

The age limits described are not absolute. They typically serve as guides in assessing whether contributory negligence did occur. The actions of school personnel, the intelligence of the student(s) involved, and the level of maturity are critical factors in the jury's deliberations. A question of prudence would also be relevant in contributory negligence cases. In any injury situation, did the student act as any other reasonable and prudent student of similar intelligence and maturity would have acted in the same situation? If the student did not exercise prudence and was injured based on unreasonable behavior, there would normally be no liability assessed by the courts. The following case illustrates the application of contributory negligence involving injury to a student.

A group of five students persuaded a custodian (who was very reluctant) to allow them access to play a game of basketball in the gymnasium during the Christmas holidays. Morris Albers was the leader of the group. After the custodian opened the door to the gymnasium, he proceeded with his cleaning duties. Morris assumed the responsibility for cleaning the playing surface while the other boys changed clothes. The boys then engaged in warm-up activities using two worn basketballs that they found lying in the gym, because the equipment room was locked. Morris was wearing standard basketball shoes and was a member of the high school basketball team, as was one of the other boys. After warming up, the boys divided into two teams to play a half-court game. Morris's statements indicated that the game was clean with respect to fouls and heavy body contact.

During the half-court game, a shot came off the backboard and headed toward the out-of-bounds line on the east side of the gym. Morris and an opposing player raced for the loose ball. As Morris reached to pick it up, the two collided, with Morris hitting his head against the opponent's hip. Morris fell to the floor on his back in a semiconscious state. On examination, a determination was made that he had suffered a fracture in the cervical area of his spine, which necessitated corrective surgery and extended hospitalization.

Morris brought suit against the district, claiming that the district breached its duty to supervise the basketball game. The facts clearly revealed that school was not in session and there was no duty to supervise. It was further determined that the boys had no authority to be in the gym but had persuaded a reluctant custodian to allow them to enter. In addition, no evidence suggested that the accident would have been avoided had there been actual supervision. Morris's injury, although accidental, was attributed to his own actions in entering the gym and engaging in playing basketball.[23]

Assumption of Risk

Assumption of risk is commonly used as a defense in situations involving various types of contact-related activities such as athletic teams, pep squads, and certain intramural activities. The theory supporting an assumption of risk is that students assume an element of risk to participate and benefit from the activity in which they wish to participate. In addition, they have knowledge and an understanding of the potential damage involved in participating in the particular activity. Even though a student assumes an element of risk, it does not relieve school personnel in cases where they fail to meet a reasonable standard of care based on the age, maturity, risk, and nature of the risk associated with the activity. The following case illustrates how a court responds to assumption-of-risk claims when evidence indicates negligence by a school district.

A New York student participated on his high school wrestling team and was instructed before a match to wrestle an opponent in the next higher weight class. The student agreed to do so and was injured when the opponent hit his jaw during a take-down maneuver. The student voluntarily continued participating in the match after a medical time-out. He later filed a personal injury lawsuit in district court against the school district, which denied the district's dismissal motion.[24] On appeal, the New York Supreme Court stated that the student had assumed the risk of incurring a blow to the jaw and that the injury was reasonably foreseeable in a wrestling match. Evidence showed that the size of the opponent had not caused the injury and that the student was aware of the risks involved in wrestling. The trial court judgment was reversed.

In assumption-of-risk cases, it must be established that the informed student knew of the risk involved and voluntarily elected to participate. Under assumption of risk, school personnel are expected to exercise prudence and to reasonably foresee that injury could result, based on either a lack of proper instruction, an absence of reasonable supervision, or improper decisions regarding the injured student.

Thus, assumption of risk does not relieve school personnel of executing their duty to instruct, supervise, and provide for the safety of students under their supervision. For example, if a wrestling coach does not properly teach sound techniques of wrestling or fails to provide proper medical support for an injured student, he or she may be charged with liability, although the activity itself carried some degree of risk. In numerous cases assumption of risk has been present, but school personnel were charged because of their own negligence. The following examples are illustrations of cases in which students were injured and school personnel found negligent for failure to meet a standard of care:

1. A woodworking instructor allowed a student to operate a table saw without the use of a safeguard, which resulted in serious damage to his proximal interphalangeal joint.[25]
2. A student dislocated his shoulder during an intramural football game when the school provided no protective equipment and improper supervision of the game.[26]
3. An eleven-year-old student suffered serious head injuries from a blow to the head during a kickball game and was without medical attention for more than an hour. The one-hour delay caused a hematoma to grow from the size of a walnut to that of an orange.[27]
4. An eight-year-old girl was seriously burned when her costume caught fire from a lighted candle on her teacher's desk.[28]
5. A twelve-year-old boy was killed when he fell through a skylight at school while retrieving a ball.[29]
6. A boy was seriously injured while playing on school grounds when he fell into a hole filled with glass, trash, and other debris, due to the absence of school officials to warn him of the dangerous condition.[30]
7. A female student was en route to class when she pushed her hand through a glass panel in a smoke-colored door, causing severe and permanent damage.[31]
8. A high school student was seriously injured when he was tackled and thrown to the ground during a touch football game in gym class, based on inadequate supervision when the players began to use excessive force.[32]

Assumption of risk is a valid defense only when school personnel met the duty of care expected in a given situation.

Comparative Negligence

Comparative negligence, a relatively new concept, has grown in popularity in many states. It differs from contributory negligence in the sense that slight negligence by the plaintiff or injured party does not relieve the defendant or persons who may have greatly contributed to the injury.

Under comparative negligence, acts of those responsible are compared in the *degree of negligence* attributed in an injury situation. Juries will normally determine the degree of negligence, which may range from slight to ordinary to gross, depending on the circumstances. The jury will make a determination regarding the degree to which each party has contributed to an injury. If one party is found to have contributed more heavily to an injury than another, then that party will be assessed a greater proportion for damages. It does not prevent recovery by the injured party but merely reduces the damages based on the fault of the injured persons. Comparative negligence may be illustrated by the following examples:

1. Two students injured each other during an off-campus fight after school.
2. Two students chased a fly ball during a softball game, causing a collision in which both received injury.

3. While one high school student was speeding in his automobile, another ran a stop sign, causing injury to both students.
4. A student was injured when he climbed a ladder that had been left leaning against the building, although he was instructed not to go near the ladder.
5. A student was injured when he ran, at an excessive rate of speed, through a glass panel at the end of the gymnasium floor.
6. A student lost two teeth in a gymnasium fall when he slipped, as a result of not using gym shoes. He had been told that he could participate in gym activities if he wished to do so.

If the jury determines that both parties, through their individual acts, contributed equally to the injury, then neither party is assessed damages. Comparative negligence will increasingly become popular in school settings based on the growing tendency of state legislatures to adopt it as a legal concept. It is considered by many legal experts to be the fairest method of assessing liability because it places proportional responsibility on both or all parties and apportions responsibility based on the degree of fault exhibited by each party involved in the injury. The following case illustrates the application of comparative negligence.

A fourteen-year-old Arkansas student exited his school bus and proceeded to walk to his family's mailbox. The bus driver turned off the bus safety devices and proceeded down the highway. As the boy attempted to cross the street, he was struck by a logging truck. The student's estate brought a wrongful death action against the school district. The jury determined that there was negligence by both the school district and the student. The jury assessed responsibility to the school district at 90 percent and the student at 10 percent.

The school district appealed to the Supreme Court of Arkansas. The district contended that the truck driver's operation of the logging truck was the primary cause of the student's death and that any negligence by the school district did not cause the student's death. The facts revealed that the Arkansas Department of Education school bus driver's handbook stated explicitly that the bus should not move until the student had safely crossed the road. The court noted that this policy was not followed. Therefore, the truck driver's operation was not independent of the bus driver's negligent acts. The court affirmed the decision of the lower court.[33]

Immunity

Immunity as a legal concept has diminished in terms of impact. It is based on the old common law of **sovereign immunity**—"The King can do no wrong"—meaning that the state or federal government is protected from suit and cannot be held liable for injuries that resulted in the proper execution of **governmental functions**. This doctrine was extended to school districts, because they are involved in state action and are agents of the state.

Some states have abrogated school board immunity, but others recognize the concept based on whether an activity is classified as *governmental* or *proprietary*. For example, if the activity is considered **proprietary**, liability may be imposed based on the facts involving negligence. Proprietary activities are normally those in which admission fees are charged.

One court defined proprietary in this manner: "In general . . . it has been said that if a given activity is one which a local government unit is not statutorily required to perform, or if it may also be carried out by private enterprise, or it is used as a means of raising revenue, the function is proprietary."[34]

Other states use the terminology *ministerial* and *discretionary* in determining whether liability may be imposed on school boards. **Ministerial** (governmental) acts are those required by state mandate or local school board policy and ones for which school personnel do not exercise choice. Examples of *ministerial acts* may include the following:

1. Providing school-sponsored transportation for certain students
2. Holding public and open board of education meetings
3. Taking and reporting attendance

4. Reporting suspected cases of child abuse
5. Developing a school calendar

In these examples, local school districts or schools are obligated to perform these duties, some of which may not be delegated.

On the other hand, discretionary acts are those for which school personnel may exercise judgment. Examples of *discretionary acts* may include the following:

1. Deciding to hold field day activities
2. Deciding whether to allow outside groups to use school facilities before or after school
3. Deciding on the nature of field trip experiences for students
4. Determining what extracurricular organizations should be sponsored by the school

These activities involve planning, assessment, and the exercise of judgment. Difficulties often arise based on the manner in which states classify these functions. Some states consider all school district activities to be governmental, whereas others do not. This sometimes creates confusion and difficulty in addressing immunity issues.

Although immunity exists to a limited degree in some states, teachers and administrators may or may not be covered by this concept. They are considered employees of the board and thus may be responsible for their individual tortious acts. They cannot rely on immunity as a defense to their individual acts that result in injury to students, unless state statutes abrogate liability when they are engaged in assigned school functions. Some courts have also waived immunity by school boards who have acquired liability insurance.

IMMUNITY COSTS.   School personnel are well advised to affiliate with their state and national educational associations, because membership carries liability protection for its members during the execution of their professional duties. This obviously should not be the primary motivation for becoming affiliated but should be considered as an important aspect of membership.

PROPER INSTRUCTION AND STUDENT SAFETY

Teachers have a legal duty to instruct students on the proper use of equipment and materials in laboratories. Instruction is extremely critical regarding activities that pose a risk to safety for students. Physical education classes, intramural sports, science, and vocational laboratories are areas that are particularly susceptible to potential injury to students. Therefore, the standard of care is greater for teachers who supervise these types of activities. Teachers must be certain that students are properly trained in the use of equipment and laboratory materials. In addition, the teacher must, to the greatest degree possible, provide sufficient supervision to ensure that students are following their instruction. Teachers have a defense only if they can adequately demonstrate that proper instruction was provided prior to allowing students to use equipment or laboratory materials and that they supervised activities to ensure that their instructions were followed. The following cases illustrate the consequences of not providing proper instruction and supervision.

The Supreme Court of Nebraska held in *Norman v. Ogallala Public School District* that a school district has a duty to ensure that students wear protective clothing while engaged in acetylene welding projects. A student was severely burned when his loose-fitting cotton shirt caught on fire while operating a welding torch. The court found that the district did not comply with standards of the American Welding Society that had been adopted by the American National Standards Institute calling for special clothing to reduce combustibility. This, along with expert testimony, was sufficient for the court to conclude that the district failed to foresee possible harm to students who did not wear protective clothing. It also failed to provide proper instruction regarding proper clothing. The school district's failure was the proximate cause of the student's injury.[35]

In a contrasting case, a shop teacher was relieved of liability when the evidence revealed that he had provided proper instruction in the use of a power saw in a shop class. A student lost several fingers when he used the saw improperly by failing to follow instruction provided by the teacher, who had given detailed instruction in the use of the machine. In fact, the teacher spent more than twenty minutes demonstrating the proper use of the saw. The court concluded that the teacher's actions were not the proximate cause of the student's injury.[36]

In another case, a teacher was held liable for failure to properly instruct physical education students on proper techniques involving various exercise routines. A sixth-grade student was injured when she attempted a vertical jump that resulted in her colliding with a wall. Based on the evidence, the teacher failed to demonstrate how the vertical jump should be performed. In addition, she failed to provide proper directions regarding this particular exercise. The teacher's action was the proximate cause of the student's injury.[37]

DUTIES OF SUPERVISION

All teachers and administrators are expected to provide reasonable supervision of students under their charge. The degree of supervision will vary with each situation. The less mature the students, the greater the need will be for supervision. The greater the potential for injury to students engaging in certain activities, the greater the need will be for supervision.

Whether school personnel have adequately fulfilled their duty of supervision is a question of fact for a jury to decide. Each case rests on its merits. Reasonable supervision is established when a jury decides it based on facts presented. Because standards of care vary depending on each unique situation, adequate supervision in one situation may be totally inadequate in a different situation. Courts will consider such factors as the nature of the activity involved, the age and number of students engaged in the activity, and the quality of supervision.

Before School

School personnel have a responsibility to provide some form of supervision for students who arrive on campus before the normal school day begins. The amount of supervision would depend on the circumstances involving early-arriving students. For example, foreseeability is established when a group of students arrives early on campus without some form of supervision. Teachers and administrators are expected to foresee that students might be harmed if no form of supervision is provided. The same principle would apply for students who are retained on campus after school, waiting for their parents to arrive. Once foreseeability has been established, it is necessary to ensure that reasonable and prudent measures be taken.

There is no expectation that teachers and administrators guarantee that students will never be injured in either case. Certainly, this would be impossible to achieve. What must be demonstrated, however, is that reasonable measures have been and are taken, based on foreseeable harm to students. For example, there would be no expectation that teachers and administrators arrive on campus during unreasonable hours to provide supervision. Although the courts have not addressed the time frame issue, per se, it would be a factor in deciding if teachers or administrators failed to meet a reasonable standard of supervision.

Certainly, parents should be informed in writing that school personnel are not available during the very early morning hours to supervise students. Parents should be discouraged from bringing their children to campus during these early hours. Although these steps should be taken, they do not in themselves totally relieve teachers and administrators of supervisory responsibilities. The courts will usually reason that students' presence on campus is not based on their own choices. They are there because of parents' decisions.

Administrators have the responsibility for ensuring that the campus is safe for early-arriving students. Students and their parents should be informed of the behavior that is expected of students when arriving before or remaining after school. Once students are informed, some type of periodic supervision should occur to ensure that students are exhibiting proper conduct and are not engaged in potentially harmful activities.

Liability involving school personnel for injury sustained before the school day begins would be based on a number of factors, such as the age and maturity of the students congregating on campus and the propensity for them to engage in prohibited activities. If the students are relatively mature and are inclined to follow directives from school administrators and teachers regarding appropriate behavior, then the standard of care would not be as high as would be the case if these students were younger, less mature, and more inclined to be involved in pranks or prohibited activities.

Titus v. Lindberg is a classic case involving on-campus supervision of students before the school day begins. Nine-year-old Robert Titus arrived at Fairview School campus at approximately 8:05 A.M. and headed toward the bicycle rack to park his bike. As he turned the corner of the building, he was struck in the eye by a paper clip shot by Lindberg, a thirteen-year-old who was not a student at Fairview at that time but was awaiting a bus to transport him to his school. The facts revealed that Lindberg had shot another student with a paper clip just five minutes earlier. Because Fairview school doors did not officially open until 8:15 A.M., the principal, Smith, provided supervision for all students who were early arrivals. On the morning of the incident, Lindberg arrived early and played around with an elastic band before he struck another student in the back and subsequently injured Titus.

Titus filed a suit, alleging that his personal injury was caused by Lindberg's negligent shooting of the paper clip and by Smith's negligence in providing proper supervision. The record shows that Lindberg had attended Fairview up to two years before and was described as a "bully."

Smith admitted that he had known of previous pranks involving Lindberg but was unaware of the incident leading to the injury of Robert Titus. Although students were supposed to be in their seats by 8:30 A.M., it was not uncommon for students to arrive on campus at or before 8:00 A.M. Smith typically would supervise milk truck deliveries as he supervised students. He sometimes walked outside the building as he moved from one part of the campus to the other, although on other occasions he walked inside. On the day Titus was injured, Smith was walking inside.

The trial court ruled for Titus and awarded him $44,000 for damages, holding Lindberg and Smith responsible for his injury. Smith sought a reversal of the trial court's ruling by the state appellate court and subsequently the state supreme court. Both courts affirmed the ruling of the trial court in holding Smith and Lindberg responsible for Robert's injury.

The state supreme court stated that school personnel are liable for injuries received by students under their supervision, when such personnel fail to exercise reasonable supervision. The fact that students arrived early did not relieve Smith of an obligation to provide reasonable supervision because he was aware of their presence on campus. Further, Smith had neither announced any rules governing student behavior before classes began, nor had he assigned other teachers supervisory responsibilities before classes began. The decision of the court of appeals was affirmed.[38]

This case illustrates what can happen when quality supervision is absent. Large numbers of students were congregating on campus, many of whom were engaged in various types of activities. It seems prudent that the principal would have foreseen possible injury to students and taken other measures, such as involving other teachers or school personnel in campus supervision.

During School

It is obvious that school personnel have a duty to supervise students during the normal school day. Because certified personnel operate *in loco parentis*, they assume the responsibility to provide reasonable supervision during the time period in which they are assigned students. Students are viewed as agents of teachers and administrators and, thus, are accountable to them for their behavior and academic performance. Because the school is considered a safe place by the courts, the presumption is that school personnel are exercising prudence in supervising students. Supervision, in this instance, covers the full range of school-related activities involving students.

Certainly, teachers have the leading responsibility to provide reasonable supervision for students to whom they have been assigned. However, they also have a responsibility to caution or warn other students attending the school if they observe these students engaged in activities that may be potentially dangerous or harmful. Although students may not be directly assigned to a particular teacher during a specified time frame, it does not relieve that teacher of responsibility.

After School

Because common law and statutory requirements vary among states regarding standards of care, it is difficult to form any generalized conclusions in tort liability cases involving the duty to supervise students after the school day ends. School personnel, in the absence of statutory or board requirements, assume no duty to supervise students who are en route to school or departing for home, unless school-sponsored transportation is involved. Courts generally do not expect school personnel to provide supervision after the school day has ended, unless students are engaged in a school-sponsored activity. However, common knowledge and awareness that students are left on campus after school require school personnel to take certain precautions.

First and foremost, parents should be informed that the school does not provide supervision after the normal school day ends. They should be further encouraged to make proper arrangements to arrive promptly at the end of the school day to transport their child home. This information should be included in the student handbook and reflected by school policy. Parents should verify by their signature that these policies have been read and understood.

These steps, although appropriate, do not completely absolve the school of any responsibility for supervision, should it be determined that unsupervised students are engaged in potentially dangerous activities on school grounds after the school day has ended. More important, a duty of care may also be established if the school has written policies and procedures for after-school supervision, especially if these are communicated to parents. Generally speaking, school personnel have no duty to provide extensive supervision beyond reasonable measures after the school day ends. Although no duty exists beyond reasonable measures, a teacher or administrator who observed students engaged in potentially harmful activities en route home after school would be expected to warn them of the impending danger and to instruct them to discontinue the potentially harmful activity. Teachers and administrators do not have the right to ignore students en route home when they observe potentially dangerous situations involving students. They must foresee that students may be harmed, even though the students involved may not be under the direct supervision of the teacher or administrator.

As long as students are enrolled in the school, teachers and administrators must take reasonable steps to protect them from harm. In some instances, the standard of care might be higher for students left on campus after the school day ends, particularly if there is evidence that unauthorized individuals are attracted to campus after hours. Particular caution should be exercised if there have been instances in which unauthorized people have attempted to abduct or assault younger students by offering them money, candy, or other inducements. Another particularly hazardous condition may exist if students are left on campus in the late afternoon. It is foreseeable that students might be assaulted more frequently if they are left unsupervised after dark. Every effort should be made to convey the potential danger to parents who have their children remain late on campus after the school day ends. As a last resort, school district security or local police officers should be engaged if parents fail to arrive in a timely fashion to transport children home after the school day ends. The school district should have well-developed policies addressing responsibilities of all parties, parents, students, and school personnel in these potentially dangerous situations.

The courts have denied recovery to parents in a number of cases where damages were sought regarding after-school injuries involving voluntary and unorganized student activities. For example, a school district was held not liable for the wrongful death of a twelve-year-old student who entered the playground after school hours, either through an unlocked gate or a hole in the fence, and suffered fatal injuries in a skateboard game. The court held that even if the school officials knew that the playground was used for such games, alleged defects in the fence or gate merely allowed access to the area and thus related to the district's duty of supervision and control over its property. The parents failed to establish that their son was a student enrolled at the school and on school grounds during the normal school day in connection with a school function. Rather, he was there for his own amusement. The court held that there was no duty on the part of the school district to supervise and control activities on school grounds at all times.[39]

In a different case, a teacher was not held liable for an injury sustained by a third-grade student that occurred while unsupervised students cleaned a classroom after school. While cleaning the room, one student rummaged through the teacher's desk and discovered a knife that subsequently resulted in injury. The facts revealed that the students had been forbidden to go near the teacher's desk. The court held for the teacher, due to the student's disobedience. The teacher did not place the knife in the student's hand. The injury occurred based on the student's actions.[40]

During Field Trips

School-sponsored field trips are considered to be mere extensions of normal school activities and therefore require a reasonable standard of supervision by school personnel. In many instances, special supervision is required, due to the fact that students visit unfamiliar places and have a greater need for supervision. These activities normally provide valuable learning experiences for students. Because schools are moving toward connecting classroom learning to real-life situations, school-sponsored field trips will likely increase in popularity and instructional value.

School personnel are expected to exercise reasonable standards of supervision during field trip experiences. Students should be informed prior to the actual activities of the circumstances surrounding the activity. Special instructions or concerns should be properly conveyed by the teacher who has responsibility for supervising the field trip activity. Students, as well as parents, particularly those whose children are enrolled in the lower grades, should be informed of rules and expected behavior during the activity.

The *standard of care* involving field trips will vary depending on the age and maturity of students and the nature of the field experience. Teachers who organize field trips and administrators who approve them should be certain that supervision is adequate in terms of *quality* and *quantity*. For example, it is foreseeable that if one teacher attempts to supervise fifty young, immature students during a trip to the zoo, some student might be harmed if a sufficient number of chaperones are not available to assist with supervisory duties.

It is an acceptable practice to request that parents serve as chaperones during these excursions, in which case parents should be fully informed of the nature of the activities involved, the type of students who will be supervised, and specific instructions regarding their supervisory duties. Students who are extremely active or have a history of misbehavior should be closely supervised by the classroom teacher, as it is foreseeable that they may be injured under certain conditions.

If field trips are well organized and supervised, they will meet the standard of care expected of school personnel as well as provide a valuable learning experience for students. The following case illustrates the court's willingness to examine factual details involving liability charges against school personnel during field trips.

An eighth-grade class consisting of 110 students took a field trip to Nashville, Tennessee. This trip included lunch at a restaurant directly across the street from a park. Teachers supervised all students as they crossed the street en route to the restaurant. Three students finished their meals early and requested permission to return to the park. The teachers granted permission, advising the three to be careful. One student reached the curb, stopped, and looked in both directions before stepping into the street and was subsequently struck by a car. The student's parents brought action against the teachers who coordinated the field trip, claiming that the teachers were negligent for not escorting the students back across the street to the park. The lower court held for the parents, finding the teachers negligent.

On review, the Tennessee Court of Appeals noted that the injured student was thirteen years of age, experienced no hearing or vision problems, and was regarded as very mature for his age. The court further noted that the street was not considered unreasonably dangerous to cross. The appellate court reversed the lower court finding by concluding that the teachers had taken reasonable measures and were not required to escort the students across the street.[41]

PARENTAL CONSENT AND WRITTEN WAIVERS. It is a common practice for school districts to require parents to sign permission slips allowing their children to participate in certain school-sponsored activities away from the school. This practice has obvious value, as parents are involved in the decision-making process regarding these activities.

In some cases, these consent forms also will contain a waiver or disclosure statement that relieves the school of any legal responsibility in the event a student is injured during a field-based, school-sponsored activity. Psychologically, this practice might discourage a parent who has endorsed such a form from raising a legal challenge in the event of an injury to his or her child, but it does not in any way relieve school personnel of their duty to provide reasonable supervision. *Such forms have very limited, if any, legal basis in law.* If a parent grants permission for the child to engage in an activity and also signs a waiver, legal action may still be brought against school personnel if negligence occurs or a lack of proper supervision is established. School personnel should be aware that permission forms, although valuable, do not abrogate their legal duty to supervise and provide for the safety of students during these excursions. Depending on the **statute of limitations**, it also is probable that a student may later bring suit against the district when he or she reaches majority age, even if the parent elects not to do so during the time in which the student actually received an injury.

FIELD TRIPS AND BUSES. It is prudent that either district-owned buses or commercial-line buses be used to transport students on field trips. Individually owned automobiles of parents or students should be avoided as both may carry liability challenges for the driver as well as the school district if accidents occur. Bus drivers are responsible for operating buses safely. The supervisory school staff and chaperones are responsible for ensuring that student conduct meets required standards. Thus, staff, chaperones, and bus drivers are jointly responsible for student safety and equipment if included on the trip.

The number of passengers on buses should not exceed the specified rated capacity. It is feasible that buses (if more than one is involved) travel together to assist the other(s) in cases of a mechanical breakdown. A passenger list should be available before buses depart school grounds. This list should include the names, home addresses, and telephone numbers of all students and chaperones involved in the trip. Appropriate parental consent should also be ascertained. In all cases, prior approval for a field trip should be granted by designated school officials. The principal generally has the responsibility to ensure that only qualified drivers who have met state commercial licensing requirements are selected for field trip excursions.

LIABILITY INVOLVING CIVIL RIGHTS STATUTES

The *Wood v. Strickland* case, involving student expulsion (discussed in Chapter 3), briefly addressed the issue of liability of school board members in relation to civil rights violations of students. The Civil Rights Act of 1871, 42 U.S.C. § 1983, prohibits denial of constitutional and statutory rights by public officials. It states:

> Every person who, under color of any statute, ordinance, regulation, custom, or usage of any state or territory, subjects or causes to be subjected, any citizen of the United States or other person with the jurisdiction thereof to the deprivation of any rights, privileges, or immunities secured by the Constitution and laws shall be liable to the party injured in an action at law, suit in equity, or other proper proceeding for redress.[42]

The significance of section 1983 was recognized by the U.S. Supreme Court in 1972: Section 1983 opened the federal courts to private citizens, offering a uniquely federal remedy against the incursion of their civil rights under the claimed authority of state law.[43]

In the school setting, this federal statute allows students to seek monetary damages from state officials for acts that violated their constitutional rights. The courts have been fairly consistent in holding public school officials and board members responsible for acts that violated students' constitutional rights. Students are successful in their suits if there is evidence that school officials or board members acted in bad faith in violating their constitutional rights.

School officials will not succeed in claiming that they were unaware of the violation. The question raised by the courts is whether school officials should have been aware, as any other reasonable person in their position, that a student's rights were violated. (See the *Wood v. Strickland* case discussed in Chapter 3 and *Doe v. Taylor* discussed previously in this chapter.)

Filing Charges Under Section 1983 of the Civil Rights Act of 1871

Section 1983 contains no administrative procedures that must be met before a suit can be made in court. A suit that alleges a 1983 violation can be filed directly with a federal court. The courts will generally apply the statute of limitations for charges alleging personal injury in the particular state in which the claim occurs. Section 1983 cases are heard by a jury. Remedies include compensatory and punitive damages based on the severity of the injury. Punitive damages are not permitted against cities or municipalities. Injunctive relief and attorney fees also are permitted under 1983 violations.

Liability Insurance for Teachers and Administrators

Educators face liability challenges by parents and students alike based on the fact that schools operate in a litigious society. Therefore, it is important that educators receive protection against potential liability charges. Most state professional organizations, as well as national organizations, provide liability insurance coverage for educators at a nominal rate. Members of these organizations may use attorney referral networks, or in some cases seek their own legal representative. The selected attorney typically will bill the insurance provider rather than the teacher or administrator. In other instances, teachers or administrators may be reimbursed when they choose their own attorney if they have elected not to accept a predetermined legal advisor. The level of coverage tends to range from $1 million to $2 million. Some states provide protection against any loss resulting from liability claims against the teachers and administrators during the execution of their assigned duties. In other states, protection is provided by the Sovereign Immunity Law and school district insurance programs.

EDUCATIONAL MALPRACTICE

Over the last several decades, educational malpractice has emerged as a formidable threat to educators. Increasingly, parents have brought suit on behalf of their children, alleging that teachers were either negligent or incapable of providing competent instruction and proper placement and classification of their children. In these cases, students have charged that they suffered academic injury by being denied the full benefits of a proper education.

Although numerous educational malpractice suits have been filed in the past, to date no such case has been won by parents or students. However, with the emergence of school-based management, national teaching standards, greater teacher accountability, and an emphasis on professionalism in education, the prospect of a successful malpractice challenge is greatly heightened. There is little doubt that somewhere in the foreseeable future a malpractice suit will be won by a student who has suffered academic injury.

Educational malpractice generally is considered to be any unprofessional conduct or lack of sufficient skill in the performance of professional duties. It represents a new kind of injury to students. This new type of injury is not physical but emotional, psychological, or educational, resulting from poor teaching, improper placement, or inappropriate testing procedures.

Because the courts have long established legal duties for teachers to instruct, to supervise, and to provide for the safety of children, a breach of these duties resulting in injury to students may form adequate grounds for a liability suit. Increasingly, students are claiming *academic injury* in cases where teachers allegedly failed or were unable to meet minimal standards of instructional competency.

In cases involving alleged academic injury to students, courts have faced the very difficult task of determining exactly where actual fault lies. Does the alleged injury rest with the student's inability to acquire basic or minimal skills due to lack of ability or motivation? Or does the alleged injury rest with the teacher's inability to meet minimal standards of teaching? Further, if the teacher is determined to be at fault, is it a single teacher, a select few, or all teachers involved in a child's educational experiences who are to be blamed? Because of these difficulties, courts have failed to support charges of malpractice. Also, because teachers historically have had no direct influence over school policies, curriculum, working conditions, or resource acquisition, they could not reasonably be held to a strict standard of liability. However, with the emergence of teacher empowerment, school-based management, and national teaching and certification standards, the courts may be better able to determine if liability has occurred and precisely where it occurred.

Professionalism in Education

The development of national teaching standards involves the establishment of quality indicators and standards of practice that should drive the instructional program. There seems to be a view that judges, who are members of a profession themselves, would understand that any program sequence ought to include certain professional standards of quality to which the instructional program subscribes. Public policy is now focused on accountability for educational outcomes. This development coupled with No Child Left Behind legislation has created even greater accountability. This increased emphasis on educational outcomes may remove historic barriers to successful malpractice lawsuits, thus allowing the courts to avoid the public policy stance they have held in malpractice rulings for decades.

Educational Malpractice Cases

In perhaps the earliest malpractice case, *Peter W. v. San Francisco Unified School District,* "plaintiffs brought suit alleging that the school district negligently failed to provide an effective education, and in doing so, violated its professional duty to educate, at least to a minimum standard." The California court, in refusing to recognize educational malpractice as an appropriate course of action, stated that the issue was a "novel and troublesome question." The *Peter W.* suit was originally filed in 1973 but was not decided until 1976. The parents filed suit against the San Francisco Unified School District, its agents, and its employees. The suit alleged intentional misrepresentation, negligence, and a violation of statutory and constitutional duties owed students and parents. The defendant school district was charged with negligently failing to use reasonable care in the discharge of its duties and failing to exercise that degree of professional skill required of an ordinary prudent educator under the same circumstances.[44]

After high school graduation, Peter W. was not able to read above a fifth grade level. Teachers had systematically promoted him each year and had told the parents he was performing at or near grade level.

The court of appeals refused to recognize a legal duty of care and decided in favor of the school district on public policy considerations. The court reasoned that it could not establish standards of care for classroom instruction and that California's education code had been "structured to afford optimum educational results, not to guard against risk of injury."

In perhaps the most revealing case, *Hoffman v. Board of Education,* the court held for the student, stating that he had experienced diminished intellectual development and psychological injury as a result of inappropriate placement. At age six years, Danny Hoffman had a speech defect. He was given a verbal abilities test by his school to determine placement. He scored 74, one point below normal. That one point resulted in his being placed, for eleven years, in programs for the mentally retarded. At age seventeen years, Danny took an intelligence test required by the Social Security Administration and scored an IQ of 94. He then sued. The trial court held for Hoffman by stating the following:

> Had [the] plaintiff been improperly diagnosed or treated by medical or psychological personnel in a municipal hospital, the municipality would be liable for the ensuing injuries. There is no reason for any different rule here because the personnel were employed by a government entity other than a hospital. Negligence is negligence, even if a defendant . . . prefer(s) semantically to call it educational malpractice.[45]

This case demonstrates one court's willingness to rule on the merits of the case rather than on public policy grounds. The lower court in this case refused to make an exception merely because a governmental entity was involved or because a new theory of educational malpractice would be created. The appellate court upheld the lower court's decision, but lowered the damages to $500,000. The New York Court of Appeals, however, reversed and held for the board of education. The appeals court in New York reached the same decision as the appellate court in California. It stated that the plaintiff had failed to establish that the school board had breached its duty, and such a cause of action should not, as a matter of public policy, be entertained by the courts of New York.

As illustrated in this case, the courts have taken a rather liberal view regarding malpractice in education. However, this position by the courts will not deter future malpractice threats. Increasingly, parents will be inclined to seek damages for injury that they conclude has resulted from poor pedagogy, particularly when educators have a legal duty to provide competent instruction.

In a more recent case, the Wisconsin Supreme Court held that a school district was not liable for "educational malpractice" when a guidance counselor's faulty advice regarding NCAA eligibility requirements resulted in a student losing a college athletic scholarship.[46] The court concluded that the district was entitled to governmental immunity from the student's negligence and breach of contract claims, because (1) the counselor's actions did not fall within the "ministerial acts" exception to the immunity statute and (2) the counselor's position could not be classified as a professional position for purposes of the "professional discretion" exception to the statute. Ryan Scott, a high school student, hoped to obtain a hockey scholarship to an NCAA Division I college. During his junior year, Scott and his parents met with guidance counselor Dave Johnson to determine what courses Ryan would need to complete to satisfy the NCAA's eligibility requirements. Johnson agreed to assist Ryan. During his senior year, Ryan took "Broadcast Communications" after Johnson assured him that the NCAA deemed the course sufficient to fulfill a core English requirement. After Ryan graduated, the University of Alaska offered him a hockey scholarship. However, when the NCAA reviewed his transcript, it found that he was not eligible because "Broadcast Communications" was not an approved core course. The court concluded that providing guidance counseling is "inherently discretionary because the statute and regulation do not impose, prescribe, and define the time, mode, and occasion for its performance" and create no school duty to provide information regarding NCAA requirements. The court refused to extend the professional discretion exception to guidance counselors, holding that to do so would allow the exception to "swallow the rule."

Administrative Guide

Educational Malpractice

1. Develop quality standards of practice as a means to guide the instructional program within schools.
2. Make certain that instructional personnel are well prepared and highly focused on their instructional duties.
3. Ensure that all required competencies and skills are taught in the classroom.
4. Provide systemwide remediation for students who fail to master required skills and competencies or for those who have difficulty learning.
5. Make informed decisions regarding the appropriateness of curricula, textbooks, and instructional policies.
6. Develop flexible and varied instructional strategies and techniques to meet individual needs of students.
7. Use well-prepared promotion and retention standards as guides to decisions affecting student progress.
8. Make certain that curricular objectives are translated into topics actually taught in the classroom.
9. Avoid inappropriate testing procedures that could result in misclassification or inappropriate placement of students.
10. Develop proper means to monitor instructional practices to improve the overall educational delivery system.

Administrative Guide

School Liability

1. School district personnel must be aware of the standard of care that must be met as they instruct and supervise students in various activities to which they have been assigned.

2. Every teacher or administrator has a responsibility to ensure to the fullest extent possible that school buildings and grounds are safe for student use.

3. The absence of foreseeability by school personnel will not be upheld by the courts when the facts reveal that school personnel were expected to foresee the potential danger of a situation resulting in injury to a student.

4. Schools may be liable for foreseeable injury to students who use school-sponsored buses.

5. School personnel have a legal duty to instruct, supervise, and provide a safe environment for students.

6. Reasonable and prudent decisions regarding student safety will withstand court scrutiny.

7. A higher standard of care may be expected during field trips and excursions involving students, especially in cases where students are viewed as licensees.

8. School grounds should be accessible and considered safe for authorized visitors.

9. School personnel must refrain from any actions that may fall under the categories of assault and battery, especially in cases involving physical punishment.

10. Personal information regarding students should be kept confidential. Only those who have a vested interest in working with a student should have access to such personal information.

11. School personnel should be mindful that qualified privilege is limited when information is shared concerning a student. They must operate in good faith with no intent to harm a student's reputation.

12. Students should not be coerced to use equipment or perform a physical activity about which they express serious apprehension. Coercion of this type could result in injury to the student and liability charges against school personnel.

13. Teachers and administrators should be reminded that the infliction of mental distress involving students may result in personal liability charges.

14. The conduct of school personnel should not be calculated to cause emotional harm to students.

15. Unorthodox and indefensible practices aimed at disciplining students should be avoided.

16. Unacceptable behavior by teachers and administrators that exceeds the boundaries of professional conduct should be clearly stated in school or district policy, with the consequences for violations spelled out.

17. Schools should develop a culture and a set of values that place a high premium on respect for the dignity of every individual involved in the school community.

18. When possible, interactions involving students that might tend to embarrass them or create mental distress should occur in private and not in the presence of their peers.

19. Board of education members may be held liable for their individual acts that result in the violation of a student's rights.

20. Students should not be detained after school for unreasonable periods of time for behavior that does not warrant detention.

21. Items retrieved from students, if not illegal, should be returned to them or their parents within a reasonable time frame and not retained permanently by school personnel.

22. Illegal items, with the administrators' consent, should be presented to law enforcement officials following notification of parents.

23. A higher standard of care is necessary in laboratories, physical education classes, and contact sports.

24. School officials should provide some form of supervision for students before the school day begins or after the school day ends.

25. Well-planned liability workshops/seminars should be offered periodically to ensure that school personnel are aware of the limits of liability.

CASE STUDIES

Liability and the Assumption of Risk

Brent Thomas, principal of Homewood High School, located in a very affluent community in the eastern part of the United States, recommended and received approval to hire George Banks as his new physical education teacher. George organized the first hockey program for the school. Students who wanted to participate were required to undergo a physical examination and submit a written permission slip from their parents. One day during practice, Ricky Watts, a fourteen-year-old student, sustained serious injuries to his mouth and jaw when he used an improper technique to block the hockey puck. His parents were upset and filed liability charges against the principal and coach.

Discussion Questions

1. What factors would determine whether the principal may be liable?
2. What factors would determine whether George Banks is liable?
3. Can either Thomas or Banks successfully use the defense of assumption of risk to avoid liability charges? Why or why not?
4. Develop a set of defensible guidelines governing supervision of competitive athletic activities.
5. What factors would determine whether assumption of risk may be used as a legitimate defense?
6. Discuss the administrative implications of this case.

Liability and the Substitute Teacher

Linda Collins was employed as a substitute teacher for Walnut Grove High School in a midsize industrial city. She generally substitutes fifteen to twenty days per month at various schools in the district. On the day she substituted in a shop class, one student was sexually assaulted by another student behind a portable chalkboard. Parents of the assaulted child filed a suit against the school district.

Discussion Questions

1. Is a substitute teacher held to the same standard as a regular teacher? Why or why not?
2. Does sexual assault of a student by another automatically result in liability? Why or why not?
3. What factors would determine whether liability claims are valid?
4. Based on factors you identified in question 3, how would the court likely view this case?
5. Defend your response regarding the court's position in this case.

Liability and Playground Supervision

Three elementary school teachers are assigned to supervise the children who are playing on the playground. There are approximately a hundred children engaged in a number of playground activities. Because these teachers do not have much opportunity to chat with each other during the school day, all of them decide to bring chairs to the playground and engage in conversation while observing the children. During this time, one child sustains a serious injury when he is struck by a rock thrown by another student.

Discussion Questions

1. What is the legal issue in this situation?
2. What factors will determine liability?
3. Can all three teachers be held liable? Why or why not?
4. How do you think the court will rule in this case? Give a rationale for your response.
5. Develop a set of guidelines regarding playground supervision.

School Liability and Student Injury

A six-year-old boarded his school bus but was allowed to leave when he thought he saw his father's car that sometimes picked him up after school. He did not find his father and was injured by a car while walking to another bus stop with other students. The child's mother filed a liability suit.

Discussion Questions

1. Should the school be held liable for the child's injury? If so, why? If not, why not?
2. Does the school have responsibility for the child after the school day ends and the student boards the bus? If yes, why? If not, why not?
3. Was the bus driver negligent in allowing the child to leave the bus? If yes, why? If not, why not?
4. What procedures should be implemented to prevent this type of liability challenge against a school district?
5. How do you feel the courts would view the child's injury in relationship to liability by the district?

Tort Liability

Jack Bellingham, an elementary school principal, has a growing tendency to call teachers to his office for various reasons.

Discussion Questions

When he does so:

1. What risks if any does Bellingham incur?
2. If a student were injured during the teacher's absence, who would be liable: the teacher, the principal, or both?
3. What factors would the courts consider in this situation if a student were injured during the teacher's absence?
4. What are the principal's obligations in this situation?
5. What guidelines would you suggest in this situation?
6. What are the administrative implications?

Playground Liability

You have learned that a number of elementary school students tend to return to your campus after school to use playground equipment with the consent of their parents. Unfortunately, two students received injuries when they fell from a slide.

Discussion Questions

1. Is the school liable for their injuries? Why, or why not?
2. Are students trespassing when they return to campus? Why, or why not?
3. What obligation, if any, does the school have regarding students' use of playground equipment after school?
4. What is the solution for handling this practice?

Bus Drivers' Protest

Bus drivers in a midsize urban school district have decided to protest against what they consider to be low pay. The district is facing significant budget challenges and does not have the capacity to address their salary demands. They are employed in a right-to-work state in the North. As a part of their protest, some drivers decided not to pick up students on their routes, leaving students stranded.

Discussion Questions

1. What is your initial reaction to this situation?
2. How would you respond if you were the superintendent of the district?
3. Is there potential liability for the district when students are left without transportation?
4. What action would you take to resolve this problem? (Be specific.)

Teachers and Facebook Friends Liability

You have been informed by reliable sources that a number of teachers in the district have students as Facebook Friends, particularly at the high school level. Your district is quite liberal.

Discussion Questions

1. As superintendent, do you have concerns regarding this situation? Why, or why not?
2. What action would you take to eliminate this situation if you agree that it should be eliminated?
3. Because teachers have freedom of association rights, do you have grounds to act? Why, or why not?
4. If you fail to act on this situation, under what conditions could you be held liable if students are harmed?

Endnotes

1. *Hosemann v. Oakland Unified School District,* No. SD11025, Supreme Court of California, 1989 Cal. LEXIS 4187, August 17, 1989.
2. *Doe v. Taylor I.S.D.,* et al. 15 F. 3d 443 (5th Cir. 1994).
3. *Mitchell v. Forsyth,* 472 U.S. 511, 105 S.Ct. 2806 (1985).
4. *Davis v. Scherer,* 468 U.S. 183, 104 S.Ct. 3012 (1984).
5. *Carey v. Piphus,* 435 U.S. 247, 98 S.Ct. 1042, 55 L. Ed. 2d 252 (1978).
6. *Priester v. Lowndes County School District,* 354 F. 3d 414, 423 N. 9 (5th Cir. 2004).
7. Restatement of Torts, Second § 339.
8. *Jackson v. Cartwright School District,* 607 P. 2d 975 (Ariz. 1980).
9. *Francis v. School Board of Palm Beach County,* 29 So. 3d 441 (Fla. Dist. Ct. App. 2010).
10. *Kilcoin v. Wolansky,* 428 N.Y.S. 2d 272 (1980).
11. *Gordon v. Oak Park School District No. 97,* 24 Ill. App. 3d 131, 320 N.E. 2d 389 (1974).
12. *Celestine v. Lafayette Parish School Board,* 284 So. 2d 650 (La. 1973).
13. *Wofford v. Evans,* 390 F. 3d 318 (C.A.4 (Va.) 2004).
14. *New Jersey v. T.L.O.,* 469 U.S. 325 (1985).
15. *Miller v. Griesel,* 308 N.E. 2d 701 (1974).
16. *Mirand v. City of New York,* 84 N.Y. 2d 44; 614 N.Y.S. 2d 372, 637 N.E. 2d 263 (1994).
17. *Mikell v. School Administrative Unit #33,* 972 A. 2d 1050 (N.H. 2009).
18. *King v. Northeast Security Inc.,* 753 N. E. 2d 10 (Ind. 2001).
19. *Wilhelm v. Board of Education of City of New York,* 227 N.Y.S. 2d 791 (1962).
20. *Tannenbaum v. Board of Education,* 255 N.Y.S. 2d 522 (1969).
21. *Hutchinson v. Toews,* Dept. 2, 4 Or. App. 19, 476 P. 2d 811 Court of Appeals of Oregon (1970).
22. *Brazell v. Board of Education of Niskayuna Public Schools,* 161 A.D. 2d 1086 557 N.Y.S. 2d 645 Supreme Court (1990).
23. *Albers v. Independent School District No. 302 of Lewis City 94,* 342 487 P. 2d (Supreme Court of Idaho 1971).
24. *Edelson v. Uniondale Union Free School Dist.,* 631 N.Y.S. 2d 391 (N.Y. App. Div. 1995).
25. *Barbin v. State,* 506 So. 2d 888 (1st Cir. 1987).
26. *Locilento v. John A. Coleman Catholic High School,* 523 N.Y.S. 2d 198 (A.D. 3d Dept. 1987).
27. *Barth v. Board of Education,* 490 N.E. 2d 77 (Ill. App. 186 Dist. 1986).
28. *Smith v. Archbishop of St. Louis,* 632 S.W. 2d 516 (Mo. App. 1982).
29. *Stahl v. Cocalico School District,* 534 A. 2d 1141 (Pa. Cmwlth 1987).
30. *Dean v. Board of Education,* 523 A. 2d 1059 (Md. App. 1987).
31. *Bielaska v. Town of Waterford,* 491 A. 2d 1071 (Conn. 1985).
32. *Hyman v. Green,* 403 N.W. 2d 597 (Mich. App. 1987).
33. *State Farm Mutual Auto. Ins. Co. v. Pharr,* 808 S.W. 2d 769 (Ark. 1991).
34. *Morris v. State District of Mt. Lebanon,* 144 A. 2d 737 (Pa. 1958).

35. *Norman v. Ogallala Public School District,* 609 N.W. 2d 338 (Neb. 2000).

36. *Izard v. Hickory City Bd. of Educ.,* 692 S.W. 2d 7566 (N.C. app. 1984).

37. *Dibortolo v. Metropolitan School Dist. of Washington Township,* 440 N.E. 2d 5076 (Ind. Ct. app. 1982).

38. *Titus v. Lindberg,* 49 N.J. 66, 228 A. 2d 65 (1967).

39. *Bartell v. Palos Verdes Peninsula School District,* 83 Cal. App. 3d 492 147 Cal. Rptr. 898 (1978).

40. *Richard v. St. Landry Parish School Board,* 344 So. 2d 1116 (La. Ct. App. 1977).

41. *King v. Kartenson,* 720 S.W. 2d 65 (Tenn. App. 1986).

42. U.S.C. § 1983 (1988).

43. *Mitchum v. Foster,* 407 U.S. 225 (1972).

44. *Peter W. v. San Francisco Unified School District,* 131 Cal. Rptr. 854 (1976).

45. *Hoffman v. Board of Education of New York City,* 64 A.D. 2d, 369 N.Y.S. (1978).

46. *Scott v. Savers Property and Casualty Insurance Co.,* 663 N.W. 2d 715 (Wisc. 2003).

Chapter 7

Liability and Student Records

The primary purpose of maintaining educational records should be to aid school personnel in developing the best educational program for each student enrolled in the school. An effective student file contains information used for counseling, program development, individualized instruction, grade placement, college admissions, and a variety of other purposes. In addition to certain types of directory information, student files typically include family background information, health records, progress reports, achievement test results, psychological data, disciplinary records, and other confidential material.

Public Law 93-380, the Family Educational Rights and Privacy Act (FERPA), protects confidentiality of student records. This act, commonly referred to as the Buckley Amendment, was enacted by Congress in 1974 to guarantee parents and students a certain degree of *confidentiality* and *fundamental fairness* with respect to the maintenance and use of student records. The law is designed to ensure that certain types of personally identifiable information regarding students will not be released without parental consent. *If a student is eighteen years of age or attends a postsecondary institution, parental consent is not required.* In that event, the student has the authority to provide consent. If the student is a dependent, for tax purposes, parents retain a coextensive access right with students over eighteen years old. Because P.L. 93-380 is a federal statute, it applies to school districts and schools that receive federal funds. Schools should develop policies and procedures, including a listing of the types and locations of educational records and persons who are responsible for maintaining these records. Copies of these policies and procedures should be made available to parents or students on request.

SANCTIONS FOR VIOLATING FAMILY PRIVACY RIGHTS

An excerpt of FERPA states the following:

> No funds shall be available under any program to any educational agency or institution which has a policy of denying access or which effectively prevents the parents of students who are or have been in attendance at a school of such agency, the right to inspect and review the educational records of their children. If any material or document in the educational record of a student includes information on more than one student, the parents of one such student shall have the right to inspect and review only such part of such material or document as related to such student or be informed of the specific information contained in such part of such material.[1]

TABLE 7.1	Content of Educational Records

Educational Records Include	Educational Records Do Not Include
Records	Instructional records
Files	Supervisory records
Documents	Records maintained by law enforcement units for law enforcement purposes
Other materials that 1. contain information directly related to a student 2. are maintained by an educational agency, institution, or person acting for agency of institution	Records on an eighteen-year-old student attending a postsecondary institution that are maintained by a physician, psychiatrist, psychologist, or other recognized professional or paraprofessional involved in the treatment of the student

Source: P.L. 93-380.

At a minimum, the school district should provide, on an annual basis, information to parents, guardians, and eligible students regarding the content of the law and inform them of their right to file complaints with the Rights and Privacy Act Office of the Department of Education. If non–English-speaking parents are affected, the district has a responsibility to notify them in their native language.[2] Annual notification must include the following information:

1. Right to inspect and review educational records
2. Right to seek amendment of records believed to be inaccurate, misleading, or in violation of student's privacy act
3. Consent to disclose personally identifiable information contained in student's records except where act authorizes disclosure without consent
4. Right to file with the department a complaint under § 99.63 and § 99.64 concerning alleged failures by the educational agency or institution to comply with requirements of the act
5. Notice must include the following:
   a. Procedures for exercising the right to inspect and review educational records
   b. Procedures for requesting amendment of records
   c. Specification of criteria for determining who constitutes a school official and what constitutes a legitimate educational interest
6. An educational agency or institution shall effectively notify parents or eligible students who are disabled
7. An educational agency or institution of elementary and secondary education shall effectively notify parents who have a primary or home language other than English

In addition, parents, guardians, or eligible students should be provided information regarding procedures for accessing educational records, if they desire to do so. The content of education records is shown in Table 7.1.

The school district may release directory information regarding students, provided that such information is published yearly in a public newspaper. Directory information normally includes the following:

1. Name
2. Address
3. Telephone number
4. Date and place of birth
5. Participation in extracurricular activities

6. Weight, height, and membership on athletic teams
7. Dates of attendance
8. Diploma and awards received

If any parents or guardians object to the release of directory information on their child, their objection should be noted in the record and honored by the school district. School policy should define what items are considered directory information and the conditions under which this information should be released.

Except for directory information, all personally identifiable records directly related to the student shall be kept confidential, unless the parent or guardian signs a consent form releasing certain such information.

RIGHTS OF PARENTS

Parents or legal guardians have the right to inspect their child's record. A school official should be present to assist a parent or guardian in interpreting information contained in the files and to respond to questions that may be raised during the examination process. Parents or legal guardians may challenge the accuracy of any information found in the files regarding their child. The school should schedule a conference with appropriate personnel, within a reasonable period of time (ten days or less although the act calls for no more than forty-five days), to discuss the information that may be deemed inaccurate, inappropriate, or misleading. If agreement is reached to the satisfaction of the parent, no further action is necessary. Appropriate deletions or corrections are executed, recorded in the student file, and communicated to parents or guardians in written form.

If the conference does not result in changes to the satisfaction of parents, they may request a hearing with the director of pupil personnel or a designee to appeal the decision reached during the conference. The hearing should be scheduled within ten days or less. The parent or guardian may be represented by legal counsel. A final decision should be rendered within ten days subsequent to the hearing. If the school official hearing the case decides that the information is accurate and correct, the parent should be informed of such and provided an opportunity to place statements of disagreement in the file with reasons for the disagreement. This explanation must become a permanent part of the record and must be disclosed when the records are released. The parent or guardian may also seek relief in civil court. If student records are subpoenaed by the courts, the parent, guardian, or eligible student should be contacted prior to the release of records.

When consent is necessary to release student records, it must be provided in written form, signed and dated by the consenting person. The consent form should include a specification of the records to be released, reason for the release, and the names of the individuals to whom the records will be released. Once records are received by the requesting party, it should be emphasized that this information is not to be divulged to others without the express permission of the parents, guardians, or eligible students. *Parents, guardians, or eligible students must be notified before a school or district complies with a judicial order requesting educational records.* School officials in another school district in which a student plans to enroll may access that student's records, provided parents or guardians are notified in advance that the records are being transferred to the new district.

FAMILY EDUCATIONAL RIGHTS AND PRIVACY ACT

Notice of Proposed Rulemaking

The Department has also released a Notice of Proposed Rule Making (NPRM) outlining proposed amendments to its regulations implementing FERPA. Over time, interpretations of FERPA have complicated valid and necessary disclosures of student information without increasing privacy protections and, in some cases, have dramatically decreased the protections afforded to students.

FERPA permits, but does not require, schools to disclose personally identifiable information from education records without consent under limited circumstances, commonly known as *exceptions*. See § 99.31 for the full list of exceptions to the consent requirement in FERPA.

Highlights of the Proposed Changes in the NPRM Consist of:

Stronger Enforcement

The Department needs stronger, more specific, and clearer enforcement authority against all entities that collect, receive, or maintain FERPA-protected data. Every entity that receives personally identifiable information from student education records has a responsibility to ensure that it is used only for authorized purposes, is protected appropriately, and is not redisclosed unless permitted by FERPA.

Ensuring the Safety of Students

Schools must have the flexibility to implement directory information policies that reflect their specific needs and policies without endangering students or opening the door for abuses of that information by allowing schools to limit the use of directory information.

Ensuring the Effectiveness of Publicly Funded Programs

Connecting K–12 and Postsecondary Data and Sharing Information to Improve Early Childhood and Workforce Programs

States and local communities must have the ability to share student data to evaluate the effectiveness of education programs ranging from early childhood through adult education. In order to evaluate the effectiveness of their own education programs, states, school districts, and high schools must be able to obtain college access, persistence, completion, and remediation data on their former students from the postsecondary institutions that those students attend.

The proposed amendments would define two terms, "education program" and "authorized representative." These terms currently are not defined in the FERPA statute or its regulations, and the NPRM proposes to define them in the following ways:

1. **An education program** would be defined as any program that is principally engaged in the provision of education, including, but not limited to, early childhood education, elementary and secondary education, postsecondary education, special education, job training, career and technical education, and adult education, regardless of whether the program is administered by an educational authority.

2. **An authorized representative** would be defined generally as any entity or individual designated by a state or local educational authority or an agency headed by an official listed in § 99.31(a)(3)—the Secretary, the Comptroller General of the United States, or the Attorney General of the United States—to conduct, with respect to federal or state supported education programs, any audit, evaluation, or compliance or enforcement activity in connection with federal legal requirements related to those programs.[3]

Student Records

An interesting case involving parental access to student records arose in Illinois. An Illinois school district violated the state School Records Act by refusing to turn over a student's biology test booklet to her parent when he requested a copy. The superintendent indicated that the information was not covered by the School Records Act because the test booklets contained no personally identifying information regarding the student. While the biology booklet lawsuit was pending, the parent made a new written request to the superintendent for copies of his daughter's advanced algebra exams. Instead, the parent was offered the opportunity to examine test booklets on school property or at home with the stipulation that they had to be returned the next day. He was allowed to hand-copy test questions. The parent sued the school district in the state court system seeking a declaration that the booklet was a student record under the state School Records Act.[4] A state trial court held that the booklets did not fall under the act, as they were devoid of any student marks or other information identifying the student. The Appellate Court of Illinois affirmed the judgment. The student's name, answers, and calculations were not contained on the algebra booklet. On appeal, the court stated that the overall intent of the act is to permit a broad right of parental access to such records. The court agreed with the parent that the algebra test booklets were covered by the act. Although the questions themselves had no information concerning the student, they were part of a document containing such information and the entire test booklet with her markings fell under the act. When student markings or other identifying information could be found on test booklets, they became student records subject to parental rights to inspect and copy. The district did not comply with the act by allowing the parent to take booklets home. The court reversed the judgment by the lower courts.

RIGHTS OF NONCUSTODIAL PARENTS

Occasionally, controversy arises regarding the rights of a noncustodial biological parent to access his or her child's educational records. School officials often find themselves caught between this request and a custodial parent's request that the noncustodial parent not be permitted to access the child's educational records. School or district policy should provide guidance in these situations. One such case arose in New York when the mother of a child requested that the school not allow the child's father to see their son's educational records. The father challenged the school's refusal to allow him access to the child's records. The district court ruled that neither parent could be denied access to the child's records under FERPA. The court held that schools should make educational records accessible to both parents of each child fortunate enough to have both parents interested in the child's welfare.[5]

RIGHTS OF ELIGIBLE STUDENTS

As previously mentioned, the student may exercise the same rights afforded parents or guardians, if he or she has reached the age of eighteen years or is enrolled in a postsecondary institution. The student may inspect confidential records and challenge the accuracy of information contained in the file. In addition, the student may determine whether anyone other than authorized individuals may have access to personal files. Students also have a right to receive a copy of their personal file, if they choose to have one. Eligible students are afforded the same due process provisions as parents are offered, if they choose to challenge the accuracy of information contained in their file. They may also, under certain conditions, bring liability charges for defamation against school personnel (discussed later in this chapter).

RIGHTS OF SCHOOL PERSONNEL

Teachers, counselors, and administrators who have a legitimate educational interest in viewing records may do so. A written form, which must be maintained permanently with the file, should indicate specifically what files were reviewed by school personnel and the date on which files were reviewed. Each person desiring access to the file is required to sign this written form. These forms should be available for parents, guardians, or eligible students, because they remain permanently with the file. If challenged, school personnel must demonstrate a legitimate interest in having reviewed the student's file.

In 1994, FERPA was amended to emphasize that institutions are not prevented from maintaining records related to a disciplinary action taken against a student for behavior that posed a significant risk to the student or others. Likewise, institutions are not prevented from disclosing such information to school officials who have been determined to have a legitimate educational interest in the behavior of the student. School districts also are permitted to disclose information regarding disciplinary action to school officials in other schools that have a legitimate educational interest in the behavior of students.

Table 7.2 summarizes the rights of all parties affected by FERPA.

A case arose in Ohio regarding disclosure of records involving student discipline specifically with respect to the use of corporal punishment. An Ohio federal district court held that records related to corporal punishment are not protected from discovery by the federal FERPA.[6] A student sued Cleveland Municipal School District over a substitute teacher's use of corporal

TABLE 7.2   Rights Under FERPA

Rights of Students Who Are Eighteen Years Old or Attend a Postsecondary Institution	Rights of Parents	Rights of School Personnel
Have knowledge of types of records and location of records and inspect confidential records	Inspect child's record if under age of eighteen years	Access to confidential information for legitimate educational purposes
Challenge the accuracy of information contained on records	Challenge the accuracy of information contained on records	Maintain personal notes on students for personal use
Have appropriate deletions or corrections executed	Have appropriate deletions or corrections executed	Disclose educational records to comply with judicial orders for state and various federal agencies
Request hearing to contest information on records thought to be inaccurate	Request hearing to contest information on records thought to be inaccurate	Disclosure of disciplinary proceedings conducted against perpetrators of a crime
Consent to disclosure of personally identifiable information contained in files	Place statement of disagreement regarding contested information remaining on the records	Disclosure of directory information on students
Determine what type of confidential information is released and to whom other than those authorized to access confidential information	Determine what type of confidential information is released, to whom it is released other than authorized personnel, and reasons to be released	Privilege against lawsuits when making truthful statements in good faith within the scope of professional duties
Place statement of disagreement regarding any contested information remaining on the records	Receive annual notice of rights under the act	Record truthful negative information on education records that should remain a part of the permanent record
Receive a copy of personal records	Receive prior notice of any records subpoenaed by the courts	Receive training on handling sensitive and confidential information on students with disabilities
Receive a copy of released record on request	File complaints with the U.S. Department of Education concerning alleged violations	Receive protection when factual references of students are provided on request
Under certain conditions, bring charges of defamation against school personnel and other appropriate parties	Seek relief in civil court if necessary	Destroy records when no longer needed after student graduates

Source: P.L. 93-380.

punishment. The student sought discovery of incident reports, student and employee witness statements, and information regarding subsequent discipline of the substitute teacher. The school district objected to the discovery request on the ground that the documents sought were protected from discovery under FERPA. The district court found that the information sought was contained in teacher records and stated, "Congress did not intend FERPA to cover records directly related to teachers and only marginally related to students." Although the records in question concern students as victims and witnesses, they are directly related to the activities and conduct of teachers. According to the court, even if the records were "education records" within the meaning of FERPA, FERPA does not prevent discovery of relevant records under the Federal Rules of Civil Procedure. The court concluded that its findings not only are consistent with FERPA's language but also operate to protect the safety of students by preventing FERPA from being used "to protect allegations of abuse by substitute teachers from discovery in private actions designed to combat such abuse."

Student Complaints and FERPA

Is a student protected under FERPA when he/she files a complaint against a teacher in public schools and colleges? Apparently not. According to a three-judge panel in *Rhea v. District Board of Trustees of Santa Fe College* in Florida who ruled that a Santa Fe college had to release the name of a student who sent an e-mail to the school complaining about a former math instructor. The appellate panel unanimously agreed that Rhea's argument suggesting that the student's name was not covered by state and federal law granting confidentiality to educational records based on the complaint does not directly relate to students. The complaint directly relates to teachers and only remotely to the complaining student. This ruling will likely have no significant impact on student complaints but will probably discourage frivolous complaints.[7]

Digitizing Student Records

Digitizing student records should present minimal concerns so long as proper controls are implemented to maintain records and assure confidentiality as well as student privacy rights protection. Students and their parents should expect that their personal information is safe, properly collected, and maintained. Digitization may create increased access for students, eligible parents/guardians, as well as authorized school personnel. It may also reduce cost and improve the overall quality of accessing student information. School leaders must ensure that user-friendly and effective hardware is utilized in the digitization process and protection is available to prevent unauthorized use or duplication of files. School personnel must act responsibly and be accountable for safeguarding students' personally identifiable information. School leaders must also weigh the benefits and challenges associated with transforming analog materials into an electronic format. Improved access, efficient space utilization, and long-term preservation are obvious advantages. Disadvantages may involve costs associated with digital transformation and staff training. School personnel must be trained to properly access and maintain confidentiality of student records. Caution must be exercised during the transformational process to ensure that reproduction of records is of high quality while preserving the integrity of the original documents. Careful examination and monitoring should be planned to ensure that vital information has not been omitted or compromised and that errors have not occurred that may distort student records or jeopardize the accuracy of information contained in the student's file. Lastly, a transitional process should be initiated to ensure that student information can be accessed during the transformational process with a strong focus on confidentiality.

Confidentiality Issues Involving School Counselors

A number of states have passed laws protecting the confidentiality of counselors. However, most states do not support confidentiality protection for counselors. Michigan and Nevada have the most complete protection. South Dakota, Ohio, Maine, Oregon, Alabama, Arkansas, Idaho, Indiana,

Kentucky, Missouri, Montana, North Carolina, Oregon, and Pennsylvania provide protection to counselors in civil and criminal proceedings. Arguably, most communication between a school counselor and a student does not rise to a civil or criminal proceeding. In states where no privilege is granted, the counselor is required to testify, if ordered by the court.

School counselors are not required to share information obtained from students with their parents. Records that remain in the sole possession of counselors are not subject to FERPA. Educational records under FERPA do not include personal files. Confidentiality, however, is not absolute. When circumstances arise in which public disclosure is in the public interest, confidentiality is lost. One of the most significant examples occurred in *Tarasoff v. Regents of the University of California* in 1976 in which a student confided to his psychologist during a therapy session that he was going to kill another student.[8] Tatiana Tarasoff was subsequently killed by the student. Her parents filed suit, claiming that the psychologist had a duty to warn their daughter and them of an impending danger. The psychologist did, however, inform campus police. The California Supreme Court ruled that the psychologist had a duty to warn the victim. Further, the psychologist became sufficiently involved to assume some responsibility for the safety not only of the patient but also of any person whom the psychologist knew to be threatened by the patient.

ENFORCEMENT OF STATE OR FEDERAL STATUTES

Federal and state officials may inspect files without parental consent in order to enforce federal or state laws or to audit or evaluate federal education programs. In these cases, personally identifiable information may not be associated with any student unless Congress, by law, specifically authorizes federal officials to gather personally identifiable data. Information may also be released without consent in connection with applications for student financial aid. Authorized representatives who may access records include (1) the comptroller general of the United States, (2) the secretary of state, (3) an administrative head of an educational agency, and (4) state and educational authorities. School district policies should address these issues so that parents, guardians, and eligible students are informed of these exceptions.

FAMILY EDUCATION RIGHTS AND PRIVACY ACT (FERPA)

Landmark U.S. Supreme Court Rulings

On February 19, 2002, the U.S. Supreme Court ruled in *Owasso ISD v. Falvo* that peer grading does not violate FERPA.[9] Student papers are not "maintained" within the meaning of FERPA when students correct them or call out grades. "Maintained" suggested that FERPA records were kept in files or cabinets in a records room at the school. The court stated further that FERPA should not be construed to prohibit techniques currently used by teachers. If homework or class work were considered educational records, a substantial burden would be placed on teachers across the country. Simply stated, an assignment is not considered an educational record as soon as it is graded by another student.

On June 20, 2002, the U.S. Supreme Court ruled in *Doe v. Gonzaga*.[10] In the *Gonzaga* case, a student brought litigation against the university for disclosing personally identifiable information, without his consent, in violation of FERPA. The Supreme Court ruled that students and parents may *not* sue for damages under 42 U.S.C. § 1983 to enforce provisions of FERPA.

U.S. Court of Appeals for the Sixth Circuit Ruling

On June 27, 2002, the Sixth Circuit Court of Appeals unanimously affirmed a lower court's ruling that university disciplinary records are "education records" under FERPA and that disclosing such records without students' consent constitutes a violation of FERPA. In 1998, the U.S. Department of Education asked a federal district court in Ohio to enjoin Miami University and

The Ohio State University from disclosing records containing the names of student victims and accused students as prohibited under FERPA.[11] On March 20, 2000, the U.S. District Court for the Southern District of Ohio permanently enjoined the two Ohio universities from disclosing their on-campus disciplinary records to the public under the state's open-records law.

In affirming the ruling, the circuit court concluded that continued release of student disciplinary records "will irreparably harm the United States" and the Department of Education. This is important for three reasons:

1. The court agreed with the lower court that the Student Right-to-Know and Campus Security Act provides parents and students with statistical information about the type and amount of crimes on campus.
2. The court reaffirmed the department's broad reading of the term "education records" and stated that Congress, in amending FERPA in 1998 to allow postsecondary institutions to disclose the final results of disciplinary proceedings, must have intended that disciplinary records be education records or this amendment would be "superfluous."
3. The court held that the Department of Education was within its rights in seeking an injunctive relief in this case because none of the administrative remedies authorized by FERPA would have stopped the violations. In effect, the court held that the department can take preemptive actions in enforcing FERPA, rather than only after violations occur.

NO CHILD LEFT BEHIND ACT OF 2002

Annual Notification Requirements

The Secretary of Education is now required to annually inform each state education agency (SEA) and each local education agency (LEA) of their obligations under both FERPA and the Protection of Pupil Rights Amendment (PPRA). This provision is found in § 1061(c)(5)(C), the amendments to PPRA (discussed below). The Family Policy Compliance Office (FPCO) is in the process of finalizing the notices to be provided to SEAs and LEAs. (See Chapter 4 for No Child Left Behind and School Safety.)

Transfer of School Disciplinary Records

FERPA currently permits schools to transfer any and all education records, including disciplinary records, on a student who is transferring to another school. See § 99.31(a)(2) and § 99.34 of the FERPA regulations. This new provision requires states that receive funds under the Elementary and Secondary Education Act (ESEA) to provide, within two years, an assurance to the secretary of education that the state "has a procedure in place to facilitate the transfer of disciplinary records, with respect to a suspension or expulsion, by local educational agencies to any private or public elementary school or secondary school for any student who is enrolled or seeks, intends, or is instructed to enroll, on a full- or part-time basis, in the school."

Armed Forces Recruiter Access

FERPA currently allows schools to designate and disclose without consent certain items of information as "directory information." FERPA regulations define "directory information" under § 99.3 of the regulations and set forth the requirements for implementing a "directory information" policy under § 99.37 of FERPA. Generally, "directory information" may be disclosed by a school to any party, provided the requirements of FERPA are followed.

Congress passed a provision in the No Child Left Behind (NCLB) Act that addresses the disclosure of directory-type information (students' names, addresses, and telephone listings) to military recruiters. Congress also included similar language in the National Defense Authorization Act for fiscal year 2002. Both laws, with some exceptions, require schools to provide directory-type information to military recruiters who request it. Typically, recruiters request names, addresses, and telephone listings of junior and senior high school students that will be used for recruiting purposes and college scholarships offered by the military.

Student Privacy and Physical Exams

NCLB contains a major amendment to PPRA that gives parents more rights with regard to the surveying of minor students, the collection of information from students for marketing purposes, and certain nonemergency medical examinations. PPRA has been referred to as the Hatch Amendment and the Grassley Amendment, after the authors of amendments to the law. School officials may also hear the law referred to as the Tiahrt Amendment, after Congressman Todd Tiahrt, who introduced to PPRA the changes regarding surveys. The statute is found in 20 U.S.C. § 1232h, and the regulations are found in 34 CFR Part 98.

DEFAMATION INVOLVING SCHOOL PERSONNEL

Defamation, discussed in Chapter 6, regarding liability applies to student records. When school personnel communicate personal and sensitive information to another unauthorized person that results in injury to the student's reputation or standing in the school or that diminishes the respect and esteem to which the student is held, they may face charges of *libel* or *slander,* depending on the manner and intent with which such information was communicated. *Defamation* is a tort or civil wrong committed against another in which recovery is appropriate with a showing that the offended party received injury based on the deliberate or malicious action of others.

Slander

Slander is oral defamation, which occurs when school personnel inadvertently communicate sensitive and damaging information contained in student files to others who have no need to be informed. Libel and slander involve communication to a third party. Information contained in student files is there for the exclusive use of the teacher, principal, or counselor who has a legitimate interest in accessing this information as each works with the student. Information should not be accessed without meeting this requirement.

Once the information is ascertained, it should be used only in providing and improving educational opportunities for the student. By no means should confidential information be discussed in a thoughtless and joking manner. Under no circumstances should the student be ridiculed. The law is very specific in indicating that personally identifiable information should not be communicated to third parties without proper consent. When this is done, not only has the law been violated, but the educator has run the risk of defaming the student. Off-the-cuff remarks and sharing sensitive information regarding a student are absolutely prohibited and may result in liability damages to those who are guilty of committing such acts.

School personnel are well advised to maintain strict confidentiality in all cases involving students' personal files. In cases involving claim of personal injury, the burden of proof rests with the student in demonstrating that actual harm occurred based on deliberate communication to a third party.

Libel

Libel, unlike slander, is written defamation. Teachers, counselors, and principals should refrain from including damaging information in the student's record for which there is no basis. Any information recorded should be factual and specific with respect to serious infractions committed by the student—for example, time and place in which infractions occurred and possible witnesses who might verify, if needed, that the incident described is an accurate account of what actually occurred.

Another consideration involves a determination as to whether certain types of information should be included in the student's permanent file. Some legal experts feel that information that is subject to change and minor disciplinary infractions should be maintained in a separate file and destroyed after the student leaves school. For example, if there is no evidence of serious and recurring behavior problems, one might question the wisdom of including a single occurrence on the student's permanent records. On the other hand, if there is a strong belief that the behavior is sufficiently serious that it needs to be passed on to those who will be working with the student in the future, it might be appropriate, under the circumstances, to do so. Sound and rational judgment is required in these cases. These decisions must be carefully drawn, due to the serious implications involved. When it becomes necessary to record a serious disciplinary infraction on the student's record, it should be executed in the presence of the student, who should be provided a copy of the document.

Schools should refrain from statements that are based on opinion, particularly those involving questions of *morality, contagious diseases, family marital conditions,* and *mental or emotional issues.* These statements are damaging, based on their content, and, if communicated to others, may result in injury to the student's reputation, self-esteem, or standing in the school. Categorical statements or stereotypical statements should be avoided. If educators adhere to confidentiality and respect for the privacy rights of students, they will avoid liability claims involving injury to students. Professionalism and ethics dictate that these practices be followed.

Privilege

On many occasions, school personnel are requested to provide either oral or written information regarding a student, some of which might be contained in the student's file. When such requests are made and school personnel respond in a truthful and reasonable manner in accordance with their prescribed duties, they are protected by *qualified privilege.* When school personnel and the recipient of the information both have a common interest, they also are protected by a qualified privilege when the communication is reasonable to achieve their objective. Those who have common interest would likely include counselors, subject matter teachers, administrators, and parents. Interestingly, this privilege is lost if the communication is transmitted to another who does not share this common interest and consequently has no need to be apprised of the information.

Good Faith

Qualified privilege is based on the premise that the educator is operating in *good faith.* When damaging or sensitive information is communicated to others who have no need to know, good faith has been violated. Good faith requires that a legitimate purpose be served by communicating the information. Common interest in the student's well-being would constitute a legitimate purpose. Good faith efforts dictate that as information is shared with other eligible parties, it is communicated for legitimate purposes and without any intent or desire to damage the student. An absence of good faith may result in personal damages against those who do not operate in a reasonable and prudent manner.

An unusual case arose in Maryland when a special education student was sexually abused by her grandfather, who was charged with child abuse. Prior to his trial, he attempted to subpoena his granddaughter's school records. The child was enrolled in a special education program for emotionally disturbed children. The school district refused to furnish the records and filed a motion for a protective order. The defense attorney argued that the records were relevant in that they could reveal mental deficiencies that affected the child's ability to control her actions. The judge examined the records privately and determined that there was nothing contained in them that would serve to impeach the child's testimony. The grandfather was convicted and then appealed his conviction, contending that his rights were violated when the judge refused to allow him access to his granddaughter's records.

Maryland requires parental consent or a court order before a student's record can be disclosed. The Sixth Amendment to the Constitution requires that a criminal defendant be allowed to confront and cross-examine his or her accusers. The defendant in this case (*Zall v. State*) argued that the information contained in personal records was needed in order to cross-examine the granddaughter. The court ruled that the defendant's right to cross-examine was not violated since it had been established by the lower court that the files contained no material evidence pertinent to the case. The Sixth Amendment only requires that the defendant receive material evidence. It is the court's role, not the defendant's, to determine material evidence. The defendant's appeal was denied.[12]

Acts of Malice

Malice exists when there is intent to harm or injure another. Intent is an important element regarding malicious behavior. When statements are communicated about a student, either written or oral, with the intent to injure his or her reputation, a tortious act has occurred, especially if these statements are false. *Truth* is a defense for liability, if no malicious intent is present. School personnel should exercise care in ensuring that statements communicated to others are free of malice, based on defensible evidence, and communicated in a professional, nonbiased, and truthful manner. When evidence reveals that school personnel acted in *bad faith* with the *intent* to injure a student's reputation and standing in the school or community, liability charges may be justified, even if statements are true. Students are entitled to a *liberty right* with respect to the expectation that their reputation be protected against unwarranted attacks.

There are essentially two types of malice. In *implied malice,* the offender has no defense for conveying harmful information. Such statements normally fall in the category of unsolicited or derogatory statements aimed at another person. In *actual malice,* the offended person must demonstrate that the person making the offensive comment had a motive for doing so and that this motive was calculated to generate ill will against the offended person. Both types may create serious legal problems for school personnel.

Since the passage of FERPA, numerous forms of litigation have surfaced, covering a full range of legal issues. The following cases summarize a number of issues faced by the courts related to the enforcement of FERPA:

1. A New York court ruled that a public school was required to release names of bilingual students with English deficiencies because complainants had demonstrated a genuine need for the information that outweighed the privacy rights of students.[13]
2. Another New York court ruled that a father's request to release third-grade test scores of other students so that they could be compared to his child's score could be honored if the test results were not identified by student names.[14]
3. A Missouri court upheld a school board member against charges of defamation who commented during a board meeting that marijuana cigarettes had been found in a student's car. His statement was held to be privileged.[15]
4. A federal court in New York ruled against a student who withheld his records from a grand jury when he could not show that they bore no relevance to the subject under investigation.[16]

In other developments, a case emerged in Illinois when a group of parents requested that their school district disclose standardized achievement scores for students for certain years, grades, and schools within the district, along with a listing of educational programs available in those schools. The district, using FERPA as its defense, refused to comply with their request. Suit was filed by parents, seeking disclosure under the Freedom of Information Act. The district court dismissed the case, which was then appealed to the Illinois Court of Appeals. The appeals court reversed the district's court decision and remanded, finding that the district had an obligation to release and mask all released information regarding students. The school district then appealed, contending that releasing masked information was in conflict with the Freedom of Information Act and would not protect the privacy rights of students. The Supreme Court held that the act was designed to open governmental records to public scrutiny. The act did not prohibit disclosure of masked student records. Because no students were identified, there is no invasion of privacy and the records must be released.[17]

Administrative Guide

Liability and Student Records

1. School districts and schools should have legally defensible policies and procedures consistent with the requirements of FERPA. Students, parents, and legal guardians should be informed of their rights under this act.
2. Accurate records should be maintained in the student's file, indicating the name, title, date, description of educational interest, specific records examined, and the place of examination of student records for those who have access.
3. Any corrections or adjustments to student records should be dated and initialed by the person responsible, with the knowledge and approval of school officials.
4. School personnel should avoid labeling children.
5. When it becomes necessary to place disciplinary infraction information on student records, the information should be specific regarding the infraction committed—time, place, and witnesses, as appropriate. The student should be present when such information is recorded.
6. School personnel should refrain from aimless chatter involving third parties regarding confidential information found on student records. Gossip or careless talk among school personnel calculated to harm a student is not protected by qualified privilege.
7. Student records should be maintained in a safe and secure place and should not be removed from school premises by school personnel unless proper authorization is secured.
8. Unless prohibited by court order, the noncustodial parent should be afforded the same right to access student records as the custodial parent.
9. To avoid allegations of malicious intent, transmit only the information that is requested by a prospective employer.
10. Refrain from releasing information over the telephone, unless identity of the other party has been firmly established.
11. Where conflict or difficulty arises regarding interpretation of FERPA, consultation with the school district's attorney would be appropriate.
12. Public disclosures of students' grades will not likely be supported by the courts. Such practices violate the intent of FERPA and should not be supported by school officials.
13. Digitization of student records must ensure high quality and not compromise the integrity and confidentiality of the records.

CASE STUDIES

Student Records and FERPA

Bernice Evans, mother of a twelve-year-old daughter, sued the board of education for releasing to a local newspaper reporter information regarding her daughter's medical condition. The newspaper article referred to a twelve-year-old female hermaphrodite with severe emotional and behavioral problems. School board members asserted that they were simply attempting to explain why the district needed to expand emergency funds to meet the needs of students with special problems. They further argued that the information did not personally identify the student because no name was revealed to the reporter.

Discussion Questions

1. Did the school board err in releasing this information? Why or why not?
2. Does Mrs. Evans have a valid claim? Why or why not?
3. Does the school board have a defensible basis for revealing the information? Why or why not?

4. How does FERPA apply in this case?
5. How do you think the court would rule in this case?
6. Provide a rationale for your response.
7. What are the administrative implications of this case?

Student Records and Breach of Confidentiality

Jamie Price, a teacher in an affluent high school in the mid-South, reviewed the educational records of one of her students and discovered some very confidential information that she shared with another teacher during their break in the teacher's lounge. Because the other teacher had not personally accessed the information, she felt comfortable sharing this information with another colleague.

Discussion Questions

1. Is there a risk in sharing confidential student information with a colleague? Why or why not?
2. What legal options might the student exercise in this situation, and under what circumstances might these options be pursued?
3. What is Price's defense if challenges about her divulging this information arise?
4. How might the courts rule in this case if a legal challenge arises?
5. What factors might influence this ruling?
6. What advice would you provide for teachers regarding sharing confidential information to a second or third party?

Defamation and Student Records

A high school principal and a tenured teacher investigated a situation regarding suspected drug involvement of students in an inner city high school. They also provided counseling for students and their parents. When they revealed their findings to the local law enforcement agency that drug involvement was present among specified groups of students, the parents sued, alleging defamation.

Discussion Questions

1. Do these parents have a valid claim? Why or why not?
2. Did releasing information on a specified group of students constitute defamation? Why or why not?
3. What defense might the principal and teacher use to justify revealing the information?
4. How would a court likely rule in this situation?
5. What criteria would the court use in reaching a decision?
6. What are the administrative implications in this case?

Disclosure of Disciplinary Action Involving a Student

An elementary student was disciplined for verbally and physically abusing other students. Parents of the victims were notified by the district of the student's actions. The assaulting student was suspended. His parent filed suit alleging a violation of FERPA by disclosing information about her son to other parents.

Discussion Questions

1. Does the complaining parent have a valid claim? If so, why or why not?
2. Does disclosure under the circumstances described constitute a FERPA violation? Why or why not?
3. Does the memorandum sent to parents constitute a release of an educational record? Why or why not?
4. How would a court likely rule on the complaining parent's allegation? Provide a rationale for your response.
5. What criteria would the court use in reaching a decision?
6. What are the administrative implications in this case?

Endnotes

1. 20 USC S. 1232 g.
2. C.F.R. § 99.6.
3. ed.gov/policy/gen/guid/fpco/ferpa/safeguarding-student-privacy.pdf
4. *Garlick v. Oak Park and River Forest High School Dist. #200,* No. 1-08-2017, 2009 WL 858866 (Ill. App. Ct. 3/30/09).
5. *Page v. Rotterdam-Mohonasen Central School District,* 441 N.Y.S. 2d 323 (Sup. Ct. 1981).
6. *Ellis v. Cleveland Municipal School District,* 309 F. Supp. 2d 1019 (N.D. Ohio, 2004).
7. *Rhea v. District Board of Trustees of Santa Fe College,* Fla. App. 109 So. 3d 851 (2013).
8. *Tarasoff v. Regents of the University of California,* 17 Cal. 3d 425; 551 P. 2d 334; 131 Cal. Rptr. 14 (1976).
9. *Owasso Independent School District No. I-011 v. Falvo,* 534 U.S. 426; 122 S.Ct. 934; 151 L. Ed. 2d 896 (2002).
10. *Doe v. Gonzaga,* 143 Wash. 2d 687, 24 P. 3d 390 (2001).
11. *United States of America v. Miami University,* 294 F. 3d 797 (6th Cir. 2002).
12. *Zall v. State,* 584 A. 2d 119 (Md. App. 1991).
13. *Rios v. Read,* 73 F. Rd. 589 (1977).
14. *Kryston v. Board of Education, East Rampano,* 77 A.D. 2d 896 (1980).
15. Springfield R-12, 447 S.W. 2d 256 (Mo. 1969).
16. *Frascas v. Andrews,* 463 F. Supp. 1043 (1979).
17. *Bowie v. Evanston Community Consolidated School District,* 538 N.E. 2d 557 (Ill. 1989).

Chapter 8

Teacher Freedoms

Public school teachers do not relinquish their rights as a condition of accepting an employment position in the public schools. Although teachers are expected to be sensitive to the professional nature of their positions and have a regard for the integrity of the profession, they do enjoy certain constitutional freedoms that must be respected by school authorities. Because teachers enter the profession with constitutional rights and freedoms, boards of education must establish a compelling reason to restrict these freedoms. In these instances, the burden rests with school authorities to demonstrate that their actions are not arbitrary, capricious, or motivated by personal and political objectives.

The courts, in addressing conflicts involving constitutional freedoms of teachers, attempt to balance the public interest of the school district against the personal rights of each individual employee. Thus, teachers are subject to reasonable restraints only if a legitimate, defensible rationale is established by the school district.

SUBSTANTIVE AND PROCEDURAL CONSIDERATIONS

As stated in Chapter 3, there are two types of due process, both of which apply to teachers: substantive and procedural. **Procedural due process** means that the state may not deprive any person of life, liberty, or property, without due process of law. Therefore, a teacher must be given proper notice that he or she is to be deprived of his or her personal rights. The teacher must be provided an opportunity to be heard, and the hearing must be conducted in a fair manner. Failure to follow procedural requirements will result in a violation of the teacher's constitutional rights. **Substantive due process** means that the state must have a valid objective when it intends to deprive a teacher of life, liberty, or property, and the means used must be reasonably calculated to achieve its objective. Most important, both procedural and substantive requirements must be met in teacher dismissal proceedings. Many administrative decisions that were correct in substance have been overturned on appeal based simply on the grounds that procedural requirements were not met. Conversely, procedural requirements may be met by school officials when the evidence reveals that a valid reason did not exist that warranted depriving a teacher of his or her rights. The administrative decision in this case would be overturned as well.

FREEDOM OF EXPRESSION

By virtue of the First Amendment to the Constitution, teachers are afforded rights to freedom of expression. Within limits, they enjoy the same rights and privileges regarding speech and expression as other citizens. Free speech by teachers, however, is limited to the requirement that such speech does not create *material disruption* to the educational interest of the school district. Material disruption, for an example, may involve an interference with the rights of others or may involve speech that creates a negative impact on proper school discipline and decorum. The level of protection provided to teachers is generally lower in cases where the teacher speaks on matters that are personal in nature, as opposed to those that are of interest to the community.

In either case, school officials may not justifiably prohibit or penalize the teacher in any manner for exercising a constitutionally protected right without showing that a legitimate state interest is affected by the teacher's speech or expression. As usual, in cases where the teacher's speech is restricted, the burden of proof justifying such restriction rests with school authorities. Districts have succeeded in their actions to restrict speech and to discipline teachers when there was evidence that the teacher's personal speech undermined authority and adversely affected working relationships. In the absence of such showing, the teacher's speech is protected.

In fact, the Supreme Court addressed the application of the First Amendment in employment situations by emphasizing the distinction between speech involving public concern and grievances regarding internal personnel matters in the *Connick v. Myers* case. Expressions regarding public concerns, according to the High Court, receive First Amendment protections, whereas ordinary employee grievances are to be handled by the appropriate administrative body without involvement of the court.[1] In this case, the issue involved a petition, circulated within an office, that was related to the proper functioning of the office. This type of personal speech did not receive First Amendment protection.

Another example involved a sarcastic, unprofessional, and insulting memorandum written by a teacher to various school officials. The teacher found that expressing his private disagreement with school policies and procedures, which he refused to follow, was unprotected speech not related to a matter of public concern. Further, he was not speaking as a private citizen but rather as an employee of the district. Another court stated that "to hold for the teacher in private expressions would be to transform every personal grievance into protected speech when complaints are raised about classroom materials, teacher aids, laboratory equipment and other related issues."[2]

Speech Outside the School Environment

Teachers are afforded First Amendment rights outside the school environment. They may speak on issues that interest them and the community, even though their speech may not be deemed acceptable by school district officials. This, of course, has not always been the case.

In the past, a commonly held belief was that public employees, including teachers, had only a limited right to freedom of expression. This restrictive posture stemmed from the commonly held view that public employment was a privilege. Although the courts have failed to support this view, many teachers in the past were restricted in their rights to freedom of expression.

Freedom of speech outside the school environment is well established; however, when exercising such speech, *a teacher should preface his or her comments by indicating that he or she is speaking as a private citizen rather than an employee of the board.* This public disclosure is significant in establishing that the teacher's speech is not the official position of the school district. This disclosure further reinforces the notion that a teacher possesses the same First Amendment privileges as regular citizens. Although teachers enjoy First Amendment rights, those rights are not without reasonable restrictions, based on the nature of the position held and the positive image teachers are expected to project. In all cases, the teacher's speech should be professional in nature and not designed to harm or injure another's reputation or render the teacher unfit, based on the content of the speech itself. These standards apply whether the speech is verbal or written.

A leading Supreme Court decision in the *Pickering* case established the limits on freedom of expression rights by school personnel.[3] This case arose in Will County, Illinois, when Marvin Pickering, a teacher in the district, was dismissed from his position by the board of education in connection with sending to the local newspaper an editorial that was critical of the school's administration and the allocation of tax funds raised by the school.

Pickering's dismissal resulted from a determination by the board, after a full hearing, that the publication was detrimental to the efficient operation and administration of the school. Hence, under relevant Illinois statutes, in the "interest of the school," dismissal was required. Pickering's claim that his speech was protected by the First and Fourteenth Amendments was rejected. He appealed the board's ruling to the circuit court of Will County, which supported his dismissal on the grounds established by the school board. On appeal, the Supreme Court of Illinois affirmed the judgment of the circuit court.

Pickering's letter criticized the school board's handling of the 1961 bond issue proposals and the subsequent allocation of financial resources between the school's educational and athletic programs. The board dismissed Pickering for writing his editorial, charging that numerous statements contained in the letter were false and that the letter unjustifiably impugned the motives, honesty, integrity, truthfulness, responsibility, and competence of the board and the school's administration. The board further claimed that the false statements damaged the professional reputation of its members and the administration.

The U.S. Supreme Court reversed the Illinois State Supreme Court's decision and held for Pickering. The High Court concluded, "To the extent that the Illinois Supreme Court's opinion may be read to suggest that teachers may constitutionally be compelled to relinquish the First Amendment rights they would otherwise enjoy as citizens to comment on matters of public interest in connection with the operation of public schools in which they work, it proceeds on a premise that has been unequivocally rejected in numerous prior decisions of this court."

Although some of Pickering's statements proved to be untrue, the High Court held that teachers are afforded First Amendment rights, which Pickering had been denied. In responding to several incorrect statements contained in Pickering's letter, the Supreme Court stated, "Absent proof of false statements knowingly or recklessly made by him, a teacher's exercise of his rights to speak on issues of public importance may not furnish the basis for his dismissal from public employment."[4]

The *Pickering* ruling represented a significant victory for public school teachers. Prior to this ruling, it would not have been uncommon to find teachers seeking new employment if they publicly criticized their school district's practices. *Pickering* also was significant in generating guidelines regarding freedom of expression issues involving teachers. If the teacher's speech disrupted superior–subordinate relationships or resulted in a breach of loyalty or confidentiality, the teacher may be disciplined. Further, if the teacher's speech created disruption of a material and substantial nature, affected the efficient operation of the school, or rendered the teacher unfit based on the content of the speech, appropriate action also may be taken against the teacher.

In addition to the *Pickering* guidelines, a Connecticut court generated the following guidelines involving freedom of expression issues regarding the operation of the public schools:

1. The impact on harmony, personal loyalty, and confidence among coworkers
2. The degree of falsity of statements
3. The place where speech or distribution of material occurred
4. The impact on the staff and students, and
5. The degree to which the teacher's conduct lacked professionalism.[5]

In a significant non-educational case, *Garcetti v. Ceballos*, the plaintiff, Ceballos, alleged that he had been denied consideration for a promotion for criticizing the legitimacy of a warrant.[6] The district attorney's office, on being informed by Ceballos, refused to dismiss the case. Ceballos then informed the defense that he believed that the **affidavit** contained false statements. He subsequently was subpoenaed to testify. The Ninth Circuit Court ruled that Ceballos was protected by the First Amendment because he had engaged in speech that addressed matters of public concern. In a 5–4 decision authored by Justice William Kennedy, the U.S. Supreme Court held that speech by a public official is protected only if he or she is engaged as a private citizen. Therefore, Ceballos's employers were justified in taking action against him based on his testimony and cooperation with the defense. His speech occurred as a part of his official duties. Consequently, his supervisors were not prohibited from evaluating his performance.

This case illustrates the level of protection afforded public school teachers by the court during the exercise of their First Amendment rights. The case arose in Mississippi when an art teacher, with twenty-one years of experience, criticized the superintendent for eliminating the art program at a historically African American junior high school while retaining the program at a historically white junior high school. The superintendent justified his action by stating that no instructors could be located for the African American school. The teacher subsequently located viable candidates for the position and joined in ongoing criticism of the superintendent by community supporters.

The teacher wrote an editorial in the local newspaper, spoke out during public forums, and sent a letter of no confidence to the superintendent. The superintendent then arranged for a demotion of the teacher to the African American junior high school. The teacher filed a suit against the superintendent and the board of education. The superintendent requested summary judgment, which was denied by the district court. The superintendent appealed to the Fifth Circuit Court of Appeals.

The appeals court, in holding for the teacher, noted that the teacher had joined in public criticism of the superintendent and was not merely expressing a personal grievance regarding his demotion. His actions were regarded as protected public speech, and the district court's ruling denying summary judgment was appropriate. Because the superintendent's actions in demoting the teacher may have been motivated by personal reasons, the teacher's First Amendment right was properly retained. The superintendent's appeal was dismissed.[7]

In a slightly different case, a teacher did not prevail based solely on First Amendment protection. In the *Mt. Healthy* case, a nontenured teacher who previously had been involved in several altercations with other teachers, employees, and students—including an incident in which he made obscene gestures to female students—phoned into a radio station the contents of the principal's memorandum to faculty regarding the dress code for teachers.[8] The radio station announced the adoption of the dress code. The board, on the recommendation of the superintendent, informed the teacher that he would not be rehired based on a lack of tact in handling professional matters and specifically referenced the obscene gesture and radio station incident. The teacher challenged the validity of the termination. The court held that in order to prevail in a First Amendment case, an employee must show that his expression is protected and that it was the motivating factor in the board's action. Also, the board must fail to show that it would have taken the same action in the absence of the employee's conduct.

Because the teacher's conduct did not disrupt the orderly operation of the school, it was constitutionally protected and could not serve as the basis for employment termination. However, by engaging in constitutionally protected conduct, a teacher should not be able to prevent an employer from assessing his or her entire performance record and reaching a decision not to rehire on the basis of the record.

As one can see, the teacher's freedom of expression rights are protected. They are, however, subject to reasonable considerations regarding order, loyalty, professionalism, and overall impact on the operation of the school. If prudence is exercised by the teacher in expressing views of public interest, he or she should not be subject to disciplinary measures or retaliation by the school district. However, if his or her overall performance record does not meet the school's expectation, dismissal may occur in spite of First Amendment privileges.

A case involving retaliation and First Amendment speech arose in Oklahoma when the U.S. Court of Appeals for the Tenth Circuit held that a school board engaged in a retaliatory employment action in violation of a teacher's First Amendment speech rights when it terminated him for making a false, but good faith, accusation and then reinstated him in a less desirable position.[9] After students discovered pornographic materials in a dumpster at Frontier Public Schools (Oklahoma), Owen Hawzipita, a high school art teacher, was told by the shipping company that the materials had been ordered by the high school's principal. Hawzipita reported his concerns to the superintendent and demanded an investigation. The local newspapers picked up the story. Eventually, the elementary school principal came forward and admitted that he, not the high school principal, had ordered the materials. The school board terminated Hawzipita, who appealed to state court and won reinstatement. When he returned to work, he was assigned to the in-school suspension program rather than to his previous position as art teacher. The Tenth Circuit concluded that Hawzipita presented sufficient evidence to establish a valid retaliation claim. Specifically, his speech was on a matter of public concern because it not only informed, but also created, the public debate. Hawzipita's reassignment was sufficiently onerous to constitute a detrimental employment action because it deprived him of the ability to utilize his specialized skills and experience and limited his interaction with members of the school community.

Academic Freedom

Public school teachers are afforded a judicially recognized academic interest in their classrooms, based on the teacher's right to teach and the students' right to learn. Academic freedom, as a concept, originated in the German universities during the nineteenth century with the express purpose of allowing professors to teach any subject they deemed educationally appropriate.

Public school teachers, of course, are not provided the same broad latitude extended to professors in higher education. *Academic freedom is a very limited concept in public schools.* It supports the belief that the classroom should be a marketplace of ideas and that teachers should be provided freedom of inquiry, research, and discussion of various ideas and issues. Because public school teachers teach children of tender years who are impressionable, their freedom of expression in the classroom is limited by factors such as grade level, age, experience, and readiness of students to handle the content under discussion.

The teacher should also be certain that the subject matter introduced into classroom discussion is within the scope of students' intellectual and social maturity levels. Public school teachers are further restrained by the requirement that *content introduced into classroom discussion be related to and consistent with the teacher's certification and teaching assignment.* Controversial material unrelated to the subject taught and inappropriate, based on content, will not be supported by the courts.

The point was clearly illustrated in the *Fowler* case, which arose when a tenured teacher was discharged for insubordination and conduct unbecoming of a teacher.[10] The basis for her dismissal was that she had an R-rated movie, Pink Floyd's *The Wall,* shown to a high school class on the last day of school. A group of students requested that Fowler allow the movie to be shown while she completed grade reports. Fowler was not familiar with the movie and asked students whether the movie was appropriate for viewing at school. One student who had seen the movie indicated that it had one bad spot in it. She instructed the student who had seen the movie to edit out any parts that were not suitable for viewing by the class. He attempted to do so by covering a 25-inch screen with an $8^1/_2 \times 11$-inch folder. The facts revealed that the movie contained nudity and a good bit of violence. Fowler testified that in spite of the fact she had not seen the movie and had left the classroom several times during its viewing, it had significant value. Furthermore, she would show an edited version again if given an opportunity. The board viewed the edited version of the movie during an executive session and voted unanimously in an open session to terminate Fowler for insubordination and conduct unbecoming of a teacher. The court recognized that Fowler was entitled to First Amendment protection under certain circumstances and that a motion picture is a form of expression that may be entitled to First Amendment protection. However, it ruled that Fowler's conduct in having the movie shown under the circumstances presented did not constitute expression protected by the First Amendment. The board was upheld in the discharge of Fowler.

Much of what is taught in public schools is influenced by state and local board curriculum policies and guidelines, as well as statutory provisions. Public school teachers must always be mindful of these considerations. *Teachers may not use their classrooms to promote a personal or political agenda.* The classroom may not be used to indoctrinate or to encourage students to accept beliefs, attend meetings, or disregard parents' wishes regarding involvement with religious groups.[11]

In light of certain restrictions, the concept of the classroom as a marketplace of ideas does apply to elementary and secondary schools. This point was well expressed in a ruling by a district court:

> Most writings on academic freedom have dealt with the universities where the courts supported the essentiality of freedom in the community of American universities. Yet, the effects of procedures which smother grade school teachers cannot be ignored. An environment of free inquiry is necessary for the majority of students who do not go on to college; even those who go on to higher education will have acquired most of their working and thinking habits in grade school and high school. Moreover, much of what was formerly taught in many colleges in the first year or so of undergraduate studies is now covered in upper grades of good high schools....
>
> The considerations which militate in favor of academic freedom—our historical commitment to free speech for all, the peculiar importance of academic inquiry to the progress of society in an atmosphere of open inquiry, feeling always free to challenge and improve established ideas—are relevant to elementary and secondary schools, as well as to institutions of higher learning.[12]

This passage adequately summarizes the importance of the recognized academic interests of elementary and secondary teachers. These privileges may not be abridged without evidence by the district that a legitimate state interest is threatened by the teacher's actions in the classroom.

The following summaries of cases reflect the court's position on various issues regarding academic freedom in public schools. One case dealt with the question of whether a teacher could, for educational purposes, assign and discuss in class an article containing a term for an incestuous son that was offensive to many. The article was written by a highly respected psychiatrist and appeared in a high-quality publication. Any student who felt the assignment to be personally offensive was permitted to choose an alternative one. The teacher would not agree, based on the district's demand, never to use the word again in the classroom. The court found the district's rule to be unenforceable. It observed that the word in question appeared in at least five books in the library, but the court did not rest its decision on this ground.[13]

In another case, the teacher had discussed the meaning of "taboo" words by using another word, deemed highly offensive to many, for sexual intercourse. The First Circuit Court affirmed the teacher's right but did indicate that teachers do not have a license to say or write whatever they choose in the classroom. The court was not in total agreement as to whether the First Amendment protected the teacher's actions, but it held for the teacher on the grounds of due process because school officials had enforced a vague rule after the incident had occurred.[14]

Teachers may not claim First Amendment protection when they make damaging and inappropriate statements in the classroom, as illustrated by the following case. A Missouri appellate court ruled that a school district did not violate a teacher's First Amendment free speech rights when it terminated her for making disparaging comments about interracial marriages and biracial children.[15] Jendra Loeffelman taught eighth-grade English at Crystal City Elementary School. When a student asked her view on interracial relationships, Loeffelman responded that she opposed them. She added that interracial couples should be "fixed" so they cannot have children who are "racially confused." Her class included biracial children. The school board concluded that it had the authority to terminate her contract on the ground that she had willfully violated board policy by engaging in discriminatory conduct and making disparaging racial comments. Loeffelman sued, alleging that the school board had erred in two ways: It lacked the authority to dismiss her because it had failed to prove she had willfully violated the board's policies, and it violated her free speech rights by terminating her for speaking on a matter of public concern. The appellate court concluded that the evidence was sufficient to show willful violation because it supported findings that Loeffelman was aware of the board policies and that she spoke with the knowledge that her comments were disparaging of interracial relationships and biracial children. The court next found that the teacher's comments did not qualify for First Amendment protection because her speech concerned private opinion rather than a matter of public concern. Even if her speech were a matter of public concern, the school board's interest in maintaining harmony and efficiency in the workplace outweighed the teacher's right to make racially insensitive and disruptive remarks.

Teachers, whether **tenured** or nontenured, do not have the latitude to deviate from the school's mission, vision, or behavioral expectations. Teachers do not operate on their own terms; rather they are expected to conform to school and district professional goals, practices, and prescribed strategies. Teachers are not expected to operate in isolation of mandated school expectations unless there is evidence of constitutional violations. Academic freedom is a limited concept and is subject to reasonable academic and curricula mandates by the school or district. Teachers do not have a right to prescribe course content. School boards are generally afforded this authority by their state legislature. Academic freedom does not permit teachers to ignore or omit prescribed course content. Examples of behavior that are not protected by academic freedom include publically shouting at co-workers, publically berating students, defaming superiors, shirking professional duties and responsibilities, failing to follow prescribed curricula, proselytizing students, and undermining district and school mission, philosophy, and culture among others.

TEACHER USE OF FACEBOOK AND SOCIAL MEDIA

Teachers enjoy rights to freedom of expression under the First Amendment. Thus, they may express their views outside the classroom as any other citizen with the awareness that their actions often affect students they teach. The courts' view is that teachers are role models for their students and must always be sensitive to and have a reasonable regard for the nature of the profession. Consequently, teachers should exercise caution when using Facebook, Twitter, Instagram, and other social media. They should refrain from messages or images that may raise questions regarding fitness to teach that may be grounds for discipline including termination. For example, a teacher was fired for posting a picture of herself holding a glass of wine and a mug of beer and using the "b" word on Facebook. The teacher was offered an option to resign or be suspended. She elected to resign and is now seeking reinstatement to her job. Dozens of teachers have been investigated, and some have been terminated for inappropriate interactions and relationships with students that began or were conducted on social media websites in New York City schools. Teachers should be mindful that if a particular type of behavior is unacceptable in the classroom, then it is also unacceptable on social media sites. It would be prudent for teachers to avoid having students as Facebook friends. To be safe and protected, teachers should refrain from using social media to communicate with their students for non-curricular purposes.

For example, the Board of Education in Paramus, New Jersey, approved restrictions on employee use of social networks and cell phones, including a prohibition against naming students as "friends" on social media and providing cell phone numbers to students without permission from supervisors. Even then, teachers cannot call students under the age of eighteen on their cell phones without the authorization of a parent.

All electronic contacts with students should be made through the district's computer account or e-mail and telephone system based on district policy. New York officials indicated that they chose not to prohibit all forms of direct electronic contact, such as providing assistance for a student in distress, but could still discipline teachers who used cell phones inappropriately. Similar policies have been passed by school districts in Ohio, Florida, Missouri, and other states.

The following represents a summary of incidents involving teacher misconduct and social media:

1. Three male high school teachers in New Jersey have been arrested and accused of having inappropriate sexual relationships with three female students. Social media were used to establish improper relationships with students. The vice principal is facing charges of official misconduct for allegedly knowing about these sexual allegations and not reporting them to law enforcement.

   Source: abc15.com/dpp/news/national/3-triton-regional-high-school-teachers-in-runnemede-new-jersey-caught-in-student-relationships

2. A female high school teacher pleaded guilty to e-mailing to a sixteen-year-old student nude pictures of herself under a screen name, "RedsoxX6606 Whore."

   Source: cbsnews.com/pictures/notorious-teacher-sex-scandals-17-7-09

3. A female Indiana teacher was arrested after allegedly having sex with a seventeen-year-old student. She was charged with child seduction. The relationship began with exchanges and messages via text and social networking sites.

   Source: cbsnews.com/pictures/notorious-teacher-sex-scandals/12

4. A high school football coach in Connecticut was sentenced to forty-six months in prison on federal child sex charges for having several online chats with a fourteen-year-old girl asking if she wanted to see him naked and learn to perform sexual acts.

   Source: boston.com/sports/football/articles/2009/01/05/former_high_school_coach_sentenced_in_sex_case

5. A twenty-three-year-old Florida female teacher was charged with statutory rape involving a fourteen-year-old male student after provocative modeling photographs had circulated on the Internet. She had briefly worked as a model when she was eighteen.

   Source: cbsnews.com/pictures/notorious-teacher-sex-scandals-17-7-09

6. A school district dismissed a tenured teacher on charges of unbecoming behavior when she posted derogative statements about her first-grade students on Facebook, such as, "I am not a teacher but a warden for future criminals."

   Source: In Re Tenure Hearing of O'Brien

7. A study by the Salt Lake Tribune revealed that two of every five teacher misconduct cases with a sexual component involve e-mails, texting, and social media sites such as Facebook.

   Source: Salt Lake Tribune, December 1, 2013

8. Two teachers were arrested in Las Vegas for sending sexually explicit messages to students.

   Source: Las Vegas Sun, September 27, 2013

FREEDOM OF ASSOCIATION

The First Amendment guarantees citizens the right to peacefully assemble. Freedom of association is included within this right of assembly, because teachers, as citizens, are entitled to the same rights and privileges provided other citizens. *Freedom of association* grants people the right to associate with other individuals of their choice without threat of punishment. Although teachers enjoy these rights, they should exercise them in light of the nature and importance of their positions as public employees. Further, they should be concerned with the "role-model image" they project and the impact of their actions on impressionable young children. The Supreme Court stated, "A teacher serves as a role model for his students, exerting a subtle but important influence over their perceptions and values."[16]

The High Court's view was further expressed in a case in which two unsuccessful applicants for teaching certification in New York filed suit enjoining the enforcement of a state statute that forbids aliens from obtaining public school teacher certification. Both teachers were married to U.S. citizens, had been in the country for more than ten years, and had earned degrees at U.S. colleges. The New York statute allowed the commissioner of education to determine a special need for the person's skills and competencies. The Court held for the state of New York, ruling that a statute that generally prohibits, with some exceptions, aliens from obtaining teacher certification is constitutional. The court further stated that a citizenship requirement for teaching bears a rational relationship to the legitimate state interest in public education because the people of New York, through their lawmakers, have determined that people who are citizens are better qualified than those who have rejected the open invitation extended to qualify for eligibility to teach by applying for citizenship in this country.[17]

Freedom of association has not always been recognized as a constitutional freedom by school districts, as countless restrictions were placed on teachers by their districts. In the early to mid-1900s, African American and white teachers were forbidden to socialize with one another. In some districts, membership in the National Association for the Advancement of Colored People (NAACP) or the Ku Klux Klan was fatal to the teacher if awareness of such affiliation became public.

In some instances, school personnel who had been involved in organized labor organizations or educational associations received questionable treatment by their school districts. This treatment was often reflected in the form of demotions, unwarranted transfers, nonrenewals, and even terminations. An example of such treatment is illustrated by the following case. A Missouri school board voted not to renew the contracts of three probationary teachers. These three teachers had publicly advocated higher teacher salaries and affiliation with the Missouri National Education Association. They alleged that their contracts were not renewed in retaliation for these activities in violation of their First Amendment rights to free speech and association. The court held for the teachers by awarding $7,500 in damages and reinstatement to their teaching positions. The district appealed. On appeal, the U.S. Court of Appeals for the Eighth Circuit agreed that despite the probationary or nontenured status of these teachers, the school board could not constitutionally refuse to renew their contracts in retaliation for the exercise of their First Amendment rights. The court remanded the issue of damages to the lower court regarding the awarding of back pay and attorney fees.[18] As illustrated by this case, school districts will not succeed when they retaliate against school personnel for the proper exercise of their rights regarding their involvement in union-related activities. They may not be legally penalized for such involvement.

Since the late 1960s, the court has shown a discernible trend toward providing teachers more freedom regarding their personal lives than was true in the past. Courts now hold that teachers, including administrators, are free to join their professional organizations, assume a leadership role, campaign for membership, and negotiate with the school board on behalf of the organization without fear of reprisal. School personnel must ensure that their participation in external organizations does not, in any manner, reduce their effectiveness as district employees or create material or substantial disruption to the operation of the district.

School personnel may also engage in various types of political activities. They may become a candidate for public office or campaign for their favorite candidate. However, school personnel may be requested to take personal leave when they run for public office. These are permissible activities, as long as they occur after school hours and do not interfere with job effectiveness.

Membership in Subversive Organizations

There has been controversy in the past regarding membership in subversive organizations by school personnel that resulted in threats of dismissal. The Supreme Court has held that *mere membership in subversive organizations is not sufficient within itself to justify dismissal.* The teacher must have demonstrated that he or she actually participated in an unlawful activity or intended to achieve an unlawful objective before punishment may be meted.

In a leading case, the Supreme Court in *Elfbrandt v. Russel* indicated, "Those who join an organization but do not share its unlawful purposes and who do not participate in its unlawful activities surely pose no threat, either as a citizen or as a public employee."[19]

This case involved an Arizona act that required an oath by employees of the state. A teacher challenged the act, refusing to take the oath based on good conscience. She further claimed that the oath was unclear in its meaning, and she was unable to secure a hearing to have the meaning clarified. The oath read as follows: "I do solemnly swear . . . that I will support the Constitution of the United States and . . . of the State of Arizona; that I will bear true faith and allegiance to the same and defend them against all enemies, foreign and domestic, and that I will faithfully and impartially discharge the duties of the office (name of office)." Anyone taking the oath was subject to prosecution for perjury and discharge from office if he or she knowingly or willfully became or remained a member of the Communist Party or any other organization that advocated an overthrow of the government.

The High Court ruled that a loyalty oath statute that carries sanction to membership without requiring specific intent to further the illegal objectives of the organizations is unconstitutional. The court stated further that the due process provision of the Fourteenth Amendment requires that a statute that infringes on protected constitutional rights, in this case freedom of association, "be narrowly drawn to define and punish specific conduct as constituting a clear and present danger to a substantial interest of the state."[20]

Another significant Supreme Court decision was rendered in *Keyishian v. Board of Regents of University of State of N.Y.*[21] This case emerged, based on a complex set of laws in New York, calling for the discharge of employees of the state education system who utter treasonable or seditious words, perform the same acts, advocate or distribute material supporting an overthrow of the government, or belong to subversive organizations. Keyishian and a number of faculty and staff at the University of New York who refused to certify that they were not and had not been members of subversive organizations were faced with dismissal from their jobs. They sought declaratory relief from the statute and sought to have it declared unconstitutional. The High Court held for the plaintiffs, stating that loyalty oaths that make membership in an organization sufficient for termination of employment are constitutionally impermissible. To be valid, a loyalty statute must be confined to knowing active members who aid in pursuing the illegal goals of the organization.

Without exception, public school employees are protected from arbitrary loyalty oaths and undue intrusion with respect to their rights of association. There must be defensible evidence of the employee's actual participation or planned participation in unlawful activities to mete any form of discipline. Mere association without an unlawful intent is not sufficient cause to penalize employees and is in violation of their First and Fourteenth Amendment rights.

Political Rights

Based on the State Interest Test, state laws prohibiting public employees from participating in all types of political activities have been deemed unconstitutional. Public school teachers have the same political rights and freedoms enjoyed by all citizens. These include, but are not limited to, running for public office, campaigning for themselves or others, developing and expounding political ideologies, and engaging in political debate. These rights, however, should be exercised with a degree of restraint inasmuch as they are not unlimited. At all times the teacher must be aware of the effect of his or her actions on others, especially children. Teachers should also ensure that engaging in political activities does not have an adverse effect on classroom performance. Teachers must limit their political activity to acts away from the classroom and outside of the normal school day. They must further ensure that their political activity in no way interferes with or infringes on their duties and responsibilities in the classroom.

An example of a teacher's political and speech rights is reflected in a case that arose in Indiana where a U.S. district court held that a teacher had a right to participate in a political demonstration by honking her horn in response to a "honk for peace" sign protesting the war in Iraq because military intervention is an issue of public importance. The teacher shared her response in class when asked by students. Because parents complained and the school principal requested that the teacher not take sides in any political controversy, her right was qualified by the requirement that the expression not disrupt an employer's business unduly.[22]

Right to Hold Office

State laws vary regarding the extent to which school personnel may legally participate in political activities and hold public office. Generally speaking, any public official (which may include a teacher) is prohibited from using his or her office or position for personal gain. The board of education may require a teacher to take a leave of absence when he or she becomes a candidate for public office. Generally, this requirement has been upheld by a number of courts. In no case, however, should a teacher's contract be canceled because he or she becomes a candidate for public office. This would be arbitrarily unjust and an indefensible act by a school board.

In recent years, however, courts tend to be somewhat divided on the teacher's right to run for political office. As stated previously, some courts support the requirement that the teacher should resign before actively campaigning for public office. Other courts view the prohibition against running for a political office as a violation of the teacher's constitutional right. For example, in the *Minielly v. State* case in Oregon, the district court held to be invalid a state law that prohibited public employees from running for political office. The court ruled that the state had no authority to limit the First Amendment rights of teachers.[23]

In an interesting ruling, a Kentucky court held that a requirement calling for mandatory leaves for all teachers who pursued a part-time public office violated the teacher's right to equal protection because no such requirements applied to teachers who were engaged in other types of time-consuming activities.[24] However, the trend by the courts seems to be toward greater political freedom for teachers, as long as the teacher exhibits prudent professional behavior, does not neglect his or her professional duties, and does not use the classroom as a political forum. School boards do have the capacity to ensure that political activity does not create material or substantial disruption to the educational process, which would constitute a legitimate state interest.

Participation in Political Campaigns

The right to campaign is afforded to teachers and other employees. However, they should understand that their professional role transcends their roles as citizens. Teachers and other employees must understand the time commitment required and be certain that it does not present any conflict of interest regarding job responsibilities. In addition, school district facilities, equipment, or supplies should not be used for campaign purposes. Districts normally adopt policies and procedures pertaining to employees who wish to run for public office. These policies generally will establish the terms and conditions that the employee must meet with respect to employment status regarding leave or continuing employment.

The employment status of the teacher or employee should not be impaired by the exercise of his or her political rights. Teachers' political rights should not be exercised in the name of the school or district. It should be very clearly established that the teacher or employee is exercising political rights as a citizen and not as a representative of the school district. The school district may not prevent, threaten, harass, or discriminate against any employee who elects to run for public office. In addition, the district should grant a leave of absence if requested by the employee based on the individual merits of each case presented for its consideration.

DRESS AND GROOMING

Numerous cases regarding personal appearance issues involving teachers have been litigated by the courts. School authorities generally contend that proper dress and decorum create a professional image of teachers that has a positive impact on students. Teachers, on the other hand, contend that dress code regulations governing their appearance invade their rights to free expression. Teachers further believe that they should enjoy freedom without undue restrictions on their personal appearance.

The courts generally have not been in disagreement regarding the authority of school officials to regulate teacher appearance that may disrupt the educational process. What has not been settled, however, is the *degree* of constitutional protection teachers are entitled to receive in disputes regarding dress and the type of evidence needed to invalidate restrictions on dress. To further complicate the issue, community standards and mores are also factors considered in dress and grooming rulings. School districts have traditionally restricted dress that is contrary to acceptable community norms.

Litigation involving dress and grooming issues reached its peak in the late 1960s and early to mid-1970s, as numerous challenges were raised by teachers and students regarding these issues. The courts established the position that school dress codes must be reasonably related to a legitimate educational purpose, which must be justified by standards of reasonableness.

Rules that restrict dress based on health, safety, material and substantial disruption, or community values generally have been supported by the courts. Rules that extend beyond these areas generally have not been supported. It seems evident that the courts recognize that teachers should be free of unreasonable restrictions governing their appearance. However, the difficulty comes with variations in standards by different communities, as well as changing societal norms. Community standards, values, and expectations play an important role in determining the legality of local school dress code regulations when considered in conjunction with these other factors.

The courts will not support restrictive dress and grooming codes that are unrelated to the state's interest. When challenged, the district must demonstrate that the code is related to a legitimate educational purpose, and not designed to place undue and unnecessary restrictions on teachers' dress. The burden of proof rests with the school district.

On the other hand, courts have assumed the posture that dress is a generalized liberty interest and is entitled to only minimal constitutional protection. One example of the court's posture is illustrated in *East Hartford Education Association v. Board of Education of Town of East Hartford.*[25] In this case, Richard Brimley, a public school teacher, was reprimanded for failure to wear a necktie while teaching his English class. With the support of the teacher's union, he filed suit against the board of education, claiming that the reprimand deprived him of his rights of free speech and privacy. Brimley further claimed that his refusal to wear a tie made a statement on current affairs, which aids him in his teaching by presenting himself as one who is not tied to the establishment, thus enabling him to establish greater rapport with his students. Brimley concluded by claiming that his refusal to wear a tie is symbolic speech and is protected by the First Amendment.

Brimley had appealed earlier to the principal and was told that he must wear the tie while teaching English but could dress more casually during film-making classes. He later appealed to the superintendent and the board without success.

The appeals court was faced with the issue of balancing the alleged interest in free expression against the goals of the school board in requiring its teachers to dress somewhat more formally than they might wish. The court, in balancing the two issues, indicated that the school board's position must prevail. The court concluded that balancing against the teacher's claim of free expression is the school board's interest in promoting respect for authority and traditional values as well as discipline in the classroom by requiring teachers to dress in an appropriate and professional manner.[26]

The appellate court did not discern in this case that basic constitutional rights were violated by the dress code and, consequently, did not weigh the matter heavily on the constitutional scale. The court presumed that the dress code was constitutional and within the scope of local authorities to decide.

In a later case, the Louisiana School Board extended its dress code to forbid school personnel from wearing beards. The board's policy was unsuccessfully challenged. The Fifth Circuit Court of Appeals, although recognizing the liberty interest of the individual in deciding how to wear his hair, held for the board. The court stated that the board had made a prudent decision in establishing the rule as a reasonable means of achieving the school board's undeniable interest in teaching hygiene, instilling discipline, and requiring uniformity in application of policy.[27]

The following case demonstrates the negative effects that result from a teacher's failure to comply with district dress code policy. David McGlothin, a high school teacher, began wearing berets and African-style head wraps to school. The principal warned her on each occasion that these items were worn, indicating that head wraps were inappropriate for the classroom. McGlothin continued to wear occasional head wraps for roughly three years, which resulted again in warnings by the principal. The district subsequently adopted a multicultural policy, which McGlothin claimed justified her head wraps. After a memorandum and lengthy discussion, McGlothin's employment was terminated. She followed the district's grievance procedure, claiming for the very first time that her head covering was in conformity with her religious beliefs. The school district did not support her grievance. She then appealed to the U.S. district court.

The court found that McGlothin had sincere religious beliefs; however, she did not convey those to the school administration at any earlier time but, instead, only in the final stage of her grievance. Because she failed to convey her religious beliefs to the district in a timely fashion, the district was under no obligation to accommodate her beliefs under the First Amendment or Title VII of the Civil Rights Act. The facts revealed that the district had offered McGlothin an opportunity for reemployment following denial of her grievance if she would agree to remove her head wraps. McGlothin refused to accept the district's offer. On the basis of those facts, the court held for the district by granting a motion to dismiss the lawsuit.[28]

RIGHT TO PRIVACY

It is commonly held that teachers and administrators enjoy a measure of privacy in their personal lives. These rights should be respected to the extent that they do not violate the *integrity* of the community or render the teacher or administrator ineffective in performing professional duties. Within the context of privacy rights, teachers and administrators are afforded an opportunity to exercise personal choices, which may range from living with a person of the opposite sex, to giving birth to a child out of wedlock, to other lifestyle choices. In many instances, school boards cite privacy issues involving teachers and administrators as the basis to dismiss them from their employment positions or recommend revocation of the teaching or administrative certificate. Although no clear distinction seems to be drawn between protected and unprotected lifestyle choices, the burden of proof resides with school boards to demonstrate that lifestyle choice adversely affects the integrity of the district or that the conduct of the teacher or administrator has a detrimental effect on his or her relations with students or parents.

In exercising lifestyle choices, teachers must also be reminded of the professional nature of their position and the impact that their behavior has on children, who often view them as role models. For example, when a teacher engages in a private adulterous activity, it does not necessarily follow that this act, within itself, forms grounds for action to be taken against the teacher. Teachers are entitled to rights to privacy, as are other citizens, and these rights must be respected. Whether a school district is successful in penalizing a teacher for private conduct would again be based on a district's capacity to demonstrate that the teacher's effectiveness is impaired by his or her conduct. The burden of proof clearly resides with school officials. A similar standard would also apply to administrators' effectiveness.

When a teacher has demonstrated a strong record of teaching, has been effective in relationships with students, and is respected in the community by his or her peers, it is unlikely that school officials will succeed in bringing serious actions against the teacher, such as removal from an employment position or revocation of certificate. On the other hand, if private conduct becomes highly publicized to the point that the teacher's reputation and relationships with parents and students have been impaired, rendering the teacher ineffective in executing his or her duties, appropriate actions may be taken by school officials and supported by the courts.

A leading case involving private, adulterous activity arose in Iowa involving Richard Arian Erb, a native Iowan and a high school fine arts teacher. He was married with two children. A complaint against Erb was filed by Robert M. Johnson, a farmer whose wife, Margaret, taught home economics at another school in the district. Johnson's goal was to have Erb removed from the school but not to revoke his certificate. Johnson read an extensive statement in which he detailed observations regarding an adulterous sexual relationship between Erb and Margaret that he and others observed in an isolated area. He and his raiding party surrounded the car and took pictures of Margaret and Erb, who were partially disrobed in the back seat. Erb and Margaret terminated their affair, and Erb offered his resignation, but the local school board unanimously decided not to accept it. The board president testified that Erb's teaching was highly rated by his principal and superintendent. He had been forgiven by his wife and the student body, and he had maintained the respect of the community. Witnesses before the board included Erb, his minister, past and present principals, parents of children in the school, and a substitute teacher.

The state board voted 5–4 to revoke Erb's teaching certificate, and without making any findings of fact or conclusions of law, ordered it revoked. Revocation was stayed by the trial court. The trial court held that Erb's admitted adultery was sufficient basis for revocation of his certificate. Erb appealed the trial court's ruling, charging that the board acted illegally in revoking his certificate without substantial evidence. This case reached the state supreme court, which ruled for Erb. The court, in ruling for Erb, stated that the private conduct of a man, who is also a teacher, is a proper concern to those who employ him only to the extent it mars him as a teacher. When his professional achievement is unaffected, when the school community is placed in no jeopardy, his private acts are his own business and may not be the basis of discipline. The court further concluded by stating, "Surely incidents of extramarital heterosexual conduct against a background of years of satisfactory teaching would not constitute immoral conduct sufficient to justify revocation of a life diploma without any showing of an adverse effect on fitness to teach."[29]

The outcome of the *Erb* case should not be interpreted to convey that adulterous acts may not result in dismissal by school boards. One such case involving dismissal occurred in Delaware when a highly successful school district administrator, who was married, developed an amorous affair with another person who was married. Their relationship grew in intensity and involved school time. The administrator took nude pictures of his lover and used them to threaten her husband by suggesting that he would disclose them to the husband's employer if the husband did not consent to allow the relationship to continue. The school district, on being informed of the situation and gathering the facts, dismissed the administrator. The administrator alleged that his acts were private and bore no relationship to his effectiveness as an administrator. He further alleged that he was not forewarned that his private conduct would lead to dismissal.

A U.S. district court rejected the administrator's claims based on the evidence that his affair resulted in gross neglect of duty. The district court held that it should have been obvious that his behavior would lead to dismissal due to the public impact of such conduct on the profession and finally that such conduct does not receive the protection of the right to privacy.

As can be seen from two contrasting cases, the courts will not support teacher's conduct that has an adverse impact on one's effectiveness or performance and will support dismissal if professional conduct and community standards are violated. The fact that school time was abused during the affair in this case and that unprofessional and illegal tactics were used to coerce the husband to support the adulterous affair were also pivotal in the court's ruling.[30] Private adulterous acts that become public and create serious community and professional concerns will not likely be supported by the courts.

In a rather unusual ruling regarding rights to privacy, the District Court of Appeals of Florida reversed the findings of the state's Education Practice Commission (EPC) when it supported a forty-eight-year-old assistant principal who married a sixteen-year-old former student. The EPC disciplined the administrator by suspending his teaching license for two years and denied him employment as an administrator. The assistant principal appealed the commission's ruling.

The court of appeals did not challenge the EPC's power to take disciplinary action but disagreed with the findings of the hearing officer in the case.

Based on the court's assessment, evidence of an inappropriate personal relationship between the two prior to marriage was neither clear nor convincing. Although both had been seen together by other individuals, it only gave rise to suspicion, which could not form the basis for disciplinary action. There was no credible evidence of sexual engagement prior to marriage or any other inappropriate activity. The EPC had taken action without the benefit of firsthand knowledge and based its ruling on inconclusive evidence alone.[31]

Although a certain aura of protection is afforded to school personnel regarding their private lives, involvement with a former student who has not reached majority age is, at best, very risky and not advisable. Privacy acts that do not involve former students will likely receive greater support by the courts than acts in which former students are implicated. In all cases, the privacy rights of teachers must be balanced against the district's need to maintain the professional integrity of its employees and the moral values of the community.

Administrative Guide

Teacher Freedoms

1. Teachers and administrators do not lose their constitutional rights when they enter the educational profession. Within limits, they possess the same constitutional rights as do other citizens.
2. School personnel should avoid personal attacks or libelous or slanderous statements when exercising freedom of expression rights or expressing concerns of interest to the community.
3. School personnel should not knowingly report false information when criticizing a district's decision or actions.
4. School officials may not penalize or otherwise discriminate against teachers for the proper execution of their First Amendment rights, especially regarding issues of public concern.
5. Academic freedom is not a right. It is a judicially recognized academic interest for elementary and secondary teachers. Teachers should introduce material in the classroom that is appropriate and related to their assigned subject matter. The classroom should never be used as a forum to advance the teacher's political or religious views.
6. Teachers and administrators may associate with whomever they wish, as long as their association does not involve illegal activity or their behavior does not render them unfit to perform their job functions effectively.
7. Teachers and administrators may face disciplinary action when they post inappropriate images or messages on their Facebook walls.
8. Teachers should refrain from engaging students as Facebook friends to ensure that the proper teacher–student relationship is preserved and maintained.
9. Dress, grooming, and appearance may be regulated by school boards if a compelling educational interest is demonstrated or if such codes are supported by community standards.
10. Teachers and administrators are entitled to rights of privacy and cannot be legally penalized for private noncriminal acts.
11. Pregnant unwed teachers may not be automatically dismissed unless there is a definite reason for doing so.

RELIGIOUS DISCRIMINATION IN PUBLIC SCHOOLS

Title VII addresses any forms of religious discrimination regarding employment. *Religion* is defined under Title VII to include "all aspects of religious observances, practices and beliefs."[32] This section also requires that an employer, including a school board, make reasonable accommodations to the employee's religion, unless the employer can demonstrate the inability to do so based on undue hardship. Consequently, school officials must respect and, where possible, make allowances for teachers' religious observances if such observances do not create substantial disruption to the educational process. Accommodations may include personal leave to attend a religious convention or to observe a religious holiday. Unless there is a showing of undue hardship, reasonable accommodation must be provided. If such requests are deemed excessive, resulting in considerable disruption to children's education, a denial would be appropriate.

In a 1986 case, a teacher was absent for approximately six school days per year because his religion, the Worldwide Church of God, required him to miss employment during designated holidays. Under the collective bargaining agreement between the school board and the teacher's union, teachers were permitted to use three days of leave each year for observance of religious holidays, but they were not permitted to use any accumulated sick leave or personal leave for religious holidays. The teacher requested that the school board adopt a policy allowing the use of three personal leave days for religious observance or to allow the teacher to pay the cost of a substitute and receive full pay for the holidays he was absent. The board rejected both proposals.

The teacher filed suit, alleging that the board had violated his rights under Title VII's prohibition against religious discrimination. The court held that the school board must make a reasonable accommodation for an employee's religious beliefs, as long as an undue hardship is not present. However, the board is not required to provide the employee preferred alternatives when more than one reasonable accommodation is possible. The alternative of unpaid leave is a reasonable accommodation if personal or other paid leave is provided without discrimination against religious purposes.[33]

In a slightly different case, a Chicago public school teacher filed suit against the superintendent, board of education, and other school officials in the U.S. district court, claiming that a 1941 Illinois statute designating Good Friday as a school holiday violated the First Amendment to the U.S. Constitution. The district filed a motion for summary judgment. The court, in its review of the case, noted that Christians observed Good Friday as one of their holiest days. However, members of other religions were required to request accommodations for special treatment on their holy days. Unlike Christmas and Thanksgiving, which have both secular and religious aspects, Good Friday has no secular aspect and is associated only with Christianity. The recognition of Good Friday was more than a mere accommodation to Christian religion. Recognition of the holiday conveyed an impermissible message that Christianity was a favored religion in the state. The court held for the teacher by ruling that the holiday designation violated the Constitution.[34]

In cases where school officials deny excessive leaves for religious purposes, the burden of proof rests with the teacher to show that the officials' decision involved the denial of certain religious freedoms. If the teacher is able to demonstrate discriminatory intent, then the burden shifts to school officials to show a legitimate state interest, such as a disruption of educational services to children. The Equal Education Opportunity Commission (EEOC) or a court would be hard pressed to challenge a legitimate state interest involving the proper education of children. (See Chapter 2 for a more comprehensive discussion of religion involving teachers in public schools.)

FAMILY AND MEDICAL LEAVE ACT (FMLA)

The Family and Medical Leave Act was passed by Congress in 1993. It is designed to allow eligible employees up to a total of twelve work weeks of unpaid leave during any twelve-month period for one or more of the following reasons:

1. Birth and care of the newborn child of the employee
2. Placement with the employee of a son or daughter for adoption or foster care
3. Caring for an immediate family member (spouse, child, or parent) with a serious health condition
4. Medical leave when the employee is unable to work because of a serious health condition

Employers with fifty or more employees are covered by this act. An eligible employee is one who has been employed for at least twelve months or for at least 1,250 hours over the previous twelve months. The law permits an employee to elect to use or the employer to require the employee to use accrued paid leave, such as vacation or sick leave, for some or all of the FMLA leave period. When paid leave is substituted for unpaid FMLA leave, it may be counted against the twelve-week FMLA leave entitlement if the employer is properly notified of the designation when the leave begins.

An employer may raise questions of the employee to confirm whether the leave is needed or being taken for qualified FMLA purposes. Periodic reports regarding the employee's status and intent to return to work after leave are permissible under the act. If an employer wishes to obtain another opinion, the affected employee may be required to secure additional medical certification at the employer's expense.

In a case involving FMLA in Florida, the U.S. Eleventh Circuit of Appeals held that to qualify as a "serious health condition" that triggers the Family and Medical Leave Act (FMLA), an employee's incapacity must entail a continuous period of more than seventy-two hours.[35] FMLA provides an eligible employee twelve weeks of leave for a "serious health condition" that renders the employee unable to perform assigned tasks. The court rejected an employee's argument that her incapacity and absence from work during seven consecutive partial days met FMLA's requirement that her incapacity be counted for more than three calendar days. The court held the U.S. Department of Labor's definition of the term *serious health condition* involving continuous treatment to be reasonable and consistent with the intent of FMLA.

CASE STUDIES

Teacher Rights—Unwed Teacher and Girlfriend Living Together

Tom Davis is a newly appointed principal in a small conservative community in the South. He has just been assigned Mark Scott, a dynamic, energetic seventh-grade math teacher. Davis later learns that Scott and his girlfriend are living together. The principal is informed of this by a group of parents who are outraged that Scott is setting a poor example for young children. They are upset and are calling for action. Davis talks with Scott, who does not deny that he and his girlfriend are living together. He further informs Scott in a very professional manner that what he does in his private life is his business.

Discussion Questions

1. Is Tom justified in approaching Mark on a personal and private matter? Why or why not?
2. How does Davis handle this situation with Scott?
3. Does the principal have a right to infringe on a teacher's private life? Why or why not?
4. Outline a plan to resolve this situation.
5. Would the courts likely support your plan of resolution?

Teacher's Freedom of Speech—Racial Content

Freddie Watts, principal, and Jimmy Brothers, assistant principal, are African American administrators assigned to administer a predominantly black high school in the deep South. Ann Griffin, a white tenured teacher, during a heated conversation with the two administrators stated that she "hated all black folks." When word of her statement leaked, it caused negative reactions among colleagues both black and white. The principal recommended dismissal based on concerns regarding her ability to treat students fairly and her judgment and competency as a teacher.

Discussion Questions

1. Is Watts justified in his recommending Ann's dismissal? Why, or why not?
2. Is the principal overreacting to Ann's statement? Why, or why not?
3. Does Ann's statement establish a basis for dismissal? Why, or why not?

4. Can Ann make the case that her statement was a private statement that does not give rise to serious disciplinary action? Why, or why not?
5. As principal, would you have made a similar recommendation for dismissal? Why or why not?
6. How do you feel the court would rule in this case? Provide a rationale for your response.

Freedom of Expression—Negative Comments

You are a middle school principal in a working-class conservative community in the Midwest. One of your tenured teachers placed a series of very negative comments about you and the school on her Facebook page. These comments were made over the weekend. A number of your students informed you that they read the teacher's comments. In fact, you heard a group of students chatting and laughing about the comments. In addition, you received phone calls from a number of parents who conveyed how negative and unprofessional the teacher's comments were.

Discussion Questions

1. How would you react to parents and students?
2. How do you approach the teacher who is allegedly responsible for the negative comments?
3. If evidence reveals that the teacher is responsible for these comments, what action would you take?
4. What options are available to you in addressing this situation?
5. What precautions must be taken to ensure that the teacher's rights are protected?
6. How do you balance the rights of the teacher against the need to protect the integrity of the school?
7. Please discuss the probable consequences of each option you identified.
8. What is your final decision?
9. Provide a rationale for your decision.

Flag Salute—A Nonconforming Teacher

As principal of Rockville Elementary in a small community in a rural district, Steve Jones finds that his community is extremely patriotic and that the school has had a long-standing practice of reciting the Pledge of Allegiance and saluting the flag every morning. He is informed by students and other teachers that Sarah Allen does not recite the pledge with her class or salute the flag. Steve Jones is obviously upset because he feels that Ms. Allen is setting a poor example for students and not conforming to community sentiments. He calls her into his office.

Discussion Questions

1. Does Steve have a justifiable reason to challenge Sarah's failure to recite the pledge? Why or why not?
2. Does Sarah Allen have a right not to participate in the morning ritual? Why or why not?
3. Are there legitimate grounds on which she may refuse to participate? If so, identify them.
4. If she fails to participate at the principal's request, could her refusal amount to insubordination? Why or why not?
5. As principal, how would you handle this situation?
6. How would the court likely rule in this case?
7. What are the administrative implications?

Religion and Teacher Freedom

Karen White, a kindergarten teacher in a strong Protestant community, informed her parents and students that she could no longer lead certain activities or participate in certain projects because they were religious in nature, according to her newly acquired affiliation with Jehovah's Witnesses. This meant that she could no longer decorate the classroom for holidays or plan for gift exchanges during the Christmas season. She also could not sing "Happy Birthday" or recite the Pledge of Allegiance. Parents protested, and Bill Ward, the school principal, recommended her dismissal based on her ineffectively meeting the needs of her students.

Discussion Questions

1. What happens next?
2. What grounds does Bill Ward have to recommend dismissal?
3. Are these valid grounds? Is so, why? If not, why not?
4. If Karen White is an otherwise competent and effective teacher, how defensible can the principal's charges be?
5. Is the school in violation of Karen's religious rights? Why? Why not?
6. How do you think the courts would rule in this case?
7. Provide a rationale for your response to question 6.

Use of Facebook by a Teacher

You are an elementary school principal in a conservative community in the "Bible Belt." A group of parents meets with you to inform you that one of your most effective tenured teachers can be seen on Facebook wearing a revealing dress and holding a beer in one hand and wine in the other. The inscription under her picture reads—"I am a bad bitch." The parents want something done, as they do not feel that her behavior reflects the values of the school and that she is a poor role model for students.

Discussion Questions

1. How do you react to their concerns?
2. What action, if any, should be taken?
3. Do you have adequate grounds to initiate disciplinary action against the teacher?
4. What is the probable solution in this case?
5. Write a draft policy that addresses teachers' use of Facebook.

Negative Comments on Facebook Posted by a Teacher

You are a middle school principal in a working-class conservative community in the Midwest. One of your tenured teachers placed a series of very negative comments about you and the school on her Facebook page. These comments were made over the weekend. A number of your students informed you that they read the teacher's comments. In fact, you heard a group of students chatting and laughing about the comments. Additionally, you receive phone calls from a number of parents who conveyed how negative and unprofessional the teacher's comments were.

Discussion Questions

1. How would you react to parents and students?
2. How do you approach the teacher who is allegedly responsible for the negative comments?
3. If evidence reveals that the teacher is responsible for these comments, what action would you take?
4. What options are available to you in addressing this situation?
5. What precautions must be taken to ensure that the teacher's rights are protected?
6. How do you balance the rights of the teacher against the need to protect the integrity of the school?
7. Please discuss the probable consequences of each option you identified.
8. What is your final decision?
9. Provide a rationale for your decision.

Caught in an Awkward Situation

One of your most popular and effective male teachers is caught in a compromising situation in a local motel with another female teacher who once taught in your school. The male teacher is tenured. Both were discovered by the former female teacher's husband, who made certain that the news was spread throughout the community. Your community is a family-oriented one.

Discussion Questions

1. What is your reaction to this development?
2. What action, if any, would you take?
3. Because this was a private act, do you have grounds to act?
4. What options do you have in addressing concerned parents who have approached you?
5. How do you resolve this situation?

Transgender Teacher

One of your male teachers returned to school in the fall as a transgender female. There is widespread alarm at school and dismay among students, faculty, staff, and parents alike. Your community is conservative and adheres to strong family values.

Discussion Questions

1. How do you handle this situation?
2. Do you speak with the teacher? If so, what do you communicate to her?
3. How do you respond to students, faculty, staff, and parents?
4. Is there a different message communicated to each group?

Endnotes

1. *Connick v. Myers,* 461 U.S. 138 (1983).
2. *Daniels v. Quinn,* 801 F. 2d 687 (4th Cir. 1986).
3. *Pickering v. Board of Education,* 391 U.S. 563 (1968).
4. Ibid.
5. *Gilbertson v. McAlister,* 403 F. Supp. 1 (D. Conn. 1975).
6. *Garcetti v. Ceballos,* 547 U.S. 410, 126 S.Ct. 1951; 164 L.Ed. 2d 689 (2006).
7. *Tomkins v. Vickers,* 26 F. 3d 603 (5th Cir. 1994).
8. *Mt. Healthy City School District Board of Education v. Doyle,* 429 U.S. 274, 97 S.Ct. 568 (1977).
9. *Burgess v. Independent School District No. I-4 of Noble County Oklahoma,* 65 Fed. Appx. 690 (Not selected for publication in the Federal Reporter), 2003 WL 21030468, 10th Cir. (Okla.), May 08, 2003.
10. *Fowler v. Board of Education of Lincoln County, Kentucky,* U.S. Court of Appeals, 6th Cir. 817 F. 2d 657 (1987).
11. *LaRocca v. Board of Education of Rye City School District,* 63 A.D. 2d 1019, 406 N.Y.S. 2d 348 (1978).
12. *Albaum v. Carey,* 283 F. Supp. 3, 10-11 (U.S. District Ct. N.Y. 1968).
13. *Keefe v. Geanakos,* 418 F. 2d 359 (1st Cir. 1969).
14. *Mailloux v. Kiley,* 448 F. 2d 1242 (1st Cir. 1971).
15. *Loeffelman v. Board of Education of the Crystal City School District,* 134 S.W. 3d 637 (Mo. App. E.D., 2004).
16. *Ambach v. Norwick,* 441 U.S. 68, 99 S.Ct. 1589, 60 L. Ed. 2d 49 (1979).
17. Ibid.
18. *Greminger v. Seaborne,* 584 F. 2d (8th Cir. 1978).
19. *Elfbrandt v. Russel,* 384 U.S. 11, 17 (1966).
20. Ibid, 18.
21. *Keyishian v. Board of Regents of University of State of N.Y.,* 385 U.S. 589, 87 S.Ct. 675 (1967).
22. *Mayer v. Monroe County Community School Corp.,* U.S. Dist. Lexis 26137 5.D.Ind (2006).
23. *Minielly v. State,* 411 P. 2d 69 (Or. 1966).
24. *Allen v. Board of Education,* 584 S.W. 2d 408 (Ky. Ct. App. 1979).
25. *East Hartford Education Association v. Board of Education of Town of East Hartford,* 562 F. 2d 838, 2nd Cir. Ct. of Appeals (1977).
26. Ibid.
27. *Domico v. Rapides Parish School Board,* 675 F. 2d 100 (5th Cir. 1982).
28. *McGlothin v. Jackson Municipal Separate School District,* 829 F. Supp. 853 (S.D. Miss. 1993).
29. *Erb v. Iowa State Board of Public Instruction,* 216 N.W. 2d 339 (Sup. Ct. Iowa 1974).
30. *Sedule v. The Capitol School District,* 425 F. Supp. 552 (U.S. Dist. Delaware 1976).
31. *Tenbroeck v. Castor,* 640 So. 2d 164 (Fla. App. 1st Dist. 1994).
32. 42 U.S.C. § 2000e(2).
33. *Ansonia Board of Ed. v. Philbrook,* 107 S.Ct. 367 (1986).
34. *Metzl v. Leiniger,* 850 F. Supp. 740 (N.D. Ill. 1994).
35. *Russell v. North Broward Hospital,* No. 02-13343 (11th Cir. October 2, 2003).

Chapter 9

Discrimination in Employment

Constitutional, federal, and state statutes prohibit discriminatory practices in employment on the basis of sex, race, age, color, or religion. A significant number of federal statutes have been enacted specifically to address discrimination in employment. The social and political movements during the early 1960s focused major attention on inequalities of employment opportunities and past discriminatory practices. Many important pieces of federal legislation were enacted during the 1960s and 1970s, one of the most significant being Title VII of the Civil Rights Act of 1964, which prohibited employment discrimination based on race, color, religion, sex, or national origin.

The equal protection clause of the Fourteenth Amendment provides protection against group discrimination and unfair treatment. It is used as a vehicle for individuals who seek relief from various forms of discrimination. A significant number of personnel practices in public schools pertaining to race, gender, age, and religion have been challenged, based on allegations of discrimination. Many school districts have responded to these challenges by noting that many of their current practices have been based on custom rather than a deliberate intent to discriminate. Nonetheless, courts have responded to challenges brought by school personnel in cases regarding alleged discrimination in employment practices based on issues involving gender, race, age, and pregnancy.

EQUAL PROTECTION PROVISIONS OF THE FOURTEENTH AMENDMENT AND EMPLOYMENT DISCRIMINATION

Due process of law includes four aspects: **procedural**, substantive, (discussed in Chapter 3) the Vagueness Test, and the Presumption Test. These tests are applied by the courts in addressing various forms of discrimination. For example, the Vagueness Test protects those who allege discrimination from arbitrary or capricious acts by the employer. Laws or policies are considered vague if a person of common intelligence has to guess at their meaning. The degree of vagueness allowed by the U.S. Constitution is contingent on the nature of the legislation and the consequences that follow. Laws involving **substantive due process** are held to higher standards than those addressing less important penalties.

Presumption Test

The presumption test essentially presumes innocence until proven guilty. This concept is basic to the U.S. system of justice. Presumption of innocence is embedded in several provisions to the U.S. Constitution, such as the right to remain silent and the right to a jury. In addition, this test supports the view that a legal basis is essential to restricting or depriving an individual of his or her constitutional rights.

DUE PROCESS STANDARDS AND EMPLOYMENT DISCRIMINATION

Courts have historically relied on a three-level balancing test to determine procedural due process: first, the test may be applied to determine whether a person is actually entitled to a hearing before action is taken; second, the test may also be used to determine if pre- or post-deprivation is necessary; and third, the test may be used to determine the standard and level of proof needed to deprive an individual. This test was enunciated in *Mathews v. Eldridge*.[1] Identification of the specific dictates of due process generally requires consideration of three distinct factors: first, the private interest that will be affected by the official action; second, the risk of an erroneous deprivation of such interest through the procedures used, and the probable value, if any, of additional or substitute procedural safeguards; and, third, the government's interest, including the function involved and the fiscal and administrative burdens that the additional or substitute procedural requirement would entail.

The primary test applied to substantive due process is the Vagueness Test. For example, cases typically involving termination of tenured teachers, teachers who are under contract, or administrators require prior notice and reasons for the proposed termination as well as an opportunity for the affected employee to respond to charges leading to the proposed termination, particularly when allegations may involve discrimination where the proposed termination is thought to be personal or political.

The equal protection clause is pivotal in cases alleging employment discrimination. It prohibits the state from showing preference to a particular class of individuals over others. When their circumstances are similar, each person must be treated equally under the Fourteenth Amendment. In discrimination cases, the initial burden rests with the plaintiff to demonstrate that a policy or law is irrational. The burden then shifts to the employer to demonstrate that a compelling reason exists for enforcement of the policy or law. The court then attempts to balance the plaintiff's contention against the employer's ability to establish a compelling reason for its action.

TITLE VII: DISCRIMINATION

One of the most extensive federal employment laws, the Civil Rights Act of 1964 Title VII, provides, in part, that

    a. It shall be an unlawful employment practice for any employer
        1. to fail or refuse to hire or to discharge any individual or otherwise to discriminate against any individual with respect to his compensation, terms and conditions or privileges of employment, because of such individual's race, color, religion, sex or national origin;
        2. to limit, segregate or classify his employees or applicants for employment in any way which would deprive or tend to deprive any individual of employment opportunities or otherwise adversely affect his status as an employee, because of such individual's race, color, religion, sex or national origin.
    b. It shall be an unlawful employment practice for an employment agency to fail or refuse to refer for employment, or otherwise to discriminate against any individual, because of his race, color, religion, sex or national origin, or to classify or refer for employment any individual on the basis of his race, color, religion, sex or national origin.[2]

The original statute, enacted in 1964, covered employers and labor unions and did not apply to discriminatory employment practices in educational institutions until 1972, when the law was amended. Since its amendment, it has been employed by educators to challenge questionable discriminatory practices in public schools. As stipulated in Title VII and Title IX, discrimination in employment based on gender is prohibited. Title VII protects males and females from gender-based discrimination.

Title VII was amended by the Civil Rights Act of 1991 (P.L. 102-166). This act provides for compensatory damages, punitive damages, and jury trial in cases involving intentional discrimination. An individual claiming discrimination under Title VII must file a complaint with the Equal Employment Opportunity Commission (EEOC) within 180 days following the alleged unlawful employment practice or within 300 days if the individual has filed a claim with a local or state civil rights agency. Failure to meet these time limits results in a loss of legal standing to challenge the alleged act. An exception to the 180-day statute of limitations was provided through the enactment of the Lilly Ledbetter Fair Pay Act of 2009, which amends the Civil Rights Act of 1964. The new statute evolved from the *Ledbetter v. Goodyear Tire and Rubber Company* case in which the U.S. Supreme Court reversed a lower court decision in ruling that the statute of limitations for presenting an equal pay lawsuit begins at the date in which the pay was agreed on rather than the date of the most recent paycheck as a lower court had previously held.[3] Ledbetter filed a discrimination suit against Goodyear based on disparity in pay between herself and fifteen male counterparts. Remedies available under Title VII include compensatory damages, punitive damages, back pay, and reinstatement for disparate treatment discrimination (discussed later in this chapter).

To succeed under Title VII, a plaintiff must demonstrate that the employer's reasons for the challenged employment decision are false and that the actual reason is discrimination. This burden often is difficult to prove because in very few instances do plaintiffs have objective evidence or proof of discrimination. Many, however, have succeeded with indirect proof of discrimination in which the pretext for discrimination is established and the defendant is unable to convince the court that the reasons for his or her actions are worthy of belief.

Under the law of discrimination, for example, a teacher or administrator must demonstrate that he or she has made application for a position, is qualified for the position, and was not given fair consideration for the position. If the teacher or administrator is able to demonstrate a bona fide case of discrimination, then the burden shifts to the school district to demonstrate that its employment decision was not based on discriminatory practices.

In two leading noneducational cases, *McDonnell Douglas Corp. v. Green* and *Furnco Construction Corp. v. Waters,* the Supreme Court developed a three-step procedure for Title VII challenges:[4]

1. The plaintiff carries the initial burden of establishing a **prima facie** case of employment discrimination.
2. The burden shifts to the defendant to refute the *prima facie* case by demonstrating that a legitimate nondiscriminatory purpose forms the basis for its actions.
3. If the defendant is successful in its contention, then the burden shifts back to the plaintiff to show that the defendant's actions were a mere pretext for discrimination. If, of course, the defendant can demonstrate the absence of a discriminatory motive, there is no need for step three.[5]

Although these are noneducational cases, the same procedures apply in all cases involving alleged discrimination, including those in public schools.

In a school-related example, a Title VII discrimination case arose in Texas when a bus driver asked another driver to punch his time card at work the morning after the night the two had been drinking at a bar. The other driver did so, but the driver later called in sick and never arrived for work. The school board discharged both drivers for misconduct. Both sued the school district in a state court for gender discrimination, claiming the district did not fire female employees who also had clocked in for their co-workers.[6] The court awarded the drivers lost wages and $175,000 each for mental anguish. The state court of appeals affirmed the judgment. The school district appealed to the Supreme Court of Texas. The court found that although female employees had been reprimanded for time card violations, and some incidents went unpunished, in no incident did a female employee fail to show up for work. In no case had female employees conspired to conceal an absence. The court held that the nature and degree of the time card violations by the female employees could not be compared with the bus drivers' conspiracy to conceal an absence. The court refused to find that the male and female employees were "similarly situated," as their misconduct was not of comparable seriousness. The court reversed the judgment and held that the drivers should receive nothing.

Retaliation

Title VII prohibits retaliation against an individual who filed a discrimination charge, who participated in a discrimination hearing, or who opposed discrimination. Retaliation may occur when an employer takes adverse action against a protected individual who engaged in a discrimination proceeding. Adverse action is taken to discourage or prevent an individual from opposing a discriminatory practice and may be manifested by termination, demotions, or refusal to employ. Adverse action may also include unjustified negative evaluations or job references as well as subtle or overt threats.

In one such case, the U.S. Court of Appeals for the Fifth Circuit held that a former school employee stated a cause of action for Title VII retaliation because, at her termination hearing, the district introduced as evidence that she was a "problem employee" because she had previously filed an unsubstantiated sexual harassment complaint.[7] Alicia Fabela was employed by Socorro Independent School District (Texas) as a secretary from 1986 to 1997. In 1991, she filed a sexual harassment complaint with the EEOC against her principal. The EEOC dismissed the complaint as unsubstantiated. Fabela was transferred to Benito Martinez School, where she spent five uneventful years. However, in 1996 a new principal was assigned to the school. Fabela clashed with the new principal, who recommended that she be terminated. Fabela appealed her termination. During the hearing, the assistant superintendent introduced Fabela's earlier complaint as evidence that she was a "problem employee." The hearing officer upheld the termination. Fabela filed suit, claiming that the district was guilty of retaliatory termination in violation of Title VII for her protected activity of filing a complaint with the EEOC. The Fifth Circuit found that the assistant superintendent's testimony was direct evidence of retaliation and that the district's claim that it would have terminated Fabela had she made no EEOC complaint created a genuine dispute of material fact to be resolved by a jury.

In a landmark case involving retaliation, the Supreme Court held that intentional discrimination against a person who files a sex discrimination complaint is a violation of Title IX. This case arose in Birmingham, Alabama, in 2001 when the girls' basketball coach, Roderick Jackson, sued the school district for what he claimed was retaliation after he challenged practices that he viewed as discriminatory toward his girls' basketball team.[8] As a result, Jackson alleged that working conditions deteriorated, resulting in his being removed from his coaching position. He further contended that he received a negative evaluation after raising questions with his supervisor regarding equity in the school's athletic program, specifically with respect to unequal access to athletic equipment, facilities, and funding that affected girls' athletics. The U.S. district court judge dismissed Jackson's case without a trial. The decision to dismiss was upheld by the U.S. Court of Appeals for the Eleventh Circuit.

The case was ultimately heard by the Supreme Court. Justice Sandra Day O'Connor, writing for the majority, and joined by Justices John Paul Stevens, David Souter, Ruth Bader Ginsburg, and Stephen Breyer, held that retaliation against a person based on complaints of sex discrimination that constitutes intentional discrimination is a violation of Title IX. The dissent, led by Justice Clarence Thomas and including Chief Justice William Rehnquist, and Justices Antonin Scalia and William Kennedy, held that a claim of retaliation is not a claim of discrimination on the basis of sex. According to the dissenting justices, Jackson did not claim that his own sex played a role in the decision to remove him from his coaching position. Justice Thomas further contended that the High Court overreacted by reading a right into Title IX that Congress clearly chose to exclude. The majority rule, according to dissenting Justice Thomas, is designed to encourage whistle-blowing regarding sex discrimination involving people who are not victims of discrimination that the law was designed to prevent. This case is very significant in that it is the only ruling to date that supports a plaintiff under Title IX who did not suffer discrimination based on sex. In a significant development, Coach Jackson retained his coaching job as head of the girls' basketball team through a settlement with the Birmingham Board of Education and also received $50,000. In addition, the school board agreed to provide equal facilities citywide for all girls' and boys' teams. In a retaliation case that clarified precisely who is covered under Title VII, the court held that a Florida teacher who resigned after filing a Title VII discrimination lawsuit against her school board could also bring a Title VII claim for retaliation against the board for denying her volunteer opportunities. Subsequent to filing her initial discrimination case against the board, the teacher resigned. She continued participating in a volunteer mentoring program in the county school district for six months, after which the board prohibited her from continuing as a volunteer. She alleged violations of Title VII. After a trial court held for the board, the District Court of the Appeals of Florida held that the lower court correctly found that volunteers are not protected by Title VII, which applies to employment relationships. However, Title VII applied in this case because of a prior relationship of the parties. The lower court committed an error in dismissing the claim, as the teacher's status as a former employee qualified her for coverage. This case was returned to the lower court for further proceedings.[9]

In a more recent landmark decision, the U.S. Supreme Court's ruling prevented employer interference with an employee's efforts to secure or advance enforcement of Title VII.[10]

Schools and Transgender Teachers

Experts estimate that there are fewer than thirty transgender teachers in classrooms across the nation. Nevertheless, they should be treated the same as any other employee. Teachers may exercise freedom of choice even in the context of a sexual transformation. School leaders with transgender teachers in their schools should hold information sessions with students and parents to respond to any questions and concerns regarding transgender issues. It is not necessary that the school embrace transgender values, but it is important to ensure that transgender teachers are treated with fairness and respect just as any other employee. It is important to note that it is illegal to discriminate against an individual on the basis of gender.

The Senate has passed the Employment Non-Discrimination Act of 2013 (S.815) that effectively prohibits discrimination on the basis of sexual orientation or gender identity. The purposes of this act are (1) to address the history and persistent, widespread pattern of discrimination, including unconstitutional discrimination, on the bases of sexual orientation and gender identity by private sector employers and local, state, and federal government employers; (2) to provide an explicit, comprehensive federal prohibition against employment discrimination on the bases of sexual orientation and gender identity, including meaningful and effective remedies for any such discrimination; (3) to invoke congressional powers, including the powers to enforce the Fourteenth Amendment to the Constitution, and to regulate interstate commerce pursuant to section 8 of article I of the Constitution, in order to prohibit employment discrimination on the basis of sexual orientation and gender identity; and (4) to reinforce the nation's commitment to fairness and equal opportunity in the workplace consistent with the fundamental right of religious freedom.

The bill must be passed by the house and signed into law by the president.

Unwed Pregnant Teachers

Courts tend to vary in rulings regarding unwed pregnant teachers. During the early 1960s and 1970s, courts were more inclined to rule against single teachers who were dismissed by school boards when they reported their pregnancy. However, during the mid-1970s and early 1980s, with increased attention focused on individual rights of teachers, courts became less inclined to rule against unwed pregnant teachers without carefully weighing all aspects of each case. In doing so, the courts considered the teacher's overall performance record, the impact of the teacher's actions on students, and, more important, the extent to which the teacher's actions adversely affect her effectiveness as a teacher. Courts may also consider community standards and the degree to which the teacher's conduct violates the ethics of the community and renders the teacher unfit to teach. Pregnancy is considered an illness and should be handled as any other illness. A pregnant teacher would be eligible for Family and Medical Leave Act if she meets the FMLA criteria. The following summary of cases shows the variance among courts in addressing pregnancy among unwed teachers:

1. In 1975, a federal appeals court ruled against a school board policy in Mississippi that automatically disqualified school employees who were parents of illegitimate children on the grounds that unwed parents do not necessarily represent improper models for students.[11]

2. In 1976, a district court upheld Omaha, Nebraska, officials in dismissing an unwed junior high school teacher because of her pregnancy on the grounds that permitting the teacher to remain in the classroom would be viewed by students as condoning pregnancy out of wedlock.[12]

3. In 1979, a federal appeals court struck down a school board practice of not renewing teachers' contracts where a foreseeable period of absence could be predicted for the next school year.[13]

4. In 1982, the Fifth Circuit Court of Appeals ruled against officials in Homewood, Alabama, for dismissal of a pregnant unwed teacher on the basis that her discharge was in violation of the Fourteenth Amendment. The school board could not demonstrate that the teacher's failure to report her pregnancy in a timely fashion would have resulted in dismissal had she been married.[14]

5. In 1986, a district court in Illinois upheld a teacher who was dismissed for being a pregnant unwed mother on the grounds that the teacher had a substantive due process right to conceive and raise her child out of wedlock without undue intrusion by the school board.[15]

Sexual Discrimination

Significant litigation has surfaced since the enactment of Title VII. The following summary describes the nature of significant rulings regarding sexual discrimination:

1. One court ruled that when a district passes over a female who has equal or more impressive credentials than a male for promotion to administrative positions, the district has violated Title VII.[16]

2. When a school board was able to defend its decision not to promote an African American female teacher on subjective but observable factors, such as the lack of interpersonal skills and an abrasive personality, the court held these reasons to constitute a legitimate nondiscriminatory decision.[17]

3. When a female teacher presented clear evidence of discrimination, the board's defense in showing that she would not have been promoted had she been a man was sufficient to counter the teacher's charges.[18]

In summation, the courts simply require gender-neutral decision making when employment opportunities are available.

Discrimination based on sex is also covered under Title IX of the Education Amendments Act of 1972, 20 U.S.C. § 1681 **et seq.**, which prohibits sexual discrimination by public and private educational institutions receiving federal funds. The basic provision of the act states, "No person in the United States shall on the basis of sex, be excluded from participation in, be denied the benefits of, or be subjected to discrimination under any educational program or activity receiving federal financial assistance."

TITLE IX

Title IX is administered by the Office for Civil Rights (OCR) of the Department of Education. The provisions of this act are similar to the provisions in the EEOC's guidelines found in Title VII. Title IX, like Title VII, makes a provision for sexual distinctions in employment where sex is a *bona fide* occupational qualification.[19] Numerous challenges were raised during the mid-1970s by educational institutions questioning the applicability of Title IX to discrimination in employment issues. After a series of highly debated cases, the U.S. Supreme Court ruled in *Northaven Board of Education v. Bell* that Title IX does apply to and prohibit sexual discrimination in employment.[20]

Following the enactment of Title IX, two local school boards in Connecticut challenged the act, contending that Title IX was not intended to address practices of school districts. The Supreme Court addressed two questions in this case: (1) whether the Title IX statute applies to employment practices of educational institutions and, if so, (2) whether the scope and coverage of Title IX employment regulations are consistent with Title IX statutes.

The court reasoned that because Title IX neither expressly nor by implication excludes employees from its reach, it should be interpreted as covering and protecting employees as well as students. The court based its decision on the wording of the statute, the legislative history, and the statute's postenactment history in Congress and at the U.S. Department of Health, Education, and Welfare.

Another highly debated issue regarding the interpretation of Title IX centered on the precise definition of *education programs and activities* with respect to sanctions. Because documented Title IX violations may result in a loss of federal funds, at issue was whether an entire educational institution is subject to a loss of funds or only the specific programs or activity affected.

This question was addressed initially in the *Grove City College v. Bell* case.[21] Grove City College, a private coeducational liberal arts college, intentionally sought to preserve its autonomy as a private institution by failing to accept state and federal financial assistance. The facts revealed that a number of students attending the college received Basic Educational Opportunity Grants (BEOGs) from the government. Based on its findings, the U.S. Department of Education concluded that the college was a recipient of federal financial assistance and would have to comply with Title IX regulations.

The college refused to execute the assurance of compliance as stipulated by the regulations, which resulted in the Department of Education's initiating procedures to declare the college and its students ineligible for the BEOG funds. The college and four students filed suit to enjoin the Department of Education from enforcing the policy as interpreted.

The court held for the college and its students by stating that Title IX applies only to specific programs that receive the federal assistance and not the entire institution. This decision was considered landmark during the mid-1980s; however, the Civil Rights Restoration Act of 1988 reversed this decision. The act now affects the entire institution or school district, even if only certain programs or activities receive state or federal financial assistance. Federal law now makes it clear that Title IX applies to everything involving the school, even if only one activity or program receives federal funds.

Although Title VII and Title IX were enacted to address many forms of discrimination, there are differences regarding legal requirements that apply to each statute. Table 9.1 summarizes the legal requirements regarding Title VII and Title IX.

TABLE 9.1	Summary of Title VII and Title IX

Title VII Civil Rights Act of 1964	Title IX Education Amendments of 1972
• Prohibits employment discrimination based on race, color, religion, sex, or national origin.	• Prohibits sex discrimination in recruiting, admissions, financial aid, athletics, textbooks and curricula, housing, facilities, counseling for careers, insurance, health care, single-sex groups and programs, extracurricular activities, and employment based on sex.
• Applies to employers with fifteen or more employees.	
• Prohibits retaliation against an individual who filed discrimination charges, who opposed discrimination, and who participated in a discrimination hearing.	• Applies to institutions receiving federal funds—public or private.
• Affects all employment practices such as hiring, firing, classifying, promoting, or referring for employment on the basis of race, color, religion, sex, or national origin.	• Requires self-study by the institution, modification of sexually discriminatory practices, and assurance of compliance with the act.
• Remedies—complainant seeks an administrative remedy through the Equal Employment Opportunity Commission (EEOC).	• One person is to be made responsible for compliance and handling grievances.
	• Remedies—complaint is investigated and an attempt is made at voluntary compliance by the Office of Civil Rights (OCR).
• Complaint is filed with EEOC either after or simultaneously with the state or local filing.	• Failure to settle may result in administrative hearing, followed by suspension or termination of federal funds.
• The normal time limit is 180 days unless the complainant has filed with the state, in which case the time is extended to 300 days.	
• If complaint is not successfully resolved, suit may be filed in district court by EEOC or the complainant.	• Complaint may be referred to the Department of Justice for court action.
	• There is no federal statute of limitations to file charges. Statute of limitations is derived from state law.
• Allows for *bona fide* occupational qualification (BFOQ)—exception and affirmative action in some allows for *bona fide*…	• Statute does not require the exhaustion of administrative remedies.
• Possible remedies include injunctive awards, damage awards, back pay, front pay, attorney's fees.	• Allows for *bona fide* occupational qualification (BFOQ)—exception and affirmative action in some allows for *bona fide*…

THE REHABILITATION ACT OF 1973 AND THE AMERICANS WITH DISABILITIES ACT OF 1990

The Americans with Disabilities Act (ADA), in conjunction with the Individuals with Disabilities Education Act (IDEA), protects individuals with disabilities against discrimination and ensures equal access and equal opportunity. Section 504 of the Rehabilitation Act of 1973 prohibits discrimination against any otherwise qualified person who has a disability with respect to employment, training, compensation, promotion, fringe benefits, and terms and conditions of employment. The act states that "no otherwise qualified individual with handicaps . . . shall solely by reason of his or her handicap be excluded from the participation in, be denied the benefits of, or be subjected to discrimination under any program or activity receiving federal financial assistance."[22] The ADA is similar to Section 504 and protects not only students with disabilities but any person who has a physical or mental impairment that substantially limits one or more major life activities, has a record of such impairment, or is regarded by others as having such an impairment.[23]

Major life activities, as interpreted by the act, may include such tasks as caring for oneself, performing manual tasks, hearing, seeing, speaking, breathing, walking, learning, and working.[24] Section 504 extends beyond the school environment and covers all people who are disabled in any program receiving federal financial assistance. Contrary to popular belief, the Rehabilitation Act does not require affirmative action on behalf of people with disabilities. It simply requires the absence of discrimination against such individuals.

Major life activities also include the operation of a major bodily function including but not limited to function of the immune system, normal cell growth, digestive, bowel, bladder, neurological, brain, respiratory, circulatory, endocrine, reproductive functions, and food allergies. ADA coverage does not apply to impairments that are transitory and minor. A transitory impairment is one with an actual or expected duration of six months or less.

The definition of disability is construed in favor of broad coverage to the maximum extent permitted by the terms of the act. For example, an impairment that is episodic or in remission is a disability if it would substantially limit a major life activity when active. The determination of whether an impairment substantially limits a major life activity shall be made with regard to the ameliorative effects of mitigating measures such as medication, medical supplies, equipment or appliances, low vision devices (not including eye glasses or contact lens), prosthetics including limbs and devices, hearing aids and cochlear implants or other implantable hearing devices, mobility services, or oxygen therapy equipment and supplies. The ameliorative effects of mitigating measures of ordinary eyeglasses or contact lenses must be considered in determining whether an impairment substantially limits a major life activity.

Regulations interpreting the Rehabilitation Act's prohibitions against disability discrimination by federal contractors have been revised to conform to ADA provisions found in 34 C.F.R. § 104.11 and 29 C.F.R. § 1641. The regulations include explicit prohibitions regarding employee selection procedures and preemployment questioning. As a general rule, the fund recipient cannot make any preemployment inquiry or require a preemployment medical examination to determine whether an applicant is disabled or to determine the nature or severity of a disability.[25] Nor can a recipient use any employment criterion, such as a test, that has the effect of eliminating qualified applicants with disabilities, unless the criterion is job related and there is no alternative job-related criterion that does not have the same effect.[26] These prohibitions are also found in the ADA and its regulations.

The ADA prohibits the use of any standard criteria or administrative method that has the effect of discriminating or perpetuating discrimination based on a disability. Section 12132 of this act includes a provision similar to Section 504. It states that no qualified person with a disability shall, by reason of such disability, be excluded from participation in or be denied the benefits of services, programs, or activities of a public nature or be subject to discrimination by any such public agency. School districts must make reasonable accommodations for people with known disabilities, including job applicants and/or employees.

Qualifications for Employment

Any individual with a disability is qualified for employment under the ADA, if with or without reasonable accommodations he or she can perform the core functions of the employment position held or desired to be held. Core job functions are not those that are considered marginal but, rather, those that are essential to successfully execute designated tasks. The act prohibits any individual with a disability to be denied a job on the basis of not being able to meet physical or mental tasks that are not essential to perform the desired job tasks.

Employers, therefore, must make reasonable accommodations to any known physical or mental impairment of an otherwise qualified individual who has disabilities. Based on the law, reasonable accommodations include the following:

1. Existing facilities used by employees must be readily accessible to and usable by individuals with disabilities.
2. Job restructuring, part-time or modified work schedules, reassignment to a vacant position, acquisition or modification of equipment or devices, appropriate adjustment or modifications of examinations, training materials or policies, the provision of qualified readers

or interpreters, and other similar accommodations must be made for individuals with disabilities.[27] An employer may be exempt if it can be demonstrated that an undue hardship is involved in making a reasonable accommodation.

The term *undue hardship* means an action requiring significant difficulty or expense, when considered in light of the following factors:

1. The nature and cost of the accommodation needed under this act
2. The overall financial resources of the facility or facilities involved in the provision of the reasonable accommodation; the number of persons employed at such facility; and the effect on expenses and resources, or the impact otherwise of such accommodation on the operation of the facility
3. The overall financial resources of the covered entity; the overall size of the business of a covered entity with respect to the number of its employees; and the number, type, and location of its facilities
4. The type of operation or operations of the covered entity, including the composition, structure, and functions of the work force of such entity; and the geographic separateness or administrative or fiscal relationship of the facility or facilities in question to the covered entity[28]

The burden of proof rests clearly with the employer.

Scope of Protection: Section 504 and the ADA

Both the ADA and the Rehabilitation Act affect public schools by prohibiting *disability-based discrimination.* When an allegation claiming discrimination is brought against school districts, individuals bringing these charges may file a complaint with the U.S. Department of Education (DOE). If a violation is found, the DOE can mandate that federal funds be terminated, subject to judicial review of such action. Affected individuals also may seek relief in the courts for such violations. Available remedies may include injunctive relief and possible monetary damages when there is evidence of malicious intent or bad faith in discriminating against individuals with disabilities.

Teachers, staff, and students with disabilities are protected in public school under both acts. For example, school employees, staff, or students with acquired immune deficiency syndrome (AIDS) would be considered disabled under both statutes. Such persons would be considered a protected class as long as they have a physical impairment that substantially limits one or more major life activities and a record of such an impairment or are regarded by others as having such an impairment.

In a leading case, *School Board of Nassau County, Florida v. Arline,* the Supreme Court addressed the issue of whether a person with a contagious disease is considered to be "handicapped" for purposes of Section 504 of the Rehabilitation Act. Arline was an elementary teacher who was hospitalized for tuberculosis. The disease went into remission for roughly twenty years, during which time she continued to teach elementary school children. She experienced a recurrence of the disease in 1977 and 1978. Responding to her condition, the board of education suspended her for the remainder of the school term and subsequently terminated her based on a recurrence of the disease.

Arline filed suit, alleging that her discharge was in violation of Section 504 of the Rehabilitation Act. The district court held for the school board, holding that the act did not apply to Arline since she was not considered a handicapped person for the purposes of the act. However, the court of appeals reversed, and the U.S. Supreme Court agreed to hear the case.

The Supreme Court upheld the court of appeals ruling by stating that a person with a contagious disease may be considered handicapped under Section 504 of the statute. The act defines a handicapped individual as any person who has a physical impairment that substantially limits one or more major life activities and has a record of such an impairment or is regarded as having such an impairment. The fact that Arline was hospitalized twenty years earlier for tuberculosis that then and now substantially limits her capacity to work clearly places her within the provisions of Section 504. The disease being contagious does not effectively remove her from coverage of the act. The Court was unable to determine whether Arline was otherwise qualified, due to the district's failure to properly inquire into the nature of the risk, the duration of the risk, the severity of the risk, and the probability that the disease may be transmitted and cause harm to others. The High Court affirmed the decision of the court of appeals and remanded.[29]

As demonstrated by the Court's ruling in *Arline,* the term *handicap* carries a broad definition, as interpreted under Section 504. As long as the person with the handicap meets the definition enumerated in the act, he or she is covered under the act and is entitled to reasonable accommodations. Failure to provide reasonable accommodations violates the spirit of the act as well as the constitutional rights of individuals with disabilities.

A similar conclusion was reached by the Ninth Circuit Court of Appeals in *Chalk v. U.S. District Court, Central District of California,* when the court ruled that a person with AIDS is considered "otherwise qualified" under Section 504 of the Rehabilitation Act and therefore afforded full protection under the provisions of the act.[30] Although individuals with a contagious disease are covered under Section 504, the courts will allow school districts to balance the rights of employees with contagious diseases against the risk that their presence might create health hazards for others who must come in contact with them. The ultimate test would rest squarely on expert medical advice, rather than unfounded fear or apprehension. Through expert medical advice regarding possible health risks to others, the rights of all parties are preserved.

Gender Discrimination

In an interesting case, the U.S. Supreme Court held that an employer's conduct need not be independently egregious to satisfy requirements for punitive damages in an employment discrimination case. In the *Kolstad v. American Dental Association* case, the plaintiff (Kolstad) sued the defendant under Title VII of the Civil Rights Act of 1964 (Title VII), asserting that the defendant's decision to promote a male employee over her was a proscribed act of gender discrimination.[31] Kolstad alleged, and introduced testimony to prove, that, among other things, the entire selection process was a sham; that the stated reasons of the company's executive director for selecting a male were pretext; and that he had been chosen before the formal selection process began. The district court denied Kolstad's request for a jury instruction on punitive damages, which is authorized by the Civil Rights Act of 1991 for Title VII cases in which the employee demonstrates that the employer has engaged in intentional discrimination and did so "with malice or with reckless indifference to the employee's federally protected rights." In affirming that denial, the court of appeals concluded that, before the jury can be instructed on punitive damages, the evidence must demonstrate that the defendant has engaged in some "egregious" misconduct and that the plaintiff had failed to make the requisite showing in this case, which was heard by the Supreme Court. The U.S. Supreme Court held that "an employer's conduct need not be independently 'egregious' to satisfy requirements for a punitive damages award, although evidence of egregious behavior may provide a valuable means by which an employee can show the 'malice' or 'reckless indifference' needed to qualify for such an award."[32]

The 1991 act provided for compensatory and punitive damages in addition to the back pay and other equitable relief to which prevailing Title VII plaintiffs had previously been limited. The High Court vacated the ruling of the court of appeals and held that the case be remanded for further proceedings consistent with its opinion. Based on this important ruling, egregious conduct by an employer is not required to pursue compensatory and punitive damages under the Civil Rights Act of 1991.

Racial Discrimination

The *Brown* case emerged when four separate cases from the states of Kansas, South Carolina, Virginia, and Delaware were consolidated and decided in this case. In each of the cases, black students sought admission to the public schools of their community on a nonsegregated basis.

Kansas, by state law, permitted but did not require segregated schools. South Carolina, Virginia, and Delaware included state constitutional and statutory provisions that required the **segregation** of blacks and whites in public schools. State residents and taxpayers who were challenging these laws were denied relief, except in the Delaware case. The courts denying relief relied on the **"separate-but-equal"** doctrine announced by the Court in *Plessy v. Ferguson (supra)*.[33] That case stated that constitutionally required equality of treatment is attained when the races are provided substantially equal, although separate facilities. The Delaware court granted relief only because the schools that black children attended in that area were substantially inferior. The U.S. Supreme Court held that students cannot be discriminated against in their admittance to public school on the basis of race.[34] Court-ordered **desegregation** since the landmark *Brown v. Board of Education*[35] case has resulted in numerous challenges of racial discrimination, as schools that were predominantly African American were closed and teachers and administrators reassigned to other schools. In many instances, African Americans who held significant administrative positions prior to court-ordered desegregation found themselves in lesser positions or in nonadministrative positions during the aftermath of the desegregation movement. Even though the courts, in their ruling, attempted to achieve some degree of equity in assignment of African Americans to predominantly white schools, their efforts fell short of achieving this objective.

The equal protection clause of the Fourteenth Amendment was relied on by African Americans to eradicate patterns of racial discrimination in public schools. The equal protection standards prohibited discrimination that can be linked with a racially motivated objective.[36] Unlike Title VII, no remedial action was attached to the equal protection clause, unless there was clear evidence that segregation was caused by **de jure** practices (official and deliberate laws or policies to promote segregation).

Perhaps one of the most compelling cases involving social discrimination, *Griggs v. Duke Power Company,*[37] did not occur in a public school setting. Although it was not public-school based, it had a profound effect on discriminatory practices in public schools. Duke Power Company had openly discriminated on the basis of race in hiring and assigning employees in one of its plants. These practices were well established before the passage of Title VII. In 1955, the company implemented a policy requiring employees to hold a high school diploma for initial assignment to any but the lowest paid, traditionally African American, departments and for transfer to the higher paying white departments. In 1965, the company began the practice of requiring that transferees to higher paying, white departments obtain satisfactory scores on professionally prepared general aptitude tests. Evidence revealed, however, that whites who met neither of these criteria had been adequately performing jobs in the higher paid departments for years.

African American employees challenged these testing requirements, which showed a disproportionate impact on African Americans. The evidence revealed that a disproportionate number of African Americans did not meet the company's eligibility requirements for employment and transfer.

The Supreme Court held that a diploma requirement and generalized aptitude test may not be used when they result in the disqualification of a disproportionate number of minority group members, unless the employer can show a direct relationship between the skills tested and adequate on-the-job performance. This ruling was profound in that it set the stage for many challenges in public school districts where various types of entry examinations were used that also showed a disproportionate impact on groups of African Americans.

Duke Power Company's practices were in direct conflict with the provisions of Title VII, which prohibited employers from using tests and diploma requirements that worked to disqualify a disproportionate number of African Americans. These practices are deemed impermissible without evidence that the requirements were job and performance related or were justified as a business necessity.

After the *Griggs* decision, a number of courts invalidated the use of the National Teachers' Examination and the Graduate Record Examination using the *Griggs criteria* of job relatedness. The burden was passed to the districts to demonstrate job relatedness in their use of these examinations.

One state succeeded in demonstrating job relatedness through its use of test scores both for certification purposes and as a salary factor. In the *United States of America v. State of South Carolina,* the state was charged with violations of the Fourteenth Amendment and Title VII of the Civil Rights Act of 1964 through the use of minimum score requirements on the National Teachers' Examinations (NTE) to certify and determine pay levels of teachers within the state. The policy had been practiced for more than thirty years as local school districts used scores on the NTE for selection and compensation of teachers. The initial minimum score was set at 975. After an exhaustive validation study by Educational Testing Services (ETS) and a critical review and assessment of this study by the Board of Education, the state established new certification standards requiring different minimum scores in various areas of teaching specialization ranging from 940 to 1198.

Plaintiffs challenged the use of the NTE for both purposes. They claimed that more African Americans than whites historically have failed to achieve the required minimum score, resulting in a racial classification in violation of the Fourteenth Amendment and Title VII of the Civil Rights of 1964.

One of the burdens faced by the plaintiffs was to prove that the state intended to create and use a racial classification. Evidence revealed that the tests could be taken an unlimited number of times. There was some evidence that the test had a disproportionate impact on African Americans. Furthermore, ETS recommended that the minimum score requirement not be used as a sole determinant of certification where other appropriate information or criteria are available. However, plaintiffs did not produce any other appropriate or reasonable criteria on which decisions could be made, nor was there a showing that the NTE examinations themselves discriminated on the basis of race.

The court held for the defendant by stating, "We are unable to find a discriminatory intent from the facts and find that there was no discriminatory intent, without independent proof, in linking the certification and salary systems."[38] The court supported the conclusion that the NTE is professionally prepared to measure the critical mass of knowledge in academic subject matters. Also, the court concluded that the state's use of the NTE for both certifications met a "rational relationship" standard and thus found the plaintiffs unable to establish a right to relief sought in their respective complaints.

In the absence of proof of a discriminatory intent, teachers will not succeed in their claims of discrimination if the state is able to establish a reasonable relationship between the examination requirement and minimal skills needed to teach. *Prima facie* evidence of discrimination rests with the plaintiff. As viewed in this case, the plaintiffs failed to meet this burden of proof.

Title VII involves two basic types of claims: disparate treatment and disparate impact. The Supreme Court addressed these two important issues in a later case involving discrimination on disparate treatment and disparate impact. *Disparate treatment* simply means that an employer treats some people more unfavorably than others regarding employment, job promotion, or employment conditions based on race, color, religion, sex, or national origin. *Disparate impact* is merely a showing that a number of people of a similar class are affected adversely by a particular employment practice that appears neutral, such as a requirement that all employees pass a test (as illustrated in the previously discussed *Griggs* case). The protected class categories usually involve race, gender, religion, and national origin. Disparate impact suits differ from disparate treatment in that they do not allege overt discriminatory action.

The Supreme Court in *International Brotherhood of Teamsters v. United States* stated that disparate treatment may be distinguished from disparate impact. "Impact involves employment practices that are facially neutral in their treatment of different groups but do, in fact, fall more heavily on one group than another and cannot be justified by business necessity . . . proof of discriminatory motive, we have held is not required under a disparate impact theory."[39]

Thus, the Supreme Court, through its rulings, has identified two avenues for plaintiffs to seek relief under Title VII: impact and treatment. Many cases regarding racial discrimination have been addressed by the courts. The following represents a brief summary of the court's responses to challenges of racial discrimination involving allegations of disparate treatment.

A teacher sued a superintendent and other district officials for wrongful discharge based on racial discrimination and denial of free speech.[40] The teacher, who was Caucasian, was hired by the school district to oversee the district's gifted program. She claimed she experienced difficulties with school officials in her attempt to change the gifted program to make it more inclusive of minorities. The officials told her she was "stirring up trouble" by meeting with minority parents, advocating changes to the gifted program, and that she "didn't understand local culture." The court held for the teacher by stating that employees are entitled to protection from retaliation for speaking out against racial discrimination, based on the Civil Rights Act of 1964 and the First Amendment.

In another case, a teacher sued a school for wrongful discharge.[41] During her three-year probationary period before she could gain tenure, the teacher was discharged at the conclusion of her second-year contract. The teacher argued that applicable law precluded her discharge without valid reasons from the superintendent. The court held for the teacher. The court found that under state law, a school could not deny contract renewal during the probationary period without valid reasons for the teacher's discharge.

The implications of the court's decisions in these cases suggest that school districts will not be supported when their rules and policies are discriminatory based on race, whether they are intentional or unintentional. Once challenged and *prima facie* evidence of discrimination is shown, school districts must bear the burden of proof to demonstrate a nondiscriminatory purpose. In cases where there is a preponderance of evidence of discriminatory intent, this becomes an insurmountable task for school districts.

Religious Discrimination

The First Amendment and Title VII provide protection to employees against religious discrimination. *Religion* is defined by Title VII to include all aspects of religious observances, practices, and beliefs. Under this act, employers are expected to make reasonable accommodations to an employee's religious observance unless a hardship can be demonstrated. The burden of proof rests with the employer to demonstrate undue hardship. Most states have enacted legislation that requires employers to make accommodations for employees' religious practices. Thus, caution must be exercised by employers to ensure that the religious rights of employees are not violated. Employers must also make sure that the establishment clause of the First Amendment is not violated.

For example, in *Estate of Thornton v. Caldor, Inc.,* the court ruled that state statutes imposing an absolute duty on employers to fashion their business practices to accommodate the religious practices of their employees was in conflict with the First Amendment. The court held further that these statutes provided no flexibility for employers and amounted to an advancement of religion in violation of the establishment clause.[42]

In a related case, *Transworld Airlines Inc. v. Hardison,* an employee challenged the company's policy that prevented him from observing Saturdays as a religious holiday. The court held for the company and stated that Title VII did not require the company to set aside special exemptions to accommodate the employee's belief. To require the airline to make special exemption for the employee—Saturdays off—is an undue hardship.[43]

The issues relating to religious discrimination involve fairness and balance. For example, an employer cannot legally require an employee to choose between his or her job and religion. Such a requirement would represent religious discrimination. In addition, employees cannot be penalized by a placement that would require that employee to ignore a religious tenet of his or her faith to preserve a job.

A job applicant sued a school district for discriminatory non-hiring based on national origin.[44] The job applicant, a member of a Native American tribe, applied for a job as either a teacher's aide or a computer specialist. During a meeting in which potential candidates for the jobs were discussed, school board members made comments regarding the applicant's affiliation with her tribe. Subsequently, the school board chose not to hire the applicant. The court held for the school district. The applicant was not qualified for either position she applied for. Because she was not qualified, she failed to meet one of the necessary elements to prove an employment discrimination case.

In a discrimination case involving employment benefits, the United States Supreme Court case determined that the state could deny unemployment benefits to a person fired for violating a state prohibition on the use of peyote, even though the use of the drug was part of a religious ritual. While states have the power to accommodate otherwise illegal acts done in pursuit of religious beliefs, they are not required to do so.[45]

Age Discrimination

Age discrimination in public schools primarily affects teachers. In past years, many districts forced teachers to retire when they reached a specified age. These policies and practices were challenged by teachers under equal protection guarantees. Many of these challenges received mixed reviews by the courts. For example, the U.S. Supreme Court supported mandatory retirement for police officers, based on the rigorous physical demands associated with their positions. Conversely, the Seventh Circuit Court of Appeals rejected a practice of forced retirement for teachers at age sixty-five, noting no justification to presume that teachers at age sixty-five lacked the academic skill, intellect, or physical vigor to teach.[46]

All challenges and uncertainties became insignificant with the passage of the Age Discrimination in Employment Act of 1967 (ADEA) as amended in 1978. These acts effectively prohibited forced retirement of employees by protecting people above age forty from discrimination on the basis of age with respect to hiring, dismissal, and other terms and conditions of employment. Prior to the act's amendment in 1978, the maximum age limit was set at sixty-five years. The 1978 amendment raised the limit to age seventy. Amendments added in 1986 removed the limit completely, except for people in certain public safety positions (e.g., police officers and firefighters). The act covers teachers and other public employees. However, there is no prohibition against failure to renew a teacher contract, as long as nonrenewal is not based on age.

Litigation under this act is similar to that involving race or gender. If a district is charged with age discrimination, it must be able to demonstrate that legitimate factors other than age affected its action. Because teachers enjoy the same constitutional rights as other citizens, the burden of proof rests with the district to demonstrate the equal protection guarantees and that the requirements of the law are respected.

Many districts, as well as universities, have instituted early retirement incentive plans. These generally are held acceptable by the courts, if they are strictly voluntary in nature. There can be no evidence that suggests that any force or coercion is used to enforce such plans. Currently, mandatory retirement plans for public schools, colleges, and universities are prohibited, as universities were exempt until 1993. They now must comply with the law.

Since the passage of the ADEA, a number of cases still have made their way into the legal arena. One such case arose in Florida when a tenured public teacher turned seventy during the school year. School officials informed him that he would subsequently be employed on a year-to-year basis under the terms of a state statute that provides that no person shall be entitled to continued employment as a public school teacher at the end of the school year following his or her seventieth birthday.

When the district failed to employ him for the next year, he filed suit, claiming discrimination based on age. The Florida Supreme Court ruled that no person over age seventy shall be entitled to continued employment with respect to tenure rights, but termination could not be made solely on the basis of age. The court held for the teacher and awarded back pay, benefits, and reevaluation of his reemployment request without reference to age.[47]

A district court held that a sixty-two-year-old social studies teacher may proceed with her suit against Washington, D.C., public schools for violating her rights under the ADEA.[48] The teacher was terminated in conjunction with a reduction in force (RIF), at which time a younger teacher was retained. The district employed a point system based on factors such as job performance, education, and longevity in determining whom to terminate. The district claimed that the younger teacher received more points than did the older teacher. The court concluded that the district's actions created a pretext for discrimination. The facts revealed that both teachers received similar evaluations during the previous year. In addition, the supervisor who assigned the points observed the younger teacher's classroom for the previous two years but failed to observe the older teacher's classroom during the same period. Last, four months after the plaintiff was terminated, the district hired another social studies teacher under the age of thirty who had no experience teaching social studies. This case illustrates that seniority is a major factor in implementing RIF policies and procedures; RIF cannot be used to remove an older teacher without defensible grounds. The fact that a younger teacher was hired suggested that the older teacher's rights were violated under the ADEA.

The evidence is quite clear that the burden of proof rests with plaintiffs to establish a *prima facie* case of age discrimination. Once established, the district must demonstrate a legitimate state interest on which to base its action. In the absence of a legitimate state interest, school districts may not discriminate on the basis of age. Stated differently, *age cannot be the sole criterion that motivates a board decision to discriminate against school personnel.* Other defensible nondiscriminatory objectives must be established by the district. The ADEA is very clear in its intent. School officials would be well served to adhere to the provisions of the law and avoid unnecessary litigation.

In a landmark ruling, the U.S. Supreme Court held in a 6–3 decision that the ADEA does not prohibit an employer from favoring an older employee over a younger employee even if both employees fall in the statutorily protected class of those aged forty and over.[49] The Supreme Court heard this case after the U.S. Court of Appeals for the Sixth Circuit held that "younger" workers who are protected by the ADEA could state a claim if they are treated less favorably than "older" workers also protected by the ADEA. The ADEA protects employees forty years and older from age discrimination. General Dynamics agreed in a new collective bargaining agreement to no longer offer retiree health benefits to employees. However, if employees were fifty and older on July 1, 1997, they were "grandfathered in" and received retiree health benefits pursuant to the past agreement. Employees between the ages of forty and forty-nine on July 1, 1997, sued, claiming that they were discriminated against in violation of the ADEA. In reversing the Sixth Circuit, Justice David Souter rejected the employees' arguments that the ADEA's age discrimination prohibition works both ways in regard to favoring older employees over younger ones. He pointed out that if Congress had been concerned about protecting younger employees against older, it would most likely not have omitted workers under forty from the act's protections.

Genetic Information Discrimination

Under Title II of the Genetic Information Nondiscrimination Act of 2008 (GINA), it is illegal to discriminate against employees or applicants because of genetic information. Title II of GINA prohibits the use of genetic information in making employment decisions, restricts employers and other entities covered by Title II (employment agencies, labor organizations, and joint labor-management training and apprenticeship programs) from requesting, requiring, or purchasing genetic information, and strictly limits the disclosure of genetic information. The law forbids discrimination on the basis of genetic information regarding any aspect of employment, including hiring, firing, pay, job assignments, promotions, layoffs, training, fringe benefits, or any other term or condition of employment. An employer may never use genetic information to render an employment decision because genetic information is not relevant to an individual's current ability to work. It is also illegal to harass a person because of his or her genetic information. Harassment can include, for example, making offensive or derogatory remarks about an applicant's or employee's genetic information, or about the genetic information of a relative of the applicant or employee. Genetic information includes information regarding an individual's genetic tests and the genetic tests of an individual's family members, as well as information about the manifestation of a disease or disorder in an individual's family members (i.e., family medical history). It is illegal to fire, demote, harass, or otherwise "retaliate" against an applicant or employee for filing a charge of discrimination, participating in a discrimination proceeding (such as a discrimination investigation or lawsuit), or otherwise opposing discrimination.

In the first lawsuit ever filed by the EEOC alleging genetic discrimination, Fabricut, Inc., one of the world's largest distributors of decorative fabrics, will pay $50,000 and furnish other relief to settle a disability and genetic information discrimination lawsuit filed by the U.S. Equal Employment Opportunity Commission (EEOC). In its lawsuit, the EEOC charged that Tulsa-based Fabricut violated the Americans with Disabilities Act (ADA) when it refused to hire a woman for the position of memo clerk because it regarded her as having carpal tunnel syndrome, and violated the Genetic Information Nondiscrimination Act (GINA) when it asked for her family medical history in its post-offer medical examination.

PREGNANCY AND PUBLIC SCHOOL EMPLOYMENT

Teachers in public schools are protected by the Pregnancy Discrimination Act of 1978 (P.L. 95-555). This law is an amendment to Title VII, which extends protection to pregnant employees against any forms of discrimination based on pregnancy. The courts have been fairly consistent in their rulings regarding issues related to pregnancy. Prior to the enactment of this law, it was not uncommon for districts to enforce policy cut-off dates in which females were required to leave their positions due to their pregnant status. In a significant case, *Cleveland Board of Education v. LaFleur,* the court held that mandatory maternity termination specifying the number of months before anticipated childbirth violated the equal protection clause of the Fourteenth Amendment, noting that arbitrary cut-off dates served no legitimate state interest in maintaining a continuous and orderly instructional program.[50]

Districts may not assume that every pregnant teacher is physically unable to perform her teaching duties and responsibilities effectively because she is at a specific point in her pregnancy. Courts have also not been supportive of district policies that bar a female teacher, after giving birth, from returning to the district until the next regular semester or year. Numerous challenges have also been brought by female teachers regarding disability benefits, sick leave, and adequate insurance coverage.

Many of these challenges led to the enactment of the Pregnancy Discrimination Act of 1978. The basic intent of the act is to ensure that pregnant employees are treated in the same manner as other employees with respect to the ability to perform their duties. The act covers pregnancy, childbirth, and related medical conditions. Under the Pregnancy Discrimination Act, no longer can a woman be dismissed, denied a job, or denied promotion due to pregnancy. Women must be able to take sick leave as other employees do for medical reasons and return to work when they are released by their physicians. Pregnancy must be treated as a temporary disability, thus entitling female employees to the same provisions of disability benefits, sick leave, and insurance coverage as any other employee who has a temporary disability. There has not been as much litigation since the passage of the act, due in large part to the consistency with which the courts have ruled on matters involving the rights of pregnant employees.

However, one interesting case arose in 1991 regarding the interpretation and intent of the Pregnancy Act regarding the use of sick leave. In 1981, a teacher employed by Leyden Community High School became pregnant. She requested, by letter to the superintendent, that she be allowed to use the sick leave she had accumulated during her employment for the period of disability relating to her pregnancy. She further informed the superintendent that following this period of disability, she would begin a maternity leave that would extend over the remainder of the 1981–1982 school year.

The superintendent responded by indicating that the collective negotiation agreement between Leyden and the teachers union barred teachers from taking maternity leave immediately following a period of disability for which they used sick leave. After obtaining a right-to-sue letter from the EEOC, she brought action against Leyden, alleging that the leave policy had the impact of preventing female teachers from using their accumulated sick leave to cover pregnancy-related disabilities and consequently violated Title VII as amended by the Pregnancy Discrimination Act.

The teacher further argued that the policy had the statistical effect of forcing females to accumulate more sick days than males, who, at retirement, were compensated at a lower rate than the teacher's per diem pay. The district court found in its ruling that the district policy did not have a disparate impact on women based on pregnancy. The teacher appealed to the Seventh Circuit Court, which was faced with determining whether the district's policy forced teachers to choose between sick leave and maternity leave, creating a disparate impact on women, in violation of Title VII.

The court ruled that the scope of the Pregnancy Discrimination Act was limited to policies that have an impact on or treat medical conditions relating to pregnancy and childbirth less favorably than other disabilities. Further, the court added that the statistical evidence focusing on the absolute number of sick days accumulated by female teachers over their career was insufficient, standing alone, to establish that the district's policy had a requisite impact on females. Therefore, the district court's ruling was affirmed.[51]

Administrative Guide

Discrimination

1. School districts will not be supported by the courts when there is evidence that districts discriminated against employees on the basis of race, color, religion, gender, or national origin.
2. Once *prima facie* evidence is presented by the employee affected, school officials must demonstrate that a compelling educational interest motivated their decisions.
3. School districts may not discriminate against employees because employees opposed practices made unlawful under discrimination laws or participated in an investigation regarding employment discrimination.
4. School officials may be held liable in any cases involving discrimination or harassment when it is determined that they were aware of these actions.
5. No employee may be coerced to retire from employment based on age, nor may the employee be denied rights and privileges afforded other employees based on age, such as promotion and other benefits.
6. Race discrimination affects all employees, not merely minority employees.
7. Punitive damages may be awarded in employment discrimination cases if the employer's conduct is not viewed as egregious.
8. Differential employment criteria may not be used that have an adverse effect on a special group of employees, even though the criteria appear to be neutral.
9. Employment examinations, if used, must bear a rational relationship to performance requirements for the position sought by the prospective employee.
10. Racial or statistical quotas are legally indefensible in rendering decisions regarding reduction of teaching staffs, unless mandated by court orders.

SEXUAL HARASSMENT

Sexual harassment is prohibited by Title VII and Title IX. In spite of these prohibitions, incidents of sexual harassment persist. Cases involving charges of sexual harassment have remained fairly constant over the past several years. Based on statistics filed with the EEOC, sexual harassment charges decreased slightly from 1997 to 2008. Since 2000 the number of cases involving sexual harassment has gradually decreased. Sexual harassment charges filed with the EEOC declined by only one percent over this same period. These trends suggest that education and awareness training are critical factors in combating harassment in the workplace.

Interestingly, sexual harassment was not included in Title VII of the Civil Rights Act of 1964 until 1980. Its primary intent is to protect employees from harassment in their work environments. Harassment is considered to be a form of sex discrimination. It can manifest itself in many forms, from verbal statements and gestures to overt behavior. The victim, as well as the harasser, may be male or female, not necessarily of the opposite sex. Sexual harassment occurs between individuals of the same sex. In a landmark case, *Oncale v. Sundowner Offshore Services*, the U.S. Supreme Court held that same-sex harassment is illegal and is a violation of Title VII.[52] The victim may not be the person harassed but may be anyone affected by the offensive conduct. Economic injury is not necessary to bring a successful case of harassment against a supervisor.

There are various levels of *verbal harassment behavior,* including, but not limited to, making personal inquiries of a sexual nature, offering sexual comments regarding a person's anatomy or clothing, and repeatedly requesting dates and refusing to accept "no" as an answer. *Nonverbal harassment* may include prolonged staring at another person, presenting personal gifts without cause, throwing kisses or licking one's lips, making various sexual gestures with one's hand, or posting sexually suggestive cartoons or pictures.

More serious levels may involve sexual coercion or unwanted physical relations. This type of behavior **quid pro quo** is commonly associated with superior–subordinate relationships in which the victim, for fear of reprisal, unwillingly participates. This relationship is best described as a power relationship. The supervisor, in this case, has the capacity to refuse to hire, promote, grant, or deny certain privileges, based on his or her position. In many instances, the promise of some job-related benefit is offered in exchange for sexual favors.

Another level of harassment involves *unwanted touching of another's hair, clothing, or body.* Undesirable acts involving hugging, kissing, stroking, patting, and massaging one's neck or shoulders are examples of physical harassment that contributes to a hostile work environment. Verbal harassment may include off-the-cuff comments, such as referring to a female as "babe," "honey," or "sweetheart," or turning work discussions into sexual discussions, including sexual jokes or stories.

Each of these levels of harassment represents a serious form of sexual discrimination for which the victim may recover damages. The burden rests with the victim to establish that the harassment is unwanted. Once established, the harasser has an obligation to discontinue such behavior immediately. Failure to do so usually creates a hostile work environment and results in charges of sexual harassment by the victim.

Sexual harassment claims are sometimes difficult for the victim to pursue in court. In many instances, embarrassing and graphic details must be revealed, which often are denied by the person(s) against whom charges are made. Many victims of various forms of discrimination have been awarded monetary damages. The dollar amounts have increased significantly in recent years.

The definition of *harassment,* under the act, is sufficiently broad to allow coverage of most forms of unacceptable behavior. Any type of sexual behavior or advance that is *unwanted* or *unwelcome* is considered covered under the act. As indicated earlier, the person affected by such behavior has an obligation to inform the party that his or her behavior is unwelcome or unwanted. If this does not occur, it is difficult to claim harassment because the accused party is unaware that his or her behavior is unwelcome. The regulation implementing sexual harassment is very broad, on the one hand, yet fairly prescriptive with respect to coverage. It defines sexual harass-ment in the following manner:

> Unwelcome sexual advances, requests for sexual favors and other verbal or physical contact of a sexual nature constitute sexual harassment when (1) submission to such conduct is made either explicitly or implicitly as a term or condition of an individual's employment, (2) submission to or rejection of such conduct by an individual is used as the basis for employment decisions affecting such individuals, or (3) such conduct has the purpose or effect of unreasonably interfering with an individual's work performance or creating an intimidating, hostile or offensive working environment.[53]

Legally, employees may not be denied promotions or other benefits to which they are enti-tled on the basis of their unwillingness to accept sexual misconduct by their superiors, nor may they be subjected to hostile, unfriendly environments by superiors or peers if they refuse to accept sexual misconduct. Under the Civil Rights Act, every person is entitled to an environment that is free of unwelcome sexual conduct and that allows the person to perform his or her duties without intimidation or fear of reprisal.

EEOC guidelines cover two types of sexual harassment: *quid pro quo* and *non–quid pro quo*. In *quid pro quo* harassment, an employee exchanges sexual favors for job benefits, promotion, or continued employment. In *non–quid pro quo* or hostile harassment, the employee is subjected to a sexually hostile and intimidating work environment that psycho-logically affects the employee's well-being and has an adverse effect on job performance.

A landmark case occurred in the private sector involving sexual harassment in which a female bank employee filed action against the bank and her supervisor. The employee alleged that she had been subjected to sexual harassment by her supervisor during her employment, in violation of Title VII. The supervisor's contention was that the sexual relationship was consen-sual and had no bearing on the employee's continued employment. The bank indicated that it had no knowledge or notice of the allegation and therefore could not be held liable.

The Supreme Court, in a landmark ruling on the case, *Meritor Savings Bank v. Vinson*, held that unwelcome sexual advances that create an offensive or hostile work environment vio-late Title VII.[54] It further held that, although employers are not automatically liable for sexual harassment committed by their supervisors, absence of notice does not automatically insulate the employers from liability in such cases.

The significance of the ruling set the stage for subsequent sexual harassment cases by provid-ing the definition of specific acts that fall within the category of harassment. The High Court sug-gested that Title VII guidelines are not limited to economic or tangible injuries. Harassment that leads to noneconomic injury also may violate Title VII. The Court considered the claim that sexual activity was voluntary to be without merit. The test, according to the Court, was whether such advances were unwelcome.

The implications suggested from this case are that employers may be held liable for sexual harassment acts involving employees when the employer knew or should have known of the undesirable conduct. If the employer knew of the conduct, the expectation is that immediate and corrective actions will be taken. Failure to take decisive action generally results in liability charges against the employer. Based on a Supreme Court decision in the *Gebser* case, students who are sexually abused by teachers cannot recover monetary damages from school officials unless officials knew of the harassment, were in a position to act, and failed to do so.[55]

In another rather unusual case, a tenured teacher in New Jersey claimed that she was fired because she refused unwelcome sexual advances from her supervisor. She further claimed that her supervisor and another lesbian teacher sought to embarrass and discredit her for rejecting the unwelcome sexual advances. The school district initiated dismissal proceedings against her. The teacher filed an unsuccessful challenge against the termination action in the state court. She subsequently filed a Title VII discrimination complaint against the school principal and school board in the U.S. District Court of New Jersey. The court granted summary judgment for the board.

The teacher appealed to the U.S. Circuit Court of Appeals for the Third Circuit. The appeals court determined that Title VII is generally inapplicable after the cessation of the employment relationship, but the act was written broadly to cover discrimination actions following the termination of an employment relationship. Because postemployment blacklisting could prove more damaging than on-the-job discrimination, the district court improperly granted summary judgment. The court reasoned that the board's continued inquiries into the revocation of the teacher's certificate were retaliatory in nature and violative of Title VII.[56]

In a significant case regarding sexual harassment and abuse involving a student, the U.S. Supreme Court in *Franklin v. Gwinnett County Public Schools* illustrates the type of risk school districts and employees face under federal statutes as well as common law. The court unanimously held that when a teacher is alleged to have harassed and abused a student by coercive sexual intercourse, unwelcome kissing on the mouth, and placing calls to the student's home requesting social meetings, damages could be available to the student under Title IX for virtually all forms of sexual misconduct. More important, these damages may be levied against the district and its supervisors as well as the accused teacher.[57]

Based on the significant ruling in the *Gwinnett* case, plaintiffs may very well be more inclined to pursue claims under Title IX, as opposed to Title VII, given the caps on damages associated with Title VII. In addition, Title IX does not require the exhaustive administrative remedies found with Title VII and generally has a statute of limitations based on state laws, thus providing a longer period of time to bring legal claims.

Sexual harassment is prevalent in the United States and likely will continue to present legal challenges. This issue continues to evolve in the courts, where the legal limits of acceptable sex-related behavior in the workplace are being defined.

A female New York City teacher sued the city, board of education, and executive faculty members after being sexually harassed and molested by another teacher, a male, at an off-campus school-sponsored social event.[58] After she reported the incident to school officials, no action was taken. Instead, she was disciplined for stating that she planned to report the incident to the media and authorities if the school failed to take action. She filed claims for negligent retention, assault and battery, and discrimination. The court held for the school district in part and for the teacher in part. The Court dismissed all but one claim for discrimination against the board of education as well as all claims against the city, and the teacher was given permission to amend her claims under city code and the state human rights law.

CASE STUDIES

Discrimination and the Interpreter for Deaf Students

Ruby Tyler, a member of the United Pentecostal Church, was employed by a school district as an interpreter and tutor for deaf students. In this capacity, she worked at an elementary school for one year and at a middle school for two years. During her interpreting, Tyler modified language she found objectionable or informed students that the speaker had used undesirable language. The school district developed new guidelines mandating that interpreters convey all information verbatim. In addition to word-for-word interpretation to hearing impaired students, the district assigned her to work at the high school. Tyler refused to work at the high school under the new guidelines and was terminated by the district. She sued, claiming discrimination.

Discussion Questions

1. Does Tyler have a valid claim of discrimination? Why or why not?
2. Was the district's action arbitrary, capricious, or in violation of Tyler's religious beliefs?
3. How would you assess Tyler's refusal to interpret personally objectionable material versus a deaf student's right to know what is communicated by speakers?
4. Is Tyler justified in her actions? Why or why not?

5. Is the district justified in its action? Why or why not?
6. How would the court likely rule in this case?
7. What are the administrative implications based on your assessment of this case?

Discrimination—Driving Under the Influence

Mary Martin, a female, tenured teacher in a rural conservative district, was stopped by the local police and charged with driving under the influence. She explained to the police that she had just left a Christmas party given by her principal and that she had consumed only a few glasses of wine. She was also aware that some of her male colleagues had been stopped in the past but not charged. Nevertheless, she was still charged. As her arrest becomes public, there is pressure from the school board for her to resign.

Discussion Questions

1. Can the board force Martin to resign? Why or why not?
2. Is the infraction serious enough to warrant dismissal? Why or why not?
3. What about male colleagues who were not charged for similar offenses?
4. What rights does Martin have as a teacher in this situation?
5. What factors would the court consider in ruling on her case?
6. What conclusion do you think the court would reach in this situation? Provide a rationale for your response.

Discrimination and a Recognized Academic Interest in Teaching

Martie Lyons, a seventh-grade teacher in a Northern industrial city, taught a course in life science using a school board–approved textbook. The course included a six-week section on human growth and sexuality. After instructing her students to get signed parental permission slips, Lyons showed two films on human reproduction and sexual development. Both films were provided by the county health department. The films were shown with boys and girls in separate rooms. When rumors spread that the films were explicit, some parents demanded that the teacher be fired. The board suspended Lyons without pay. Lyons subsequently filed a § 1983 lawsuit alleging a violation of her constitutional rights.

Discussion Questions

1. Was the board's action justified? Why or why not?
2. Does Lyons have a legitimate claim? Why or why not?
3. Is the challenge by parents an invasion of Lyons's academic interest in teaching her subject matter? Why or why not?
4. Is there evidence of discrimination against Lyons? If so, when did it occur? If not, why not?
5. How do you think a court would rule in this case? Provide a rationale for your response.
6. What are the administrative implications of this case?

Age Discrimination and Teacher Employment

Beth Stuart, a fifty-five-year-old teacher, applied for a position in an upper-middle-class community in the eastern part of the United States. She had recently relocated and had accumulated over twenty-five years of teaching experience in another state. In fact, she had served for six months as a substitute teacher in the district in which she applied. She was interviewed for a permanent position to fill a sudden vacancy. The superintendent asked her to be prepared to begin teaching on August 28. Meanwhile, the superintendent continued to interview candidates for the vacant position. Stuart had decorated her classroom and was prepared to begin teaching when, three days before school opened, she was informed that another teacher had been hired instead. Stuart learned that the new hire was twenty-five years old.

Discussion Questions

1. Did Stuart err in decorating her room in the absence of a contract? Why or why not?
2. Does Stuart have legal recourse? Why or why not?
3. Did the superintendent breach a verbal contract with Stuart?
4. Does Stuart have defensible grounds to file suit based on age discrimination? Why or why not?
5. How do you think a court would rule in this case?
6. What are the administrative implications of this case?

Discrimination and a Reduction in Force

Your district must implement a Reduction in Force (RIF) based on declining enrollment and budget cuts. You have recommended a list of teachers from your school to the superintendent. One of the teachers on the list had previously filed an EEOC suit against you alleging discrimination regarding a department chair's position that she was not awarded. You know that she will allege retaliation as the basis for her layoff.

Discussion Questions

1. How do you counter her charge?
2. What data do you need to justify your recommendation?
3. Should you allow her to retain employment based on the previous EEOC suit?
4. How do you legally defend your recommendation?

Endnotes

1. *Mathews v. Eldridge,* 424 U.S. 319, 96 S.Ct. 893, 47 L.Ed.2d 18 (1976).
2. 42 U.S.C. § 2000e et seq.
3. *Ledbetter v. Goodyear Tire and Rubber Company,* 127 S. Ct. 2162 (2007).
4. *McDonnell Douglas Corp. v. Green,* 411 U.S. 792 (1973).
5. *Furnco Construction Corp. v. Waters,* 438 U.S. 567 (1978).
6. *Ysleta Independent School Dist. v. Monarrez,* 177 S.W. 3d 915 (Tex. 2005).
7. *Fabela v. Socorro Independent School District,* 329 F. 3d 409 (C.A.5 [Tex.], 2003).
8. *Jackson v. Birmingham Board of Education,* 309 F. 3d 1333 (11th Cir. 2002).
9. *Gates v. Gadsden County School Board,* 45 So.3d 39 (Fla. Dist. Ct. App. 2010).
10. *Burlington Northern & Santa Fe Railway Co. v. White,* 548 U.S. 53 (2006).
11. *Andrews v. Drew Municipal Separate School District,* 507 F. 2d 611 (5th Cir. 1975).
12. *Brown v. Bathke,* 416 F. Supp. 1194 (D Neb. 1976), rev'd 566 F. 2d 588 (8th Cir. 1977).
13. *Mitchell v. Board of Trustees of Pickens County School District,* A. 599 F. 2d 582 (4th Cir. 1979).
14. *Avery v. Homewood City Board of Education,* 674 F. 2d 337 (5th Cir. 1982).
15. *Eckmann v. Board of Education of Hawthorn School District,* 636 F. Supp. 1214 (N.D. Ill. 1986).

16. *Spears v. Board of Education of Pike County, Kentucky,* 843 F. 2d 822 (6th Cir. 1988).
17. *Patterson v. Masem,* 774 F. 2d 751 (8th Cir. 1985).
18. *McCarthney v. Griffin, Spalding County Board of Education,* 791 F. 2d 1549 (11th Cir. 1986).
19. 34 C.F.R. § 106.61.
20. *Northaven Board of Education v. Bell,* 456 U.S. 512 (1982).
21. *Grove City College v. Bell,* 465 U.S. 555 (1984).
22. 29 U.S.C. § 794 (A) (1988).
23. 29 U.S.C. § 706 (8) (B) (1988).
24. 34 C.F.R. § 104.3 (i) (2) (ii) (1991).
25. Ibid., 104.14 (a).
26. Ibid., 104.13 (a).
27. 42 U.S.C. § 12111(9).
28. Ibid. (10).
29. *School Board of Nassau County, Florida v. Arline,* 480 U.S. 273, 107 S.Ct. 1123 (1987).
30. *Chalk v. U.S. District Court, Central District of California,* U.S. Court of Appeals, 840 F. 2d 901 (1988).
31. *Kolstad v. American Dental Association,* 527 U.S. 526, 119 S.Ct. 2118; 144 L. Ed. 2d 494 (1999).
32. Ibid.
33. *Plessy v. Ferguson,* 163 U.S. 537 (1896).
34. *Brown v. Board of Education,* 347 U.S. 483, 74 S.Ct. 686 (1954).
35. Ibid.
36. *Keyes v. School District No. 1,* 413 U.S. 189, 93 S.Ct. 2686 (1973).

37. *Griggs v. Duke Power Company,* 401 U.S. 424, 91 S.Ct. 849 (1971).

38. *United States of America v. South Carolina,* 445 F. Supp. 1094, affirmed 434 U.S. 1026, 98 S.Ct. 756 (1978).

39. *International Brotherhood of Teamsters v. United States,* 431 U.S. 324, 97 S.Ct. 1843 (1977).

40. *Peters v. Jenney,* 327 F. 3d 307 (4th Cir. 2003).

41. *Palmer v. Louisiana St. Bd. of Elem. and Secondary Educ.,* 842 S. 2d 363 (La. 2003).

42. *Estate of Thornton v. Caldor,* Inc., 472 U.S. 703 (1985).

43. *Transworld Airlines Inc. v. Hardison,* 432 U.S. 63, 97 S.Ct. 2264 (1977).

44. *Ramey v. Twin Butte School District,* 662 N.W. 2d 270 (N.D. 2003).

45. *Employment Division, Department of Human Resources of Oregon v. Smith,* 494 U.S. 872 (1990).

46. *Massachusetts Board of Regents v. Murgia,* 427 U.S. 307 (1976).

47. *Morrow v. Duval County School Board,* 514 So. 2d 1086 (Fla. 1987).

48. *EEOC v. District of Columbia Public Schools,* 2003 WL 21982925 (DDC August 13, 2003).

49. *General Dynamics Land Systems Inc. v. Cline,* 540 U.S. 581 (2004).

50. *Cleveland Board of Education v. LaFleur,* 414 U.S. 632 (1974).

51. *Maganuco v. Leyden Community High School Dist. 212,* 939 F. 2d 440 (7th Cir. 1991).

52. *Oncale v. Sundowner Offshore Services,* 523 U.S. 75 (1998).

53. 29 C.F.R. § 1604.11(a) (1991).

54. *Meritor Savings Bank v. Vinson,* 106 S.Ct. 2399 (1986).

55. *Gebser v. Lago Vista Independent School District,* 524 U.S. 274; 118 S.Ct. 1989; 141 L. Ed. 2d 277.

56. *Charlton v. Paramus Board of Education,* 25 F. 3d 194 (3rd Cir. 1994).

57. *Franklin v. Gwinnett County Public Schools,* 112 S.Ct. 1028 (1992).

58. *Linder v. City of New York,* 263 F. Supp. 2d 585 (E.D.N.Y. 2003).

Chapter 10

Recruitment, Tenure, Dismissal, and Due Process

RECRUITMENT OF PERSONNEL

School officials should recognize and value the need for a diverse workforce within their districts. Therefore, efforts should be made to recruit and retain the most diverse pool of qualified candidates the district can afford to compensate. With the critical shortage of teachers across the country, especially minorities, the recruitment and retention process becomes increasingly competitive. Many districts have created incentives to attract the brightest and best personnel through low-interest mortgages, forgivable college loans, discounts on certain purchases, and signing bonuses.

However, one important dimension of the recruitment and retention process is the image that the district projects through the recruitment process. A district that projects a professional image and has well-defined processes to support its mission generally is more appealing to prospective candidates. Therefore, it is important to create a positive impression on candidates as school officials assess them and they assess the district. A well-organized and legally defensible interview process contributes significantly to the candidates' overall impression of the district and further protects the district from allegations of unfair treatment.

The Employment Interview

An important component of the recruitment and selection process is the employment interview. The interview process is most effective when each candidate is assessed by a select panel of interviewers. The panel should resist judging candidates until the interview has been completed. Time should be allocated between interviews for all interviewers to complete an evaluation of each candidate. A scoring system, particularly one that is linked to competencies, may enhance the process enormously. Those conducting interviews should be trained to avoid racial and other biases. Written guidelines should be developed for all persons conducting interviews. Checklists also are valuable tools to ensure that all relevant areas are covered.

Questions raised during the interview should relate to the position each candidate is pursuing. Any questions needed to determine whether the candidate meets the job requirements with respect to hours, overtime, and mobility should be raised equally of men and women. The assessment of candidates, wherever possible, should be based on factual evidence of past performance, behavior, and achievements. Open-ended questions should be raised by using such words and phrases as *who, what, tell us more,* and *describe* to encourage candidates to express themselves as much as possible. Questions regarding age, marital status, credit rating, number of children, spouse employment, and arrest record are potentially discriminatory questions and should be avoided. Questions dealing with pregnancy, plans for a family, or intent to marry should be avoided. Questions regarding religious beliefs or affiliation are illegal and should be avoided. Inquiries regarding the type of military discharge a candidate received may be potentially discriminatory, as well as questions about organizations with which a candidate is affiliated. Employment applications typically should not include requests for the following:

- Race
- Age
- Birth date
- Birthplace
- National origin
- Marital status
- Number of children
- Gender
- Height
- Weight (unless demonstrably necessary as a requirement for certain jobs)
- Home ownership
- Religious affiliation
- Type of military discharge
- Photography

A record should be maintained regarding why each candidate was or was not recommended. This type of documentation may prove useful in the event that a candidate files a legal challenge if he or she was not recommended for an employment position.

When an applicant is under serious consideration for employment, a thorough reference check is appropriate and should be expected. A background check regarding criminal convictions also is appropriate and should be initiated to ensure that students are not exposed to undesirable personnel.

Vague Interviews

Personnel interviews should be as specific as possible so that sufficient information is gathered regarding an applicant to facilitate an informed decision by employers. Focused interviews also allow the applicant to understand what type of response is required. However, there are many instances in which vague questions are raised that do not provide sufficient guidance to applicants. Consequently, it sometimes is difficult for them to respond in an organized and logical manner. The following questions typically are raised during personnel interviews:

- Tell us about yourself.
- What significant challenges have you faced?
- Where would you like to be in the foreseeable future?
- What are your proudest accomplishments?
- Tell us about your most frustrating job experience.
- Tell us about your major weaknesses.
- What do you know about our organization?
- Are you pursuing other types of positions?

Some of these questions may prove challenging for applicants because they provide little direction regarding the specific response that is sought by interviewers. Interview questions should be raised that are purposeful, direct, specific to the position for which the applicant has applied, and not structured in a manner that provides guidance to the applicant.

Retention of Personnel Data

The Data Protection Act of 1998 does not mandate a particular retention period for employment data and records. It does indicate that these data are not to be maintained longer than necessary. Retention time should be assessed based on the types of employment data. For example, interview records might only be minimally maintained for six months after the unsuccessful candidate is notified of the employment decision. This six-month period provides adequate opportunity (180 days) based on EEOC guidelines for an applicant to file charges of alleged job discrimination. However, a two-year period is recommended based on federal agencies such as Title VII, ADA, and ADEA requirements. Personnel resumes may be maintained for future job opportunities. If so, the applicant must be informed and consent to have his/her resume maintained on file. There should be an indication regarding the length of time the resume will be maintained on file.

Hiring Discrimination

School districts that develop a well-defined and focused process that is legally defensible tend to have a greater opportunity to attract and retain quality personnel while minimizing legal challenges. Legal challenges do arise during the employment process.

One such case involving religious discrimination arose in California when two Jehovah's Witnesses applied for positions with the California community college district.[1] In accordance with state-mandated preemployment procedures, the district required applicants to sign an oath swearing allegiance to the U.S. and California constitutions. The applicants refused to take the oath because it conflicted with their religious beliefs. The district rejected their applications. They then filed suit against the district under the Religious Freedom Restoration Act (RFRA) in the U.S. District Court for the District of California, challenging the validity of the loyalty oath. The district moved for summary judgment. The court held that requiring applicants to take a loyalty oath placed an undue burden on their right to free exercise of religion. Although employee loyalty was a compelling state interest, the evidence failed to establish that a loyalty oath was an effective way to achieve this goal. An alternative oath directed to an applicant's actions rather than his or her beliefs would be equally effective and less restrictive. Because the loyalty oath could not be justified under the compelling interest test articulated in the RFRA, the court enjoined the district from administering the oath.

Another case involving employment discrimination was filed by a black Florida man who applied for a full-time teaching position with a county school district.[2] He was not hired. He then filed a complaint with the Florida Commission of Human Relations, alleging that he had been denied employment because of his sex and race. A formal hearing was conducted. The hearing officer determined that the teacher had presented a *prima facie* case of discrimination and that the school board had failed to present a legitimate, nondiscriminatory reason for not hiring the teacher. The commission then ordered the school board to cease discriminating on the basis of race and sex, to offer the teacher the next available full-time position for which he was qualified, and to award the teacher back pay. The school board appealed to the District Court of Appeal of Florida.

The appellate court first noted that the evidence supported the commission's determination that the teacher had been discriminated against. However, it stated that the teacher had presented no evidence that he had been economically damaged by the discriminatory actions of the board. Therefore, the commission did not have the authority to permit an award of back pay to the teacher. The court affirmed that part of the commission's decision that ordered that the teacher be hired to the next available full-time teaching position, but it reversed the commission's authorization of back pay.

TENURE

Tenure in public schools is prescribed by state statute. Although variations among states are many, most tenure laws are designed to protect teachers. The *tenure contract* is designed primarily to provide a measure of security for teachers and to ensure that they are protected from arbitrary and capricious treatment by school authorities. Tenure also is viewed as a means of providing a degree of permanency in the teaching force from which students ultimately benefit.

Any teacher who earns tenure or continuing service status also acquires a property right or a legitimate claim to the teaching position. Once a property right is acquired, the teacher may be dismissed only for cause. Tenure does not guarantee continued employment, but it does ensure that certified school personnel may not be arbitrarily removed from their employment positions without due process of law.

A continuing service status case arose in South Dakota when the Supreme Court of South Dakota held that a school district was not required to provide a hearing or other due process protections to a retired teacher who claimed she retained her continuing contract status on returning to the district under a probationary contract.[3] In a related case, the Court of Civil Appeals of Alabama held that a retired teacher who tried to rescind his retirement and later signed a probationary contract accepted probationary status. The property and tenure rights he enjoyed were terminated before retiring.[4]

The intended purpose of tenure laws has been described by the courts. One court described it in this manner:

> While tenure provisions . . . protect teachers in their positions from political or arbitrary interference, they are not intended to preclude dismissal where the conduct is detrimental to the efficient operation and administration of the schools of the district. . . . Its objective is to improve the school system by assuring teachers of experience and ability a continuous service based upon merit, and by protecting them against dismissal for reasons that are political, partisan or capricious.[5]

Through this protection, teachers are insulated from special-interest groups and political factions, thereby enabling them to perform their professional duties without undue interference. When this occurs, the educational system is improved and students derive the benefits of quality education.

Acquisition of Tenure

Tenure is increasingly becoming an issue in a number of states. Some states have revised tenure laws through increasing the number of years required to attain tenure. For example, a law was passed in Ohio that requires seven years of service before a teacher becomes eligible to earn tenure. Florida is considering abolishing tenure whereas Delaware is considering linking tenure to student achievement.

The *probationary period* is one in which the nontenured teacher is seeking tenure. In a number of states, tenure may be attained only after the teacher has successfully completed three successive years (the probationary period) and receives an offer for reemployment for the succeeding year. School boards are provided broad latitude in determining whether tenure should be granted as illustrated in a case in Mississippi. A Mississippi Junior ROTC instructor worked for three school years, left for a year, then returned to his job for a week. The U.S. Court of Appeals, Fifth Circuit, held that he had no protected property interest in employment. The school board never approved a recommendation by the principal to rehire the instructor. State law codified the procedures for hiring teachers and limited the role of principals to recommending candidates. Any expectation for reemployment held by the instructor was based on statements allegedly made by the principal. The principal's actions were not sufficient to create a property interest in employment, and the district was entitled to judgment.[6] During the probationary period, a teacher may be nonrenewed at the end of the contract year without cause or dismissed during the year with cause. In the case of the latter, the teacher must be afforded full due process rights. There is no requirement for due process provisions in cases involving nonrenewal, unless the teacher is able to demonstrate that nonrenewal was based purely on personal or political motives or motivated by arbitrary and capricious actions involving infringement on constitutional rights. This is usually a difficult burden of proof to meet, but the ultimate burden rests with the probationary teacher. However, school leaders may not recommend nonrenewal based on arbitrary and capricious decisions.

Because state laws prescribe that certain substantive and procedural requirements be met regarding tenure, it is essential that school districts adhere to these requirements (see Chapter 8). Generally, state statutes identify a specific date in which a probationary teacher must be informed that employment opportunities will no longer be available for the succeeding year. This notice informing the teacher of nonrenewal is normally forwarded to the teacher by certified or registered mail to the latest known address on or before a specified date. If the district fails to meet this requirement, the teacher may have gained employment for the following year. When a teacher has completed three consecutive years in the same district and does not receive timely notice of nonrenewal, the teacher may have acquired tenure by *default*. It is essential that school officials meet statutory requirements in matters involving proper notification.

An interesting case arose in New Jersey regarding the interpretation of requirements for attaining tenure. The case involved a New Jersey learning disabilities teacher who was later classified as a school psychologist. She had worked as a psychologist for over two years, until a work-related injury forced her to take an involuntary leave of absence. Her employment was terminated by the board six months after her leave was approved. The psychologist alleged that she was wrongly terminated and had, in fact, accumulated the necessary thirty months to attain tenure, even though she had worked for only twenty-eight months at the time of her injury. She filed an appeal with the state board of education, which agreed that the termination violated her tenure rights.

The New Jersey Superior Court, Appellate Division, affirmed the state board's decision. The school district then appealed to the Supreme Court of New Jersey. The court held that employees who took sick leave remained school district employees for the duration of their leave.[7] Therefore, the psychologist was not prohibited from completing her probationary period while on leave. The use of the leave did not prevent the psychologist from attaining tenure.

In reviewing this case, it is apparent that an official and sanctioned sick leave may not prevent a teacher from accumulating time toward statutory tenure. Boards of education must be aware of the specific provisions of their state's tenure law to avoid costly and unnecessary litigation.

In sum, nontenured status involves the following:

- No expectation for employment beyond the contracted year
- No right to be provided reasons for nonrenewal
- No right to due process
- No hearing

These conditions are valid unless the nontenured teacher produces evidence that a liberty or property right exists, in which case due process must be provided. A *liberty right* exists when damaging statements are communicated that may limit the teacher's range of future employment opportunities.

In a leading case, the U.S. Supreme Court addressed contract nonrenewal with respect to the legal dimensions impacting the process. In the *Roth* case, a nontenured teacher was hired by a state university for a fixed term of one year. He was later notified that he would not be rehired for the following year. State statute, university policy, and the teacher's contract did not provide for a pretermination hearing or require that reasons be given for nonrenewal. The teacher challenged the constitutionality of the university's action in dismissing him without notice of the reasons for its decisions and without the benefit of a hearing. The Supreme Court held that the state may opt not to renew a nontenured teacher's contract at the end of the fixed period of employment without providing reasons for the decision or without a pretermination hearing if he has not been deprived of liberty or property. In this case, no liberty or property interest was impaired; consequently, no due process or Fourteenth Amendment right had been violated.[8]

Nonrenewal

The primary reason due process does not apply to probationary status centers around a limited property interest. During the probationary period, the teacher typically is offered a one-year contract, which is renewable each year, if the school board elects to do so. The probationary teacher, then, only has a property right for the duration of the one-year contract. When the contract period ends each year, the teacher loses the inherent property right because both the teacher and the district have met contractual obligations to each other. Due process and cause are necessary only if there is evidence that a property interest continues to exist. A property interest does not exist if no legal contract is in force. (*Mt. Healthy v. Doyle* represents a classic case of nonrenewal in Chapter 8.) As stated previously, if a district decides to dismiss a probationary teacher during the contract period, then full due process provisions are required, including notice, cause, and a formal hearing because the teacher has a property right for the contract year.

Table 10.1 summarizes legal dimensions related to tenured and nontenured status.

Two interesting cases have arisen, in New York and Michigan, regarding nonrenewal of a teacher's contract. In the first case, a teacher who was denied tenure brought § 1983 action challenging the school board's refusal to allow her attorney to raise tenure issues during a public session.[9] On the school district's motion to dismiss, and the teacher's motion for partial summary judgment, the district court held that the teacher had no First Amendment right to appear through her agent at regularly scheduled, nonadversarial board meetings at which no action was going to be taken with respect to her property rights.

In that case the teacher, Prestopnik, was employed with the Greater Johnstown School District from September 1, 1999, through June 30, 2002. The district superintendent did not recommend her for tenure, and the board of education affirmed the superintendent's recommendation. Prestopnik then hired an attorney to represent her in connection with her denial of tenure and termination of employment. Her attorney attended a public board meeting and attempted to request that the board reconsider the tenure decision concerning his client. The district attorney informed

TABLE 10.1 Legal Requirements Involving Tenured and Nontenured Teachers	
Tenured Teachers	**Nontenured Teachers**
• Earns property right to the teaching position	• Contract may be nonrenewed after it expires during the probationary period or without cause
• Earns continued service status	
• May only be dismissed for statutory cause	• May or may not be provided reasons for nonrenewal, depending on state statutes
• Full due process procedures must be met	
• Is entitled to a formal and fair hearing	• May or may not be provided a hearing based on state statute
• Must receive prior notice of intent and grounds for proposed dismissal by registered or certified mail	• Written notice of nonrenewal must be received on or before the statutory date required by law
• Must be provided information regarding time, place of hearing, with option of public or closed hearing	• Failure to meet the statutory date by the school board may result in continued employment by the teacher
• Has right to legal counsel	• Receives hearing if contract is cancelled before contract date expires or if required by state law
• Has right to be provided names of witnesses	• Hearing not provided unless stipulated by state law
• Must be provided transcript of the hearing if requested	• Does not have right to appeal unless stipulated by state statute
• May appeal decision to higher authority or the courts if decision is not favorable	• May be provided hearing if there is evidence of a liberty right violation—injury to good name or information communicated that affects future employment opportunities

him that he would not be permitted to raise the issue of Prestopnik's tenure during the public session of the meeting. He was invited to address the board in writing on behalf of the plaintiff.

In the Michigan case, Flaskamp was a physical education teacher at Fordson High School from 1997 until 2001.[10] Teachers employed in the Dearborn public school system are eligible to receive tenure after a four-year probationary period. The board voted to deny Flaskamp tenure at the end of her four years because of an alleged sexual relationship with a former student that the board found to be inappropriate and the principal's statement that he could no longer trust her. Flaskamp brought § 1983 action against the school district and school board based on the board's denial of tenure due to her alleged intimate relationship with a high school student. On the parties' cross-motions for summary judgment, the district court held that (1) Flaskamp had qualified immunity from the right-to-privacy claim, (2) a constitutional right to intimate association did not extend to teacher–student relationships, and (3) her substantive due process rights had not been violated. The district court granted the school board's motion. Under Michigan law, a teacher in probationary period who is denied tenure is not entitled to a hearing.

The United States Court of Appeals for the Seventh Circuit held that a school district administrator had no property interest in continued employment that was entitled to due process protection.[11] Even if she had such a property interest, the court held, her due process rights were not violated when the school board, rather than an outside decision maker, conducted her contract renewal hearing. The court also rejected her claim that she had a protected liberty interest that was violated by a press release the board issued after the hearing. Karen Beischel entered into a two-year contract with Stone Bank School District (WI) to serve as district administrator and principal of its only school. After a difficult first year, the school board notified Beischel that it was considering not renewing her contract. Following a hearing, the board voted to not renew the contract. Beischel sued, claiming that she was deprived of property and liberty interests in violation of her right to due process under the Fourteenth Amendment. She argued that her property interest in continued employment was denied because the board conducted the hearing. Even though the board was vested under state law with the power to employ and dismiss teachers, she contended that the hearing should have been conducted by an outside decision maker because the board was biased and could not render an impartial decision. The court rejected this argument, concluding that she had no legitimate expectation in continued employment that would warrant a protected property interest. Even if she had such an interest, her evidence of bias could not overcome the presumption that board members carried out their duties with honesty and integrity. There was no proof that the board had a pecuniary interest in the outcome. Consequently, the board was not required to recuse itself and relinquish its authority to an outside hearing officer "unaccountable to the voters of the Stone Bank school district." The court disposed of the deprivation of liberty claim on the grounds that, although the press release may have damaged Beischel's reputation, it did not implicate a liberty interest because it did not make it "virtually impossible" for her to find new employment.

Administrative Guide

Tenure

1. Teachers are entitled to fundamental fairness, irrespective of tenure status.
2. Tenure is not designed to protect teachers who are inept or ineffective.
3. Tenure should protect competent and effective teachers.
4. Teachers may be dismissed only for specified reasons that are based on objective and documentable evidence.
5. Due process procedural safeguards, as established by state statutes, should be followed to ensure that dismissal decisions are legally defensible.
6. Nonrenewal of a nontenured teacher's contract does not generally require due process or reasons, unless an alleged constitutional violation is involved.

School Leader (Principal) Evaluation

Most states have developed evaluation systems for educational leaders with increased emphasis on teacher effectiveness and student performance outcomes. Increasingly, these two aspects of an evaluation are critical to the district's capacity to achieve its mission and vision. Principals as educational leaders are expected to implement effective leadership strategies that focus on student success. They should be judged, in part, on the basis of how well teachers implement classroom strategies that yield high levels of student achievement. The principal is expected to assess existing practices working with teachers to develop and implement new strategies to optimize student learning. Additionally, they are expected to provide overall leadership and manage resources efficiently and effectively.

An effective evaluation system should contain standards and rubrics that describe the level of proficiency expected for each standard. Minimally, at least four rubrics should be used that reflect the desires of the district. The evaluation system should include performance standards, benchmarks, or performance indicators for each standard rubric to measure the extent to which the leader is meeting leadership expectations. Some of the more common rubrics are outstanding (exemplary), proficient or effective, improving, unsatisfactory, or unmet with statements that describe the leader's behavior under each rubric.

Performance outcomes should be thoroughly documented, discussed with the principal, and include evidence that supports each level of performance. This documentation usually is recorded on some type of assessment form. Many districts engage external consultants who work with principals to ensure that everyone involved understands all aspects of the evaluation system.

At the district's discretion, the evaluation system may include a self-evaluation component that allows the principal to assess his or her effectiveness when measured against prescribed standards. This method allows the principal and evaluator to compare the self-evaluation to the evaluator's assessment. Differences in each should be discussed with a focus on reaching agreement regarding why differences exist and steps that may be taken to facilitate improved performance. The evaluation plan may, at the district's discretion, include both formal and informal assessments designed to establish a composite picture of the principal's performance or behavior in a variety of settings. A thorough and well-developed plan holds the key to improved leadership effectiveness, teacher performance, and student achievement. Consistent evaluation data may be used to determine the employment status of school principals based on the extent to which district performance outcomes are met. It should also be used to develop a professional development plan as well. However, if the evaluation is administered to accomplish any objective other than performance improvement, the school leader should be informed of the purpose of the evaluation prior to its execution.

The evaluation process should be sufficiently specific so that the principals and the evaluator clearly understand what is expected of each other. The evaluation plan should form the basis for professional growth and overall leadership effectiveness, particularly with respect to the school's instructional program.

Tenure for Principals

Some states provide tenure protection for principals based on principals' meeting certain statutory requirements. Most requirements for principal tenure are similar to those required of teachers—that is, three successive years of employment in the same district with an offer of reemployment at the end of the third year. Considerable debate has been waged regarding the merits of tenure protection for principals. Advocates of tenure contend that school administrators need protection against arbitrary and capricious actions of school boards. They also cite tenure as providing incentives to attract prospective candidates into administrative positions. Opponents argue that school administrators who are performing their jobs effectively need not be concerned with job security and that tenure tends to protect principals who are not effective as school leaders. Nationwide, only thirteen states provide some type of tenure for principals:

Alabama	New York
Hawaii	North Dakota
Iowa	Pennsylvania
Minnesota	Utah
Montana	Washington
Nebraska	West Virginia
New Hampshire	

Fixed-term contracts for principals appear to be growing in popularity among legislatures across the country. These contracts generally offer some degree of protection with respect to procedural safeguards if dismissal is recommended by school boards. Although these fixed contracts vary in length from one to five years, the most common term appears to be three-year renewable contracts. Thirty-six states offer fixed-term contracts for principals.

Trends across the nation tend to support fixed-term contracts that are renewed based on performance. The intent of fixed-term contracts centers on creating increased accountability among principals based on the quality and effectiveness of their performance. Tenure as a concept for principals appears to be rapidly disappearing.

Administrative Guide

Principal Tenure

1. Principals on fixed-term contracts are entitled to due process hearings if their contract is cancelled prior to the contract expiration date.
2. If a principal is nonrenewed with timely notice at the end of the contract period, reasons need not be provided for the nonrenewal.
3. Principals may challenge nonrenewal if they believe such action was based on arbitrary or capricious action by the school board.
4. The burden of proof rests with principals who challenge nonrenewals to demonstrate arbitrary and capricious action by school boards.

Teacher Evaluation

With increased emphasis on student performance and learning outcomes, teachers are expected to perform at very high levels in a classroom environment that is peaceful, orderly, and conducive for teaching and learning. The teaching process has been transformed within school districts throughout the United States. States have included student performance outcomes as a component of the teacher's overall evaluation. There are numerous methods used to evaluate teachers including observation scales, appraisal instruments, video productions, self-appraisal, peer evaluation, and teaching portfolios, among others. In all cases, teacher evaluations should be characterized as fair, objective, and free of distortions. Valid documentation is critical to an effective appraisal of teaching performance. It is highly desirable to include teachers in the design of the evaluation system as an effort to facilitate a comprehensive, objective, unbiased review process. Teachers should be informed that the purpose of the evaluation is to improve the quality of instruction and optimize student growth and development. If the evaluation is conducted for any other purpose, the teacher should be informed prior to initiating the process.

A teacher evaluation system should incorporate performance standards, which would include the core duties performed by the teacher, observable behavior regarding each standard, and rubrics for measuring performance. Multiple data sources should be used to assess performance including but not limited to the teacher's self-assessment, informal observations by the evaluator, student assessment data, formal evaluation, teacher portfolios, and video production of the teacher's classroom performance.

Documentation of Teaching Performance

A documentation log may be included that will note specific evidence that the teacher's performance has or has not met performance standards incorporated in the assessment instrument. The teacher's verbal ability should be assessed; his/her ability to think critically and diagnostically; ability to explain and clarify subject content, which suggests that the teacher should possess strong content knowledge; and be able to present it in a manner that is understood by students. A wide array of instructional materials, supplies, and electronic equipment should facilitate teaching effectiveness. Additionally, classroom content should fully relate to real-life situations as much as possible. Students should understand the relevance of content shared in the classrooms by the teacher and should be fully engaged in learning by the teacher. This means that the teacher must have a strong concept of learning and understand students' growth and developmental learning stages while recognizing that all students do not learn in the same manner. This knowledge will assist teachers in understanding interventions that may be needed to assist students in their development. Teaching performance should be documented and shared with each teacher at the end of each evaluation. Because documentation is critical to improving the quality of teaching and student learning and development, all components of the evaluation system should be documented in the documentation log including multiple data sources to measure student academic progress. Observations may occur through drop-by classroom visits—formal or pre-planned observational review—some of which may be announced or unannounced based on teacher evaluation policy.

DISMISSAL FOR CAUSE

Dismissing a teacher for cause is a serious matter, because the teacher has an inherent property right to hold the employment position. State statutes prescribe permissible grounds on which dismissal is based. In these cases, the burden of proof resides with the board of education to show cause based on a preponderance of evidence. The obvious benefit of tenure is that dismissal cannot occur without a formal hearing and the presentation of sufficient evidence to meet statutory requirements. This assures the teacher that procedural and substantive due process requirements are met.

Tenure laws include grounds for dismissal in virtually all states. Although laws vary among states, these grounds normally include incompetency, insubordination, neglect of duty, immorality, justifiable decrease in the number of teaching positions, or financial exigency, and a statement indicating "other good and just cause." This latter phrase provides the board with broader latitude to address other grounds that may not be specified in the statute. A board of education may dismiss a teacher for almost any reason, as long as the reason is valid and meets the substantive and procedural due process requirements.

Incompetency

One of the more frequently used grounds for dismissal involves charges of incompetency. *Incompetency* is a vague term in many respects. In some states, incompetency is the sole grounds for dismissal, using almost any reason to comprise this category. Most commonly, *incompetency* refers to inefficiency, a lack of skill, inadequate knowledge of subject matter, inability or unwillingness to teach the curricula, failure to work effectively with colleagues and parents, failure to maintain discipline, mismanagement of the classroom, and attitudinal deficiencies. Because the court views the teaching certificate as *prima facie* proof of competency, the burden of proof challenging a teacher's competency rests with the school board. The competent teacher is generally viewed as a person who has the knowledge, skills, and intelligence of the average or ordinary teacher.

Courts often view incompetency as a term characterized by a lack of knowledge, skill, intelligence, and, in some instances, professionalism. These characterizations may impede the teacher's effectiveness in the classroom, his or her teaching methods and strategies, as well as the teacher's overall ability to create a proper learning environment for students. It is very difficult to sustain charges of incompetency in the absence of a systematic and continuous evaluation process with feedback designed to assist the teacher in improving performance.

Fundamental fairness dictates that an evaluation process be employed. For example, a case involving charges of incompetency arose in Missouri when an elementary administrator determined that a teacher had numerous communication problems. After giving her warnings, the administrator created a professional development plan, requiring her to attend teaching workshops and read materials on communication and instruction. After a number of evaluations, the principal determined that the teacher's performance was still unsatisfactory. Classroom management problems also were evident. After further meetings and warnings, the administrator issued a letter to the teacher, in compliance with the state tenure act, informing her that formal charges would be forthcoming unless she showed improvement within 120 days.

The administrator videotaped classes held by the teacher and followed them with discussion meetings with the teacher. Although the teacher's deadline was extended, the administrator eventually recommended termination. The board approved the dismissal, which was affirmed by the Missouri Court of Appeals. The appellate court recognized that the tenure act mandated reasons and procedures for removing teachers—incompetency, insubordination, or inefficiency—and, further, that a written warning specifying grounds for actions was initiated by the administrator consistent with the law. The court held for the district and against the teacher, stating that the board did act in good faith in contradiction to the teacher's argument. The evidence revealed that the administrator had made many efforts to assist the teacher in improving her performance and had provided additional time beyond what was legally required to comply with the development plan. The court affirmed the board's decision.[12]

It is clear from this case that proper evaluation, documentation, assistance rendered, and timely notice were crucial to the district's efforts to remove an ineffective teacher. Furthermore, all conditions of the tenure act were met. This case challenges the misconception that a tenured teacher cannot be dismissed. Tenured teachers can, in fact, be dismissed on incompetency charges when proper evaluation, defensible documentation, and procedural guidelines are followed consistent with the state's tenure laws.

If charges of incompetency are brought against a teacher, these charges should be preceded by systematic evaluations and documentation of performance as well as a thoroughly developed teacher improvement plan. Proper documentation and a reasonable time frame designed to allow the teacher to meet expected performance standards are critical to sustain charges of incompetence should it become necessary to do so.

There are many excellent examples of professional improvement plans, but any plan should minimally include the following components (see Figure 10.1):

- Teacher's name
- Teacher's position
- Evaluator's name
- Date of evaluation
- Competencies and skills to be addressed
- Professional development goals related to each competency and skill
- Specific objectives to be met under each goal for a specific competency and skill
- Recommended activities to meet professional goals and objectives
- Time frame in which goals and objectives are to be met
- Types of support systems provided by the school and district to assist the teacher in improving performance

School _____ School District _____

Teacher _____ Grade Level(s) _____ Evaluator _____ Date _____

Performance	Professional Development Goals/Objectives	Proposed/Planned Activities/Strategies	Designated Time Frame		Support Services Provided by the School District	Assessment Method	Progress Checkpoints (Dates)		
			Dates Started/Finished				1	2	3

Summary of Assessment Results/Improvements

Strengths	Weaknesses

Evaluator's Responses

Recommendations for Continued Growth and Development—Areas of Improvement

• • • • • • •

Steps to Measure Progress

Follow-Up Modifications

Agreement on Plan as Developed

Teacher _____ Date _____ Evaluator _____ Date _____

Confirmation of Discussion Regarding Assessment Results/Improvements—Steps to Measure Progress

Teacher _____ Date _____ Evaluator _____ Date _____

Resources Provided the Teacher

FIGURE 10.1 Sample Teacher Improvement Plan

- Performance assessment methodology and documentation that the teacher-improvement plan was agreed on by the teacher and the evaluator
- Documentation that the teacher and the evaluator discussed assessment results and improvements based on clearly defined goals and objectives

When these components are present in the absence of an unfair or arbitrary teacher performance assessment, school officials will likely succeed in sustaining charges of incompetency against a teacher who has consistently failed to meet required performance standards.

In an interesting case involving incompetency, disciplinary charges were brought against a school district's secondary supervisor and high school principal.[13] A high school principal and the secondary supervisor for a school district encouraged teachers to clarify test questions, allowed the use of a student accountability scale, and scheduled extended time for test sessions during the annual KIRIS assessment testing within the high school. The Kentucky Education Professional Standards Board (EPSB) found that these actions showed incompetence and misconduct on the part of the employees. The circuit court, however, found that although the actions of the employees amounted to incompetence, they did not rise to the level of misconduct or willful neglect. The court held for the EPSB. The high school principal and secondary supervisor failed to follow the guidelines in the instruction manual for assessment coordinators of the KIRIS test by performing the actions stated above. Such actions rose to the level of incompetence and misconduct under applicable Kentucky statutes.

Insubordination

Insubordination is generally viewed as the willful failure or inability to obey a reasonable and valid administrative directive. In most cases, a discernible pattern in the teacher's behavior reveals that the teacher has been insubordinate. However, in other instances one serious violation may form the basis for charges of insubordination. Most cases involving insubordination are those in which the teacher has been given distinct warning regarding the undesirable conduct and has failed to heed the warning. In such cases, charges of insubordination are usually sustained.

To succeed with insubordination charges, administrators must have documented evidence of the alleged misconduct with further evidence that the administrative order or directive was valid. Insubordination charges are more likely to succeed when they are linked with teaching performance or related academic issues. If the evidence reveals that the directive or administrative order was biased against the teacher or unreasonable, insubordination charges will be difficult to defend. Also, there should be no evidence that the order or rules violated the teacher's personal rights.

Insubordination is a serious charge and should be handled based on state statute and/or district policy. Substantiated insubordination may result in serious disciplinary actions, not excluding termination; therefore, it is essential that insubordination charges be handled in a legally defensible manner. Certain steps should be taken to ensure that the employee in question receives fair treatment and that insubordination charges are appropriate:

- Determine if the order was valid and communicated in a clearly written manner.
- Determine if the employee clearly understood the order and understood what should be done in response to the order.
- Determine if the directive was reasonable and appropriate; for example, was the directive questionable from a legal standpoint or would execution of the order create a safety risk for the employee.
- Determine if the employee was capable of executing the directive based on skill and experience.
- Determine if the employee was provided adequate opportunity to execute the directive.
- Determine if the employee willfully disregarded the order.
- Determine if the employee understood the consequences of not executing a valid directive.

TABLE 10.2	Insubordination

Insubordination terminology varies among states; however, the most common definition for insubordination is failure to follow a reasonable and valid administrative directive. An important component of insubordination charges revolves around whether the directives given were clear and reasonable so as to eliminate broad and nebulous interpretation. There is concern among school personnel regarding acts that constitute insubordination and those that do not. This table summarizes the difference between these acts.

Insubordination Involves:	**Insubordination does not Involve:**
• Willful and persistent failure to follow clear, reasonable, and valid administrative directives	• Disagreements with the supervisor
	• Professional and wholesome debate regarding school or educational issues
• Consistent failure to comply with school and district policy	• Disagreement between employee and supervisor over performance evaluation results
• Complying with some school policies and disregarding others	• Failure to endorse a performance evaluation concerning a disagreement between the teacher and supervisor
• Willful refusal to complete required program evaluation forms	
• Repeatedly introducing unauthorized content into class instruction	• Critical editorial regarding school issues that affect the citizens of the community
	• A rule that is unreasonable
• Excessive attendance problems coupled with other school policy violations	• The inability to and failure to return to work based on fear, intimidation, and stress involving school incidents
• Failure to report to a newly assigned school	
• Repeated failure to work on school or district-wide committees	• Behavior that is not proven to have occurred
	• Alleged behavior that occurs in the absence of a pertinent school or district rule unless it is egregious
• Repeated failure to perform reasonable nonteaching assignments	
• Failure to take daily student attendance	• A teacher who attempts to, but is unsuccessful in complying with a reasonable rule
• Failure to teach an assigned course	• A teacher who does not possess the skill or experience to comply with an order
• A single or substantive incident involving policy violations	
• Rude behavior coupled with consistent disrespectful behavior	• A rule that is invalid and beyond the authority of the supervisor
• Impertinence, rebelliousness, and defiance of authority	• A rule that is discriminatory or biased against the teacher

At a minimum, these steps should be followed to determine if acts of insubordination are valid and if the intended discipline is justified.

A teacher was dismissed for insubordination for repeated failure to provide lesson plans during her absence. She was also excessively absent and repeatedly failed to provide emergency lesson plans for substitute teachers. The court held for the school district in stating that the teacher's conduct demonstrated gross insubordination based on her continued refusal to obey a reasonable and direct request by her principal.[14]

Neglect of Duty

Neglect of duty occurs when a teacher fails to execute assigned duties. Neglect may be intentional or unintentional based on ineffective performance. One court defined neglect of duty as the failure to carry out professional obligations and responsibilities in connection with classroom or other school-sponsored activities.[15] Another court held that neglect of duty involving performance is not measured against a standard of perfection but must be measured against the standard required of others performing the same or similar duties.[16]

Just Cause

Just cause is found in statutes as a basis for employment termination. These statutes identify specific grounds for termination such as incompetency, insubordination, neglect of duty, immorality, justifiable decrease in the number of employment positions, and other good or just cause. Good and just cause provides school boards the latitude to terminate employees for valid reasons aside from the specific reasons listed in state statute. Just cause termination may occur if there is a legally defensible reason that warrants termination. In its most basic form, just cause requires that an employee's termination meet the substantive requirement (valid reason and valid means to terminate), which means that employment termination may not be based on arbitrary or capricious actions by the school board. The board, if challenged, must be able to demonstrate that its actions were fair and objective and that it acted in good faith (legitimate purpose served by its action) in reaching a termination decision. Some states refer to good and just cause as a "zipper clause," which recognizes that an employee may be dismissed for valid reasons not specifically identified in statute.

The term good and just cause is purposely broad so as to provide latitude for school boards to act in cases where termination of employment is warranted. The courts tend to support good and just cause termination so long as reasons for termination are not irrational, arbitrary, or capricious.

Examples of behavior that may constitute good and just cause include serious violation of district policy, chronic absenteeism or misrepresenting reasons for absenteeism, theft, fraud, verbal abuse of colleagues, refusal to discontinue irreparable damage to the employer–employee relationship, and verbal and physical abuse of students, among others. The key element of good and just cause termination is that the employee's actions must be provable. The following questions should be addressed prior to establishing just cause as the basis for employee discipline:

- If dismissal is based on just cause, was the employee warned of the infraction and made aware of the consequences of his/her behavior?
- Did the employee's behavior create substantial disruption to the education process?
- Did the employee willfully violate a school or district policy?
- Did sufficient evidence exist that warranted dismissal?
- Did the discipline received by the employee reasonably relate to the severity of the documented offense?
- Did the employee's behavior cast a negative image on the school or district?
- Did the employee receive a fair and objective hearing prior to (procedural and substantive due process) contemplating dismissal?

Documenting Teacher Misconduct

Teacher misconduct regarding school issues must be thoroughly investigated and documented. If the alleged misconduct is strictly private, no investigation may be necessary unless there is substantial evidence that the alleged behavior has a negative impact on students or the school. When misconduct is alleged, the date of the incident should be documented along with a summary of specific facts related to the teacher's behavior. If there are any other documents supporting the alleged misconduct, they should be included. Witnesses should also be identified where possible. Documentation should be substantial enough to clearly describe the behavior exhibited by the teacher. Additionally, if school or district policy is involved, the documentation should note the specific policy or procedure that has been violated.

When documentation is completed, the teacher should be provided an opportunity to respond in writing or refute any information associated with the alleged misconduct. Documents to support the teacher's position also should be included. A conference should be held with the teacher, at which time the alleged misconduct is discussed. If it is established that the claims against the teacher are valid, they should be duly documented. The teacher should be provided directions in writing regarding future behavior and the expectations associated with improved behavior. The teacher should receive a written copy of the behavior that gave rise to the misconduct, school policy or procedures that were violated, and consequences associated with the violation. Additionally, the teacher should receive a follow-up letter summarizing the content of the conference with a statement indicating the adjustments the teacher should make and consequences of future violations. Sufficient time must be provided the teacher to remedy the behavior based on the nature of the misconduct. The teacher should subsequently remedy the undesirable behavior. Close supervision may be needed based on the nature of the infraction. Each time an incident occurs, it should be properly documented. Each act of misconduct should be documented using a similar process. The documentation process and subsequent conferences should provide minimal due process provisions for the teacher by assuring that the teacher has been treated fairly both substantively and procedurally.

At a minimum, the following steps should be followed in addressing teacher misconduct:

1. Determine if the teacher was aware of the alleged misconduct.
2. Identify a school or district policy associated with the alleged misconduct.
3. Determine if the policy in question was clearly understood.
4. Conduct a thorough investigation to validate if a policy violation actually occurred.
5. Ensure that the investigation was fair, objective, and complete.
6. Identify evidence that clearly substantiates that a school or district policy was or was not violated.
7. If a policy was violated, confirm that the discipline applied to the teacher was reasonable and commensurate with the nature of the misconduct.

Immorality

Immorality is cited in relevant state statutes as grounds for dismissal and involves conduct that violates the ethics of a particular community. Some state laws refer to *immorality* as "unfitness to teach" or behavior that sets a poor example for students and violates moral integrity. One court has held that the conduct in question not only must be immoral under the particular community standards test but also must be found to impair the teacher's ability to teach.[17] This latter statement seems to reflect the consensus of court decisions regarding issues of immorality in that there must be a showing that the conduct in question impairs the teacher's effectiveness in the classroom.

Other acts that have fallen under the category of immorality include homosexual conduct, unprofessional conduct, criminal activity involving moral turpitude, and sexual activities involving students. Any act or behavior that substantially interferes with the education of children and has a direct impact on the teacher's fitness to teach usually forms the basis for immorality charges. One fundamental issue courts seek to address is a determination of whether the teacher's alleged conduct adversely affects teaching performance and effectiveness. The response to this issue, in many cases, will determine whether a teacher should be dismissed.

Homosexuality and Employment in Public Schools

State statutes, in many instances, cite unprofessional conduct as grounds for teacher dismissal. Because homosexual lifestyles may call into question concerns regarding professional conduct, courts have been consulted, with increasing frequency, to adjudicate issues regarding homosexual behavior involving public school teachers. The courts have not been altogether consistent in their rulings regarding employment rights of homosexual public school teachers. A few state laws, however, have become more liberal by not regarding homosexual relationships among consenting adults as a violation.

There seems to be a growing trend toward liberalizing state statutes based on the national recognition of gay rights and greater acceptance of lifestyle issues across the country. In fact, eight states and more than a hundred municipalities prohibit discrimination based on sexual orientation. Even though there is disparity among the courts in ruling on homosexuality, one pivotal issue seems to involve *private acts versus public acts*. If the act is private and does not involve students, there is a greater tendency to be supported by the courts. However, if the act becomes public knowledge or if it is committed in public, there is a greater likelihood that the courts will uphold dismissal on grounds of immorality. The following examples illustrate the disparity among the courts on the issue of homosexuality:

1. The U.S. Sixth Circuit Court of Appeals held that the Constitution permitted dismissal of a teacher who divulged to her colleagues that she was homosexual and in love with another woman.[18]
2. A teacher admitted, when asked, that she was homosexual. She was promptly dismissed on grounds of immorality when it became known to the public, who became very agitated. The teacher filed suit, alleging wrongful dismissal. The court ruled that immorality as a ground for dismissal was unconstitutionally vague. Strangely, the teacher was awarded monetary damages but not reinstatement to her teaching position.[19]
3. A district court held that a teacher's private homosexuality would not be permissible grounds for dismissing him from his teaching position. On appeal, the Fourth Circuit Court ruled that even when the teacher made public comments on television regarding his homosexuality, such statements were protected by First Amendment freedoms.[20]

However, the Supreme Court has recently ruled on the constitutionality of private consenting homosexual acts. Although this case did not involve teachers, it has implications for teachers who enjoy most of the personal rights of average citizens.

A recent landmark 7–2 U.S. Supreme Court ruling grew out of a case in Texas when John Geddes Lawrence and Tyron Garner were arrested by police officers who entered Lawrence's apartment and observed Lawrence and Garner engaging in intimate sexual conduct.[21] The two men were arrested, held in custody overnight, charged, and convicted before a justice of the peace. The arresting officers were responding to an anonymous call regarding an alleged weapons disturbance in a private residence. Texas maintained a statute making it a crime for two persons of the same sex to engage in certain intimate sexual conduct. In this case, the statute applied to adult males who had engaged in a consensual act of sodomy in the privacy of home.

One similar Georgia statute was upheld in a previous U.S. Supreme Court case, *Bowers v. Hardwick* (1986), when the High Court held that school boards may validly dismiss teachers for homosexual activity. Justice John Paul Stevens dissented by concluding that (1) the fact that a state's governing majority has traditionally viewed a particular practice as immoral is not sufficient reason for upholding a law prohibiting the practice and (2) individual decisions concerning the intimacies of physical relationships, even when not intended to produce offspring, are a form of liberty protected by due process.

The two petitioners in Texas argued that they had equal protection under both the equal protection and due process clauses of the Fourteenth Amendment. The U.S. Supreme Court heard this case and held that the Texas statute making it a crime for two persons of the same sex to engage in certain intimate sexual conduct violates the due process clause. Prior to the U.S. Supreme Court's ruling, the Court of Appeals for the Texas Fourteenth District considered the petitioners' federal constitutional arguments. After hearing the case **en banc**, the court, in a divided decision, rejected the petitioners' constitutional arguments and affirmed the convictions, which called for a $200 fine for each petitioner in addition to court costs.

The question facing the U.S. Supreme Court involved a determination as to whether the petitioners were free as adults to engage in private conduct in the exercise of their liberty under the due process clause of the Fourteenth Amendment. The High Court noted that laws prohibiting sodomy do not seem to have been enforced against consenting adults acting in private.

A substantial number of sodomy prosecutions and convictions involve predatory acts against those who could not or did not consent, as in the case of a minor, the victim of an assault.

The Supreme Court, in handing down its ruling, stated that:

> The present case does not involve minors. It does not involve persons who might be injured or coerced or who are situated in relationships where consent might not easily be refused. It does not involve public conduct or prostitution. It does not involve whether the government must give formal recognition to any relationship that homosexual persons seek to enter. This case does involve two adults who, with full and mutual consent from each other, engaged in sexual practices common to homosexual lifestyle. The petitioners are entitled to respect for their private lives. The state cannot demean their existence or control their destiny by making their private sexual conduct a crime. Their right to liberty under the Due Process Clause gives them full right to engage in their conduct without intervention of the government. It is a promise of the Constitution that there is a realm of personal liberty which the government may not enter. The Texas statute furthers no legitimate state interest which can justify its intrusion into personal and private life of the individual. The judgment of the Court of Appeals for the Texas District is reversed and the case is remanded for further proceedings not inconsistent with this opinion.[22]

Although this case did not involve public school employees, it does have serious ramifications for school districts. Private sexual relations between consenting adults are now viewed as a liberty right that receives Fourteenth Amendment protection. Therefore, punishment for these acts violates the equal protection and due process rights of those involved. Based on this ruling by the U.S. Supreme Court, school officials will not be able to approach this issue under the guise of immoral or illegal conduct, as was the case in *Bowers v. Hardwick*. School officials will increasingly need to focus on verifiable knowledge of the act and whether the act rendered the employee, particularly a teacher, ineffective in meeting his or her teaching responsibilities. School officials can no longer validly dismiss teachers for private homosexual activity. Thus, the nexus between private homosexual activity and teaching effectiveness becomes increasingly pivotal in cases when school officials bring dismissal charges against consenting adults who engaged in sexual relations with persons of the same gender. The burden of proof likely will rise to a higher standard and rest squarely on the shoulders of school officials.

As early as 1969, California's Supreme Court held that a teacher who had engaged in a limited noncriminal homosexual relationship could not have his teaching certificate revoked unless there was a showing that he was *unfit* as a teacher. The court indicated that the board may consider the likelihood that the teacher's conduct may have adversely affected students or fellow teachers. The degree of the adversity anticipated, the remoteness in time of such conduct, and the extent that the board's action may adversely affect the constitutional rights of the teacher or other teachers involved in similar conduct are relevant considerations.[23] The courts generally recognize the state's authority to consider moral conduct of public school teachers and allow them by statute to determine if just cause warrants dismissal proceedings based on issues involving moral conduct. As stated previously, the weight centers around the teacher's acts and whether they render the teacher ineffective or unfit in performing his or her duties and responsibilities as a professional.

A historical case that addressed the question of fitness to teach arose in the state of Washington, where James Gaylord was discharged from his employment as a high school teacher by the school district. Gaylord had engaged in homosexual relationships for more than twenty years. He actively sought homosexual company and participated in homosexual acts. He was aware that his status as a teacher would be jeopardized, his reputation damaged, and his parents hurt if his homosexual lifestyle were revealed.

Gaylord's school superiors first became aware of his sexual status on October 24, 1972, when a former Wilson High School student informed the vice principal that he thought Gaylord was a homosexual. The vice principal confronted Gaylord at his home the same day with a written copy of the student's statement. Gaylord admitted he was a homosexual and attempted, unsuccessfully, to have the vice principal drop the matter.

On November 21, 1972, Gaylord was notified by the board of directors of the Tacoma School Board that it had found probable cause for his discharge, due to his status as a publicly known homosexual. His status was contrary to a school district policy that provided for discharge of school employees for immorality. After a hearing, the board of directors discharged Gaylord, effective December 21, 1972.

The court ruled against Gaylord, finding that an admission of homosexuality connotes illegal, as well as immoral, acts, because sexual gratification with a member of one's own sex is implicit in the term *homosexual.* After Gaylord's homosexual status became publicly known, it would and did impair his teaching efficiency. A teacher's efficiency is determined by his relationship with students, their parents, the school administration, and fellow teachers. If Gaylord had not been discharged after he became known as a homosexual, the result would be fear, confusion, suspicion, parental concern, and pressure on the administration by students, parents, and other teachers.

The court concluded, "Appellant was properly discharged by respondent school district upon a charge of immorality based on his admission and disclosure that he was a homosexual" and that relief sought should be denied.[24] Even though there is a discernible trend toward national acceptance of gay rights, no court has yet held that homosexuals must be allowed to teach in public schools.

As previously mentioned, there is a lack of consistency in court rulings involving homosexual behavior, and the basic standard centers on *fitness to teach.* The overriding issues in recent years seem to evolve on the question of whether a homosexual lifestyle prevents the teacher from effectively executing his or her teaching duties. Courts have shown a reluctance to support or prohibit certain types of questionable conduct, based solely on conformity. Instead, they have required that there be a nexus between the questionable conduct and teaching effectiveness.

An unusual case involving homosexual behavior arose in the Tenth Circuit Court of Appeals of Oklahoma. The court addressed the question of whether a state may constitutionally mandate the firing of a public school teacher who engages in public homosexual conduct that poses a substantial risk of coming to the attention of school children or employees. An Oklahoma statute provided that its public schools could dismiss teachers for engaging in *public homosexual conduct,* which was defined as indiscreet same-sex relations not practiced in private. Public homosexuality was considered to involve advocating, soliciting, or promoting public or private homosexual activity in a manner that created substantial risk that the conduct would come to the attention of schoolchildren or employees.

The Gay Rights Task Force, a national organization promoting homosexual rights, some of whose members included teachers in the Oklahoma City Public School District, challenged the statute on constitutional grounds, claiming that the statute violated its members' rights of free speech, privacy, and equal protection. The district court held for the district, although indicating that the statute did restrict protected speech and that it was constitutionally valid, given the Supreme Court requirement in the *Tinker v. Des Moines* ruling. The National Gay Rights Task Force appealed.

The Tenth Circuit Court also held for the district, stating that a state may constitutionally require the discharge of a public school teacher who engages in public homosexual activity— such as public acts of oral or anal intercourse—that poses a substantial risk of coming to the attention of schoolchildren or employees. The court further stipulated that the equal protection clause does not, at this time, view homosexuals as a suspect classification warranting strict scrutiny of laws that treat homosexuals differently from other groups. However, the Oklahoma statute does penalize free speech concerning homosexuality, without limiting the firing sanction to advocacy or inciting imminent breaking of the law. The First Amendment does not permit a person to be punished for advocating illegal conduct at some indefinite future time.

Consequently, the part of the statute requiring dismissal or suspension for speech alone is severed as unconstitutional, whereas the remainder is permitted to stand. The decision was reversed.[25]

This case supported the state's right to constitutionally mandate the dismissal of a public school teacher who engages in public homosexual conduct, but it disallowed the state to do so on the basis of speech in which one may advocate illegal conduct at some time in the unforeseeable future. A penalty cannot be imposed prior to the actual engagement in illicit behavior.

Conduct Involving Morality

Public school teachers serve in highly visible and significant positions. In many instances, they exert important influence on the views of students and the formation of their values. Based on their roles, the expectation is that a teacher's character and personal conduct will be elevated above the conduct of the average citizen who does not interact with children on a daily basis. Questions involving teacher morality often involve personal behavior and lifestyle issues, as communities have developed expectations that teachers serve as positive role models for their students, particularly in such areas as dress, grooming, and moral and social behavior.

The U.S. Supreme Court sodomy ruling in Texas supports greater acceptance of diverse lifestyles. However, in a significant number of cases, community norms, standards, and expectations are pivotal considerations in determining acceptable professional conduct. Due to variations among communities, court rulings have been fairly inconsistent. Although there is inconsistency among court rulings, it has been determined that teachers need not be viewed as *exemplary* in certain areas regarding their personal conduct. In fact, there appears to be a noticeable trend toward providing teachers more freedom in their private lives than has been provided in the past.

As previously mentioned, eight states currently prohibit discrimination on the basis of sexual orientation: California, Connecticut, Hawaii, Massachusetts, Minnesota, New Jersey, Vermont, and Washington recognize the rights of individuals to determine their particular lifestyles. Conceivably, other states may assume a similar posture regarding lifestyle issues. It will be interesting to determine the precise impact of sexual orientation on employment decisions rendered by school districts in the future. As emphasized previously in this chapter, there has to be a nexus between an act committed by the teacher and his or her efficiency and effectiveness in the classroom to succeed in dismissal proceedings. Other examples of teacher morality may involve issues such as dishonesty, pregnant and unmarried teachers, unmarried teachers of the opposite sex living together, homosexuality, adulterous conduct, sex change operations, sexual advances toward students, and other related behaviors.

One of the most quoted definitions of the term *immorality* was established by the Supreme Court of Pennsylvania in 1939. It was defined as "a course of conduct as offends the morals of the community and is a bad example to the youth whose ideal of a teacher is supposed to be fostered and elevated."[26]

This course of conduct is sometimes referred to as *immorality* or *unfitness,* depending on state statutes. The courts have taken the position that immorality is not considered unconstitutionally vague in most jurisdictions. Although a high degree of vagueness is involved, courts have supported charges of immorality when it is related to fitness to teach.

The following summary illustrates the inconsistent nature of court decisions in the area of unprofessional conduct:

1. The Court of Appeals of California upheld the dismissal of a teacher who had executed an affidavit recounting her long and beneficial use of marijuana, which attracted national publicity.[27]
2. The Fifth Circuit held that being an unwed mother does not, per se, constitute immorality. The court invalidated a rule prescribing the employment or retention of unwed mothers.[28]
3. Lying was considered immoral when a tenured teacher was denied permission to attend a

conference but did so anyway and on her return submitted a request for excused absences due to illness.[29]

4. A female teacher was not dismissed for writing letters to a former student. The mother of the male student discovered the letters and turned them over to the police and subsequently to a newspaper, which printed the letters. According to the court, the letters contained language that many adults would find gross, vulgar, and offensive. The court noted the teacher's excellent record and also noted that the letters did not adversely affect the welfare of the school community until public disclosure, which was not the result of any misconduct by the teacher.[30]

5. The Eighth Circuit Court of Appeals held for a teacher who was charged with unbecoming conduct for having allowed men not related to her to stay overnight in her apartment. The guests were friends of her sons.[31]

6. A court upheld the dismissal of a male teacher who underwent sex change surgery to alter his external anatomy to that of a female.[32]

7. A schoolteacher appealed the final decision permanently revoking her educator's certificate.[33] This middle school teacher sent several students e-mails and audio files over the Internet that contained sexually suggestive material and profanity. Because the teacher failed to show a lack of remorse for her actions, the teacher's license was permanently revoked at an informal hearing before the Education Practices Commission. The court held for the commission. The Florida statute in question authorized permanent revocation for the teacher's actions, and the court refused to substitute its judgment for that of the commission in a discretionary matter. Further, the teacher did not prove that the penalty was excessive when compared to previous rulings of the commission.

These cases clearly illustrate the difficult task courts face in ruling on issues involving proper conduct of teachers. Again, given the changing dynamics of society and a general acceptance of various lifestyles in the United States, it is anticipated that the courts will face greater difficulty in the future as they attempt to balance the rights of the teacher with the interest of the state.

Criminal Activity

Charges of criminal activity committed by public school teachers will normally result in dismissal, based on general unfitness, immorality, and unprofessional conduct. Depending on the severity and specifics of the criminal act, revocation of the teaching certificate also may be appropriate, especially in cases where a conviction occurs. In a number of states, conviction of a **felony** or crime of moral turpitude will form defensible grounds for the revocation of the teacher's certificate. In other instances, a series of convictions for misdemeanors may also prove sufficient to remove a teacher from an employment position by revocation of the teaching certificate.

It is well established that dismissal for unfitness may not necessarily be dependent on criminal conviction. The fact that a teacher is charged with a criminal activity and is not subsequently convicted does not imply that the teacher cannot be dismissed from an employment position. The school district may address the teacher's behavior from the standpoint of fitness to teach, irrespective of whether a conviction is sustained through the courts, simply because the standard of proof is higher to sustain a conviction than it is to dismiss a teacher.

In a leading case, a school board dismissed a teacher for immorality and unfitness when he was charged with a criminal act involving oral copulation with another man. Even though he was acquitted of criminal charges, the school district dismissed him for immorality and unfitness. State statute permitted the board to dismiss teachers for sex offenses. The court held for the board, indicating that it was the board's purview to determine overall fitness of its employees, even in cases where the teacher has been acquitted of criminal charges.[34]

In another case, a tenured teacher was arrested and charged with disturbing the peace while under the influence of alcohol. He was also charged with attempting to fight and displaying a gun.

The board dismissed the teacher for "other good and just cause." The board's decision was supported by the court as reasonable, based on the evidence.[35]

Drug possession convictions also have resulted in dismissals by school boards. Most state statutes make no specific reference to drugs as grounds for dismissal, but "other good and just cause" found in most statutes is sufficient to cover issues involving drug possession, use, and convictions. For example, a case arose in Georgia in which a tenured teacher was arrested for possession of cocaine and marijuana. The teacher pleaded guilty to violating the state's Controlled Substances Act. The evidence revealed that this was the teacher's first offense, and the court was lenient in placing her on probation. Due to the publicity surrounding the case, the district transferred her to two other teaching positions during the remainder of the school term. The board later brought charges against the teacher, resulting in her dismissal for immorality and other good and just cause based on her plea of guilty for possession of controlled substances. The court held for the board, stating proven facts supporting drug possession charges by the teacher that were sufficient to support charges of immorality, even in the absence of criminal purpose or intent.[36]

It is important to note that when criminal activity involving teachers does not result in a conviction, school boards may still bring charges against the teacher strictly for school-related purposes. If the behavior associated with the criminal act is such that it meets the standards for *unprofessional conduct or unfitness,* the teacher may be dismissed.

In an interesting case involving dismissal, teachers sued a school district after being fired for reporting to work while under the influence of marijuana.[37] After observing behavior and physical symptoms that were out of character for both teachers, they were tested for drug use and both tested positive for marijuana. After administrative hearings, both teachers were fired without written notice because their behavior was deemed to be "irremediable." The court held for the school district. One of the school board's options for a teacher who reports to work under the influence of drugs, alcohol, or any controlled substance is to terminate the employee. It was at the school board's discretion to determine whether the teachers' conduct was irremediable. Given the weight of the evidence, the board found the conduct to be irremediable and therefore written notice was not required before the teachers could be terminated.

Sexual Advances Toward Students

Courts have left little doubt that they will deal judiciously with matters involving improper sexual conduct toward students. The courts support the general view that teaching is an exemplary professional activity and those who teach should exhibit behavior that is above reproach in their dealings with students. Many state statutes include provisions that require teachers to impress on the minds of their students principles of truth, morality, temperance, and humanity. These are very high standards that teachers are expected to meet in their professional roles. Given the position of the courts and the provisions in many state laws governing teacher conduct, it is not surprising to find that courts consistently uphold school districts when they produce evidence that a teacher has engaged in unlawful sexual involvement with students.

One of the most flagrant cases, *Doe v. Taylor,* arose in Texas involving improper sexual conduct with a student. This case involved a Texas teacher who sexually abused a fifteen-year-old female student. Over a two-year period, the teacher cultivated a relationship with the student through overt favoritism and assignment of grades she did not earn. He sent her love letters and cards and encouraged a friendly relationship with his daughter. The relationship with his daughter led to the student's spending time at his home. He attempted to convince her to engage in sexual intercourse after kissing and caressing her over a period of time. After continuous efforts, she finally submitted to his advances, feeling that he was becoming angry and upset with her.

The principal received complaints from students and parents, as it became common knowledge that the teacher and student were having an affair. When news of the teacher's misconduct reached the superintendent, he instructed the principal to speak to the teacher. The superintendent was unable to substantiate the rumors until an incident occurred six months later during which the teacher danced with the student in the presence of his wife at a school-sponsored activity, took the student to a field, and engaged in sexual intercourse with her.

When the victim's parents reported the abuse to the superintendent, the teacher was immediately suspended. The teacher subsequently resigned, after pleading guilty to criminal activity. The court held that school officials should have known that the student's constitutional right was violated. The superintendent was granted immunity, but the principal was denied immunity by the Fifth Circuit Court.[38]

The U.S. Court of Appeals for the Tenth Circuit ruled that a school district is not liable for the negligent retention and supervision of a teaching paraprofessional who sexually molested a disabled student.[39] The court concluded that the employee's actions were not foreseeable because they occurred after school hours off school property and because the employee took steps to deceive school officials regarding the nature of her relationship with the student. David Gann, a learning-disabled student, was receiving speech therapy from speech pathologist Pamela Hart and speech and language paraprofessional Sandra Zolman. At some point during or after the school year, Zolman and David developed an intimate relationship. School officials were unaware of the nature of the relationship, as all inappropriate contact occurred off campus. In fact, after informing Hart that David had made an "inappropriate sexual advance" toward her at her home, Zolman agreed to end all contact with David and to report the incident to his mother. She did neither, although she told Hart that she had. The court, finding that nothing in these facts suggests that school officials knew or should have known that Zolman was abusing David, affirmed the lower court's granting of summary judgment in favor of the district.

In a contrasting case, the New Jersey Supreme Court held a school district liable for a principal's molestation of students.[40] The court concluded that Elmwood Park School District negligently failed to fulfill its most basic duty of properly supervising children "because it failed to implement rudimentary reporting procedures that would have informed it of [the principal's] misconduct" and disregarded readily available information that should have prompted it to scrutinize the principal's behavior. During Samuel Bracigliano's eight-year tenure as a principal, he photographed male students in sexually suggestive poses and retained the photographs for his gratification. He obstructed the view into his office by placing a paper picture over the window in his door, even though this violated the state's administrative code. When state monitors told him to remove the picture, Bracigliano replaced it after they left. The school board was aware of the state monitors' instructions and failed to ensure removal of the picture. In addition, on more than one occasion, school personnel observed Bracigliano touching male students in a sexually suggestive manner, but they were unaware of procedures for reporting these types of incidents. After Bracigliano's arrest on child pornography charges, the parents of two students filed suit against both him and the district. Although a default judgment was entered against Bracigliano, the district contested the negligence claims. The New Jersey Supreme Court agreed with the trial court that the evidence overwhelmingly demonstrated that the district negligently ignored signs of the principal's misconduct and failed to implement reporting procedures and to train school staff in those procedures.

The following case illustrates deliberate indifference to allegations of sexual abuse by school officials in Ohio. The case arose when a ninth-grade student at Mansfield High School informed school officials that Donald Coots, a teacher, had touched her inappropriately and made sexually explicit comments to her. After investigating her complaints, the principal concluded that she was lying. Consequently, no action was taken and no reports were sent to child services or the police. Three years later, Coots became sexually involved with another ninth-grade student at Mansfield. When the principal became aware of this relationship, he informed the police and the student's parents. Coots was forced to resign and was subsequently convicted of felony sexual battery. The student's parents sued, alleging that Ashley was injured as the proximate result of the board's negligent failure to report the previous incident and its negligent retention of Coots as a teacher in the school. The trial court granted summary judgment for the board based on grounds of sovereign immunity. The Ohio Court of Appeals affirmed the trial court's ruling that sexual abuse reporting statutes did not constitute an exception to sovereign immunity because the duty to report sexual abuse ran only to the specific victim and not to subsequent victims.

The Supreme Court of Ohio reversed and held that a local board of education can be held liable for sexual abuse of a student by a teacher. The evidence indicated that the board failed to report a previous alleged incident of sexual abuse by this same teacher involving another student. The court further reasoned that the board's failure to report could have proximately resulted in the second incident of abuse.[41]

Courts in other jurisdictions have taken strong positions in ruling against teachers for sexual misconduct, as illustrated by the following rulings:

1. A teacher was dismissed for immoral conduct when he placed his hands inside the jeans of a student in the area of her buttocks and on other occasions squeezed the breast of a female student. The court determined the teacher's conduct to be grossly inappropriate.[42]
2. A male teacher was dismissed for professional misconduct when he tickled and touched female students on various parts of their bodies while engaged in a field trip experience. He also touched them between the legs. He was found lying on a bed, watching television with one of the female students. The court determined that his activities were sufficient to sustain charges of unfitness to teach.[43]
3. A tenured art teacher was dismissed for immoral conduct when he placed his hands on female students by giving back rubs, which resulted in further sexual contact. Evidence was also presented that he had engaged in sexual intercourse with two students at various places in the building.[44]

Administrative Guide

Dismissal

1. The teacher must be informed if an evaluation is conducted for any purpose other than the improvement of performance.
2. School authorities should avoid any actions regarding evaluation for dismissal that may be viewed as harassment or intimidation by the affected teacher.
3. School officials should be knowledgeable of their state's statutory definition of insubordination and ensure that cases involving insubordination are well documented. Professional disagreements between superiors and subordinates do not normally constitute insubordination.
4. Community norms and expectations regarding professional conduct of teachers are important considerations in cases involving alleged immoral conduct and dismissal.
5. Private acts of homosexuality and adultery may not form grounds for dismissal, unless there is evidence that such acts rendered the teacher ineffective in performing assigned duties.
6. There must be a showing that lifestyle choices adversely affect the teacher's fitness to teach and his or her effectiveness to perform assigned duties before disciplinary action can be taken by the school district.
7. Conviction of a felony or a series of misdemeanors may form grounds for dismissal and revocation of the teaching certificate.
8. Sexual misconduct involving students by school personnel will almost always result in dismissal.

Financial Exigency (Abolition of Positions)

Financial exigency occurs when the district faces a *bona fide* reduction in its budget that results in abolishing certain employment positions. Positions may also be abolished when the district encounters reductions in student enrollment. The courts will generally support districts that demonstrate the need to reduce their teaching force, commonly called *reduction in force (RIF),* when there is evidence that a legitimate financial problem exists. Obviously, districts should implement RIF policies and procedures that ensure that substantive and procedural due process requirements involving school personnel are met. Generally, these due process expectations are not as stringent, because dismissal decisions are based on financial concerns as opposed to personal or performance issues. The courts, in supporting financial exigency, usually require school districts to demonstrate the following:

1. A *bona fide* financial crisis exists.
2. A rational relationship between the benefits derived from dismissal and the alleviation of the financial crisis exists.
3. A fair and uniform set of due process procedures is followed in dismissal decisions.

School districts attempt to use objective criteria in building their RIF policies. Districts will generally use the following criteria in making RIF decisions:

1. Subject matter needs
2. Teacher's length of experience (seniority) in the district
3. Teacher's length of experience in the teaching profession
4. Highest degree or certificate earned
5. Length of time in which the degree or certificate has been held
6. Subject matter qualifications
7. Teaching performance

School districts should also attempt to achieve staff reduction through voluntary retirements, resignations, leaves of absence, and transfers. These areas normally should be addressed before action is taken to implement an RIF plan.

In implementing an RIF policy, the name of an employee who has been terminated usually is placed on a recall list and remains on such list for a minimum of one year. Any teacher desiring to be placed on the recall list for an additional year may apply in writing, by registered mail, for retention of his or her name on such list on or before a specified date as determined by the district's RIF policy.

No new employee may be hired to fill a position for which an employee on the recall list is qualified and certified or immediately certifiable. In cases where more than one employee on the recall list is qualified, certified, or immediately certifiable for a particular position to be filled, employees with tenure must be given preference.

Any teacher on the recall list should receive, by registered letter, a written offer of reappointment, at a reasonable period of time prior to the date of reemployment. The teacher may accept or reject the appointment in writing, by registered letter, within a required period after receipt of the offer, or the offer is deemed rejected. A teacher may refuse to accept an offered assignment and remain on the recall list.

An employee who is reappointed should be entitled to reinstatement of any benefits earned or accrued at the time of layoff, and further accrual of salary increments and fringe benefits should resume at the point where they ceased. No years of layoff will normally be credited as years of service for compensation or retirement purposes. It should be understood that a layoff is a termination of employment subject to administrative and judicial review in the manner set forth in the relevant state statutes.

The courts view RIF policies favorably that include seniority as one of the major criteria in rendering termination decisions. School districts would be hard pressed to defend dismissal of a seasoned teacher with a longer record of seniority in favor of one with considerably less seniority when both are teaching in the same teaching area or the senior teacher is qualified to teach in an area in which the younger teacher is assigned.

A case of this nature arose in Oklahoma. This case involved a tenured teacher who had completed nine years as a classroom teacher in the same district. After a few parents complained about her teaching style, the district reassigned her to the position of elementary librarian.

During the following school year, after the district's enrollment dropped, the superintendent recommended to the board that an RIF plan be implemented for the school term and that the elementary librarian position be eliminated. Further, the special education program had to be decreased by one staff member. The board voted to implement the policies, which resulted in nonrenewal of fifteen teachers. When the board met to consider nonrenewal, the tenured teacher was provided an opportunity to state her case. The board voted not to renew her as librarian in accordance with its RIF policy. During the same meeting, however, the board voted to reemploy fifteen nontenured teachers.

The tenured teacher filed suit in district court, seeking reinstatement. The Oklahoma Supreme Court held that the state's tenure law gives tenured teachers priority over nontenured teachers during an RIF in those instances where the teacher is qualified to teach the subject for which the nontenured teacher is retained. Further, the board's RIF program violated the statutory tenure system. The court specifically found that even though the teacher had been reassigned to an elementary librarian's position, she had tenure at the time but, because of RIF procedures, she was locked into a nonteaching classification. This classification prevented her from priority consideration for employment over nontenured teachers with less seniority.

The court stated that when a school board's RIF plan gives tenure-like priority to nontenured teachers, the board, in effect, has elevated its nontenured personnel to the status of tenured teachers. Whether taken in good faith or not, the court cannot support a school board's action that manipulates job assignments in a manner that defeats the rights of tenured teachers with seniority and circumvents the purpose and spirit of the state's tenure law.[45] RIF policies should make allowances for teachers with longer lengths of service who might hold certification in other areas to be considered for those positions held by teachers with less seniority. When a district is able to demonstrate that objective and verifiable criteria were used in its decisions and all persons affected were provided full due process rights consistent with state statutes, they should encounter few problems with the courts.

Administrative Guide

Financial Exigency

1. All employees affected by an RIF must be afforded full due process provisions.
2. The burden of demonstrating *bona fide* financial exigency rests with the board of education.
3. School districts may not use financial exigency as a means to remove an employee who has exercised a constitutionally protected right.
4. Seniority and job performance should receive priority in RIF decisions.
5. School district policy and/or state statutes should be followed judiciously in implementing RIF policies.

Just Cause

Just cause is designed to provide the district broader latitude in dismissing teachers for causes not specifically identified in state statutes. It is not designed to allow the district to dismiss a teacher for personal, political, arbitrary, or capricious reasons. The same due process provisions must be met under this category as would be met under the more specific causes for dismissal. As long as the board can justify its actions as being fair and reasonably related to a legitimate state interest, there should be no challenge by the courts. Just cause is not a category used frequently by school districts; most tend to rely on the more specific causes previously identified.

Occasionally, a case involving other just cause is addressed by the courts. Such a case was decided by a Colorado court when a fourth-grade teacher encouraged boys to come to his home for homework assistance and game play. Over a period of time, the teacher developed a close relationship with a ten-year-old student, who gradually began to spend most of his time at the teacher's home, with his mother's consent. Within the year, a father–son relationship had developed between the teacher and the child wherein the teacher engaged in a custody battle with the student's illiterate Spanish-speaking mother. The custody became widely publicized, appearing in the local newspaper. Dependency and child neglect charges were filed against both the teacher and the mother, after which six sets of parents requested that their children be reassigned to a different teacher.

The school superintendent, after having assessed the situation very carefully, recommended dismissal of the teacher. The school board supported the recommendation of the superintendent. On investigating the situation, a hearing officer also determined the presence of adequate grounds for dismissal. After an unfavorable ruling at the district court level, the teacher filed an appeal with the Colorado Court of Appeals. The appeals court affirmed the decision of the district court, upholding the hearing officer's findings.

The court observed that the student had experienced no academic or behavioral problems prior to his close relationship with the teacher. Further, the teacher had taken advantage of his position to foster a relationship with the child. "Good cause" for dismissal was found under Colorado statute. Because the teacher's actions were reasonably related to his overall fitness to execute his duties and they had adversely affected his performance as a teacher, the court supported termination. The trial court decision was affirmed.[46]

Good cause may be used to bring dismissal charges against a teacher, particularly when there is a showing that performance and effectiveness are impaired and a question of fitness to teach arises as a major concern. Because this category is covered by many state statutes, school districts may use it as long as due process provisions are met. As with all charges, the burden of proof rests with school officials. In this particular case, the district met this burden.

In a related good or just cause case, a middle school teacher who was also an accomplished band director was terminated for sending vulgar, crude, racist, and pornographic/sexually oriented e-mails to a student.[47] She also told patently offensive jokes. She referenced another student as a "f_____ bitch." She also denigrated and humiliated a fellow teacher in the presence of a student and referred to her as a "turd." A referee appointed to the case determined the existence of sufficient grounds to terminate the teacher's contract. The court agreed. Even the undisputed evidence of the teacher's otherwise exemplary employment history and achievements did not outweigh the clearly inappropriate conduct that at the very least constituted a serious lapse in judgment.

Administrative Guide

Good or Just Cause

1. Good cause provisions should not be used to arbitrarily dismiss a teacher from an employment position.
2. Good cause should never be motivated by actions that affect the constitutional protection rights of teachers, such as free speech and association.
3. The burden of proof should always reside with school officials to demonstrate that just cause is valid.
4. Evidence should indicate that the teacher's performance and effectiveness are adversely impaired based on his or her conduct.

FAIR LABOR STANDARDS ACT

School personnel who do not occupy administrative, teaching, or other professional positions are classified as nonexempt and normally include clerical personnel, food service personnel, custodial services, campus security, and such. Such employees receive hourly wages and are subject to both federal and state work-hour laws. School officials must be certain that all requirements of the Fair Labor Standards Act (FLSA) are met. The FLSA has been amended many times since 1938. The act essentially:

- Establishes minimum wage and overtime pay for nonexempt employees.
- Provides overtime pay for hours worked beyond forty hours per work week.
- Places no limits on the number of hours employees may work in any work week.
- Defines hours worked as those that ordinarily include all times during which an employee is required to be on the employer's premises, on duty, or at a prescribed workplace.
- Requires employers to display an official poster outlining the requirements of FLSA.
- Requires the employer to maintain employee time and pay records.

The basic intent of the law is to ensure that nonexempt employees receive fair treatment and appropriate compensation for performing their assigned duties.

Source: Department of Labor dol.gov/whd/flsa/index.htm

COLLECTIVE BARGAINING

Collective bargaining has grown in popularity and appeal in public education. Although collective bargaining has always provoked controversy, many educators view it as a mechanism to achieve a greater role in management and operation of public schools. Because many of the issues involving collective bargaining focus on the rights of employees as well as terms and conditions of employment, its very nature sometimes evokes conflict and adversarial relationships between school boards and union representatives.

It is well recognized that collective bargaining has not always enjoyed the popularity it does today. In fact, it did not gain legal protection until the early 1930s in the private sector. The evolution of this concept in the public sector developed very slowly, due primarily to the belief and acceptance of governmental sovereignty. Public schools, as agents of the state, exerted almost complete control of school operations as well as terms and conditions of employment consistent with their state's statutory mandates and local district policy. The prevailing view among state lawmakers was that this sovereign power should not be abrogated.

Collective bargaining gradually emerged in the public sector in the late 1940s, when Wisconsin became one of the first states to enact legislation allowing bargaining to occur. However, it was not until the 1960s that teachers launched a major effort to gain a greater level of involvement in the administration and operation of their schools. Most states currently permit some form of bargaining between teachers and school boards. These agreements may vary from required bargaining to some form of *meet and confer provision.*

Irrespective of these variations, the basic intent is to create teacher empowerment and shared power between teachers and school boards. Obviously, some states are more liberal than others in deciding on items that are negotiable. For example, arbitration is mandated in some states yet prohibited in others. In any case, the primary objective is to create conditions within which school employees are afforded the opportunity to affiliate with a union without fear of reprisal for their participation. One common element found in most state statutes is a *good faith* requirement imposed on employers, which implies that they must bargain with the recognized bargaining unit with the sincere intent to reach a reasonable agreement. In fact, this good faith provision affects both parties during the bargaining process.

Private Sector Versus Public Sector Bargaining

The differences between private sector and public sector bargaining are obvious. One of the most notable differences is that private sector employees do not enjoy constitutional protections, as do public sector employees. Public sector employees are afforded equal protection rights under due process as well as certain rights enacted by state statutes for their protection.

Private sector rights were severely restructured in 1947 with an amendment to the National Labor Relations Act (NLRA), which had passed in 1935 to support collective bargaining as an effort to improve management and labor relations. The National Labor Relations Board was formed during this time to remedy unfair labor practices. With the amendments to the NLRA, limitations were imposed on various union practices after widespread evidence of union corruption surfaced. The amended version resulted in the Labor Management Relations Act, commonly called the Taft-Hartley Act. This act was subsequently amended in 1959 with the Labor Management Reporting and Disclosure Act (LMRDA), which provided protection to private sector employees who faced various forms of union abuse. It also invoked penalties for misappropriation of union funds.

Another significant difference is that, in many instances, public school teachers are not permitted to strike. Proponents of public sector negotiations view this restriction as a real limitation in the sense that bargaining strength is weakened regarding the capacity to reject the terms and conditions offered during the negotiation process. In the private sector, rejection of an offer is most often followed by a strike when an impasse occurs. In states where strikes are not permitted by law, penalties are imposed on teachers and union officials, which may range from loss of salary to dismissal for teachers and stiff fines for union officials. When an impasse occurs, public sector bargaining is also affected by state and local budget restraints. Because funding is determined by state legislatures and dependent on tax projections and revenue, regulations regarding salary issues are limited by state appropriations to education, irrespective of bargaining agreements.

RIGHT TO WORK STATUTES

Right to work statutes effectively prohibit union security agreements between labor unions and employers that determine to what extent a union can require employees to pay membership dues as a condition of employment. Essentially, right to work statutes prevent employers and unions from excluding nonunion employees or requiring them to pay a fee to the union that negotiated an employment contract for all employees.

Right to work statutes emerged after the National Labor Relations Act of 1935 that required every individual covered by the collective bargaining contract to pay dues to the negotiating labor union. The Taft-Hartley Act of 1947 amended the NLRA by allowing individual states to enact laws that prohibit union security agreements. These states are known as *right to work states*. Right to work laws tend to weaken labor unions based on fewer resources, resulting in less power, influence, and ability to launch significant organized drives. Twenty-four states currently have passed right to work statutes that might suggest in a broader context that the remaining pro-union states are not immune from right to work legislation.

TEACHER STRIKES

Teacher strikes are prohibited in a number of states. Some states permit limited statutory rights to strike provided state procedures are followed for resolving an impasse. An impasse is reached when there is a breakdown in negotiations resulting in failure to reach an agreement and neither party is willing to compromise. State statutes vary regarding limited strikes and may include specific conditions such as the inability to reach an agreement after fact-finding, mediation, and arbitration processes have been exhausted. Some states also permit limited strikes when the union contract expires, with the provision that written notice is given of the intent to strike with no threat to public safety. The following thirteen states actually permit strikes: Alaska, California, Colorado, Hawaii, Illinois, Louisiana, Minnesota, Montana, Ohio, Oregon, Pennsylvania, Vermont, and Wisconsin. Certain statutory conditions must be met in these thirteen states prior to initiating a strike. The conditions normally include the steps involved when negotiations reach an impasse. In states where no-strike laws have been challenged, courts have been quite consistent in upholding them. For example, serious penalties have been imposed in Georgia, Tennessee, and North Carolina. Even though not legally sanctioned, districts in Indiana, Michigan, and Massachusetts have initiated illegal strikes. Penalties for illegal strikes vary among states and may involve fines, dismissal, demotion, lack of pay for days missed based on the strike, or a loss of recognition for the recognized union.

An interesting incident involving an illegal strike occurred in the Wayne-Westland School District. Health care insurance and class size were critical issues that led to the alleged strike. School was cancelled when Westland teachers refused to report to work after five hours at the bargaining table the night before. The district requested that they return; however, teachers began picketing before school began. Buses arrived, but because teachers decided to strike, students were forced to return to their homes. The school district and union were close on compensation but split on health care insurance and class size. The union accused the district of not bargaining in good faith. Governmental strikes are illegal in Michigan. A district judge ordered striking teachers to return to work but did not exact penalties. The penalty to the teachers for illegal striking was a fine equal to their pay for each day they refused to work.

State Involvement

A number of states have passed permissive legislation to aid recognized union organizations. Some states support an *agency shop* measure, which stipulates that teachers must be members in good standing with the union through dues payment or some form of service charge, if the teachers are not affiliated with the recognized bargaining unit. A few state laws make union affiliation mandatory for teachers as a condition of continuing their employment. This agreement is commonly referred to as *union shop*. Other states require teachers to affiliate with the recognized bargaining unit when they make application for a teaching position. This arrangement is commonly referred to as *closed shop*. Still other states have enacted legislation that protects employees from harassment by other employees and union officials because they elect not to affiliate with the bargaining unit. When a bargaining unit is granted the exclusive right to represent employees, it must do so on a fair and equitable basis, irrespective of whether the employee is a member or not. State law in most cases will require the union to do so.

Scope of Collective Bargaining

State laws vary regarding issues that are deemed negotiable. These issues normally fall under the categories of mandatory, permissive, and illegal. Issues involving compensation conditions of employment—such as length of workday, school, teaching workload, extra-duty assignments, leaves of absences, and other fringe benefits—are almost always considered mandatory, which means that bargaining issues must involve both parties. A compensation dispute was settled in Hawaii when the Hawaii Supreme Court struck down an attempt by the state legislature to prohibit public employers and employee associations from bargaining over "cost items," including wages for the 1999–2001 bienniums.[48] The framers of the Hawaii Constitution did not intend for the legislature to deny public employees the right to organize and collectively bargain. This decision was the result of a challenge to a law enacted by the Hawaii legislature in 1999 prohibiting state and county governments, including public schools and the state university system, from negotiating over "cost items" during the 1999–2001 biennium. Cost items included wages, hours, contributions to public employee pensions, and other terms and conditions of employment that required legislative appropriations. Permissive subjects generally are based on common agreement between both parties and would not constitute a breach of duty to bargain in good faith. Issues involving personnel recruitment, selection, and induction are considered administrative prerogatives not subject to mandatory negotiations. Because these areas vary among states, there is an obvious lack of a clear distinction among these areas.

In areas involving mandatory bargaining, school boards are required to bargain in good faith. As previously indicated, state statutes establish the framework regarding the scope of collective negotiations in public schools. Several basic issues emerge in relation to negotiation agreements.

These normally cover areas that a school board can and cannot negotiate. Also covered are issues that must be negotiated until agreement is reached by both parties. Some issues are neither mandatory nor permissive in some states; they are a function of negotiations between the teacher's union and the school board and include areas such as teacher's planning periods, changes in the length of class periods, nonteaching assignments, sick leave banks, academic policies, and much more.

By way of illustration, a case arose in Pennsylvania in which the local education association challenged the school board on an honor roll policy change. The association contended that such change required bargaining between the board and the association. The controversy arose when the school board raised the requirements for achieving honor roll status by 0.25 grade point as part of a statewide effort by the state department of education to improve statewide education quality and accountability. A grievance was filed by the association against the board under the collective bargaining agreement. The arbitration held that its board violated the collective bargaining agreement by not involving the association in the policy amendment decision. The trial court, however, supported the district in holding that the new policy was the school board's inherent managerial prerogative. The association appealed to the commonwealth court, which held that the district was not required to bargain away matters of inherent managerial policy, particularly those dealing with academic standards, personnel matters, organizational structure, budgeting, and technology. The decision clearly established the prerogatives that the school board has that are not subject to negotiations. Whereas negotiable items vary among the states, there is a great deal of consistency with respect to managerial prerogatives that must remain under the purview of the school boards.[49]

Impasse and Bargaining

On numerous occasions, the parties involved in negotiations fail to reach an agreement, and it becomes obvious that no further progress toward resolution is possible. When this occurs, an *impasse* has emerged. Some state laws include provisions that require both parties to continue to bargain beyond the termination date of the previous contractual agreement when an impasse is reached, which means that certain commitments must be honored by the school board before the expiration of the previous contract.

The regular negotiation process calls for a series of options designed to resolve the dispute. These options are as follows:

1. *Mediation* occurs when a neutral party is engaged to assist both parties in reaching objective solutions to the dispute at hand. The mediation normally is chosen by common agreement between parties. If mediation fails, another option is to engage a fact finder.
2. A *fact finder* is a third party who attempts to analyze facts and determine where compromise might occur. The fact finder offers solutions that are not binding on either party. If the fact-finding process fails to resolve the dispute, the final step involves arbitration.
3. *Arbitration* occurs when a third party performs similar functions to those performed by the fact finder. If the arbitration is *binding,* then what is recommended as a resolution to the dispute is binding on both parties.

Legal Issues

Numerous legal challenges have had an impact on collective bargaining in public schools. These challenges cover a broad range of issues, such as the right to strike, preferential treatment regarding the exclusive bargaining agency, preferential layoffs, free speech rights of teachers not affiliated with the union, good faith issues involving school boards, and many others. The courts have found it necessary to intervene in an attempt to settle disputes involving teachers, school boards, and union officials.

An interesting case arose in Wisconsin during negotiations toward a collective bargaining agreement when the union demanded that a provision be enacted to require all teachers within the bargaining unit to pay dues irrespective of their affiliation decision. During the discussion of this issue in an open meeting, one teacher, who was not a union affiliate, spoke briefly, urging that a decision be delayed pending further study. The state had passed a law prohibiting school boards from negotiating with individual teachers once an exclusive agent had been chosen. Thus, the state employment relations committee charged the district with violating state law by allowing the teacher to speak and further ordered that the board disallow this practice in the future. This ruling was challenged by the school board.

The court, in ruling against the board, indicated that an order that prohibits teachers who are not union representatives from speaking during public meetings is unconstitutional. Further, teachers enjoy First Amendment rights to express their views during public meetings when speaking on issues of common interest, and such speech by the teacher was not an attempt to negotiate with the board but rather to express public concern.[50]

A case involving preferential treatment reached the Supreme Court when a layoff policy was challenged as discriminatory based on an agreement between the board of education and the teacher's union. The bargaining agreement between the board and the union included a clause that provided protection to members of certain minority groups against layoffs. The board did not comply with this provision until it was challenged to do so. When layoffs occurred, minority teachers were maintained, whereas nonminority teachers were not. This policy was challenged by the nonminorities, alleging discrimination.

The Court held that this action amounted to reverse racial discrimination, which must be justified by a compelling state interest. The board responded by suggesting the importance of maintaining a diverse workforce and providing minority role models for students. The High Court ruled that the board's rationale did not constitute a compelling interest and could not be justified. The district's policy was held unconstitutional.[51]

In a later case involving a strike by public school teachers, the Supreme Court of Pennsylvania held that such a strike presented a threat to the health and safety of the public welfare. This case arose when teachers voted to strike after only four days of instruction. The Jersey Shore Area School District filed for an injunction, requesting that teachers return to work. After a successful hearing for the district, the Court of Common Pleas issued an injunction, ordering teachers to return to work. The Jersey Shore Association subsequently filed for reconsideration and an additional hearing on the matter. When the chancellor of the Court of Common Pleas refused to lift the injunction, the association appealed to the Supreme Court of Pennsylvania.

The state supreme court held for the district on a preponderance of evidence, which revealed that senior high school students were placed at a competitive disadvantage with respect to instruction that would assist them in preparing for national tests for college admissions. Furthermore, many faced deadlines with respect to filing for scholarship aid with no direction provided by the counseling and guidance services. Other students at lower grades also were placed at competitive disadvantages with respect to state-mandated tests to determine whether remediation was needed. Finally, with only four days of instruction, students would be forced into remedial courses that they otherwise would not have needed. These findings, coupled with the threat of the district losing roughly $27,000 per day in state subsidies for each day it fell short of the mandated 180 days of school, resulted in the court's conclusion that such a strike created a threat to the health, safety, and welfare of the public. The court therefore upheld the commonwealth's order that teachers return to work.[52]

Teachers' Union National Strike Strategy

A rather interesting strategy emerged in a teachers' strike in Washington State, which was the longest teachers' strike in the state's history. Many parties were involved in this prolonged strike as factions formed on either side—local parent associations, the attorney general's office, along with the school board and union affiliate.

Teachers were not compensated initially for time, responsibilities, and incentives (TRI) contracts for work outside the instructional day. School districts were permitted to make these settlements in addition to teachers' regular pay.

TRI was intended solely to improve student achievement when the Washington Education Association failed to secure cost of living increases from the legislature. The union pressured the district to inflate TRI contracts to compensate for illegal cost of living increases. The school district elevated contracts to unreasonable levels to provide cost of living increases until resources ran out and financial reserves were relied on. When the legislature refused to fund the districts to rebuild their reserves, the districts refused to renew TRI contracts, resulting in turmoil and a prolonged strike. Regrettably, this model has gained momentum across the United States, as associations are demanding more union control over TRI pay and pushing districts toward approving unsustainable budgets. Because of strained factions and unlimited resources that were wasted, a superintendent and three school board members were relieved of their responsibilities.

Workers' Compensation

Teachers are protected by workers' compensation in most states when they are injured during the course of performing their professional duties. The theory supporting workers' compensation is that the employing agency should assume responsibility for injury suffered by employees during the conduct of the agency's business. Workers' compensation does not normally apply in situations where an employee is willfully or wrongfully injured by the employer or a colleague. The injured employee does not need to prove that any injury resulted from a certain incident.

In recent years, increased flexibility and latitude have been provided in allowing compensation for a job-related injury that developed over time. For example, a teacher might incur an injury over time for lifting heavy equipment or performing routine tasks, such as rearranging furniture in the classroom. In some instances, an employee is covered by workers' compensation if he or she aggravates a preexisting condition. In all cases, there must be supportive evidence that the injury grew out of the executing of professional duties and responsibilities. It is very difficult, in most instances, to receive coverage for psychological or mental illness unless the employee can adequately demonstrate that he or she was involved in an unusually and unavoidably stressful work environment. An employee normally will not succeed in cases of self-induced stress that grows out of his or her ineffectiveness in performing expected job duties and responsibilities. Most states have explicit processes and procedures that employees must follow to receive workers' compensation for injury situations covered by state statutes, including a specified time within which injury must be reported. Virtually every state has an agency that administers the program. As a last resort, employees may resort to the courts in cases where they are denied workers' compensation benefits once the state's procedures have been exhausted.

Administrative Guide

Collective Bargaining

1. The collective negotiations process should always be guided by a good faith effort involving both parties: school boards and union officials.
2. School boards should not negotiate items for which they have no legal authority to negotiate (e.g., setting salaries and employing personnel) unless there is express statutory authority to do so.
3. Any sustained action taken by striking teachers that may disrupt educational opportunities for students will not likely receive court support.
4. Constitutionally protected rights and freedoms of teachers should not be impaired by collective bargaining agreements.

CASE STUDIES

Dismissal of Tenured Teachers

As the principal, you have recommended that two of your tenured teachers be terminated for cause. (You may determine cause.)

Discussion Questions

1. Outline the procedure that must be followed in this situation.
2. Write a legally defensible letter to both teachers informing them of possible termination.
3. Cite relevant court rulings to document your written response.

Nontenured Teacher and Liberty Interest Claim

Mary Glendale was a ninth-grade social studies teacher. She completed her second year with Millsdale High School, which is located in a moderate-size middle-class community.

She received notice from the superintendent and school board that her contract would not be renewed for the following year. Glendale later learned from reliable sources that she had been described by her principal as anti-establishment and was unable to relate well to colleagues. Mary filed charges claiming that her liberty interest was affected by her principal's comments.

Discussion Questions

1. What does liberty interest involve?
2. Based on the definition, has a liberty interest been affected in this case? Why or why not?
3. If so, what steps should be followed to address liberty interest?
4. If not, does the district have any obligation to Mary Glendale?
5. How would the court rule in this case?
6. What are the administrative implications of this case?

Incompetency and Questionable Performance

Gloria Williams, a well-respected tenth-grade social studies teacher, has taught at Johnson High School for over fifteen years. Her formal evaluations were quite good under the previous administration. She was informally evaluated each year during her fifteen-year tenure. The new principal, Bob Mason, who has held his position for only two years, recommended dismissal for incompetency based on two informal assessments of Williams's performance.

Discussion Questions

1. What are the chances that Williams may be dismissed for incompetency?
2. Is there sufficient evidence to sustain such a charge? Why or why not?
3. Ideally, what process should be used to successfully remove a teacher for incompetence? Outline the process.
4. Based on information provided in this case, has Gloria Williams been treated fairly? Why or why not?
5. How would the court likely rule in this case? Provide a rationale for your response.
6. What are the administrative implications of this case?

Insubordination—Failure to Change a Student's Grade

Alice Hill, an eleventh-grade English teacher at Fairview High School, located in a fairly progressive school district, assigned the grade of F to a star basketball player, Tom Benson, who had failed to turn in assigned work. Hill encountered considerable criticism from coaches and other colleagues at school. A request was made by the principal, Jim Martin, for Hill to return to school and change the grade. Due to stress associated with this event, Hill was unable to do so and arranged for a substitute to cover her classes for two days. The principal recommended dismissal based on charges of insubordination for failure to return to change the grade.

Discussion Questions

1. Was Alice Hill justified in not returning to change the grade? Why or why not?
2. Does the principal have sufficient grounds to recommend insubordination? Why or why not?

3. Did Alice Hill's failure to return constitute insubordination? Why or why not?
4. As principal, would you have taken the position the principal took in this situation? Why or why not?
5. How would the court likely rule in this case? Provide a rationale for your response.

Unprofessional Conduct—Sexual Activity

Paula Gibson, an elementary school teacher in an upscale progressive city, was arrested by an undercover policeman for openly engaging in sexual activity with two men at a singles' club party. She was recommended for dismissal by her principal, Hank Doss, based on this conduct. Her defense was that these acts took place at a private party and should have no impact on her capacity to teach.

Discussion Questions

1. Is the principal justified in recommending dismissal? Why or why not?
2. Should acts that occur in private be held against teachers? Why or why not?
3. Does Paula have a justifiable defense in this situation? Why or why not?
4. What standards would the court use in ruling in this case?
5. What do you feel the court's ruling would be? Provide a rationale for your response.
6. What are the implications for teachers and administrators in this case?

Recruitment of Teachers

You have very few male teachers in your elementary school. Because many of your students are products of single-parent households, you have a strong desire to provide male role models for them. You are situated in an inner-city urban environment and feel very firmly that you are doing what is best for your students.

Discussion Questions

1. Are you justified in focusing recruitment solely on male teachers when your school has teaching vacancies? Why or why not?
2. What legal issues, if any, are involved?
3. Is the desire to meet the needs of single-parent children a compelling reason to use this strategy?
4. What is the most feasible method of achieving your goal in a legally defensible manner?

Horns of a Dilemma

You have just been named to the central office administrative position that you have always dreamed about in a city school district composed of forty-one schools. Additionally, the district is located in your home town. You are obviously excited to hold this position for two reasons:

1. The salary is phenomenal compared to your current salary as a teacher.
2. It will greatly assist you in advancing your administrative career.

However, two months after you accepted the position, to your amazement, their values and views are totally inconsistent with your values and the manner in which you feel people should be treated in the organization. You confide in a trusted colleague, who tells you to "keep your mouth shut. Do your job and you will be fine!"

Discussion Questions

1. How do you react to your colleague's suggestion?
2. What do you do about this obvious conflict in values?
3. What factors do you consider before you make a decision?
4. What is your decision?

Endnotes

1. *Bessard v. California Community Colleges,* 867 F. Supp. 1451 (#. D. Cal. 1994).

2. *School Board of Leon County v. Weaver,* 556 So. 2d 443 (Fla. App. 1st Dist. 1990).

3. *Wirt v. Parker School Dist. #60-04,* 689 N.W.2d 901 (S.D. 2004).

4. *Kilgore v. Jasper City Board of Educ.,* 624 So.2d 603 (Ala. Ct. Cit. App. 1993).

5. *Pickering v. Board of Education,* 225 N.E. 2d 16 (Ill. 1967).

6. *Watson v. North Panola School Dist.,* 188 Fed.Appx. 291 (5th Cir. 2006).

7. *Kletzkin v. Board of Education of the Borough of Spotswood,* 136 N.J. 275, 642 A. 2d 993 (1994).

8. *Board of Regents of State College v. Roth,* 408 U.S. 564, 92 S.Ct. 2701 (1972).

9. *Prestopnik v. Johnstown School District,* 2003 WL 1678580 (N.D.N.Y. 2003).

10. *Flaskamp v. Dearborn Schools,* 232 F. Supp. 2d 230, 687, 172 Ed. Law Rep. 651 (E.D. Mich. 2002).

11. *Beischel v. Stone Bank School District,* 362 F. 3d 430 (7th Cir. 2004).

12. *Johnson v. Francis Howell R-3 Board of Education,* 868 S.W. 2d 191 (Mo. App. E.D. 1994).

13. *Kentucky Education Professional Standards Board v. Gambrel,* 104 S.W. 3d 767 (Ky. App. 2002).

14. *Dolega v. School Board of Miami-Dade Co.,* 840 S. 2d 445 (Fla. App. 2003).

15. *Blaine v. Moffat County School District Region No. 1,* 748 P. 2d 1280 (Colo. 1998).

16. *Sanders v. Board of Education of South Sioux Community School District No. 11,* 263 N.W. 2d 461, Neb. (1978).

17. *Thompson v. Southwest School District,* 483 F. Supp. 1170 (Mo. 1980).

18. *Rowland v. Mad River Local School District, Montgomery County,* 730 F. 2d 444 (6th Cir. 1984), cert. denied, 470 U.S. 1009 (1985).

19. *Burton v. Cascade School District Union High School No. 5,* 353 F. Supp. 254 (U.S. District Court, Oregon 1973), cert. denied, 423 U.S. 879 (1977).

20. *Acanfora v. Board of Education of Montgomery County,* 359 F. Supp. 843 (D. Md. 1973).

21. *Lawrence v. Texas,* 123 S.Ct. 2472 (2003).

22. *Bowers v. Hardwick,* 478 U.S. 186, 106 S.Ct. 2841, 92 L. Ed. 2d 140 (1986).

23. *Morrison v. State Board of Education,* 461 P. 2d 375, 386-387 (Cal. 1969).

24. *Gaylord v. Tacoma School District No. 10,* 88 Wash. 2d 286, 559 P. 2d 1340 (1977).

25. *National Gay Task Force v. Board of Education of Oklahoma City,* 729 F. 2d 1270 (10th Cir. 1984).

26. *Horosko v. Mt. Pleasant School District,* 335 Pa. 369 6 A. 2d 866 (1939), cert. denied, 308 U.S. 553 (1939).

27. *Governing Board of Nicasio School District of Marin County v. Brennan,* 18 Cal. App. 3d 396, 95 Cal. Rptr. 712 (1971).

28. *Andrews v. Drew Municipal Separate School District,* 507 F. 2d 611 (5th Cir. 1975).

29. *Bethel Park School District v. Krall,* 67 Pa. Cmwlth. 143, 445 A. 2d 1377 (1982).

30. *Darvella v. Willoughly by East Lake City School Dist. Board of Education,* 12 Ohio Misc. 288, 233 N.E. 2d 143 (1967).

31. *Fisher v. Synder,* 476 F. 2d 375 (8th Cir. 1973).

32. *In re Grossman,* 127 N.J. Super. 13, 316 A. 2d 39 (1974).

33. *Wax v. Home,* 844 S. 2d 797 (Fla. App. 2003).

34. *Board of Education v. Calderon,* 35 Cal. App. 3d 490, 110 Cal. Rptr. 916 (1973), cert. denied, and appeal dismissed, 414 U.S. 807, 95 S.Ct. 19 (1974).

35. *Williams v. School District No. 40 of Gila County,* 4 Ariz. App. 5, 417 P. 2d 376 (1966).

36. *Dominy v. Mays,* 150 Ga. App. 187, 257 S.E. 2d 317 (1979).

37. *Younger v. Board of Education of City of Chicago,* 788 N.E. 2d 1153 (Ill. App. 2003).

38. *Doe v. Taylor Independent School District,* 15 F. 3d 443 (5th Cir. 1994).

39. *Kurtz, et al. v. Unified School District No. 308,* 39 IDELR 61 (10th Cir. 2003).

40. *Frugis v. Bracigliano,* 177 NJ 250, 282 (2003).

41. *Yates v. Mansfield Board of Education,* 2004 WL 1124474 (Ohio June 2, 2004).

42. *Fadler v. Illinois State Board of Education,* 153 Ill. App. 3d 1024, 106 Ill. 840, 506 N.E. 2d 640 (5 Dist. 1987).

43. *Weissman v. Board of Education of Jefferson County School District No. R-1,* 190 Colo. 414, 547 P. 2d 1267 (1976).

44. *Johnson v. Beaverhead City High School District,* 236 Mont. 532, 771 P. 2d 137 (1989).

45. *Babb v. Independent School District No. 1–5,* 829 P. 2d 973, 74 Ed. Law Rptr 977 (1992).

46. *Kerin v. Board of Ed Laman School Dist No. Re-2 Prowers County,* 860 P. 2d 574 (Colo. App. 1993).

47. *Oleske v. Hilliard City School District Board of Education,* 764 N.E. 2d 1110 (Ohio App. 2001).

48. *United Public Workers, AFSCME, Local 646, AFL-CIO v. Yogi,* 62 P.3d 189 (Haw. 2002).

49. *Rochester Area School District v. Rochester Education Association,* No. 2915 C.D. 1999 (Pa. Commw. Ct. 2000).

50. *Madison v. Wisconsin Employment Relations Commission,* 429 U.S. 167, 97 S.Ct. 421 (1976).

51. *Wygant v. Jackson Board of Education,* 476 U.S. 267, 106 S.Ct. 1842 (1986).

52. *Jersey Shore Area School District v. Jersey Shore Education Association,* 519 Pa. 398, 438 A. 2d 1202 (1988).

Chapter 11

The Instructional Program and School Attendance

CONTROL OF PUBLIC SCHOOLS

It is well established that citizens of the United States have no federal constitutional right to public education. In fact, the U.S. Constitution makes no reference to education. By virtue of the Tenth Amendment to the U.S. Constitution, the powers not delegated to the United States by the Constitution, nor prohibited by it to the states, are reserved to the states respectively, or to the people. The Tenth Amendment essentially places the responsibility on each state to provide free public schools. Thus, each state constitution places the responsibility on its legislature to provide schooling for all children within the state at public expense.

The legal authority for defining the curriculum of public schools resides with the state legislature. Based on constitutional provisions in a few states, this duty is shared between the legislature and the state board of education. The legislature may, at its discretion, prescribe the basic course of study, testing, and graduation requirements. In most cases, state legislatures delegate curriculum matters to state boards of education and to local school districts. Many local school districts in turn have the latitude to establish local school-based management councils that are empowered to make decisions in matters regarding curriculum and instructional practices and selection of textbooks and other instructional materials.

The state's responsibility for public education was clearly established as early as 1890, in *State v. Haworth,* when the court enunciated the following:

> Essentially and intrinsically, the schools . . . are matters of state, and not local jurisdiction. In such matters, the state is the unit and the legislature the source of power. The authority over schools and school affairs is not necessarily a distributive one to be experienced by local instrumentalities; but on the contrary, it is a central power residing in the legislature of the state. It is for the law-making power to determine whether the authority shall be exercised by a state board of education, or distributed to county, township, or city organization throughout the state.[1]

An example of legislative control is further demonstrated by the court in the following case:

> The legislature has entire control over the schools of the state . . . the division of the territory of the state into districts, the conduct of the school, the qualifications of teachers, the subjects to be taught therein, and all within its control.[2]

Children who enroll in public schools are subject to state laws and local regulations governing the operation of public schools. The state has **police powers**, which allow it to exercise rules and regulations designed to protect the health, safety, and well-being of all citizens. It is in this context that children are provided a free public education. The Supreme Court in *Prince v. Massachussetts* held that the government has broad authority to regulate the actions and treatment of children. Parental authority is not absolute and can be permissibly restricted if doing so is in the interests of a child's welfare. While children share many of the rights of adults, they face different potential harms from similar activities.[3]

COMPULSORY ATTENDANCE

Every state requires children between certain ages, usually six or seven through sixteen or seventeen years old, to attend public, private, or home school. States operating under the doctrine of **parens patriae**, which literally means the state has sovereign powers over persons such as minors, was enacted during the years 1852 through 1918 and was designed to protect children from unlawful labor abuse. Today, parents who willfully fail to comply with compulsory attendance laws face criminal charges.

An example of a compulsory attendance requirement is illustrated in a West Virginia case. An eighteen-year-old West Virginia student missed five days of school without an excuse. He was warned that continued absences could result in criminal prosecution. After continuing unexcused absences, the county prosecutor's office filed a criminal complaint against the student. After he was convicted of violating a state compulsory attendance statute, the student petitioned the Supreme Court of Appeals of West Virginia for review.[4] The court observed that the compulsory attendance statute mandated school attendance for children between the ages of six and sixteen and provided enforcement sanctions against parents, guardians, or custodians but not against individual students. There was no possibility of liability under the statute for a nonattending student regardless of age.

Compulsory attendance laws today are enacted to ensure that students receive a suitable education. Students who violate compulsory attendance requirements may be suspended or expelled, depending on the severity of their absenteeism. Compulsory attendance is based on the common law responsibility that the parent has an obligation to the child and the state to ensure that the child receives an appropriate education. Therefore, parents do not have a right to be totally free from state laws affecting the upbringing of their children.

In an early compulsory attendance case, *State v. Hoyt*, the state charged Oscar Hoyt, Richard Daniels, Lucius Covey, and Truman Covey for failure to cause a child of the defendant to attend public school. Each defendant filed a statement of defense alleging that on that day the child was instructed and taught by a private tutor in his home in the studies required to be taught in the public schools. The defendants prayed for dismissal of the charge. The court denied the motion and fined each defendant a $10 fee.[5]

In an early case, the U.S. Supreme Court affirmed the right of a state to require compulsory attendance but indicated that school attendance may be met through attending private schools. In 1922, Oregon voters amended their state constitution, which required all residents to send their children between the ages of eight and sixteen to public schools only. A statute that declared violating this act to be a misdemeanor subsequently was passed, to take effect in 1926. A Catholic school corporation and a military school that operated academies in the state sued state officials in a federal district court under the U.S. Constitution, seeking an injunction to prohibit enforcement of the act. The court ruled for the schools. State officials appealed to the U.S. Supreme Court. The High Court ruled that the Oregon statute unreasonably interfered with parental liberty rights to direct the upbringing and education of their children. "The fundamental theory of liberty on which all governments in this Union repose excludes any general power of the state to standardize its children by forcing them to accept instruction from public teachers only." The Court noted that the schools could not claim this liberty guarantee for themselves, inasmuch as they were corporations. However, the schools sued to vindicate their own business and property interests, and they were clearly threatened by arbitrary and unlawful interference by the statute. Because of the immediate threat of harm to the two schools, they were entitled to relief in the form of a court order preventing state officials from enforcing the invalid statute. The Court affirmed the district court's order for the schools.[6]

In a New York case, the school's policy required students to attend 90 percent of all classes in each course to receive credit. The policy also required schools to drop students from any course in which they had been deliberately absent. A group of students brought action against the district challenging the constitutionality of the attendance policy. Students claimed that the denial of credit for a class is tantamount to dropping a student from enrollment, which is contrary to New York law. The school district filed a motion for summary judgment, which was granted by the court. The students appealed to the New York Supreme Court, Appellate Division. The court rejected the students' arguments and held that the denial of credit was not equivalent to being dropped from enrollment because it did not prevent a student from attending class or attending makeup classes. The court upheld the lower court's entry of summary on behalf of the school.[7]

Compulsory Attendance Exceptions

The state's right to require school attendance was the subject of considerable controversy during the twentieth century. In *Wisconsin v. Yoder,* the U.S. Supreme Court reversed its earlier position by stating that the state's interest regarding universal and compulsory education is by no means absolute to the exclusion or subordination of all other interests.[8] The plaintiffs in this case challenged Wisconsin's compulsory education statute, which required children between the ages of seven and sixteen to attend school on a regular basis. Parents of one child challenged the statute by refusing to send their child to school after she reached the eighth grade. They believed that continuation in school violated the basic tenets of their Amish religious beliefs. The parents were convicted of violating the state's compulsory law. They appealed the conviction by stating that the statute infringed on their free exercise of religion rights. The Wisconsin Supreme Court held for the parents. The U.S. Supreme Court affirmed this decision in holding that the First Amendment prohibits state action that interferes with a parent's right to control the religious upbringing of his or her child. It is important to note that this decision did not invalidate compulsory attendance requirements beyond the eighth grade—it only suggested minimum literacy as a compelling state interest, which does not have to be manifested by completing high school. Furthermore, only students who have strong religious beliefs that conflict with a continuing public school education are permitted to be exempted from compulsory attendance beyond the eighth grade.

In a related case, *Church of God v. Amarillo School District*, the Church of God sought to enjoin the enforcement of the Amarillo School District's absence policy that limits the number of excused absences for religious holidays to two days each year. The fundamental tenets of the Church of God require that members abstain from secular activities on seven annual holy days based on the Book of Leviticus in the Old Testament. Students who are members of the church miss from eight to ten days each year observing annual holy days. The district formulated a new policy that allowed make-up work for absences whether they were excused or unexcused; however, students readmitted with unexcused absences received a zero for a grade. Plaintiffs contended that the policy was unconstitutional because it violated the free exercise of religion. The court recognized the school's district interest in academic development of its students but held that the district's policy violates the free exercise of religion guaranteed by the First and Fourteenth Amendments.[9]

A number of states also make provisions for exemptions to their compulsory attendance laws for married students who are **emancipated** and are no longer under their parents' care.

Truancy

Truancy represents a significant challenge for school districts throughout the United States. Students are truant when they have an unexcused absence from school without the parent's knowledge. The legal school age of students varies among states. With most states, compulsory attendance laws typically apply to students between the ages of six to seventeen and some instances between five and eighteen. Exceptions are Pennsylvania with compulsory ages of five to eighteen and Illinois with ages seven to sixteen. Most state statutes define the number of absences that students accumulate in order to be classified as truant. In some states, school attendance is tied to school funding with average daily attendance a major component of the funding formula. Consequently, low daily attendance may result in less funding, a loss of teaching positions, and other funding limitations.

The theory behind compulsory attendance supports the view that an educated society serves the public interest. According to the U.S. Department of Labor, students who fail to earn a high school diploma tend to have low-paying jobs, experience increased health problems, and place a strain on social services. School districts, in their attempt to curb truancy, have employed truant or attendance officers to pursue truant students and to refer them to juvenile court. Some states, such as Arizona and Virginia, impose sanctions on students as well as their parents when students are truant. Virginia also mandates jail time for parents of truant students. The intent of these sanctions is to hold parents accountable and to motivate them to take a more active role in preventing truancy. Other states have implemented diversion programs aimed at identifying root causes of truancy.

In most jurisdictions, local police are given the authority to check and determine whether school-age children are truant. If they find truants, they are directed to send them to school or to arrest those who are habitual truants.

McKinney-Vento Homeless Assistance Act

The McKinney-Vento Homeless Assistance Act was reauthorized by Title X, Part C of the No Child Left Behind Act. The statute effectively ensures immediate enrollment and educational stability for homeless children. Federal funds are provided to each state to support programs that serve homeless students. The McKinney-Vento Act defines homeless children as "individuals who lack a fixed, regular, and adequate nighttime residence." The act provides examples of children who would fall under this definition:

- Children and youth sharing housing due to loss of housing, economic hardship, or a similar reason
- Children and youth living in motels, hotels, trailer parks, or camp grounds due to lack of alternative accommodations
- Children and youth living in emergency or transitional shelters
- Children and youth abandoned in hospitals
- Children and youth awaiting foster care placement
- Children and youth whose primary nighttime residence is not ordinarily used as a regular sleeping accommodation (e.g., park benches)
- Children and youth living in cars, parks, public spaces, abandoned buildings, substandard housing, and bus or train stations
- Migratory children and youth living in any of the situations cited above

Enrollment and Transportation

The McKinney-Vento Act requires schools to enroll homeless children and youth immediately, even if they lack normally required documents, such as immunization records or proof of residence. The Act ensures that homeless children and youth have transportation to and from their school of origin if it is in the child's or youth's best interest.

Home Schools

Increasingly, parents who are not satisfied with public schools are electing to provide instruction for their children at home. It is estimated that roughly 1.3 million students receive home schooling. Virtually every state in the nation makes provisions for home schooling. Minimum standards for home schooling vary among the states based on the individual state's compulsory attendance laws. Minimal standards for curriculum and instruction, length of instruction time, and the number of days in which instruction should be provided are generally prescribed by state statute or state board of education policies. All such requirements must be met by parents offering home instruction.

Although requirements for home schools vary among states, some of the more common components include a requirement that the home school operative be a parent or legal guardian who possesses a high school diploma. All children who are home schooled must be identified by name and age. The address where the program is offered is typically required. Also mandated by law is a calendar indicating that the children are taught the minimum number of days required by law (usually 180 days). Parents or legal guardians should have on file copies of diplomas or degrees earned. Children's immunization records should also be maintained in a file. Information from these files is normally submitted to the appropriate state official. An annual progress assessment report is typically required in each subject area. If parents or legal guardians intend to continue home schooling, most states require written notification by a specified date.

Parents who fail to comply with state statutes regarding home schooling may be brought to trial for failure to comply. In most cases, the burden of proof rests with the parents to demonstrate that home instruction is essentially equivalent to instruction offered in public schools. In fact, in *New Jersey v. Massa,* the New Jersey Supreme Court held that equivalent education other than that which is offered in public schools only requires a showing of academic equivalence.[10]

A home-schooling challenge emerged in South Carolina when a group of parents brought suit to enjoin the enforcement of a state law requiring parents who only possessed a high school diploma to pass a basic skills examination to be approved for home schooling. The examination in question had been used to test the reading, writing, and mathematics of entry-level education students. This examination did not assess teaching ability. The district engaged a company to evaluate the test's suitability to assess home-schooling instructors. A thirty-three-member panel consisting of home schoolers, public school teachers, and college professors was formed to determine whether the knowledge needed to succeed on the basic skills examination was a necessary prerequisite to offering home schooling. Although there was a wide range of opinion among the panelists regarding suitability of the examination, it was validated for use. A trial court found the test to be properly validated. The parents appealed. The state appellate court disagreed, finding that the validation process was unreasonable based on disparities among panelists. The court noted further that sixteen panel members were not familiar or experienced with home schooling and found that it was manifestly unreasonable to rely on their evaluation. Last, home schoolers had a high pass rate on state tests. Consequently, they should not be required to pass a test as a prerequisite.[11]

The following cases reflect the requirements imposed by various states regarding home schooling:

1. Michigan passed a law requiring home schools to comply with teacher certification requirements. Parents who objected to the law based on religious grounds were exempted.[12]
2. In West Virginia a statute was passed by the legislature, making children ineligible for home schooling if their national standardized test scores fell below the fortieth percentile and did not improve after receiving remedial home instruction.[13]
3. A Virginia court upheld the state's compulsory attendance law requiring home schoolers to be "tutors or teachers" but did not require private instructors to meet similar qualifications.[14]
4. A Maryland law was upheld that required the state to monitor home education when a parent challenged the required curriculum by arguing that it promoted atheism, paganism, and evolutionism by diminishing the importance of Christian holidays.[15]
5. In North Dakota, the state supreme court allowed parents to choose home-based instruction exception rather than a private school exception to comply with state compulsory

attendance laws and minimum state standards. The private school exception required compliance with health, fire, and safety laws applicable to private buildings.[16]

A home-schooling case arose in Michigan when several parents decided to educate their children at home using a home-based education program, which they had purchased from a private-school corporation. These parents were charged with truancy. They, along with the private-school corporation, sued the superintendent of public instruction and various school officials, claiming that their constitutional rights had been violated. Specifically, they stated that they had a constitutional right to educate their children at home and that they had been denied due process of law.

The case was heard before a federal district court. The district court held that the private-school corporation could not bring the lawsuit because it had not demonstrated economic loss. The corporation also was not considered an association of members but, rather, a business marketing a service to customers. The court stated that because the parents were able to assert their own rights, the corporation need not bring an action on their behalf. The court ruled further that the right to educate children at home is not a fundamental right guaranteed to parents. Although parents have a constitutional right to send their children to private schools and to choose private schools that offer specialized instruction, private school education can be regulated by the state as long as it is reasonable. Because the state merely required that a certified teacher provide instruction in courses comparable to those offered in the public schools, the court ruled that the regulation was reasonable. Finally, the court held that the parents were not members of a class of people federal discrimination statutes were enacted to protect. They were merely a group of people who wished to educate their children at home. The court denied the parents' claims.[17]

Charter Schools

According to the U.S. Department of Education, charter schools are public schools that emerge through a contract with a state agency or a local school board. The charter establishes the ground rules regarding the operations of the school. The primary advantage of charter schools is autonomy over their operations; they are relieved of rules and regulations that govern public schools. In exchange for flexibility, charter schools are held accountable for achieving outcomes established by the charter, including student achievement as a primary goal. The charter school concept is sound. It encourages innovation and creativity without bureaucratic barriers in exchange for measurable and positive student learning outcomes. It is too early to determine if charter schools are effective. In recent years, however, they have experienced a range of problems, including audit findings, failure to follow state guidelines in expending funds, ineffective record-keeping practices, and poor student achievement results, among others.

Charter schools are funded by local, state, and federal tax dollars based on school attendance. They are free and do not assess tuition fees. Charter schools may choose their own organizational and management structure. These schools are required to meet federal and state educational standards just as regular public schools are. Additionally, they are judged based on the extent to which they meet achievement goals established by their charter contracts. Charter schools have received mixed reviews. Many studies suggest that they are out-achieving traditional public schools while others suggest that students in charter schools perform no better than students in traditional schools.

FUNDING. State educational agencies with specific statutes authorizing charter schools may apply for federal grant funds. Charter school program (CSP) funds are used by state educational agencies to award subgrants to eligible applicants to allow them to plan and implement charter schools within the state. State educational agencies may reserve up to five percent of CSP grant funds for administrative expenses related to operating the state charter school program and up to ten percent of their CSP grant funds to support dissemination activities. Initial implantation costs may cover the following:

- Acquiring necessary equipment and educational materials and supplies.
- Acquiring or developing curriculum planning materials.
- Other initial operational costs that cannot be met from state or local sources such as implementation of office functions, accounting systems, installation of computers, data systems, networks, and telephone.
- Personnel expenses incurred before or after the school's opening that are associated with initial implementation activities.[18]

FACILITIES.   States fund charter school facilities through dedicated facilities funding state grant programs, tax-exempt bond programs, or state credit enhancement. The particular method of funding varies among states because charter schools have limited access to local school district tax and bond revenues regarding school facilities. They rely on alternative sources of public and private funds to cover facility costs. Some states provide direct cash assistance based on per-pupil funds related to facilities. Some states award grants while other states permit charter schools to apply for tax-exempt bonds to cover facility costs. Numerous federal programs provide assistance to public schools for facility improvements. State charter school facilities and incentive grant programs provide grants for qualifying states to support charter school facilities. One popular trend has emerged involving the use of abandoned school buildings or the use of unused space in existing facilities. Charter schools may also rent facilities at market rate.

SCHOOL VOUCHERS

School vouchers have and continue to evoke debate regarding their use, particularly by public school advocates. Vouchers, in principle, allow parents to use them to support their child's private school education. Funds to support vouchers may be derived from city, state, or federal sources. The amount of a voucher generally parallels the same amount allocated to public school for a child's education.

In some instances, parents in low income brackets or whose child is attending a low-performing school are issued vouchers to allow them the freedom to choose a better school. In other cases, vouchers can be used by any parent who desires to choose another educational alternative. There is strong support for vouchers as well as strong opposition. Those who support vouchers suggest that they create increased accountability for public schools. The overarching belief among those who support vouchers is that parents should have a right to decide where their child attends school. In addition, vouchers create competition and should result in better schools both public and private. School officials in poorly performing schools suggest that vouchers draw needed resources from public schools that would enable them to perform more effectively. In addition, the loss of funds leads to deteriorating conditions in public schools.

Added to the debate is the issue of religion. Critics of voucher programs allege that state funds are allocated to sectarian schools and in doing so create separation of church and state violations. Interestingly, the U.S. Supreme Court in *Zelman v. Harris* in a 5–4 vote rejected the argument in an Ohio case that vouchers violate the First Amendment's separation of church and state.[19] The Supreme Court ruled that the Ohio program did not violate the Establishment Clause of the First Amendment to the United States Constitution because it passed a five-part test developed by the Court in this case, titled the Private Choice Test. Under the Private Choice Test developed by the court, for a voucher program to be constitutional it must meet *all* of the following criteria:

- The program must have a valid secular purpose.
- Aid must go to parents and not the schools.
- A broad class of beneficiaries must be covered.
- The program must be neutral with respect to religion.
- There must be adequate nonreligious options.

The court held that the Ohio program met the five-part test. However, some states have rejected vouchers for parochial schools based on state constitutional violations. States have embraced vouchers for various reasons. For example, Vermont uses them in rural towns where students do not have their own high schools. In Cleveland, Ohio, and Milwaukee, Wisconsin, vouchers are provided to students of low-income families.

No Child Left Behind (NCLB), which is a federal initiative, closely parallels the voucher concept by allowing parents of children in low-performing schools to transfer their children to better performing schools if these schools fail to meet state standards. The exodus of students from any public school may affect funding for that school. The debate will likely continue regarding voucher programs. Time will reveal the extent to which children benefit from parental choice.

HEALTH REQUIREMENTS

States typically require medical examinations and certain immunizations as a prerequisite for school admission. Because the state, through its police powers, shares a primary responsibility to protect the health and safety of students enrolled in public schools, states have been supported by the courts in establishing health requirements for public school students.

The most common challenge faced by school districts has involved First Amendment objections by parents who claimed that mandatory immunization violates their rights to a free exercise of religion. However, courts have been fairly consistent in supporting the state in requiring specific immunizations to prevent communicable disease and have viewed the state interest to be more compelling than parents' interest. Parents have been convicted and fined for failure to have their children vaccinated as a condition for admission to public schools. Some states provide for certain exemptions as long as the health and welfare of other students are not jeopardized, although others have not been quite as lenient.

For example, a court refused to grant religious exemption from school immunizations in New York when a New York couple refused to comply with the school district's enforcement of the state's health law regarding immunization. This case arose when a rural New York couple who were members of the Universal Life Church, which advocated a natural existence, refused to comply with the state's immunization requirements. They claimed their son was entitled to a religious exemption from immunization under New York law. The exemption required affiliation with a *bona fide* religious organization. The school district found no conflict between the family's religious beliefs and vaccination. The couple unsuccessfully appealed to the state education commissioner. They then filed a lawsuit in a federal district court for a declaration that their beliefs were within the religious exemption, plus $1 million for civil rights violations. The court ruled that their beliefs did not exempt them from immunization.

On appeal to the U.S. Court of Appeals, Second Circuit, the couple argued that their beliefs were sincere and that the term *religious* expanded beyond belief in a deity. The court held for the school district, finding that the couple's belief was not essentially religious but primarily scientific in nature. Strong conviction did not convert their scientific beliefs into religion. The court affirmed the refusal to grant the religious exemption. Because there was no violation of the couple's First Amendment rights, there was no basis for any damage claim.[20]

In *Brown v. Stone,* a religious exemption also was disallowed. The court in this case held that an exemption based on religious grounds would discriminate against the vast majority of children whose parents did not subscribe to a religious conviction.[21] In a rather unusual case, *Lewis v. Sobel,* the court held that a state law requiring a student whose parents' religious convictions conflicted with state health requirements be provided an exemption. Although the parents were not members of an organized church, their beliefs caused them to reject preventive medicine. The court found that the parents' beliefs were sincere in that these beliefs permeated every facet of their lives and the immunization requirement placed a burden on their religious beliefs even though they had on one occasion relinquished their opposition to immunization. The district was ordered to admit the child to school. In a very rare move, the court awarded monetary damages to the family for emotional distress.[22]

RESIDENCE

Public schools generally are required to educate students who reside within the district's boundaries. Residence is a student's actual dwelling place. A student may also have a domicile, which is where the student intends to remain indefinitely. It is conceivable that a student may have a number of residences but only one domicile. At one time, common law suggested that a student's domicile be associated with his or her father. In recent years, this view has changed. A student's domicile follows that of his or her legal guardian. If the child is emancipated (free of parental control) his or her domicile is determined by where the student intends to remain indefinitely. Domicile is basically determined by intent. When a student intends to remain in a certain location, domicile is established. Courts have taken the position that public school officials are required to educate school-age students who reside within their district with the intent to remain. In the past, a student was not allowed to establish residence within a district for the primary purpose of attending a school within the district. This practice is highly questionable today if there is evidence that the student has an intent to establish permanent residence and is actually living within the district with a degree of permanency. The student is entitled to a public school education even though his or her parent or guardian may live elsewhere. School districts may impose reasonable tuition costs when a student attends school within a district in which he or she has not established legal residence.

A case arose involving proper residence when the grandmothers of three young children filed a lawsuit against a Texas school district, seeking an order that the children be allowed to attend public schools. A federal district court issued an order to compel their enrollment. The children had resided with their grandmothers for considerable lengths of time but not for the primary purpose of attending public school in the local school district. The grandmothers were not the legal guardians of the children. Texas laws require that the presence of the child in the school district not be for the primary purpose of attending their free public schools.

The school district took the position that children could not establish residency apart from their parents or legal guardians and that persons having lawful control or custody of children must initiate some type of judicial proceeding. The district court issued a permanent order instructing the school district to allow the children to enroll in their schools. The court ruled that these children living apart from their parents or legal guardians must be admitted to school to prevent violation of the federal Constitution. The children had established their residence by physical presence and an intention to remain in the district.[23]

Another case involving residence arose in New York. A New York state law has a provision that allows a homeowner whose property or dwelling intersects adjoining school districts to choose either district in which to send his or her children. A homeowner who desired to send his children to a school in another district purchased a small parcel of land adjoining his lot in order to meet the law's intersection provision. The other school district sued the homeowner, seeking tuition payment. A trial court held for the school district, concluding that the homeowner's motivation in purchasing the parcel disqualified him from using the other school district tuition free. The homeowner appealed to an appellate division court, which reversed the trial court decision. The homeowner's motivation in purchasing the adjoining parcel was immaterial, and his children could attend the new district school without paying tuition.[24]

In a significant case regarding nonresidence for homeless children, the court held that homeless children must be provided a right to be educated under New York law. This case arose when Diane Harrison and her two school-age children had been homeless since 1986 after a fire destroyed their apartment. They moved to a motel and later to various residences. At one point, the children lived with their father in Peekskill and enrolled in the district. In October 1987, they were required by the landlord to leave his residence, and they moved back with their mother at the hotel in which they had lived previously. The hotel was not located in the Peekskill district. Harrison was notified that her children could no longer attend Peekskill schools unless they found an apartment in Peekskill. She received no written notice detailing factual or legal grounds for the expulsion. She also was not notified of any right to a hearing pursuant to New York Education Law § 301. The court held that the expulsion clearly denied children their right to an education under New York law. In the case of a homeless child, the New York Commissioner of Education had previously found that, for the purpose of residence, children are entitled to continue to attend in their previous home district. Because the children had resided in Peekskill and enrolled in their schools, Peekskill represented their previous home district. In addition, the court observed that after the suit was filed and prior to rendering a decision, a new regulation was implemented allowing parents of homeless children to designate either the school district in which the child resided at the time he or she became homeless or the district where the child was temporarily living. Under this regulation, districts that deny a child admission based on nonresidence must provide written notification to parents and allow parents to produce evidence that the child has a right to attend school.[25]

CURRICULUM STANDARDS

Minimal curriculum standards in public schools are established by state statute and policy. In almost all cases, certain courses and minimum achievement standards are determined through state policy. Local school districts may establish other standards as long as they do not contradict state requirements. Federal aid programs such as Title I, Goals 2000, the Educate America Act of 1994, Education for Disabled Students, and most recently NCLB specify certain standards that must be met to receive federal funds. Also, under Goals 2000 and the Educate America Act of 1994, states receive funds if they agree to develop plans to meet certain national goals. Generally, courts are very reluctant to intervene in matters involving public school curricula based on the view that states retain the authority to establish curriculum standards as long as there is no federal constitutional infringement involved. State legislation requires that certain subjects be included in school curricula throughout the state and that instruction be provided in subjects such as American history, state government, civics, and U.S. and state constitutions. State legislatures generally prescribe broad guidelines and delegate authority to determine the specifics of the curriculum to the state board of education and local school districts. Except for issues involving religious matters, courts are reluctant to interfere with school officials' authority to prescribe curriculum. School officials tend to develop a common secular curriculum to avoid the assertion that the curriculum advances a particular or specialized sectarian interest to the exclusion of others.

Most conflicts involving curriculum center around special interest groups that register objections to the school's use of certain textbooks, courses, or programs. Courts generally have supported schools as they advocate knowledge expansion rather than knowledge restriction. Although school boards generally have prevailed in matters regarding curriculum disputes with parents, their powers are not absolute. If legitimate constitutional issues emerge, the courts will intervene to determine the constitutionality of the issue under review and will rule appropriately based on the facts involved in the case.

COMMON CORE STANDARDS

Common Core Standards are designed to provide consistent and focused understanding regarding what students are expected to learn. This awareness ultimately provides guidance for teachers and parents so that they are able to assist students in acquiring relevant knowledge and skills that will enable them to succeed in college and their professional careers. Common Core Standards reflect high expectations regarding what students should know to achieve success. These standards tend to be more rigorous than previous standards and are designed to prepare students effectively in a global and competitive marketplace.

To date, forty-seven states are members of the Common Core Standards Initiative. A group of governors representing the National Governor's Association (NGA) and State Commissioners representing the Council of Chief State Officers worked collectively with teachers, parents, and subject matter experts to develop standards in response to the decline in student achievement nationally as compared to other industrial countries.

Common Core Standards establish benchmarks for English and Mathematics for each grade level from kindergarten through high school. The Common Core Standards do not adversely affect teaching methodology or lesson plan development. They do, however, require students to think more critically, to develop stronger reasoning and problem-solving skills.

States began to adopt new standards in 2010. Some states are phasing these standards in over a period of time. However, other states are adopting these standards as a means of preparing students for college or careers, which is a condition identified by the U.S. Department of Education to qualify for Race to the Top competition. The Race to the Top funds provide competitive grants to encourage and reward states that are creating conditions for education innovation.

Those who oppose Common Core Standards argue that they reduce control at the school district level by establishing a national curriculum and federal control of education, which amounts to a federal mandate. A number of states have initiated efforts to eliminate these standards or reduce the pace at which these standards are implemented. The Republican National Committee passed a resolution indicating that the standards were inappropriate and represented an effort to standardize school curriculum and control education at the federal level. The National Republican Committee is involved in rewriting the No Child Left Behind Legislation and has encouraged states to make independent decisions regarding Common Core Standards without influence from Washington.

SPECIAL INTEREST GROUPS AND PUBLIC SCHOOL CURRICULUM

Special interest groups through their advocacy have effectively censored textbook versions of many of the classical works in public schools across the United States. These groups tend to represent either ultraconservatives or ultraliberals, and many of these groups have significant funds to support their causes. Consequently, they exert influence on textbook publishers when they object to certain content or the manner in which content is presented. Publishers anxious to meet the demands of state education boards in order to promote and sell their products tend to be willing to modify texts based on strong objections from parents and special interest groups.

These groups tend to be specific in identifying items that they find objectionable such as the inclusion of "witches" in *The Wizard of Oz,* teenage sex in Shakespearean plays, and a major focus on slavery in history textbooks. Many states have implemented textbook adoption programs in which school districts are permitted to choose books from the state adopted list. However, when pressures are exerted on state boards, they often will respond to protests by removing objectionable books from the approved list because they represent constituents who elected them.

Special interest groups and parents expect to have a voice in what is taught in public schools. This increased desire to be involved in curricular matters stems, in part, from the fact that certain topics invoke emotional responses. Topics such as intelligent design, the theory of evolution, human sexuality, homosexuality, and black history are among many of the hot topics provoking debate among various groups.

In reality, parents, community leaders, and special interest groups do exert considerable influence on curriculum content in public schools. No longer are school boards, school leaders, and subject matter specialists the sole curricular decision makers. This is because of the emergence of school-based management councils, school choice, and charter schools. Parents and community leaders have played a greater role in curricula decisions and school policies. Thus, they have exerted greater influence in these areas due in part to the view that school boards are expected to be more responsive to parents and communities under school choice, charter schools, and school-based management.

Religious tensions have fueled debate for decades and have become infused in curricular decisions. Many of the controversial topics such as homosexuality, atheism, and evolution are in conflict with religious doctrines of certain groups. For example, two local community and special interest groups sued Montgomery County public schools in Maryland over teaching materials that were planned for the district's health class units on different lifestyles.[26] Interestingly, these groups were successful in their lawsuit. The judge ruled that some of the material was biased against certain religions. In addition, the school board was required to reimburse these groups $36,000 in legal fees and was subsequently required to eliminate the sex education unit. A citizen's committee was formed to recommend a new curriculum.

School boards find themselves caught in a major dilemma with respect to supporting teachers and content specialists in curricular decisions while attempting to be responsive to parents, communities, and special interest groups. The National School Board Association recommends that school boards develop policies on how the board will receive input from special interest groups in their communities. It might be prudent to involve parents and community leaders in the policy development process to ensure that these policies, once implemented, receive their support.

Many special interest groups attempt to censor schoolbooks based on political (conservative or liberal) and religious viewpoints. They tend to target books that are inconsistent with their philosophy or values. Some of the most popular books that have been targeted include those by Shakespeare, Rowling, Hawthorne, and Steinbeck. Courts have supported adult involvement in textbook selection but have not supported boards of educations in their attempts to censor books based on strictly unpopular points of view. The *Counts* case reflects the courts' position.

In *Counts v. Cedarville School District*, the school board of the Cedarville, Arkansas, school district voted to restrict students' access to the Harry Potter books on the grounds that the books promoted disobedience and disrespect for authority and dealt with witchcraft and the occult. As a result of the vote, students in the school district were required to obtain a signed permission slip from their parents or guardians before they could borrow any of the Harry Potter books from school libraries. The district court overturned the board's decision and ordered the books returned to unrestricted circulation on the grounds that the restrictions violated students' First Amendment right to read and receive information. In so doing, the court noted that while the board necessarily performed highly discretionary functions related to the operation of the schools, it was still bound by the Bill of Rights and could not abridge students' First Amendment right to read a book on the basis of an undifferentiated fear of disturbance or because the board disagreed with the ideas contained in the book.[27]

NO CHILD LEFT BEHIND ACT OF 2001

Over the past two decades, the federal government has taken a more active role in public education through the passage of major acts designed to improve P–16 public education such as Title I and Goals 2000 and the Educate America Act of 1994. Perhaps the most comprehensive and sweeping act since the Elementary and Secondary School act was passed in 1965 is the No Child Left Behind Act.

On January 8, 2002, President Bush signed into law the No Child Left Behind Act of 2001 (NCLB). This new act redefines the federal government's role in K–12 education and is designed to close the achievement gap between disadvantaged and minority students and their peers. It is based on four principles:

- Stronger accountability for results
- Increased flexibility and local control
- Expanded options for parents
- An emphasis on teaching methods that have been proven to work

Increased Accountability

NCLB strengthens Title I accountability by requiring states to implement statewide accountability systems covering all public schools and students. These systems must be based on challenging state standards in reading and mathematics, annual testing for all students in grades three through eight, and annual statewide progress objectives ensuring that all groups of students reach proficiency within twelve years. Assessment results and state progress objectives must be broken out by income, race, ethnicity, disability, and limited English proficiency to ensure that no group is left behind. School districts and schools that fail to make adequate yearly progress (AYP) toward statewide proficiency goals will, over time, be subject to improvement, corrective action, and restructuring measures aimed at getting them back on course to meet state standards. Schools that meet or exceed AYP objectives or close achievement gaps will be eligible for state academic achievement awards.

More Choices for Parents and Students

NCLB significantly increases the choices available to the parents of students attending Title I schools that fail to meet state standards, including immediate relief, beginning with the 2002–2003 school year, for students in schools that previously were identified for improvement or corrective action under the 1994 Elementary and Secondary Education Act (ESEA) reauthorization.

Local education authorities (LEAs) must give students attending schools identified for improvement, corrective action, or restructuring the opportunity to attend a better public school, which may include a public charter school, within the school district. The district must provide transportation to the new school, and must use at least 5 percent of its Title I funds for this purpose, if needed.

For students attending persistently failing schools (those that have failed to meet state standards for at least three of the four preceding years), LEAs must permit low-income students to use Title I funds to obtain supplemental educational services from the public- or private-sector provider selected by the students and their parents. Providers must meet state standards and offer services tailored to help participating students meet challenging state academic standards.

To help ensure that LEAs offer meaningful choices, the new law requires school districts to spend up to 20 percent of their Title I allocations to provide school choice and supplemental educational services to eligible students.

In addition to helping ensure that no child loses the opportunity for a quality education because he or she is trapped in a failing school, the choice and supplemental service requirements provide a substantial incentive for low-performing schools to improve. Schools that wish to avoid losing students, along with the portion of their annual budgets typically associated with those students, will have to improve; otherwise, if they fail to make annual progress for five years, they run the risk of reconstitution under a restructuring plan.

Greater Flexibility for States, School Districts, and Schools

One important goal of NCLB was to breathe new life into the "flexibility for accountability" bargain with states first struck by President George H. W. Bush during his 1989 education summit with the nation's governors at Charlottesville, Virginia. Prior flexibility efforts have focused on the waiver of program requirements; NCLB moves beyond this limited approach to provide states and school districts with unprecedented flexibility in the use of federal education funds in exchange for strong accountability for results.

New flexibility provisions in NCLB include authority for states and LEAs to transfer up to 50 percent of the funding they receive under four major state grant programs to any one of the programs or to Title I. The covered programs include Teacher Quality state grants, Educational Technology state grants, Innovative Programs, and Safe and Drug-Free Schools.

The law also includes a competitive state flexibility demonstration program that permits up to seven states to consolidate the state share of nearly all federal state grant programs, including Title I, Part A grants to local educational agencies, while providing additional flexibility in their use of Title V innovation funds. Participating states must enter into five-year performance agreements with the Secretary of Education, covering the use of the consolidated funds, which may be used for any educational purpose authorized under the ESEA. As part of their plans, states also must enter into up to ten local performance agreements with LEAs, which will enjoy the same level of flexibility granted under the separate Local Flexibility Demonstration Program.

The new competitive Local Flexibility Demonstration Program would allow up to eighty LEAs, in addition to the seventy LEAs under the State Flexibility Demonstration Program, to consolidate funds received under Teacher Quality state grants, Educational Technology state grants, Innovative Programs, and Safe and Drug-Free Schools. Participating LEAs would enter into performance agreements with the Secretary of Education and would be able to use the consolidated funds for any ESEA-authorized purpose.

Summary and Implications

ACCOUNTABILITY.   Each state will implement a statewide accountability system that will be effective in ensuring that all districts and schools make adequate progress. The accountability system includes rewards and sanctions. Students cannot be left behind based on any of the following:

- Race/ethnicity
- Disabilities
- Limited English proficiency
- Economic status (disadvantaged)

PARTICIPATION

- Students with disabilities who take alternative assessment must participate.
- Schools and districts must have a 95 percent participation rate for all students.

ADEQUATE YEARLY PROGRESS

- The same high academic achievement standards will be applied to all students.
- Academic improvement should be continuous and demonstrated for all students.
- Separate measures and annual achievement objectives may be used for all students, including those in racial and ethnic groups, the economically disadvantaged, those with disabilities, and those with limited English proficiency.

PUBLIC SCHOOL CHOICE.   Under NCLB, children attending public schools who have not made AYP for two or more consecutive years and have thus been designated for needs improvement have the option of moving to a higher performing public school.

SUPPLEMENTAL SERVICES.   Under NCLB, children in schools that have been in needs improvement status for two or more years may receive supplemental services that include before- and after-school tutoring or remedial classes in reading, language arts, and mathematics.

UNSAFE SCHOOL CHOICE OPTION (USCO).   Under NCLB, states must develop a definition of "persistently dangerous" schools and allow public school choice for students who have been victims of a violent criminal offense or who attend a school that meets the definition.

EXCEPTIONAL STUDENTS.   Ensuring that no student with disabilities is left behind under NCLB, all students, including students with disabilities, must meet Georgia's proficient level of academic achievement by 2013–2014.

SCHOOL IMPROVEMENT.   Schools are required to design and implement an effective system of support to enhance school improvement with an intense focus on schools that fail to make adequate yearly progress.

LIMITED ENGLISH PROFICIENCY STUDENTS.   Under NCLB, all students, including students with limited English proficiency (LEP), must meet their state's proficiency level of academic achievement by 2013–2014. LEP students will become proficient in English and reach high academic standards, at a minimum attaining proficiency or better, in reading/language arts and mathematics.

NCLB strengthens Title I requirements for state assessments, accountability systems, and support for school improvement. The law also establishes minimum qualifications for teachers and paraprofessionals in Title I programs.

ASSESSMENTS.   By the 2005–2006 school year, states must have developed and implemented annual assessments in reading and mathematics in grades three through eight and at least once in grades ten through twelve. By 2007–2008, states also must have administered annual science assessments at least once in grades three through twelve. These assessments must be aligned with state academic content and achievement standards and involve multiple measures, including measures of higher order thinking and understanding.

- *Alignment with State Standards.* State assessments must be aligned with challenging academic content standards and challenging academic achievement standards. States were required under the previous law to develop or adopt standards in mathematics and reading/language arts, and the new law requires the development of science standards by the 2005–2006 school year. NCLB standards require that all students meet the same expectations in science in grades three through five, grades six through nine, and grades ten through twelve.
- *Inclusion.* State assessments must provide for the participation of all students, including students with disabilities or limited English proficiency. Students enrolled in schools in the United States for three consecutive years must be assessed in English in the area of reading and language arts.
- *Accommodations.* State assessments must provide for reasonable accommodations for students with disabilities or limited English proficiency, including, if practicable, native-language versions of the assessment.
- *Annual Assessment of English Proficiency.* Beginning with the 2002–2003 school year, states were required to ensure that districts administer tests of English proficiency—which measure oral language, reading, and writing skills in English—to all limited English proficient students.
- *Reporting.* State assessment systems must produce results disaggregated by gender, major racial and ethnic groups, English proficiency, migrant status, disability, and status as economically advantaged. The assessment system must produce individual student interpretive, descriptive, and diagnostic reports. States must report itemized score analyses to districts and schools.
- *Prompt Dissemination of Results.* States must ensure that the results of state assessments administered in one school year are available to school districts before the beginning of the

next school year. The assessment results must be provided in a manner that is clear and easy to understand and must be used by school districts, schools, and teachers to improve the educational achievement of individual students.

As of 2002–2003, states must participate in biennial National Assessment of Educational Progress (NAEP) assessments in reading and mathematics for fourth- and eighth-graders. State-level NAEP data will enable policymakers to examine the relative rigor of state standards and assessments against a common metric.

STRONGER ACCOUNTABILITY FOR RESULTS.   Under NCLB, states are working to close the achievement gap and ensure that all students, including those who are disadvantaged, achieve academic proficiency. Annual state and school district report cards inform parents and communities of state and school progress. Schools that do not make progress must provide supplemental services, such as free tutoring or after-school assistance; take corrective actions; and, if still not making adequate yearly progress after five years, make dramatic changes in the way the school is run.

PROVEN EDUCATION METHODS.   NCLB places emphasis on determining through rigorous scientific research which educational programs and practices have been proven effective. Federal funding is targeted to support these programs and teaching methods that work to improve student learning and achievement. In reading, for example, NCLB supports scientifically based instruction programs in the early grades under the Reading First program and in preschool under the Early Reading First program.

TEACHER QUALITY

- All core academic teachers were required to be highly qualified by 2005–2006.
- Core academics include the following:

  a. English, reading, or languages
  b. Mathematics, science, foreign languages, civics, and government
  c. Economics, the arts, history, and geography

QUALIFIED TEACHERS.   The following measures will be used in part to assess qualified teachers:

- A teacher's license
- Success in passing a test
- Content area knowledge:

  a. Academic major or graduate degree in content area
  b. Credits equivalent of academic major (24 hours)
  c. Success in passing tests such as Praxis

PARAPROFESSIONALS.   Paraprofessionals must meet the following requirements:

- Two years of higher education
- Associate's degree
- Test (Parapro through ETS)
- High school diploma or its equivalent
- Translators and parent liaisons

Each group of students should meet or exceed annual objectives, except as follows:
- The number of students who are below proficiency standards should be reduced by 10 percent from the prior year.
- Other indicators may be used to measure progress for subgroups.

RESTRUCTURING (CORRECTIVE ACTION).   If a school fails to make adequate yearly progress after one full year of corrective action, the district must do the following:

- Continue to make public school choice available
- Continue to make supplemental services available
- Prepare a plan to restructure the school

ALTERNATIVE GOVERNANCE.   By the beginning of the following school year, the district must implement one of the following alternatives:

- Reopen the school as a public charter school
- Replace all or most of school staff, including the principal
- Enter into a contract with an entity, such as a private management company with a proven record of effectiveness, to operate the school
- State takeover
- Any other major restructuring of the school's governance plan

No Child Left Behind Act of 2013

This legislation was introduced in the Senate as Senate Bill S 1306 113 Congress (2013–2014) on July 20, 2013. The No Child Left Behind Act of 2013 amends the Elementary and Secondary Act of 1965 (ESEA) to direct the Secretary of Education to award grants to states and through them, competitive subgrants to eligible partnerships to support implementation of state environmental literacy plans that include environmental and educational standards and teacher training. These subgrants involve the eligible partnership, a local educational agency (LEA), and at least one institution of higher education, another LEA, an elementary or secondary school, or a government or nonprofit entity.

The bill requires the use of subgrants for one or more of the following activities:

- Providing targeted job-embedded professional development that improves teacher environmental content knowledge and pedagogical skills
- Establishing and operating education and summer workshops for teachers
- Developing or redesigning more rigorous environmental education curricula
- Designing programs that prepare teachers to provide environmental education, mentoring, and training to other teachers in their schools
- Establishing and operating programs to bring teachers and students into contact with working professionals in environmental fields
- Creating initiatives that incorporate environmental education with teacher training programs or accreditation standards
- Promoting the integration of outdoor environmental education lessons into regular school curriculum and schedules.

The bill authorizes the Secretary of Education to award competitive matching grants to eligible partnerships for one or more of the following activities:

- Developing and implementing state curricula frameworks for environmental educators that meet challenging state academic content and achievement standards for environmental education
- Replacing or disseminating information about proven and tested model environmental programs
- Developing and implementing new approaches to advancing environmental education and the adoption and use of environmental education content standards.

The bill amends Part B (Mathematics and Science Partnerships of Title II) of the ESEA to include the following:

1. Nonprofit environmental education organizations and government science environmental or natural resource management agencies among the entities eligible to participate in Part B Partnerships
2. The use of Part B funds to train teachers to provide environmental education that enhances students' understanding of science and mathematics
3. An amendment to Part B (21st Century Community Learning Centers) of Title IV of the ESEA to include environmental literacy activities among the before- and after-school activities that such programs fund at community learning centers.

It directs the Secretary of Education to do the following:

- Request all federal departments and agencies to provide information on any environmental literary assistance program that they operate or support
- Make that information searchable and accessible through the Department of Education's website and cross reference with the U.S. Green Ribbon School application information
- Coordinate environmental literacy activities between the Department of Education, the Environmental Protection Agency (EPA), the Department of Interior, and the Department of Commerce
- Appoint an advisory panel of stakeholders to advise and support interagency environmental literacy planning and assessment activities.

This bill was assigned to a Congressional Committee on July 16, 2013, which will consider it before sending it to the House and referred to the Committee on Health, Education, Labor and Pensions. The bill is still pending at the time of the writing of this edition.[28]

INTELLECTUAL PROPERTY AND FAIR USE

Intellectual property covers four basic areas: patents, trademarks, designs, and copyright materials. The Copyright Act prohibits unauthorized use of copyrighted material for profit or public display without appropriate payment to or permission from the copyright proprietor. Under the act, the owner of a copyright has the exclusive rights to do and to authorize any of the following:

1. To reproduce the copyrighted work in copies or phonorecords
2. To prepare derivative works based on the copyrighted work
3. To distribute copies or phonorecords of the copyrighted work to the public by sale or other transfer of ownership, or by rental, lease, or lending
4. In the case of literary, musical, dramatic, and choreographic works, pantomimes, and motion pictures and other audiovisual works, to perform the copyrighted work publicly
5. In the case of literary, musical, dramatic, and choreographic works, pantomimes, and pictorial, graphic, or sculptural works, including the individual images of a motion picture or other audiovisual work, to display the copyrighted work publicly

   a. The act permits educators and libraries to make "fair use" of copyrighted material. Section 107 specifically permits "reproduction in copies or phonorecords . . . for purposes such as . . . teaching (including multiple copies for classroom use), scholarship or research. . . ."[29]

The guidelines are liberal with respect to producing single copies for teaching or research purposes but fairly restrictive regarding the reproduction of multiple copies. For example, reproduction of a poem should not exceed 1,000 words or 10 percent of the work, whichever is less. In addition, copies should be reproduced by the specific teacher who intends to use the materials for teaching purposes. These guides are not based on law but rather are widely acceptable as meeting the legal intent of the Copyright Act.

The Copyright Act specified four factors that should be used to determine fair use:

1. The purpose or use relative to whether use is commercial in nature or for nonprofit, educational purposes
2. The nature of the work

3. The amount of material extracted from the work in relation to the work as a whole
4. The impact of the use on the potential market in relation to the value of the copyrighted work[30]

Teachers are allowed to produce single copies of copyrighted materials for teaching purposes only; therefore, multiple copies are not permitted. Specialty and extracted materials must be brief in the context of the type of work involved and should be initiated by the teacher who intends to use the materials. In addition, the use of the materials must be applied in a manner that makes it unreasonable to seek permission by the authors to use the materials. Copies should be restricted to one course. Care must be exercised by the teacher to avoid extracting all materials from a single author. Duplicating materials should not be produced to avoid purchasing a book or any other consumable work.

Copying Computer Software

Copyright laws also affect computer software. Teachers should not reproduce copies of software for students from an original program to serve as a backup copy. This is prohibited under the Copyright Act. Most school districts have purchased site licenses to provide protection for the use of software. This license is essentially a contractual agreement with a software company in which a fee is negotiated for the use of educational software. Under the contractual agreement, a reasonable number of copies may be reproduced for educational purposes.

Copyright laws also apply to the use of media. Table 11.1 provides information regarding fair use of media materials.

TABLE 11.1   Copyright and Fair Use Guidelines for Teachers

This chart was designed to inform teachers of what they may do under the law. Feel free to make copies for teachers in your school or district, or download a PDF version at www.techlearning.com. More detailed information about fair use guidelines and copyright resources is available at www.halldavidson.net.

Medium	Specifics	What You Can Do	The Fine Print
Printed Material (short)	• Poem less than 250 words; 250-word excerpt of poem greater than 250 words • Articles, stories, or essays less than 2,500 words • Excerpt from a longer work (10 percent of work or 1,000 words, whichever is less) • One chart, picture, diagram, or cartoon per book or per periodical issue • Two pages (maximum) from an illustrated work less than 2,500 words, e.g., a children's book	• Teachers may make multiple copies for classroom use, and incorporate into multimedia for teaching classes. • Students may incorporate text into multimedia projects.	• Copies may be made only from legally acquired originals. • Only one copy allowed per student. • Teachers may make copies in nine instances per class per term. • Usage must be "at the instance and inspiration of a single teacher," i.e., not a directive from the district. • Don't create anthologies. • "Consumables," such as workbooks, may not be copied.
Printed Material (archives)	• An entire work • Portions of a work • A work in which the existing format has become obsolete, e.g., a document stored on a Wang computer	• A librarian may make up to three copies "solely for the purpose of replacement of a copy that is damaged, deteriorating, lost, or stolen."	• Copies must contain copyright information. • Archiving rights are designed to allow libraries to share with other libraries one-of-a-kind and out-of-print books.

(continued)

TABLE 11.1	Copyright and Fair Use Guidelines for Teachers (*continued*)		
Medium	**Specifics**	**What You Can Do**	**The Fine Print**
Illustrations and Photographs	• Photograph • Illustration • Collections of photographs • Collections of illustrations	• Single works may be used in their entirety, but no more than five images by a single artist or photographer may be used. • From a collection, not more than 15 images or 10 percent (whichever is less) may be used.	• Although older illustrations may be in the public domain and don't need permission to be used, sometimes they're part of a copyright collection. Copyright ownership information is available at www.loc.gov or www.mpa.org.
Video (for viewing)	• Videotapes (purchased) • Videotapes (rented) • DVDs • Laserdiscs	• Teachers may use these materials in the classroom. • Copies may be made for archival purposes or to replace lost, damaged, or stolen copies.	• The material must be legitimately acquired. • Material must be used in a classroom or nonprofit environment "dedicated to face-to-face instruction." • Use should be instructional, not for entertainment or reward. • Copying OK only if replacements are unavailable at a fair price or in a viable format.
Video (for integration into multimedia or video projects)	• Videotapes • DVDs • Laserdiscs • Multimedia encyclopedias • QuickTime Movies • Video clips from the Internet	• Students "may use portions of lawfully acquired copyright works in their academic multimedia," defined as 10 percent or three minutes (whichever is less) of "motion media."	• The material must be legitimately acquired (a legal copy, not bootleg or home recording). • Copyright works included in multimedia projects must give proper attribution to copyright holder.
Music (for integration into multimedia or video projects)	• Records • Cassette tapes • CDs • Audio clips on the Web	• Up to 10 percent of a copyright musical composition may be reproduced, performed, and displayed as part of a multimedia program produced by an educator or students.	• A maximum of 30 seconds per musical composition may be used. • Multimedia program must have an educational purpose.
Computer Software	• Software (purchased) • Software (licensed)	• Library may lend software to patrons. • Software may be installed on multiple machines, and distributed to users via a network. • Software may be installed at home and at school. • Libraries may make copies for archival use or to replace lost, damaged, or stolen copies if software is unavailable at a fair price or in a viable format.	• Only one machine at a time may use the program. • The number of simultaneous users must not exceed the number of licenses; and the number of machines being used must never exceed the number licensed. A network license may be required for multiple users. • Take aggressive action to monitor that copying is not taking place (unless for archival purposes).

Medium	Specifics	What You Can Do	The Fine Print
Internet	• Internet connections • World Wide Web	• Images may be downloaded for student projects and teacher lessons. • Sound files and video may be downloaded for use in multimedia projects (see portion restrictions above).	• Resources from the Web may not be reposted onto the Internet without permission. However, links to legitimate resources can be posted. • Any resources you download must have been legitimately acquired by the Web site.
Television	• Broadcast (e.g., ABC, NBC, CBS, UPN, PBS, and local stations) • Cable (e.g., CNN, MTV, HBO) • Videotapes made of broadcast and cable TV programs	• Broadcasts or tapes made from broadcast may be used for instruction. • Cable channel programs may be used with permission. Many programs may be retained by teachers for years—see Cable in the Classroom (www.ciconline.org) for details.	• Schools are allowed to retain broadcast tapes for a minimum of 10 school days. (Enlightened rights holders, such as PBS's *Reading Rainbow*, allow for much more.) • Cable programs are technically not covered by the same guidelines as broadcast television.

Source: http://www.halldavidson.net/. Used by permission of the author, Hall Davidson.

Note: Representatives of the institutions and associations who helped to draw up many of the above guidelines wrote a letter to Congress dated March 19, 1976, stating; "There may be instances in which copying that does not fall within the guidelines stated [above] may nonetheless be permitted under the criterion of fair use."

USE OF THE INTERNET FOR INSTRUCTION

Another important component of the instructional program is the use of electronic technology. Information technology has drastically altered teaching and learning as well as the school's administrative processes. It has changed the fabric of school operations. Internet access has increased by almost 70 percent in public schools and roughly 80 percent in public school class-rooms during the period between 1994 and 2005, as illustrated in Table 11.2. Given the wide-spread use and application of the Internet and the potential for abuse, students and parents should be required to review and agree on rules governing access and use of the Internet.

School Officials' Responsibility

School officials should include procedures for accessing the Internet and identify resources that are well suited to the school's learning objectives. These components may be included under "student acceptable use for electronic network." Filtering software should be used to block access to visual images that are obscene, pornographic, or otherwise deemed unsuitable for children. The software is required under the Children's Internet Protection Act of 2000 (discussed later in this section). Students should be expected to exhibit good behavior on school-owned computer networks. Furthermore, they should be made aware that communications on the network most often are public. School officials must stress that access to the school's information network is not a right but a privilege. Parental consent should be required for minors to access the school's network. School officials should clearly communicate by policy which acts are permissible and which are not. Specific disciplinary action should be clearly defined and communicated to students and parents alike when violations occur. Millions of pages of information have been posted to the Internet by all types of individuals and organizations, so students must be cautioned that many of these pages contain offensive, sexually explicit, and inappropriate materials.

TABLE 11.2 Number and Internet Access of Instructional Computers and Rooms in Public Schools, by Selected School Characteristics: Selected Years, 1995 through 2008

Instructional Computers and Rooms, and Access	All Public Schools	Instructional Level[1]		Size of School Enrollment			Community Type[2]				Percent of Students Eligible for Free or Reduced-Price Lunch[3]			
		Elementary	Secondary	Less Than 300	300 to 999	1,000 or More	City	Suburban	Town	Rural	Less Than 35 Percent	35 to 49 Percent	50 to 74 Percent	75 Percent or More
1	2	3	4	5	6	7	8	9	10	11	12	13	14	15
Computers for Instructional Purposes														
Number (in thousands)														
1995[4]	5,621 (—)	3,453 (—)	2,021 (—)	850 (—)	3,600 (—)	1,171 (—)	1,497 (—)	1,526 (—)	1,404 (—)	1,195 (—)	2,905 (—)	806 (—)	950 (—)	882 (—)
2000	8,776 (174)	5,296 (149)	3,271 (113)	1,135 (73)	5,524 (121)	2,117 (103)	2,537 (179)	3,396 (213)	1,155 (132)	1,689 (131)	4,394 (147)	1,373 (93)	1,606 (112)	1,384 (107)
2005	12,672 (281)	7,701 (251)	4,783 (148)	1,566 (98)	7,966 (243)	3,139 (163)	3,132 (177)	4,058 (242)	1,819 (193)	3,663 (255)	5,352 (261)	2,193 (185)	2,687 (244)	2,440 (152)
2008	15,434 (193)	9,711 (159)	5,415 (125)	1,746 (68)	9,486 (144)	4,202 (130)	3,611 (155)	5,787 (255)	2,062 (159)	3,974 (180)	6,195 (174)	2,364 (155)	3,805 (190)	3,070 (175)
Average number per school														
1995[4]	72 (—)	60 (—)	112 (—)	41 (—)	72 (—)	164 (—)	84 (—)	83 (—)	72 (—)	54 (—)	78 (—)	59 (—)	74 (—)	67 (—)
2000	110 (2.0)	89 (2.4)	178 (5.3)	57 (3.1)	106 (2.3)	259 (9.0)	120 (4.9)	128 (4.3)	97 (5.6)	82 (3.6)	120 (3.4)	111 (5.9)	94 (5.7)	99 (5.5)
2005	154 (3.4)	124 (3.8)	253 (6.8)	75 (4.2)	149 (4.2)	388 (13.5)	165 (7.2)	170 (6.3)	154 (13.4)	132 (5.9)	166 (5.5)	153 (9.3)	147 (6.9)	139 (7.4)
2008	189 (2.9)	157 (2.8)	301 (6.5)	87 (3.4)	179 (2.9)	486 (10.4)	205 (7.5)	221 (6.1)	189 (8.0)	147 (4.2)	209 (5.6)	182 (7.7)	181 (6.8)	170 (8.2)
Number with Internet access (in thousands)														
1995[4]	447 (—)	232 (—)	187 (—)	59 (—)	315 (—)	73 (—)	96 (—)	131 (—)	126 (—)	94 (—)	286 (—)	46 (—)	57 (—)	36 (—)
2000	6,759 (174)	3,813 (136)	2,779 (113)	882 (69)	4,191 (114)	1,686 (97)	1,782 (148)	2,688 (178)	955 (111)	1,335 (91)	3,608 (139)	1,064 (80)	1,215 (93)	858 (87)
2005	12,245 (274)	7,361 (246)	4,706 (151)	1,515 (98)	7,642 (239)	3,089 (162)	3,009 (173)	3,912 (238)	1,784 (193)	3,541 (239)	5,239 (259)	2,090 (176)	2,583 (228)	2,332 (146)
2008	15,162 (204)	9,508 (169)	5,356 (128)	1,710 (69)	9,308 (153)	4,144 (130)	3,517 (154)	5,716 (253)	2,028 (154)	3,901 (178)	6,131 (174)	2,321 (153)	3,739 (188)	2,971 (175)
Percent with Internet access														
1995[4]	8 (—)	7 (—)	9 (—)	7 (—)	9 (—)	6 (—)	6 (—)	9 (—)	9 (—)	8 (—)	10 (—)	6 (—)	6 (—)	4 (—)
2000	77 (1.1)	72 (1.5)	85 (1.2)	78 (2.6)	76 (1.3)	80 (1.8)	70 (2.1)	79 (1.7)	83 (2.5)	79 (2.1)	82 (1.2)	77 (2.9)	76 (2.6)	62 (3.1)

2005	97 (0.4)	96 (0.5)	98 (0.4)	97 (0.7)	96 (0.5)	98 (0.5)	96 (0.7)	96 (1.1)	98 (0.6)	97 (0.7)	98 (0.6)	95 (1.0)	96 (1.0)	96 (0.8)
2008	98 (0.2)	98 (0.3)	99 (0.2)	98 (0.7)	98 (0.3)	99 (0.4)	97 (0.5)	99 (0.3)	98 (0.7)	98 (0.4)	99 (0.3)	98 (0.5)	98 (0.4)	97 (0.7)
Ratio of Students to Instructional Computers with Internet Access														
2000	6.6 (0.10)	7.8 (0.20)	5.2 (0.20)	3.9 (0.30)	7.0 (0.20)	7.2 (0.30)	8.2 (0.40)	6.6 (0.20)	6.2 (0.30)	5.0 (0.30)	6.0 (0.20)	6.3 (0.40)	7.2 (0.40)	9.1 (0.70)
2005	3.8 (0.10)	4.1 (0.10)	3.3 (0.10)	2.4 (0.10)	3.9 (0.10)	4.0 (0.10)	4.2 (0.20)	4.1 (0.10)	3.4 (0.20)	3.0 (0.10)	3.8 (0.10)	3.4 (0.20)	3.6 (0.20)	4.0 (0.20)
2008	3.1 (0.04)	3.2 (0.05)	2.9 (0.05)	2.2 (0.07)	3.2 (0.05)	3.2 (0.06)	3.4 (0.12)	3.2 (0.08)	2.7 (0.09)	2.9 (0.07)	3.1 (0.06)	3.2 (0.08)	2.9 (0.08)	3.2 (0.14)
Instructional Rooms[5]														
Number (in thousands)														
2000	2,905 (35)	1,864 (28)	972 (24)	377 (22)	1,871 (23)	657 (23)	866 (56)	1,086 (61)	413 (47)	541 (39)	1,380 (46)	465 (28)	570 (36)	482 (29)
2005	3,283 (71)	2,152 (70)	1,078 (27)	426 (23)	2,152 (70)	705 (30)	849 (62)	1,050 (61)	439 (41)	945 (67)	1,339 (50)	593 (51)	695 (56)	655 (39)
2008[5]	2,663 (21)	1,723 (20)	887 (15)	282 (9)	1,692 (20)	689 (18)	639 (26)	1,003 (35)	338 (24)	683 (28)	1,053 (27)	425 (26)	653 (27)	532 (22)
Percent with Internet access[6]														
1995	8 (0.7)	8 (1.0)	8 (1.0)	9 (1.6)	8 (1.0)	4 (1.0)	6 (1.3)	8 (1.4)	8 (2.0)	8 (1.5)	10 (1.2)	6 (1.4)	6 (1.9)	3 (1.0)
2000	77 (1.1)	76 (1.5)	79 (1.6)	83 (2.8)	78 (1.5)	70 (2.2)	66 (2.2)	78 (2.0)	87 (2.6)	85 (1.7)	82 (1.5)	81 (2.9)	77 (2.8)	60 (3.3)
2005	94 (1.3)	93 (1.9)	95 (0.9)	92 (1.9)	94 (1.9)	94 (1.5)	88 (3.7)	96 (0.8)	98 (0.7)	95 (1.8)	96 (0.8)	88 (4.3)	96 (0.8)	91 (2.5)
2008	— (†)	— (†)	— (†)	— (†)	— (†)	— (†)	— (†)	— (†)	— (†)	— (†)	— (†)	— (†)	— (†)	— (†)

—Not available.
†Not applicable.

[1] Data for combined schools are included in the totals and in analyses by other school characteristics, but are not shown separately.

[2] Due to definitional changes for community type, estimates for years prior to 2005 may not be directly comparable with estimates for later years.

[3] Free or reduced-price lunch information was obtained on the questionnaire and supplemented, if necessary, with data from the Common Core of Data (CCD).

[4] Includes computers used for instructional or administrative purposes.

[5] In 2008, instructional rooms included classrooms only and excluded computer labs and library/media centers. Prior to 2008, instructional rooms included classrooms, computer labs and other labs, library/media centers, and other rooms used for instructional purposes.

[6] Some data differ slightly (e.g., by 1 percent) from previously published figures.

Note: Detail may not sum to totals because of rounding. Standard errors appear in parentheses.

Source: U.S. Department of Education, National Center for Education Statistics, Fast Response Survey System (FRSS), Internet Access in U.S. Public Schools and Classrooms: 1994–2005 and Educational Technology in U.S. Public Schools: Fall 2008; and unpublished tabulations. (This table was prepared August 2010.)

Children's Internet Protection Act

School officials also must understand their responsibilities under the Children's Internet Protection Act (CIPA). This act was enacted by Congress at the end of 2000 as part of House Appropriations Bill H.R. 4577. Under this law, schools and libraries are required to adopt an Internet safety policy and install filtering technology if they are to receive certain federal funds. This law applied to all schools and libraries that receive discounted rates for the purchase of equipment and services used to access the Internet under the E-Rate Program or through the Library Services and Technology Act (LSTA) or Title III of the ESEA. Although the act required libraries to install filtering technology, this requirement has been ruled unconstitutional by a special three-judge district court. The court held that filtering technology erroneously blocks a massive amount of speech that is protected by the First Amendment. *This ruling affects only libraries.* The portion of the law that applies to schools remains intact. Section 1703 of the act requires the National Telecommunication and Information Administration no later than eighteen months after its enactment to initiate a notice and comment proceeding for the purpose of (1) evaluating whether current available technology protection measures, including commercial Internet blocking and filtering software, adequately address the needs of educational institutions, (2) making recommendations on how to foster the development of measures that meet such needs, and (3) evaluating the development and effectiveness of local Internet safety policies that are currently in operation after community input. Local education agencies covered under the act shall certify their compliance during each annual program application cycle.

Schools without Internet safety policies and technology for the first program year after the effective date of the act in which the agency is applying for funds shall certify that it is undertaking such actions, including any necessary procurement and procedures to implement an Internet safety policy that meets the requirements of the act. During the second year of the program, after the effective date in which the LEA is applying for funds under the act, the LEA shall certify that the school is in compliance with such requirements. Any school for which the LEA is unable to certify compliance during the second year shall be ineligible for all funding under the act, in this and all subsequent years, until the school comes into compliance. Any school subject to certification for which the LEA cannot make the required certification may seek a waiver if state or local procurement rules or regulations or competitive bidding requirements prevent certification required by the act.

The LEA shall notify the Secretary of Education of the applicability of that clause to the school. The notice shall certify that the school will be brought into compliance before the beginning of the third year after the effective date in which the school is applying for funds under the act. Whenever the Secretary has reason to believe that any recipient of funds under the act is failing to comply substantially with its requirements, the Secretary may withhold further payments, issue a complaint to compel compliance through a cease and desist order, or enter into a compliance agreement to bring the school into compliance with the requirements of the act.

The primary focus of the act is to protect children from undesirable content accessed through the Internet. An administrator, supervisor, or other person authorized by the certifying authority may disable the technology protection measure during use by an adult to enable access for *bona fide* research or other lawful purpose. The determination regarding subject matter that is inappropriate for minors shall be made by the school board, LEA, library, or other authority responsible for making the determination. Each Internet safety ruling adopted by LEAs shall be made available on request to the Federal Communications Commission for review.

School or District Responsibility

Schools or school districts should develop and enforce an acceptable use policy. This policy should govern all electronic programming, such as e-mail and general access to the Internet, by students and employees. The board of education generally will not incur liability if it has filtering software installed that may inadvertently fail. However, measures must be taken to correct the failure. By standard practice, each district or school should establish a process for modifying the filtering system or defiltering Internet access for students when it is educationally appropriate.

At a minimum, the filtering system should restrict access to Internet sites or chat rooms that contain any of the following:

- Offensive messages
- Obscene language
- Sexuality
- Sexual acts
- Violence
- Sexual attire
- Crime
- Nudity
- Intolerance
- Harassing messages

Students or employees who violate board policy may be banned from using the Internet. Students who are banned should not be otherwise excluded from participation in the educational program. Minimal due process requirements should be met if a student or employee is banned from Internet use. These procedures should be communicated to students, parents, and employees. Disciplinary actions for students should be tailored to the severity of the violation and to further assist the student in gaining knowledge and developing reasonable judgment in the use of the Internet. Employee violations resulting in disciplinary action should be based on defensible policy.

Teacher's Responsibility

Teachers have a responsibility to select material that is appropriate based on the age and maturity of students and consistent with course objectives. Consequently, teachers must preview material and sites that students are required to access to determine the appropriateness of material contained on the site. Teachers should also provide guidance by identifying and listing resources to assist students in their learning activities. They should monitor content that students access on the Internet and follow approved procedures when student violations occur.

Parent's Responsibility

Parents should be aware of guidelines and instructions for student protection while using the Internet. Although the board or school acceptable use policy will restrict access to inappropriate material, a wide range of material is available to students on the Internet. Parents must assume a leadership role in instilling proper values to their children and instructing their children regarding which materials are acceptable and which are not acceptable. Parents also should monitor Internet use at home to ensure that their children are following their directives. Home monitoring by parents will reinforce acceptable use policies implemented by school officials. Cooperation and coordination of Internet use between parents and the school generally will yield more favorable results regarding Internet use by students.

GRADING AND ACADEMIC REQUIREMENTS

As stated previously, courts traditionally have been reluctant to interfere in cases involving academic matters. The prevailing view held by the courts is that professional educators are better prepared to make decisions regarding student evaluation. Requirements regarding progress from one grade to another typically are not reviewable by the courts unless there is substantial evidence of unreasonableness. For example, the Fourth Circuit Court of Appeals refused to intervene in the failure of a school district to promote to the third grade those students who failed to pass a reading level test.[31] The court respected the educational judgment of professional educators even though the students' intelligence indicated that they were capable of reading at the third-grade level; the students could not be promoted until they had demonstrated mastery of the requisite

---

Administrative Guide

Use of the Internet

1. Involve parents and students in drafting Internet use policies.
2. Make certain that Internet use policy is clearly written and communicated to parents and students.
3. Policies should inform teachers, students, and parents of their responsibilities regarding enforcement of Internet use policies.
4. Due process and fundamental fairness should be observed in enforcing Internet use policies.
5. School districts have a responsibility to develop acceptable use policies regarding the use of the Internet by students and employees.
6. Specific disciplinary measures for inappropriate use of the Internet should be spelled out in the district's acceptable use policy.
7. Students should be cautioned that personal contact information about themselves or others should not be posted on the Internet without prior written consent from the parent or legal guardian.
8. Students should be informed that they should promptly disclose to their teachers inappropriate messages they receive on the Internet.
9. Users should be informed by policy that the following activities are prohibited:
   a. Subverting network security
   b. Bypassing restrictions established by school officials
   c. Using the Internet for illegal purposes such as drug transactions, obtaining alcohol for minors, and gang-related activities
   d. Seeking information about passwords of others
   e. Using obscene, vulgar, rude, threatening, or abusive language
   f. Taking writings of others and presenting them without prior written permission (plagiarizing)
   g. Using the Internet to promote personal or commercial enterprises

---

reading skill. One court observed that academic matters by their very nature are more subjective and evaluative than typical issues presented in disciplinary decisions and that such academic judgments should be left to professional educators.[32]

Student Testing

It is well established that the state has the authority to promulgate promotion and graduation requirements. Often, standardized tests are used to determine student competencies. If the measures are reasonable and nondiscriminatory, they generally will be supported by the courts. School officials are provided considerable discretion in matters relating to appropriate academic requirements. By and large, courts do not feel equipped to evaluate academic performance issues.[33] Because courts are not equipped to evaluate academic performance issues, they limit themselves to addressing issues relating to due process, discriminatory impact, or arbitrary or capricious acts by school officials. Therefore, the state's authority to develop and assess student performance standards is not debatable. However, challenges may be raised regarding the fairness of certain assessment programs. These challenges most frequently involve minimal competency tests used to determine whether students met requirements for high school graduation.

In an early challenge, the state of Florida was unable to demonstrate that the school's curriculum actually reflected concepts included on the test and whether the literacy test actually covered material taught in the classrooms. Tests also cannot be defended if there is a showing of discrimination based on race. The most common challenge regarding testing programs is whether tests are used to track students, which results in discrimination and a violation of the Fourteenth Amendment's equal protection clause. The issue becomes more profound when there are few or no opportunities for students to move from one track to another. The key issue involves intent. Tests will not be supported by the courts if there is discriminatory intent. Therefore, school officials must be able to demonstrate a compelling state interest to support tests if they resulted in separation of students by race. Testing programs must be fair and equitable to all students. There must be a regard for due process rights of students. Special areas such as inadequate phase-in periods, inadequate matches between tests and instructional materials, racially discriminatory tests, and other arbitrary and capricious practices should be given special consideration to ensure that individual rights of students are not violated.

Oregon was the first state to establish minimum competency requirements for graduation. In the fall of 1975, New York administered to its ninth-graders the first statewide competency test. Arizona was the first state to formulate minimum competency standards as a condition of graduation for its senior class of 1976. Florida was the first state to provide major funding for remedial programs for students who did not achieve the minimum score required for passage of the test.

Grade Reductions for Absences

Excessive absenteeism by students poses a challenge for school officials who often resort to grade reductions as a means of limiting excessive absences. Courts generally will support reasonable policies regarding grade reduction for excessive absences if they do not conflict with state statute, as illustrated by a case in Michigan. A Michigan high school student was absent from school for five days during the first of six grading periods for the school year. Her absences were due to an injury and thus were excused. The local board of education's policy required that any student with more than three excused absences in a grading period make up the missed time at after-school study sessions; failure to comply would result in a reduction in the student's letter grade. The plaintiff attended only one of the five required make-up sessions. Consequently, her grades were lowered by one full letter grade.

The student filed suit against the school board, claiming that the grading policy was beyond the scope of the board's authority and that the policy violated her due process rights. The circuit court dismissed the case. The student appealed to the Michigan Court of Appeals. The court held that the grading policy was not beyond the board's scope of authority because the attendance policy was impliedly authorized by statute and was not arbitrary or unreasonable. The court also held that due process protections require a property right. The court ruled that the student's right to due process was not violated because the student had no vested property interest in any grade higher than those she actually received. The court of appeals affirmed the trial court's decision.[34]

Grade Reduction for Unexcused Absences

School rules that penalize students academically for unexcused absences, or truancy, are not uncommon. Courts have been more supportive of schools on this type of rule than on one that mandates grade reduction based on general misconduct. In fact, since the mid-1970s courts have been quite consistent in ruling against school districts for grade reduction related to misconduct. Thus, school districts must be certain that their rules in this area are carefully drawn. The following cases illustrate this point.

In a New Jersey school district, school board policy mandated that a student receive a zero in all subjects on those days he or she was truant from school. The student could make up any tests missed on such days, but the zero had to be used when grades were averaged for the term. In ruling for a student who challenged the rule, the New Jersey Commissioner of Education found the penalty to be excessive.[35] In some instances a student could receive a failing grade in a class for even a single absence. A major reason the school board lost its case appears to be related to the severity of the penalty, rather than the policy of grade reduction in general.

In a Colorado school district, students who had more than seven absences for any reason from a given class were denied academic credit. The court ruled against the school district in this case because the school board regulations violated the state's attendance statute.[36] State law specified that students should be in attendance at school for a minimum of 172 days. Days of absence because of illness or suspension were to be counted as days of attendance for the purpose of meeting the requirement of 172 days. On the basis of the state statute, the court concluded that a school district was prohibited from imposing sanctions on students who were absent from school based on illness or school suspension.

In Illinois, a school district was upheld in a case in which a student's grades were lowered as a result of his having unexcused absences.[37] The school board's policy mandated that grades be lowered one letter grade per class for unexcused absences. Kevin Knight was truant two days. Thus, his grades were reduced in accordance with the rule. In one of his classes his grade was not reduced, and in three of his other classes the grade reductions were less than the one letter grade required by the board's policy. These inconsistencies apparently had a bearing on the court's decision. The board of education rescinded the rule that had been applied to Kevin. The court, after expressing its reluctance to interfere with the school's judgment regarding grades, held that the rule, as applied to Kevin Knight, was not so harsh as to deprive him of substantive due process of law. The court pointed out that the rule was not fully applied to Knight. The court also noted that the possibility of damage to Knight was remote because the following year he was admitted to a junior college. It would have been interesting to observe what the court might have decided had the rule been applied fully and Kevin Knight had been unable to enter college.

In a related case, Roberta Raymon, a high school student, was penalized for an unexcused absence from class by the deduction of three points from her six-weeks algebra grade. This penalty did not alter her grade point average significantly and did not change her class standing. She remained second in her class. Arguing that the penalty was arbitrarily imposed in violation of the Fifth and Fourteenth Amendments, her parents brought this action for damages and injunctive relief under 42 U.S.C. § 1983. The district court, without deciding the federal constitutional issue, exercised jurisdiction over state law claims and ordered the three points restored to Raymon's algebra grade. The court refused to award attorneys' fees, and plaintiffs appealed that denial to the Fifth Circuit Court of Appeals.[38]

In its ruling, the Fifth Circuit Court of Appeals stated that federal courts are proper forums for the resolution of serious and substantial federal claims. They are frequently the last and often the only resort for those who are oppressed by the denial of the rights afforded them by the Constitution and laws of the United States. Fulfilling this mission and the other jurisdiction conferred by acts of Congress has imposed on the federal courts a workload that taxes their capacity. Each litigant who improperly seeks federal judicial relief for a petty claim forces other litigants with more serious claims to wait for their days in court. When litigants improperly invoke the aid of a federal court to redress what is patently a trifling claim, the district court should not attempt to ascertain who was right or who was wrong in provoking the quarrel but should dispatch the matter quickly.

Accordingly, the court reversed the judgment and ordered the district court to dismiss the complaint for lack of subject matter jurisdiction. The Fifth Circuit Court considered the plaintiff's claim to be petty and a misuse of the court's time given the litigation of more serious cases before the court.

Grade Reductions for Academic Misconduct

A number of school districts have formulated policies requiring grade reductions for misconduct. An example of the courts' position regarding this was illustrated in the following case.[39] Shaun Dunn and Bill McCullough were both fine musicians who participated as guitar players in the high school band program at Fairfield Community High School. Fairfield prohibited its band members from departing from the planned musical program during band performances, and it specifically forbade guitar solos during the performances. In direct defiance of those rules and their teacher's explicit orders, Dunn and McCullough played two unauthorized guitar pieces at a February 10, 1995, band program. The discipline they received for this infraction caused them both to receive an F for the band course, and that F prevented McCullough from graduating with honors. Dunn and McCullough appealed the district court's decision to grant summary judgment for Fairfield. The court concluded that the school's actions violated no right under the federal civil rights statutes.

Every rehearsal and concert were assigned a point value. Points were awarded for presence at the event, appropriate dress, and appropriate conduct. In addition, there were at least two playing evaluations per quarter for points. The point scale worked as follows:

Daily rehearsal: 5 points

Performances: 20 points

Playing evaluations: 25 points

The policy also warned that conduct at performances had to be professional and that conduct not meeting that standard would give rise to serious consequences.

The court rejected the students' contentions, noting also that they had failed to address the Eighth Amendment component of their case in their summary judgment motion. The disciplinary action in question, the court concluded, bore a rational relation to the school's interest in maintaining order and providing an education. The court also commented that if the plaintiffs were to prevail, "almost every disciplinary action could become a federal case." The court then considered the students' claim that Fairfield had violated Illinois state law. Because the complaint did not invoke the court's supplemental jurisdiction under 28 U.S.C. § 1367, the court expressed doubt that the claim was properly before it. The court decided that the undisputed facts showed that no violation of Illinois law had taken place.

A different case arose in Indiana in which a student's grade was reduced as punishment for alcohol-related misconduct. The student's parents brought suit against the district and moved for summary judgment. The district court held that a high school rule mandating a 4 percent reduction in grades for each day a student had been suspended for alcohol use during school hours was invalid and a violation of substantive due process. The court stated further that the policy was arbitrary and that the school failed to demonstrate a reasonable relationship between the use of alcohol during school hours and a reduction in grades.[40]

Physical Punishment for Poor Academic Performance

Physical punishment of public school students for failure to maintain acceptable academic standards has not received support by the courts. Courts have consistently ruled against school officials for the use of physical punishment when the student's behavior did not involve improper conduct. For example, one court ruled against physical punishment of a student who failed to perform athletically at a desired level even though the coach considered the punishment to be instructive and a source of encouragement to the student.[41]

A teacher in Iowa was found guilty of assault and battery when he inflicted punishment on a child who was unable to complete studies in algebra.[42] The courts have also held that it was improper to physically punish a student who was unable to solve a mathematics problem at the blackboard.[43] U.S. courts have consistently held that public school students should not be physically punished for conduct not related to disciplinary infractions. An Indiana court held that it was not proper to physically punish a child for accidentally breaking school objects and for failure to pay for such damages. The court reasoned that students must rely on their parents for financial resources. Consequently, if parents refused to pay or were not able to pay, the student then would be punished for not having met an obligation he or she had no power to meet.[44] School officials would be ill advised to physically punish a child for not paying school debts. Furthermore, students should not be physically punished for failure to complete homework or other assignments. School officials may adopt policies calling for academic penalties, such as a loss of credit for failure to meet academic assignments, but under no circumstances should physical punishment be inflicted in cases involving academic matters.

Withholding Diplomas

School officials are delegated the authority to determine when a student has completed the required curriculum entitling him or her to be awarded a diploma. It is well established that when

---

Administrative Guide

Instructional Program

1. The state legislature has a responsibility to provide schooling for all children within the state at public expense.
2. The legal authority for defining curriculum resides with the legislature.
3. Courts typically do not intervene in curriculum matters because each state retains the authority to establish curriculum standards. They will intervene only if legitimate constitutional issues emerge.
4. Secular curricula are developed by school officials to avoid First Amendment religious conflicts involving church and state.
5. All schools should be held accountable for ensuring that the achievement gap between disadvantaged and minority students is close to that of their peers under NCLB.
6. Competency tests are supported by the courts where there is no evidence of discriminatory intent.
7. Students may be penalized academically for unexcused absences or truancy if state statute permits. However, policies in this area should be carefully drawn to ensure fairness.
8. Compulsory attendance policies are legally defensible. Parents are accountable and may be penalized for failure to comply with compulsory attendance laws.
9. Exceptions to compulsory attendance policies may be justified based on religious grounds.
10. Home schooling is generally permissible as long as minimal state requirements are met. However, parents do not have a fundamental right to educate their children at home.
11. Public schools generally are required to educate students who reside within their boundaries if the students establish a degree of permanency.
12. Reasonable tuition fees may be imposed on students who attend school outside of their legal residence.
13. Students who are emancipated (not under parental control) are not subject to compulsory attendance requirements.
14. School districts may establish mandatory immunization requirements under the state's police powers, even over parents' religious objections.

---

a student has met prescribed academic requirements for graduation, he or she must be awarded a diploma. However, a student may be denied participation in the graduation ceremony if his or her conduct significantly deviates from acceptable standards of behavior. There is no direct relationship between earning a diploma and participation in the graduation ceremony. The awarding of a diploma is a ministerial act that must be performed by school officials. There have been instances in which a student has been denied a diploma for nonacademic reasons, primarily misconduct. The courts have been very consistent in ruling that the student must be granted his or her diploma if all academic requirements have been met.

An early court case, which is most often cited, regarding withholding a diploma is *Valentine v. Independent School District of Casey.*[45] This case involved students who refused to wear the caps and gowns required for participation in the ceremony. These students indicated that the gowns smelled, even though they had been cleaned. They were denied diplomas based on their refusal to wear the prescribed dress. The court, in holding for the students, stated that these particular students had earned their diplomas based on their academic performance. Consequently, participation in the actual ceremony was not prerequisite to receiving a diploma. The court further stated

> that a diploma, therefore is *prima facie* evidence of educational worth, and is the goal of the matriculate. . . . The issuance of a diploma by the school board to a pupil who satisfactorily completes the prescribed course of study and who is otherwise qualified is mandatory, and, although such duty is not expressly enjoined upon the board by statute, it does arise by necessary and reasonable implication. . . . This Plaintiff . . . having complied with all the rules and regulations precedent to graduation, may not be denied her diploma by the arbitrary action of the school board subsequent to her being made the recipient of the honors of graduation.

CASE STUDIES

Immunization and Religion

Tom Banks is the principal of a large elementary school in an urban district. The school includes students from kindergarten through sixth grade. The district requires all students to be immunized before enrolling in school. Two kindergarten children, whose parents hold sincere and genuine religious beliefs against immunization, were not allowed to enroll. The parents, who were Jewish, based their belief on a passage from the Bible that they interpreted as forbidding immunization. The parents requested an exemption. Based on information Banks received from a local rabbi, nothing in Jewish teaching prohibits immunization for children.

Discussion Questions

1. Is an exemption warranted? Why or why not?
2. How should Banks respond to the parents' request?
3. The parents have sincere and genuine religious beliefs against immunization for their children. Should the school or district respect their beliefs?
4. What is the relative weight of parental rights versus the powers of the school or district?
5. If you were facing this issue, how would you respond?
6. How do you think the court would view this issue?
7. How should this issue be resolved?

Instructional Program and Questionable Curriculum Content

Gary Stone is the principal of a middle school in a steel mill town in the northeastern United States. The town is small, and parents are united and quite vocal regarding school issues. One issue that has emerged involves the school's use of a series of English and literature books that the parents consider Godless, profane, and inappropriate for use in the school. They have organized boycotts and public prayer meetings calling for the death of the principal and school board members who supported the series.

Discussion Questions

1. What rights do parents have to determine curriculum or course content?
2. How should Stone respond to these irate parents?
3. Should the superintendent and board intervene on behalf of the school? Why or why not?
4. If you were Gary Stone, how would you attempt to resolve this issue, given the very strong emotional position taken by parents?
5. If the court was called into this conflict, how do you think it would rule?
6. How would you assess the relative value of continuing the use of the series versus the disruptions that have been created by the parents?

Strict Internal Policy Regarding Internet Usage

Your school, a midsize high school located in a rural district, has a very strict policy that limits internal use of the Internet by teachers to school purposes only. You have discovered that several of your most talented tenured teachers have defied this policy and periodically employ the Internet for their personal use. Other teachers are aware of this situation.

Discussion Questions

1. How do you respond?
2. Do you ignore this situation because it is a minor occurrence?
3. These teachers are among your best teachers who consistently work late and go beyond the call of duty. Do you wish to alienate them on this issue? Why? Why not?
4. What is the most feasible solution?

Endnotes

1. *State v. Haworth,* 23 N.E. 946, 947 (Ind. 1890).
2. *Child Welfare Society of Flint v. Kennedy School District,* 189 N.W. 1002, 1004 (Mich. 10922).
3. *Prince v. Massachusetts,* 321 U.S. 158 (1944).
4. *State ex rel. Estes v. Egnor,* 443 S.E. 2d 193 (W. Va. 1994).
5. *State v. Hoyt,* 146 A. 170 (N.H. 1929).
6. *Pierce v. Society of Sisters,* 268 U.S. 510, 45 S.Ct. 571, 69 L. Ed. 1080 (1925).
7. *Bitting v. Lee,* 564 N.Y.S. 2d 791 (A.D. 3d Dept. 1990).
8. *Wisconsin v. Yoder,* 406 U.S. 205 (1972).
9. *Church of God v. Amarillo School District,* 511 F. Supp 613 (1981).
10. *New Jersey v. Massa,* 231 A. 2d 252 (N.J. Sup. Ct. 1967).
11. *Lawrence et al. v. S.C. State Board of Education,* 412 S.E. 2d 394 (1991).
12. *People v. Bennett,* 501 N.W. 2d 1067 (Mich. 1993).
13. *Null v. Board of Education,* 815 F. Supp. 937 (W. Va. 1993).
14. *Gregg v. Virginia,* 297, 2. E. 2d 799 (Va. 1982).
15. *Battles v. Anne Arundel County Board of Education,* 904 F. Supp. 471 (Md. 1995).
16. *Birst v. Sanstead,* 493 N.W. 2d 690 (N.D. 1992).
17. *Clonlara v. Runkel,* 722 F. Supp. 1442 (E.D. Mich. 1989).
18. U.S. Department of Education, Charter Schools Program, Title V, Part B of the ESEA, *Nonregulatory Guidance,* April 2011.
19. *Zelman v. Harris,* 536 U.S. 639 122 S.Ct. 2460; 153 L.Ed. 2d 604 (2002).
20. *Mason v. General Brown Cent. School District,* 851 F.2d 47 (2d Cir. 1988).
21. *Brown v. Stone,* 378 So. 2d 218 (Miss. 1980), cert. denied, 449 U.S. 887 (1980).
22. *Lewis v. Sobel,* 710 F. Supp. 506 (S.D.N.Y. 1989).
23. *Byrd v. Livingston Independent School District,* 67 F. Supp. 225 (E.D. Tex. 1987).
24. *Crowe v. MacFarland,* 515 N.Y.S. 2d 429 (A.D. 3d Dept. 1988).
25. *Harrison v. Sobol,* 705 F. Supp 870, 52 Ed. Law Rptr. 91 (S.D.N.Y. 1988).
26. *Citizens for a Responsible Curriculum, et al. v. Montgomery County Public Schools, et al.,* Not Reported in F. Supp. 2d, 2005 WL 1075634 (D. Md. 2005).
27. *Counts v. Cedarville School District,* 295 F. Supp. 2d 996 (W.D. Ark. 2003).
28. *Source:* Congress.Gov
29. 17 U.S.C. § 101 et seq. (1996).
30. Ibid.
31. *Sandlin v. Johnson,* 643 F.2d 1027 (4th Cir. 1981).
32. *Board of Curators of the University of Missouri v. Horowitz,* 435 U.S. 78, 985 S.Ct. 948 (1978).
33. Ibid.
34. *Slocus v. Holton Board of Education,* 429 N.W. 2d 607 (Mich. App. 1988).
35. *Minorities v. Board of Education of Phillipsburg,* N.J. Commissioner of Ed. (1972).
36. *Gutierrez v. School Dist.* R-1, 585 P. 2d 935 (Colo. App. 1978).
37. *Knight v. Board of Education of Tri-Pt. Comm. Unified School District,* 348 N.E. 2d 299 (Ill. 1976).
38. *Raymon v. Alvord Independent School District,* 639 F. 2d 257 (N. Tex. 1981).
39. *Dunn and McCollough v. Fairfield Community High School District No. 225,* 158 F.3d 962; U.S. App. (1998).
40. *Smith v. School City of Hobart et al. Defendants,* 811 F. Supp. 391, 80 Ed. Law Rept. 839 (Ind. 1993).
41. *Hogenson v. Williams,* 542 S.W. 2d 256 (Tex. App. 1976).
42. *State v. Mizner,* 50 Iowa 145 (1878) in 89 A.L.R. 2d 457.
43. *Melen v. McLaughlin,* 176 A. 297 (BT. 1935).
44. *State v. Vanderbilt,* 18 N.E. 26 (In. 1888).
45. *Valentine v. Independent School District of Casey,* 191 Iowa 1100, 183 N.W. 434 (1921).

Chapter 12

School Desegregation

DE JURE SEGREGATION

Historical Background

Racial segregation sanctioned by law persisted in the United States until the 1950s and 1960s, when the courts took a firm position that separation of children based on race was constitutionally impermissible. Although the Fourteenth Amendment, passed in 1868, provided for equal protection under the laws, the majority of U.S. schools remained segregated. Until the mid to late 1960s most school boards held the view that separate but equal was acceptable, when in reality separate facilities for minorities were not equal to those for nonminorities. This view of separate but equal was reinforced by the 1896 *Plessy v. Ferguson* case, in which the U.S. Supreme Court held that a Louisiana statute providing for "equal but separate" accommodations for the white and "colored" races on passenger trains was not illegal. Plessy, a black passenger, had entered a coach designated for whites and refused to leave. He challenged the constitutionality of the law after he was arrested, claiming that discrimination on the basis of color violated the Fourteenth Amendment. The U.S. Supreme Court affirmed that Louisiana's law was not discriminatory, thereby sanctioning the concept of separate but equal. Although this case did not involve schools, its decision established the legal basis for segregated public facilities that was embraced by most public schools.[1] In a related case in 1942, *Briggs v. Elliott*, which was one of the five cases combined into *Brown*, a district court decided that constitutional and statutory provisions of South Carolina requiring separate schools for the white and colored races did not, of themselves, violate the Fourteenth Amendment. However, the court ordered the school officials to proceed at once to furnish equal educational facilities and to report to the court within six months what action had been taken. After an appeal to this court had been docketed, the required report was filed in the district court.[2]

In 1954, in the landmark *Brown v. Board of Education* case, the principle of separate but equal was struck down by the U.S. Supreme Court, which stated:

> Segregation of white and colored children in public schools has a detrimental effect upon the colored children. The impact is greater when it has the sanction of the law; for the policy of separating the races is usually interpreted as denoting the inferiority of the Negro group. A sense of inferiority affects the motivation of a child to learn. Segregation with the sanction of the law therefore has a tendency to retard the educational and mental development of Negro children and to deprive them of some of the benefits they would receive in a racially integrated

school system. We conclude that in the field of education, the doctrine of separate but equal has no place. Separate educational facilities are inherently unequal. Therefore, we hold that plaintiffs and others similarly situated for whom this action has been brought are, by reason of the segregation complained of, deprived of the equal protection of the law guaranteed by the Fourteenth Amendment.

Brown v. Board of Education arose when black children in Kansas, South Carolina, Virginia, and Delaware challenged state statutes requiring racial segregation in public schools. Each group challenged the laws in federal district courts on the basis that these laws violated the equal protection clause of the Fourteenth Amendment. Subsequently, each court affirmed that as long as school facilities for blacks were equal to those for whites, segregation was permissible. The U.S. Supreme Court granted *certiorari.* Plaintiffs argued successfully that segregated public schools were not and could not be made equal because they are separated from white facilities. The court examined the effects of separated facilities on children enrolled in public schools and concluded that separate but equal facilities are inherently unequal. Where the state undertakes to provide education, it must make it available to all persons on an equal basis.

Although *Brown* was a landmark decision rendered by the Supreme Court banning *de jure* segregation, the decision did not provide a remedy for removing the vestiges of segregation in the public schools. It provided no guidance and mandated no time frame to achieve desegregated schools. Specific issues unaddressed in *Brown I* were not clearly addressed in *Brown II,* which was decided on May 17, 1954. The prevailing message was that the conversion from a dual to a unitary school system must occur with all deliberate speed. Because very little guidance was provided and virtually no direction regarding a specific timetable in which the conversion should occur, there was wide disparity among school districts across the country in complying with the Court's mandate. The High Court essentially returned the cases to the local federal courts to fashion remedies that would permit desegregation with all deliberate speed, because the Fourteenth Amendment applies only to the states. Consequently, the U.S. Supreme Court ruled on the day of the *Brown* ruling that segregation in the public schools of Washington, DC, was a denial of due process of law guaranteed by the Fifth Amendment.[3]

BROWN II IMPLEMENTATION

After its ruling in *Brown I,* the Supreme Court ruled in *Brown II* to ensure proper implementation of the ruling in *Brown I.* The Court remanded the cases to the federal district courts because of their close proximity to local school districts. It further held that school authorities should be delegated the primary responsibility for implementing its ruling, in good faith and with all deliberate speed. However, the court stated that each district could, in reviewing implementation plans, consider problems related to administration, transportation, personnel, and other issues that might arise during the transition to a nondiscriminatory school system. District courts were mandated to supervise the transition from dual segregated systems to unitary desegregated school systems.[4]

By the 1960s, the Supreme Court recognized that the test of good faith and all deliberate speed was not moving as rapidly as it had mandated. Consequently, the Supreme Court became more aggressive by ordering immediate desegregation of students and facilities in the *Rogers v. Paul* case in 1965 in which a desegregation plan adopted by the school system was a grade-a-year plan. Black students in high school did not have the range of courses offered at white schools because the plan started at the lower grades. The Court ruled that where equal course offerings are not available to black students in grades that have not yet been desegregated under a grade-a-year plan, the black students must be admitted immediately to the white school, which had a superior curriculum.[5] In the *Green v. County School Board of New Kent County,* the High Court held that the school board had a leading responsibility to develop a defensible system of determining admission to public schools on a nonracial basis. The Court placed the burden on school districts to develop realistic and workable plans to achieve desegregated schools.[6] The Supreme Court did not support "freedom of choice plans," which allowed students to choose their own school because they were not effective in achieving desegregation. The only exception involved a clear demonstration by a school district that proper results were achieved. By and large, freedom of choice plans were not deemed to be appropriate remedies to eliminate segregated facilities. In a leading case, the Supreme Court held that continued operation of segregated schools under a standard allowing all "deliberate speed" for desegregation was no longer constitutionally permissible. An obligation was placed on every school district in the United States to eliminate dual school systems immediately and thereafter to operate only unitary schools.[7]

The *Swann* case was a leading case in defining the scope of the duty to eliminate *de jure* segregation and a dual school system.[8] Chief Justice Warren Burger delivered the opinion of the Court:

> This case and those argued with it arose in states having a long history of maintaining two sets of schools in a single school system deliberately operated to carry out a governmental policy to separate pupils in schools solely on the basis of race. That was what *Brown v. Board of Education* was all about. These cases present us with the problem of defining in more precise terms than heretofore the scope of the duty of school authorities and district courts in implementing *Brown I* and the mandate to eliminate dual systems and establish unitary systems at once. Meanwhile district courts and courts of appeals have struggled in hundreds of cases with a multitude and variety of problems under this Court's general directive. Understandably, in an area of evolving remedies, those courts had to improvise and experiment without detailed or specific guidelines. This Court, in *Brown I*, appropriately dealt with the large constitutional principles; other federal courts had to grapple with the flinty, intractable realities of day-to-day implementation of those constitutional commands. Their efforts, of necessity, embraced a process of "trial and error," and our effort to formulate guidelines must take into account their experience.

Racial Balances or Racial Quotas

Our objective in dealing with the issues presented by these cases is to see that school authorities exclude no pupil of a racial minority from any school, directly or indirectly, on account of race; it does not and cannot embrace all the problems of racial prejudice, even when those problems contribute to disproportionate racial concentrations in some schools.

In this case, it is urged that the district court has imposed a racial balance requirement of 71 percent to 29 percent on individual schools.

We see therefore that the use made of mathematical ratios was no more than a starting point in the process of shaping a remedy, rather than an inflexible requirement. From that starting point the district court proceeded to frame a **decree** that was within its discretionary powers: an equitable remedy for the particular circumstances. As we said in Green, a school authority's remedial plan or a district court's remedial decree is to be judged by its effectiveness. Awareness of the racial composition of the whole school system is likely to be a useful starting point in shaping a remedy to correct past constitutional violations. In sum, the very limited use made of mathematical ratios was within the equitable remedial discretion of the district court.

For the reasons herein set forth, the judgment of the court of appeals is affirmed as to those parts in which it affirmed the judgment of the district court. The order of the district court, dated August 7, 1970, is also affirmed.

It is so ordered.

In this landmark case, the U.S. Supreme Court affirmed the broad discretionary powers of federal district courts to implement desegregation plans.

One-Race Schools

The record in this case reveals the familiar phenomenon that in metropolitan areas minority groups are often found concentrated in one part of the city. In some circumstances certain schools may remain all or largely of one race until new schools can be provided or neighborhood patterns change. Schools all or predominately of one race in a district of mixed population will require close scrutiny to determine that school assignments are not part of state-enforced segregation.

An optional majority-to-minority transfer provision has long been recognized as a useful part of every desegregation plan. Provision for optional transfer of those in the majority racial group of a particular school to other schools where they will be in the minority is an indispensable remedy for those students willing to transfer to other schools in order to lessen the impact on them of the state-imposed stigma of segregation. In order to be effective, such a transfer arrangement must grant the transferring student free transportation and space must be made available in the school to which he desires to move.* * * The court orders in this and the companion *Davis* case that these options be provided.[9]

Remedial Altering of Attendance Zones

The maps submitted in these cases graphically demonstrate that one of the principal tools employed by school planners and by courts to break up the dual school system has been a frank—and sometimes drastic—gerrymandering of school districts and attendance zones. An additional step was pairing, clustering, or grouping of schools with attendance assignments made deliberately to accomplish the transfer of Negro students out of formerly segregated Negro schools and transfer of white students to formerly all-Negro schools. More often than not, these zones are neither compact nor contiguous; indeed they may be on opposite ends of the city. As an interim corrective measure, this cannot be said to be beyond the broad remedial powers of a court.

We hold that the pairing and grouping of noncontiguous school zones is a permissible tool and such action is to be considered in light of the objectives sought. Judicial steps in shaping such zones going beyond combinations of contiguous areas should be examined in light of what is said in subdivisions (1), (2), and (3) of this opinion concerning the objectives to be sought. Maps do not tell the whole story since noncontiguous school zones may be more accessible to each other, in terms of critical travel time because of traffic patterns and good highways, than schools geographically closer together. Conditions in different localities will vary so widely that no rigid rules can be laid down to govern all situations.

Transportation of Students

The scope of permissible transportation of students as an implement of a remedial decree has never been defined by this court and by the very nature of the problem it cannot be defined with precision. No rigid guidelines as to student transportation can be given for application to the infinite variety of problems presented in thousands of situations. Bus transportation has been an integral part of the public education system for years, and was perhaps the single most important factor in the transition from the one-room schoolhouse to the consolidated school. Eighteen million of the nation's public school children, approximately 39 percent, were transported to their schools by bus in 1969–1970 in all parts of the country.

An objection to transportation of students may have validity when the time or distance of travel is so great as to either risk the health of the children or significantly impinge on the educational process.* * * It hardly needs stating that the limits on time of travel will vary with many factors, but probably with none more than the age of the students. The reconciliation of competing values in a desegregation case is, of course, a difficult task with many sensitive facets but fundamentally no more so than remedial measures courts of **equity** have traditionally employed.

The Court of Appeals, searching for a term to define the equitable remedial power of the district courts, used the term *reasonableness*. In *Green*, supra, this court used the term *feasible* and by implication *workable, effective,* and *realistic* in the mandate to develop "a plan that promises realistically to work, and . . . to work now." On the facts of this case, we are unable to conclude that the order of the district court is not reasonable, feasible, and workable. However, in seeking to define the scope of remedial power or the limits on remedial power of courts in an area as sensitive as we deal with here, words are poor instruments to convey the sense of basic fairness inherent in equity. Substance, not semantics, must govern, and we have sought to suggest the nature of limitations without frustrating the appropriate scope of equity.

It does not follow that the communities served by such systems will remain demographically stable, for in a growing, mobile society, few will do so. Neither school authorities nor district courts are constitutionally required to make year-by-year adjustments of the racial composition of student bodies once the affirmative duty to desegregate has been accomplished and racial discrimination through official action is eliminated from the system. This does not mean that federal courts are without power to deal with future problems; but in the absence of a showing that either the school authorities or some other agency of the state has deliberately attempted to fix or alter demographic patterns to affect the racial composition of the schools, further intervention by a district court should not be necessary.

For the reasons herein set forth, the judgment of the court of appeals is affirmed as to those parts in which it affirmed the judgment of the district court. The order of the district court, dated August 7, 1970, is also affirmed.

It is so ordered.

Intra District Segregation

ATTENDANCE ZONES.   School officials and courts alike viewed gerrymandering (altering) of school districts' attendance zones as a useful tool to alleviate segregated schools. Pairing, clustering, and grouping of noncontiguous school zones were considered by the courts to be permissible remedies to achieve desegregated schools. These initiatives were designed primarily to move black students out of segregated schools and to transfer white students to historically black schools. The objective of **zoning** plans was to create racially neutral student assignments. However, these plans were not always viewed as acceptable by the courts. For example, if they failed to counteract the continuing effects of past school segregation resulting from the discriminatory location of schools to achieve racial separation, they were not supported by the courts. School officials are not permitted to create racially identifiable schools by establishing school locations through drawing attendance zones. In cases where school officials created unlawfully segregated schools in one segment of the district, the Supreme Court held that the constitutional remedy was limited to that part of the district that produced *de jure* segregation. The courts may order reassignment of teachers and students to remove vestiges of segregation. They may also remedy the adverse effects of past discrimination by ordering segregated districts to implement and fund certain educational programs, such as remedial reading and writing, as well as staff development training for minority teachers.

A student assignment plan was not acceptable to the courts simply because it appeared to be neutral. Evidence was needed to ensure that the plan counteracted the continuing effects of past school segregation. An example of the court's position arose in an extended case involving intra district segregation in 1977 when the Kansas City, Missouri, School District (KCMSD), its school board, and a group of students who resided within the district sued the state and a number of suburban school districts in U.S. district court. They contended that the state had caused and perpetuated racial segregation in Kansas City schools. Following a realignment of parties to establish KCMSD as a nominal defendant, the district concluded that the state and KCMSD were both liable for an intra district constitutional violation. Both defendants were ordered to eliminate all vestiges of state-imposed segregation. Because the district's student population was approximately 70 percent black, the district court ordered a wide range of education plans that resulted in magnet schools for all high schools, middle schools, and some elementary schools that were designed to attract white students from the suburbs. The court's action was based on a finding that KCMSD students' achievement levels still lagged behind national averages in some grades. The state contested its court-ordered responsibility to assist in funding capital improvements for Kansas City Schools. It also contested district court orders requiring it to share the cost of teacher salary increases and quality education plans. The U.S. Court of Appeals for the Eighth Circuit affirmed the district court's orders.

On appeal by the state, the U.S. Supreme Court observed that the district's remedial plan had been based on a budget that exceeded the KCMSD's authority to tax. There also was no compelling evidence in the district court's records to support the theory that the continuing lack of academic achievement in the district resulted from past segregation. The High Court held that the district court had exceeded its authority by ordering construction of a superior school system to attract white students. Its mandate was to eliminate the racial identity of Kansas City Schools. The intra district remedy exceeded the intra district violation. The magnet concept could not be supported by the existence of white flight. The district court's orders for state contributions to salary increases, quality education programs, and capital improvement were thereby reversed.[10]

BUSING AND DESEGREGATION

Historically, the courts have viewed **busing** as an effective means of achieving desegregated schools. It has met opposition by parents and taxpayers who considered busing to be a threat to the neighborhood school concept, time-consuming for students, and an added expense on taxpayers. Parents and taxpayers advocated that money be expended on improving neighborhood schools rather on busing. Several states passed anti-busing legislation to prohibit the use of busing. Blacks involved with the *Swann* case sought injunctive and declaratory relief against the statute. North Carolina law prohibited busing children to achieve racial desegregation during the conclusion of the *Swann* case. A three-judge federal district court declared the anti-busing law unconstitutional. The state board of education and school officials sought review by the U.S. Supreme Court.

The Court held that busing based on race was a necessary and legitimate manner in which to carry desegregation. Although busing was not required by the district, a blatant prohibition against it conflicted with the obligation of school officials to implement an effective desegregation plan. The district court's decision was upheld.[11]

Federal courts were challenged when their rulings called for busing to remedy segregated schools. For example, California passed Proposition One, barring busing to achieve desegregation, and voters in Washington approved legislation restricting busing. However, in *Washington v. Seattle School District No. 1,* the U.S. Supreme Court upheld an appellate court's ruling that mandated the use of busing to achieve a racial balance in schools within the district. The Supreme Court held that an anti-busing initiative would result in impermissible racial classification of students for the purpose of achieving segregated schools.[12] However, in a California case, *Crawford v. Board of Education of Los Angeles,* the Supreme Court upheld a state constitutional amendment barring the use of mandatory busing except where there was evidence of Fourteenth Amendment violations. California was not required to adhere to more stringent standards than were mandated by the Fourteenth Amendment because, by state law, *de facto* and *de jure* segregation were prohibited.[13]

Involuntary busing emerged as a major issue during the height of the courts' efforts to achieve nonracially identifiable schools. Busing has been imposed by the courts and legislation as one solution to eliminate segregated schools. It has been viewed as an affirmative effort to correct inequities as a result of past discrimination. Consequently, many districts, as a component of their desegregation plan, implemented programs requiring students to be transported to schools outside their neighborhoods. The intent was to create equal educational opportunities for all children regardless of race, national origin, or socioeconomic background. Interestingly, busing was initiated almost as a one-way concept simply because black students were bused to allegedly better schools in white neighborhoods. Busing was opposed by many citizens, including parents of minority children. A number of minority parents felt that one-way busing supported discriminatory attitudes toward black children and that their children were bearing the burden by having to be transported great distances from their neighborhoods. Similar views were also expressed by nonminority parents whose children were transported from their neighborhoods.

A number of district courts concluded that allowing students to attend schools near where they lived would not effectively dismantle dual school systems. Busing was considered one viable measure used by the courts to achieve desegregated schools.

Busing for racial balance was implemented to affect class and status through reallocating educational services to minority students. This overarching goal of busing was to achieve racial balance, protect the civil rights of black students, and foster equality. Busing was based on the view that America has on society that excluded blacks. Consequently, the goal of providing equal opportunity to all students, particularly those who had been denied, was the desired goal. Equal opportunity suggests that black and white students have equal status and equal opportunity to succeed. Furthermore, success should not be a function of skin color.

FREE TRANSFER AND FREEDOM OF CHOICE PROGRAM

Although some courts had held that free transfers and freedom of choice plans were not effective ways to achieve desegregation, many districts adopted these plans as a means to avoid desegregation. The implementation of free transfers led to students being assigned to racially identifiable schools. School officials were not able to avoid court-ordered desegregation by permitting students to select any school they wished to attend within the district. A number of districts adopted minority-to-majority transfer plans in an effort to avoid desegregation orders. These plans permitted a student to transfer from a school where he or she was in the racial minority to a school where he or she would be in the racial majority. The plan had the effect of resegregating schools, as virtually no students sought transfers. Consequently, these plans were not supported by the courts.

As an example, a group of black children in Tennessee challenged the school board's desegregation plan in a federal district court.[14] The plan provided for rezoning of school districts without reference to race. However, the plan also provided that a student could request to transfer from the school to which he or she was reassigned back to his or her former segregated school where his or her race would be in the majority. The plan was approved by a federal district court and by the U.S. Court of Appeals, Sixth Circuit. The U.S. Supreme Court granted certiorari.

The black children contended that the district's transfer policy perpetuated racial segregation. They pointed out that although transfers were available to those who chose to attend school where their race was in the majority, there was no provision for a student to transfer to a school in which his or her race was in the minority, unless he or she could show "good cause" for the transfer. The Court agreed and struck the plan down as constitutionally insufficient to fulfill the *Brown* requirements of desegregation. The Court ruled that if the plan had provided for transfer provisions regardless of the students' race or of the schools' racial composition, it would have been constitutional. Classifications on the basis of race for transfer purposes between schools violate the Fourteenth Amendment. The Court invalidated the plan.

Freedom of choice plans met the same resistance by the courts when used to perpetuate segregated schools. Freedom of choice plans resulted in a sparse number of black students attending predominantly white schools and no whites attending predominantly black schools. The court held in *Green v. County School Board of New Kent* that

> The burden on a school board today is to come forward with a plan that promises realistically to work. . . . Now we do not hold that the Freedom of Choice Plan might of itself be unconstitutional . . . rather, all we decide today is that a plan utilizing freedom of choice is not an end in itself . . . If the means prove effective, it is acceptable, but if it fails to undo segregation, other means must be used.[15]
>
> The only school desegregation plan that meets constitutional standards is one that works.[16]

Prior to the passage of *Brown I* and *II,* the equal protection clause of the Fourteenth Amendment was subject to customs and traditions as determined by state legislative interpretation, irrespective of the impact of the law on a particular class of people.

De Jure Segregation

Because the equal protection clause essentially covers state action, it prohibits state-endorsed discrimination. Racial segregation derived from the enforcement of law is called *de jure* segregation and is illegal and unconstitutional and does not exist today. Conversely, segregation or racial imbalance created by housing patterns independent of government influence is called *de facto* segregation and is generally deemed permissible. The following elements are usually present in cases involving *de jure* segregation:

1. It has been initiated or supported by government action
2. With an intent or motive to discriminate, and
3. The action must result in creating or increasing segregation.[17]

Although unconstitutional *de jure* segregation may lack a precise definition based on factors that surround each case, it has consistently been held unconstitutional by the courts. Although the Supreme Court has come under enormous criticism, it has been fairly consistent in approving the *de jure–de facto* distinction in its rulings involving segregated facilities.

> What is or is not a segregated school will necessarily depend on the facts of each particular case. In addition to the . . . composition of a school's student body, other factors such as the racial and ethnic composition of faculty and staff and the community and administration's attitudes toward the school must be taken into consideration.[18]

De Facto Segregation

De facto segregation is present when a substantial number of students enrolled in a school represent a racial or ethnic minority. This situation developed through no action taken by the school district designed to encourage or require it. However, the courts, and especially *Brown,* mandate that corrective actions be taken in instances where school officials gerrymander school attendance zones to create zones with large concentrations of black students assigned to historically black schools within the district. These actions represent deliberate efforts to create segregated schools by governmental action. Although often referred to as *de facto* segregation, it is in reality a form of covert *de jure* segregation.

An example of false *de facto* segregation emerged in New Rochelle, New York. The board of education realigned several school attendance boundaries and permitted transfers only of white students who lived within the boundaries of the school in question. Approximately 90 percent of the students attending the school were black. According to the Second Circuit Court of Appeals, the primary objective of the school redistricting was to produce a substantially segregated school. Such conduct clearly violated the Fourteenth Amendment and the *Brown* holding, and it was deemed to be *de jure* segregation.[19]

A very different case arose in Connecticut when a suit was filed on behalf of public school children alleging denial of equal educational opportunities based on racial and ethnic segregation. The facts suggested that such segregation was *de facto* rather than *de jure* (based on law). Consequently, the defense requested that the case be dismissed. Plaintiffs asserted that their rights under the state constitution were violated because it provided a right to a free public elementary and secondary education as well as a right to protection from segregation. The Supreme Court of Connecticut held for the plaintiffs. The court stated:

> We direct the legislature and the executive branch to place the search for appropriate remedial measures at the top of their respective agenda. . . . We are confident that with energy and good will, appropriate remedies can be found and implemented in time to make a difference before another generation of children suffers the consequences of a segregated public school education.[20]

Nonetheless, the court mandated a remedy to segregation in this case whether it was based on *de facto* or *de jure* segregation.

It is important to understand that school districts generally are not required to take corrective action in cases where racial imbalances have developed within the schools of the district as a result of housing patterns and the uniform application of school zoning and student transfer policies. However, it also does not mean that the courts will support unequal facilities, programs, and staffs in predominantly black schools. These deficiencies will necessitate responsive corrective action to ensure equality of educational opportunity. The posture of the courts regarding de facto segregation has been to correct educational inequalities without requiring racial mixing.

Faculty Desegregation

The issue involving faculty desegregation did not surface until the mid to late 1960s. Teacher race had not been challenged during the initial desegregation cases. Plans involving desegregation of faculty had not been required by the courts as they addressed plans involving desegregation of students. However, two black students filed suit in a federal district court to enforce pupil and teacher desegregation in an Arkansas school district's high schools.[21] The district court refused to grant the order by holding that the students had no standing to challenge desegregation among faculty. The U.S. Court of Appeals, Eighth Circuit, affirmed. During the proceedings, one of the students had graduated and the other had reached the twelfth grade. Two other black high school students petitioned the U.S. Supreme Court to be added as plaintiffs in the suit. It further held that blacks could not be assigned exclusively to black high schools. The court ruled that the students did in fact have legal standing to challenge faculty segregation in the district because it denied them equal educational opportunities. The case was remanded to courts of appeal for further deliberations.

Because desegregation plans involving faculty were not addressed during the height of school desegregation plans, progress came very slowly in achieving a desegregated faculty. Added to this development was the fact that no test was to be applied to achieve a racially mixed faculty. The absence of a test created difficulties for the courts to fashion remedies without creating untimely delays. However, one tangible remedy was ordered by a lower court and upheld by the U.S. Supreme Court. The plan established a goal for each school within the district that called for assigning approximately the same ratio of black and white teachers as the ratio existing in the school district as a whole.[22]

The following year this concept was adopted by the Fifth Circuit Court of Appeals as a guide for integrating faculty throughout the circuit.[23] Some district courts had accepted a slow **integration** of black and white faculty based on the view of boards of education that a rapid pace would result in white flight among their faculties. The court of appeals was not very sympathetic to this view and held that faculty resistance cannot form the basis for not moving ahead to achieve a unitary school system.

A problem arose in integrating faculty with respect to tenure status, especially in cases where a disproportionate number of black faculty were not retained. Courts scrutinized cases where large reductions occurred among black faculty based on a long history of racial discrimination and resistance among districts to move aggressively with the implementation of desegregation plans. Consequently, school boards were required to justify their action with clear evidence when there was an inference of discrimination. School districts were required to formulate nonracial objective criteria for retention and employment of teachers and to apply them equally to all teachers.

Student Classifications and Desegregated Public Schools

Public schools in the United States appear to be gradually resegregating. Segregated schools produce racial isolation for black students and Latino students who typically attend schools that are separate and unequal. These schools are poorly funded and enroll many students from low socioeconomic backgrounds. According to The Civil Rights Project,[24] the following ten states have the lowest percentage of black students attending schools with white students: New York, Illinois, Michigan, California, Maryland, New Jersey, Mississippi, Louisiana, Texas, and Wisconsin.

In terms of black students attending highly segregated schools (90 to 100 percent minority students), the list is almost identical: New York, Illinois, Michigan, Maryland, New Jersey, Pennsylvania, Alabama, Wisconsin, and Mississippi. With respect to Latino students' exposure to white students, the ten most segregated systems are located in New York, California, Texas, New Mexico, New Jersey, Illinois, Rhode Island, Arizona, Florida, and Maryland. The states with the highest percentages of Latino students attending highly segregated schools (90 to 100 percent minority) are New York, Texas, California, Illinois, New Jersey, Arizona, Rhode Island, Florida, New Mexico, and Maryland. Critics of segregated schools suggested that the lack of continual court supervision has resulted in increased racial isolation of minority students. In addition, the Rehnquist Court held that policies that consider race in creating integrated schools were suspected of requiring districts to demonstrate a compelling reason to prove that their goals could not be achieved without a consideration of race. The net effect of this conclusion by the Rehnquist Court resulted in lower courts demonstrating apprehension in supporting school district policies calling for voluntary desegregation.

In solidifying the Rehnquist position, a major ruling issued by the U.S. Supreme Court in a 5–4 decision in *Parents Involved in Community Schools v. Seattle School District No. 1*[25] and *Meredith v. Jefferson County Board of Education*[26] affirmed the importance of racial diversity but limited options that school districts may choose.

Latino Students and Racial Diversity

Challenges faced by Latino students can be traced to classification of students based on language. Public schools in the United States consist of many different minorities, some of whom experience language barriers. This point was emphasized in an early case, *Lau et al. v. Nichols,* when the U.S. Supreme Court held that San Francisco schools failed to make provisions for non-English-speaking students.[27] This prohibition violated the equal protection clause of the Fourteenth Amendment as well as Title VI based on the absences of appropriate remedial English instruction. Thus, students who are deprived of English instruction are denied an opportunity for meaningful education.

Latino students who attend public schools face language barriers that impede their educational progress. Roughly one in every five students in the United States is Latino, which suggests that public schools must take appropriate steps to address inequities in educational opportunity based on language barriers. In a development regarding equal education opportunity, parents of students who filed a suit in *Flores v. Arizona* received a setback when the U.S. Supreme Court decided in a 5–4 decision to remand the case to the Ninth Circuit Court of Appeals with instruction to determine whether the state of Arizona was in compliance with Civil Rights law by improving English learners programs and students' overall education.[28] The majority opinion written by Justice Samuel Alito questioned the need for schools and states to continue to remain under the supervision and direction of courts. The High Court considered that the *Flores* case was initially based on the Equal Opportunities Act of 1974, which required states to take appropriate steps to assist students attempting to master skills in English to keep pace with their English-speaking classmates. The High Court, however, emphasized that it is left to the states to determine how they will meet this requirement.

Critics of the *Flores* ruling suggest that this decision effectively narrows the civil rights of Latino students. This ruling is significant considering the fact that Latinos represent the largest minority group in America. Added to the growth in population is the view that schools have done very little to provide a desegregated educational experience for Latino students. In addition, many non-English-speaking students are tested under No Child Left Behind (NCLB) in English, which they have not mastered, thereby producing invalid and unreliable assessment of their academic achievement. These students tend to perform poorly in mathematics and reading. Their scores on invalid tests are included in adequate yearly progress reports, resulting in these students not meeting AYP goals.

NO CHILD LEFT BEHIND AND CIVIL RIGHTS

Because the passage of NCLB reauthorized and amended the Elementary and Secondary School Act of 1965 (ESEA), there is a view that it is an integral component of the U.S. Civil Rights Movement, which focuses on equal educational opportunity for all children irrespective of race or socioeconomic status. However, the statute focused specifically on disadvantaged, high-poverty, high-minority students as well as students with disabilities. The statute directs states to define major racial and ethnic subgroups that traditionally have been underserved and focus their attention on improving academic achievement of these groups. There is disagreement regarding whether the act advances civil rights or whether it creates greater disadvantages for the students to whom the act is directed. The group that advocates for NCLB views it is as a measure that mandates school officials to focus their efforts on students who have traditionally been neglected. Some teachers' unions and civil rights groups who oppose the act cite school choice, high stakes testing, and punitive sanctions as measures that place students farther behind. In the past, civil rights advocates pursued equal educational opportunity for minority students. They demanded effective teachers, good facilities, and relevant educational programs. NCLB focuses on closing the achievement gap, improving student achievement, and changing the culture of schools in America. The effectiveness of this act will be determined by the extent to which it attains its goal of having every child meet state-defined standards by the end of the 2013–14 school year.

Seeking Unitary Status

After years of fashioning remedies for segregated schools, school districts across the country are currently filing for unitary status, in which school officials are claiming that good faith efforts have been initiated to achieve desegregated schools; therefore, they should be relieved of court supervision. Desegregation orders have been lifted in Denver, Colorado; Buffalo, New York; Dallas and Austin, Texas; Indianapolis, Indiana; Savannah, Georgia; and Nashville, Tennessee. Many more districts are currently filing for unitary status. Two U.S. Supreme Court decisions during the 1990s provided some direction in addressing judicial supervision.

In *Board of Education of Oklahoma City Public Schools v. Dowell* in 1972, a federal district court issued an injunction mandating a school desegregation plan for Oklahoma City. In 1977, the court found that the district had achieved unitary status. Consequently, an order was issued by the court terminating the case. In 1984, there was an increase in young black students that necessitated them being bused farther away. Based on this development, the board adopted the Student Reassignment Plan (SRP), which assigned students in grades K through four to their neighborhood schools and continued busing for grades five through twelve. Parents who initiated the desegregation suit filed a motion requesting that the case be reopened because SRP was a return to segregation. The federal district court refused to reopen the case and held that the district was unitary and would not be relitigated. Parents appealed to the Tenth Circuit Court of Appeals, which held that the court's 1977 finding was binding but did not mean that the 1972 injunction should necessarily be lifted. The case was remanded to determine whether the injunction should be lifted. The trial court, on remand, found that the SRP did not have a discriminatory intent and ordered that the injunction be lifted. The case was again appealed to the U.S. Court of Appeals, which reversed the lower court's decision. The school district petitioned the U.S. Supreme Court for a review.

The High Court held that the 1977 order did not dissolve the desegregation decree. Furthermore, the district court's finding that the district was unitary was too ambiguous to prevent parents from challenging the later actions by the board. The Court emphasized that supervision of the district by federal courts was intended to serve as a temporary remedy to past discrimination. The U.S. Supreme Court remanded the case to the trial court to determine whether the district had shown sufficient compliance with constitutional requirements when it adopted the SRP. The trial court was to determine whether the district had acted in good faith to eliminate vestiges of past discrimination—to the extent possible.[29] In essence, the U.S. Supreme

Court held that the federal court's regulatory control over an unlawful segregated district is limited to the necessary time needed to remedy vestiges of past discrimination.

In another case involving unitary status, *Freeman v. Pitts,* the DeKalb County, Georgia, school system was cited for unlawful segregated schools in 1969 and placed under supervision by the court. The district implemented a variety of measures to achieve unitary status, then requested that judicial control be removed. A federal district court held that unitary status had been achieved to the extent practicable regarding student assignments, transportation, physical facilities, and extracurricular activities. However, unitary status had not been achieved regarding faculty assignments and resource allocation. The district court relinquished control in the four areas found to be unitary but retained control of the remaining two areas. On appeal, the U.S. Court of Appeals rejected the incremental approach and held that unitary status in some areas could not lead to relinquished judicial control until all areas under review were unitary. On certiorari, the U.S. Supreme Court reversed the court of appeals decision in holding that the incremental approach was constitutional. The Court ordered no further remedy in areas found to be unitary, thus allowing the district to focus on areas in need of correction.[30] The implication of this case is that the federal district court, which supervises court-ordered desegregation, has the latitude to order incremental withdrawal of its supervision and control.

The U.S. Court of Appeals for the Tenth Circuit in *Brown v. Board of Education of Topeka* (*Brown III*) expressed its view of unitariness and the standards for determining whether it has been achieved. It stated that the court must assess what a school district has or has not done in good faith to meet its obligation to desegregate. Once it has been established that the district is intentionally segregated, the burden of proof rests with the district to demonstrate that it has eliminated all vestiges of segregation to the fullest extent possible. Racially identifiable schools must first be present to satisfy the court that segregation exists, which commonly is demonstrated by the assignment of students to one-race schools. However, if one-race schools are present due to no fault of the district but based on shifts in demographics beyond the control of the district, they are not necessarily illegal as long as *de jure* segregation is not present. In such cases, the district is not held accountable. If a district can demonstrate effective results in moving from a segregated district to a desegregated district, it generally will meet the approval of the courts. In cases where there is a substantial record of evidence demonstrating that school officials have acted in good faith to achieve a desegregated school system, the courts are inclined to grant the request. The burden of proof that unitary status has been achieved rests with the school district. Absent proof of a good-faith effort and effective results, many districts have not been relieved of court supervision.

A case challenging removal of court supervision arose in Alabama. The Talladega County school district was under federal court-ordered supervision from 1967 to 1985. A group of black parents contended that after dismissal of the original lawsuit, the district engaged in action that had a disparate impact on black students attending schools in the district. The group alleged that the district closed an all-black school, constructed a new school in the white community, allowed white students to transfer to other public school systems, and ignored the black parents' concerns at school board meetings. Parents filed suit against the school district in the U.S. District Court for the Northern District of Alabama, claiming violations of the Fourteenth Amendment, Title VI of the Civil Rights Act of 1964, state laws such as the Open Meeting Act, and a breach of contract of the 1985 stipulation of settlement. When the court dismissed the case, the parents appealed.

The U.S. Court of Appeals, Eleventh Circuit, ruled that the district court had properly dismissed the constitutional and Title VI complaints based on the failure of the parents to prove that the board's action had been motivated by racial discrimination. The rationale provided by the board for closing and constructing new facilities was supported by substantial evidence that its actions met legitimate educational goals. Evidence was insufficient to support the claim that the board could have taken action against white students who transferred to schools outside the district. The district court had properly dismissed the breach of contract and state law claims, but its decision stated no reason for ruling against the parents regarding their complaint that the board had prohibited recordings of its public meetings. That portion of the district court's decision was vacated, and the remainder was affirmed.[31]

Summary of Challenges Involving School Desegregation

1. In 2007, black parents challenged a school rezoning plan in Tuscaloosa, Alabama. This plan resulted in all but a handful of the hundreds of students required to move in the fall being black—with many sent to virtually all-black, low-performing schools.

2. In *Comfort v. Lynn School Committee*, the U.S. Court of Appeals for the First Circuit held that a Massachusetts school district's use of race as a factor in its student assignment plan violated the Fourteenth Amendment's Equal Protection Clause.[32]

3. A federal district court in Wisconsin ruled that a school district, which admittedly violated a white student's equal protection rights by denying the student's transfer request, was not liable because the violation occurred as a result of the school district complying with a state law prohibiting it from allowing transfers that increase racial imbalance.[33]

4. An African American teacher in Louisville, Kentucky, has sued the Jefferson County public school district in federal court, challenging the teacher assignment policy as discriminatory. Lorraine D. Hill alleges she was denied interviews and a transfer to elementary schools that were close to her home because they already had too many black teachers. She is contesting the district's use of a longstanding ratio requiring that the percentage of black teachers within a school remain within five percent of the overall average for elementary, middle, or high schools.[34]

5. The U.S. Supreme Court held that a school district having implemented a student reassignment plan to comply with a court order did not have an affirmative duty to revise remedial efforts annually when demographic shifts resulted in some schools becoming more than 50 percent minority.[35]

Administrative Guide

De Jure Segregation

1. *De jure* segregation is illegal and will not be supported by the courts.

2. Involuntary segregated schools deny black students equal protection under the law.

3. "Separate but equal" schools for blacks and whites are inherently unequal.

4. Lack of funds cannot be used by school districts as a basis for failure to create a desegregated school district.

5. *Brown* was a pivotal case in establishing the civil rights of black Americans not only in education but also in public transportation and housing.

6. Court-ordered quota systems and busing have not been totally effective in achieving desegregated schools and may have precipitated white flight.

7. During the late twentieth and early twenty-first centuries, the discernible trend has been toward resegregated schools where many blacks are attending inferior inner city schools whereas whites attend more affluent suburban schools.

8. School authorities should be committed to providing an equal educational opportunity for black and white students even in the absence of court-ordered desegregation rulings. Pairing and clustering are allowable as means of achieving desegregation in an effort to remove vestiges of segregated schools.

9. Busing, although not a popular option among parents and citizens, was one remedy by which school officials could affirm desegregated schools.

10. Court supervision may be lifted in part or in whole where a school district can show that it has acted in good faith to remedy past discrimination in its schools.

11. Once unitary status has been achieved by a school district and no deliberate action has been taken to recreate segregated schools, the school district *is not required to seek remedies* in situations involving segregation *that may evolve* that are beyond the district's control.

12. Race may be used as a factor in university admissions decisions.

13. Point systems or quotas are disallowed in university admissions decisions and violate the Fourteenth Amendment's equal protection clause.

CASE STUDIES

Desegregation—An End to Busing

An affluent Southern school district was subject to a court-ordered desegregation plan involving busing. After receiving the court order recognizing that the district had achieved unitary status, the district decided to discontinue elementary school busing and move toward a neighborhood plan that would bus sixth-graders to a middle school. Parents and citizens challenged the end of elementary school busing, alleging that it would re-create segregated schools.

Discussion Questions

1. Do parents and citizens have a valid claim?
2. Are the district's actions designed to create segregated schools?
3. Does the district have a right to discontinue elementary school busing and implement a neighborhood plan after it has achieved unitary status?
4. Did the district use its new status to engage in *de jure* segregation? Why or why not?
5. How do you think the court would rule in this case? Provide a rationale for your response.
6. What are the administrative implications of this case?

Desegregation and Teacher Transfer

A board of education in an urban school district of 160,000 students adopted a teacher-transfer policy in each of its schools to establish a racial composition that was within 10 percent of the racial composition of the district population as a whole. This policy was not mandated by the court. Essentially, this policy restricted voluntary transfer of black and white teachers to other schools within the district but also required reassignment of other teachers. The policy was challenged by the teachers' association, which claimed a violation of teachers' Fourteenth Amendment rights.

Discussion Questions

1. Does the teachers' association have a valid claim? Why or why not?
2. Is the district justified in the formulation of this transfer policy? Why or why not?
3. Can teachers make a valid claim of disparate impact in this case? Why or why not?
4. Should the policy be race neutral? Why or why not?
5. Do you feel that such a policy is arbitrary and capricious? Why or why not?
6. How would the court likely view this policy?
7. What are the administrative implications?

Endnotes

1. *Plessy v. Ferguson,* 163 U.S. 537 (1891).
2. *Briggs v. Elliott*, 342 U.S. 350 (1952).
3. *Brown v. Board of Education,* 349 U.S. 294, 75 S. Ct. 753 (1955) (*Brown I*). 753, 99 L. Ed. 1083 (1955) (*Brown II*). *Brown v. Board of Education,* 892 F.2d 851 (10th Cir. 1989) (*Brown III*).
4. Ibid.
5. *Rogers v. Paul,* 382 U.S. 198 (1965).
6. *Green v. County School Board of New Kent,* 391 U.S. 430 439-40 (1968).
7. *Alexander v. Holmes County Board of Education,* 396 U.S. 1218, 90 S. Ct. 14 (1969).
8. *Swann v. Charlotte Mecklenburg Board of Education,* 402 U.S. 1, 91 S. Ct. 1267, 28 L. Ed. 2d 554 (1970).
9. *Davis v. County School Board of Prince Edward County,* 103 F. Supp. 337 (1952).
10. *Missouri v. Jenkins,* 115 S. Ct. 2038, 132 L.Ed. 2d 63 (1995) (*Jenkins III*).
11. *North Carolina State Board of Education v. Swann,* 402 U.S. 43, 91 S. Ct. 1284 2d L. Ed. 2d 586 (1971).
12. *Washington v. Seattle School District No. 1,* 458 U.S. 457; 102 S. Ct. 3187; 73 L. Ed. 2d 896 (1982).
13. *Crawford v. Board of Education of Los Angeles,* 458 U.S. 457; 102 S. Ct. 3187; 73 L. Ed. 2d 896 (1982).

14. *Goss v. Board of Education,* 373 U.S. 683, *3 S. Ct. 1405, 10 L. Ed. 2d 632 (1963).

15. *Green v. County School Board of New Kent,* op. cit.

16. *United States v. Jefferson County Board of Education,* 372 F.2d 836, 847 (5th Cir. 1966).

17. *Alexander v. Youngstown Board of Education,* 675 F. 2d 787, 791 (6th Cir. 1982).

18. *Keyes v. School District No. 1,* 413 U.S. 189, 196 (1973).

19. *Taylor v. Board of Education of City School District of New Rochelle,* 294 F.2d 36 (2nd Cir. 1961), cert. den., 368 U.S. 940, 82 S. Ct. 382, 7 L. Ed. 2d 339 (1961).

20. *Sheff v. O'Neill,* 238 Conn. 1, 678 A.2d 1267 (1996).

21. *Rogers v. Paul,* 382 U.S. 198 (1965).

22. *United States v. Montgomery County Board of Education,* 395 U.S. 225, 89 S. Ct. 1670; 23 L. Ed. 2d 263 (1969).

23. *Singleton v. Jackson Municipal Separate School District,* 419 F.2d 1211 (5th Cir. 1970), cert. den., 396 U.S. 1032, 90 S. Ct. 612, 24 L. Ed. 2d 530 (1970).

24. The Civil Rights Project, University of California at Los Angeles. Retrieved October 1, 2010, from civilrightsproject.ucla.edu.

25. *Parents Involved in Community Schools v. Seattle School District No. 1,* 551 U.S. 701 (2007).

26. *Meredith v. Jefferson County Board of Education,* 127 S. Ct. 2738 (2007).

27. *Lau et al. v. Nichols,* 414 U.S. 563 94 S. Ct. 786; 39 L. Ed. 2d 1; 1974 U.S. LEXIS 15.

28. *Flores v. Arizona,* 405 F. Supp. 2d 1112 (D.Ariz. 2005).

29. *Board of Oklahoma City Public Schools v. Dowell,* 498 U.S. 237, 111 S. Ct. 630, 112 L. Ed. 2d 715 (1991).

30. *Freeman v. Pitts,* 503 U.S. 467, 112 S. Ct. 1430, 118 L. Ed. 2d 108 (1992).

31. *Elston v. Talladega County Board of Education,* 997 F.2d 1394 (11th Cir. 1993).

32. *Comfort v. Lynn School Committee,* No. 03-2415, 418 F.3d 1, 27–29 (CA1 2005).

33. *N.N. v. Madison Metropolitan Sch. Dist.,* No. 08-581 (W.D. Wis. Nov. 24, 2009).

34. *Hill vs. Jefferson County Public Schools et al.* (Undecided)

35. *Pasadena City Board of Education v. Spangler,* 427 U.S. 424 (1976).

Chapter 13

Public School Finance

The state has the inherent power to levy taxes on its citizens to support public education. The U.S. Constitution imposes no legal obligation on the federal government to operate a public education system. In fact, no such obligation is placed on state government by the U.S. Constitution; however, this right is reserved to the states. State support of public education is a voluntary activity, by virtue of the Tenth Amendment, which states that "the powers not delegated to the United States by the Constitution, nor prohibited by it to the states, are reserved to the states respectively or to the people."

Because powers regarding education are not expressly delegated to the federal government but rather reserved to the states, it becomes a function of the state to establish, support, and maintain public schools. State constitutions generally authorize the legislature to provide for a public education system. State legislatures are also empowered to levy taxes and to develop a systematic method of distributing school funds. However, the federal government does support various education initiatives through categorical grants, block grants, and various other funding initiatives. The authority to provide assistance to education by the federal government was handed down by Congress when it decided that Article I, Section 8, the General Welfare Clause, provided Congress the power to tax and spend for activities not expressly mentioned in the Constitution.[1] Consequently, the General Welfare Clause allows the federal government to offer an array of federal programs that support elementary and secondary schools in the United States. In so doing, the federal government exercises significant influence over public education through certain requirements that school districts meet to qualify and receive federal funds.

TAXATION FOR PUBLIC SCHOOLS

State and local taxes account for over 90 percent of educational expenditures. There appears to be a move toward increased state control of education funding. Sales taxes and income taxes are primary sources of state funding whereas property tax represents the most abundant source at the local level. Property taxes are generally characterized as real property or personal property and contribute the major source of funding for public schools. Property taxes typically are calculated in mills. For example, 1 mill equals 1/10 of one cent; therefore, if property were assessed at $200,000 and the state collected 10 mills, then the owner would pay $2,000 in property tax. There is no total agreement on the use of property tax as a major source of funding for public schools. Critics of property tax suggest that the state should take a more active role in funding public schools because education, by virtue of the Tenth Amendment, is a jurisdiction of the state. Those who support property tax view low volatility of property tax as an advantage, particularly when there is a significant spending decline in the economy. Those who oppose property tax cite the disparity that it creates between more affluent districts and less affluent districts, where property values are high in the former and low in the latter. Obviously, no tax levied is without criticism.

The three basic types of taxes are progressive, regressive, and proportional. With progressive tax, the rate of tax increases as the base increases. Consequently, a larger percentage of income is taken as taxpayer income increases. Personal income and property tax are examples of progressive tax. In regressive taxes, tax rates decrease when the tax base increases, with higher income residents paying a smaller percentage than lower income residents. Gasoline and cigarette taxes are examples of regressive taxation. In proportional or flat tax, the rate remains the same irrespective of income or wealth. Sales tax and estate wealth are examples of proportional tax. The debate over tax and funding formulas likely will continue and become a primary source of ongoing litigation. The exception is Hawaii. Hawaii is the only state with a single, statewide school district. Consequently, no property is levied for education, and no prescribed formula is used to fund public schools. State support for public schools is derived from the general fund.

TAX RATE

When a local district formulates its budget based on anticipated needs of the district, it may be necessary to levy taxes to generate needed funds. Tax rates generally are based on estimated revenue needed by the district to meet its financial needs. Estimated revenue projections must be realistic, made in good faith, and based on defensible grounds. Local school districts may not use their taxing authority with the express purpose of creating a surplus fund. It is not unusual for taxpayers to challenge the validity of a tax levy for local schools based on a claim that the tax levy is excessive and extends beyond the needs of the district.

For example, in a very early case, the Supreme Court of Illinois held that it was unconstitutional for a school district to levy taxes with the purpose of accumulating a fund to be used at some point in the future to construct a school building.[2] Because revenue projections are not absolutely precise, other state courts have permitted districts to levy taxes that may result in small surpluses should all taxes be collected. The courts have consistently held that a legislative act will not be deemed invalid unless it clearly violates basic provisions of the constitution.

The courts have consistently held that school districts are agents of the state created by the legislature to provide educational opportunities for students within the state, based on express state constitutional mandates. School districts do not possess broad powers but rather are subject only to the powers delegated to them by the legislature.

In an early case, *Pironne v. City of Boston,* a state court held that local school districts had no inherent power to levy taxes, which applied to the kind of taxes as well as the rate of taxes.[3] It held further that the power to tax is a special one that must be expressly conferred on a subordinate governmental agency by the legislature. The legislature does have the power to delegate taxing authority to local school districts if it chooses, as long as state constitutional tax limitations are met.[4] Taxing authority cannot be delegated to subordinate bodies unless clear limitations or restrictions are placed on the delegated power.

The courts have supported this delegated power in cases where the purpose of the tax is clearly expressed and the tax rate is specified. Because local school districts are agents of the state, school taxes are viewed as state taxes rather than local taxes. Therefore, local school districts may be required to meet certain standards with respect to establishing and maintaining schools. School districts may also be required to issue bonds to construct school buildings as long as the levied tax is used specifically for the purpose for which it was intended.

EQUITY FUNDING IN EDUCATION

Equity may be defined differently among state lawmakers. However, it typically means that per-pupil expenditures are equally distributed throughout a local school district. Because property tax is most frequently used to support local education, there are disparities throughout a state based on the level of local revenue generated by property tax. Most states attempt to generate funding formulas that subsidize local effort to compensate for disparities among wealthy and less wealthy districts. Typically, the equity formula includes state aid minus local effort as a means of creating parity in funding schools throughout the state. Some states refer to such formulas as power equalization formulas or district equalization formulas. The theory behind this approach is grounded in the need to provide equal educational opportunities for all students irrespective of socioeconomic status. Equal educational opportunity occurs when all school districts within a state have equal access to resources that are necessary to provide an education up to a prescribed level. Equity formulas by definition are input based and have been the target of legal challenges over several decades based on **funding disparities**.

LEGAL CHALLENGES TO SCHOOL FUNDING

Public School Finance programs have been challenged under federal and state constitutions. These challenges have centered around claims that tax systems designed to generate school revenue are unfair and do not apply equally to all taxpayers. Other challenges involve assertions by parents that their children are denied the benefits of an equal educational opportunity based on disparities in tax revenue and distribution of revenue among school districts within the state. Challenges by parents most frequently are based on the equal protection clause of the Fourteenth Amendment to the U.S. Constitution as well as the equal protection provisions found in state constitutions. Most states have adopted minimum foundation programs or basic educational programs with average daily attendance or average daily membership formulas that distribute funds on a per-pupil basis based on the district's wealth and its ability to pay. Wealth is not distributed equally among school districts. Some districts are located in wealthy communities, and others are located in poor communities. The funding gap between wealthy districts and poor districts creates disparities that affect per-pupil expenditures. Hawaii is the only state in the union that provides full state funding. It also has a statewide system of education, which means that schools are funded entirely from state taxes.

Most of the legal challenges regarding public school funding are addressed through state courts. Litigation most often involves issues surrounding the methods of regulating and distributing funds to support education. In instances where local school districts or local governments are authorized to provide funding to support public schools, challenges to local entities generally involve a claim that they are not operating within the powers granted to them by the legislature or issues regarding the constitutional rights of students with respect to equity of funding decisions.

Very few remedies are available for taxpayers who succeed in their claims that a tax law is invalid, particularly when it is in conflict with a state or the federal constitution. Generally speaking, if an illegal tax was paid without coercion by a citizen, the underlying presumption by the courts is that the taxpayer knew that the tax was invalid. Therefore, no recovery is permitted. The tax, if illegal, may be enjoined by the courts, thus preventing collection of such taxes.

Numerous legal challenges have surfaced since the early 1970s regarding state finance systems for education. Many of these challenges have been brought by citizens representing poor school districts who challenged funding formulas based on inequities. In a number of these cases, state courts have ruled that state funding systems were unconstitutional, particularly in cases where inequalities in spending were found between wealthy and poor districts. Challenges have also surfaced based on issues involving adequacy of education. Plaintiffs in these cases alleged that students in poor districts failed to receive an adequate education based on inadequate funding.

In most cases, however, plaintiffs' challenges have been based on equal protection provisions of the Fourteenth Amendment. The methods of financing schools have been held unconstitutional by state supreme courts across the nation in such states as Alabama, Kentucky, Missouri, Tennessee, Texas, California, Ohio, Washington, and Vermont. Challenges involving equity usually address concerns regarding differences in per-pupil expenditures that result in unequal expenditures for children in poor districts.

In ruling on these cases, the courts tend to focus on supplemental state funding to correct these disparities. Because property taxes are the most common source of revenue to support local schools, many of the disparities are linked to differences in local property values. States attempt to address this issue by establishing a minimum foundation program that provides a minimal level of funding for each child, followed by state subsidy to support local efforts in order to achieve a minimum level of funding for all school districts.

Plaintiffs have also challenged states on the issues of adequacy of results for students. In these cases, the focus shifts from per-pupil expenditures to outcomes such as achievement levels and graduation rates. Students in poor districts tend to lag behind students in wealthy districts. Plaintiffs argue that insufficient resources largely contribute to low quality of education for students in poor districts.

Serrano v. Priest was one of the early cases that supported the equal protection challenge regarding disparities in funding.[5] The state court recognized that education was a "fundamental interest." Although the basic state finance program's intent was to equalize funding among school districts, the total system including a combination of state and local funds did in fact create great disparities in school revenue. When taken as a whole, the system generated school revenue that was proportional to the wealth of the individual school. It concluded further that property wealth was a suspect classification. The funding system was found to be unconstitutional.

The basic view held by the court in *Serrano* was that the quality of a child's education should not be a function of the wealth of the district in which the child resides. This case emerged when plaintiffs alleged that under the state finance system they were required to pay taxes at a higher rate than were taxpayers in many other districts to provide essentially the same or lesser educational opportunities for their children. They based this challenge on the notion that the amount of revenue available for education effectively denies students equal protection of the laws under both the U.S. Constitution and California's constitution. The *Serrano* case was instrumental in establishing the fiscal neutrality standard that was used by the court to address wealth disparity.

A state superior court reached a similar ruling in *Robinson v. Cahill* in New Jersey during this same period, when it held that funding of public schools that relied heavily on local property taxes violated the state constitution as well as the equal protection clause of the Fourteenth Amendment.[6] The court observed that a large number of children throughout the state were not getting an adequate education based in large measure on insufficient funds in many districts despite high taxes. The court recognized the gross inequities that the property-tax-based system created as well as many deficiencies in poor school districts. The legislature was given a deadline to enact a new and equitable system for funding public schools. The legislature, in responding to the court's mandate, passed the public Education Act of 1975 with a goal of developing a thorough and efficient system of free public schools for all children irrespective of socioeconomic status or geographic location. The court, in its ruling on the constitutionality of the law, reaffirmed that the state must meet its continuing obligation if the local government is unable to do so. Although the new act did not identify the sources of new funds, the court upheld the constitutionality of the law, assuming that it would be fully funded. Based on the legislature's failure to fund the new bill, the case was again presented to the state supreme court, which closed the unconstitutionally funded public school system. In response, the state initiated the state's first income tax that was earmarked for public education. The state supreme court lifted the injunction, thus allowing the public school system to operate for a number of years before another legal challenge emerged as a class action suit in *Abbott v. Burke,* challenging the disparity in spending and achievement between the richest and poorest school districts.[7] The state supreme court ruled in *Abbott v. Burke* that the current funding system was unconstitutional, and the state was charged with resolving the disparities.

A flurry of suits was filed following *Serrano,* attacking school funding schemes. Many plaintiffs succeeded in their efforts to have courts embrace the fiscal neutrality standard adopted in *Serrano* to remedy wealth disparity.

THE LANDMARK *RODRIGUEZ* CASE

One significant fiscal neutrality case, *San Antonio Independent School District v. Rodriguez,* reached the U.S. Supreme Court, which resulted in the High Court's reaching a landmark decision affecting Public School Finance programs across the nation.[8]

In *San Antonio Independent School District v. Rodriguez,* Mexican American parents whose children attended urban elementary and secondary schools in the Edgewood Independent School District filed a class action equity suit on behalf of minority children throughout the state who were poor and resided in a school community that had a low property tax base. A three-judge district court held that the Texas finance system was unconstitutional under the equal protection clause of the Fourteenth Amendment. The state appealed. The U.S. Supreme Court, in a 5–4 decision, reversed the ruling by the district court. The court did note the discrepancies created by the funding system in which great disparities existed regarding *ad valorem* taxes from one district to another. In spite of these discrepancies, the court indicated that the Texas funding system did not work to the disadvantage of any class or group because the disadvantages occurred only between districts regardless of the relative wealth of any family within the district. Consequently, poor citizens throughout the system were not disadvantaged as a class. The Texas system of funding schools did not interfere with a right to an education, because, although undeniably of highest importance, this is not recognized by the court as being among those rights guaranteed by the Constitution. Therefore, the Texas school financial system was deemed to be constitutional.

LITIGATION FOLLOWING *RODRIGUEZ*

The *Rodriguez* decision essentially removed litigation from the federal courts in the Public School Finance arena. State courts became the court of choice to address claims based on state constitutions' equal protection provisions rather than Fourteenth Amendment grounds. State courts also addressed issues involving educational quality as influenced by teacher quality and appropriate instructional materials. Children, particularly those who reside in poor communities, tend to earn lower test scores and have lower graduation rates than those in more affluent communities. In addition, states tend to define equity differently. State courts have not reached the same conclusions in many of these challenges regarding equity in funding based on differences in their constitutions as well as their state statutes. Because of these differences, state court decisions have not been altogether consistent. Litigation has occurred in forty-nine states regarding Public School Finance challenges. (Hawaii is excluded based on its provision for full state funding of all schools.) State courts are virtually even in their rulings with half supporting plaintiffs and the other half supporting defendant states. (Please refer to the National School Boards Association Public School Finance Litigation Table for a listing of relevant Public School Finance cases at nsba.org.)

POST-*RODRIGUEZ* CASES

One significant case that emerged after *Rodriguez* was *Williams v. California,* which addressed the issue of educational quality that affected educational outcomes of poor students.[9] Two basic issues were presented in this case: First, does the state of California provide all students the basic resources needed to learn, such as qualified teachers, sufficient instructional materials, and adequate facilities? And second, should all students have a fundamental right to an equal education?

Williams, the plaintiff, argued that California's public education failed on both measures by not providing students the necessary educational resources, leading to unequal results across schools in the state. Williams further claimed that the state should be responsible for ensuring that classrooms contained qualified teachers and needed textbooks for students. He urged the state to create standards for basic educational materials along with an accountability system that schools must meet. Williams was supported by parents and students who described the terrible conditions they faced in their schools daily.

Based on the pressure it received, the state of California decided in August 2004 not to challenge Williams's claims but to enter into a settlement. The state agreed with every issue presented by Williams and formally acknowledged its responsibility for ensuring quality and equal education to the students of California. The key aspects of the agreement involved a commitment from the state to ensure that sufficient numbers of textbooks and learning materials are available for all children, that safe buildings in good condition are provided, and that teachers are appropriately trained to teach students in their classes. The state further agreed to post these new standards in every school. Each year officials from each county in California agreed to visit schools with the greatest needs, based on low test scores, to ensure that appropriate resources are available to support teaching and learning. The measures taken by the state of California represented an important victory for poor students of color because it created new standards for measuring whether students learned and whether students were provided the basic resources and conditions to enhance learning.

In a landmark fiscal equity case, *CFE v. State of New York,* the court of appeals in a 4–1 decision held that New York City schoolchildren were not receiving the constitutionally mandated opportunity for a sound basic education.[10] The court further directed the governor and the legislature to ensure that every school in New York City has the resources necessary to provide the opportunity for a sound basic education. Consequently, the governor and the legislature were ordered to determine the cost of providing a sound basic education and enact appropriate funding and accountability reforms by July 30, 2004. This ruling overturned the decision of the appellate court, which ruled that New York City had not failed in its constitutional obligation to provide students with an opportunity for a sound basic education.

In a related case, *Montoy v. State of Kansas,* involving educational adequacy, a state district court held that the state's Public School Finance plan violated the state constitution.[11] The court found that the state failed to distribute resources equitably among children who are equally entitled to a suitable education, which dramatically and adversely impacts the learning of the most vulnerable and protected Kansas children. The court found a 300 percent funding disparity between poor and wealthy districts. The No Child Left Behind Act (NCLB) was cited as mandating that public schools eliminate achievement gaps among groups of students impacted by this case. Some legal experts believe that more objective standards that define an adequate education will be beneficial in educational adequacy lawsuits. Traditionally, judges are reluctant to substitute their judgment in academic matters, particularly those involving what constitutes an adequate education.

In a contrasting Illinois case, *Lewis E. v. Spagnolo,* the issue facing the court focused on whether the Illinois Public School Funding System violated students' rights under the state constitution and the U.S. Constitution with respect to the due process clauses.[12] Plaintiffs argued that the Illinois State Constitution granted them the right to a minimally adequate education. The court in ruling against the plaintiffs held that questions and issues relating to the quality of education are solely the responsibility of the legislature to answer.

The issue regarding education quality and its relationship to school funding is a difficult one due primarily to differences among public school students. Students require different levels of resources based on background, preparation, and other factors to achieve prescribed educational outcomes. In addition, the cost of providing educational services varies from state to state based on geographical location and demographics.

Funding distribution schemes to achieve quality and equity will be continuously debated due to the many variables involved in determining precisely what constitutes quality and the level of funding necessary to achieve quality. To date, there is no universal quality education model that has distributive applications for school districts throughout the nation.

EQUITY AND ADEQUACY OF FUNDING FOR PUBLIC SCHOOLS

In recent years, many states have commissioned studies to determine the adequacy of their public education systems. The focus on adequacy is a departure from their traditional focus on equity. Equity denotes fairness, which suggests that all communities, rich or poor, are taxed at similar rates and have equal access to similar amounts of revenue per student—which, of course, does not occur in most states. Adequacy, on the other hand, focuses on a minimal level of funding needed for every school to teach its students, thus subscribing to an education that is adequate rather than excellent. Public schools across the United States are facing increased pressure to improve the overall quality of education provided for students and have commissioned adequacy studies. Data generated by adequacy studies are often used to increase state aid to local school districts. Lawmakers in Texas, Ohio, Kentucky, South Carolina, Colorado, Missouri, Montana, Arkansas, Wyoming, Arkansas, and New Hampshire have commissioned educational adequacy studies. In states such as Texas, New York, and Kansas, courts have mandated increases in state appropriations for public school funding based on such studies. States with the aid of NCLB are focusing their attention on output measures such as graduation rates and student achievement, which is a departure from input-based issues such as teacher–student ratios.

DeRolph v. State of Ohio was a leading case that involved an adequacy study methodology, which attempted to establish a basic foundation level by determining specific conditions that will enable the state to provide all children a sound and defensible educational opportunity. The case involved a class action suit representing over five hundred school districts who sued the state for failure to provide an efficient education system based on the state's constitution.[13] They alleged further that the state relied too heavily on local property taxes to fund schools. This reliance created disparities in the districts located in communities where high property values could more readily meet student needs than could districts located in communities with lower tax values. The judge in this case ruled that public education is a fundamental right and that the legislature must provide an improved and more equitable means of financing schools. However, the lower court's decision was overturned on appeal by the legislature. The Ohio Supreme Court subsequently held that the state's current method of funding school violated the Ohio Constitution. Although additional appropriations were allocated to schools, the overall system of funding was not overhauled.

In contrast, the legislature in Maryland enacted a new system of finance that increased state funding for schools by 1.3 billion annually to be phased in over a six-year period. A larger portion of increased revenue targeted lower-wealth districts with high-need students. Maryland's overhaul of its funding system linked funding with standards-based education. The new funding program grew out of *Bradford v. Maryland State Board of Education,* from allegations that the current system of finance violated students' constitutional rights based on its inability to provide an adequate education to students within the state.[14] The Court of Appeals held in June 2005 that the legislature should appropriate extra funds to the Baltimore City School District to manage budget shortfalls.

For example, Texas faced ongoing litigation involving funding inequities in the landmark case of *Edgewood Independent School et al. v. Kirby.* This case arose when a suit was filed by the Mexican American Legal Defense and Educational Fund against the Commission of Education in May 1984, with Kirby alleging discrimination against students in poor districts.[15] Plaintiffs asserted that the state's method of funding public schools minimally violated four principles of the state constitution, which obligated the legislature to provide an efficient and free public school system. They further argued that the current funding system violated the equal protection clause as well as the state constitution. The trial court held for the plaintiffs in 1987 by ruling that the state's system of funding schools was unconstitutional. However, on appeal, a state appellate court reversed the trial court's decision. The Texas Supreme Court heard the case in 1989, unanimously confirmed the trial court's ruling, and ordered the legislature to develop an equitable system to finance schools by the 1990–1991 school year.

Pivotal to the state supreme court's decision was the revelation that large disparities in property wealth existed that impacted per-pupil expenditures across districts throughout the state. The legislature passed a bill that increased state funding by more than $500 million. The plaintiffs immediately challenged the constitutionality of the new legislation, arguing that the basic structure of the system of finance had not changed.

In 1991, the state supreme court, in *Edgewood II*, supported the plaintiff's contention by mandating that the legislature devise a new funding system. The legislature enacted new legislation that combined the state's existing independent school districts into county education districts. These new districts would levy a state-mandated property tax of $1 per $100 of property value per pupil. This revenue would be distributed on an equal per-pupil basis within each district. The new legislature was then challenged by a group of wealthy school districts in 1992 in *Edgewood III*. The state supreme court held that the new bill was unconstitutional because it violated the state's constitution, which required local voter approval of school property tax levies. The legislature was granted an additional year to devise a new funding system.

In 1993, the legislature enacted another bill designed to create a more equitable funding system as well as a statewide system of accountability based on student performance as measured by the Texas Assessment of Academic Skills Test. In 1995, the Texas Supreme Court held in *Edgewood IV* that the new system was in fact constitutional. In its ruling, however, the court noted inequities in financing school facilities based on limited support by the state, thereby leaving local districts with the responsibility to bear the cost. The court cautioned that this problem, if not addressed, could result in an unconstitutional funding system. The legislature passed legislation that provided additional state revenue for facilities.

In 1998, the system was challenged again in *Edgewood V*, contending that equity was eroding by allowing property-rich districts to escape the recapture provision of the new bill. The suit alleged furthermore that no equalization revision existed regarding the retirement of old debt. The legislature responded by increasing tier-level funding. The *Edgewood V* suit has not been heard by the state supreme court.

Summary of Public School Finance Court Decisions

1. A district court held that Montana's funding system failed to provide adequate funding for its public schools. Further, the state has shown no commitment to preserve American Indian culture.[16]

2. The Wyoming Supreme Court declared that the state's funding system was unconstitutional on equity and adequacy grounds. In its second decision, the state's new cost-based finance system was held to be capable of fulfilling the state's constitution's guarantee of an appropriate education.[17]

3. The intermediate Colorado Court of Appeals held that educational adequacy was an unjustifiable political question. In addition, the state constitution's education clause did not provide judicially manageable standards for discerning the definition of educational adequacy. The plaintiffs' challenge involved a lack of resources for educating students with disabilities and English language learners.[18]

4. The Indiana Court of Appeals held that the state's constitutional language imposes a duty on the state to provide an education that equips students with the skills and knowledge that enable them to become productive members of society. The state was denied a motion to dismiss the plaintiff's complaint.[19]

5. Plaintiffs challenged Iowa's funding statute, which was described as shortchanging school districts in non–retail-rich counties. In response, the legislature charged the funding system, resulting in a withdrawal of the suit, thus preventing school districts from generating sufficient funds to provide safe and healthy learning environments. Iowa is one of six states in which no court has decided on a legal challenge alleging a school funding system that violates the state's constitution. The other five states are Delaware, Hawaii, Mississippi, Nevada, and Utah.[20]

Administrative Guide

Public School Finance

1. The power of taxation for education resides with the state limited only by federal and state constitutions.
2. State constitutional provisions allow the legislature to make provisions for a system of public schools and to tax citizens for support of public education.
3. The legislature has the inherent power not only to tax citizens for support of education but also to distribute funds for the operation of public schools.
4. The Equal Protection Clause establishes a minimum standard of uniformity to be met by state tax legislation.
5. Tax distribution formulas are determined by the legislature based on the needs of various types of school districts and the ability of citizens in those districts to support public education.
6. The view held by the court in the *Serrano* case is that the quality of a child's education should not be a function of the wealth of the district in which the student resides.
7. The U.S. Supreme Court held in *Rodriguez* that there is no loss of a fundamental right since education in itself is unprotected by the U.S. Constitution.
8. According to the *Rodriguez* ruling, a funding system based on local property tax that provides a minimum education to all students is constitutional.
9. The *Rodriguez* decision removed Public School Finance litigation from the federal courts to state courts.
10. Following the *Rodriguez* decision, courts have been more inclined to focus their attention on educational quality as influenced by teacher quality, appropriate instructional materials, student achievement scores, and graduation rates as a means of addressing equal opportunity provisions for students.
11. Based on different conclusions reached by state courts in matters involving equity in funding as well as differences in state constitutions, there is no uniformity among courts in their decisions regarding adequacy of funding for public schools.
12. Generally speaking, courts will not deem an act of the legislature unconstitutional without a showing that the legislature exercised its authority in an arbitrary and capricious manner.
13. The state may collect tax funds from wealthy school districts and redistribute them to poorer districts to achieve a measure of equity.

Endnotes

1. *United States v. Butler,* 279 U.S. (1936).
2. *Cleveland C.C. and St. L. Ry. Co. v. People,* 208 Ill. 9, 69 N.E. 832 (1904).
3. *Pirrone v. City of Boston,* 364 Mass. 403, 305 N.E. 2d 96 (1973).
4. *Hurd v. City of Buffalo,* 34 N.Y. 2d 628 355 N.Y.S. 2d 369, 311 N.E. 504 (1974).
5. *Serrano v. Priest,* 487 P. 2d 1241 (Cal. 1971), *Serrano v. Priest,* 557 P. 2d 929 (Cal. 1976).
6. *Robinson v. Cahill,* 303 A. 2d 273 (N.J. 1973).
7. *Abbott v. Burke,* 798 A. 2d 6702 (N.J. 2002).
8. *San Antonio School District v. Rodriguez,* 411 U.S. 1, 93 S. Ct. 1278, 36 L. Ed. 2d 16 (1973).
9. *Williams v. California,* 372, U.S. 713 (2000).

10. *Campaign for Fiscal Equity v. State of New York,* 2003 N.Y., slip op. 15615 (N.Y. 2003).

11. *Montoy v. State of Kansas,* No. 99-1738 (Kan. Dist. Ct. Dec 2, 2003).

12. *Lewis E. v. Spagnolo,* 710 N.E. 2d 798 (Ill. 1999).

13. *DeRolph v. State* (2001), 91 Ohio St.3d 1274.

14. *Bradford v. Maryland State Board of Education,* Case No. 95258055/CL20251 (Cir. Ct. Balt. City Oct. 18, 1996).

15. *Edgewood Independent School District et al. v. Kirby,* 777 S.W. 2d 391 (Tex. 1989).

16. *Columbia Falls Public Schools v. State of Montana,* 326 Mont. 304, 109 P.3d 257 (Mont. 2005).

17. *Campbell County School Dist. v. State,* 907 P. 2d 1238 (1995).

18. *Lobato v. State of Colorado,* 218 P.3d 358 (2009).

19. *Bonner v. Daniels,* 885 N.E. 2d 673 (Ind. Ct. App 2008).

20. *King v. State of Iowa,* 258 Iowa 1339, 1351 (142 NW 2d 444) (1996).

APPENDIX

The Constitution of the United States and Selected Key Provisions and Amendments Affecting Education

CONSTITUTION OF THE UNITED STATES

We the People of the United States, in Order to form a more perfect Union, establish Justice, insure domestic Tranquility, provide for the common defence, promote the general Welfare, and secure the Blessings of Liberty to ourselves and our Posterity, do ordain and establish this Constitution for the United States of America.

Article I

Section. 1. All legislative Powers herein granted shall be vested in a Congress of the United States, which shall consist of a Senate and House of Representatives.

Section. 2. The House of Representatives shall be composed of Members chosen every second Year by the People of the several States, and the Electors in each State shall have the Qualifications requisite for Electors of the most numerous Branch of the State Legislature. . . .

Section. 7. All Bills for raising Revenue shall originate in the House of Representatives; but the Senate may propose or concur with amendments as on other Bills.

Every Bill which shall have passed the House of Representatives and the Senate, shall, before it becomes a Law, be presented to the President of the United States; If he approve he shall sign it, but if not he shall return it, with his Objections to that House in which it shall have originated, who shall enter the Objections at large on their Journal, and proceed to reconsider it. If after such Reconsideration two thirds of that House shall agree to pass the Bill, it shall be sent, together with the Objections, to the other House, by which it shall likewise be reconsidered, and if approved by two thirds of that House, it shall become a Law. But in all such Cases the Votes of both Houses shall be determined by yeas and Nays, and the Names of the Persons voting for and against the Bill shall be entered on the Journal of each House respectively. If any Bill shall not be returned by the President within ten Days (Sunday excepted) after it shall have been presented to him, the Same shall be a Law, in like Manner as if he had signed it, unless the Congress by their Adjournment prevents its Return, in which Case it shall not be a Law.

Article II

Section. 1. The executive Power shall be vested in a President of the United States of America. . . .

Section. 2. The President shall be Commander in Chief of the Army and Navy of the United States, and of the Militia of the several states, . . .

He shall have Power, by and with the Advice and Consent of the Senate, to make Treaties, provided two thirds of the Senators present concur; and he shall nominate, and by and with the Advice and Consent of the Senate, shall appoint Ambassadors, other public Ministers and Consuls, Judges of the supreme Court, and all other Officers of the United States, whose Appointments are not herein otherwise provided for, and which shall be established by Law: but the Congress may by Law vest the Appointment of such inferior Officers, as they think proper, in the President alone, in the Courts of Law, or in the Heads of Departments. . . .

Section. 4. The United States shall guarantee to every State in this Union a Republican Form of Government, and shall protect each of them against Invasion; and on Application of the Legislature, or of the Executive (when the Legislature cannot be convened) against domestic Violence.

Article III

Section. 1. The judicial Power of the United States, shall be vested in one supreme Court, and in such inferior Courts as the Congress may from time to time ordain and establish. The Judges, both of the supreme and inferior Courts, shall hold their Offices during good Behaviour, and shall, at stated Times, receive for their Services, a Compensation, which shall not be diminished during their Continuance in Office.

Section. 2. The judicial Power shall extend to all Cases, in Law and Equity, arising under this Constitution, the Laws of the United States, and Treaties made, or which shall be made, under their Authority;—to all Cases affecting Ambassadors, other public Ministers and Consuls;—to all Cases of admiralty and maritime Jurisdiction;—to Controversies to which the United States shall be a Party;—to Controversies between two or more States;—between a State and Citizens of another State;—between Citizens of different States;—between Citizens of the same State claiming Lands under Grants of different States, and between a State, or the Citizens thereof, and foreign States, Citizens or Subjects. . . .

The Trial of all Crimes, except in Cases of Impeachment, shall be by Jury; and such Trial shall be held in the State where the said Crimes shall have been committed; but when not committed within any State, the Trial shall be at such Place or Places as the Congress may by Law have directed.

Article IV

Section. 1. Full Faith and Credit shall be given in each State to the public Acts, Records, and judicial Proceedings of every other State. And the Congress may by general Laws prescribe the Manner in which such Acts, Records and Proceedings shall be proved, and the Effect thereof.

Section. 2. The Citizens of each State shall be entitled to all Privileges and Immunities of the Citizens in the several States.

Article V

The Congress, whenever two thirds of both Houses shall deem it necessary, shall propose Amendments to this Constitution, or, on the Application of the Legislatures of two thirds of the several States, shall call a Convention for proposing Amendments, which, in either Case, shall be valid to all Intents and Purposes, as Part of this Constitution, when ratified by the Legislatures of three fourths of the several States, or by Conventions in three fourths thereof, as the one or the other Mode of Ratification may be proposed by the Congress; Provided that no Amendment which may be made prior to the Year One thousand eight hundred and eight shall in any Manner affect the first and fourth Clauses in the Ninth Section of the first Article; and that no State, without its Consent, shall be deprived of it's equal Suffrage in the Senate. . . .

Article VI

This Constitution, and the Laws of the United which shall be made in Pursuance thereof; and all Treaties made, or which shall be made, under the Authority of the United States, shall be the supreme Law of the Land; and the Judges in every State shall be found thereby, any Thing in the Constitution or Laws of any State to the Contrary notwithstanding.

The Senators and Representatives before mentioned, and the Members of the several State Legislatures, and all executive and judicial Officers, both of the United States and of the several States, shall be bound by Oath or Affirmation, to support this Constitution; but no religious Test shall ever be required as a qualification to any office or public trust under the United States.

Article VII

The Ratification of the Conventions of nine States, shall be sufficient for the Establishment of this Constitution between the States so ratifying the Same.

AMENDMENTS TO THE CONSTITUTION
OF THE UNITED STATES OF AMERICA

Articles in Addition to, and Amendment of, the Constitution of the United States of America, Proposed by Congress, and Ratified by the Several States, Pursuant to the Fifth Article of the Original Constitution

Amendment [I.] [1791]

Congress shall make no law respecting an establishment of religion, or prohibiting the free exercise of thereof; or abridging the freedom of speech, or of the press; or the right of the people peaceably to assemble, and to petition the Government for a redress of grievances.

Amendment [IV.] [1791]

The right of the people to be secure in their persons, houses, papers, and effects, against unreasonable searches and seizures, shall not be violated, and no Warrants shall issue, but upon probable cause, supported by Oath or affirmation, and particularly describing the place to be searched, and the persons or things to be seized.

Amendment [V.] [1791]

No person shall be held to answer for a capital, or otherwise infamous crime, unless on a presentment or indictment of a Grand Jury, except in cases arising in the land or naval forces, or in the Militia, when in actual service in time of War or public danger; nor shall any person be subject for the same offence to be twice put in jeopardy of life or limb; nor shall be compelled in any criminal case to be a witness against himself, nor be deprived of life, liberty, or property, without due process of law; nor shall private property be taken for public use, without just compensation.

Amendment [VIII.] [1791]

Excessive bail shall not be required, nor excessive fines imposed, nor cruel and unusual punishments inflicted.

Amendment [IX.] [1791]

The enumeration in the Constitution, of certain rights, shall not be construed to deny or disparage others retained by the people.

Amendment [X.] [1791]

The powers not delegated to the United States by the Constitution, nor prohibited by it to the States, are reserved to the States respectively, or to the people.

Amendment [XIV.] [1868]

Section 1. All persons born or naturalized in the United States and subject to the jurisdiction thereof, are citizens of the United States and of the State wherein they reside. No State shall make or enforce any law which shall abridge the privileges or immunities of citizens of the United States; nor shall any State deprive any person of life, liberty, or property, without due process of law; nor deny to any person within its jurisdiction the equal protection of the laws.

Section 5. The Congress shall have power to enforce, by appropriate legislation, the provisions of this article.

Note: Refer to loc.gov/law/help/statutes.php for further information about federal statutes.

GLOSSARY OF RELEVANT LEGAL TERMS

A

abatement   Termination of a law suit.

action   A lawsuit proceeding in a court of law.

advisory opinion   An opinion generally rendered by a lower court when no actual case is before it.

affidavit   A written statement made under oath.

affirm   To uphold a lower court's decision or ruling.

allegation   A statement in the pleadings of a case that is expected to be proven; usually brought by the plaintiff.

amicus curiae   A friend of the court. A party that does not have a direct interest in a case who is requested or offers information to the court to clarify an issue before the court.

appeal   An application to a higher court to amend or rectify a lower court's ruling.

appellant   One who causes an appeal to a higher court. The appellant may be the plaintiff or the defendant.

appellate court   A higher court that hears a case on appeal from a lower court.

appellee   A person or party against whom an appeal is brought.

arbitrary   An act or action taken without a fair and substantial cause.

assault   An offer to use physical force in a hostile manner.

B

battery   Making physical contact with another person in a rude and hostile fashion.

bona fide   Acting honestly and in good faith.

breach   Failure to execute a legal duty.

brief   A written argument presented to a court by attorneys.

busing   The transporting of students across school-district boundaries, usually court ordered, to create more racially balanced schools.

C

case law   A body of law created by decisions of the judicial branch.

cause of action   The basis for a legal challenge.

certiorari   A judicial process whereby a case is moved from a lower court to a higher one for review. The record of all proceedings at the lower court is sent to the higher court.

civil action   An action in court with the express purpose of gaining or recovering individual or civil rights.

civil rights   The personal freedoms of citizens guaranteed by the Thirteenth and Fourteenth Amendments to the U.S. Constitution.

class action   Legal action brought by one or more individuals on behalf of themselves and others who are affected by a particular issue.

code   A systematic compilation of statutes usually arranged into chapters and headings for convenient access.

common law   A system of law in which legal principles are derived from usage and custom as expressed by the courts.

compensatory damages   Damages awarded to compensate an injured party for actual losses incurred.

complaint   A formal plea to a court seeking relief and informing the defendant on the basis for a legal challenge.

concurring opinion   An opinion written by a judge expressing the will of the majority in a court ruling.

consent decree   Agreement by parties to a dispute and the admission by parties that the decree is a just determination of their rights based on facts related to the case.

contract   A legal agreement between parties involving an offer and acceptance to perform certain duties that are enforceable by courts of law.

contributory negligence   Negligence by the injured party that, when combined with the negligence of the defendant, resulted in the proximate cause of the injury.

court of record   A court that maintains permanent records of its proceedings.

D

damages   Compensation or indemnity claimed by the plaintiff or ordered by the courts for injuries sustained resulting from wrongful acts of the defendant.

declaratory relief   An opinion expressed by the court without ordering that anything be done; it recognizes the rights of the parties involved.

decree   An order issued by a court in an equity suit.

de facto   In fact; in reality a state of affairs that is accepted without the sanction of law.

defamation   Scandalous words or expression, written or spoken, that result in damages to another's reputation for which legal action may be taken by the damaged party.

defendant   The party against whom a legal action is brought.

de jure   Sanctioned by law.

de minimis   Something that is so insignificant that it does not warrant judicial attention.

demurrer   Objection to a pleading that is viewed as legally insufficient.

de nova   New; a preceding that ignores all previous proceedings. It is usually associated with a second trial mandated by a higher court to a lower court for a new trial.

deposition   A statement of a witness taken under oath obtained before the actual trial.

desegregation   The ending of the separation of children of one race from children of another race.

dicta   Statements in a judicial opinion that have no bearing on the decision of the case.

dictum   An opinion expressed by a judge in a proceeding that is not relevant in reaching a court's decision.

discretionary power   Involves the exercise of judgment in deciding whether to take action in a certain situation.

discrimination   The unfair treatment of a group of people by another because of race, gender, religion, culture, or national origin.

disposition   A final determination or outcome of a case or motion by a court.

dissenting opinion   An opinion written by a judge in disagreement with the decision of the majority hearing a case.

due process   A course of legal proceedings in accordance with principles of law designed to protect individual rights.

E

emancipated   Free of parental authority and control and free to make independent decisions.

emancipation   Legal release from another's control (e.g., married child from parents).

en banc   By all judges of the court.

enjoin   To require an individual by writ of injunction to perform or refrain from a certain act.

equity   A system of law that provides a remedy where no adequate remedy is available at law.

et al.   And other unnamed parties involved in legal proceedings.

et seq.   And those following.

executory   That which is yet to be fully executed or performed.

ex parte   A proceeding for the benefit of one party.

ex rel.   On behalf of.

F

felony   A crime that is punishable by imprisonment or death.

fiduciary   A special relationship between individuals in which one person acts for another in a position of trust.

finding   The conclusion reached by a court regarding a factual question.

functional exclusion   The provision of equal access without special provisions to disabled students that will enable them to benefit from instruction, although they are physically exposed to the same experience as nondisabled students.

fundamentality   A requirement to obtain redress under the equal protection clause regarding state constitutions through a claim that alleged discrimination affects a fundamental right.

funding disparity   Unequal funding of schools based on tax distribution.

G

governmental function   Function required of an agency for the protection and welfare of the general public.

H

hearing   An examination of a legal or factual issue by a court.

holding   A ruling or decision by the courts on a question or issue properly raised in a case.

I

implied   Inferred; not expressed.

infra   Following; below.

injunction   A court order prohibiting a person from committing an act that threatens or may result in injury to another.

in loco parentis   In place of parents.

integration   The process of bringing together different races of students so that all may enjoy the same educational benefits.

inter alia   Among other things.

invitee   A person who is on the property of another by express invitation.

ipso facto   In and of itself.

J

judgment   A decision reached by a court.

L

liable   Bound or obligated by law; responsible for actions that may involve restitution.

licensee   A person granted the privilege to enter into property by actual or implied consent for his or her own purpose rather than the purpose of the one who owns the property.

litigation   Formal challenge involving a dispute in a court; a lawsuit.

M

malfeasance   Commission of an unlawful act.

malice   The intentional commission of a wrongful act without justification.

mandate   A legal command.

material   Important to a case.

ministerial acts   Required usually by public officials in which there is no discretion.

misfeasance   Improper performance of a lawful act.

motion   A request for a court ruling.

N

negligence   A lack of proper care; failure to exercise prudence, which may result in injury to another.

nolens volens   With or without consent.

nuisance   A condition that restricts the use of property or creates a potentially dangerous situation for the user.

O

original jurisdiction   The legal capacity of a court to accept a case at its inception.

P

parallel citations   A reference to the same court case that is published in two or more sources.

parens patriae   In place of parents; the state's guardsmanship over those unable to direct their own affairs (e.g., minors).

per curiam   An opinion rendered by an entire court rather than by any one of several justices.

petition   A written application to a court for the redress of a wrong or the grant of a privilege or license.

plaintiff   The party who brings action by filing a complaint.

pleadings   Formal documents filed in court containing the plaintiff's contention and the defendant's response.

plenary   Full; complete.

police powers   The inherent power of the government to impose restrictions to protect the health, safety, and welfare of its citizens.

precedent   A decision relied upon for subsequent decisions in addressing similar or identical questions of law.

prima facie   At first view; a fact presumed to be true if not rebutted or proven untrue.

procedural due process   Guarantees that a prescribed set of steps be followed that allows individuals an opportunity to seek redress for alleged violations before any action is taken against them.

proprietary function   Those functions not normally required by statutes or law and usually involving a state or governmental agent.

punitive damages   An award intended to punish the wrongdoer.

Q

quid pro quo   A consideration; giving one valuable thing in exchange for another.

R

ratio decidendi   Reasoning applied by a court regarding crucial facts related to the case in rendering a judgment.

relief   Legal redress sought in the court by the plaintiff.

remand   To send back; the act of an appellate court when it sends a case back to the lower court for further proceedings.

remedy   A court's enforcement of a right or the prevention of the violation of such right.

respondeat superior   The responsibility of a master for the acts of his servants.

respondent   The party against whom an appeal is taken; the defendant.

restrain   To prevent or prohibit from action.

S

segregation   The separation of one group of people from another through laws or personal discrimination.

"separate but equal"   A concept that gave states the right to segregate races of people in public transportation. This idea was extended to allow races to have separate but similar quality schools. It was subsequently ruled unconstitutional.

sine qua non   A thing that is indispensable.

slander   Oral defamation.

sovereign immunity   A doctrine providing immunity from suit of a governmental body without its express consent.

standing   The right to raise an issue in a lawsuit.

stare decisis   To stand by a decided case.

statute   An act of the state or federal legislative body; a law.

statute of limitations   A statute that established the time period in which litigation may be initiated in a particular cause of action.

substantive due process   Ensures that a valid reason exists before an individual is deprived of life, liberty, or property and that the means used to achieve this objective are reasonable.

substantive law   The proper law of rights and duties.

suit   A proceeding in a court of law initiated by the plaintiff.

summary judgment   A court's decision to settle a dispute or dispose of a case promptly without conducting full legal proceedings.

T

tenure   A security measure for those who successfully perform duties and meet statutory or contractual requirements; a continuous service contract.

tort   An actionable wrong committed against another independent of contract; a civil wrong.

trespass   The unauthorized entry upon the property of another; taking or interfering with the property of another.

U

ultra vires   Outside of the legal power of an individual or body; exceeding the power of authority.

V

vacate   To rescind a court decision.

vested   Fixed; not subject to any contingency.

vicarious liability   A form of liability in which school districts are held liable for negligent or intentional wrongdoing of their employees when the act is committed within the scope of the district employment position, even though the district may not be directly at fault.

void   Null; without force or a binding effect.

W

waive   To forgo, renounce, or relinquish a legal right.

warrant   A written order of the court; arrest order.

writ of mandamus   A command from a court directing a court, officer, or body to perform a certain act.

Z

zoning   A strategy used by school districts to create desegregated schools.

CASE INDEX

SUBJECT INDEX